THE WOMEN'S LIBERATION MOVEMENT IN RUSSIA

WITHDRAWN

WITHDRAWN

D0145683

THE WOMEN'S LIBERATION MOVEMENT IN RUSSIA

Feminism, Nihilism, and Bolshevism
1860–1930

RICHARD STITES

PRINCETON UNIVERSITY PRESS
PRINCETON, NEW JERSEY

Copyright © 1978 by Princeton University Press
Published by Princeton University Press, Princeton, New Jersey
In the United Kingdom: Princeton University Press,
Guildford, Surrey

ALL RIGHTS RESERVED

Library of Congress Cataloging in Publication Data will
be found on the last printed page of this book

Printed in the United States of America
by Princeton University Press,
Princeton, New Jersey

TO MY WIFE,
TANYA

CONTENTS

LIST OF ILLUSTRATIONS
(following page 154)

VOICES OF THE 1860'S

N.G. Chernyshevsky. E.N. Vodovozova, *Na zare zhizni*. 3d ed. 2 v. Moscow, 1964.

E.N. Vodovozova. E.N. Vodovozova, *Na zare zhizni*, 3d ed. 2 v. Moscow, 1964.

CONFLICTING VIEWS OF WOMEN'S WORK

In the Print Shop. ("V tipografii," graviura P. Kurenkova po risunku N. Stepanova v No. 22 zhurnala "Iskra" za 1864 god.) from Vodovozova, *Na zare zhizni*, II, 304.

HEROINES OF TERROR

Vera Zasulich. *V.I. Zasulich*. SPB, 1906.

Vera Figner (Soviet Postcard). Soviet postcard in author's possession (n.d.).

Sofya Perovskaya. E. Segal, *Sofya Perovskaya*. Moscow, 1962.

FEMINIST LEADERS

Anna Filosofova. *Sbornik pamyati Anny Pavlovny Filosofovoi*. 2 v. Petrograd, 1915, I.

Organizers of the Women's Congress of 1908. *Trudy Pervago Vserossiskago Zhenskago S"ezda . . . 1908*. SPB, 1909.

COMPETING ISSUES OF FEMINISM:
PROSTITUTION AND POLITICS

A Nine-Year-Old Prostitute of Kiev (1904).
  M.K. Mukalov, *Deti ulitsy*. SPB, 1906.
Suffragist Cartoon. *PZhK*, VIII (1906) 335–43.

PROPHETS AND ORGANIZERS OF
BOLSHEVIK LIBERATION

Inessa Armand
  Kommunistka, 8–9 (Jan.–Feb. 1921).
A.V. Artyukhina
  Svetlyi put. Moscow, 1967.
Nadezhda Krupskaya
  Kommunistka, 8–9 (Jan.–Feb. 1921).
Sofya Smidovich
  Svetlyi put. Moscow, 1967.
K.I. Nikolaeva
  Svetlyi put. Moscow, 1967.
Alexandra Kollontai
  Kommunistka, 8–9 (Jan.–Feb. 1921).

ABBREVIATIONS

Bib. chten. Biblioteka dlya chteniya
BSE Bolshaya sovetskaya entsiklopediya
CDSP Current Digest of the Soviet Press
ES Entsiklopedicheskii slovar
GM Golos minuvshego
GMCS Golos minuvshego na chuzhoi storone
ICW International Council of Women
IISHA International Institute of Social History, Amsterdam
IWSA International Women's Suffrage Association
KS Katorga i ssylka
Lit. nasled. Literaturnoe nasledstvo
NEP Novaya Ekonomicheskaya Politika (New Economic Policy)
OZ Otechestvennye zapiski
PZhK Pervyi zhenskii kalendar
RB Russkoe bogatstvo
RM Russkaya mysl
RS Russkoe slovo
RV Russkii vestnik
Sov. Sovremennik
SV Severnyi vestnik
SZh Soyuz zhenshchin
TsGIAL Tsentralnyi Gosudarstvennyi Istoricheskii Arkhiv, Leningrad
VE Vestnik Evropy
WIC War Industries Committee
ZAGS Otdel zapisi aktov grazhdanskogo sostayaniya (Office of Civil Registry)
ZhD Zhenskoe delo
ZhM Zhenskaya mysl
ZhV Zhenskii vestnik

NOTE ON TRANSLITERATION
AND DATES

I have used a modified Library of Congress system of transliteration (minus the soft signs and diacriticals), with Я and Ю rendered as *ya* and *yu* rather than *ia* and *iu*. I have also used the more familiar -sky as a personal name ending. All dates up to February 1918 are given according to the old (Julian) calendar which was behind the Western (Gregorian) calendar by twelve days in the nineteenth and thirteen days in the twentieth century. In February 1918, the Soviet government shifted to the Western calendar. Dates thereafter are given in the new style.

PREFACE

The most important and concise thing to say by way of introduction about this volume is that it is not a history of Russian feminism *per se*, but rather a history of the women's movement in Russia of which feminism was but a component. Since this movement can be seen in two different historical contexts—that of nineteenth-century European feminism and that of twentieth-century communism—it may be useful to summarize these at the outset. Modern European feminism was initially sounded by a few isolated voices—von Hippel, Wollstonecraft, the French women of 1789—and died rather quickly from social undernourishment. When it was revived in the 1830's and 1840's, it was usually synchronized (as earlier) with "larger" causes and momentous events (revolution, national ferment, the emancipation of other subjugated groups); and—of equal importance—it intersected with problems of economic change and social adjustment for the middle- and upper-class women who launched the movement. Clusters of educated females, possessing both leisure and awareness of their restricted status, advanced from the abstract debates over the "woman question" to organized activity. The first phase of this was usually concerned more with charity, self-help, and the improvement of educational, professional, and legal status than with securing the vote—though suffragism did burst forth sporadically in France in 1848 and in Britain in the 1860's. As the century turned, "political" feminism was revived and exalted to a central place in the feminist struggles. Almost simultaneously, in response to real and perceived needs of the growing class of working women in industry, socialist women attempted to build a "proletarian women's movement" whose political goals were democratic but often at loggerheads with so-called "bourgeois" feminism. The three major international organizations of women reflected these phases: the International Women's Council, formed in 1888 to coordinate world feminist charity and organizational efforts; the International Women's Suffrage Association (1904); and the international women's socialist movement begun in 1907. The Russian experience followed this pattern rather closely.

If the perspective is changed sharply and the Russian Soviet emancipation of women is viewed from the vantage point of modern communist revolution—as in China, Vietnam, Cuba, or Yugoslavia—similarities of a different order are seen. In all these societies, both feminists and socialists had to fight against deeply embedded antifeminist value systems. Feminist movements, as in Europe, appeared in the wake of major political events and social dislocations, sooner or later dividing into radical detachments of women and straight feminists—though seldom in a neat or decisive way. As in Russia, non-Marxist radical women played a historically interesting role in a variety of physical struggles against internal regimes or alien over-lords. Although the memory of their exploits and their revolutionary style were usually folded into the radical ethos of Marxist women, they differed from Marxists in their unwillingness or inability to make contact with working women. Marxist women in China, Vietnam, and (partially) Yugoslavia, on the other hand, differed somewhat from both their Russian and European counter-parts by placing more emphasis on organizing rural, as opposed to urban, women. As with the Bolsheviks, women's mobilization organs in these societies faced the forbidding postrevolutionary task of educating and politicizing masses of largely illiterate (except in Cuba) and passive women. The results—though mixed—have been impressive when viewed in a historical context, but very different in character from the results of feminist movements in the West.

Classical feminism—a justifiable term in spite of the rich variety in the movement—finally came to focus on the vote as the capstone of emancipation in the West. This does not mean that the vote was seen as the end of feminist aspirations. The evidence is clear enough that most feminists envisioned political equality as a means, a continuance of the emancipation process at a higher level: female voters would elect women; women would effect the desired reforms not only for their own sex (law, divorce, education and the rest) but also (via an argument for female sensitivity which sometimes contradicted mainstream feminist rhetoric) contribute to national regeneration, and insure the abolition of such evils as alcoholism, prostitution, and war. The feminist record on these matters after achieving the vote was, to put it in the best light, also mixed. Indeed the styles and milieus of the two different approaches to women's emancipation (Western and communist) were—and are—so different as to make flat comparisons of them difficult, often misleading, and sometimes even inappropriate.

The purpose of this volume is to examine historically the origins of the communist variety of women's liberation in Russia. Parts One and Two deal with the status of educated women in Russian society, the appearance of the "woman question" there, and the major active responses to it. The chapter on the early feminists (III) focuses on their charitable activities and on the meaning of their triumph in opening the doors of university courses to women. The so-called nihilist approach to women is treated separately (Chapter IV) because it differed from feminism and radicalism in stressing personal liberation, sexual freedom, intellectual fulfillment, and a visibly experimental lifestyle. The chapter on the radical response (V) examines revolutionary impulses and roles of women and it describes those attitudes toward sex, feminism, and politics which induced some women to subordinate female emancipation to the more sweeping mission of social revolution. This phase of female radicalism ended with the defeat of the People's Will in the 1880's and was punctuated by the first execution, in 1881, of a female political criminal.

Part Three (1881–1920) explores the impact of industrialization and urbanization upon women and upon the shape of the women's issues and movements which emerged at the opening of the twentieth century. Chapter VI describes the influx of peasant women into the cities, the resulting "female proletariat," the related growth of prostitution, and the formation of a new female professional class from which both feminist and radical leaders were drawn. Chapter VII plots the transition in feminist interest from philanthropy and educational-professional opportunity to women's suffrage and traces the course of the suffrage movement. The Marxist theory of the woman question and the Proletarian Women's Movement based upon it is the nucleus of Chapter VIII that also treats socialist predictions about the family and sex as well as the new roles of women in the various radical and terrorist movements. Chapter IX is an antiphonal treatment of feminist and Bolshevik responses to the War of 1914, the Revolutions of 1917, and the Civil War.

In the belief that a clear understanding of social history is impeded by the traditional obeisance to the year 1917 as a watershed, Part Four interprets the Soviet liberation of women and its self-styled resolution of the woman question in the light of pre-revolutionary aspirations, achievements, and failures; and in the light of the furious, if often untangential, debates between feminists and Marxists. This part assesses the limits of female equality achieved by and granted to Russian women up to about 1930 and relates the "sexual revolution" of the 1920's and its outcome to the larger question of women's role in Soviet society. Chapter XII attempts to weave together current Western and Soviet opinions on the status of women in Soviet life with some personal observations made during numerous visits to the USSR over the past decade.

The present study advances no single unifying argument or thesis, and it is doubtful that a serious treatment of such a complex movement could do so fairly. There is a good deal of "intellectual history" in this account, but it is not meant to be *Ideengeschichte* in the sense of a genealogy of ideas. It is really more the history of a morality or of an ethos than the history of an idea, in the formal sense employed by intellectual historians; and it endeavors to show the effects of ideals and values upon certain groups and representative figures. Again, although the subject is eminently social, the approach is not strictly speaking "social history" either, at least as that term is currently understood. It is more concerned with small groups, biography, personality, and personal interaction than with rigorous sociological and statistical analysis of large segments of the population. Descriptive narrative is balanced with biographical portraiture (without which histories of social movements appear to me quite lifeless and unreal) and a running analysis.

Although the number of people who need to be thanked for their role in the creation of this book (and acquitted for any responsibility for its shortcomings) is too large to be listed here, I wish to acknowledge my gratitude to the following: Hilary Conroy and Richard Barlow who encouraged my interest in history years ago at the University of Pennsylvania and Roderic Davison who did so at George Washington University; Richard Pipes, my thesis director at Harvard, who encouraged research in a topic that was none too topical at the time and Robert Wolff, my second reader, whose stern but kindly critical remarks on style I have never forgotten; and the staffs of the New York Public Library, the Library of Congress, and the Widener Library at Harvard where I researched the dissertation (roughly coterminous with parts One and Two of this book) in 1964–1967.

Research for the balance of the book was done mostly in Europe in the years 1967–1973. For access to the Soviet archives and a memorable semester in Leningrad, I wish to thank the Inter-University Travel Grants Committee (now IREX) and my Soviet advisor, Professor Nahum Grigorevich Slad-kevich. Then, and in subsequent years, I benefited from the rich collections in the University, the Academy of Sciences, and the Saltykov-Shchedrin public libraries in Leningrad and from the kind and competent assistance of their staffs, particularly Anatoly Terentevich Bystrov and Natalya Sergeevna Batalova of the last named library. In 1968, through generous grants from the National Endowment for the Humanities and the American Philosophical So-ciety, I was able to use archives and published works in the International Insti-tute of Social History in Amsterdam and to draw on the expertise of Boris Moiseevich Sapir, Liane Kist, and Leo van Rossum. A grant from Lycoming College in 1969 helped me finance four months of research in the magnificent Slavic collection of the University of Helsinki Library where my investiga-tions were facilitated by the vast bibliographical knowledge of the late Dr. Maria Widnäs. I also wish to thank Knud Rasmussen and Eigil Steffansen of the Slavisk Institut in Copenhagen, the staff of the Royal Library in the same city, especially Carol Gold and Charles Benoff, and the staffs of the British Museum Library and the Millicent Fawcett Library in London.

Since returning from Europe, I have further indebted myself to a number of institutions, groups, and individuals: to the Russian Research Center at Har-vard for an associateship in 1974–1975 that enabled me to study the Smolensk Archives and to check my notes; to the history department at Brown Univer-sity for, among numerous other kindnesses, enabling me to give a seminar on the substance of this book in 1974; to Dorothy Atkinson and Alexander Dallin of Stanford and Gail Lapidus of Berkeley for an enriching conference on Women in Russia in 1975; to Dean Arthur Adams, Professor Marvin Zahniser, and Dr. James Biddle of The Ohio State University who gave strong moral and financial support in the final stages; to Judy McBride and Catherine Bigelow of the same university for their expert typing of a big and difficult manuscript; to Robert Daniels of the University of Vermont, Kaare Hauge of the University of Oslo, and Henryk Lenczyc of the University of Uppsala for sharing bibliographical and other data about Kollontai with me; and to Bar-bara Clements of the University of Akron, Robert Drumm of Columbia, Ruth

PREFACE

Dudgeon of George Washington University, Vera Dunham of Queens University, Barbara Engel of the University of Colorado, Beatrice Farnsworth of Wells College, Xenia Gasiorowska of the University of Wisconsin, Susan Heumann of Columbia, Bernice Madison of San Francisco State, Roberta Manning of Boston College, Charles Schlacks of the University of Pittsburgh, and Reginald Zelnik of Berkeley for stimulating comments and conversations about the subject matter of this book.

Professor Leo Winston of Lycoming College was very helpful with some Russian terms in the early chapters. Chapters II/2 and X/2 have previously appeared, in different form, in *Canadian-American Slavic Studies* and *Russian History*, whose editors and publishers I wish to thank. Parts of the manuscript were read by Rose Glickman, currently at Leningrad University, Rochelle Ruthchild of the Cambridge-Goddard Graduate School, Noralyn Neumark of the University of Sydney, Carole Eubank of Berkeley, and Amy Knight of the University of London. The entire work was read by Abbott Gleason of Brown, Cyril Black of Princeton, Sheila Fitzpatrick of Columbia, and David Joravsky of Northwestern. Whatever virtues the book has owes much to the constructive comments and advice of these friends and colleagues. I am also indebted to those people at Princeton University Press whose interest transformed the manuscript into a book: Carol Orr who processed it; Lewis Bateman who skillfully edited it; and especially Pamela Long who believed in it. A large measure of personal thanks is due to my oldest friends and supporters, Thomas MacMahon and Joseph Wagner of Philadelphia; to Abbott Gleason who helped me when I needed it most; to my aunt, Florence Stites, who started me on my way; to my father; and, most of all, to my wife Tanya who is as much a part of the book as I am.

Leningrad,
September 1976.

PART ONE

On The Eve

I

Women and the Russian Tradition

Kuritsa ne ptitsa,
Zhenshchina ne chelovek.
—*Traditional Russian Saying*

1. THE GENTRY WOMAN AND HER WORLD

In Russia, as in the rest of Europe, the woman question did not emerge from among the ranks of working and peasant women. Except as the distant objects of revolutionary vision, the female masses at the bottom of the social order played almost no role in the women's movement until the beginning of the twentieth century. The impulses of self-emancipation in Russia appeared first among educated gentry women. Until the 1860's, they were almost the sole beneficiaries of the limited facilities for female education. After that, they dominated in numbers and influence both the legal feminist movement and the female sector of the underground revolutionary movement that emerged simultaneously with it. In both cases, the dominance persisted with only minor diminution almost up to the Revolution of 1917. The following pages present a brief sketch of the gentry woman, of the educational, legal, and domestic environment that served to fashion her way of life, and of the various modulations that public opinion about her underwent in the generations preceding her rather sudden awakening to consciousness in the midddle of the nineteenth century.

Russian education in the early nineteenth century was status-oriented, as it usually is in traditional societies. For women this meant an education "appropriate" to their future social roles and in accordance with their station, a view deeply rooted in European culture. It received classic articulation in the seventeenth century when Fénelon insisted that sex, with rank and function, be a determinant of how much and what kind of education a person received, and that girls be trained for modest wifehood, motherhood, and domestic concerns. This had obvious implications: first, that few women would be educated at all; second, that the education of these would be vocational training to prepare mothers, wives, and housekeepers of the privileged classes. The idea, fashioned for a landed, highly stratified class society, has proved to be one of the sturdiest principles of social conservatism.

3

In the Russian Empire, there was no higher or professional education for women until the 1870's. There was no secondary education for girls of all classes until the late 1850's. Between 1764 and 1858, secondary schools were few in number and accessible only to gentry girls and to a smattering of merchants' daughters. Private tutors, preferred by many gentry families, were more expensive. Of the two kinds of girls' "high schools"—to use the term loosely—those operated by the government (*instituty*) were the more exclusive. They were created in 1764 when Catherine II founded the Society for the Training of Well-Born Girls, with its headquarters in the old village of Smolny, then on the fringe of the capital. The attached school was known as Smolny Convent or Smolny Institute—ironically the headquarters of the Bolsheviks in 1917 and presently housing the Leningrad Party organization. Similar institutes, about twenty in all, sprang up in the main cities of the Empire. In the nineteenth century, these shelters of aristocratic Russian girlhood were not part of the Ministry of Education but, reflecting their august birth, of an imperial welfare complex known as the Charitable Institutions of Empress Mariya Fëdorovna, a division of the Imperial Chancery.

Daughters of the upper ranks of the military and the bureaucracy were eligible for admission to the institutes, one of the primary criteria being the service that the applicant's family had rendered to the Empire. A girl whose father had been killed in action was given preference in the best institutes—provided of course that the deceased hero had been well born and highly placed. Often enough, admission was gained merely on the basis of family name or influential connections, a situation hardly peculiar to Russia or to that time. Merchants and non-hereditary nobles could insinuate their offspring into certain institutes, but had to pay a fat tuition fee for the privilege of doing so. The enrollments were kept small and select. Smolny, queen of the institutes, graduated an average of seventy girls a year in its first century of existence. In addition to the institute, there was the private boarding school (*chastnyi zhenskii pansion*) modeled after the French *pension* or *pensionnat*. Most of these were owned and operated by foreign-born women who endeavored to emulate the class appeal of the government institutes.[1]

Education in both kinds of schools was artificial and remote from everyday life. Gogol, who had reason to know, was not merely being funny when he wrote in *Dead Souls*: "It is a well-established fact that a proper upbringing is obtained in boarding schools at which three subjects are considered the foundation of all human virtue: the French language, indispensable to family hap-

---

[1] Vladimir Ovtsyn, *Razvitie zhenskago obrazovaniya* (SPB, 1887); V. N. Lyadov, *Istoricheskii ocherk stoletnei zhizni Imperatorskago Vospitatelnago Obshchestva Blagorodnykh Devits* (SPB, 1864), a panegyric; D. Semënov, "Stoletie Smolnago Monastyrya," *Otechestvennye zapiski*, CLIV (May 1864) 288–409; and the articles "Zhenskoe obrazovanie" and "Instituty zhenskie" in *Entsiklopedicheskii slovar* (Brokgaus-Efron), XII (XIA) 867 and XXV (XIII) 245.

4

piness; the pianoforte, to afford pleasant moments to one's spouse; and, finally, the subject which touches directly upon the running of one's future
home—the knitting of purses and other presents with which to surprise one's
husband." Twenty years later, an institute graduate complained that things
had not improved appreciably since the time of Gogol. More like convents
than schools, the institutes and pensions allowed their charges almost no contact with the outside world except under the strictest supervision. They were
"closed institutions," lamented an elderly lawyer in 1906, "which strove to
fashion their pupils into 'ladies,' strangers to the reality of life and to serious
scholarly knowledge."[2]

In a personal memoir, written in the 1860's, a former *institutka* recalled the
aridity of the instruction, the institutionalized hostility toward enthusiasm for
learning or "inordinate curiosity," and the absence of any meaningful preparation for life, even in its simplest forms. The emphasis was on obedience,
strict adherence to the curriculum, and parietal rules. Violating the rule about
hair style brought loss of the Sunday visit with parents. Under such a regimen,
the memoirist observed, the young woman had lost her sense of family by the
time she had reached womanhood, but had failed to gain preparation for life.
Genuine pursuit of knowledge was frowned upon. "It got so bad finally," she
said, "that the pupils were not only lazy but prided themselves on it, putting
their idleness and insouciance on display." An institute pupil of a later period
was told by her teacher that "a well-educated girl needs above all to have
good manners and to speak French impeccably; this is the *sine qua non* of her
future happiness." Morality, she admonished, consisted in unconditional
obedience and keeping the hair uncoiffed.[3]

Women shaped in such a hothouse atmosphere hardly could be expected to
evince much passion for intellectual "self-development." The *institutka* was a
standing joke in Russian society, and the word became a veritable synonym
for the light-headed and ultra-naive female. Elena Ghica, the Russian-reared
Dalmatian princess who wrote under the name Dora d'Istria, observed that the
only aspiration held by ladies of the highest rank in Russian society was to be
close to the imperial presence; Kropotkin, who spent part of his childhood at
court, made the same observation. These were the values of the "best" ladies;
the level of consciousness possessed by their provincial cousins is well
known. Dora d'Istria tells of a ten-day sojourn at the home of a provincial

[2] The Andrew MacAndrew translation of *Dead Souls* (New York, 1961), p. 33; Nadezhda D.
[Destunis], "Chemu my, zhenshchiny, uchilis?" *Russkaya beseda*, 3 (1859) 21–50, 27; N. V.
Davydov, *Zhenshchina pered ugolovnym sudom* (Moscow, 1906) 5.

[3] M. Dol—eva [Dolgomosteva], "Institutki," *Epokha* (Oct. 1864) 1–40 (p. 40). A. L.
Lukonina, "Iz detstva i shkolnykh let," *Severnyi vestnik* (Feb. 1886) 65–96; (Mar. 1886) 94–
129; (Apr. 1886) 87–144 (quotation, Mar. 1886, 96). For similar episodes and judgments, see V.
Stoyunin in *Razsvet*, VII (1860) 21–31; N. A. Dobrolyubov, *Sobranie sochinenii*, 9 v., ed. B. I.
Bursov *et al.* (Moscow, 1961–1964) II, 363–65; and a review of Marko Vovchuk's "Institutka,"
Razsvet, VI (June 1860) 15–23.

lady friend—a deadly dull round of "female" functionless existence: sewing, cards, a walk, tea, bed.[4]

But education, after all, is a relative thing. In spite of the oppressive regimen and the rote learning—features by no means unique to Russia and to that age[5]—a number of girls who were bred in these hothouses transcended their limited training. Dora d'Istria, survived the deadening pall of institute life and became a well-known writer. She was not the only one. At the very least, institute pupils acquired there the reading and linguistic skills that enabled them, if they so desired, to acquire the fruits of Western culture, including its teaching about women's rights. A few of them rebelled wholly against their environment, devoured the best literature, journalistic and belletristic, and, after the fashion of their alienated brothers, discovered therein the frightening contrast between what was and what ought to be.

As in the rest of Europe, the well-born woman of early nineteenth-century Russia usually married a man of her own class, approved if not chosen by her parents. "We do not marry, but we are given in marriage," said Olga in Goncharov's *Oblomov*. This was not strictly true in law. Although the daughter was not permitted to marry without her parents' consent, she could not be coerced into a marriage she did not desire. In practice, of course, few women availed themselves of or even knew about this provision of the Russian code. The wedding ceremony was a sacrament of the Orthodox Church, solemn and binding, in the presence of God, family, and friends. Once married, the function of the bride was to care for her husband, oversee domestic affairs, and, most important, bear and rear children. "The education of children is the duty of the citizen," wrote Karamzin at the beginning of the century; it was the duty of both parents, and especially the mother "to rear worthy sons of the fatherland," a sentiment echoed in an 1827 marriage manual which stressed the maternal role of women and their duty in raising healthy, religious, service-minded patriots.[6]

"The woman must obey her husband, reside with him in love, respect, and unlimited obedience, and offer him every pleasantness and affection as the

[4] Dora d'Istria [Elena Koltsova-Masalskaya, née Ghica], *Les Femmes en Orient*, 2 v. (Zurich, 1859, 1860) II (*La Russie*), 94–95, 107–109; Peter Kropotkin, *Memoirs of a Revolutionist*, ed. J. A. Rogers (New York, 1962) 113.

[5] Compare, for example, the atmosphere at Lowood, the girls' school in Charlotte Brontë's *Jane Eyre*, with that described in these Russian memoirs: "If Bessie's accounts of school-discipline . . . were somewhat appalling, her details of certain accomplishments, attained by these same young ladies were, I thought, equally attractive. She boasted of beautiful paintings of landscapes and flowers by them executed; of songs they could sing and pieces they could play, of purses they could net, of French books they could translate" (ch. 3).

[6] *Svod zakonov Rossiiskoi Imperii*, 16 v. in 2, ed. I. D. Mordukhai-Boltovsky (SPB, 1912). Volume X, on women, children, and the family, is the 1887 version. See cols. 1–3. *Zhenskoe pravo* (SPB, 1873) 98–108 reproduces relevant sections of the earlier code on women's rights. Karamzin quoted by Stoyunin in *Vestnik Evropy* (Jan. 1884) 67. The manual: Illarion Vasilev, *Femida* (Moscow, 1827).

6

ruler of the household." This article from the 1836 Code of Russian Laws, resounding like the fundamental law of an absolute monarchy, was the legal basis of the subservience of married women to their husbands in nineteenth-century Russia. The wife was obliged to conform to her spouse's wishes while under his roof, to cohabit with him, and also to accompany him wherever he happened to go or be sent. The only exception to this was when a husband was branded as a criminal, stripped of his civil rights, and sent to Siberia; in such cases the wife had the right to refuse to accompany him into exile. But she had almost no separate civil identity; without her husband's express permission, she could not work, study, trade, or travel. The noble husband, needless to say, possessed his own passport and suffered no such restrictions. Before marriage, the girl's movements and activities were similarly guarded by her parents, particularly the father.[7] In many ways, the wife-daughter's status under the husband-father was analogous to that of the landlord's serf.

The only escape from marriage, aside from death or arrest, was divorce. Since the time of Peter the Great, the church had increased its influence in marital affairs and gradually had tightened up the bonds of holy matrimony. The only grounds for its dissolution were sexual impotence over a period of three years, adultery as proven by witnesses, five years unexplained absence of a spouse, or deprivation of civil rights. For most Russians, even of the upper classes, the lumbering, expensive, and publicity-laden divorce proceedings were much too agonizing to go through—and for women virtually impossible.[8]

But again, if we view women's status from a more spacious perspective, we perceive at once that the Russian woman was not unique in her lack of mobility and her absence of rights. European codes, many of them modeled on the influential Code Napoléon, exerted similar coercion and control of women, married and single alike. There was, of course, great variation in practice. The feverish economic growth and the loosening of class distinctions allowed the side-stepping of legal blocks to female employment and mobility in Western Europe before they did so in Russia, but the offensive laws were there, capable of being invoked at any time. Moreover, the juridical status of the Russian woman was superior to most of her European sisters in one important respect: that of property and inheritance rights. A wife could possess her own property and inherit from her husband one-seventh of his real and one-fourth of his movable property. Daughters also inherited, though not on an equal basis with sons. These provisions of the laws contrasted sharply with

[7] *Zhenskoe pravo*, 110–111. But again, in practice, it was not always possible for the husband to enforce the law of cohabitation. On this see Ya. Orovich [Kantorovich], *Zhenshchina v prave*, 3d ed. (SPB, n.d. 1895) 92.

[8] *Svod zakonov*, X, arts. 45–60. For the development of divorce custom see: A. D. Sposobin, *O razvode v Rossii* (Moscow, 1881); M. A. Filippov, "Vzglyad na russkie grazhdanskie zakony," *Sovremennik*, XV (Feb. 1861) 523–62 and (Mar. 1861) 217–66; L. N. Zagursky, *Rechi* (Kharkov, 1904), 159–204.

those of most European countries where female rights to property were severely curtailed or nonexistent. Opponents of women's liberation in Russia often alluded to these laws as "proof" that their women did not need it.[9]

There will be, in the coming pages, occasional references to the so-called "domestic despotism" in the Russian family. There were landlords like Sergei Aksakov's grandfather and officials like General Perovsky (the father of Sofya) who tyrannized their families and servants. But it is a distortion to view the typical gentry family as a prison, with the father holding unlimited sway over his cowering household. There are too many indications in literature and in memoirs of families headed by a kind and cultivated country squire—Kirsanov of Turgenev's *Fathers and Children*, for example—who is warm and benevolent to his servants and relations. And numerous gentry husbands were effectively ruled by domineering wives. The plays of Alexander Ostrovsky, inspired chiefly by life in the Moscow merchant quarter, have all too often been cited as images of family despotism among all classes. The true despotism in the gentry family was juridical and potential rather than pervasive. It came into prominence on a large scale only in the 1860's when the wishes of a wife or daughter who wanted to work and study came into conflict with the power of the head of the family. At that moment, we shall see many an omnipotent despot worsted by his humble subjects.

A word about gentry women who did not marry. Whatever one might, from our present-day vantage point, imagine about the agonizing nature of married life under the unequal conditions described above, one would have to concede that the lot of the "old maid" was worse. Certainly it was in the eyes of society. *Ne zhenat, ne chelovek*, the Russian saying goes; not married, not human. And though the saying refers to bachelorhood, the object of real pity in Russian society, as in most, was the unmarried female rather than the male. The maiden "Auntie" was a familiar figure on the social landscape, and the literature is full of references to her eccentricities and foibles. D. M. Wallace, a British observer of Russian life, tells about the maiden aunt of the old school who whiled away her time playing patience and predicting the advent of a stranger or the imminent occurrence of a wedding. Sofya Kovalevskaya, the well-known mathematician, described with sad irony the departure of her old English governess with her "battery of little boxes, little baskets, little bags, and little parcels, without which no old maid can set out on a journey." But most Russians seemed to sense, with a humanity not often displayed elsewhere, that the quirks of the old maid were her substitute for sexual life.

[9] *Zhenskoe pravo*, 168–81; Orovich, *Zhenshchina*, 102; V. I. Sinaisky, *Lichnee i im-ushchestvennoe polozhenie zamuzhnei zhenshchin* (Dorpat, 1910) 42; Jerome Blum, *Lord and Peasant in Russia from the Ninth to the Nineteenth Century* (New York, 1964) 41, 378. Property disabilities of married women in Europe and America are discussed in Orovich, *Zhenshchina*, 29–31 and throughout Theodore Stanton, ed., *The Woman Question in Europe* (New York, 1884). A favorite example used by smug Russian anti-feminists was England where, until the Married Woman's Property Act of 1882, wives were wholly propertyless.

However patronizing married folk were to unmarried women, the latter usually were well provided for by their families and were often a permanent member of the ménage.[10]

The childhood of a girl in a gentry family was a dream-world. She played with girlish toys, skated, went mushrooming in summer, sleigh-riding in winter, and occasionally broke unwanted into her brothers' game of Cossacks and Bandits. She learned Russian from her nurse, a house-serf, and French from her governess, who also taught her to sew, to sing, to plunk out little Schubert songs on the piano. The world was her father's estate; its capital the manor house. Its sovereign, at once kind, awesome, and stern, was a distant and mysterious man whom she seldom saw. With her mother there was more contact, though little enough—and never enough for the child to learn the intimate secrets of life. The pitiful and typical sister-in-law of Anna Karenina, Dolly Oblonskaya, poignantly recalled her own experience, "With *maman's* upbringing," she said, "I was not merely innocent, I was stupid. I knew nothing."[11]

One of the psychological byproducts of the relative absence of contact between daughter and parents might have been a development in many young girls of a feeling of "otherness." By this is meant not simply isolation or alienation from family nurture but also a turning toward others for intimate friendship and ego support. In the structure of middle and well-off gentry household, this meant nannies, nursemaids, and other servants. Excessive neglect or formal manipulation by parents (and tutors) led many a gentry child into the consoling arms of his or her favorite domestic, who would frequently provide the warm and unstructured pampering that sensitive children sometimes need. We hear of this relationship again and again in the childhood memoirs of Russian women. In return for this affection, the child would often "side with" the servants in cases of friction between the household authorities, usually the mother and father. As we shall see later, a good many Russian women raised in a manorial environment experienced the first delicious and painful impulses of altruism through the mechanism of "social daydreaming"—fantasies in which the privileged gentry girl comes to the aid of the oppressed, and defends them against the common enemy: cold and loveless authority. The mechanism was complex and led in diverse directions—not only radical ones; but its prevalence raises some interesting problems about the relationship of upbringing and society as a whole.[12]

[10] Donald Mackenzie Wallace, *Russia on the Eve of War and Revolution*, ed. Cyril Black (New York, 1961) 124–25; Sofya Kovalevskaya, *Vospominaniya detstva i avtobiograficheskie ocherki* (Moscow, 1945) 74.

[11] Leo Tolstoy, *Anna Karenin*, tr. Rosemary Edmonds (Harmondsworth, Middlesex, England, 1954) 82.

[12] For related speculation on this topic, see Patrick P. Dunn, " 'That Enemy is the Baby': Childhood in Imperial Russia," in Lloyd de Mause, ed., *The History of Childhood* (New York, 1975) 383–406. Cf. the childhood recollections of, for example, Vera Zasulich, Sofya

Unless tutored at home, eight crucial years of the gentry girl's life, from age ten to eighteen, were spent in an institute or its equivalent. Here she learned some arithmetic, "the law of God," and a few domestic skills; here she perfected her French and was introduced to upper-class notions of dress, the dance, and social behavior. Deprived of its natural object, the parents, her adolescent urge to love was deflected into pathetic and innocent "crushes" on teachers and older pupils. At eighteen, her "finishing" was complete: having entered school a child, she returned to her estate a *baryshnya*—a young lady, or, in the affectionate and gently scornful epithet of the time, a "bread-and-butter miss." Resembling like nothing else the Southern Belle of the American plantation—sweet and helpless, child-like, and surrounded by the most capacious crinolines—she awaited her first ball, her first dance, her first taste of life.

But in the years between graduation and marriage, life was still a reverie as she wafted between two worlds that she did not know: beneath her, the servants and the serfs, always there but unreal and of a different species; beyond her, the world of men, of wars, of "affairs." Even if she had journeyed to the spas of Europe, those worlds were beyond her ken. Thus suspended between girlhood and womanhood, she was enveloped by a sense of malaise and anticipation. She was ready for life. In coming generations her adolescent counterparts would construct elaborate visions of the future—"social daydreams" inspired by the daily spectacle of the suffering and inequality that surrounded them. But in more tranquil times, the spell could be broken only by a man. Usually it was one of the dashing young officers who passed through her parents' drawing room. "The Count and the Countess," wrote Kovalevskaya in a fictional portrait of a gentry family, "knew that in good time, in two to three years, some Hussar or Dragoon would inevitably appear on the scene and take Lena away; then, a little later, another Hussar would take Liza. Then would come Vera's turn."[13] And so it went. If the supply of officers was low, then local landowners, her brother's student friend, or Rudin-like talkers from the city would be marshaled. In the end, she would marry: seldom to someone below her rank, and just as seldom to the first romance of her youth.

After the wedding, the bride would throw herself sincerely into the game of matrimony, thoroughly enjoying the first year or so of freedom from the family and her sense of authority as chatelaine of her new domestic empire, however modest it might be. Children would be born regularly, and life would become a busy round of hiring domestics, overseeing the education of her young, and entertaining her husband's friends. On reaching thirty, she would likely feel a vague sense of longing for the lost romance of her youth. If circumstances and income permitted, she might find compensation for this and a

---

Kovalevskaya, Catherine Breshkovskaya, Angelica Balabanoff, and Alexandra Kollontai cited in the following chapters.

[13] Kovalevskaya, *Vospominaniia detstva; Nigilistka* (Moscow 1960) 146.

degree of personal fulfillment by hurling herself into society—by becoming a "woman of the world":

> What does she think about? [asks Sollogub in his *Life of a Woman of the World*] She thinks that Lyadov plays the violin well, that the color pink becomes her, that in such a shop she can get such a gown, that this woman has beautiful jewelry, that this man used to pursue her, that one still does, and a third soon will. Sometimes her tedious domestic concerns confuse her. But she does not think about them—nor does she want to. Home to her is a strange place. She has no home. Her home, her very life is the world: restless, stylish, garrulous, dancing, frolicking, glorious, troubled, and trivial. This is her sphere, her lot, her purpose in life.[14]

Outside Petersburg and Moscow, few Russian ladies could become "women of the world," for there was little of the glitter of society even in the provincial capitals. Life would be confined largely to home, to guests, and to visits with other families on name days and holy days. Indeed the world of the *barynya* had broadened but little since her dreamy days as a *baryshnya*. At most, the languid musings of her youth might give way to a bittersweet nostalgia and to a gnawing awareness that something had passed her by. That "something" would later be defined and redefined by her daughters and granddaughters as life, work, knowledge, freedom, or action. But the gentry woman of pre-reform Russia, though often possessed of great will and strong character, was not yet ready to give voice to her feelings in terms of the terrible question which heralds the beginning of woman's consciousness: Is there nothing more to life?

2. CHANGING IMAGES

By the middle of the seventeenth century, the popular image of the Russian woman of whatever class had reached the antipode of what the liberators would require that image to be two centuries later. Although there is evidence that many Russian women of the pre-Kievan and Kievan periods had possessed a certain amount of prestige, power, and even equality in a number of endeavors, including military ones, all this had disappeared in the centuries of Muscovite rule. The sources do not tell us exactly when, how, and why this relatively important change had taken place. Historians generally agree that the tendency began taking shape in the thirteenth century and became rigid in the sixteenth century; and that its cause was a combination of the spread of the Byzantine church tradition and the "militarization" of Muscovite society resulting from the so-called Tatar Yoke. Most sources and interpretations agree, however, that by the end of the period man's working perception of women was that they were impure by nature and thus a standing temptation to sinful-

---

[14] V. A. Sollogub, *Zhizn svetskoi zhenshchiny*, quoted by Dobrolyubov in *Soch.*, I, 535.

11

ness; were inferior in every possible way to men; were best kept isolated from the outside world and subservient to husband or father; and had as their principal function the satisfaction of man's natural desires and the bearing of children.[1]

The doctrine of the impurity of the female sex was implicit in Byzantine Christianity and was transferred gradually to Russia after the conversion. Slavic Orthodox Christianity, like its Byzantine model, taught that coitus was unclean: the icons had to be covered during the act and ablutions made after it. And there was no question that the uncleanness arose from the female sexual organs rather than from the male. After parturition or menstruation, an interval had to elapse before the woman was permitted entry into a house of worship. The Russians were hardly different from other medieval people in fearing, despising, and at the same time, being greatly attracted to the place from where they all issued.[2]

The corollary, though hardly logical, to the notion of feminine impurity was the universal belief that women were inferior to men. Gone were the pre-Kievan days when Amazons, and later Slavic women, marched out to battle the foes of the steppe. Among the upper classes, the family became the only focus for the Russian female. And within the family, she sat lowest on the scale. Love your wife but give her no power over you—the defensive words of Vladimir Monomakh (a twelfth-century ruler of Kiev)—were translated into the Domostroi's advice to beat her and give her no power at all. The harsh judgment of *The Bee*, the misogynous Byzantine collection that appeared in Russia in the twelfth century proclaiming that "a bad man is always better than a good woman" was imparted to a score of Russian popular sayings.[3]

The social institution which embodied these ideas was the Terem, the female quarter, or tower, of the houses of the well-to-do. Such elaborate architectural proof of the inferiority and untouchability of women was, of

---

[1] The relevant sources for the Muscovite period, Herberstein, Fletcher, Kotoshikhin, and the rest, are discussed in N. I. Kostomarov, *Ocherk domashnei zhizni i nravov velikorusskago naroda v XVI i XVII stoletiyakh* (SPB, 1860). See also the Stoyunin article cited above, VE, XIX (Jan. 1884) 22ff.; I. E. Zabelin, "Zhenshchina po ponyatom starinnykh knizhnikov," *Russkii vestnik*, IX (1857) 5–47; A. Shchapov, "Polozhenie zhenshchin v Rossii do-petrovskomu vozzreniyu," *Soch.*, II, 105–53. The most informed and intelligent discussion in English is Dorothy Atkinson, "Society and the Sexes in the Russian Past," in D. Atkinson, A. Dallin, and Gail Lapidus, eds., *Women in Russia* (Stanford, 1977).

[2] An introduction to the influence of Byzantine Christianity on Russian socio-religious customs is G. P. Fedotov, *The Russian Religious Mind: Kievan Christianity, the 10th to the 13th Centuries* (New York, 1960).

[3] V. Shulgin, *O sostoyanii zhenshchin v Rossii do Petra Velikago: istoricheskoe isledovanie* (Kiev, 1850) 4–67; E. N. Shchepkina, *Iz istorii zhenskoi lichnosti v Rossii* (SPB, 1914) 17–27; C. Claus, *Die Stellung der russischen Frau von der Einführung des Christentums bei den Russen bis zu den Reformen Peter des Grossen* (Munich: Doctoral Dissertation Microcopy, Basel University, 1959) 53–54; P. Grimal, ed., *Histoire mondiale de la femme*, 4 v. (Paris, 1965–1967) III, ch. 2 (A. Gieysztor "La femme dans la civilisation des peuples slaves") 11–43.

course, far beyond the means of the lowly peasant and he was content to prove his point by clubbing his wife with a bottle from time to time or breaking her teeth with his fists. But for him who could afford it, the Terem served to keep the womenfolk out of harm's way, out of his own way mostly; and even as a place of exile or imprisonment when the need arose. There was none of this in pagan times, but with the advent of Christianity, women were isolated from the men in the churches. Later, probably in the twelfth century, this was extended to the home. The word itself was not, as has sometimes been stated, borrowed from the Tatars; although they, as Muslims also practiced seclusion and masking of women. The custom as well as the term is Greek, coming from the Byzantine practice of "rigorous seclusion of women in polite society." Their word *teremnon* meant home or house or building; in Russian it became both *tyurma* (prison) and *terem* (keep or tower of a lord). The original term *zhenskii terem*, women's tower, was a section of the house reserved for them. It was probably used as much to protect women from the dissolute habits of the menfolk in the family as it was to quarantine the morally contagious females from the rest of the world.[4]

From all this flowed the general principle that girls and women should do less, be less, and get less (as inheritance, for example) than men or boys. From the principle came the practice, prevalent among boyar, merchant, and peasant, of treating the wife, or its equivalent, as nothing more than a *samka*, a brood mare upon whom the sexual act could be performed at any hour. It is little wonder that the women themselves, conditioned by their masters, began behaving in a manner as dissolute as the men.

It would be wrong to date the beginning of a "woman question" from the time of Peter the Great's reforms. But it is undeniable that its emergence was impossible without the social bases laid down by him. In this case the foundation was imported European culture and custom. However superficial and eclectic the borrowing, and however narrow the base, upon it was built a very thin stratum of educated and cultivated Russian men and women. The subsequent development of woman's self-awareness and of man's image of woman was to be conditioned closely by the kind, the volume, and the origin of the "culture" imported into Russia from Europe. In less than a century, the isolated and inferior sexual chattel of the boyars was transmuted into the sociable, well-mannered, respected—even exalted—Russian lady, and in another half-century, even the cloying notion of inferiority-in-all-but-morals was being assaulted.

Peter's innovations were designed to reduce the glaring differences between Russian domestic customs (*byt*, or "way of life") and those of Western

---

[4] For the terem, see the sources listed above; *The Cambridge Medieval History*, v. IV, *The Byzantine Empire*, pt. II, 88–91; V. Dal, *Tolkovaya slovar zhivago velikorusskago yazyka*, 3d ed. 4 v. (SPB, 1903–1909) IV, 751–52; D. N. Ushakov, *Tolkovyi slovar russkago yazyka* 4 v. (Moscow, 1934–1940) IV, 688.

Europe. Shortly after returning from Europe in 1700, he invited the leading figures of Russia of both sexes to mingle socially at evening affairs. Eighteen war-filled years later, he tried again, this time by fiat rather than invitation (the 1718 Decree on Assemblies). On December 2 of that year "Messieurs et Mesdames"—as the hefty boyars and their ladies were quaintly called—were invited to Peter's residence where they danced and chatted away uncomfortably until eleven o'clock. Other such events followed, although the habit of socializing publicly with the opposite sex was adopted at first with great pain and reluctance. The de-isolation of women had begun, but much beyond this Peter could not go, try as he might. A decree of 1702 required brides-to-be to have a six-week period of personal acquaintance with their betrothed before the wedding; another of 1714 prohibited mate selection by parents without consent of the parties involved. Peter opened no schools for girls though he did send his own offspring abroad to be educated, a gesture that a few members of the *dvoryanstvo* (gentry) copied. The really lasting educational technique introduced by Peter was the employment of foreign governesses and tutors for well-born girls.[5]

From this point on, Russian women of the now well-defined gentry class began to share attitudes and social values as well as the costumes of their Europeanized husbands. In the best circles, the refined manners and fashionable gowns of western cities and courts were quickly donned. After about 1750 Russian women delved more deeply into the trunk of European ways and discovered salon free thinking and subtle flirtation—*zhenskaya intriga* as it was called. By then France had become the major supplier of imported cultural and life-style commodities, and the courtiers and courtesans of Versailles became the models for the leisured classes of Russia. This in turn wrought a profound change in the "official" attitudes of men toward the female sex. Instead of sex objects to be rudely thrown into bed at the command of desire, they were now deft and delicate prey to be conquered in games of intrigue and "dangerous liaisons." Many good Russians, notably Prince Shcherbatov, thought the new version of Russian womanhood much worse than the old one.[6]

The history of eighteenth-century Russia was studded with examples of telescoped development and sociologically freakish phenomena. One of these was the number of highly educated women of European culture. Beginning in the age of Empress Elizabeth and reaching their numerical zenith during the reign of Catherine II, scores of well-read, witty, polyglot, literary-minded women appeared in both the capitals, eagerly emulating the Russian gentle-

---

[5] Z. Librovich, *Pëtr Velikii i zhenshchiny* (SPB, 1904) 100–13; Stoyunin's article in VE (1884) 30ff.

[6] M. Kuznetsov, *Prostitutsiya i siflis v Rossii* (SPB, 1871) 54–55; D. Mordovtsev, *Russkiya zhenshchiny novago vremeni* 3 v. (SPB, 1874) I, xii–xiii; Librovich, *Pëtr*, 115–18; Shchapov *Sochineniya*, 3 v. (SPB, 1906–1908) III, 590ff.

men who sought to be more Gallic than the Gauls. Catherine, herself a foreigner, became the model for women who aspired to reach the very heights of European culture and learning—although the learning was often superficial and was acquired more for social than for creative purposes. Princess Dashkova, whom the tsarina appointed as president of the Academy of Science in 1782, was only the most spectacular and highly placed of this bright cluster of women. Their ready erudition became so renowned that foreign visitors were willing to testify, at the end of the century, that women in Russian high society tended to be better read and generally more cultivated than men.

But, like much else in the Russian enlightenment, the appearance was misleading and the promise deceptive. Catherine and Dashkova were both self-taught, and most of the brilliant women of the salons were privately tutored by expensive imported personnel. Although women of high culture were exceptionally visible to those who traversed the orbit of the Russian *haut monde*, their numbers were really minute. They were in no way representative even of gentry women as a whole. Elena Likhachëva's monumental study of women's education in the eighteenth century shows that Russian society had little interest in it at the beginning of Catherine's reign and practically none at the end of it. And the institutes, though multiplying in number, continued to turn out naive bread-and-butter misses whose only purpose in attending school, as far as the public was concerned, was learning "savoir vivre," in the patrician sense of the term. Moreover, with the onset of the sentimental romantic movement in literature, launched by Karamzin in the 1790's and followed closely by a resurgence of conservative, religious, and national thought and feeling, the whole idea of the flashy and witty lady of learning became somewhat repugnant to the official custodians of society's new moral ethos. The ideal woman, said Karamzin in 1802, "does not blind you at first glance, for her mind is not so much brilliant as it is refined and solid. She is sufficiently vibrant, charming, and ready with a sharp reply; but all this is concealed beneath a veneer of incomparable diffidence." Society belles, salon wits, and even women writers continued to grace gentry drawing rooms, but they would know their limits and their place. In Russia, as in the rest of Europe, both the erotic and the ultra-intellectual sides of woman—recently exalted—were now to be subordinated to her more "natural" role.[7]

The early nineteenth century witnessed a conscious attempt by Russia to reject "French" values. With the rejection came a romantic idealization of the Russian woman as the embodiment of Virtue and Maternity. Fidelity rather than intrigue became her hallmark. Pushkin's heroine, Tatyana, in the poem *Eugene Onegin*, has often been cited by critics as the purest example of this

---

[7] E. Likhachëva, *Materialy dlya istorii zhenskago obrazovaniya v Rossii, (1086–1796)* (SPB, 1890) chs. 3–10 and *1796–1828* (SPB, 1893) (Karamzin quotation, p. 267).

ideal. "To another husband I am tied/And stand forever by his side" are her last words in rejecting the tardy attentions of Onegin whom she still loves. Dostoevsky called Tatyana the apotheosis of duty and constancy, the chief virtues of the Russian woman. The woman as "citizen-mother," the bearer and molder of patriotic sons-of-the-fatherland was another aspect of this image. Woman's influence, said a popular translation of a pious English tract, was wrought through raising children and infusing men with modesty and propriety. Glorying in the great honor women held in the society of his day (1850), the historian Shulgin wrote that woman "was a representative of morality, love, modesty, and constancy"; while man represented "law, duty, honor, thought."[8]

The official exaltation of Russian female purity was adopted, indeed taken to its metaphysical limits, by some of the earliest representatives of the Russian intelligentsia. By then German idealism and romanticism had come to exercise an overwhelming influence on Russian thought and feelings. From organicism in legal philosophy and historicism in the social sciences to the bohemianism of E.T.A. Hoffman and the *Schönseeligkeit* of Schiller in literature, German thought seeped into every pore of the consciousness of Russian educated society. Goethe's "elective affinities," Schiller's "Beautiful Soul," and Fichte's metaphysical concept of love, as expressed in *Die Anweisung zum seligen Leben* (1806), were among the major currents of philosophical idealism, emotional religiosity, and imaginative romanticism that reached Russia by 1830. The German idea-world appealed mightily to the delicate mystic, Nikolai Stankevich, and his Moscow circle. The compulsion to embrace all living experience in terms of an "absolute" led Stankevich and his most exalted and emotionally volatile disciple, Mikhail Bakunin, to view love between a man and a woman as no more and no less than parts of some collective consciousness of the absolute.[9]

In practice, this meant that privacy in love was somehow identified with the atomism and egoism of the rational tradition that the Russians were in the process of repudiating. Love, in order to be real, that is whole, had to transcend the ordinary pleasures of the man-woman relationship; and to insure its wholeness and purity, it had to be subjected to the literal soul-searching of one's fellow metaphysicians of love. The result of such totalism in the realm of individual love and personal relationships—a realm scarcely fitted for the eyes of peering exaltés—was a series of tragicomic and stillborn love affairs, bewildering in their complexity, distressing in their futility. Stankevich, for whom love "was above all a world-force which has endowed the world and its inhabitants with life," was unable to cope with the physical presences that housed the "beautiful souls" of his attachments and he escaped abroad.

---

[8] F. M. Dostoevsky, *Pushkin* (SPB, 1899) 9; *Prizvanie zhenshchiny*, tr. from English (anon.) (SPB, 1840) 67; Shulgin, *O sostoyanii*, iii–v.

[9] M. Gershenzon, *Istoriya molodoi Rossii* (Moscow, 1923) ch. III; for Stankevich, 182–209.

Bakunin, who was apparently incapable of normal sexual life, destroyed, in the name of the absolute, his own, his sisters', and Stankevich's affairs of love in the same devastating manner in which he would later, in the name of anarchism, set out to destroy God, the state, the church, and private property. For him, love was "a reward for the objective activity of men"; and "love existing outside general conditions must necessarily be either a *poussée* of sensualism or a phantom and morbid sentiment."[10]

The lofty notion of love as a metaphysical web that must embrace all beings (as well as the Absolute) clearly had little to do with any idea of the emancipation of women. Although it could be argued that the doctrines of the Stankevich circle implied the complete equality of men and women at the very highest levels (that is, in the realm of holy feeling), there could be few practical consequences to what was essentially a philosophy of nonaction. The deification of woman and the worship of her soul could take little account of her more conventional socio-sexual needs, to say nothing of a more ambitious program of human fulfillment. Woman was gripped in "romantic immobility" in the words of Nestor Kotlyarevsky, who summed up the male image of her in the Russian literature of this age:

> She spoke little or not at all, but rather whispered or sang. The meaning of her words in song and speech was unclear, but in them one could feel much sadness. Why? Who can say. In any case it was not her lack of equal rights which saddened her. Her gentle grief was not of this earth, but it was as if she yearned after some distant mountainous clime. To earth's matters, except for love, she was indifferent; ready for any sacrifice, she never initiated any but went where she was led in humble submission. In the end she preferred to perish early, exchanging terrestrial life for heaven, and in the full flower of her strength already hinted at the immiment parting.[11]

Although German idealism continued to inflict its "metaphysical pogroms" upon the Russian mind for a while longer, the 1840's witnessed a gradual return of French intellectual influence to Russia. French thought at that moment was immersed deeply in "the social question." Whether expressed in blueprints for harnessing the new industrialism to social justice, as with the romantic utopian socialists; or in novels with a heavy strain of anti-bourgeois social criticism, such as those of Balzac, Hugo, and Sand; or simply in the frantic attempts to infuse traditional Catholicism with new elements of social and political consciousness, French "ideology" began increasingly to dispel

[10] The personal details are given in E. H. Carr, *Michael Bakunin* (New York, Vintage, 1961) 20–61. Quotations: P. Milyukov, *Iz istorii russkoi intelligentsii* (SPB, 1902) 76; B.-P. Hepner, *Bakounine et le panslavisme révolutionaire* (Paris, 1950) 113.

[11] N. Kotlyarevsky, "Zhenshchina shestidesyatykh godov," *Sbornik pamyati Anny Pavlovny Filosofovoi*, 2 v. (Petrograd, 1915) II, 77. For the social impotence of the Stankevich worldoutlook, see A. Veselovsky, *Zapadnoe vliyanie v novoi russkoi literature*, 5th ed. (Moscow, 1916) 224.

the murky vapors of Germanic philosophy that hung over much of Europe, and to serve as inspiration to social thinkers all over the continent.

French writers of the period, particularly the Utopians, paid a good deal of attention to the problem of women's emancipation. Out of the bizarre and fantastic assortment of ideas on the subject offered up by the social dreamers of those days, two notions stand out as most problematic for the future: "rehabilitation of the flesh" and "rehabilitation of the heart." The former was associated with the so-called Saint-Simonians, disciples of the departed Claude-Henri de Saint-Simon, who formed a well-organized and highly effective propaganda circle in the early years of the July Monarchy. Their leader, a young man of some wealth and education calling himself Father Enfantin, wore a Christ-like beard in an age of the shaven chin; preached religious collectivism in a secular age of unfolding competition; and asked for honesty and equality between the sexes in the classic era of bourgeois hypocrisy. Building on Saint-Simon, Enfantin elaborated a form of mystical socialism not uncommon in that era of social experimentation and quasi-religious ardor.

Enfantin's central idea was "rehabilitation of the flesh"—the need to reaffirm the nature of man as a sensual creature and to negate the ascetic model that Christianity, since Augustine, had tried to impose upon its believers. Criticizing "bourgeois" marriage as a hypocritical farce in which one half dominated the other, Enfantin proposed complete equality between the sexes. It was not true, he said, that men were the sensualists, requiring variety in sexual life in contrast to fundamentally monogamous women. Rather, mankind was divided into two major psychosexual types—Othello and Don Juan—which cut across sex lines. Othello types were loyal to a single mate, Don Juans in constant need of new liaisons. Why then, asked Enfantin, shouldn't the new social order cater to this basic need of mankind: an adequate sexual existence in consonance with a person's own particular nature? Othellos would presumably care for themselves, after proper matching. But for Don Juan men and women Enfantin envisaged a Priest Couple, a kind of male-female sexual coadjutator who would "regulate, sanctify, and lubricate the relations of the sexes through the grace of abandon." Further particulars on the place of marriage in society and definitive answers to other questions raised by his suggestions, Enfantin categorically refused to offer. They would have to await the appearance of his counterpart—the other half of the supreme priest couple, so to speak, a "woman messiah," who would herself answer these burning questions.[12]

It was hard for Europeans not to laugh at Enfantin and his weirdly costumed disciples of both sexes taking turns scrubbing the floors of their commune in Ménilmontant and performing neo-pagan rituals. Enfantin's chief rival,

[12] B. P. Enfantin and C. H. de Rouvroy, count de Saint-Simon, *Oeuvres*, 47 v. (Paris, 1865–1878), XIV (*Enseignements*) 23, 26–29, 39, 42, 148–52, 154–62. The standard older work on the Saint-Simonians is S. Charléty, *Histoire du Saint-Simonisme (1825–1864)*, 2d ed. (Paris, 1931).

Bazard, outraged by the former's advanced sexual program, withdrew from the sect and caused a serious schism; the police and Parisian ridicule did the rest, and the colony of Ménilmontant dispersed. In Russia, Enfantinism repelled not only the blunt-minded conservative, Faddei Bulgarin, but also a basically sympathetic soul, Alexander Herzen; and Enfantin had no disciples among the budding Russian intelligentsia.[13] But echoes of his carnal mysticism, after thorough purification by Nietzsche, can be heard at the end of the century among such mystical sensualists as Rozanov and others. More important, the tension between Enfantin and Bazard—both self-proclaimed advocates of woman's emancipation—was reflected also in Russian radicalism's attitude toward sex and its relation to emancipation. Lenin, as we shall see much later, was a fairly faithful preserver of the tradition of Bazard; and though we cannot really call Alexandra Kollontai the latter-day counterpart of Enfantin, it might be said that she was one of the few women in European history up to her time who would have satisfied his requirements for the woman messiah.

Of more immediate consequence for Russian life was "rehabilitation of the heart," the idea of freedom in love, vaguely and romantically formulated in the works of the novelist and publicist, George Sand. For Enfantin, passion of the flesh played the leading role; passion of the heart—love, affection, commitment—took care of itself. For George Sand, it was the opposite: the free expression of feeling—the spiritual and physical attraction that we clumsily try to define as love—was the burning necessity. Sex was simply the normal and necessary culmination of that feeling, whether before, after, or outside of marriage. In spite of what her critics said at the time, loveless promiscuity had no place in her teachings.[14]

Her sexual ideas and a sincere, if haphazard, socialist creed were exhibited in a series of extraordinarily popular novels and some articles in *Revue independante*, which she edited with the socialist Pierre Leroux. Beginning in 1836, her novels virtually flooded Russia and by the end of the reign of Nicholas I, were familiar fare to readers, male and female, of the "thick journals," then the leading medium for new ideas. Dostoevsky later recalled how, when he was sixteen years old, he had been put into a nocturnal fever after reading *Uscoque*. Characteristically, he was impressed most by those works that portrayed womanhood in colors of "elevated moral purity," recognition of duty, pride of chastity, hatred of compromise, and thirst for sacrifice—precisely those traits that the intelligentsia came to revere in Russian women.

[13] The commune at Ménilmontant: *Rétraite de Ménilmontant* (1832) in Enfantin and Saint-Simon, *Oeuvres*, VII, 94–133; Bulgarin's comments: *Biblioteka dlya chteniya*, VI (1834) 88–99, a masterpiece of boring invective.

[14] The standard biography is by a Russian, Wladimire Karénine (the pseudonym for Varvara Komarova), *George Sand*, 4 v. (Paris, 1899–1924); the Russian original, *Zhorzh Sand* (SPB, 1899–). For her influence in Russia, see K. Skalkovsky, "Zhorzh Sand," *Razsvet*, XI (1861) 353–80; Veselovsky, *Zapadnoe vliyanie*, 225ff.; N. Venkstern *Zhorzh Sand* (Moscow, 1923).

Vladimir Pechërin admired her religiosity and the stoic virtue of her characters, admitting that she had a "decisive influence" on his conversion to Roman Catholicism. The "westernizers" Belinsky, Herzen, and Bakunin came to revere Sand as a new kind of socialist Christian savior. Their friend Botkin called her a female Christ.[15]

But it was not so much the moral sweetness or the sentimental populism that cast its spell on so many Russian writers of George Sand's generation. It was rather her fearless confrontation of the eternal and seemingly insoluble problem of the love triangle. In *Jacques* (1843), the hero sacrifices his own deep love, through suicide, in order to free his woman's heart for her beloved. *Jacques* became the prototype for a whole series of triangles, real and fictional, that Russian men and women managed to square, one way or another. In Druzhinin's *Polinka Saks*, the married heroine falls in love with an old flame and when given her freedom by the unselfish Saks, falls in love with him again, only to die of consumption as she realizes her "error." Avdeev's *Underwater Stone* treats the theme in a similar way. The most famous variants of the Jacques dilemma were Chernyshevsky's *What Is To Be Done?* and Sleptsov's *Step by Step*. It was not, of course, her solution to the problem which so impressed Russian writers and readers with George Sand. It was her relentless pursuit of happiness and emotional honesty for her heroines. Implicit in all her writings was the idea of the absolute right of a woman to the achievement of romantic fulfillment with the object of her love without regard to convention or public opinion.

How did Russian society react to the ideas of George Sand in the 1830's and 1840's? The first and least ambiguous response was conservative disapproval. The intrepid defenders of morality, Bulgarin and Grech, warned the reading public against Sand even before the appearance of her first novel in Russian translation. Senkovsky, another "reptile," called her Mrs. Egor Sand or Gospozha Speredka, a pun on her real name, Dudevant ("from the front"), and dwelled on sordid scandals about her affairs, her trousers, and her cigars. (Eighty years later, Western journalists would use similar devices to ridicule and defame the Bolshevik Alexandra Kollontai, often compared by enemies as well as admirers to George Sand.) Ridicule and fear would remain handy weapons of anti-feminist Russians from that moment onward. So would the refusal to distinguish radically different ideas in favor of woman's emancipation from one another.[16]

In Belinsky and Herzen we find a second viewpoint—that of the early Russian intelligentsia. Of that small but brilliant Moscow-based coterie of male social critics, only these two wrote anything worth noting on the emancipation

[15] Dostoevsky, *Diary of a Writer*, tr. B. Brasol, 2 v. (New York, 1949) I, 344–49; V. S. Pechërin, *Zamogilnye zapiski* (Moscow, 1932) 107–13; Carr, *The Romantic Exiles* (Harmondsworth, Middlesex, England, 1949) 74; P. V. Annenkov, *Literaturnye vospominaniya* (Moscow, 1960) 9.

[16] The anti-Sand campaign: S. S. Shashkov, *Sobranie sochinenii*, 2 v. (SPB, 1898) I, 484; Skalkovsky, "Zhorzh Sand."

of women. Vissarion Belinsky, at one stage of his tortured philosophical quest, was an arch-conservative worshiper of the Absolute who found reasoned order in the reality around him. But by the early 1840's, he had shifted abruptly and drastically on philosophical and, consequently, social questions. This shift was reflected in his modulating attitude to George Sand and the problems of love and marriage. As late as 1840, in pious outrage, he scornfully summarized what he took to be "the social teachings of the Saint-Simonians" as distilled in the novels of George Sand:

All differences between sexes must be abolished, allowing women into all the burdensome concerns and admitting her, along with men, to the exercise of civil obligations, and especially giving her the enviable right to change husbands for reasons of health. The unavoidable result of these profound and excellent ideas is the dissolution of the holy bonds of matrimony, parenthood, and family—in short, the total transformation of the state first into a beastly and outrageous orgy, and then into a phantom, fashioned out of words written on air.[17]

The "reptile press" could hardly have matched this effort of Belinsky to lump Enfantin together with Sand and to liken both of them with the residents of Sodom and Gomorrah.

But within a year he had turned full circle intellectually. "What humanity breathes in every line, every word of this writer of genius," he exclaimed of George Sand in 1841. He praised "her hatred for crude falseness legitimized by ignorance as well as her vital sympathy for the pure, however obscured by prejudices. George Sand is the advocate of woman just as Schiller was the advocate of mankind." For Belinsky, George Sand, the erstwhile courtesan, was now the accuser, the exposer, and the conscience of French society. Belinsky even adds a touch of Saint-Simonianism in a prediction made elsewhere in his writings: "When people become human and Christian, when society has at last allowed its ideal development, then there will be no more marriages. Away with these frightful bonds. Give us life, freedom." In the meantime, unions ought, he said, to be based upon mutual personal respect and equality of the partners. And this meant as much sexual freedom for women as for men. Belinsky stated plainly that neither woman nor man could live by love alone, and that woman deserved human rights broader than those given her in the kitchen and the boudoir, but about these rights and how to achieve them he said nothing.[18]

Alexander Herzen, an illegitimate child, thought more profoundly and ex-

---

[17] V. G. Belinsky, *Polnoe sobranie sochinenii*, 13 v. (Moscow, 1953-1959) III, 398. In another review of the same year, Belinsky was still of the opinion that women were made to be wives and mothers, and he opposed equality of the sexes. *Ibid.*, 493–94.

[18] *Ibid.*, V, 175–76; VII, 649; Martin Malia, *Alexander Herzen and the Birth of Russian Socialism* (Cambridge, Mass., 1961), 259 (Belinsky's words on marriage); Shashkov, *Soch.*, I, 851. Belinsky's scattered ideas on education for women are given in N. A. Konstantinov, *Istoriya pedagogiki*, 2d ed. (Moscow, 1959) 87–93.

tensively than Belinsky about love and the relations between the sexes. He was one of the first in Russia (1833) to comment intelligently on Enfantin's rehabilitation of the flesh. "These great words," he wrote, "contain a whole new world of new relationships among people—a healthy world, a world of spirit and beauty, a world which is naturally moral and thus morally pure. Much sneering has been done at the free woman, at the recognition of sensual demands—sneering which lends only dirty meanings to these words; our monastically debauched imagination fears the flesh and fears woman." But Herzen was repelled by the behavior of the colony at Ménilmontant and during the 1830's he retreated into the convoluted idea-world of the German romantics, particularly Schiller's *Schönseeligkeit* and its exaltation of woman. A Schillerian romantic web, binding the Herzens and the Ogarëvs with exotic emotional ties, was the result of this new direction. After its destruction and pathetic aftermath, Herzen, disillusioned with German idealism, discovered George Sand and, in Martin Malia's felicitous phrase, "Realism in Love."[19]

The chief literary fruit of this encounter was Herzen's novel, *Who Is To Blame?* (1846), whose plot was partly inspired by Sand's *Horace* (1842) and by *Jacques*. It was again the triangle, set in provincial Russia, wherein the "romantic" lover departs and the married principals are left to continue cohabitation in grief and boredom. The critique of matrimony implicit in the novel is supplemented by the author's diary entry of June 30, 1843:

> Marriage is not the result of love, but its Christian result; it brings with it the terrible responsibility of the education of children, of life in an organized family, etc. . . . In the future there will be no marriage, the wife will be freed from slavery; and what sort of word is wife anyway? Woman is so humiliated that, like an animal, she is called by the name of her master. Free relations between the sexes, the public education of children and the organization of property, morality, conscience, public opinion, and not the police—all this will define the details of family relationships.

And in his diary of the following year, Herzen leads woman even further from the traditional concerns of wedlock. In the new communal society, "woman will be more involved in general interests; she will be strengthened morally by education, she will not be so one-sidedly attached to the family."[20]

Here is everything, or almost everything, that one will find in Marx, Bebel, and their Russian followers up to the 1930's. Not only the programmatic dogma: freedom in sexual life, equality in those relationships including the right of the woman to retain her own name, the public rearing of children, and a role for woman in the common work of the new society; but also the unspo-

[19] Quotation: A. I. Herzen (Gertsen), *Sochineniya*, 9 v. (Moscow, 1955–1958), IV, 164. Malia, *Herzen*, 257–312; Carr, *Romantic Exiles*.

[20] Gertsen, *Kto vinovat?*, 2d. ed. (London, 1859). Herzen's diary entries: Malia, *Herzen*, 268, 274–75. For more on Sand and the Russian literary triangle, see M. Elizarova, "Zh.-Zand v russkoi kritike i literature," *Uchenye zapiski Moskovskogo Gosudarstvennogo Pedagogischeskogo Instituta im. V. I. Lenina*, XXXI, 5 (1941), *Kafedra Zapadnoi Literatury*, 41–63.

ken contradictions as well: abolition of marriage and comments on the family almost in the same breath and the absence of any clear idea of how woman will take up her role in society and how much of a role that will be. Herzen's diary entries did not add to the public debate on the emancipation of women; but the ideas he expressed gained currency and were shared by generations of the Russian intelligentsia. Few of them recognized how fatal those contradictions, first adumbrated by Herzen, were to be when it came time to piece together a new society.

The final reaction to George Sand was that of women themselves. This was varied. Its boldest form was the *zhorzhzandshchina*: a series of female exploits carried out in the name of individualism and "free feeling," a euphemism for adultery. Russian ladies, frustrated by an oppressive domestic regimen and nurtured, like Emma Bovary, on tales of romance and love in "Scottish cottages and Swiss chalets," fell headlong into the arms of seducers and casual conquerors. Armed with the half-digested ideas of George Sand, such women found it stylish to tear off the veil of hypocrisy and the chains of domestic "tyranny" for a little self-indulgence, all the while being considered chic and advanced. Alexandra Smirnova, wife of the governor of Kaluga in those days, complained in her memoirs that highborn ladies, after reading Sand, cavorted around Europe with Italian lovers and returned to Russia to don the mask of decency. Similar gossip was recorded in the recollections of Praskoviya Tatlina whose daughter became "infected with so-called George Sandist ideas." The novels as well as the ideas even penetrated the walls of that virginal sanctuary, Smolny, and, if we can credit the gossipy Smirnova, caused scandals and divorces when they were carried out again and applied to life by Smolny graduates.[21]

But the *zhorzhzandistka*, a comic type of the period, soon disappeared, leaving little in the way of general consciousness. The real worth of George Sand was the deepening of social and sexual awareness among sensitive women. One example of this was Nadezhda Stasova who recalled how she was captivated by Sand's works, "My sister and I, I recall, used to stay up all night reading her novels one after another, discussing and arguing about them until dawn. When one of us got tired reading, the other would continue so as not to stop in the middle of a book or article. We were brought up on her works." Like the men of the intelligentsia, she was impressed as much by the moral tone of the writer as by her naive unraveling of sexual problems. And Stasova, far from turning to promiscuity, later became a devoted and always prim founder of Russian feminism.[22]

Elena Gan, salon figure and writer of the 1840's, was only one of a

[21] Shashkov, *Soch.*, I, 849–50; "Zapiski Aleksandry Osipovny Smirnovoi," *Russkii arkhiv*, II, 5 (1895) 17–27 and III, 9 (1895) 77–90 (see 86); P. N. Tatlina, "Vospominaniya," *ibid.*, III, 10 (1899) 190–224 (*passim*); V. F. Botsyanovsky, "Zhorzh-Zand v Rossii," *Novyi zhurnal inostranoi literatury, isskustva, i nauki*, II, 4 (Apr. 1899) 2–11.

[22] Karenin, *Zhorzh-Zand*, I, 15–16. Karenin does not actually name the woman so affected by George Sand but her description clearly points to her aunt, Stasova.

number, larger than is commonly held, of cultivated women—the Bakunins, the Passeks, Pavlova, Rostopchina, and others—who passed the ordinary limits of women's consciousness of their age to look at the larger world around them. "Like strange exotic plants," wrote the Slavophile, Ivan Kireevsky, "these thinking women flourished in the midst of family despotism, urban frivolity; in the country in the midst of barbarousness and boorishness, side by side with the cruelty and depravity of the landowners." Elena Gan, daughter of Princess Dolgorukaya, sister of the noted Panslav, Rostislav Fadeev, and mother of the founder of Theosophy, Elena Blavatskaya (Mme. Blavatzsky), was exceptionally well educated at home. She never stopped learning until her untimely death at the age of twenty-eight. "Inactivity would make me insane," she said. But she married a man twice her age who had little in common with her. "The life of men of superior intellect who live in the country is intolerable; but that of a woman of a similar level is really horrible," she once wrote, describing the drab existence of one of her characters much like herself.[23]

To escape the drabness, she wrote novels. Since they were written about love and from a woman's point of view, she has often been compared to George Sand. But the comparison is superficial, for most of her heroines were *odnolyubki*, women of one love. She rejected the idea—Saint-Simonist, she calls it—of the equality of sexes. Woman had her own special function as wife, mother, and rearer of children, "of sons with strength and firmness of spirit," and of daughters to be future wives and mothers. For Gan, adultery or sexual equality was no answer to the problem of women's superfluousness. But she recognized that the problem existed, and she faced it honestly by making most of her *odnolyubki* unhappy, if faithful, wives. In doing so, she touched upon the painful truth that love itself was not enough to endow life with meaning.

What then was missing? No analysis is required to perceive at once that she hit upon the answer to the question in a brief passage from the novel *Ideal*, written in 1837, twenty years before the Russian public would "discover" the same answer.

It is true [the heroine laments] that sometimes it seems as though God made the world only for men; to them, all its secrets are revealed; for them its glory, its art, its knowledge; for them freedom and all the joys of life. From birth, woman is chained by propriety, enmeshed by the fear of "what the world will say"—and if her hopes for family happiness are not realized, what remains for her? Her poor, limited education does not even allow her to devote herself to important things and she must, willy-nilly, throw herself into the whirl of society or drag out a wretched, colorless existence.[24]

[23] The Kireevsky quotation: Shchepkina, *Iz istorii*, 253; For Gan, see T. Khitrovo, "Nashi babushki," *Zhenskoe delo* (Jan. 1, 1913) 17–21; Gan's quotations: *ibid*, 18 and E. A. Gan, *Polnoe sobranie sochinenii* (SPB, 1905) 4.
[24] Gan, PSS, xiv–xv, and "Ideal," 1–47.

The coming debate on the "poor, limited education" of women would lead directly to a larger discussion of what came to be called the "woman question." The educational debate was hardly new; it had begun a century earlier. But in previous generations it had concerned itself mostly with the relative importance of home, love, and social success as the ends of education. Like most pedagogical arguments, it was cyclical, repetitive, boring, and largely irrelevant; for it ignored the obvious truth that a school system is a creature of the society which surrounds it, not its creator. Such debates can go nowhere unless and until broader forces of social change are on the move. The crucial importance of the post-Crimean debate would lay not in its terms, its format, or its voices, but rather in its timing. For it was to be synchronized with the massive socio-economic and ideological transformation that Russia was about to undergo. In the autocratic Russia of Nicholas I, the isolation and limited education of upper-class women, together with the rightlessness and immobility of all subjects, meant that voices like Elena Gan's were disembodied ones echoing in a social void.

PART TWO

The Woman Question 1855–1881

II

The Birth of the Woman Question

Women cannot be expected to devote themselves to the emancipation of women, until men in considerable number are prepared to
join with them in the undertaking.—JOHN STUART MILL

1. A QUESTION OF LIFE

The woman question emerged in Russia at a crucial turning point in the history of modern Russia: the half-decade which followed the Crimean War.
Russia's humiliating defeat had demolished what Ivan Aksakov called the
"façade-ness" of the pre-Crimean empire, and had revealed the essential
weaknesses of an archaic socio-political system, previously obscured by a
seemingly efficient bureaucracy. The immediate effect of the defeat and the
death of the rigid Nicholas I was to open what the intelligentsia liked to call
Russia's "social sores" to public gaze. A bright young woman of the period,
Elena Stackenschneider, wrote in her diary in 1856: "Thank God they no
longer talk of war; that this horrible time is past. All our wounds are healing
except those wounds which the war has just opened and which the war itself
did not cure." There was a widespread conviction that much good would issue
out of the terrible evil of humiliation and defeat. "The enemy found Sevastopol a bloody ruin," wrote the liberal jurist, Anatol Koni, some years afterward, "but Russia found in it the seed of her resurrection." From another part
of the ideological spectrum, Nikolai Dobrolyubov wrote in 1857: "Two years
ago the war stirred us and convinced us of the power of European education
and of our own weaknesses. It seemed as though we had awakened after a
long sleep, had opened our eyes to our domestic and social life, and had
guessed that all was not well with us. Hardly had we realized this than we
began, with rare conscientiousness and sincerity, to expose our 'social
sores.' "

A joyous time that was [he continues], a time of widespread euphoria
and enthusiasm. . . . It seemed somehow that everybody's soul was more
receptive to the good in this world; everything around us looked brighter. It
was as though the warm breath of spring had blown upon the hard frozen
earth, and every living creature happily began to breathe in this spring air.

29

Our breasts expanded and our speech flowed sonorous and smooth like a river freed from the ice. It was a glorious time![1]

The relaxation of the oppressive censorship measures enacted by Nicholas toward the end of his reign gave rise to a whole range of debates on the causes of the recent catastrophe, on the urgent need of reform, and on the possible directions in which Russia might now move. Out of these debates arose what the intelligentsia called the "burning questions" or, after Heine, "accursed questions" ranging from problems of specific reform suggested by the liberals to the more fundamental questions of life and social reorganization posed by the radicals. The "woman question" (zhenskii vopros) was one of these questions, taking shape first as a limited probe into the problem of improving education for women, and later amplifying into a full-scale anthropological discussion of woman's peculiar genius and destiny.

The man who initiated the debate on women's education was Nikolai Pirogov (1810–1881), the noted surgeon and educator. His dual career in education and medicine revealed to him both the gross inadequacies of the philosophy of vocational education—with its stress on preparing for a fixed career rather than on the development of one's peculiar capacities—and the acute shortage of medical skills in Russia. At the beginning of the Crimean War he was asked by Elena Pavlovna, sister-in-law of the tsar, about the possibility of sending female nurses to the front. Elena Pavlovna, a court "liberal" and a friend of reformers, had two goals in forming a female auxiliary corps: marshaling needed personnel for the aid of Russia; and calling attention to the capabilities of women and promoting a greater role for her sex in "public life." She suggested that Pirogov supervise the unit of nurses, adding that, although women were competent, they had to be directed by men. "Quite so," answered Pirogov, "but only as long as they are educated according to the present methods and as long as they are treated in an archaic and inane way. But this must change and women must take a role in society more nearly corresponding to their human worth and their mental capabilities." This casual reply contained the seeds of the argument he was to elaborate a few years later in "Questions of Life."[2]

Pirogov was convinced that women were capable of front-line work and set about organizing and training his group of volunteers, the "Sisters of Mercy of the Society of the Exaltation of the Cross." Of its 163 members, about 110 were of the privileged order (wives, widows, and daughters of officials and of landowners), about twenty-five from the petty bourgeoisie (meshchanstvo), five of clerical origin; and there were five nuns, two domestics, and a nurse. One of them, Alexandra Krupskaya, has left a moving ac-

---

[1] Stackenschneider (Shtakenshneider), Dnevnik i zapiski (Moscow, 1934), 136; A. F. Koni, Na zhiznennom puti, 5 v. (Reval, 1914–1929), IV, 298; Dobrolyubov, Soch. II, 120, 123.

[2] On Elena Pavlovna: A. Kornilov, Obshchestvennoe dvizhenie pri Aleksandre II (Paris, 1905) 28. E. Likhachëva, Materialy dlya istorii zhenskago obrazovaniya, 2 v. (SPB, 1899–1901) II, 1–2.

count of the women's first reaction to the sound of the artillery fire that banished from them all memories of the discomforts of the journey, producing fear in the hearts of some and stoicism in others. Across the Black Sea, Florence Nightingale and her English sisters remained in the base hospital at Scutari. Pirogov sent the Russian nurses to bandage points and field hospitals near the fighting. The soldiers, according to Krupskaya, were happy with the arrangement, appreciating, as she put it, the warmth of women's care after the cold ministrations of the male medical personnel. Tolstoy, in his *Sevastopol Tales*, described "the sisters with peaceful faces and with an expression not of futile, female, lachrymose pity, but of active useful participation, stepping here and there among the wounded. . . ." They were commended privately and publicly by the tsar and other high officials. Some volunteered for perilous missions in danger areas; at least two of them died of typhus. The apogee of horror, Krupskaya recalls, was the Mikhailovsky Battery with its clusters of wounded and its mounds of limbless and headless corpses.[3]

From the beginning there was opposition to the presence of women at the front. An army doctor, initially horrified by the idea, was converted by witnessing their outstanding performance. A number of high-ranking officers objected to the Society on moral grounds—the presence of women, they maintained, could only lead to "intrigue" and thus an increase in syphilis. More serious than this was the institutionalized opposition of the professional medical corps, a formidable combination of traditional army bureaucratism and professional exclusiveness and jealousy. Pirogov and his nurses, like their counterparts in Scutari, survived the abuse heaped upon them. At the end of their tour of duty, the nurses were sent home and were fêted and decorated for their valor. In leaving the service, Krupskaya, voicing the feeling of many of her colleagues, observed that women who had seen suffering and war and had actively helped relieve the pain of other human beings had "lived a full life, had loved and suffered themselves."[4]

Princess Elena Pavlovna was warmly pleased by the successes which came of her idea, but she played no further role in promoting the cause of women. In fact, according to her friend Baroness Rahden, she was deeply hurt by the turn which the emancipation struggle took a few years later. But Pirogov was immensely gratified at the brilliant showing made by his charges. He spoke effulgently of their tenderness, endurance, and "superhuman exploits." He was convinced that Russia had "completely ignored the miraculous gifts of

[3] Pirogov's memoirs: *Istoricheskii vestnik*, VII (Nov. 1886) 249–80 and reprinted in Pirogov, *Sochineniya*, 2d ed., 2 v. (SPB, 1900) I, 496–525; *idem. Sevastopolnye pisma i vospominaniya* (Moscow, 1950) 621–23. A. Krupskaya, "Vospominaniya sestry Krestovozdvizhenskoi Obshchiny," *Voennyi sbornik*, XX (Aug. 1861) 417–48. J. S. Curtiss, "Russian Sisters of Mercy in the Crimea, 1854–1855," *Slavic Review* (Mar. 1966) 84–100; L. N. Tolstoy, *Sobranie sochinenii*, 11 v. (Moscow, 1958) II, 125.

[4] A. Krupskaya, 424, 448; Pirogov, *Sobranie sochinenii*, 8 v. (Moscow, 1957–1960) VI, 391; Koni, *Na zhiznennom puti*, IV, 287.

our women" and that "if woman received the proper education and upbringing, she could also construct for herself an artistic, scientific, and social consciousness as highly developed as that of the man." At the close of the war,
Pirogov published a widely discussed article entitled "Questions of Life,"
which focused on the purpose of life, the nature of education, and its relation
to human society.[5]

In a charming metaphor, Pirogov offered a sharp comment on current
upper-class women's education: "Her education usually turns her into a doll.
It consists of dressing her up, putting her on display before a class of idlers,
keeping her behind a curtain, and having her perform like some marionette.
But as the rust eats away the wires, she begins to see through the holes and
tears in the curtain what has been so carefully hidden from her." Heretofore,
would-be reformers of women's education had the very limited goal of giving
woman enough knowledge to enable her to converse intelligently with her
husband and oversee her children's upbringing. The most recent version of
this position was expressed in *The Physiology of Woman*, a medical-moral
work of a Russian physician that appeared shortly before Pirogov's article. In
her capacity as wife, mother, housekeeper (she had no other function), the
author conceded, a woman needed the final polish of good schooling, but beyond this she need not go. Even Pirogov put limits on the educational aspirations of women: "Not all will be doctors. Not all need uselessly examine the
poisons of society, . . . dig into garbage pits."[6]

But women certainly deserved better education than they were getting,
Pirogov concluded. They needed independent opinions in order to share
"man's struggle" (not merely, be it noted, his amateur interests in agronomy
or butterflies). "It is not the position of woman in society, but her
education—including as it does the education of all humanity—which needs
to be changed. Let the idea of educating herself for this goal and of living for
the inevitable struggle and sacrifice thoroughly penetrate the moral fiber of
woman; let inspiration illumine her will. Then she will know where she must
seek her emancipation." Pirogov casually suggested that the mission of
women might soon become far more formidable than the pedestrian concerns
of married life. In the future, some Russian women would be called from on
high to perform lofty deeds of self-sacrifice; he urged such women to answer
the summons by saying "Yes, I am ready."[7]

To modern ears, Pirogov's style seems pompous and turgid and his suggestions about women's capacities excessively diffident and amorphous. But contemporary readers were struck by the application of the exalted and progres-

[5] *Ist. vest.*, VII (Nov. 1886) 276; Likhachëva, *Materialy*, II, 2–3; Pirogov, "Voprosy byta,"
reprinted in *Soch.* (1900) I, 1–44.

[6] *Ibid.* 42; V. V. Deriker, *Fiziologiya zhenshchiny* (SPB, 1854); and a similar position taken in
"O vospitanii," *Morskoi sbornik*, XX (Jan. 1856) 1–68.

[7] Pirogov, "Voprosy," *Soch.* (1900) I, 44.

sive outlook of the intelligentsia to an issue that had rarely attracted the attention of serious people in the past. There is no doubt, given the response he evoked, that many women were intrigued by allusions to "struggle and sacrifice." The article caused a furor among women, according to Elena Stackenschneider; and Nadezhda Belozerskaya, an early feminist, even claimed that the woman question in Russia achieved total and immediate acceptance in society and literature from the time of Pirogov's article. From that moment onward, the issue of woman's education became one of the hottest in the Russian press.[8]

In the spring of 1857, there appeared in the pages of a journal recently founded by the students (all male) of the University of St. Petersburg an anonymous letter from a young woman describing her reactions as she witnessed the formation of a student organization and the eager talk of the young men planning their new journal. Like the liberal women of Europe who watched in frustration as their husbands agitated for political rights, she felt sympathetic and left out. In tones that were both self-pitying and angry, she urged the editors to devote a few words to the plight of woman, to her suffering, her lack of education and lack of self-respect; to tell their readers that woman was "the teacher of mankind, above all a citizen-mother, and not a fashionable doll," and that it was time for action as well as words. The voice was weak, dependent, and indecisive; but it was the first voice of woman's consciousness addressing itself publicly to men.[9]

Remarks, letters, and articles by women now began to flow into the journals. In 1858, "A Woman's Plaint" appeared in the pages of *The Contemporary*, the chief radical organ of the time. Bewailing the uselessness of girls' private school education that did not prepare them for life and that was passed on, willy-nilly, to the next generation of daughters, the author suggested that mothers be more realistic in the education of their children of both sexes, contending that it would neither weaken the virility of the future man nor destroy the femininity of the future woman but would make them both the wiser. An "Echo of 'A Woman Plaint' " followed soon after in the same journal. The author, a gentrywoman reduced to straitened circumstances, told a despondent tale of raising her children alone and without assistance. But as a result of this, her family was more close-knit and "realistic" she said: her daughters read Gogol, Aksakov, Turgenev, and Tolstoy and were frankly informed about how children were conceived and born. "In my opinion," she said, "poor daughters have to learn early that there is bitterness and suffering in the world, and that there are not only good people but ridiculous and stupid ones as well;" and they must learn to judge these things for themselves. "Help us,"

[8] Likhachëva, *Materialy*, II, 17; Stackenschneider, *Dnevnik*, 136; V. V. Stasov, *Nadezhda Vasilevna Stasova* (SPB, 1899) 48.
[9] Likhachëva, *Materialy*, II, 467.

she appealed, in the still familiar tones of dependence, "whoever can, and let my poorly expressed ideas stimulate some bright mind to the solution of the most important question of life: the education of woman."[10]

A brief flurry of debate arose over this issue between a minor publicist, G. Ya. Appelroth, and a major radical writer, Dmitry Pisarev. The former, arguing that women's education needed improvement, repeated the old belief that its ultimate purpose was to heighten the tone of domestic life, and that it be roughly complementary (but not equal) to that of a man. Appelroth regarded equality of learning as out of the question; "Women in general are more capable of feeling with the heart than of judgment; imagination is more developed in them than consciousness; and faith more developed than conviction." Pisarev flatly rejected these assumptions—and was the first man in Russia to do so publicly—saying that the goal of human education was "to develop a person's physical, intellectual, and moral potential, and to allow for the completely free and natural inclinations; any limitation in education, any directing toward a preconceived and narrow goal (such as that of housewife) leads to harmful consequences, especially if only one goal is allotted to half the human race." And if woman seemed less developed now, it was not due to her "natural" disability but rather to the lack of growth that comes of disuse.[11]

Nadezhda Destunis, a woman publicist of the period—a species which was evolving naturally side-by-side with public interest in the woman question—linked the arguments about women's education directly to the reform atmosphere: "Can it be that in our time when everywhere, in all of Russian society, there is so much activity, so much seething, so much striving forward—can it be that the Russian woman alone remains a passive, non-participating spectator to all this activity? Cannot some role for her in this common endeavor be found?" What would be the new role? The question was for the moment left unanswered, but the feminist Nadezhda Stasova was right in her terse characterization of the new Russian Woman: "she desired not the moonlight, but rather the sunlight."[12]

The moon, however, continued to hang over Russia. Questions of love, sex, marriage, and the family that had been treated somewhat *in vacuo* during the literary reign of George Sand, were now related to the general problem of woman's nature. The best known and longest remembered comment on the family made in his generation was Nikolai Dobrolyubov's "The Realm of Darkness," a review of Ostrovsky's major plays. Dobrolyubov already had added his voice to those in favor of improving women's schools. But literary

[10] *Ibid.*, 456–57; V—ya, "Otgolosk na 'zhalobu zhenshchiny,' " *Sovremennik*, LXVII (Feb. 1858) 366–74. For other complaints and answers, see Evgeniya Tur "Parizhskiya pisma," *Russkii vestnik*, XVII (1858) 5–75 and Likhachëva, *Materialy*, II, 460.

[11] Appelrot, "Obrazovanie zhenshchin srednago i vysshago sostoyanii," *Otechestvennie zapiski*, CXVI (Feb. 1858) 653–90; Pisarev, review in *Razsvet*, I (Jan. 1859) 26–35.

[12] Nadezhda D. [Destunis], "Chemu my, zhenshchiny, uchilis?" *Russkaya beseda* (Mar. 1859) 49; Stasov, *Stasova*, 45.

criticism was still the best vehicle for social comment and Dobrolyubov found in Ostrovsky's works a world of social evil waiting to be exposed, particularly the harsh domestic life and the subjection of women in Moscow merchant families—a "realm of darkness," where the domestic atrocity was a feature of everyday life. It was, in the critic's eyes, a loveless realm, where paternal tyranny, generational hatred, ignorance, and brutishness flourished in the dark. Dobrolyubov traced almost every species of depravity among the merchants, including prostitution, to the distortions within the family, particularly the hypertrophied power of the father and the near total economic dependence upon him of the women. Pavel Buryshkin, a latter-day member of that class and one of its few articulate voices, has maintained that Dobrolyubov exaggerated greatly. But for the intelligentsia, the Russian family—merchant, gentry, peasant—as "dark kingdom" would be a major social cliché for generations.[13]

Women's need for economic independence received its first full statement at the hands of Mariya Vernadskaya (*née* Shigaeva, 1831–1860). Educated at home by her father and trained in political economy (which she called "the gospel of life") by her professor-journalist husband I. V. Vernadsky, she became the first woman economist in Russia. With her husband she edited *The Economic Index*, the main organ of Manchester liberalism in Russia. The Vernadskys were warm advocates of free trade, *laissez-faire*, and a free labor force, and thus in favor of emancipating the serfs without land in order to release a huge force of employable labor that could be harnessed in the surge toward industrialization. They hoped for an increase in female labor that, it had been shown in the West, was cheaper than male labor and could be used effectively in the factories. Vernadskaya avoided this line of reasoning in addressing women, stressing instead the liberating possibilities of work. In a series of intelligent and well-written articles composed in the last two years of her life, she made an impassioned plea for women's work.[14]

Specialization of labor and free trade, she wrote, would ultimately solve most economic problems; and free choice of employment (as opposed to hereditary designation) was the *sine qua non* for economic development. Women would have to abandon their exclusive roles as wife-mother, free themselves as people, and thus free invisible economic energies. As long as the husband made the living and bore the financial responsibility for his fam-

---

[13] 15 Dobrolyubov, *Soch.*, I, 493–514; II, 360–73, 428–56; III, 217–24; and V, 7–139 ("Tëmnoe tsarstvo"). P. A. Buryshkin (the celebrated half of the 1917 industrial non-comedy team, Shishkin-Buryshkin), *Moskva kupecheskaya* (New York: Chekhov, 1954), 28. For a divergent reading of Ostrovsky, see Terti Filippov in *Russkaya beseda*, I (1856) 70–100; Khomyakov, "Pismo k T. I. Filippovu" *Russkaya beseda* (Apr. 1856) reprinted in *Polnoe sobraniya sochinenii*, 8 v. (Moscow, 1900) III, 243–59; and A. Savelev's review of Paul Janet, *La famille* (1855) in *Russkoe slovo* (Nov. 1859) 23–49.

[14] S. O. Seropolko, "Vernadskaya," *Zhenskoe delo* (Oct. 10, 1910) 3–4; Stasov, *Stasova*, 30; N. V. Shelgunov, *Sochineniya*, 3d ed. 3 v. (SPB, 1904) II, 690.

ily, he would expect obedience from those he supported. A realist, Vernadskaya noted that some women looked upon working as socially shameful. "A person can of course dishonor any calling," she answered; "but no honorable calling can dishonor a person." Her tone was reminiscent of the European bourgeois defense of trade and its criticism of idle landowners at the beginning of the industrial revolution. Vernadskaya refused to accept the excuse of mothers unwilling to leave their children, particularly from women who spent most of their waking hours gadding about St. Petersburg, gossiping, and going to balls. "Mesdames! grow up. Stand on your own two feet, live by your own mind, work with your hands, study, think, *work* just as men do; and then you will be independent or at least in less dependence on your tyrants than is now the case."

With more optimism than accuracy, Vernadskaya assured her readers that there were more than enough opportunities for women in the economy; not in the cavalry or in government service, she conceded, but in trade, factory work, agriculture, literature, science, teaching, and medicine. The last, in view of woman's intimate knowledge of women's, children's, and family needs was particularly suitable for her, and perhaps more for her than for a man. Vernadskaya was speaking largely in the abstract and for the future. She could not foresee the enormous battles that would take place before women were to enter the labor force above the level of farmhand or factory worker. But she did see that women would command wages lower than those for men, at least until they abandoned the attitude of dilettantism and improved their education. She had no doubt of woman's ability to perform tasks traditionally associated with "male" skills. Tersely summarizing one of the central arguments of European feminism—the argument of civilization and technical progress—she said that a woman with a revolver could kill a man with an axe and that a woman in a carriage could outstrip a man on foot. Regarding marriage, Vernadskaya suggested that if women had the opportunity to earn a living, fewer of them would rush headlong into unions which often produced only unhappiness and personal tragedy. And those who remained unmarried could no longer be held in such contempt and pity by patronizing relatives as were the helpless spinsters of old.[15]

Vernadskaya had gone beyond Pirogov in giving specific answers to the unasked question: education for what? By the time of her untimely death at twenty-eight, economic independence through work was assuming its rightful place beside education as a fundamental approach to the emancipation of women. Even a writer for the conservative *Reader's Library* admitted that better education by itself was insufficient. He insisted that the scope of women's occupations be infinite and, with unassailable logic, asked whether

[15] M. N. Vernadskaya, *Sobranie sochinenii* (SPB, 1858–1862) I, 71–146.

prohibiting women from performing jobs beyond their capacity made any more sense than prohibiting men from breast-feeding children.[16] In the literature of reform, the worried frown of fear for the collective fate of one's class often can be observed behind the mask of general concern. Vernadskaya, in her forthright apologia for a new economic ethos, may also have been voicing the as yet unarticulated anxieties of those thousands of gentry women whose economic security and familiar way of life was about to be challenged by the new agrarian order arising out of the emancipation of the serfs.

In an age when the "thick journal" played such an outsized role in the dissemination of ideas and the raising of consciousness, the appearance of a journal devoted to the formation of women's opinions was a natural event. In one sense the idea of a journal *for women* was a negation of the underlying philosophy of equality of the sexes: that women were equals of men in every intellectual respect including reading habits and tastes. On the other hand, there was at this early stage a genuine need for a transitional publication that would offer the natural attractions of a "ladies' journal" combined with more general material normally found in the thick journals. The latter offered almost nothing of special feminine interest, and the older women's journals were either light and airy fashion magazines full of dreamy illustrations, such as *The Ladies' Journal*, 1823–1833, and *Fashion* of the 1840's, or saccharine and trivial delights such as *Little Star*, 1845–1863, and *Ray*, 1850–1860 for young girls. Occasional notices by Russian journals of the success of English women's magazines of the 1850's, especially *English Woman's Journal*, showed what might be done at home to create a more mature publication for women. *Daybreak (Razsvet)*, founded in 1859, hoped to fill this role.[17]

The founder was Valerian Krempin, a former artillery officer who was able to attract radicals and liberals and a handful of otherwise unknown budding women writers. In the first issue, whose cover displayed a sleeping girl being awakened by the figure "Knowledge," the editor wrote that women, like the rest of society, were coming out of a long slumber. *Daybreak* was "to create a feeling among young readers for the direction which society had been taking in recent times; to show them that contemporary ideas are fully in accord with the spirit of Christian learning." A preface by the pedagogue, Aleksei Razin, spouted similar platitudes about women's role in harmonizing the world by her love and maternalism. In its two-and-a-half years of life, *Daybreak* suc-

---

[16] I. G. Slavinsky "Obzor razlichnykh uchennii ob obshchestvennykh otnosheniyakh zhenshchin k muzhchinam," *Biblioteka dlya chteniya*, XXVII (Apr. 1860) 1–62. See also: *Syn otechestva* (Mar. 15, 1859) 293–94.

[17] Pisarev, in 1867, wrote: "Most of the public reads only journals; this is a fact which is obvious to anyone who has lived in the provinces and has moved in the society of some district towns." *Soch.*, I. 97. See *OZ*, CXX (Sept. 1858) 35–36 of "miscellany." *Damskii zhurnal*, *Mod*, *Zvëzdochka*, *Luch* are the Russian names of the journals listed.

ceeded in adhering to these pious goals. It was, in Pisarev's words, "sugary but all right."[18]

Daybreak served to alert female readers in Russia to the fact that they were not alone in their musings about the future of their sex. Certain items, such as the biography of the highly influential Anglo-American doctor, Elizabeth Blackwell, introduced foreign models of behavior that so often played a crucial role in pushing Russian women (and men) in certain directions. But most of the material was distinctly middle-brow and patronizing. It was full of trivia, and even the "serious" articles on history, geography, and science were considerably watered down. That *Daybreak* went far beyond the syrupy women's journals of the old style there was no doubt, and it pulled together some of the current ideas on women in Russia and in Europe. But as one of its contributors later pointed out, the younger generation by 1862 had gone beyond the transitional appeal of *Daybreak* and was satisfied with nothing less than serious classics and the more adult thick journals of the period. In the meantime, others were probing much deeper into the "woman question."[19]

2. MIKHAILOV AND THE WOMAN QUESTION

The first serious discussion of the "woman question" in Russia was undertaken by a man, the poet and radical publicist, M. L. Mikhailov.[1] In a series of articles published between 1859 and his death in 1865, Mikhailov established this issue as a major item in the ideological constellation of the Russian intelligentsia. Although not an original thinker and not the first to speak publicly on these matters, he was the first to synthesize the separate strands of the problem (work, education, love) into an anthropological argument. Like J. S. Mill, Mikhailov possessed the ability to organize data, to analyze and refute his opponents' positions, and couch his conclusions in clear, reasoned, convincing prose. He was the publicist-apologist of women's emancipation. By the time of his arrest for radical activities in 1862, Mikhailov had transformed the loosely connected *ad hoc* arguments of the preceding decade into a compact and perennial, though still problematical, feature of Russia's intellectual life.

Mikhailov's ideas on the woman question were aroused by the anti-feminist writings of the liberal nationalist Jules Michelet and the socialist P.-J.

---

[18] M. A. Skabichevsky, *Literaturnye vospominaniya* (Moscow, 1928), 132; *Razsvet*, I (Jan. 1859) i–vi, 1–10; Pisarev, *Soch.*, II, 175–76. The journal was recommended by the government as "morally useful reading for students of the higher classes of women's secondary schools." Likhachëva, *Materialy*, II, 457.

[19] For a sampling, see: *Razsvet*, I (Mar. 1859) 437–50; II (May 1859) 311–26; III (Mar. 1860) 475–78; XIII (Mar. 1862) 301–10, 311–12; XI (Sept. 1860) 457–61. *Razsvet* ceased publication in June 1862. See Skabichevsky, *Lit. vosp.*, p. 174 and D. Seménev in *Zhurnal Ministerstva Prosveshchenii*, CXIII (Feb. 1862) 75–94 and CXIV (Apr. 1862) 23–43.

[1] For a more detailed treatment, see R. Stites, "M. L. Mikhailov and the Emergence of the Woman Question," *Canadian Slavic Studies* (Summer 1969) 178–99.

Proudhon. Michelet, increasingly concerned over what he saw as the degeneration of French morality, the rapid disintegration of the family, and a declining birth rate, had written *L'amour* (1858), which contained his ideas on women, love, and marriage. Believing in the biological inferiority—indeed infirmity—of woman, he spoke of the "physical fatalism in which she is held by nature" and of her weakness in comparison with man, a weakness caused by "the great malady of maternity" and "the eternal wound" of menstruation. Whenever she avoided these natural disabilities by hard physical labor, he explained, her sexuality was blotted out. Serious education and work were ruled out for women by nature itself, according to Michelet. Her husband would "instruct her and elevate her in things pious and holy." No serious undertaking could be open to a species that was subject to such debilitating distractions as the menstrual cycle and pregnancies. What could woman do, then? Love her husband and serve him, bear his children, and serve as the source of love for all of society, answered Michelet. France needed an infusion of love and a resurgence (but not freedom) of the heart—a new mystical bond that would keep together what was being pulled apart by the atomistic egoism of urbanization and industrial capitalism. What others sought in religious revival, in socialism, in *palingénésie sociale*, Michelet found in love—romantic and familial. And the bearer of that love was woman.[2]

The other major defence of the traditional status of women was Proudhon's *La justice dans la révolution et dans l'église* (1858). Proudhon's ideas on women centered around the ownership of personal property, the preservation of the hearth, the monogamous conjugal household, and a belief in male superiority. But he was more bluntly anti-feminist than Michelet, whose work he called erotic and obscene babbling. Proudhon pointed to the physical smallness of woman and her passivity in the sexual act as proof of her weaker nature; to her large hips, pelvis, and breasts as proof of her sole function as child-bearer; and to the relative smallness of the female brain (an undeniable, though irrelevant, fact) as proof of her intellectual inferiority. Using a curious system of numerical values that he assigned to both sexes, Proudhon suggested that since man's relation to woman was physically 3:2 (his own premise), this ratio must also prevail in initiative, educability, potential, and so forth: man was master and woman must obey, "dura lex, sed lex." "Genius," he proclaimed, "is virility of spirit and its accompanying powers of abstraction, generalization, creation, and conception; the child, the eunuch, and the woman lack these gifts in equal measure." And as if to refute the sentimental slobberings of Michelet, Proudhon assailed women's propensity to love as mere idolatry and "idéalisme érotique."[3]

Such dogmatic and unscientific opinions on women were doubly disturbing

[2] J. Michelet, *Pages choisies*, ed. H. Chabot, 2 v. (Paris, 1935) I, 67; *idem, Oeuvres complètes* (édition définitive) 40 v. (Paris, 1839–1899) XXXIV (*L'amour*) 32–33, 44, 18, 334–35.

[3] P.-J. Proudhon, *Oeuvres complètes*, ed. C. Bouglé, 12 v. (Paris, 1923–1946); VIII, 4 (*La justice*), 183–85, 197, 47, 201–15.

to feminists because they were made not by reactionaries, who of course shared them, but by so-called progressive elements. The two books caused an uproar in Paris. In feminist-socialist circles, such as the neo-Saint-Simonian group around the *Revue philosophique*, Proudhon for a while was as hated as Napoleon III. Out of this circle emerged an intrepid feminist, and one of Europe's first woman doctors, Eugénie (Jenny) d'Héricourt, to defend the rights of women against their latest defamers and false idolaters. Her *La femme affranchie* (1860) called Michelet's work "perfumed prurience," and warned that his physiological myths were more insidious than the crude and blatant attacks on womanhood made by Proudhon. The latter, she said, considered woman "a perpetual invalid who should be shut up in a gynocaeum in company with a dairymaid." Upon him she turned her major arguments, effortlessly exposing his lack of logic and an intuitionism as indefensible as that of Michelet. She pointed to her own medical career as an example of what woman could do if not trammeled by the archaic web of traditions and restrictions imposed by a prejudiced society.[4]

The controversy made only minor waves in Russia before the appearance of Mikhailov's articles. A bizarre collection of articles was published anonymously in St. Petersburg entitled *Man and Woman Individually and Together in Various Epochs of their Lives* (1859). Its contents were lifted almost wholly from the recent works of Michelet and Proudhon as was its verdict on woman's fate: "As a child she loves her doll; as a wife she loves her children and her husband; in old age she devotes herself to God." But the progressive journals sided with d'Héricourt. *Notes of the Fatherland* could not agree with Proudhon that a woman had to be either wife or whore. Michelet's *L'amour* was reviewed in *The Russian Herald* by a prominent salon figure, Evgeniya Tur who, while admitting that women were intellectual inferiors of men and often illogical, accused Michelet of having no logic at all. Michelet, she observed, was capable of calling woman the queen of the earth and of condoning wife-beating on certain occasions. Tur never became a feminist but she caught the utter falsity in Michelet's mystical concept of love. In terms that were soon to become familiar, she described love as an active, living force that gave energy to life and was capable of banishing the stale and the deadening.[5]

D'Héricourt had met Mikhailov and other Russians in Paris in the 1850's and she followed the Russian coverage of the controversy closely and even planned to give a series of lectures in Petersburg on the emancipation of women, though she never did so. One of her pieces on women's education

[4] On d'Héricourt and her circle, see N. V. Shelgunov, L. P. Shelgunova and M. L. Mikhailov, *Vospominaniya*, 2 v. (Moscow, 1967)—cited hereafter as Shelgunovs-Mikhailov, *Vospom.*—I, 82, 119-20 (Shelgunov) and II, 75 (Shelgunova). Her book has been translated as *A Woman's Philosophy of Woman* (New York, 1864) quotation, 17.

[5] *Muzhchina i zhenshchina vroz i vmeste v razlichiya epokhi ikh zhizni* (SPB, 1859); OZ, CXII (May 1857); Evgeniya Tur (pseudonym of the Countess de Sailhas de Tournemire), "Zhenshchina i liubov po ponyatiyam G. Mishle," *RV*, XXI (Jun. 1859) 461–500.

was published in *Daybreak* in 1861. In France her voice, the last feminist voice there for some time to come, was drowned out by the hubbub of other concerns. But her friend Mikhailov returned to Russia and transformed her feud with Michelet and Proudhon into a major "burning question" for a long time to come.

Mikhailov (1829–1865) was the son of a government official whose father had been a serf on the Orenburg estate of the Aksakovs and who had worked his way into the gentry. Mikhail Larionovich trod a path that was typical for many men of the 1860's: study at St. Petersburg University, a brief fling at government service, disillusionment with Russian life, and the apocalyptic journey to Western Europe. He had read Belinsky and Herzen and had written a few tales of his own in which the status of women was a minor leitmotif. But aside from this, Mikhailov showed no particular interest in the woman question. In 1853 he met Nikolai Vasilevich Shelgunov and fell in love immediately and permanently with his wife, Lyudmila Petrovna (née Mikhailis). When the affair became intimate, Shelgunov accepted it and remained the close friend and political collaborator of Mikhailov until their arrest in 1862, as well as the undaunted friend and admirer of his nominal wife. From his position in this triangle, Mikhailov had his first view of the practical implications of women's freedom. And from his partners in it, he derived some of his subsequent ideas.[6]

Lyudmila Shelgunova's father was a government administrator, and she was well educated in a Petersburg private school. But her chief training came from her mother, a talented and independent woman, who constantly spoke of "women's rights" and the need for financial independence. Though far from needy, she gave lessons and did translations, and she taught Lyudmila how to do the same. When the latter was being courted by her cousin, Shelgunov, she made it clear to him that she expected, at the very least, complete equality in all matters. Her suitor, a man of poorer gentry background who had studied at the Forestry Institute, was at first appalled by the ideas of his fiancée. "The idea of equality was alien to the creator," he wrote her in 1849; later he relented and agreed to give her marital freedom. After marriage and a few years of provincial boredom, they settled down in Petersburg where they met Mikhailov and where Shelgunov's promise was put to the test. The three were already warm supporters of the woman's cause when in 1858 they converged on the Hôtel Molière in Paris, headquarters of Jenny d'Héricourt and her friends. The Shelgunovs had met her on a previous visit and now Mikhailov

---

[6] There is an adequate, if uninspiring, biography by P. S. Fateev: *Mikhail Mikhailov: revoliutsioner, pisatel, publitsist* (Moscow, 1969). A shorter sketch by M. Dikman and Yu. Levin in Mikhailov's *Sochineniya*, ed. B. P. Kozmin *et al*. 3 v. (Moscow, 1958) I, 5–47. On the triangle see A. Panaeva, *Vospominaniya*, ed. K. Chukovsky (Moscow, 1956) 197 and Tatyana Bogdanovich, *Lyubov lyudei shestidesyatykh godov* (Leningrad, 1929).

became her ready advocate, spending long evenings excitedly discussing Proudhon's *Justice*. Shelgunova, inspired by d'Héricourt, yearned to become a doctor; Mikhailov retired to Trouville to begin his articles; Shelgunov gave him a few pointers on economics.[7]

Mikhailov's work was partly a refutation of Michelet and Proudhon and partly a suggested program for reform; his arguments, rarely original, were drawn largely from European works on anthropology, medicine, and feminism.[8] He suggested that the current wave of anti-feminism in Europe was a reaction to a reaction. Social reformers and moralists in France, reacting to bourgeois hypocrisy in sex, had proposed elaborate forms of social reorganization, freedom for women, and recasting of the family. These sincere notions had been taken to lewd extremes by those who only half understood them. Mikhailov mentioned George Sand as "a sorry though sympathetic phenomenon of the transitory temper of the times." This had produced the reaction of Michelet and Proudhon who were using the feminist peccadilloes of the past to discredit any kind of reform in the present. But most of their arguments, he correctly observed, were drawn from analogies with pre-civilized societies, analogies much in vogue among popular essayists of the time. In such "natural" societies, he admitted (this time incorrectly) females were always subservient to males. This was appropriate, he further conceded, in societies characterized by violence, conflict, and brute strength. But conservatives refused to see that the "natural" state had passed and man had become civilized. Brute force was no longer a virtue. Yet women continued in subjection and bondage. Why?

To Proudhon's argument on the weakness and smallness of the female organism, Mikhailov answered that science was making strength obsolete; reading a book or adjusting a telescope required far less energy than one round of a waltz. Household and "society" concerns of the upper-class wife demanded more activity than study or simple office routine. Physical weakness was no drawback in the "modern" world. It was the argument of civilization again: a woman with a gun could kill a man with an axe. Michelet's argument of "biological infirmity"—an early version of Freud's "anatomy is destiny"— was more serious, and remains to this day to haunt feminists. With some intellectual inconsistency, Mikhailov suggested that "civilization" (which he had just used in an opposite way) was responsible for the delicacy and thus the sickness of the menstruating and pregnant woman. Sexual maladies were not the cause of woman's inactivity, but were the result of it. Arguments for the natural inferiority of women he said, were similar to those used by American

[7] Shelgunovs-Mikhailov, *Vospom*. I, 82; II, 17, 35, 41–43, 97, 70 and *passim* (Shelgunova); Shchepkina, *Iz istorii*, 267–78; Fateev, *Mikhailov*, 168–98. Mikhailov's writings on the subject (except for the less important Berlin Letters) are collected in Mikhailov, *Zhenshchiny: ikh vospitanie i znachenie v seme i obshchestve* (SPB, 1903) which is also the title of the major article. His *Soch.*, III, contains some of these works but omits the fifth Paris Letter.

[8] For specific page references, see the article cited in note 1 above.

planters and their scientific-racist apologists—he mentioned Agassiz—who argued for the racial inferiority of the Negro. But, he continued, if the pregnant woman and the Negro seemed unable to compete with the man and the white man respectively, it was because neither had been allowed to do so.[9]

Was woman intellectually inferior to man by nature? Many prominent women writers of the nineteenth century believed so. (Proudhon's contribution to the subject was his claim that woman was incapable of reasoning while in love and did not even possess free will when menstruating or pregnant.) Where were the female Homers, Shakespeares, and Donatellos? Mikhailov answered that creative genius required experience and observation of the world and contact with life. Women had been chained to the house, isolated from society, and denied creative possibilities. Man had blinded them, deafened them, imprisoned them, and excluded them from intellectual activities, feeding them instead on romantic novels and sentimental tripe. The critics of women, he said, had once again confused the cause with the effect.

The allegation of woman's moral inferiority distinguished Proudhon from most other anti-feminists. As proof, he had referred to the sexual libertinage of emancipated women during the July Monarchy; to coquetry, the abominable and specifically feminine vice; and to prostitution, the institutionalized manifestation of woman's obscene nature. All of these Proudhon maintained, were traceable to woman's "perpetual heat" and her atavistic urge to bear children. Mikhailov answered by turning the indictment the other way. Were the sex-heroes of Paul de Kock's novels and their real-life models morally superior to the *cocottes* of Paris? The inventor of coquetry, he said, was man, not woman: in a man's world, where woman had no other function than to snare a husband or lover, and where man's vanity invited feminine wiles, what else was there to expect? And prostitution? Its luxuriant history only proved that *man* would purchase what *few women* would sell. It was *man* who had the perpetual heat and *man* who constantly sought gratification of his most depraved desires.

Mikhailov saw education as the key problem in Russia. The female institutes and pensions, such as the one his mistress Shelgunova had attended, were breeding places of naiveté and barriers to social and sexual consciousness and were responsible for most of women's subsequent "inferiority." The natural maladies of woman were rooted in the lack of a realistic and healthy education. Her unworldly upbringing induced her leap for freedom from an intolerable school and family life into marriage with the first man she met, and thus to later disappointment and the "Balzacian family life." The need was clear: education equal at all stages to that of men. The husband could not educate the wife, as Michelet claimed; by that time it was far too late. Coeducation was necessary in order to familiarize a girl with the opposite sex at an

---

[9] The slave-slaveowner analogy was popular among feminists all over the western world in these years. See, for instance, the passage from Fanny Lewald quoted in *Die Geschichte der Frauenbewegung in den Kulturländern*, ed. H. Lange and G. Bäumer (Berlin, 1901), 42.

early age and save her from unreal fantasies about sex and love. Finally, the woman's education should be liberal not vocational. To train women to be wives or mothers to the exclusion of all else was just as absurd, in his opinion, as the preselection of doctors and engineers from among the ranks of the unborn.

Mikhailov's critique of the family was tied closely to education, the lack of which resulted in mismatching, a shaky family, and badly educated children. To Proudhon's insistence that woman had no other function but the domestic one, Mikhailov answered that if so, she was unfit even for that because of her poor training. Mikhailov was a champion of the family, but of the family based upon mutual respect and equality rather than on the sexual nexus alone. He was opposed to one-sided unions that forced the wife to live by cunning, but also to promiscuity, libertinism, or the dissolution of the family. What he envisioned was marriages or unions—in view of the censorship, he could only say marriages—of well-matched mates, based upon equal education and equal status. Only this could unite the sexes in common causes and interests. Divorce would be rare in such marriages, he thought, and they would be a shining example for the coming generation.

Given the conditions in Russia, Mikhailov made no mention of political rights for women. The franchise, for both sexes, was practically nonexistent until 1864 at the local level and until 1905 at the national. But Mikhailov cautiously raised the question of women's ultimate right to representation by translating an article by John Stuart Mill and Harriet Taylor on "The Enfranchisement of Women." Mikhailov had come across it in the midst of his own work in 1858 and decided to present it to the Russian reading public as an example of a dispassionate and logical approach to the subject. Harriet Taylor, whom Mill later married, was a remarkable woman who played a role somewhat analogous to that played by Shelgunova to Mikhailov in attracting his attention to the plight of women. Their article, based largely on her ideas but written by him, appeared in 1851. It was a plea for the female vote argued on the basis of the old English right of the taxed to be represented in Parliament. It had no immediate relevance to the Russian scene except to dramatize the ultimate possibilities of the women's rights movement and to link women's emancipation to the whole tendency of extending rights and abolishing the old privileged monopolies of monarchy, aristocracy, and church.[10]

Mikhailov's writings met with immediate response in Russia. Pisarev heartily recommended the articles to all techers and mothers: "upon these ideas the younger generation should be raised." The pedagogue, V. Stoiunin, saw

[10] In Russian law, a woman landowner (possédante fief) could proxy her vote in local gentry elections. Michael St. John Packe, *The Life of John Stuart Mill* (London, 1954) 63, 87–90, 124, 137–38, 313, 370; Mill, *Autobiography*, ch. vii on Harriet Taylor's role in the article which first appeared in *The Westminster Review* and is reprinted in *Dissertations and Discussions*, 4 v. (Boston, 1865-1868) III, 93–101; Mikhailov's translation with preface and afterword: "Ob emantsipatsii zhenshchin," *Sov.*, LXXXIV (Nov. 1860) 221–50.

in the ideas of Pirogov, Mikhailov, and Mill the beginnings of a new epoch of equality and free development for women. In the capital ladies began demanding Mikhailov's portrait. His articles had, recalled Shelgunov, "produced an earthquake in Russian minds." But the main reason for his subsequent fame and his status among radicals was the fact that he became a revolutionary martyr. With Shelgunov—and probably with some help from Shelgunova—he composed the illegal pamphlet "To the Younger Generation" and was arrested during the reaction against the "era of proclamations" of 1861–1862. Mikhailov confessed his sole guilt in composing the pamphlet, was condemned, and sent into exile. His fame preceded him to Siberia: on arrival at Irkutsk, a priest warned him that God would punish him for wanting "to take the harness off women." Penal servitude also was enlivened by a group of young women who, having read his articles, visited him seeking advice on matters romantic, matrimonial, and political. After a few years of struggle with poor health, Mikhailov died in 1865.[11]

Mikhailov's arguments were not only convincing but also in the main correct. Even in the light of what was known then, his statements about women's capacities were sounder than the subjective, *a priori* notions of Michelet and Proudhon; and the subsequent development of woman's emancipation has made most of his conclusions seem like truisms, especially those concerning woman's ability to learn and to work in responsible positions. Equality of education and economic opportunity for both sexes became the stated goal in his own country after the Revolution. Mikhailov's writings in *The Contemporary* were the first to approach the problem as a whole with frankness, as well as with tact and reason. Obfuscation by silence and innuendo no longer would do. Earlier pleas for the reform of women's education, vague critiques of "family despotism," and economic arguments for female labor now were brought together by Mikhailov in a synthesis that asked the greater question: what is woman's significance "in the family and in society?" Such a sweeping formulation of the question was the sort that always appealed to the Russian intelligentsia.

Mikhailov's views on love and marriage merit a comment. His affair with the wife of his friend and the happy triangle that ensued would seem to contradict his self-righteous rejection of George Sand and so-called free love. But Mikhailov was rejecting the one-sided solution to life's problems, especially women's, through simple adultery or "following the heart," a solution all too often adopted by the followers of George Sand. Mikhailov patently had no reverence for the formalities of matrimony, holy or otherwise, though he showed in action as well as in word that he was basically monogamous, that

[11] For these and other reactions, see *Razsvet*, IV (Nov. 1859) 48–53, VII (1860) 11–19; IX (1860) 1–15; *OZ*, XXIII (Apr. 1861); Shelgunovs-Mikhailov, *Vospom.*, I, 121. His fate: introduction to *ibid.* by E. Vilenskaya and L. Roitberg in I, 5–46; Mikhailov *Soch.*, III, 601 (*Zapiski*); M. Lemke, *Politicheskie protsessy v Rossii v 1860-kh gg.* (Moscow, 1923) 144; and Fateev, *Mikhailov*, 158–369.

he preferred living in fleshly and spiritual partnership with the one woman of his choice to endless compulsive campaigning on the sexual battlefields. But the partnership had to be equal: an egalitarian contract, as he put it, insuring mutual respect and comradeship throughout life and a cooperative approach to the higher tasks of life. This was the seed of "revolutionary friendships" of the 1870's and the "comrade marriages" of the early Soviet epoch. Mikhailov assumed that the pairing of humanistically oriented men and women would insure, not undermine, the stability of the family. So we have in Mikhailov, as in Herzen before him, the beginnings of two notions of marriage that would eventually face each other in bitter competition for the souls of Russians: that of the free union of two comrades contracted and broken in the light of their consciences alone; and that of the enduring partnership of equals whose mutual commitment was for life. Three generations would pass before the contradictions between these concepts became fully and tragically apparent.

Mikhailov did not seek to make the woman question *the* burning question of the Russian intelligentsia. Writers of the radical camp always tended to look at the woman question as only a portion of the entire human question; and their first concern in those days was the imminent emancipation of the serfs. "Away with these erotic questions!" was Chernyshevsky's well-known remark, and he largely ignored them until his own arrest in 1863. The contributions of Pisarev and Dobrolyubov to the subject were few and incidental to their major concerns. Mikhailov and Shelgunov shared this attitude. Mikhailov's sense of priorities was clearly revealed in the proclamation "To the Younger Generation," which did not mention women at all but focused on political and revolutionary tasks of the new generation.[12] In this, Mikhailov foreshadowed a whole generation and more of revolutionaries who placed the "woman question" on the agenda for the day after the Revolution. But Mikhailov's immediate influence on women's consciousness was nevertheless great. He advanced a new image of woman: "there should be nothing feminine in women except their sex. All other traits should be neither masculine nor feminine, but purely human." The New Woman, in his view, was one who renounced the "eternally feminine" attributes of the traditional lady, allowing these human characteristics that she held in common with men to emerge. This would be the gospel of the nihilists and radicals who soon would appear on the Russian scene.

How far had the cause of women's emancipation advanced by the time of Mikhailov's efforts to promote it? Not very far, according to Mikhailov himself. Russia was still wavering, he observed, between obsolete ways of looking at the subject and the alluring innovations of the West. Only a few of the best minds shared healthy convictions about women, he admitted, concluding somewhat prophetically that it would take another seventy years before these

---

[12] "K molodomu pokoleniyu," in Shelgunovs-Mikhailov, *Vospom.*, I, 332-50.

convictions filtered down to the people. On the other hand, even as Mikhailov was writing these words (1861), feminism and nihilism were both emerging, as well as the political radicalism that would draw thousands of women into its orbit in the coming decades. Though Mikhailov had not provided the definitive theoretical solution to the woman question, he had certainly inscribed upon the consciousness of the new generation an image of Woman that was far in advance of any that had preceded it in Russian history.

The years 1860–1861 were a turning point: an end of incubation and a beginning of application. What of women's consciousness at this critical moment in the history of Russian woman? The active minority has left rich evidence in the memoirs that we shall examine. But we also hear distant but distinct tremors of the impending change in Russian literature. The so-called strong woman of Russian *belles lettres* was going through a psychic change. Pushkin's Tatyana (*Eugene Onegin*) and Turgenev's Natasha (*Rudin*) had already established the type of resolute woman as foil to the superfluous man. Three heroines of works that appeared at the end of the 1850's continued this tradition, but displayed a stage of consciousness not shared by earlier ones: Olga in Goncharov's *Oblomov*, Elena in Turgenev's *On the Eve*, and Lëlenka in Krestovsky's *The Boarding-School Girl*. Olga, constantly "striving" toward something not quite defined, was the least developed of these fictional women. But the critics noted that she was in advance not only of Oblomov, the quintessential superfluous anti-hero but also of the energetic Stolz whom she finally married after failing to mobilize the immobile Oblomov. Dobrolyubov admired Olga as a "living person, but one we haven't met as yet" and suggested that such a woman, if disillusioned with her second choice, would desert him as well.[13]

Turgenev's Elena was more clearly defined. Her early stirrings, so lovingly described by the author, strongly resembled those felt by real-life women revolutionaries of the 1860's and 1870's: "the reading alone did not satisfy Elena; she had longed for action, for good deeds ever since her childhood." Her budding consciousness found girlhood expression in her emotional sympathy for sufferers, and particularly for suffering animals. "Whoever has given himself up to something heart and soul," she said, "has nothing to worry about, nothing to account for. Nothing for the ego, everything for the cause." Before meeting the Bulgarian patriot Insarov, however, Elena had not yet identified the cause. "What is it I want? Why is my heart so heavy, so anguished? Why do I look with envy at passing birds? I feel like flying away with them, I know not where, only it would have to be far, far from here. . . . A heavy hand seems to weigh upon me. It is as if I were in a prison and the

---

[13] Dobrolyubov, *Soch.*, IV, 307–43; see Pisarev's less sympathetic remarks in his *Soch.*, I, 231–73 (esp. 242–48).

walls were about to tumble down upon me." Dobrolyubov, in his famous review ("When Will the Real Day Dawn?"), expressed the view that Elena's longing for action and reality was shared by the best elements in Russian society. Elena was clearly ahead of her time (1859) in terms of her embracing a "cause" and her sharp break with the Russian tradition ("And as to going back to Russia," she wrote her mother, "why should I? What is there to do in Russia?"). Like many inhabitants of the fictional world she was as much a model to be emulated (the "ideal of the woman-citizen," Shashkov called her) as she was a representation of her living contemporaries. But her longings and misgivings, her sensation of being slowly entrapped, her yearning to fly like the birds are flawless replicas of the feelings churning inside countless educated women around the years in question.[14]

Nadezhda Dmitrievna Khvoshchinskaya (1824–1889) composed a long story in 1860 entitled *The Boarding-School Girl*. It is a compact and effective tale of a naive provincial girl, Lëlenka, who met and was enchanted by a verbose intellectual named Veretitsyn, a man of Rudinesque dimensions (his name is a pun on turnabout), who chattered endlessly about the need for progress and science, condemning all traditions of Russian life indiscriminately. Moved by his speeches, Lëlenka rebelled against her family and went to live in the capital where she found employment and an independent existence. When Veretitsyn sees her again, he is appalled at the extremes to which she has taken some of his facile notions. He reproaches her and compares her unfavorably with their mutual friend, Sofya who married without love and settled into dull but tranquil domesticity. Lëlenka rejects both love and marriage and in her climactic final speech, utters, for the first time in Russian literature, the philosophy of the New Woman: "I swear that I will give no one authority over me and that I will not serve that barbaric old law in word or in deed. . . . On the contrary, I say to all: do as I am doing. Liberate yourselves, all of you who have two hands and a strong will! Live alone. Work, knowledge, and freedom—this is what life is all about."[15]

One feature of the period just reviewed—one that no woman reader will have missed—was that the propagation of women's emancipation was done almost exclusively by men. Pirogov, Mikhailov, Pisarev and a host of others were the Russian counterparts of advanced men all over the Western world in the mid-nineteenth century who, like Mill, Léon Richer, Frederik Baer, and Carl Almqvist, lent their talents and sensibilities to a cause that they perceived

[14] I. S. Turgenev, *On the Eve* (1859) (Moscow, n.d.), 35, 89, 85, 178. Dobrolyubov, "Kogda zhe pridët nastoyaschii den?" *Sov.* (Mar. 1860) in *Soch.*, VI, 96–140. Other reactions: *Razsvet*, V (Mar. 1860) 42–45; Pisarev, *Soch.*, I, 239–41; R. Zh. [i.e. Russkaya zhenshchina (A Russian Woman) or N. P. Grot] in *Nashe vremya*, 13 (1860) quoted in Likhachëva, *Materialy*, II, 460; Shashkov, *Soch.*, I, 856.

[15] N. D. Khvoshchinskaya (V. Krestovsky-Psevdonim) *Povesti i rasskazi* (Moscow, 1963) 92–188 (186).

as far transcending the apparent limits of its sexual dimensions. Their impulses were hardly distinguishable from those of white abolitionists or of socialist intellectuals of bourgeois backgrounds. If Russian pro-feminist men were more numerous, more active, and more sweeping in their advocacy of women's rights, this is because the Russian intelligentsia, by its nature and from its inception, exhibited a social and intellectual style dominated by the compulsion to live a life that was fully consistent with its ideas.

It was still a man's world in journalism as well as in letters. "In these years," wrote Kotlyarevsky with only a bit of exaggeration, "the Russian girl trustingly and impetuously followed the young male generation, fearing the thought of being left behind, and consoling herself with the realization that this was necessary in order to catch up to those who were ahead."[16] But things were changing. Women were no longer content to sit back and read about the settlement of their destinies by well-meaning men. In 1860, an anonymous woman (how many we have heard from in these years!) made an ironic but hopeful comment on a patronizing article by a man. "While the brilliant and satirical male mind is distracted solely by the negative side of social protest, while it waxes indignant, complains, pushes, and breaks through the old without the means to create the New—could it be possible that, in the midst of these emergent opinions, enlightened convictions are quietly maturing somewhere deep in the recesses of the woman's soul, or that a robust and true Ideal is gestating and a new mode of activity is being prepared?" The answer of course was "yes." And she further foresaw a new breed of women, not of the *beau monde* but sufficiently educated and idealistic to infuse life with their convictions, ideas, and actions.[17]

3. DIMENSIONS OF THE PROBLEM

The emancipation of the serfs in 1861 ushered in a new age for Russian society. The social fact itself and its failure to satisfy the radical youth tore a searing wound in the rough solidarity of educated Russians that had prevailed since the Crimean War. The emancipation had a double effect on women of the privileged classes: the feared dissolution of the traditional family economy, based on serfdom, induced many to seek gainful employment; and the vision was raised among them that the very nature of Russian society was undergoing rapid and thoroughgoing change, and that their aspirations for a wider role in life would find fulfillment in the near future. Because of the rapid spread of new ideas in educated society, the second had an even broader impact than the first. Women sensitive to their status were quick to contrast the liberation of fifty million illiterate serfs (and two years later of four million Negro slaves in the United States) to their own lack of liberation. Elizaveta

[16] N. Kotlyarevskii, *Kanun*, 415.
[17] A. R., "Pismo k redaktoru," *Russkii vestnik*, XXVIII (Jul. 1860) 183–85.

Vodovozova, an alert observer, recalled the mood of the times. "Never before had I encountered such unrestrained joy, such pealing laughter! And this was quite natural: after the abolition of serfdom came further changes, all of which inspired great hopes for a better future. Everything seemed to be pointing clearly to the inauguration of a completely new and unfamiliar civil and public life, wherein anyone really interested could render service to the country in accordance with one's talents."[1]

A young institute pupil wrote in her diary (1861) after reading Herzen: "I didn't know that so much evil existed in Russia. How I should like to bring about social good someday." Enthusiasm among youth was contagious and self-confident. Young men and women and those not so young did not ask "can anything be done?" but rather "what is to be done?" "what path shall I take," "which is *the* correct path?" The belief was widely shared that there was *one* correct solution to the complex problems of life, a comprehensive solution which, if only it could be found, would provide a resolution of all the burning questions of the day. A young girl friend of Vodovozova, when told by her old-fashioned aunt that it was impossible to reform the status of women, angrily answered that "if the nature of woman is so vain and worthless, if her thoughts are primarily directed toward triviality, then we had better find out how to change this nature for the better."[2]

The debate on "whether" to improve women's education soon dried up in the press, being quickly replaced by the question "how far?" Opinion now took the form of reactions to specific events and reforms. The first of these was the reform of girls' secondary education. Public uproar over this issue at the end of the Crimean War had not missed the attention of official Russia. The new Minister of Education, Avraam Norov, though no liberal, was sensitive to the sorry conditions prevailing in the institutes. In a memorandum to Alexander II, he alluded to their hothouse atmosphere and asked for public schools open to commuting day students from other social classes.[3] When the tsar agreed, Norov made a preliminary survey of officials and educators to see how such schools could be organized, staffed, and financed. The responses to this survey could serve as a small object lesson to those historians who measure the depth of a society's commitment to an issue solely by the treatment that the issue receives in the press. The "best people" in Russia may have endorsed the arguments of Pirogov and Mikhailov; but the nation's educational establishment and the parents whose views they may have reflected showed the pragmatic wariness that always suspects a "new" idea.

[1] *Na zare zhizni i drugie vospominaniya*, ed. B. I. Kozmin, 2d ed., 2 v. (Moscow, Leningrad, 1934) II, 44; see Mikhailov, *Zhenshchiny*, 80.

[2] Quotations: N. A. Konstantinov, *Ocherki po istorii srednei shkoly* (Moscow, 1947) 16; Vodovozova, *Na zare zhizni*, 2d ed., II, 40; the spirit is also captured in the memoirs of Elizaveta Yunge: "Iz moikh vospominaniya, 1843-1860" in *VE*, XL (May 1905) 256-91.

[3] *Polnoe sobranie zakonov rossiiskoi imperii*, XXX (1857) 266-67; Likhachëva, *Materialy*, II, 4-5.

The resistance that Norov encountered was not simply a manifestation of bureaucratic Oblomovism. It was a local example of the public reaction to mass education that one finds everywhere in nineteenth-century Europe. The privileged resented opening the gates to the lower orders; and the taxpayers resented the spending it entailed. In Russia some officials, after they had digested the full meaning of Norov's plan, registered their fear that parents would not patronize schools in which social classes were to be mingled, and they proposed separate-and-not-even-equal old-style institutes for each social class. An Odessa schoolmaster kindly suggested that Odessa's winters were too cold and her streets too muddy to allow little girls to commute back and forth to day schools; and that perhaps parents would object to exposing them to the outside world and "would prefer the preservation of pure morals to a definitive education of their daughters and their further intellectual development." Another educator, in a fit of honesty, exclaimed that "nowadays girls are learning too much."[4] The crowning objection to the project was financial: Interior Minister Lanskoi, who made everything his business, said the Empire simply could not afford it.

It is a tribute to the reforming zeal of the day that the resistance was overcome. Decrees of 1858 and 1860 established secondary or middle schools for women of all social classes, though in practice this meant "city people of moderate means." They were to be financed by public and private funds. The schools were of two levels: the first, so-called Class I (later gymnasium), with six years; the second, Class II (pro-gymnasium), with three years. No concession was made to sweeping concepts of sexual equality: the stated goal at the schools was to provide pupils with "that religious, moral, and mental education which is required of every woman, and especially of future mothers." But the curriculum was substantial enough for its time: religion, Russian, arithmetic, geometry, physics, geography, natural history, history, drawing, sewing, and the options of modern languages, music, and dance. By 1870 about 150 of these schools had opened with perhaps 10,000 students. The "Fourth Section," which had presided for a century over the institutes, opened its own nonexclusive girls' high schools ("Mariya Schools"), and democratized all but six of the institutes. Even Smolny, the last preserve of girlish aristocracy, felt the brooms and mops of the reformers.[5]

The opening of a network of public girls' high schools was very salutary.

---

[4] Compare the remark of a Victorian mother, "You can't send a girl into the drawing-room repeating the multiplication table," quoted in Ray Strachey, *Struggle* (New York, 1930) 125. This paragraph is based on Likhachëva, *Materialy*, II, 7–14 (quotations, 8, 14).

[5] On earlier efforts to reform girls' high schools, see Sophie Satina, *Education of Women in Pre-revolutionary Russia* (New York, 1966) 39; Konstantinov, *Srednaya shkola*, 14, 25; and *Istoriya pedagogiki*, 2d ed. (Moscow, 1959) 296. The schools were renamed in 1870: Nicholas Hans, *History of Russian Educational Policy* (London, 1931) 127–28. On the Mariya Schools see A. Chumikov, "K voprosu ob osnovanii zhenskikh gimnazii v Rossii, 1856–1858," *Russkaya starina*, LVIII (Apr. 1888) 277–80 and Likhachëva, *Materialy*, II, 42–95; on the Smolny reform, Vodovozova, *Na zare zhizni*, 2d ed., I, 407–34 and 534ff.

By the middle of the 1870's, some 27,000 girls were attending them.[6] But there were some blemishes in the picture. It may seem trite to say that the schools were almost always in perilous financial straits and therefore suffered from a paucity of good teachers; in which school system, in any age or culture, can we not find the same complaint? But the complaining, individual and official, continued throughout the imperial epoch. Although the old boarding-schools were aired out and new ones built on sounder principles, unimaginative teaching and mindless discipline prevailed right up to the Revolution. For the more ambitious female pupils, these schools were a dead end. A full university education still was denied to women.[7]

Since the establishment of the university system by Alexander I at the beginning of the century, women had not been permitted to enroll. Harsh regulations concerning professors and students enmeshed the universities in the reign of Nicholas I. With the accession of Alexander II and the freer atmosphere that ensued, many of these heavy-handed measures quietly were ignored or removed. Norov replaced the troglodytic Shirinsky-Shakhmatov, new curators were appointed, and the students began to organize and publish periodicals. The old practice of admitting the public to lectures was restored. Among those who now began to frequent the lecture halls of the university were young women, the first being an architect's daughter, Nataliya Korsini, who wished to hear the great jurist, Konstantin Kavelin. Receiving permission, she was escorted personally by the rector, Pletnëv, who said a few words to the students in favor of women auditing university courses. Korsini continued to attend, modestly dressed, and attracted little attention. Others followed her, and women auditors soon became a common sight. How many there were is not quite clear, though one student recalled that by 1860–1861 there were as many women students in some courses as men.[8]

The professors were divided in their attitudes: some welcomed the newcomers, some resented them. One professor, Mikhailov recalled, "wearing a smile of cynicism," succeeded in embarrassing a young woman in one of his lectures by giving details of a particularly delicate aspect of natural science. The students, with some exceptions, accepted the women with pleasure.

[6] Pavel Milyukov, *Ocherki po istorii russkoi kultury*, Jubilee Edition, 3 v. (Paris, 1931) II, 813.

[7] Reform of girls' secondary education was slow in coming all over the West in the nineteenth century. In England, however, it was tied from the beginning to the possibility of the universities' opening their doors to high school graduates, and the curriculum was oriented towards university preparation. No such standards were employed in Russian girls' schools, and when university courses did open to them, the gaps in their knowledge became painfully apparent. Marie Zebrikoff [Mariya Tsebrikova] "Russia" in Stanton, *Woman Question*, 390–423; Strachey, *Struggle*, 138–40.

[8] On Korsini: *Zhenskoe delo* (May 25, 1910) 17–18, Shchepkina, *Iz istorii*, p. 287. Witnesses: Shelgunov, *Soch.*, II, 663; Pisarev, *Izbranye pedagogicheskie sochineniya* (Moscow, 1951) p. 127; N. G. Chernyshevsky, *Polnoe sobranie sochinenii*, ed. B. I. Kozmin *et al.* 15 v. (Moscow, 1939–1950) XI, 718 (note); and S. Ashevsky, "Russkoe studenchestvo v epokhu shestidesyatykh godov (1855–1863)," *Sovremenyi mir* (July to November, 1907), see August, 19–36.

Elizaveta Junge, who went to hear her idol Kostomarov was greeted warmly. Chernyshevsky claimed that the women students had a healthy influence on male students, who, he said, had had no previous knowledge of girls other than prostitutes. "Young women and girls of our society feel the need to study," wrote Pisarev, summing up the view of the students and the intelligentsia; "intellectual activity is awakening inside them. The question is whether or not to put books in their hands and let them into the universities. By [doing so] we men are not really doing anything at all. We are merely reducing our influence on them and disavowing responsibility. By [not doing so] we are grossly infringing upon someone else's freedom. Now tell me: in what educated society is such a question even possible? It is like asking publicly 'Should one strike women with the fist or not?' "[9]

The honeymoon did not last. The new expansive feelings of the student body led them to seek further expression in political activity. Disappointment with the decree freeing the serfs and the bloody events in Bezdna and in far off Poland led to demonstrations and demands; these were countered by new rules and restrictions. Women attending the courses were embroiled quickly in the resultant disputes. Since many of them showed open and vocal sympathy with the disorderly students, women auditors as a group were compromised in the eyes of certain officials, and not only those of a reactionary stamp. Nikolai Milyutin, for example (known among the die-hard landowners as a Mirabeau or even a "red"), described these young women as "*révolutionnaires* in crinoline, who are of all the most fanatical."[10] When, therefore, a commission was appointed to write a new university statute, the question of permitting women to attend the universities as students was in serious jeopardy from the beginning.

The commission, including such liberals as Kavelin, Savich, Stasyulevich, and Golstunsky, supported the right of women to attend not only as auditors but also as matriculated students. To the objection that "nobody else allowed it"—a widely employed anti-feminist argument—they replied that foreign universities were enshrouded with prejudice and tradition and that there was no "basis for the exclusion of women." To the concern that some lectures were not suitable for feminine ears, they pointed out that most lectures were printed anyway. Drawing on the experience of the few preceding years, the commission judged that women were not only serious about their studies but (unfortunate irrelevance) also tended to improve the decorum of the male stu-

[9] On professors' attitudes: Likhachëva, *Materialy*, II, 471 and (for Moscow University) B. I. Kozmin, *Iz istorii revolyutsionnoi mysl v Rossii* (Moscow, 1961) 145. For the students: Kornilov, *Obshchestvennoe dvizhenie*, 123; Yunge, "Iz moikh vospom.," 258; Ashevsky, "Russkoe studenchestvo," 20; Chernyshevsky's remark to Pantaleev cited in Ludwig Kulczycki, *Geschichte der russischen Revolution*, tr. A. Schapier-Neurath, 2 v. (Gotha, 1910) I, 346. Pisarev's remarks (1861) from *Soch.*, I, 105.
[10] Quoted from one of Milyutin's letters in Wallace, *Russia*, 453. Further details on these events will appear in Chapter V/1.

dents. The recommendation was made to the Council of Universities that passed it on to governing bodies of the universities. Moscow University voted 23 to 2 against the report, and this was followed by Dorpat. The most Russian and the least Russian universities opposed having women students in their corridors. All the others accepted the report. Thus the university system, as a whole, endorsed full university education for women as early as 1863. But the Minister of Education Golovnin, by no means a reactionary, sided with the minority against the admission of women. When the new statute was published, women were expressly forbidden (for the first time) to enroll as students or to attend lectures. In the capital, women flocked to lectures given by off-duty professors at the great hall of the City Duma. But university days for them were over.[11]

It was a bitter blow. So was the accompanying news that the women studying medicine could now only hope to be midwives and not doctors. Medicine had become a favorite subject of study for many "striving" women. For some, notably Sofya Kovalevskaya's sister who imported trunks full of medical books and filled her room with hopping frogs and cringing moles, it was part of their science-worship ritual; others thought medical practice an ideal way to fulfill their own aspirations to "help society" in a country where doctors were few in number and tended to cluster in the cities amid wealthy clienteles. Women doctors might also, as Elizabeth Blackwell had suggested, bring an extra dimension of care and intuition that male doctors did not possess. Here, where the bland topic of women's education impinged upon an established profession, the debate took flesh once again.[12]

Conservative wags made the most of the situation by conjuring up ladies who danced with skeletons and drank tea from a skull; or suitors who came calling and found their darlings with hands buried in a bloody cadaver. But these charming images could not obscure the fact, witnessed by a male medical student, that women could withstand the rigors of the dissecting room while some males vomited or transferred to other faculties at the first sight of a corpse. More serious objections to women doctors were raised by a certain Dr. Onatsevich in the pages of *St. Petersburg News*. Could a woman doctor be on call at all hours and in all seasons? Was she physically able to travel the long miles through mud and snow by horse and sleigh? Had she the capacity for sustained intellectual effort, and the endurance for long sieges and bedside vigils? No, a doctor "had to be as cold as a colonel before a battle," and woman was too tender and sympathetic for that. A dissenting writer for *Day-*

[11] Likhachëva, *Materialy*, II, 472–78; the report of the Commission is from G. A. Dzhanshiev, *Epokha velikikh reform*, 6th ed. (Moscow, 1896) 257–58. Kavelin had made a trip to Western Europe to examine university life and rules there.

[12] Sh [A. N. Shabanova], "Zhenskie vrachebnye kursy," *VE*, XXI (Jan. 1886) 345–57 (345); Stepniak [Sergei Kravchinsky], *Russia under the Tzars*, tr. W. Westall (New York, 1885) 255–56; Kovalevskaya's sister was Anna Korvin-Krukovskaya. See I. S. Knizhnik-Vetrov, *Russkie deyatelnitsy Pervogo Internatsionala i Parizhskoi Kommuny* (Moscow, 1964) 143.

break suggested that abundance of feminine sympathy would be a marked improvement over the cold-as-a-colonel indifference and commercialism of many male doctors; and that a woman doctor's "distractions" might be no more serious than the rites of Bacchus which distracted men of the profession. Among some male doctors, he concluded, quoting Onatsevich's words with withering scorn, the shibboleths science, work, and sacredness of duty, really meant good position, large practice, and fat fees. In a rather gentler tone, a doctor correspondent admitted that "medicine ought to be introduced into the life of the common people and not merely be the affair of the few."[13]

In the meantime young women had already infiltrated the halls and laboratories of Russia's most prestigious medical institution, the St. Petersburg Medical-Surgical Academy. Among them were Nadezhda Suslova, Russia's first woman doctor, and Mariya Bokova, the prototype for Vera Pavlovna of Chernyshevsky's *What Is To Be Done?* They found approving mentors in such professors as Gruber and Sechenov, and in later years Leshaft and Borodin. The university council's commission of inquiry also smiled favorably on them and reported that on the question of women's ability to learn medicine the answer was *ab non esse ad non posse consequentia non valet*—the fact that they *do* not practice does not mean that they *can*not; and that women patients might benefit from treatment by women doctors. But this had no effect; the decree that closed the universities also closed the medical schools to women. Only midwifery courses were available, attached to hospitals or medical schools. Although no degrees could be had there, science-starved young women flocked to them anyway. One of them recalled years later without a trace of irony how she and her eager friends labored in the dissecting theater from morning till night, cutting away at the cadavers, unperturbed by fatigue or hunger.[14]

Faced with an obstacle to further medical training in Russia, and unwilling to accept less than a full degree, some Russian women decided to avail themselves of opportunities for study in Switzerland. The first was Nadezhda Prokofevna Suslova, the daughter of one of Count Sheremetev's serfs. He had become a factory owner, and she was able to attend good schools in Moscow and Petersburg. She began auditing at the university in 1860 and at the medical academy in 1861. When the restrictive statute was published, Suslova went abroad to Zurich where she earned a doctorate in medicine, surgery, and midwifery. On setting out for a career in medicine, Suslova, with a keen sense of prophecy, proclaimed that she was "the first but not the last. After me

---

[13] A. E. Kaufman, "Pionerki," *Solntse Rossii* (Feb. 1913) 6–7; Student meditsiny, "Zhenshchiny i anatomiya" *Severnaya pchela* reprinted in *Razsvet*, XI (Nov. 1861) 461–62; I. Shishkin, "Po povodu voprosa o tom, dopuskat li zhenshchin k nauchenyu meditsiny," *Razsvet*., XIII (Feb. 1862); Likhachëva, *Materialy*, II, 472–73.

[14] The Commission report: Dzhanshiev, *Epokha*, 260–63; the midwifery students: Ekaterina Nekrasova, "Zhenskie vrachebnye kursy v Peterburge: iz vospominanii i perepiski pervykh studentok," *VE*, XVII (Dec. 1882) 807–45 (810).

thousands will come." When she returned to Russia, the medical authorities, after some debate, recognized her degree. After this, a steady stream of Russian women made their way to Swiss universities.[15]

Less important, though noteworthy, was the isolated success of the midwifery student, Varvara Kashevarova-Rudneva who received an invitation from the chief of a Bashkir tribe to pursue a medical education at his expense on the condition that she specialize in venereal diseases and then bring her skills to the treatment of the infected Bashkir women. These women, being Muslims, would not permit male physicians to treat them. Kashevarova accepted and was permitted to finish her studies at the medical academy, becoming in fact if not in name the first woman doctor educated in Russia.[16] But these were exceptions and the doors of medical academies remained locked to women for a decade after the statute of 1863.

Economic hardship was a familiar condition to the vast majority of females in the Russian population, both before and after the emancipation of the serfs. But this fact made it no easier for those proud young gentry women whose economic status was changed by domestic financial disruptions that came in the wake of the emancipation. "Fate had played a cruel joke on them," wrote Kovalevskaya in a fictional portrait of a gentry family caught in a downward turn of fortunes. "What of all their bright hopes? Their whole childhood, their whole upbringing, so to speak, had prepared them for nothing except that happy day when they would don their long gowns and make their debut. And now, nothing but boredom." Many old "gentry nests" that had sheltered large families with extended kinship groups, unmarried females, and retainers were no longer economically viable. For the women in such families, this meant a major change in life-style. Wives replaced their husbands as breadwinners. Daughters, no longer assured of support up to their wedding day, sought work both as relief for their hard-pressed parents and as the means to their own independence. Women who possessed no visions of marriage came to realize that the old dependent way of spinster life was quickly disappearing.[17]

[15] Herzen, *Sobranie sochinenii*, 30 v. (Moscow, 1954–) XX/1, 325; On Suslova see: A. Ya. Panaeva, *Vospominaniya*, ed. K. Chukovsky (Moscow, 1956) 333; "Pervaya russkaya zhenshchina-medik," *Zhenskii vestnik* (Oct. 1867) 80–84; A. Smirnov, *Pervaya russkaya zhenshchina-vrach* (Moscow, 1960). J. M. Meijer, *Knowledge and Revolution: the Russian Colony at Zuerich (1870–1873)* (Assen, The Netherlands, 1955) 25–26; Bogdanovich, *Lyubov*, 424–25. Suslova quot. from Smirnov cited in Noralyn Neumark, "The Consciousness of Russian Women, 1860–1914," Ph.D. thesis, U. of Sydney, 1975, 74.
[16] "Zhenskii vopros," *Vsemirnaya illyustratsiya*, V (Feb. 20, 1871) 122–23; (Mar. 6) 158–59; (Mar. 13) 171–74.
[17] Kovalevskaya; *Nigilistka*, 156; Shashkov, *Soch.*, I, 858; Vodovozova, *Na zare zhizni*, 2d ed., II, 326; V. N. Shchegolov, *Zhenshchina-telegrafist v Rossii i za granitsyu* (SPB, 1894) 8; Zebrikoff, "Russia." Professor Roberta Manning, a close student of the Russian gentry, suggests an alternative—and less direct—mechanism: Emancipation forced some gentry out of state service and back to their estates; this in turn generated new and constrictive attitudes toward gentry women at home and at the same time reduced their traditional role in the household. (Comments at a panel of the American Assoc. for the Advancement of Slavic Studies Conference, Atlanta, Georgia, October, 1975; personal communication, Oct. 26, 1975).

The number of such women was not massive but their problem was none the less acute, for however few they may have been, the number of suitable jobs was much smaller. Those who migrated from home tended to congregate in the cities. In 1858 there were some 204,527 women in Petersburg; a dozen years later the estimated figure was 320,832. Observers on all sides agreed that there was a growing number of women in need of work, a new "female proletariat," as one of them put it, of aunts, sisters, old maids, divorcees, and widows, cut loose from the patriarchal family and left to their own economic devices. Women were caught between the blades of a pre-industrial scissors: no rapid industrialization to absorb them into the economy, and an insufficiency of governess positions—a traditional occupation for the poor but proper lady all across Europe—due to the economic decline of the gentry. What was to be done?[18]

Answers to this ran the gamut from a plea for full-scale capitalist industrialization to the total rejection of capitalism. In spite of their variety, these responses agreed on one thing: that women ought to work, that there was no going back to old-style dependence. The classical "industrializing" position already had been laid out by the Vernadskys and others in the late 1850's. But their optimism was challenged in the 1860's by a new "laborist" point of view: hostile in spirit to but conditionally accepting capitalist industrialization. Its European spokesmen in the Russian press were Jules Simon and Elisée Réclus; and its Russian spokesman, Shelgunov. Réclus, in a review of Simon's *L'ouvrière*, dwelt upon the poisonous effects of the factory system on the woman worker and her family: long hours, wages lower than men's (which were also low), sexual exploitation by employers and foremen, lack of sanitation, and separation from children. Even more vivid was Shelgunov's series, based largely on Engels' *Condition of the Working Class in England* (1845). Together, the works of Réclus and Shelgunov presented a grim picture of the working woman's life in Western Europe at mid-century, and thus, by implication of Russia's future female industrial force. Both challenged the sanguine belief that "more work" was in itself the answer to women's problems; reform of the factory system was required as well. But they also agreed with the "capitalist" school that work for women was not only inevitable, particularly for single women, but also salutary. Work, not "romanticism," as Shelgunov crisply put it, would bring emancipation to women.[19]

[18] The steady rise in the St. Petersburg female population may be traced in the following works: *Statisticheskiya tablitsy Rossiiskoi Imperii: vypusk vtoroi. Nalichnoe naslenie imperii za 1858 god* (SPB, 1863) 170; *Statisticheskii vremennik Rossiiskoi Imperii*, II, vyp. 1 (SPB, 1871) 24; and *ibid.*, vyp. 10 (SPB, 1875) 15. Between 1858 and 1863, the increase in the number of gentry-women (hereditary and personal) in the capital averaged 3,833 a year: see A. P. Korelin, "Dvoryanstvo v poreformennoi Rossii (1861–1904 gg.)," *Istoricheskie zapiski*, 87 (1971) 91–173 (118, 130, tables 1 and 3). For more numerical data and for evidence of economic difficulties among upper-class educated women, see E. Karnovich, *O razvitii zhenskago truda v Peterburge* (SPB, 1865), *passim* and 64–67. For other contemporary observations, see Stasov, *Stasova*, 215; Shashkov, *Istoricheskiya sudby zhenshchiny: detoubiistvo i prostitutsiya* (SPB, 1871) 312–313 (comment on a "female proletariat").

[19] Jules Simon, *L'ouvrière*, 3d ed. (Paris, 1861) pt. I, ch. 1–3, pt. II, ch. 3 (translated as

The first application of Marxist theory to the woman question in Russia was an 1863 article by the economist Yuly Zhukovsky. Committed to a rather crude materialist interpretation of social phenomena, he brushed aside current debates about marriage, education, and social duty. These required leisure, said Zhukovsky: the "woman question" was fundamentally an economic one. "I doubt at this juncture," he wrote, "that the woman question is identified, in the minds of the majority of female readers, with the resolution of the marriage problem or with permission for women to wear men's clothing, smoke cigars in the street, or sit in parliament." Zhukovsky was one of those patronizing radicals who liked to put women down a bit while telling them the answers to their problem. He continued: "The soil in which [woman's status] grows and from it which it gets its nutrients is economic. The elements in this soil have to be changed in order to provide material security for woman." But when it came to giving practical advice to women, he was as far from reality as the women who allegedly wanted to smoke cigars or sit in parliament. Rejecting untrammeled industrialization with its attendant abuses, he adopted instead the proposals of the German socialist, Ferdinand Lassalle, for large government-sponsored cooperatives.[20]

Peter Tkachëv (in 1866) went much further than Zhukovsky's fuzzy Lassaleanism. To Tkachëv, capitalist industrialism was totally evil and incapable of being reformed or modified through cooperatives. In a study of the impact of "economic progress" upon the position of women, he also brushed aside arguments for female equality as being irrelevant truisms. The task, particularly in Europe, was to rescue women from the economic fate that awaited them: functionlessness, a fate far worse than slaving in the modern factory. Machine production, he explained, had robbed women of their traditional domestic work, and by weakening the family, had also deprived them of their domestic function. Women now were "without any claim to independent existence, because in our time the right to live is almost wholly synonymous with the right to work. The only path to independence and self-realization was work." The vicious malpractices of the factory system were no excuse for denying women their right to earn a living. Was the female population thus doomed to perpetual exploitation in the dark Satanic mills? No, said Tkachëv, but one must not rely on piecemeal reforms of the system or on small-scale cooperatives to end this evil. Exploitation of men as well as women could end only with the abolition of capitalism and the private ownership of the means of production. To the criticism that he had excluded the woman question

---

Rabotnitsa v Evrope, SPB, 1874); E. Rekliu [Elisée Réclus] review of the above in *RS*, III (May, 1861) 28–37; Shelgunov, "Rabochii proletariat v Anglii i vo Frantsii," *Sov.* LXXXIV (Sep. 1861) 131–72; (Oct. 1861) 485–518 (see the section "zhenshchiny i deti"), and XC (Nov. 1861) 205–70; *idem.*, "Zhenskoe bezdele," *RS*, VII (May, June, Aug. 1865) reprinted in *Soch.*, II, 217–60.

[20] Yu. G. Zhukovsky, "Zatrudneniya zhenskago dela," *Sov.*, XC (Dec. 1863) 275–96 (quotations, 279, 288); Zhukovsky later became an anti-Marxist economic liberal.

"from the influence of the intellectual development of humanity," Tkachëv replied: "I maintain that all political, moral, and intellectual phenomena boil down, in the last analysis, to one thing: the phenomenon of the economic world and 'the economic structure' of society, as Marx put it."[21]

The theories of a "female proletariat" had evolved rather quickly in the course of a decade from Vernadskaya's idea of a capitalist free labor market to Tkachëv's insistence that only the abolition of capitalism would permit the true liberation of women. Behind all these assertions was the belief that the economic status of women was the essence of the problem and that marriage, love, and education were merely elements of a superstructure which would be properly built as soon as the economic base was modified in the right direction. Tkachëv's thesis though radical in its long-range implications, scarcely provided a thoroughgoing socialist solution to the problem at hand. He did not pursue the implications of Marxism for the woman question as a whole. There were no answers to the unspoken questions: what effect would the abolition of capital have upon the status of women? or how would it ameliorate the parlous condition of the family? These questions would be answered later by Engels, Bebel, Krupskaya, and Kollontai. For the moment, Tkachëv had only succeeded in being the first Russian to tie the liberation of women to the abolition of capitalism. But his thinking, as we shall observe later, was in perfect synchronization with that of the radical intelligentsia in respect to women's liberation.

The real world of female employment in this period shows at once how distant these debates were from reality. Jobs were hard to find. The influx of the educated class into the cities, especially Petersburg, after the emancipation swelled the pool of jobless women. Employers were slow to accept the idea of upper- and middle- class women working. Once hired, usually in the white collar or artisan trades, women were often subjected to intolerable behavior and foul language by male employees who resented the competition and scorned women. Friends and relatives, who could not understand the need to "lower oneself" by working, made things worse by their criticism. Lack of proper training and sometimes of a work ethic also contributed to the difficulties of landing and holding a job for any length of time. Women soon discovered that even when employed, their wages were lower than men's for the same work, and high rents made it all but impossible to find decent living quarters reasonably close to their jobs.

Factory work, at the lowest level, was out of the question for most educated

[21] P. N. Tkachëv, "Vliyanie ekonomicheskago progressa na polozhenie zhenshchiny i semi," *ZhV*, I (Sep. 1866) 61–114; his preface to the Russian version of Alphonse Daul, *Die Frauenarbeit oder der Kreis ihrer Erwerbsfähigkeit* (Altona, 1867); "Zhenskii vopros" in Daul, *Zhenskii trud* (SPB, 1869), quotations, xli, xlv; a rejoinder to *OZ*, CLXXXII (Jan. 1869) 110–111; Tkachëv, *Izbrannye sochineniya na sotsialno-politicheskie temy*, ed. B. I. Kozmin, 7 v. (Moscow, 1932–1937) I, 445, note 54 (reprinted from *Delo*, No. 2, [1869]). The impact of Marxism on the woman question in Russia will be taken up in Chapter VIII.

women, for reasons too obvious to belabor; only in the 1870's, when political consciousness had spread widely among them, would they desert their culture and move into the factory labor force, but then it would be for ideological not economic reasons. A cut higher than factory work were embroidery, glove- and hatmaking, garments, and decorative crafts. But even these more "gen- teel" occupations were being pushed out by the tremendous competition of the machine.[22] The most suitable occupation for an intelligent young woman was still teaching. But, as elsewhere in Europe, that profession had its own disabilities: a shortage of posts, low and unequal wages, an ambiguous though respectable social standing, marital restrictions, and an insufficient opportu- nity to use one's education.

One bright note was that even slow and superficial modernization some- times made it possible to label emerging occupations as women's. An exam- ple of this occurred in the 1860's when the Russian government began hiring women in the telegraph service. The Hughes Telegraphy system, a complex operation, was one which women handled well. In 1865, wives, daughters, and widows of the Telegraph Service's employees were allowed to apply; these were thought to be more responsible (read: less independent) than ordi- nary married women. The educational requirements were minimal: Russian, arithmetic, and good penmanship. An average of fifty-six women per year worked in the service from 1865 to 1881 (an interesting plunge from ninety to fifty-three in 1866–1867 may have reflected an "anti-nihilist" attitude which worked against women in those years). A cross-section of the telegraph- women in the Petersburg office, where most of them were employed, showed them largely gentry by origin, with the gymnasium graduates running well ahead of the *institutki*. Russia's utilization of women in this area ran almost parallel to the experience of the West. American women entered the service in the 1850's; Europeans in the 1860's (Norway, 1858; Sweden, 1863; Baden, 1864).[23] But the creation of new women's jobs was a slow business. In the government, as in the commercial world, clerical, stenographic, and account- ing positions did not begin to answer the needs of Russian women.

Prostitution, as a legal, medical, and potentially serious social and eco- nomic problem won public attention for the first time in the 1860's beginning with a series of medical reports on venereal disease, and ending with the pub- lication of some interpretive historical tomes. The institution was as old as Russia, but had not been a public issue. In 1843 Nicholas had created a medi- cal inspection apparatus, designed less to control the practice than to minimize its contagious effects. The *Archive of Forensic Medicine* showed that the number of Petersburg's registered prostitutes had grown by 20 percent between 1853 and 1867 while the population of the city had grown only by 6

[22] "K voprosu o zhenskom trude," *OZ*, CLI (Nov.-Dec. 1863) 122–42.
[23] Shchegolov, *Zhenshchina-telegrafist*.

percent. And these figures did not include women who worked without a license, estimated to equal the number of licensed ones. Since three-fourths of the registered prostitutes were diseased, it is likely that even more of the unregistered ones were also infected. Syphilis led all other diseases in Petersburg hospitals. In numbers of "official" prostitutes, St. Petersburg and Moscow (about 2,000 each) ranked below London, New York, Paris, and Liverpool and above Glasgow, Marseilles, Lyons, Brussels, and Berlin.[24]

Who were they? A rough profile of Petersburg prostitutes reveals that they derived equally from three groups: *meshchanstvo* or petit bourgeoisie, soldiers' wives and daughters, and the peasantry; the gentry constituting a small proportion. An 1868 sampling shows 508, 492, 658, and 55, respectively for those four classes. Foreigners were few in number, mostly German. The age range was exceedingly wide—in both directions, dipping downward even into prepuberty ages. Moscow listed a number of eleven-, twelve-, and thirteen-year-olds even among the registered prostitutes.

As everywhere else, a prostitute either joined an established brothel or acted as an independent freelance or "loner" (*odinochka* in Russian). There were about 150 houses in the capital, varying greatly in their accommodations and their human merchandise. Deluxe establishments, catering to gentry, officials, and anyone who could afford them, employed the more physically attractive women. After age and the ravages of their profession reduced their economic value, these usually would drift downward to the lowest brothels or to the streets. Conditions in lower establishments were dreadful. One of them, a Moscow tavern called The Crimea, had a basement-whorehouse (popularly known as "Hell") where the trade was plied "under bestial conditions." Loners, who refused to affiliate with a house of prostitution, paraded the main streets in the cities of the Empire—Nevsky in Petersburg, the Kreshchatik in Kiev, or the Odessa waterfront—freer than the house women and better able to control their own revenue. But they were hardly better off. Many of them ended sadly as aged, painted streetwalkers, doing their business in courtyards and staircases and under bridges in the small hours of the morning for a handful of kopeks.[25]

Prostitution was hardly a secret to Russians who had ever ventured onto the Ligovka in Petersburg or into the Khitrovka in Moscow or their own local equivalents.[26] But now the sordid details, the attested large numbers, and the

---

[24] Mikhail Kuznetsov, *Prostitutsiya*; Shashkov, *Ocherk istorii russkoi zhenshchin*, rev. ed. (SPB, 1872) 245–75. K. I. Babikov, *Prodazhnyia zhenshchiny* (Moscow, 1871) was little more than a plagiarism of Shashkov. See also the latter's *Istoricheskiya sudby*. Figures are interpreted from Kuznetsov, 90, 92, 95, 99–103, 115–16, 125–26 and Shashkov, *Ocherk*, 267–68, 270, and from *OZ* CLXXV (Jul. 1869) 187–208. European estimates: Shashkov, *Ist. sud.*, 584.

[25] Shashkov, *Ocherk*, 258–67, 271; *idem. Ist. sud.*, 587; *OZ* CLXXVI (Sep. 1869) 139–41.

[26] The Ligovka (now Ligovsky Prospekt) ran southward from the Nicholas (now Moscow) Station and was the main red-light thoroughfare. The Khitrovka (Khitrova Market) was a topographical and moral depression in Moscow which housed myriads of thieves, beggars, outcasts, and whores.

specter of disease combined to qualify prostitution as a fully accepted "social cancer." The government's attitude, like that of the tsars towards chastity and adultery, was two-faced. Before 1843, the police had contributed little to the inspection and control of prostitution except brutality, incompetence, and extortion. After 1843 these did not cease but a new law provided for a system of compulsory medical inspection and registration of prostitutes by combined forces of approved physicians and the police. The registered women were given the well-known "yellow passport" as the badge of their profession and a control on their activities. Brothel women were subjected to regular physical examination—their clients, needless to say, were not—and loners were required to visit a station periodically if they wished to retain their licenses. Thus the tsarist administration, morally opposed to prostitution on religious grounds, and outlawing it in the letter of the Russian Code, found itself the sole licensing bureau, inspector, and protector of the sexual traffic in its cities.[27]

What could be done? Periodically, one official or another would produce a scheme for reducing the volume of prostitution. In 1868 it was proposed that all prostitutes be isolated, reregistered, and taxed out of business. But this and similar schemes for the total elimination of the vice had been tried before, elsewhere, and had resulted only in upward spiraling infection statistics. "Public opinion" was hardly more helpful. Dobrolyubov in 1859 had written that the road to depravity could be blocked only by upgrading women's moral education and ending family tyranny. In a similar and equally pious vein, the journal *Time* suggested civic training in the "true human worth" of the female sex. Even the harder-headed Nikolai Mikhailovsky, though facing the issue squarely, could suggest nothing better than to make the government's role in vice total and monopolistic. Since sex and poverty, the parents of prostitution, could not be soon eliminated, he said, clean state-inspected whorehouses, "the safety valve, so to say, for immorality," must be retained in order to obviate the spread of degradation and disease.[28]

By the end of the decade, the economic factor began to come into focus as the major, though not exclusive, contributor to the prevalence of prostitution in Russia. Nadezhda Stasova, a prominent feminist, was shocked by the crisp rationale of a mother who allowed her daughter to sell herself: "Last night my daughter brought home fifty kopeks." Kuznetsov and Shashkov, the writers most responsible for bringing attention to the topic, asserted that poverty was

---

[27] For the legal status of prostitution, see *Zhenskoe pravo*, 320. State regulation of vice (*police des moeurs*) had first been systematized in Napoleonic France. The custom, along with its vocabulary (*carte*, *dispensaire*, *visit forcée*), spread through Europe, reaching Russia in 1843 and Britain in 1864. In the latter country, it immediately met with a campaign by the feminists to abolish it and its legal foundation, the Contagious Diseases Acts. See Stanton, "France," in *idem. Woman Question*; and Strachey, *Struggle*, 194ff.

[28] *OZ* (Apr. 1868) 252; Dobrolyubov, *Soch.*, V, 113; *Vremya* (Aug. 1862) 60–80; N. K. Mikhailovsky, "O merakh protivodeistviyu prostitutsii," *OZ*, CLXXXV (Jul. 1869) 187–208.

a major cause of prostitution; more important, they both tried to moor the issue to its social base, the status of woman. "The root of the evil, prostitution, is to be found at the base of social life [*byt*] . . . ," wrote Shashkov. "The prevalence of prostitution and its constant companion, syphilis, requires us to face categorically the problem of basic social changes and, especially, of the freedom and equality of woman." Kuznetsov put it more directly: "There can be no doubt that, with the education of woman and the extension of her sphere of activity, both secret and public prostitution will gradually decrease."[29] The publicity surrounding prostitution at the turn of the decade no doubt helped the cause of women's rights, for it dramatized an issue with which the public was rapidly becoming bored. By tying a specific public evil to large-scale social and economic causes, Kuznetsov, Shashkov, and others were expressing sentiments shared by three generations of Russian radicals about the nature of problems of this sort. And by couching the issue in these terms, they also helped to draw that ideological line which divided those who were anxious to help the victims of the social cancer and those who wanted to find the permanent cure. This division was to be neatly illustrated in the history of the major responses to the woman question: feminism, nihilism, and radicalism.

[29] Stasov, *Stasova*, 79; Kuznetsov, *Prostitutsiya*, 41; Shashkov, *Ocherk*, 265–66 and (quotation) 275.

III

The Feminist Response

> To render mankind more virtuous, and happier of course, both
> sexes must act from the same principle; but how can that be ex-
> pected when only one is allowed to see the reasonableness of it?
> To render also the social compact truly equitable, and in order to
> spread those enlightening principles which alone can ameliorate
> the fate of man, women must be allowed to found their virtue on
> knowledge, which is scarcely possible unless they be educated by
> the same pursuits as men.
>
> —MARY WOLLSTONECRAFT

1. THE FEMINISTS

Of the three major responses to the woman question to emerge during the
reign of Alexander II—feminism, nihilism, and radicalism—it was feminism
that first enunciated a philosophy and initiated specific action. Feminists
searched for solutions within the framework of the Russian social system, accepted its basic assumptions, and, though wishing to change this or that aspect
of it, refrained from suggesting its total renovation or reorganization. Their
outlook was liberal and moderate; their goal was gradual, peaceful, and legal
reform of the status of women, particularly their economic and educational
position. Questions of sex, marriage, and family played a minor part in their
public discussions and activities. In most respects the Russian feminists
shared the basic goals and employed the same tactics as their counter-parts in
Europe and America throughout the nineteenth century. In all these ways,
they set themselves off strikingly from nihilists and revolutionaries.[1]

What were their governing ideological assumptions? Taking their cue from
Clara Balfour and other English feminists, these women believed first of all
that the improvement of woman's lot was the mission of women themselves,
not of men. They needed to develop "the faculty of self-help" as Balfour put
it. That meant women helping other women; the cultivation of concern for the

[1] The historical use of the term "feminism" here has little in common with the meaning given
to it by the contemporary Neo-Feminists or "Radical Feminists" of the women's liberation
movement in the United States, except that it denotes women working in the cause of women.
Modern feminists differ from their forebears in at least two ways: first, they reject cooptation by
male dominated hierarchies for whatever noble cause; secondly, they see the sexual aspect of the
problem as not only important but as central to their fate. See the concluding chapter for further
comments on this issue.

unfortunate members of one's sex by the "more fortunate." These notions were outgrowths of the Protestant, Anglo-Saxon philanthropic tradition that had transformed *noblesse oblige* into a modern urban variety of "social duty." Much of the early feminist movement in the West was built on a psychologically sound principle that allowed its practitioners to continue enjoying the fruits of the system while salving their consciences with gestures of social charity. Acts of kindness toward unfortunate women are not at first differentiated from similar acts toward Negro slaves, beggars, savages, "heathens," prize-fighters, lunatics, seamen, orphans, and drunks. It took some time before the woman as such was extricated from this company. But when enlightened women became more conscious of what they were doing, they realized that, by a single kind of activity, they could improve their moral performance here on earth—or at least burnish the image of that performance—and help their sisters as well.[2]

Traditional "charity" among Russian ladies was embellished, as in other countries, by the conspicuous leadership of tsarinas, empress-dowagers, and princesses. Activities usually were limited, refined, and impersonal; one is tempted to say ritualistic. The feminists of the 1860's introduced an element of genuine enthusiasm for charity. They would help their sex by helping others. V. V. Stasov, the brother and biographer of one of them, contrasted their motivation with that of the court ladies who joined the Visitation Society. "Membership in it was *comme il faut. Grandes dames* wearing a sympathetic smile would say 'my poor,' 'I must go and visit my poor,' and 'oh please contribute something for my unfortunates.' The feminists' attitude was something quite different. At the bottom of it all was an unfeigned respect for those visited and helped, and an interest in their physical and intellectual condition."[3] Ironically, nihilists would accuse the feminists of precisely the same sort of smugness and hypocrisy that the feminists found in the court ladies.

The women under consideration in this chapter did not use the term "feminist," but it is the only term that accurately describes them. Words like "female moderate" or "liberal" are inadequate both because they fail to denote the special mission of the feminists and because they imply a political stance that was largely absent until 1905. Feminists were as "liberal" as the male segment of the critical intelligentsia, but in terms of activity, they were apolitical. The label "progressive" frequently was used by conservatives to describe these women, but it was applied indiscriminately to nihilists and feminists alike. It was often difficult to draw the distinction between the two camps, because in the early 1860's they tended to intermingle, to participate in the same activities, and sometimes even to dress alike. The nihilists, on their part, used the term "*aristokratka*" for the more elegant feminist leaders

[2] Clara Lukas Balfour, *Working Women of the Last Half-Century* (London, 1856; 1st ed. 1853); excerpted in *Razsvet*, V (Mar. 1860) 447–78; Strachey, *Struggle*, 219.

[3] Stasov, *Stasova*, 73–74.

but spoiled the effect by applying it as well to nihilist women who retained vestiges of their pampered past. The stunning irony of this semantic confusion was that these vestiges were contemptuously called "bourgeois." The word feminism connotes activity for women and by women, avoiding the more sweeping anthropological and political considerations found in nihilism and radicalism. The feminists' life-style, conditioned by their temperaments and social background, led them quite naturally into areas more philanthropic than philosophic.[4]

The Russian feminist leaders were well educated members of the privileged classes, past their first youth[5] when they began their work. This may help explain their preference for caution and their refusal to break completely with the past, their traditions, and their families, as the nihilists were to do. But some of the most prominent nihilist and revolutionary women were also from very wealthy and highly placed families, and some were even mature wives and mothers when they took up a new life. And, although some feminists suffered from emotional instability it cannot be said that feminism itself owed its existence to the deep psychological inadequacies of its founders. The fact that, of the three major figures in the movement, Filosofova, Trubnikova, and Stasova, one was happily married, one was unhappily married, and one was unmarried, does not support a theory of sexual frustration as the impetus of feminism.

Mariya Vasilevna Trubnikova (1835–1897) was the first on the scene as well as the first to leave it. Daughter of the Decembrist exile V. P. Ivashëv and his mistress, Camille Ledentu, she was born in Chita and raised in an atmosphere of pious reverence for the defeated rebels. Her education, at the hands of her aunt, was superb, embracing European languages, literature, and history as well as Russian culture. At nineteen, she married K. V. Trubnikov, later editor of the *Stock Exchange News*, who had won her heart by reading passages of Herzen to her. From 1855 her Petersburg salon was the meeting place for liberals and radicals. "A born social worker" as one contemporary described her, she launched her first efforts to help the poor well before she became a fiery advocate of women's rights. Jenny d'Héricourt's book fell into her hands during an 1861 tour of Europe. She never met the author or translated the book into Russian as she intended to do, but she corresponded with d'Héricourt and through her was put into contact with the European feminists, Josephine Butler and Marie Gögg. One hardly can fail to note the difference in the effect that d'Héricourt had upon Trubnikova and upon Mikhailov and the Shelgunovs. With the aid of Stasova and Filosofova, she led the first feminist

---

[4] Compare for example the Russian words *chelovekolyubie* (philanthropy) and *vse-chelovechnost* (a term untranslatable by a single word, denoting the tendency to look at the world from an all-human, universalist point of view, or *sub specie humanitatis*). One ought to avoid Kollontai's anachronistic practice of calling these feminists a "bourgeois women's movement." See her *Polozhenie zhenshchiny v evoliutsiya khozyaistva* (Moscow, 1922) 115.

[5] All of them around twenty-five except Stasova who was thirty-eight in 1860.

social enterprises of the 1860's, eschewing any radical solutions to the problems that confronted her.[6]

The Stasov family hardly needs an introduction. Its most famous member was V. V. Stasov, Russia's leading music critic in the nineteenth century. His two nieces were the biographers of George Sand, Wladimir Karénine, and the Bolshevik, Elena Stasova. His sister, Nadezhda Vasilevna Stasova, was the second in what was called "the triumvirate" of Russian feminism. Older than her two colleagues (born 1822), she was reared in the cultivated atmosphere of Tsarskoe Selo where her father served as court architect. As a girl, she suffered a severe emotional crisis when her fiancé married someone else. The blow was so shattering that she had to be treated by hypnosis. Later she folded her own sorrow into that of her sister, who had lost an only child and was inflicted with an incurable disease. Nadezhda Vasilevna nursed her sister until her death abroad in 1858. She then returned to Russia determined to "help others." Her suffering, her training in the art of self-effacement and altruism, her early schooling in Byron, Heine, Karamzin, George Sand, and Rousseau, and her own physical unattractiveness, undoubtedly combined to channel her natural tenderness and romanticism into the resolution that she should devote her life to the cause of mankind. "To love for oneself only was impossible," she realized. "For me the attraction of family disappeared. I now felt a love for the universal family: this became my cause." Her meeting with Trubnikova at this point in her life converted the amorphous "universal family" into the women's cause.[7]

The family of "Nonochka" Dyagileva, who later became Anna Filosofova, was hardly less eminent than the Stasovs. To it belonged not only herself, a prominent feminist leader for two generations, but also her son and nephew, "Mitya and Serëzha," who would revolutionize Russian culture at the turn of the century as Dmitry Filosofov and Serge Diaghilev. Like her contemporary, Shelgunova, she received a fine education in a spacious home on Vasilevsky Island in the capital. Unlike Shelgunova, she confined her sexual attentions to one husband throughout her life, the high-ranking official, V. D. Filosofov, whom she married in 1855. In her first years of marriage, she thought "only of balls and gowns," but an unwanted sojourn in a Russian village quickly opened her eyes to the contrast between her life and that of the peasants. Later, heated conversations about the imminent emancipation of the serfs reached her ears as her salon became a "liberal" center. But it was only after

[6] Stasov, *Stasova*, 61–64; *Sbornik pamyati Anny Pavlovny Filosofovoi*, 2 v. (Petrograd, 1915) I: A. V. Tyrkova, *Anna Pavlova Filosofova i eya vremya* (to be cited as Tyrkova, *Filosofova*) 111–118; V. Cherkesova, "Mariya Vasilevna Trubnikova," *Zhenskoe delo*, XII (Dec. 1899) 15–37; Satina, *Education*, 95.

[7] Stasov, *Stasova*, 1–60; Tyrkova, *Filosofova*, 118–20. Josephine Butler, the noted British crusader, was converted to the cause of women after her small daughter was accidentally killed before her eyes. She was thereafter consumed with the burning desire to find pain sharper than her own. Strachey, *Struggle*, 193.

she met Trubnikova that she began to learn, as she put it, "the ABCs of self-consciousness." She worked closely with Stasova and Trubnikova throughout the 1860's and 1870's. In a letter to the Russian jurist, Koni, she interpreted her goal in those years as "giving woman the opportunity for an autonomous path to employment and a morally and materially independent status." Filosofova was the only member of the trio to survive into the twentieth century.[8]

Others moved in and out of the feminist organizations: Anna Engelhardt, 1835–1903, an alumna of a Moscow institute, who married the radical chemist Alexander Engelhardt; Countess Rostovtseva, wife of the adjutant-general to the tsar; and Mariya Tsebrikova, a leading writer for *Notes of the Fatherland*. Only the last was to achieve notoriety outside feminist circles. Beyond these, the triumvirate could depend on perhaps twenty-five to thirty regular supporters and could enlist the aid of up to a hundred for larger undertakings. Their organizations were chartered legally and most of the time composed exclusively of females. Officers were elected and the membership accepted the decisions of the voting majority. As frequently happens in small clubs and service groups, those with natural "leadership"—social prominence, enthusiasm, an ability to speak, or simply a pleasant personality—were elected again and again.

The feminists began with charity, employing the talents of a few women to help large numbers of the poor of both sexes. This added little impetus to a women's movement as such, but it did provide experience in leadership, nurtured a feeling of self-respect, and aroused a consciousness of women's ability to function in public life. Most important, these efforts brought together many women of similar backgrounds in new situations that transcended the salons and the other established forms of social intercourse that prevailed among ladies. Philanthropy blended easily into feminism, and in a short time their efforts were pointed in the direction of helping women to live, to study, and to work.

Initially, feminists seemed to have had no clearer purpose than to bring women together in a more democratic atmosphere than that of the salons, which were perhaps early responses to the letters of women appearing in the thick journals. A Vologda Women's Club was founded in order "to bring together educated women without distinction of class or condition into a single society for inexpensive entertainment." A few officers were elected and the club was underway. Although it charged only five rubles a year and stipulated that simple dress be worn, its reference to "educated women" and its decision to hold its meetings in the hall of the Gentry Assembly gave little hope that it would draw women of every "class or condition." In the same spirit, a Soci-

[8] Tyrkova, *Filosofova*, 1–118; M. Chekhova, "Anna Pavlovna Filosofova," in *Sbornik: Filosofova*, II, 144–47 (quotation, 145); Koni, *Na zhiznennom puti*, IV, 322–34.

ety of Cotton Dresses was organized, according to *Daybreak*, whose members agreed to eschew silk and other costly materials.[9]

The organization that launched the St. Petersburg feminists on their way was the Society for Cheap Lodgings, organized by Trubnikova, Stasova, and Filosofova in the spring of 1859. Its purpose was to provide needy families, especially fatherless ones, with respectable, clean, and inexpensive places to live. It also tried to keep indigence away from their doors. The Society divided over how far its supervision of the poor should go. The so-called German faction—meaning some baronesses of German or Baltic extraction—wanted strict control over the recipients of their aid, while the Russians, including the founders, favored a less restrictive mode of activity. The "Germans" withdrew and established their own society. After two years of planning and experimentation, the original Society was formally chartered. Its main agents were soon attracted to the dismal Vyborg Side, a poor quarter of the capital and later a great proletarian zone from which the Bolshevik women's movement drew many supporters in 1917. The feminists set up dressmaking workshops, communal kitchens, and a school for working mothers, staffed chiefly by Society members.[10]

The same groups founded a Women's Publishing Cooperative early in 1863 designed to provide educated women with interesting and useful work corresponding to their intellectual abilities—writing, copying, editing, translating, or binding—and at the same time produce "good reading for the younger generation." The latter included Darwin's *Origin of Species*, some of H. C. Andersen's didactic tales, and Tkachëv's edition of Daul's *Women's Work*. Some forty members pooled their money, produced and sold the books, and divided and/or reinvested the profits. The Cooperative was a resounding success because it offered sensitive, educated women, too cautious to become nihilists and too serious to be satisfied with gestures of munificence, not only satisfying intellectual work but also the warm feeling of participating in a cooperative enterprise. It was also a boon to women's consciousness, tied as it was to "the idea of uplifting the status of women in the eyes of society (and in her own eyes) to an appropriate level," as Stasova put it.[11]

One of the most ambitious of the feminist projects in the 1860's was a Society for Women's Work. Although it never actually got under way, its broader aims and the circumstances of its stillbirth are of some interest. The idea originated in a small circle of men close to the feminist leaders, including Engelhardt and Lavrov, who was at that time a moderate. Lavrov composed a charter for the Society and the men persuaded the feminists to accept it. The draft charter alluded to the practical evils of the underemployment of women: the social loss of women's "moral and intellectual forces," the waste of male

[9] Likhachëva, *Materialy*, II, 468; "Obshchestvo sitsevykh platev," *Razsvet*, XI (Aug. 1861) 325.

[10] Stasov, *Stasova*, 67.   [11] *Ibid.*, 118–46 (quotation 129).

effort on unsuitable labors, the national burden of supporting unproductive women, and prostitution. The Society was to act as an employment agency for women, to open new fields of work for them through cooperatives and private enterprises, to train them for new trades, and to help support them during periods of unemployment. It was to be financed by dues and contributions of members, fees from clients, interest on loans, and profits from Society-run enterprises. All members—men and women—were eligible to hold office in an executive committee that would make policy and run the Society's business between the triannual meetings of the general body.[12]

The charter was typical for private social organizations in nineteenth-century Russia, and future feminist organizational projects resembled it closely. The feminist leaders adopted Lavrov's charter at once and the government gave its stamp of approval in 1865. Filosofova called a meeting in her home to elect officers of the new Society. A schism arose at once between what an eye-witness, Stackenschneider, called the "nihilists" and the "aristocrats." Stasova and the other well-established feminists supported the candidacy of Countess Rostovtseva for president. The nihilists, including Zhukovskaya, whom we shall meet later, opposed Rostovtseva because her husband was the Decembrist-turned-informer of 1825. They opposed her name and its implications, and demanded that a working girl be made president. Stackenschneider detected a visible distinction between the well-groomed and modish aristocrats and the hatless, short-haired nihilists who wore plain black woolen dresses. Efforts to heal the breach were of no avail and the Society faded away. The schism, while foreshadowing the great rivalries of the twentieth century between radicals and feminists, was not serious enough to prevent the feminists of Petersburg from spawning other labor and cultural organizations for women, such as the Society for Helping Needy Women. A Society for Circulating Useful Books, and a Society for Stimulating a Love for Work also appeared in Moscow in the same period.[13]

Contact with the poor eventually put the feminists face to face with prostitution. "When I read *Crime and Punishment*," wrote Stasova, "I cried together with the unfortunate Sonya." Tearful pity and hopeful piety were the main ingredients in the feminists' attitude toward prostitutes, and their response was to care for the fallen women and to provide them with the spiritual strength to resist a return to the streets. Stasova worked with Princess

[12] "Proekt ustava Obshchestva Zhenskago Truda," *RS*, VI (Apr. 1864) 57–62; for Lavrov's role, see his *Izbrannye sochineniya po sotsialno-politicheskie temy*, 8 v., ed. I. A. Teodorovich (Moscow, 1934–), I, 34–35, 80.

[13] For the events, see: Stackenschneider, *Dnevnik*, 239–56; Stasov, *Stasova*, 68–69; *Sov.*, XIX (Mar. 1865), 173–76, and *OZ*, CLII (Feb. 1864), 302–20 on the charter. For Rostovtsev as Decembrist, see M. V. Nechkina, *Dvizhenie Dekabristov*, 2 v. (Moscow, 1955) II, 264. A women's employment bureau had been organized in England in 1858; a German one in the early 1860's, the Lette Union; and an all-German one in 1865. For the other enterprises see: *Sov.*, CVII (Mar. 1865) 171ff; *ZhV* (Oct. 1867) 52; *Ustav Obshchestva dlya Posobiya Bednym Zhenshchinam v S. Peterburge* (SPB, 1865); Stasov, *Stasova*, 69, 127–28, 167; Dobrolyubov, *Soch.*, VII, 563.

Dondukova-Korsakova, a noted philanthropist who had renounced her position at court to live and work among the venerally diseased women and to open a shelter for them. Princess Lambert, daughter of the former finance minister Kankrin, opened her St. Mary Magdalene Shelter in 1865. These supplemented the work of the official Petersburg House of Mercy. Though the motives of high born ladies were usually more religious and charitable than feminist, their activities blended in well with those of the feminists. But philanthropy as a cure for prostitution was a failure. The dull regimen of work and religious training in the shelters and the patronizing care in the venereal wards merely served to hasten the women back into active duty again. At best the shelters reduced the number of prostitutes by keeping some of them out of circulation for a while and lowered the incidence of infection.[14]

Another mode of activity popular among feminists was the Sunday School movement that had a brief but vigorous existence in Russia in the years 1859 to 1862. The idea of giving free, adult education for all social classes on Sunday so that working people could attend was European in origin. It was introduced into Russia by Professor P. V. Pavlov of Kiev University in October 1859. The idea quickly took hold of the Russian intelligentsia, and Sunday Schools began to open all over European Russia. In 1860 the Ministry of Education ordered that the schools be supervised, thus sanctioning the spontaneously created institutions. By the end of the year there were twenty-three such schools in St. Petersburg alone. Sunday schools offered feminists a chance to give women education that would be difficult to obtain elsewhere; and they provided mature and fortunate women the chance to organize, finance, and teach in them. A typical effort was Stasova's women's Sunday School founded in the fall of 1860 for shopgirls and factory hands. M. S. Shiplevskaya, daughter of a government official, opened a school accommodating some 200 wives and daughters of factory workers. The teachers—some women and one priest—taught religion, the three R's, and drawing, and wore simple clothes in order to impress their pupils that the "real" values in life had nothing to do with fashion. In the country, wealthy ladies and their daughters opened similar establishments for their peasants.[15]

Opposition was not long in coming. The conservative journal, *Household Conversation*, accused one of the schools of disrespect to a visiting priest, of deemphasizing religious instruction, and—*horribile dictu*—of allowing the pupils to read *Oblomov*. Conservative bureaucrats were disturbed at the tremendous enthusiasm and popular initiative which accompanied the movement

---

[14] Stasov, *Stasova*, 84 (quotation), 75–82, 120–22; Kuznetsov, *Prostitutsiya*, 97, 120–22; *OZ*, CLXXXVI (Sep. 1869) 139–41.

[15] Reginald Zelnik, "The Sunday-School Movement in Russia, 1859–1862," *Journal of Modern History*, XXXVII (Jun. 1965) 151–70. For earlier British efforts, see Strachey, *Struggle*, 77; *Sov.*, LXXXI (May, 1860) 165ff. Stasov, *Stasova*, 87–115; *Sov.*, LXXXIII (Sep. 1860), 140–41; Skabichevsky, *Lit. vospom.*, 124. See also comments by Kropotkin in *Memoirs*, 175 and Stepniak, *Russia*, 276–77.

(there were some 500 schools in operation in 1862). An excuse to close the schools presented itself in 1862 when it was discovered that some of them were sheltering nihilist and radical elements among the younger teachers. In July two of these were tried in a political case. Soon after that the movement came to an end by government decree.[16] For the feminists it was a bitter disappointment, followed in the next year by the government decision to bar women from the universities.

In 1868, an ephemeral female versifier of the period depicted the sad fate of "the woman question" in a poem of that name. Born, she wrote, of the union of freedom and progress, it consistently had been ignored by peasant, official, merchant, and society lady. Though adopted by the journalist in whose home it flourished, the child soon suffocated for lack of space. This was a reasonably accurate picture of the status of the problem in Russian public opinion as of that moment. The social action of the feminists, though satisfying to its sponsors and admirable in itself, did little to further the cause of greater equality for women. Worse, the 1866 attempt to murder the tsar, and the persecution of nihilists, male and female, which succeeded it, threw a shadow over spontaneous public activities conducted by women. The issue was moribund, attracting the attention only of those who either attacked all women activists as immoral accomplices of assassins, or who endeavored to refute these charges by repeating the pro-feminist clichés of the early 1860's. Even the short-lived *Women's Messenger* (1866–1867), whose title seemed to promise serious treatment of the problem, offered little that had not been written years before, even though it employed such talented writers as Tkachëv, Lavrov, Sleptsov, and Gleb Uspensky.[17]

Hardly more impressive were the voices from elsewhere in the "democratic" press. Shelgunov tried to soften the image some people had of advanced women by reminding them that the issue was not whether or not girls would wear men's clothes or try to be doctors and professors, but simply one of developing their potentialities. Mariya Tsebrikova, reviewing Goncharov's *Precipice*, criticized the author for implying that women like his heroine Vera had no choice in life except falling over the "precipice"—that is, becoming nihilists—or turning into domesticated *babushkas*. There were, she said, other honorable ways out of a modern woman's dilemma. The exiled radical Serafim Shashkov, an ethnographer and one of the first historians of Russian women, assaulted the enemies of women's emancipation: the clergy and old-school gentry, the defenders of obsolete family laws, "the old guard of European science" with their frock coats and heavy tomes, and all the "English lords, Russian libertines, French bankers, German sausage-makers, bigoted

[16] *Razsvet*, VIII (Aug. 1860), 13–22; Milyukov, *Ocherki*, II, 181; Meijer, *Knowledge*, 16.
[17] Olga Lenko, "Zhenskii vopros," *OZ*, CLXXIX (Jul. 1868), 179–82. *Zhenskii vestnik*, Sept. 1866–Nov. 1867, nine issues.

and sanctimonious matrons, Famusovs and Skalozubs, Chichikovs and Noz-drëvs." Such people, he said, could not understand that women's rights did not mean nihilism, socialism, communism, or the sharing of women and property, but simply the full equality of sexes in education and in marriage. Polemical tidbits of this sort demonstrated that it was terribly difficult to keep the issue of women's emancipation on a reasonably serious level of public debate.[18]

Deliverance arrived in the form of two events: a renewed campaign for women's higher education and the appearance in Russia of John Stuart Mill's *Subjection of Woman* (1869). In 1867, Mill had startled his fellow M. P.'s by proposing a bill granting women political rights equal to those of men. Hearing through his correspondent, Trubnikova, that the feminists were pushing for a women's university in Russia, he wrote to them, speculating percep-tively that perhaps Russia would "prove that a nation relatively recently civilized grasps the great ideas of amelioration sooner than the older ones." He then published *Subjection* that was an elaboration of the thoughts first set down by him and Harriet Taylor in 1851, now buttressed with the sturdy out-erworks of Mill's political philosophy and enriched by the experience he had undergone both as a husband and as a public figure. Mill's view of the woman question was embedded in his larger belief that as a human being the woman, like the slave, the abject vassal, and the impressed seaman, deserved, by the very nature of her humanity, the same rights as those enjoyed by all free men. Her right to an autonomous civil identity as well as to full political rights were simply logical extensions of his central premise. Conceding that it was impos-sible to know the genuine possibilities of either sex under present conditions, he suggested that the "free play of competition" would sort the talents of both sexes into appropriate social roles. "Nobody thinks it is necessary to make a law that only a strong-armed man shall be a blacksmith." He predicted that the result of emancipation would be "doubling the mass of mental facilities available for the higher service of humanity." Only a full and equal education for women, of course, would make it possible. And if all this induced some women not to marry, he explained, that in itself would tend to transform the family, now "a school of despotism" into a more democratic organism capa-ble of attracting women to it on its own merits.[19]

In spite of some repetitiveness and occasional pieties and inconsistencies, *Subjection* is a powerful and logical book. Anyone accepting its underlying liberal assumptions would have a difficult time refuting its arguments for women's rights. It captured public attention in Russia at once. Published in

---

[18] T. Z. [Tyuremnyi Zaklyuchenik (prisoner), i.e. Shelgunov, who was still in exile], "Zhenskii vopros," *Luch* (No. 2, 1867) pp. 361–96; "Psevdonovaya geroinya," *OZ*, CXC (May 1870) 24–53; Shashkov, *Istoricheskiya sudby*, 1, 337–40 (first printed in *Delo*, Sept.-Dec., 1869).

[19] Mary Wollstonecraft, *The Rights of Woman* and John Stuart Mill, *On the Subjection of Woman* (London, 1955). Mill's letter in Stasov, *Stasova*, 205.

England in the spring of 1869, it enjoyed four Russian editions in less than two years; prior to their appearance, the English edition was hungrily devoured. Four young daughters on a provincial estate told an English visitor a few months after publication that it was their Bible. One of them slept with it under her pillow. Blagosvetlov, editor of the leftist journal *The Cause*, and translator of *Subjection*, lavished praise on Mill's viewpoint that he happily contrasted to the "eastern decrepitude" (his ironic rendition of *samobytnost*) of the Slavophiles. He told his Russian readers that the goal of emancipation was to transform woman "from a simple nurse to a genuine mother, from a household servant to a free member of the family, from a harem odalisque to an authentic, loving wife, and from a piece of dead matter in society to a living and active force."[20]

Mill's book had evoked a number of rebuttals from eminent thinkers all over Europe. To this barrage, the Russian conservative Nikolai Strakhov contributed a little article, sardonically entitled "The Woman Question." Strakhov, like his friend Dostoevsky, was a "man of the soil" (*pochvennik*), a conservative Russian nationalist who resented the Russian intelligentsia's habit of posing all of life's little problems as philosophical "questions" whose solutions were then imported from the West. The woman question he saw as the latest such absurdity, succeeding the "réhabilitation de la chair" of a generation before. Westernized Russians, he said, always chose the wrong answers, preferring nature to God, matter to spirit, organism to soul, beast to Man, hedonism to morality, and the useful to the beautiful. In the case of Mill and his Russian admirers, the "purely English" stress on human rights overshadowed the Russian tendency to avoid aspiring to too many rights because of the obligations attached to them. Strakhov had no sympathy whatever with Mill's central political theory; and, like his friend, Tolstoy (but unlike Dostoevsky), no particular sympathy with advancing women's rights. But the reasons he adduced were woefully inadequate and failed to mask the fact that they stemmed from deeper political and anthropological positions. He claimed, for example, that Russian women did possess ample civil rights, citing the favorite example of inheritance rights. A look at the Code would have told him that this made up only a minor part of woman's civil existence. He sidestepped Mill's proposals for more education and opportunity by accusing him (falsely) of sloppy epistemology and expressed the fear that giving women more work would encourage nonmarriage and thus immorality.[21] The fundamental difference between the Mills and the Strakhovs, of course, was not in their attitude toward the woman question as such, but in their attitude

[20] Packe, *Mill*, 496. The Russian editions: *Podchinenie zhenshchiny*: ed. Marko Vovchuk (SPB, 1869), 2d ed. 1870; *O podchinenii zhenshchiny*, ed. G. E. Blagosvetlov (SPB, 1869), 2d ed. 1870 (see his preface to 1st ed., iii–xv, and *OZ*, CXII [Oct. 1870], 216–34).

[21] Nikolai Strakhov, *Zhenskii vopros: razbor sochineniya Dzhona Styuarta Millya "O podchinenii zhenshchiny"* (SPB, 1871), a reprint of his 1870 article in *Zarya*.

toward the nature of social evolution and the possibility of man's consciously changing his lot for something better. It is an argument that still divides mankind in the twentieth century.

2. VICTORY IN A BACKWARD SOCIETY

From 1868 onward, Russian women mounted an intensive drive toward higher education. A few months after Olga Lenko's elegy on the demise of the woman's rights debate, the streets of St. Petersburg were buzzing with young women carrying petitions for the creation of a women's university. Inspired by the opening of Vassar College for women in the United States and by the agitation of the English and American feminists for higher education, Russian feminists, writers, and knowledge-hungry young women copied their techniques and began an assault on government positions and on public opinion. The new campaign was launched by the journalist, Evgeniia Konradi (1838–1898). The daughter of a wealthy Tula landowner, she had received a good education, and was, with her husband, Dr. Pavel Konradi, editor of the journal *Week*. After their estrangement, she became sole manager. Her successes and her awareness of the women's movement abroad prompted her to attend a conference of naturalists in December 1867 in order to present a motion in favor of a women's university. Although the conference did not formally accept her motion, most of the delegates privately offered their support. Konradi, the feminist leaders, and the professors joined forces and some thirty women and forty-three scholars met in the apartment of Trubnikova. Among the professors were Mendeleev, Borodin, Sechenov, and Orest Miller. It was resolved that they would petition the University administration and persuade it to approach the Ministry of Education.[1]

Ten days after the meeting, some 400 names had been collected and both the petition and its organizers received ample publicity. Elena Likhachëva, a feminist writer for *Notes of the Fatherland*, later a historian of women's education, filled her columns with news of feminist victories abroad and of the current agitation in Russia. The petition requested that special coeducational courses be established at the University of St. Petersburg. The rector, supported by his council, favored the idea and sent it on to the Ministry for approval. Mill and André Léo, the French poet and feminist, congratulated the Russian women in glowing and optimistic terms for their efforts to open the first European university for women.[2]

But two obstacles delayed the struggle and distorted its outcome. The first

[1] On Konradi and these events, see: Stasov, *Stasova*, 161–77; Skabichevsky, *Lit. vospom.*, 258, 343–48; Stackenschneider, *Dnevnik*, 370, 417; Kornilov, *Obshchest. dvizh.*, 195; Peskovsky, "Ocherk istorii vyssh. zhen. obraz.," *Nablyudatel*, I (Apr. 1882) 77–82.

[2] *OZ*, CLXXXI (Dec. 1868) 361–85; CLXXXII (Jan. 1869) 176–204; CLXXXIV (May 1869) 118–26; CLXXXV (Oct. 1869) 345–51; *VE*, IV (Feb. 1869) 958–68; III (May 1869) 318–35. The idea of women petitioning was popularized by the English feminists in the 1860's.

was discord among the women organizers. Konradi apparently displayed excessive impatience and lack of tact. Stackenschneider, a witness, claimed that if the whole matter had been handled from beginning to end by Trubnikova or Stasova, the courses would have opened in the fall of 1868. One wonders, however, whether the patient and tactful feminist leaders would ever have broached the issue at all without the "tactless" efforts of Konradi. More damaging was the fact that the feminists, in attempting to draft large numbers of women into the petition campaign, had attracted some nihilists and radicals who were also interested in higher education. One of them, who had earlier been arrested and questioned by the police, grew tired of the constant bickering and took it upon herself to appeal directly to the Minister of Education, Dmitry Tolstoy, and outline for him the educational needs of Russian women. She was dismissed at once and the whole effort now appeared faintly tinged with nihilism. Recriminations among the women followed. "The nihilists spoil everything for us," lamented the feminist leaders. "Who needs philanthropists and patronesses?" asked the nihilists. But the campaign did not founder, and cooperation between the two factions continued. One of the nihilist participants made the cogent observation that the "aristocrats" were distinguished by their close ties with officialdom through family and social relations, while the nihilists were much closer to the young women who were actually seeking to enroll in the university courses.[3]

The second obstacle, partly conditioned by the first, was government hostility. Minister Tolstoy initially had little sympathy for female higher education; his functional, service-oriented view of education—amply suited for a relatively static bureaucratic-agrarian state—did not include educating certain segments of the population simply because some of their representatives voiced a desire to have that education. He offered all sorts of reasons why it was impractical and undesirable to initiate the courses, but these did not satisfy the petitioners. Tolstoy was also incensed by the fact that, as he claimed, half of the signers' names were to be found in the records of the secret police. His final argument, and the one possessing the most validity, was that most Russian women were insufficiently prepared for university subjects. Despite the reform, the Ministry and the Mariya schools and the Institutes all fell far short of preparing their graduates for higher studies. There were some private schools whose curricula matched that of men's secondary schools, but they were few, expensive, and required a seven-year residence. What women needed was a relatively quick way to fill the gaps in their education and prepare them for the university.[4]

[3] Stackenschneider, *Dnevnik*, 418–21; A. Annenskaya, "Iz proshlykh let," *Russkoe bogatstvo* (Jan. 1913), 63–65.

[4] Stasov, *Stasova*, 183; L. D. Filippova, "Iz istorii zhenskogo obrazovaniya v Rossii," *Voprosy istorii* (Feb. 1963) 209–18; Likhachëva, *Materialy*, II, 510–14. A first-rate study of government attitudes and policies towards women's higher education in these years, based upon archival records, is Cynthia Whittaker, "The Women's Movement During the Reign of Alexander II: A Case Study in Russian Liberalism," condensed in *Journal of Modern History* (June 1976).

While the authorities were pondering over the problem of a women's university, the women directed their energies toward opening preparatory schools. They persuaded Professor Paulsohn, who taught pedagogy at the university, to provide preparatory courses for them in the evenings. After obtaining permission from the government, which had unwittingly suggested the idea, he and his colleagues began holding courses in April 1869 at the Fifth Men's Gymnasium, located near the place where the Alarchin Bridge crosses the lower reaches of the Catherine (now Griboedov) Canal. Thus appropriately named, the Alarchin Courses (*alarchinskie kursy*) became Russia's first "bridge" to women's higher education as well as an incubator for a later famous band of populist women. In Moscow, groups of women held noisy meetings that summer, drew up petitions, and caused so much uproar that the police banned further meetings. A month after the opening of the Alarchin Courses, they received permission for a similar venture in Moscow known as the Lubyanka Courses (*lubyanskie kursy*) after the street on which they were located.[5]

In the same year, the Ministry arrived at a decision on the establishment of the university courses for women. It was a compromise: courses taught by university professors, but at a popular level, were to be offered to members of the public of both sexes. The feminists, after two years of hope and work, were dismayed; but over 700 women crowded into the lectures during the first year. After a time men simply stopped coming. In January 1870, the courses were given a permanent home in the district surrounding the Church of St. Vladimir on Sadovaya Street, and were dubbed "Vladimir Courses" (*vladimirskie kursy*), though the official name was Public Lectures for Men and Women. Such academic luminaries as the historian, Bestuzhev-Ryumin, the chemist Mendeleev, and the physiologist, Mechnikov, lectured to the female auditors, but had to water down their material in order to communicate with an audience of widely divergent educational background. Facilities were so limited that Stasova, one of the patronesses of the school, maintained its library in her apartment. To the government, it represented a generous concession to its women; to the women themselves, it represented little more than a step along the way to their ultimate goal: equality of education.[6]

Two conditions contributed to the victory that the feminists and their supporters won in higher education for women in the 1870's: one was the climate of public opinion, which favored the cause; the other was the government's fear that women would go abroad and become infected with radicalism if not permitted university education at home. In the early 1870's, the thick journals

---

[5] Likhachëva, *Materialy*, II, 514–18; Peskovsky, "Ocherk," 86; Satina, *Education*, 73–78, 98 (with some errors in chronology).

[6] *Ibid.*, 94–99; Peskovsky, "Ocherk," 85–86; Likhachëva, *Materialy*, II, 519–21; and S. N. Valk *et al.*, eds., *Sankt-Peterburgskie vysshie zhenskie (bestuzhevskie) kursy (1876–1918): sbornik statei* (Leningrad, 1965) 9, 170 (hereafter cited as Valk, *Kursy*).

maintained a constant barrage of articles in favor of full university rights for women and argued persuasively that this was the only way to wean women away from the extremist revolutionary activity that was growing among them. The furthest left of these was *The Cause*, whose contributors—Shelgunov, Lavrov, Tkachëv, Shchapov, and Shashkov—saw the woman question not only as a worthy cause in itself but also as a vehicle for exposing the very nature of rightlessness without evoking the frown of the censor. A bit further to the right stood *Notes of the Fatherland*, the successor to *The Contemporary*, and described variously as liberal-populist and democratic. Its staff included some notable friends of women's emancipation: Nekrasov (the editor), Elena Likhachëva, its women's affairs writer, the scientists Sechenov and Leshaft, and the prophet of populism, Mikhailovsky. Their writings were mild and focused mostly on women's higher education.[7]

Mikhailovsky, however, struck a note that revealed a deeper gulf among the intelligentsia over the proper mission of feminism. It was unwise, he asserted, "to single out the woman question or any other question from the general social question"; a veiled reference to the coming social reconstruction of Russia (by revolution if necessary), and an implication that women could be liberated only after the dawn of socialism. The *Messenger of Europe*, with its bright pleiade of liberal writers—Sergei Solovëv, Kavelin Pypin, Koni, V. V. Stasov, and others—took the opposite view. Its general attitude was expressed in an 1874 article which hinted that if the government did not supply outlets in education and employment for young women, they would be drawn into the "nihilist" underground. Sensing perhaps that the bureaucracy was amenable to such arguments, the liberals on the *Messenger* endeavored to distinguish between a feminist emancipation of women and a general social upheaval.[8]

Reactionaries like Prince Meshchersky and Mikhail Katkov, who presided over the right wing of Russian journalism, opposed feminism on principle and adhered to the traditional notions of the female role. Katkov, conceding that teaching was a suitable alternative to a full-time career as wife-mother, added that "there is no basis in fact for the purported need of women specialists in medicine," and that "we cannot permit the question of feminine education to arise in our fatherland, if the demand is occasioned only by the occurrence of *shorthaired women students*" (original italics). Among the major conservative literary figures, Dostoevsky alone championed the broadening of

[7] B. I. Esin, *Russkaya zhurnalistika 70-80-kh godov XIX veka* (Moscow, 1963) 52. For some samples of Shashkov, see *Delo*, V (Nov. 1871) 145–60; VI (May 1872) 1–18 and (June 1872) 139–154; for some of Likhachëva's work: *OZ*, CCIII (Aug. 1872) 296–304 and CCXII (Jan. 1874) 104–23.

[8] Mikhailovsky, *Sochineniya*, 6 v. (SPB, 1896–1897) I, 884–89 (see 884–86); *VE*, IX (Aug. 1874) 792–807 (see 806–807). A series of articles in *Wheatfield* argued that the *niglistka* with her man's coat, blue glasses, and short hair had hurt "the real woman's cause:" better schools and jobs (*Niva*, I [May 1, 1870], 279–82 and [May 8, 1870], 296–99).

women's intellectual horizons. "Educated women need a wider thoroughfare," he had written back in the early 1860's, "one which is not cluttered up with needles, threads, chain stitches, and sewing." In his highly influential column of the 1870's, "The Diary of a Writer," he praised the efforts of woman to improve her mind: "In her resides our only great hope, one of the pledges of our revival. The regeneration of the Russian woman in the last twenty years has been unmistakable." But Dostoevsky's support of a "wider thoroughfare" for women did not allow for harmful "male" ideas such as "the debauch of acquisition, cynicism and materialism," which had occasionally lured women from their "pure worship of the idea." For the scores of Russian women who identified further education with the mastery of western science and "materialism," Dostoevsky's blessings may have been somewhat less than welcome.[9]

The feminists, as they entered the 1870's, had to steer a tight course between the hostility of the government and the conservatives on the one hand and the radicals on the other. Their attitude was similar to the one symbolized in the character Katya in Khvoshchinskaya's novel, *Ursa Major* (1871). A maturer version of the author's 1860 *Boarding-School Girl*, Katya gives up all political involvement and embraces the philosophy of "small deeds." "To do what is needed, however small," she says, "to finish it, struggle, die doing it. Things are accomplished not by large individual efforts but by all the little ones. One at a time they are drops; together—they are waves." Writing many years later, Alexandra Kollontai scornfully described Katya's activity as the "monetary donation" of dawning gentry conscience.[10] In a literal sense, this was true. The feminists devoted most of their efforts to winning and then financing higher education for women, while continuing to pour their "monetary contributions" into famine relief (in 1873–1874) and their own charitable enterprises. Like the overwhelming majority of the population, they were unwilling to break with society and throw themselves into the revolutionary maelstrom. Instead they directed their efforts toward achieving what was possible within the context of the life and society they knew. What they did achieve was impressive. The obstacles placed in their path were as imposing as any faced by Russian reformers in the nineteenth century. For these and other reasons, Soviet writers of the present time have ignored Kollontai's venomous (though not always altogether irrelevant) remarks, and have tended to treat the feminist pioneers with historical respect.

Like their counterparts in Berne, Leipzig, London, and Boston, the Russian feminists engaged in fund-raising, speech-making, signature-gathering, lobbying, and keeping each other informed. Such clubbing may have seemed

[9] For the remarks by Katkov about women, see Marvin Katz, *Mikhail N. Katkov: a Political Biography, 1818–1887* (The Hague, 1966) 5–8, 23–29, 39. The earlier Dostoevsky quotation is cited in Bogdanovich, *Lyubov*, 16. The others in Dostoevsky, *Diary*, I, 340–41.

[10] Quotation from Khvoshchinskaya in the introduction to her *Povesti*, 17. Kollontai's comment: *Novaya moral i rabochii klass* (Moscow, 1918), 4, n.1.

inane to the women of the underground who risked their lives daily in the revolutionary struggle. But there was no time for aiming shafts at the "mere feminists"—that would come later. And, indeed, feminists themselves sometimes incurred political risks almost unknown to nineteenth-century Western feminism. Filosofova, for instance, held benefit performances on behalf of political prisoners, raised funds for underground groups connected with Land and Liberty, and even had the audacity to give her husband's military greatcoat (he was a general) to an exile departing for Siberian internment. Her husband suffered a tongue lashing from the tsar; and Filosofova, for this and other shady activities, was forced to leave the country from 1879 to 1881. But for all this, Anna Filosofova was no "red" or even a "Madame Roland," as Dmitry Tolstoy was wont to call her. There was very little contact between the feminist women and the women of the revolutionary movement; and very little animosity. Manifesting a position resembling the familiar *pas d'enemis à gauche*, the feminists seemed, as Kropotkin saw it, to be saying: "We shall wear our velvet dresses and chignons, because we have to deal with fools who see in a velvet dress and a chignon the tokens of 'political reliability,' but you revolutionary girls, remain free in your tastes and inclinations."[11]

The greatest and perhaps only substantial victory for the Russian feminists in these years was won in the realm of higher education. It was by no means an easy one because the regime was always cautious about educating its daughters. Like most governments, it would do nothing until prodded by public opinion and influential persons; then it would grudgingly roll into action, while voicing the complaint that there was not enough money for such novelties. When action was taken, it was always done so in terms of specific and limited goals. The official view can be discerned in a report of a government commission on girls' secondary education. "A proper education for a woman," it declared, "ought to include only those subjects which would not distract the pupil from her main purpose and would not require her to put an undue strain upon her mental efforts exclusively, at the expense of preserving those feminine qualities (most important for social well-being) which should grace the modest hearth."[12] Such a guideline, though not strictly enforced, served as a brake upon the efforts of the feminists to advance the cause of unlimited educational opportunity. Furthermore, the imperial administration, no more consistent than most governments, could never quite make up its mind whether higher education acted as a stimulus to or a check upon female radicalism.

In any case, its pious remark about gracing the modest hearth did not have

---

[11] Kropotkin, *Memoirs*, 174. On Filosofova: Koni, "Pamyati," 326–29; Knizhnik-Petrov, *Russkie deyatelnitsy*, 211–12; Valk, *Kursy*, 168. For some sketchy data on Filosofova's illegal connections, see *Arkhiv "Zemli i Voli" i "Narodnoi Voli"*, ed. S. N. Valk (Moscow, 1930), 215, 216, 221.

[12] Quoted in Konstantinov, *Ocherki*, 25.

much relevance for an increasing number of women who crowded into the cities to make their own way. By 1871, unattached females in Moscow outnumbered males in every class except merchants (many of whom had families elsewhere) and peasants. Commercial employment absorbed some of them in telegraphy, bookkeeping, cashiering, photograph retouching, engraving, and watchmaking; but these hardly sufficed to accommodate the bulk of independent women. Nor did they satisfy well-born or well-educated women who aspired to professional or cultural and literary work. With few exceptions, entrée to the active intellectual world required exposure to university courses if not a degree. The main exception was teaching: here, an additional year of pedagogical training after high school enabled a woman to become a teacher. But the scope of opportunity was small, women graduates being allowed to teach only in certain kinds of schools and at the lowest grades. Clearly, the road to professional life led through the university corridor.[13]

Until 1872, this path was blocked off. There were, to be sure, many different kinds of "higher" specialized schools for girls. But these catered to those with innate talents (art, music, the ballet) or to subprofessionals (midwifery, for example). And there were also the "public lectures" in St. Petersburg and Moscow. But these were a partial success at best. Because of the heterogeneous character of the audience, they were too difficult for some and too superficial for others. Since there was no equivalent to the liberal arts college, women desiring a higher education must acquire it at the established universities or at their "own" universities, with instruction from accredited professors. Details such as matriculation, coeducation, and the earning of degrees were all marginal to the main concern of getting an education; and the women of Russia, like those elsewhere, felt that if they could get a foot inside the doors, the rest would follow in due time. Only three things were needed to set the process going: the cooperation of some professors, the permission of a university (this meant the sanction of the government), and money to cover expenses. In this way, the first real institution of higher education for women was born in Moscow in 1872.

The move was initiated by a group of Moscow women who had gained experience as well as sharpened aspirations in the feminist campaign for higher courses of the late 1860's. They approached the Moscow University professor, Vladimir Guerrier (Gere), a historian who had, like many conservative reformers, become convinced that the then prevalent girls' education did not give them an adequate preparation to be teachers, tutors, and mothers. With the help of the rector, Sergei Soloviëv, he won the support of the governor general of Moscow and received formal permission in May 1872 to open "Higher Courses for Women" (*vysshie zhenskie kursy*). An additional request

[13] V. Guerrier [Gere] in "Teoriya i praktika zhenskago obrazovaniya," *VE*, XII (Mar. 1877), 663; *Niva*, I (May 1, 1870), 297–98; *VE*, IX (Aug. 1874), 792; M. V. Kechedzhi-Shapovalov, *Zhenskoe dvizhenie v Rossii i zagranitsei* (SPB, 1902) 140, 174; Ovtsyn, *Razvitie*, 40–41. Peskovsky, "Ocherk," 175–76.

to add the words "of the University of Moscow" was denied. The courses opened in November with Guerrier as director. The limited financial resources assigned to the school were augmented by private donations from feminists and philanthropists and even from the "realm of darkness" in the form of an annual gift of 500 rubles from the Moscow Merchants' Society. Natural sciences, the *bête noire* of the minister of education were not allowed, and the course of study was restricted to two years. But additional years were gradually added and the Higher Course became, in all but name, a liberal arts college, or annex, like Newnham of Cambridge or Radcliffe of Harvard. Sixty-five women enrolled in the first year and an average of about 160 per year until its demise in 1886.[14]

One door had been opened and a principle had been conceded. It was only a matter of time before the government would extend its accommodating policy beyond the limits of Moscow. From 1870 to 1872 a large number of Russian women, dissatisfied with the pace of educational reform is Russia, had swarmed into Switzerland, chiefly the university and the Polytechnic School in Zurich, in order to pursue their education. As we shall see, many of them became infected with "dangerous" ideas. The Russian government, through its network of police spies abroad, was painfully aware of this from the beginning; it may have been a factor in the decision to allow the opening of the Moscow Courses and a women's medical institute in St. Petersburg. It was certainly the major consideration in the decree that allowed women's higher courses to be opened in all university towns in Russia. At first, the government had tried to entice the women home by an 1873 order to leave Zurich. Some of them simply went elsewhere to study; others returned home as fully developed revolutionaries and propagandists. By 1876, Tolstoy, who had originally opposed the idea, became its ardent supporter and decided that it was safer to provide women with a higher education in the homeland than forcing them abroad for a rapid training course in radicalism. Thus the decree that established women's universities in Russia was the result not only of feminism but also of fear of radicalism.[15]

Kazan University was the first to avail itself of the new opportunity and women's courses were founded in 1876, the year of the decree. St. Petersburg and Kiev followed in 1878. The Guerrier Courses in Moscow were elevated to a higher status. Other women's courses were established or planned at the universities of Odessa, Kharkov, and Warsaw. Some of these were stillborn; all of them, except at St. Petersburg, were to be closed down by the government in the middle of the 1880's. The Petersburg Higher Women's Courses were the most famous of these women's universities, as well as the most en-

[14] Peskovsky, "Ocherk," 91; Tsebrikova, "Russia," 410; Likhachëva, *Materialy*, II, 530–35; Satina, *Education*, 78–82.

[15] On the decree, see Peskovsky, "Ocherk," 168; Valk, *Kursy*, 10; "Zhenskoe obrazovanie," *ES* (Brokgaus-Efron), XIA, 871. Whittaker, "Women's Movement."

during. Popularly known as "the Bestuzhev Courses" after K. N. Bestuzhev-Ryumin, professor of history and first director, they opened their doors in the fall of 1878 to women of all social classes, and granted degrees four years later to a class of ninety-nine. In 1883 the Courses were given a permanent abode in the middle of Vasilevsky Island, about a mile from the main buildings of the university.

The Courses had two faculties: History-Philology, and Mathematics-Natural Sciences, the ban against the latter having been dropped by the Ministry. Some of the best professors from the university, Bestuzhev, Sechenov, Orest Miller, and Ovsyaniko-Kulikovsky, contributed time and money or else taught for a modest fee. The students, though mostly of gentry background, came from all social classes: of the 938 attending in 1881, 610 were gentry, 133 merchant, 113 clerical, 102 *meshchanstvo*, 9 peasants, 8 wives or daughters of soldiers. Though by upper-class standards the tuition fees seemed modest enough (50 rubles a year), they were too high for many deserving aspirants; but they were too low to allow the school to finance itself through tuition alone. Since the government was not particularly munificent, contributing only 3,000 rubles a year to the enterprise, the balance had to be raised from private sources.

Having seen their dream of higher education for women come true, Filosofova, Stasova, and their colleagues were determined that it would not perish from lack of financial support. In 1883 they received official permission to found the Society for Providing Means of Support for the Higher Women's Courses. It boasted 1,000 members with an executive committee composed largely of the feminist leaders and honorary figures such as Sofya Kovalevskaya. The executive committee organized book sales, lotteries, lectures, and concerts for the benefit of the courses; scholarships were awarded to deserving women. The Society eventually expanded its range of activities and became the protectress, patroness, and godmother of the Bestuzhev Courses.[16] Similar groups of feminists and philanthropists attached themselves to women's universities in other towns. Undramatic as all this activity appeared, it was of enormous importance to the progress of women's emancipation in Russia. In the face of the government's niggardly attitude toward women's universities, the committees and societies offered valuable moral and financial support for thousands of women who were to make up the major part of the female professional class and the female intelligentsia of the early twentieth century.

From the 1860's until the present moment, Russian women have exhibited a strong attraction for the study of medicine. From the very beginning, medicine and radicalism have been elements of the liberation movement that

[16] For this and the above paragraph, see Valk, *Kursy*, 7, 10, 16, 30–73, 167–72.

have frequently competed with each other for the attention of enterprising women. To us of "the West" who have not had our share of Sun Yat-sens, Rizals, Fanons, and Guevaras, the juxtaposition may seem strange indeed. But in "backward" societies, if we may again apply that overused term to the Russia of the nineteenth century, medical education and practice often serves as an introduction to social maladies deeper than those which can be treated clinically. In Russia, there was a tradition of social consciousness in the medical profession, which produced figures as diverse as Pirogov the reformer, the women suffrage leaders of 1905–1917, and the long line of radical doctors from Suslova to Fëdor Dan. During the most intensive moments of the revolutionary struggle in the nineteenth century, many had to choose between medical practice and full-scale revolutionary activity, because the initial impulse for them to devote their lives to medicine was the social one of serving the people.

In the early 1870's, scores of Russian women, inspired by the successes of Suslova, migrated to Zurich where they were admitted to the university and the Polytechnicum. Of the 120 Russian women enrolled at the university from 1864 to 1874, 85 or about 71 percent were engaged in medical studies. Since less than a quarter of all the women students in Zurich were radicals, it is clear that the large majority of the female medical students were there for serious study alone. But the difference was not one of pure radicalism versus pure medicine: radicals like Vera Figner and Adelaida Lukanina persisted in their medical studies long after they had taken a radical path. For them it was difficult to separate these two intimately related modes of personal expression. The more committed radicals joined revolutionary circles and returned to liberate their country. The others continued their studies abroad at Berne, Paris, or Philadelphia, or returned to Russia to join the courses newly opened there. "This type of woman student," observed Vera Figner, "was not drawn to socialism and to active struggle for freedom, but was perhaps more closely related to those pioneers of the women's movement who fought for equality in higher specialized education and won a spectacular success in this fight." Figner herself was the prime example of one who evolved gradually from a feminist-minded consciousness to that of a lifetime revolutionary.[17]

It is difficult to say how much of a role female radicalism in Zurich played in the government's decision to open a medical school for women in 1872. In its decree ordering the women out of Zurich, it referred to this school as the best reason why the women should return home to study. But its counsels were divided. Minister of Education Tolstoy was opposed to the idea, happily endorsing the opinion of Professor von Bischoff of Munich who, on the basis

[17] Figner, "Studencheskie gody (1872–1873)," *Golos minuvshego*, X (Oct. 1922) 180–81. The Zurich figures are drawn from the tables in Meijer, *Knowledge and Revolution*, 208–12. For radicalism in Zurich, see Chapter V, 2 below.

of "scientific investigation," had concluded that women were physiologically unfit for the study and practice of medicine. The liberal journals and the feminists raised a storm of protest, pointing to the shameful shortage of doctors in Russian society. They found their champions in the Ministry of War, then under the enlightened direction of Dmitry Milyutin, who wished to improve the military medical services. The Military Medical-Surgical Academy in St. Petersburg was headed by Dr. N. D. Kozlov whose daughter, Praskoviya Tarnovskaya, later became one of Russia's best known women doctors. His plan to open courses for women at the Academy was approved and, with the aid of a 50,000 ruble donation from a wealthy supporter, Mme. Rodstvennaya, brought to fruition in November 1872.[18]

Ninety women enrolled in the first semester, mostly of gentry and official families, with a sprinkling of middle class girls and a relatively high percentage of Jews. The entrance requirement was a diploma and, for those under twenty, permission from parents and a character reference; the entrance examination, curiously enough, an essay on the Tartar Yoke and another on Belinsky. The regimen of academic life was severe and the setting intensely formal. The students had to sit up straight in their benches, wear formal dresses and long hair, and endure being treated as children, though most of them were over twenty and some of them even mothers. Talking with male students, even relatives, was forbidden. Day-to-day life was hard for those who had no family in the city. They took cheap rooms near the Academy (located about a block from the Finland Station). Whenever possible they enlivened their book-filled lives with evenings of music and poetry. The general outlook of the students was intensely serious. One alumna glumly recalled that the relations between male and female students were always "perfectly correct," notwithstanding the dirty insinuations made against them by people incapable of understanding decent feelings.[19]

Economic conditions were eased somewhat through the efforts of the feminists and sympathetic professors who founded the Society for Aiding Women Students at the Medical and Pedagogical Courses. The chemistry professor and part-time composer, Alexander Borodin, a member of the committee, gave freely of his time and energy to educating sincerely interested young women. More important, the staff of the courses quietly ignored the original limitations of the program (pediatric and gynecological subjects) and eventu-

[18] For the debate, see: Lange, *Frauenbewegung*, I. 72–73; *Delo*, VI (Sept. 1872) 119–22; *VE*, VII (Sept. 1872) 357–83; *OZ*, CCI (Apr. 1872) 260–64 and CCV (Nov. 1872) 31–49. For the origin of the courses: E. S. Nekrasova, "Zhenskie vrachebnye kursy v Peterburge: iz vospominanii i perepiski pervykh studentok," *VE*, XVII (Dec. 1882) 807–45 (810–18); Peskovsky, "Ocherk," 91, 164–65; Likhachëva, *Materialy*, II, 536–53. Kozlov's other daughter was the grandmother of Vladimir Nabokov: *Speak Memory* (New York, 1966) 50–51.
[19] See Nekrasova's reminiscences, cited above and those of Shabanova, "Zhenskie vrachebnye kursy," 345–57.

85

ally presented a full five-year program of medical training. When the first class reached graduation in 1877, the rigor of their life had taken its toll. Twelve of the original ninety had died: seven of consumption; two by suicide; and one of typhus in the Turkish War.[20]

The War of 1877, like the Crimean War before it, was a great boon to women's advancement in medicine. Their suitability for the profession was dramatized by their professional conduct as well as by their heroic sacrifices. The entire graduating class of twenty-five women went to serve in the Turkish campaign, twenty as medical assistants with the army, and five with the Red Cross. The usual resistance to having women at the front was quickly brushed aside, and women were soon performing major surgical operations without the assistance of male physicians. One woman doctor, Mariya Siebold (Sibold) of St. Petersburg, organized and directed a military hospital for the Serbs before Russia entered the war in the Balkans. At the University of Zurich, she had been black-balled by a radical library because "she had come to Zurich to study medicine and nothing more." When the war ended the Military Medical Inspector praised their accomplishments and they were decorated. More important, they were given the title "woman doctor" (zhenskii vrach), which now replaced "learned midwife" as the designation of future graduates of the medical courses.[21]

All of this was the beginning of a social trend in Russia that has persisted up to the present: the utilization of women's talents and inclinations in one of the most difficult and useful of all social services. The leaders of local government bodies (zemstva) were quick to perceive the advantages in augmenting their notoriously understaffed medical points with women doctors, and invitations to serve in the zemstvo medical establishments were received by students even before graduation. But despite the enthusiasm of some of the women and the crying need for rural doctors, most of the women doctors ended up emulating their male colleagues and staying in the cities. In 1886, for every sixty women serving in zemstvo medicine, there were forty in Moscow and Petersburg. This was more the fault of the bureaucracy than it was of the women, however, for provincial governors possessed the right, and often used it, of prohibiting women from practicing medicine in their provinces, whatever the wishes of the zemstvo officials.[22] Wherever they worked, city or country, their success would depend largely on whether their superiors wanted them there or resented them.[23] But the pattern of women in medicine

[20] Nekrasova, "Vospom.," p. 840. For the Society, see VE, XII (Jul. 1877), 401–13. For Borodin, T. Popova, Borodin, 2d ed. (Moscow, 1960), 113–16.

[21] P. A. Ilinsky, Russkaya zhenshchina v voinu 1877–1878 g. (SPB, 1879); Peskovsky, "Ocherk," p. 166; Ovtsyn, Razvitie, 30. On Siebold, see M. P. Sazhin, "Russkie v Tsyurikhe (1870–1873 gg.)," Katorga i ssylka (No. 10, 1932), 20–78 (43).

[22] -!-, Za Zhenshchin, 2d ed. (SPB, 1886), 238–39.

[23] M. I. Pokrovskaya, Kak ya byla gorodskim vrachem dlya bednykh (SPB, 1903) 67. A valuable personal memoir by a woman doctor who became a feminist leader in 1905. See Chapter VII of this study.

was set by the end of the 1870's in Russia; by then Russia was far ahead of Europe in the number of practicing women doctors. The tendency continued right up to the revolution and was to be one of the most precious of the social accomplishments inherited by the Bolsheviks from the feminists.

"How is it that Russia, which by no means occupies the foremost rank in European civilization, is first in the matter of woman's emancipation? for no country in the Old World can vie with Russia in this respect." Writing in the early 1880's, Mariya Tsebrikova tells us that such questions were often put to her by her European friends. She agreed. So did Likhachëva who announced in 1880 that "Russia has outstripped other countries and Russian women have achieved greater results."[24] If by "results" they meant a wide range of educational opportunity for those women who could avail themselves of it, Tsebrikova and Likhachëva were right. The efforts of the feminists and their sympathizers, combined with the government's fear of radicalism, had made possible the establishment of a women's medical school and a handful of women's universities whose number would be augmented after 1905. In quality and range of women's higher education, Russia had no peer in Europe. Only England came close; in the world at large, only America was further ahead.

The Russian "government" was not a monolithic entity, but a complex organism. Its position on women's education was shifting and often contradictory. The simplistic belief that education led women automatically into political temptations appeared regularly every decade from 1860 to 1917. The liberal belief that enlarging the horizons of women was simply a good thing for backward Russia was pronounced less frequently in the government, but asserted itself vigorously in practice nonetheless. Between these lay the more traditional conviction that providing a solid education for the women who insisted on it could after all provide the nation with loyal and reliable citizens—a modern application of the well-rooted "citizen-mother" concept. The 1885 proclamation on the establishment of a Gentry Bank described the function of that class in the following words. *The gentry of the Russian Empire must preserve a leading place in the military, in matters of local administration and justice, and in spreading by their example the rule of faith and loyalty and the sound principles of popular education."*[25] Could better words than these last be chosen to describe the function of women and mothers educated by the Russian state?

It would be too much to credit the "spectacular success" referred to by Figner to the feminists alone. At work here were many varied and even conflicting forces inside the government, in society, and among the radicals. But the feminists began the campaign, saw it through to the end, and performed

[24] Tsebrikova, "Russia," p. 291; Likhachëva in *OZ*, CCXLIX (Mar. 1880) 1.
[25] Cited by Aleksandr Kornilov in *Kurs istorii Rossii XIX veka*, pt. III, 2d ed. (Moscow, 1918) 298 (italics in the original).

many unseen but crucial services that made it possible for courses to open and to survive the political and financial pressures besetting them. The encomiums heaped upon them, particularly Stasova and Filosofova, by historians and memoirists, both Soviet and anti-Soviet, are richly deserved. But the feminist victory as of 1881 was a narrow one indeed. At most it affected only a few thousand women a year, a minuscule slice of even the gentry population of females. It made almost no impact upon the peasant women, except that some women doctors went into village *zemstvo* work to supplement or replace the archaic ministrations of *baba* midwives. The feminist solution was classically liberal, deriving unconsciously from the eighteenth-century English Whig tradition of liberalizing from the top and slowly spreading the benefits of reform down the social ladder. Russians of a radical persuasion, being radical in their very special Russian way, could hardly have been expected to be even remotely satisfied with this model and this philosophy of social reform.

IV

The Nihilist Response

Volos dolog,
Da um korotok.
—*Traditional Russian Saying*

1. WHAT IS TO BE DONE?

In the broadest sense, Chernyshevsky's novel, *What Is To Be Done?* (1863) was a Bible for all advanced Russian women with aspirations toward independence, whether they thought and acted as organized feminists, as revolutionaries, or as "nihilist" women. To the feminists it reinforced their ideas on education and economic independence and on the moral imperative of helping other women struggle for these things. To the radical women whose life interests transcended the narrower aspiration of women's emancipation in order to embrace the cause of liberating the "people," the influence of the book was more subtle. Though necessarily muted by the problem of censorship, the theme of the radical remaking of Russian society was vividly implicit as was its summons to women to free themselves from social incarceration in order to join the ranks of the "new people" who would one day effect the social revolution. But the most direct impact of the novel was upon what came to be seen as the nihilist outlook on women and sex—a doctrine of personal emancipation and sexual freedom that was not only psychologically alien to the moderate feminism of Stasova and Trubnikova but also distinguishable (if not always distinguished) from female political radicalism.

By all accounts, the work exerted a colossal influence on the radical intelligentsia. On women's consciousness and on men's awareness of "the problem," it had both a short and a long range effect. To contemporary men and women of the so-called nihilist persuasion, it offered attractive and apparently rational solutions to such immediate problems as parental despotism, incompatible marriages, conflicting loves, and the true road to a life of fulfillment and meaning. These solutions are clearly mapped out in the rapidly developing consciousness of the central character, Vera Pavlovna. But beyond this, it also advanced a broader program of relations between the sexes and a view of erotic love that would command the unspoken allegiance of generations of revolutionaries.

Chernyshevsky, son of a priest, and hero of the radical "hot-heads" of the

89

day, was best known for his essays on philosophy, politics, and economics, and, during the halcyon days of *The Contemporary*, was the leading radical spokesman in Russia. His open contempt for liberalism and "small deeds" precluded any sympathy for the feminist approach to women's subjection. His major views on women had been fashioned years before, chiefly under the suggestive influence of George Sand and Fourier, whose teachings he first encountered from friends in the Petrashevsky Circle. Shortly before his marriage to Olga Sokratovna Vasileva—a most suitable subject for his theories—Chernyshevsky drafted a personal "program" of future relations with women. The program called for submission to his wife, full freedom of action for her, and unflagging fidelity for himself. He voiced the hope that the marriage would be a partnership of two intellectuals, but he also argued that women "occupied an insignificant place in the family," and that now "the reed should be bent back the other way." In line with this, he was prepared to offer his wife the freedom that he would deny to himself—inconstancy and adultery. As it happened, Olga Sokratovna was perfectly willing to avail herself of Chernyshevsky's broad-minded generosity.[1]

This was a calculated moral act and not merely an indulgent gesture. It was meant to be an act of "rational egoism" resting on the supposition that his cuckolded feeling created less pain than that caused by his wife's lack of freedom.[2] But Chernyshevsky felt pain none the less, and this perhaps induced him to avoid writing about the subject until his arrest. While endorsing Mikhailov's conclusions, he disagreed with his undue emphasis on the woman question, and told Shelgunov that such an emphasis was well enough when there were no other problems. But faced with the prospect of unlimited leisure in the Peter-Paul Fortress, Chernyshevsky turned once again to those enduring personal issues and sought to find answers for them. What prompted him? Retrospection? The novels of George Sand? Mikhailov's recent articles and their warm reception? We do not know. Perhaps all of them, combined with his personal acquaintance with advanced "nihilist" women striving for that consciousness he was about to describe in the person of Vera Pavlovna.[3]

The unfolding of Vera Pavlovna's consciousness as a full human being is the dominant theme of *What Is To Be Done?* Its direct artistic inspiration may

[1] Georges Sourine, *Le Fourierisme en Russie* (Paris, 1936) 89; Chernyshevsky, *Polnoe sobranie sochinenii*, ed. B.P. Kozmin. 15 v. (Moscow, 1939–50) I, 444; Bogdanovich, *Lyubov*, 23–28.

[2] The full elaboration of this theory, drawn largely from Helvétius and the English Utilitarians, may be found in Chernyshevsky's *Antropologicheskii printsip v filosofii* (Geneva, 1875), first written in 1860. For a modern critique of such theories, see C. D. Broad, "Egoism as a Theory of Human Motives," in *Ethics and the History of Philosophy: Selected Essays* (New York, 1952) 218–31.

[3] See the note in *OZ* (Apr. 1861) 146 and Shelgunovs-Mikhailov, *Vospom.*, I, 121. His prison books included Sand's *Rudolstadt*, *Piccinino*, and *Aldini*, Pomyalovsky's *Molotov*, and various works by Dickens, Rousseau, Heine, Vogt, Lyell, and Darwin. N.A. Alekseev, ed., *Protsess Chernyshevskogo: arkhivnye dokumenty* (Saratov, 1939) 356.

have been Pomyalovsky's *Molotov* (1861), which Chernyshevsky had with him in the cell. That story's main female character, her conversations with Molotov, and the author's soliloquies to the reader, all have their counterparts in Chernyshevsky's novel. Vera, like Pomyalovsky's Nadya, is a sensitive and well-educated girl, trapped in an obscurantist household, and seeking "her own way." Her mother is a model of crude ambition and ignorance ("Young girls shouldn't know about such things; it's their mother's business"), and is endeavoring to marry Vera to a well-heeled libertine. Vera's consciousness begins with one of those dreams that play such a crucial role in her development. In an allegory of her deliverance, she is released from a dark and stifling cellar by a figure who calls herself "Love of Mankind," then hastens to the myriads of dream prisons to liberate her sisters from their bondage. But at her level of development—and given the Russian legal code—she cannot extricate herself without the aid of an outside force. A medical student, Dmitry Lopukhov, offers her what came to be called a "fictitious marriage," a legal convenience to enable her to leave the house of her parents but with no connubial obligations.[4]

The device of the "fictitious marriage" was already in use among Russian youth by the time Chernyshevsky wrote the novel. One of his real life models for Vera Pavlovna was Mariya Obrucheva, sister of a well-known radical. At Chernyshevsky's suggestion, the medical student Peter Bokov agreed to tutor her; later he offered her a fictitious marriage (1851), so that she could break with her family and study medicine in St. Petersburg. Vera Pavlovna, like her prototype, fell in love with her obliging liberator, though this was by no means part of the agreement. But, in spite of an ideal arrangement of marital equality, including separate rooms, Vera later fell in love with her husband's best friend, Kirsanov, an instructor at the medical academy. In real life, this was the noted physiologist, Ivan Sechenov, who won the heart of his student, and settled down with the Bokovs in a *ménage à trois* in the early 1860's. This, the Mikhailov-Shelgunova-Shelgunov triangle, and his own broodings provided ample material for Chernyshevsky's literary triangle.[5]

Vera had advanced to the point where she could recognize that Lopukhov did not love her (a combination of friendship and sex was not enough for her), and that she was attracted to the more sociable Kirsanov. But she could not

[4] The domestic hell of Pomyalovsky's Nadya, a serious young girl, was her Institute where the headmistress segregated cocks from hens during Lent and then bewailed the lack of Easter eggs. For a Soviet edition, see *Meshchanskoe schaste; Molotov* (Moscow, 1957). *Chto delat?* (Moscow, 1963) 46.

[5] Bogdanovich, *Lyubov*, 426–38; S. Kara-Murza, "Geroi i geroini romana *"Chto delat?*," *Krasnaya niva*, VI (July 22, 1928), 8–9; I. M. Sechenov, *Avtobiograficheskiya zapiski* (Moscow, 1907) 117–18. Bokov eventually withdrew from the menage and married. Years later his wife, who had kept his name while living with Sechenov, obtained a divorce and married her lover. She outlived them all and died in 1929 at the age of ninety. In her will she wrote: "I have neither money nor objects of value. I ask to be buried beside my husband, without church services, as simply and as cheaply as possible." Kovalevskaya, *Vospom.*, 180–81, n. 123. See also M.T. Pinaev, *Kommentarii k romanu N. G. Chernyshevskogo "Chto delat?"* (Moscow, 1963) 93, 94.

solve the problem; this was still left to the initiative of the male principles. After a brief struggle with the arcane complexities of "rational egoism," Lopukhov cut the knot neatly, if melodramatically, by feigning suicide and disappearing. His motivation was the same utilitarian theory that had undergirded Chernyshevsky's own marital "program." The latter had once hinted to Olga Sokratovna that if he were too much in the way, he might emulate the hero of George Sand's *Jacques* and do away with himself.[6]

In the course of her struggle for freedom to love, Vera discovers that love, marriage, and even total erotic fulfillment are not enough to make her a free woman. Like many women in Russian life at that moment, she sensed that economic independence was even more fundamental than sexual freedom and equality. "Everything is based on money," her first husband tells her. "He who has money has power and rights"; and "as long as woman lives off a man, she is dependent on him." Julie Letellier, the lady of easy virtue, put it another way: "I am depraved not because they call me an immoral woman; not for what I have done or what I have lost or what I have suffered; not because my body has been desecrated. No, I am depraved because I have become accustomed to idleness and luxury without being able to live independent of others." Vera already knows this. "I want to be independent and live in my own way," she says. "I do not want to submit to anyone. I want to be free, to be obligated to no one, so that no one dare say to me: you must do this or that for me."[7]

Vera's second dream shows her that work, the social equivalent of motion in nature, is the central force in life. Drawing partly on socialist theory and partly on the practice of Russian *artels*, Chernyshevsky constructs for her a fictional sewing cooperative, which begins as a limited profit-sharing enterprise and develops into a full-scale residential producers' and consumers' commune in the heart of St. Petersburg. Vera Pavlovna, recalling her dream-given injunction to liberate other women, uses the sewing *artel* to raise the consciousness of her female employees. She makes partners of them, shares the profits, draws them into the administration, and gradually educates them to self-reliance through carefully programmed readings of "progressive" literature. She is the fictional predecessor of the Zhenotdel organizers who, sixty years later, were using similar techniques in "consciousness raising" throughout the length and breadth of the Soviet Republic. It is here among the needles and the brochures of her sewing establishment that Vera Pavlovna reaches that level of awareness and activism that makes her one of the earliest agents of women's liberation in European fiction.

Yet even this activity, together with her household duties (performed with

[6] PSS, XI, 716. The difference in spirit between Chernyshevsky's and George Sand's solutions to the love triangle is analyzed by A. Skaftymov in "Chernyshevskii i Zhorzh Sand," *Stati o russkoi literature* (Saratov, 1958) 203–27.

[7] *Chto delat?*, quotations, 144, 67.

92

the aid of a servant!) and her lessons, is not sufficient to absorb her self-generating energies and sublimate her confessed surplus of passion. She needs "a personal occupation, something important, on which [her] whole existence would hang." But she realizes the obstacles to a higher role for women: "The rule of force has deprived her both of the means for development and the motivation for it." Her level of consciousness will not allow her to be content with a governess job, an overcrowded occupation in any case. She decides to study medicine, with the aid of her husband, just as the real Bokova studied with Sechenov before the academy excluded her. "It would be very important," says Vera Pavlovna, "if we finally had women doctors. They would be very useful for all women. Women can talk with other women much better than they can with men. How much suffering, pain, and sorrow could be avoided. It must be tried." Will power, social consciousness, action—the salient features of the New Woman—are all on display. In pursuing medicine, Vera Pavlovna was following, not setting, a trend; but her imitators in the next two decades would be legion.[8]

Chernyshevsky's approach to women's liberation has a different style from that of the organized feminists. In education, his stress was on individual effort: books, tutoring by friends, and circles. No scenes in university halls, no struggling female students, no petitions. As for charity, the author's view is given subtle expression in the following passage about Polozova, a minor character: "Her father gave her a good deal of pocket money and she, as any good woman would do, gave to the poor. But she also read and thought, and she began to notice that what she did give had a much smaller effect than it ought to have had; that too many of her 'poor' were fakers and good-for-nothings, and that the really deserving . . . almost never received enough to have any long-range effect on their condition."[9] The *artel* was meant to be the nucleus of a fundamental reordering of society that would give decent work to all, and thus obviate the need for such demeaning activity as philanthropy. But even to some contemporary readers, the contrast was not entirely convincing in the novel, for a good deal of patronizing took place even in the egalitarian atmosphere of the *artel*. This was especially apparent in the parable of the redeemed prostitute, Nastya Kryukova. Chernyshevsky's teaching, reduced to its essentials, is this: men must cease being the clients of prostitutes and thus eliminate the market; women must help the victims by giving them work. Any feminist from 1860 right up to the Revolution could have said (and did say) the same thing.

Commenting both on the bleakness of the Russian social landscape and on the significance of his heroine, Chernyshevsky says of Vera Pavlovna that she is "one of the first women whose life is well arranged. First examples possess historical interest; and 'a first swallow' is of special interest to us denizens of northern climes." She is to be the harbinger of a warm springtime in human

---

[8] *Ibid.*, quotations, 373, 369, 377.   [9] *Ibid.*, 443–44.

relations that will succeed the harsh winter of class and sexual subjugation. Her well-ordered life is rooted in her ability to make social activity a pendant to her erotic life, to counterpoise will against passion. In a scene, cunningly interrupted by intervals of sexual intimacy, Chernyshevsky has her utter the following words to her husband: "If a person thinks to himself 'I can't,' then he can't. It has been suggested to women that they are weak; so they feel weak, and then actually become weak." Vera's strength lies in her profound consciousness of the power of her will and her ability to act. Throughout the story, she endeavors to impart this same consciousness to other members of her sex. The novel thus becomes, among other things, a celebration of the latent power of woman, and a flattering summons to take her life into her own hands. Vera Pavlovna's positive outlook and her towering self-confidence constituted a legacy to the nihilists of the 1860's who would see in her the proper model of action, will, and sexual identification. This was Chernyshevsky's parting gift to the women of his generation.[10]

In view of the great debates on sex and marriage that occupied his revolutionary grandchildren some sixty years after he wrote *What Is To Be Done?*, Chernyshevsky's views on these matters, strewn through the novel, need to be brought into sharper focus. Some of these required little comment on his part; for example the ideas of freely contracted unions and of equality in marriage that included privacy and "a room of one's own."[11] Others, like his unqualified rejection of possessiveness and jealousy, evoked a storm of verbal emotion. "O filth, filth! 'to possess.' Who dares possess a human being? A robe or a pair of slippers, yes. But this is nonsense! Almost all of us men possess some of you, our sisters. But this is nonsense too. How can we call you our sisters? You are our lackeys! Some of you, even many of you, dominate us. But that means nothing; don't lackeys dominate their masters?" As to jealousy: "A developed man shouldn't have it. It is a distorted emotion, a false emotion, a vile emotion; a phenomenon of that social order under which I let no one wear my linen or smoke my pipe; it is a vestige of that view of man which sees him as property, as a thing."[12]

Thus divorce or its non-juridical equivalents is not only permissable but also necessary in Chernyshevsky's sexual world. When two halves of a union do not "fit," there should be neither blame nor guilt nor any effort to cripple the personality of one by remodeling it to fit the other. Indeed, Chernyshevsky unabashedly tells his reader that the "secret" of enduring and loving partnerships is the awareness of both members that the other is free "at any moment"

[10] *Ibid.*, quotations, 83, 370.

[11] Vera tells Lopukhov that people should not live as they do now "completely together, completely," but "only when they want to or when they have a reason for it." *Ibid.*, 148. The idea of separate rooms was drawn from Chernyshevsky's life with Olga Sokratovna, who first suggested it: G. Plekhanov, *N.G. Chernyshevskii* (SPB, 1910) 72.

[12] *Chto delat?*, quotations, 68–69, 326–27.

to bid farewell, without regret or rancor, once the free bond of love has eroded. Only in the case of children, he says, should the parents make every effort to avoid separation if such an act would have harmful consequences for them.[13] These remarks and the lives of his characters leave no doubt that Chernyshevsky looked upon divorce as an exception, a necessary escape hatch for those who had come together through error. Divorce, or its nihilist equivalent, was not to be construed as an everyday convenience to be invoked repeatedly in order to satisfy promiscuous inclinations.

What of sex itself? Does Chernyshevsky ignore it, as some commentaries and abridged translations would lead us to believe?[14] Was the puritanical Rakhmetov, who eschewed wine and women, the *alter ego* of Chernyshevsky? Hardly so. For the author does not merely rail against "abnormal thirst" and loveless carnal possession; against them he poises an acutely sensitive appreciation of amorous eroticism. It is given first utterance when he describes how Kryukova, the ex-prostitute, achieves sensual arousal for the first time in the arms of the loving Kirsanov. And it reaches its apogee in Vera Pavlovna's triumphant depiction of sexual ecstasy as an act of love:

> The power of sensation is commensurate with the depth of the organism out of which it rises. If aroused only by an external cause, an external object, it is fleeting and it embraces only a limited portion of life. He who drinks wine only because someone offers him the glass will not have much appreciation of its taste and will derive little satisfaction from it. Pleasure is much more intense when it is rooted in the imagination, when the imagination seeks out the object and agent of its pleasure. Then the blood rises more noticeably and you can feel its warmth, a feeling which heightens the impression of ecstasy. But even this is very weak in comparison with what happens when the root of the relationship is planted deep in the soil of a moral life. Then passion penetrates the entire nervous system with extraordinary force over a long period of time.[15]

Chernyshevsky moors the idea of erotic love to other aspects of a healthy social life in essentially Fourierist terms. "Unless work precedes them," says Lopukhov, "diversion, relaxation, fun, and festivity have no reality." And elsewhere: "A person who manages his life correctly divides his time into three parts: work, pleasure, and rest or recreation." This notion is given full play in the great commune of Vera's fourth dream, with its futuristic visions of golden fields, fertile valleys, workers singing in the sun and returning home to their glass and crystal communal dwellings to receive bounteous meals pre-

---

[13] *Ibid.*, 342, 385. Legal divorce was generally unacceptable to the people of the new dispensation, as Pisarev pointed out (*Soch.*, IV, 38) because of its humiliating character.

[14] For example, *What Is To Be Done? Tales About New People*, tr. Benjamin Tucker, rev. and abr. Ludmilla B. Turkevich (New York, 1961) manages to delete all the erotic passages in the book.

[15] *Chto delat?*: Kryukova's experience, 239; Vera's words, 390.

pared by the children and the old people. Hard work has prepared them for an augmented enjoyment of pleasure. And here Vera's guide, now "the beautiful tsaritsa" now the "Goddess of Sexual Equality" speaks with the voice of Eros: "I rule here. Here all is dedicated to me: Work—to prepare fresh feelings and energy for me; Play—to get in readiness for me; Rest—to enjoy after me. Here I am the goal of life. Here I am life itself."[16]

Thus we have in Chernyshevsky not only the moral mechanics of sexual freedom, equality, and mobility but also the centrality of sex itself. Even Lenin, who admired him deeply, might have admitted that the author of *What Is To Be Done?* had spent more than a little time in ventilating questions which Lenin felt to be too much in the forefront. As a matter of fact, Chernyshevsky's basic views are not greatly different from those of Alexandra Kollontai whose writings were to bring down upon her the moral wrath of Leninists in the 1920's, and neither Chernyshevsky nor Kollontai were on the extreme sexual left of their respective revolutionary cultures. Chernyshevsky would not have dreamed of allowing the communitarian couples of Vera's fourth dream to emerge from their connubial alcoves in order to change partners.[17]

But the line between promiscuity and ease of divorce is a difficult one to draw. Like Herzen, Mikhailov, and the others who wrote before him, Chernyshevsky, by insisting on freedom in love and at the same time celebrating the joys of a lasting union, left the door open for conflicting interpretations. Otherwise it could not be. Chernyshevsky knew this. He was writing for New People who were endowed with realism, rational egoism, and the "correct" moral vision. For the still corrupted generality no program, no credo, no novel could chart the way to a new sexual basis for society. Nor, as it happened, could either the fortified monogamy of tsarist society or the permissive atmosphere of post-revolutionary Russia bring and keep together what the laws of ordinary psychology would rend asunder.

Reactions to the novel were immediate and strong. Fëdor Tolstoy, a conservative writer for *The Northern Bee*, accused Chernyshevsky of recommending "every comfort and seduction for shopgirls and streetwalkers, removing all obstacles for them, and giving them the right to take lovers into their rooms." Askochensky, in *Household Conversation*, suggested that Chernyshevsky's characters belonged in a workhouse where the meager diet and hard labor would help them unlearn their stupid emancipatory notions. A conservative priest, N. Soloviëv, used his review of *What Is To Be Done?* as an occasion to strike at the entire phenomenon of women's emancipation in Russia, including higher education. His major concern was the moral laxness of "modern" women who, he claimed, had adopted the harmful idea of

---

[16] *Ibid.*, quotations, 186, 338, 410.
[17] For the views of Lenin and Kollontai, see Chapter XI.

George Sand that since men have sexual freedom, women should have it too. Soloviëv insisted that Chernyshevsky's *What Is To Be Done?* preached a brand of "free love" that was hardly distinguishable from prostitution and "the debasement of woman's noble nature by means of cunning theoretical positions." He concluded from the drift of the novel that Vera Pavlovna would fall in love with Rakhmetov and then cohabit with all three of her admirers, or so the philosophy of the author would allow.[18]

One of the most violent critical reactions was a polemical tract entitled *What They Did in "What Is To Be Done?"* written in the 1870's by Professor Tsitovich of Odessa University. In a deliberate effort to distort and discredit the meaning of the book, by means of a dubious exegesis of the Russian law codes, Tsitovich accused the characters of committing abduction, bigamy, pimping, and fornication, among other things. His bitterest comments, including some vile remarks about the heroine, were directed at the alleged Darwinian spirit of the novel. Vera Pavlovna's choice of Kirsanov over Lopukhov, he said, was no more than a mechanical act of sexual selection, a human version of the beastly behavior described in *The Origin of Species*.[19] Tsitovich was particularly distressed by the fact that, as he said, every schoolgirl and student knew the book intimately and was "considered a dunce if she was not acquainted with the exploits of Vera Pavlovna." From this no doubt accurate observation, he concluded that the female defendants in the recent political trials were the latest embodiments of the characters in Chernyshevsky's book.[20]

Conservatives were unanimous in imputing to the novel an open endorsement of sexual licence. The term "free love," used all over the Western world as a weapon against emancipation, was defined as complete promiscuity. But of course neither George Sand's "freedom of the heart" nor Chernyshevsky's version of it was any such thing. It simply meant that a young woman should be allowed to follow her romantic (not merely physical) inclinations, including, if necessary, the desertion of one man for another. But the love knot of each relationship would be as binding on the members as that made by any matrimonial contract, indeed more so. Freedom of love could only be sequential, never simultaneous. Even Enfantin stopped short of polygamous behavior for his Don Juan types. But most conservatives could not or would not see this truth. The cynical obscurantists, as Plekhanov pointed out years later, understood full well the real morality of the novel which menaced their Philistine life style of secret affairs and "boudoir visits." Thus the identification of the moral formulas of *What Is To Be Done?* with the worst kind of debauchery

---

[18] The first two reviews are described by the editor in Chernyshevsky, PSS, XI, 707; N. Soloviëv, "Zhenshchinam," *Epokha* (Dec. 1864) 15–24.

[19] Strakhov with more justice observed that there was hardly any difference at all between Lopukhov and Kirsanov. "Schastlivye lyudi" (1865), reprinted in *Iz istorii literaturnogo nigilizma* (SPB, 1890).

[20] P. Tsitovich, *Chto delali v romane "Chto delat?"* 5th ed. (Odessa, 1879) iv–vii, 6, 19, 39, 53.

and carnal license was to be the hall-mark of anti-nihilist criticism for decades.[21]

Reviews of the novel in the "progressive" camp were generally favorable. Pisarev's "Thinking Proletariat," the most influential, welcomed the heroes to the world of Russian letters and praised Vera Pavlovna as "the new woman." He defended them against the critics' charge of immorality by contrasting their honest behavior to that of the conventional cad, Storeshnikov, who lewdly dreams of seducing Vera. But Shelgunov, was not so enthusiastic. He saw Vera Pavlovna as an undeveloped woman, still moving in the rarefied atmosphere of love that suffuses the works of Turgenev and George Sand, a transitional figure, trained for love and not for work rather than a New Woman. Being one of the real life models for the novel, Shelgunov also found fault with the "chivalrous relations" among the principals. "Even our best people have not yet been able to free themselves from their false relations with women. . . ." Among simple people, he said, were simple desires, based on physiology and not on the exalted and excessively "feminine atmosphere" of this book.[22]

But it was Pisarev's view which prevailed overwhelmingly among the young radicals and nihilists. Skabichevsky recalled the impact that Chernyshevsky's novel made upon his circle:

> We read the novel almost like worshippers, with the kind of piety with which we read religious books, and without the slightest trace of a smile on our lips. The influence of the novel on our society was colossal. It played a great role in Russian life, especially among the leading members of the intelligentsia who were embarking on the road to socialism, bringing it down a bit from the world of drama to the problem of our social evils, sharpening its image as the goal which each of us had to fight for.

Vodovozova recalled how the gentry, returning from their summer homes in the fall of 1863, were greeted everywhere with discussions of *What Is To Be Done?*. Young girls would pay up to twenty-five rubles for a copy composed of serial issues of *The Contemporary* bound together. Although most of its ideas were already current, she said, its literary form provided a synthesis that opened people's eyes and "gave a vigorous push to the mental and moral development of Russian society." As the literary historian, Ovsyaniko-Kulikovsky observed many years later, "Vera Pavlovna symbolized the

---

[21] On reading the book, Prince Odoevsky exclaimed: "But how this *promiscuité des femmes* must attract the young folk." "Dnevnik V. F. Odoevskogo, 1858–1869 gg.," in *Lit. nasledstvo*, XXII–XXIV (1935), 79–308 (176–78).

[22] Pisarev, *Soch.*, IV, 7–49; Shelgunov's 1865 review is reprinted in N. K. Piksanov, ed., *Shestidesyatye gody: materialy po istorii literatury i obshchestvennomu dvizheniyu* (Moscow, Leningrad, 1940) 173–86.

women's movement of the 1860's; in her aspirations and her enterprises were reflected the stage which the woman question had reached at that time."[23]

When Chernyshevsky was led out of the fortress to his place of civil execution in 1864, two young women, one the sister of Lyudmila Shelgunova, threw bouquets of flowers at him.[24] This act of gratitude and admiration symbolized the belief of a large number of women in the Russia of the 1860's that he had shown them "the right path" to future emancipation. Although it is true that Chernyshevsky had worked up themes and techniques already in use among the younger generation, it was clear that he had offered the most comprehensive set of answers to date to the "burning questions." Even Shelgunov admitted that in *What Is To Be Done?*, Chernyshevsky was describing life and not creating it. What Sergei Aksakov, Goncharov, and Turgenev had done to describe the ethos of the pre-emancipation gentry, Chernyshevsky had done for the would-be destroyers of that ethos. Herzen, no great friend of Chernyshevsky at the time (1866), named him and Mikhailov as those who had done the most to help liberate women from the humiliating yoke of the family.[25]

2. NIHILISM AND WOMEN

Although cultural anthropologists might not agree, the concept of ethnicity need not be confined to national, regional, or linguistic groups but ought to be applied to any category of human beings that constitutes a more or less clearly defined cultural community visibly distinguishable from the surrounding society. Indeed, when applied to communities with a homogeneous culture—whether political, social, or religious—it can have far more meaning than when used to conceptualize such internally diverse categories as "Jews," "Southern Blacks," or "Irish Catholics." The term "nihilists" has long been employed by both sympathizers and critics to describe a large, diffuse group of Russians who made their appearance in the late 1850's and early 1860's and who formed the pool out of which radical movements emerged. There have been many attempts to define Russian nihilism, but I think Nikolai Strakhov came close to the truth when he said that "nihilism itself hardly exists, although there is no denying the fact that nihilists do."[1] Nihilism was

---

[23] Skabichevsky quoted in Bogdanovich, *Lyubov*, p. 16; Vodovozova, *Na zare zhizni*, 2d ed., II, 216–28; D. N. Ovsyaniko-Kulikovsky, *Istoriya russkoi intelligentsii*, 2 v. (Moscow, 1907–1908) II (2d ed.), 130. Even the unlikely Kuropatkin, sometime Minister of War, recalled that the novel "was read and reread . . . Lopukhin's [*sic*] resolution of the woman question vis-à-vis Vera Pavlovna delighted us." Quoted by Knizhnik-Vetrov in *Russkie deyatelnitsy*, 22.

[24] Lemke, *Polit. Protsess*, 495.

[25] Shelgunov, *Soch.*, II, 663; Herzen's remark cited in Yu. M. Steklov, *N.G. Chernyshevskii: ego zhizn i deyatelnost, 1828–1889*, 2d ed., 2 v. (Moscow, Leningrad, 1928) I, 206.

[1] *Iz istorii literatornogo nigilizma*, 201.

not so much a corpus of formal beliefs and programs (like populism, liberalism, Marxism) as it was a cluster of attitudes and social values and a set of behavioral affects—manners, dress, friendship patterns. In short, it was an ethos.

The origin of the term *nigilistka* (female nihilist) is just as difficult to trace as that of the word *nigilist*. One thing is certain: it was a derivative of the masculine word and followed it into the language of popular usage. But just as nihilists existed before the word was popularized in Turgenev's *Fathers and Children* (1861), so the women nihilist was on the scene before the birth of Kukshina, the caricature of her from the same novel. Although the word had been used previously in Russian thought,[2] it was in the 1860's that it assumed its familiar meaning. "In those days of national renewal," wrote Elizaveta Vodovozova, a representative woman of the 1860's, "the young intelligentsia was moved by ardent faith, not by sweeping negation."[3] For many young women of the 1860's, embarrassed by the restrictions, real or imaginary, which Russian society imposed upon them, and impatient with the pace of feminism, the philosophic posture and the social attitudes of the people who were called nihilists had an enormous attraction. Only they, it seemed, were trying to put into practice the grandiose notions of equality and social justice which the publicists of recent years had preached.

Lev Deutsch, the well-known revolutionary and pioneer of Russian Marxism, made the following observation:

> By rejecting obsolete custom, by rising up against unreasonable opinions, concepts, and prejudices, and by rejecting authority and anything resembling it, nihilism set on its way the idea of the equality of all people without distinction. To nihilism, incidentally, Russia owes the well-known and remarkable fact that in our culturally deprived country, women began, earlier than in most civilized states, their surge toward higher education and equal rights—a fact which already [as of 1926] has had enormous significance and which in the future will obviously play a great role in the fate of our country and even perhaps throughout the civilized world.

"The idea of the equality of all people without distinction" was the magnet which drew so many young idealistic women into the "nihilist" camp. When it became clear that nihilism was the only intellectual movement which emphatically included women in its idea of emancipation, the way was opened for a coalition of the sexes.[4]

Nihilist women, whatever their age or costume, approached the problem of their rights as women with an outlook basically different from that of the

---

[2] Professor Bervi in 1858 used the word nihilist to mean skeptic: Dobrolyubov, *Soch.*, II, 332.

[3] Vodovozova, *Na zare zhizni*, 3d ed., 2v. (Moscow, 1964) II, 38.

[4] Lev Deutsch (Deich), *Rol Evreev v russkom revolyutsionnom dvizhenii* (Moscow, Petrograd, 1926), 17. See also Pisarev, "Realisty" in *Soch.*, III, 7–138 (50–51).

feminists. If the feminists wanted to change pieces of the world, the nihilists wanted to change the world itself, though not necessarily through political action. Their display of will and energy was more visible; and their attitude toward mere charity was similar to that of Thoreau—that it was better to *be* good than to *do* good.[5] The feminists wanted a moderate amelioration of the condition of women, especially in education and employment opportunities, assuming that their role in the family would improve as these expanded. The nihilists insisted on total liberation from the yoke of the traditional family (both as daughters and as wives), freedom of mating, sexual equality—in short, personal emancipation. Better education and jobs were simply the corollaries of this. Though they thirsted after learning, nihilist women often preferred to seek it abroad than to join the slow struggle for higher education in Russia itself. Where the feminists may have seen complete liberation as a vague apparition, the nihilists saw it as an urgent and realizable task. This is one reason why the social and personal behavior of the *nigilistka* was more angular and more dramatic than that of the feminist.

The outlook of the woman-as-nihilist has been differentiated here from that of the woman-as-radical whom we shall encounter in the following chapter. This differentiation is only slightly artificial for, while it is true that many women nihilists of the 1860's were drawn to radical causes, political radicalism as such was not a necessary condition for choosing "nihilist" solutions to the woman question. The techniques employed by the nihilists did not in themselves imply a politico-revolutionary view of life. Indeed there were some nihilists of both sexes whose extreme individualism, though drawing them to socially and sexually radical attitudes, actually prevented them from embracing causes, ideologies, or political action. Like the individualist sexual rebels of early nineteenth-century Europe, many women nihilists avoided organized movements, whether feminist or radical. Their "feel-yourself orientation" was at odds with the imperatives of underground activity.[6] "Inner rebellion" and personal identification were sufficient, and they avoided revolutionary circles out of fear, lack of awareness, or plain distaste. Sexually emancipated behavior in a woman—to say nothing of a man—has never been a necessary indication of her political "modernity."

Precisely when the people of St. Petersburg began using the word *nigilistka* to describe the progressive, advanced, or educated woman is difficult to say.

---

[5] The comparison to Thoreau was made by Yunge, "Iz moikh vospom.," 265. The reference is to Thoreau's critique of philanthropy at the end of the first chapter of *Walden*.

[6] Celestine Ware, *Woman Power: the Movement for Women's Liberation* (New York, 1970) 12, uses this term to describe the outlook of nonpolitical liberated women of the 1960's in America. In the early 1860's, some Moscow women classified *nigilistki* in the following way: those who worshipped progress and socialism (in the abstract) and who scoffed at religion, customs, and convention; those who busied themselves exclusively with studying the exact sciences; and political radicals. (Karnovich, *O. razvitii*, 109–11).

We can only be sure that after the publication of *Fathers and Children*, the image of the "female nihilist" (Turgenev did not use the word) was firmly fixed in the public eye. Much has been written about Turgenev's attitude to his hero, Bazarov, and the nihilists he seemed to represent; but there was no doubt that Evdoksiya Kukshina was an unflattering caricature. She surpassed the ludicrous in her attitudes and behavior. Her cigarette smoking, her slipshod attire, and her brusque manner were affected gestures of modernity, accompanying her shallow passion for chemistry. When asked why she wanted to go to Heidelberg, her answer was the hilarious "How can you ask! Bunsen lives there!" She is beyond George Sand ("a backward woman, knows nothing about education or embryology") and correctly denounces Proudhon, but in the same breath praises Michelet's *L'amour*![7]

Dostoevsky called Kukshina "that progressive louse which Turgenev combed out of Russian reality." Pisarev pointed out that her counterparts in real life were not nihilists, but "false nihilists" and "false *emancipées*." The radical critic, Antonovich, however, blasted the novel in *The Contemporary*, and berated the author for his unfair portrayal of contemporary women. Seeing that the cartoon figure of Kukshina would be used as a weapon of ridicule against all advanced women, he suggested that, however ridiculous the unripe, progressive female might appear, the traditional upper-class woman was even more ridiculous. "Better to flaunt a book than a petticoat," he said. "Better to coquette with science than with a dandy. Better to show off in a lecture hall than at a ball."[8]

The nihilist view of women was further crystallized in the following year by the discussion of a satirical anti-nihilist play, *Word and Deed*, by Ustryalov. Its hero is stern, unbending, thoroughly unromantic; his credo is "to believe what I know, acknowledge what I see, and respect what is useful." Like Bazarov, he scorns love, only to be swept off his feet by a conventional young damsel. This buffoonery prompted Andrei Gieroglifov, a member of Pisarev's circle, to face the issue squarely in an essay bearing the title "Love and Nihilism," written just as Chernyshevsky was completing his novel, and drawn largely from Schopenhauer's "Metaphysics of Love." Gieroglifov proposed a thoroughgoing anti-idealistic explanation of love as no more than the awakening of the reproductive instinct, however innocent it might appear. Going well beyond Chernyshevsky, he insisted that love was not to be seen as

[7] *Fathers and Children*, tr. R. Hare (New York, 1957) 75–79. The name "Kukshina," as well as that of her foolish friend, Sitnikov, was still used as a polemical term in 1905 by people as different as Milyukov and Plekhanov to designate brash and unripe radicals: Milyukov, *God borby: publitsisticheskaya khronika, 1905–1906* (SPB, 1907) 466–71.

[8] Dostoevsky, *Winter Notes on Summer Impressions*, trans. R. Renfield (New York, 1955), p. 68; Pisarev, "Bazarov," *Soch.*, II, 7–50 (33–36); M. Antonovich, "Asmodei nashego vremeni," *Sov.*, XCII (Mar. 1862) 65–114. Vodovozova (*Na zare zhizni*, 3d. ed. II, 46–49) described an obnoxious woman of her circle, Mariya Sychova, who thought that a sloppy appearance and rude manners sufficed to make her "advanced." On this, see also P.G. Pustvoit, *Roman I.S. Turgeneva "Ottsy i dety" i ideinaya borba 60-kh godov XIX veka* (Moscow, 1964) 108.

a purely personal and individual pleasure. In it "the will of each person becomes the agent of the race," and "there is no participation by the individual will of man." All mating and the feelings that accompany it were based on nature's need to continue the species. Can a nihilist love? Yes, answered Gieroglifov, "for reason does not negate feeling;" but the nihilist must recognize love's relationship to nature. What kind of woman can he love? Not a doll or a plaything, says Gieroglifov, but a woman of knowledge who rejects the archaic, the passive, and the impotent and embraces the new, the creative, and the forceful. "Then there will be a greater correspondence and harmony between the men and women of the new generation. Without this it is impossible to reach that mutual happiness which nature itself demands."[9]

One of the most interesting and widely remarked features of the *nigilistka* was her personal appearance. Discarding the "muslin, ribbons, feathers, parasols, and flowers" of the Russian lady, the archetypical girl of the nihilist persuasion in the 1860's wore a plain dark woolen dress, which fell straight and loose from the waist with white cuffs and collar as the only embellishments. The hair was cut short and worn straight, and the wearer frequently assumed dark glasses. This "revolt in the dress" was part of the *nigilistka's* repudiation of the image of the "bread-and-butter miss," that pampered, helpless creature who was prepared exclusively for attracting a desirable husband and who was trained at school to wear *décolletée* even before she had anything to reveal. These "ethereal young ladies" in tarlatan gowns and outlandish crinolines—the phrase is Kovalevskaya's—bedecked themselves with jewelry and swept their hair into "attractive" and "feminine" coiffures. Such a sartorial ethos, requiring long hours of grooming and primping, gracefully underlined the leisure values of the society, the lady's inability to work, and a sweet, sheltered femininity. The *nigilistka's* rejection of all this fit in with her desire to be functional and useful, and with her repugnance for the day-to-day existence of "the superfluous woman."[10]

But it was also a rejection of her exclusive role as a passive sexual object. Long luxuriant tresses and capacious crinolines, so obviously suggestive of fertility, were clearly parts of the feminine apparatus of erotic attraction. The

---

[9] G—fov, "Lyubov i nigilizm," *RS* (Jan. 1863) 25–44. The chapter on sexual love of Schopenhauer's *Die Welt als Wille und Vorstellung* (1818) appeared in the following year in Russian translation: Shopengofer, *Metafizika lyubvi* (SPB, 1864).

[10] Quotation from Tolstoy's *Anna Karenin*, tr. R. Edmonds (Harmondsworth, Middlesex, 1954) 225. Of the myriad descriptions of such attire, see: Vodovozova, *Na zare zhizni*, 3d ed. II, 40; Stasov, *Stasova*, 58; A. F. Koni, "Peterburg," in *Vospominaniya o pisatelyakh* (Leningrad, 1963) 65–66; N. V. Davydov, *Zhenshchina pered ugolovnym sudom* (Moscow, 1906) 6; Kovalevskaya, *Vospom.*, 82. The term "muslin miss" or "bread-and-butter miss" (*kiseinaya devushka*) was given greater currency at the time by Pomyalovsky's story *Meshchanskoe schaste* (1861) and Pisarev's review of it (*Soch.*, III, 185–216). Stackenschneider recalls that the term *nigilistka* was held in high regard among women of the sixties, while *kiseinaya devushka* was a pejorative term (*Dnevnik*, 292). The Smolny costume is described and pictured in Stefanie Dogorouky [Dologorukaya], *La Russie avant la débâcle* (Paris, 1926) 86–87. Both Kotlyarevsky (*Kanun*, p. 443) and Koni ("Peterburg," 66) date the appearance of the new women in public at the beginning of the 1860's.

traditional results were romance, courtship, and marriage, followed by years of disappointing boredom or domestic tyranny. The machinery of sexual attraction through outward appearance that led into slavery was discarded by the new woman whose nihilist creed taught her that she must make her way with knowledge and action rather than feminine wiles. Linked to the defeminization of appearance was the unconscious longing to resemble the man, for the distinctive garb of the nihilist girl—short hair, cigarettes, plain garments—were boyish affectations. These, together with intensity of interest in academic and "serious" matters, tended to reduce the visible contrasts between the sexes and represented the outward form of her inner desire—to diminish the sharp social and cultural difference between men and women.

Beneath her new costume, the nihilist of the 1860's also assumed a new personality and self-image. The sickly romanticism and sentimentality are gone. She realized that true personal autonomy required psychological independence, though not separation, from men. To establish her identity, she needed a cause or a "path," rather than just a man. So, in rejecting chivalric or tender attention from men, she often seemed blunt, for she deeply longed to be received as a human being, not simply as a woman. This also explains why she cut or hid her pretty hair beneath a cap and covered her eyes with smoked lenses. "Value us as comrades and fellow workers in life," she seemed to be saying to men; "as your equals with whom you can speak simply and plainly."[11]

The new attitude was vividly reflected in her social behavior. The typical *nigilistka*, like her male comrade, rejected the conventional hypocrisy of interpersonal relations and tended to be direct to the point of rudeness, unconcerned with the ordinary amenities, and often enough unconcerned with cleanliness as well.[12] The insistence upon complete equality of the sexes also induced men of the new generation to cast overboard the ballast of chivalry and stylized gallantry. As one of Kropotkin's acquaintances observed, they would not stand up when a woman entered the room, but they would often travel halfway across the city to help a girl in her studies. The new woman was anxious to be respected for her knowledge and not for the size of her bust or the plenitude of her skirts.[13]

The costumes and customs of the new culture were assumed, sometimes

[11] Kotlyarevsky, "Zhenshchina," in *Sbornik: Filosofova*, II, 79 (the description, as well as the imaginary quotation, is his).

[12] Not only disarray, but downright dirtiness was often noted as a prominent feature of the nihilist, the woman even more than the man. This is not strange: scorners of the conventions in every generation (including our own) since the early nineteenth century, beginning with the "bohemians," have looked upon neatness and cleanliness as part of the mantle of bourgeois hypocrisy. For a typical Russian reaction to this, see the diary entry of Prince Odoevsky in *Lit. nasled.*, XXII–XXIV (1935) 211.

[13] Kropotkin, *Memoirs*, 197. In Vera Pavlovna's fourth dream, the Beautiful Tsaritsa expounds at length about the need for equality, respect for the whole person, the unimportance of physical beauty, and the loathesomeness of hypocrisy (*Chto delat?* 391–411).

temporarily, by so many faddists that it was often difficult to tell the nihilist from the *poseur*. The term nihilist was flung about as indiscriminately then as it was in the 1870's and 1880's when it became a synonym for assassin. Leskov, for instance, reported in 1863 that "short haired young ladies who married at the first chance" were considered nihilists.[14] Like many such terms, it was loosely applied and was fluid enough to serve many purposes—most of them pejorative: A *nigilistka* could be an auditor at the university, a girl with bobbed hair, a grown woman with "advanced" ideas (whether or not she understood them), or a volunteer in one of the feminist or philanthropic bodies, depending upon the point of view of the describer.

What Is To Be Done? bequeathed to the woman of the 1860's not only a self-image but also some specific devices for liberation as well, particularly the fictitious marriage as a means of escape, and the *artel*-commune as a mode of social action. Though both pre-dated the novel, their incidence increased with its publication and with the growth of family discord that formed its social background. The great schism between fathers and sons, which has received much scholarly attention, also affected the daughters and drew them into a "struggle between the Domostroi and the nineteenth century," as Pisarev neatly if oversimply put it. That there was a genuine family upheaval among the gentry, there can be no doubt. "Girls, bred in the most aristocratic families," wrote Kropotkin, "rushed penniless to St. Petersburg, Moscow, and Kiev, eager to learn a profession which would free them from the domestic yoke, and some day, perhaps, from the possible yoke of a husband." Sofya Kovalevskaya recalled the same phenomenon from the days before her own deliverance: "Children, especially girls, were seized by a virtual epidemic of running away from home . . . we would hear how the daughter of this or that landowner had fled, perhaps abroad to study, or to Petersburg—to the 'nihilists'."[15]

The adventures of Kovalevskaya's circle offer an array of influences and motivations that were fermenting among the privileged young ladies of the time. Her sister, Anna Korvin-Krukovskaya, grew up in the sheltered idyll of a country estate, far from "the stream of new currents." Spoiled and petted, she roamed like a "free cossack" through her childhood, untouched by any ideas other than an adolescent spell of religious mysticism. But in the summer of 1862, when she was nineteen, the son of the village priest, on vacation from his scientific studies in Petersburg, regaled her with the "materialist" theories of Darwin and Sechenov, and introduced her to the thick journals. Anyuta was transformed. She donned a black dress and stuffed her hair into a

---

[14] N. S. Leskov, *Sobranie sochinenii*, ed. B. G. Bazanov, 11 v. (Moscow, 1956–1958) X, 21.

[15] Pisarev, *Soch.*, I, 104; Kropotkin, *Memoirs*, 198; Kovalevskaya, *Vospom.*, 68. Other observations of this phenomenon in Vodovozova, *Na zare zhizni*, 3d ed. II, 221–22, and Shelgunov, *Soch.*, II, 667.

severe net; she started teaching village children, refused to attend balls, and filled her room with the acoutrements of scientific learning. When her father, the stern commanding general of the St. Petersburg Arsenal, denied her plea to study medicine in the capital, she turned her hand to fiction and, after titanic battles with her family, eventually freed herself.[16]

Sofya Kovalevskaya's childhood was as unhappy as her sister's was carefree. The feeling of being unloved haunted her early years and was the key to her subsequent emotional difficulties. Envy of her sister filled her with malaise and was given expression in possessive puppyloves and sexual longing in the form of a three-legged man who pursued her in dreams. But by the time she was eighteen, she was under Anyuta's nihilist spell and had developed her own consuming passion for mathematics. The sisters with a friend hatched a plan to secure a "fictitious" husband for Anyuta who would take them to Europe. Their first candidate, Sechenov himself, refused at the insistence of his "wife" Bokova, who opposed the project despite her reputation as the inventor of fictitious marriages. They found a "brother"—code word for fictitious husband—in Vladimir Kovalevsky, who agreed to marry, not Anyuta, but Sonya. She expressed her regret "that brother is not a Muslim," so that he could marry all three of them. Kovalevsky agreed, in accordance with the code, that he would not exercise his conjugal rights. The marriage took place, over strenuous objections from the family, in 1868. All the parties hastened abroad to carve out for themselves separate careers in literature and science. Sonya and her husband remained friends, but only after the death of her adored father did she allow him "full" relations with her.[17]

Anna Evreinova (1844–1919), offered another variant. Though the daughter of the high-ranking commandant of Pavlovsk, she acquired an early aversion for balls and gowns and refused to become "a drawing-room lady." Closely guarded by her imperious father who abhorred "superfluous" learning, she would study classical languages by candlelight after returning from the hated galas. She tried to acquire a fictitious husband, writing to her cousin that "we are seeking people like ourselves, warmly devoted to a cause and whose principles are identical to ours, who would not so much marry us as liberate us, and who would understand our needs and be useful to us in our present circumstances." Failing to find one, she crossed the frontier illegally and, after a few years study at the University of Leipzig, became the first woman doctor of laws in Russia. Like Kovalevskaya, she avoided radical activity and in later years became an active proponent of women's rights and publisher of *The Northern Messenger*.[18]

Vodovozova described some of the difficulties of fictitious marriages in the

[16] Kovalevskaya, *Vospom.*, 65–72; Knizhnik-Vetrov, *Deyatelnitsy*, 138–47.

[17] Kovalevskaya, *Vospom.*, 7–109 (her comment, 138); Anna Carlotta Leffler, *Sonya Kovalevsky* (New York, 1895) 159–297 (see 159–92). For a sensitive and beautifully written analysis of Kovalevskaya's childhood, see Beatrice Stillman, "Sofya Kovalevskaya: Growing Up in the Sixties," *Russian Literary Triquarterly*, 9 (Spring 1974) 277–302.

[18] Kovalevskaya, *Vospom.*, 179–80, n. 120; Evreinova's letter in Knizhnik-Vetrov, *Deyatelnitsy*, 153.

1860's. A young man, hearing of a woman who wished to leave home in order to study and develop herself, would offer himself as a fictitious husband. After the wedding there was immediate separation, without consummation of the marriage, and often without any contact at all. The girl would typically go abroad; the man would fall in love with someone else and wish to marry. A long correspondence and a drawn-out divorce would ensue. In the meantime, both couples might have illegitimate children. For those who continued to reject conventional morality, of course, such conditions offered little hardship, especially if they dwelt in the half-world of underground or émigré circles. But for "May nihilists" who later returned to the world of more conventional norms—and there were many—the situation was more painful. Sometimes a "fictitious" husband, hiding his real designs, would attempt to extract his conjugal rights from the deceived girl after the ceremony had taken place. But the fictitious marriage remained for a long time a favorite method among women who wished to escape from uncomfortable nests.[19]

There were also wives who left husbands for failing to offer them the kind of life promised by the teachings of the New People. Sleptsov's novel, *A Difficult Time*, accurately portrays an advanced woman, disillusioned with her husband from whom she had expected "significant things" and a partnership in a life of excitement. About to leave him to go to St. Petersburg, she says:

When you wanted to marry me, what did you tell me? Just remember! You said, "We will work together and do great things which might even bring us and our dear ones to ruin, but I'm not afraid of that. If you feel you have the strength, then let's go on together"—and I went. Of course then I was just a foolish girl and didn't fully understand what you were talking about; I simply felt and guessed. And I would have gone anywhere . . . because I thought and believed that we would do real things. And what has it all amounted to? You curse at your peasants for every copeck; and I stand here salting pickles.[20]

A real life example was Ekaterina Maikova (1836–1920), wife of the well-known literary figure Vladimir Maikov. The marriage was a happy and stable one, but there was clearly something missing in Maikova's life. In the early 1860's, she began re-examining her married life in the light of ideas, particularly those of *What Is To Be Done?*. Her life no longer fulfilled her needs. In the end she went off with a student, bore him a child, and began to study at the Alarchin Courses in Petersburg. Her case was a common one in those days.[21]

[19] Vodovozova, *Na zare zhizni*, 3d ed. II, 223–24.
[20] The passage is quoted from Pisarev's review of *Trudnoe vremya* in *Soch.*, IV, 50–85 (70).
[21] O. M. Chemëna, "I.A. Goncharov i semeinaya drama Maikovykh," *Voprosy izucheniya russkoi literatury*, Ed. B. P. Gorodetsky (Moscow, Leningrad, 1958) 185–95. Maikova has been taken by some as the partial inspiration for Olga in Goncharov's *Oblomov*: Stackenschneider, *Dnevnik*, 210, 507–508n. For references to large numbers of married women in St. Petersburg not living with their husbands, see Shashkov, *Ist sudby.*, 558–59.

There was a rumor abroad among the provincial gentry in the middle of the 1860's about a communist community in St. Petersburg to which all young girls of good family were invited after escaping from home. There both sexes and all classes lived together in "complete communism" with well-born ladies taking their turns washing the floors.[22] At the root of this rumor was the fact that both the nihilists and the radicals had adopted the *artel* and the commune as a means of assisting women along their new path. This development preceded *What Is To Be Done?* by about two years. Since 1861, Petersburg was rapidly filling up with women and most of them did not find suitable outlets for their energies through the feminist organizations. Most were too poor to act as leaders in these enterprises and too proud to play the passive role in feminism by accepting charity from the grand ladies of the capital. What they wanted desperately was intellectual work, freedom, and a decent place to live. None of the ordinary channels of female employment could offer this combination to all the recent immigrants to the city. Rents were high, wages low, jobs, especially white collar ones, very hard to get—for men as well as women.[23] The cooperative and its variants emerged as a partial solution to this problem.

The best-known commune, which appeared before Chernyshevsky's novel, was the Grech Commune. According to Nikolai Leskov, who fictionalized it in "The Enigmatic Man," a number of journalists who favored women's emancipation decided to put their theories into practice and extend a hand to the numerous unemployed, educated women in the capital by hiring them as typesetters, translators, and writers. Most of these men, said Leskov, a tendentious witness, were mainly interested in seducing their female clients. An exception was Arthur Benni, a Polish-born British citizen, who moved in and out of radical circles in the 1860's until his death on a Risorgimento battlefield in 1867. In 1862 he conceived of the idea of hiring women as translators, and established a "commune" for them in his quarters in the Grech lodging house—thus the "Grech Commune" or "Grech Phalanstery," a share-the-expense living arrangement with take-home work. Again according to Leskov, the communalists spent most of their time debating the woman question and very little time translating. Benni was forced to do most of the work himself and pay the women out of his own pocket until he could do so no longer. Then the commune dissolved.[24]

Far more famous was the commune organized by Benni's friend, Vasily Sleptsov (1836–1878), the author of *A Difficult Time*. His yearning to help the "working masses" fused with his growing interest in the woman question,

[22] Kovalevskaya, *Vospom.*, p. 68.

[23] Chukovsky, *Lyudi*, 171; Vodovozova, *Na zare zhizni*, 3d ed. II, 195–96.

[24] Leskov, *Sob. soch.*, III, 350–53; Solomon Reiser, *Arthur Benni* (Moscow, 1933) 63–64; Chukovsky, *Lyudi*, 244–45. On the relations between Leskov and Benni, see Hugh McLean "Leskov and his Enigmatic Man," *Harvard Slavic Studies*, IV (Cambridge, Mass., 1957) 203–24.

and he played a leading role in giving education, work, and independence to young women of the capital. Some critics have stressed that it was only the *young* women of the capital who attracted his attention, but other accounts do not seem to bear this out. He organized popular lectures for women on scientific subjects. They drew large crowds, until rumors of a police raid and the hostility of some of the female auditors to the presence of *aristokratki* (i.e., well-dressed ladies) hurt the attendance. He also founded bookbinding workshops for women and set up mutual aid funds to supply them with cheap credit. In short, Sleptsov, though not the first to take up the problem of women's independence as his mother claimed, was the most energetic example of the advanced man of the 1860's who endeavored to help women without patronizing them.[25]

In 1863, he established a residential commune, inspired directly by *What Is To Be Done?* and partly also no doubt by Fourier whose works on women he had studied. The commune consisted of seven men and women in a large apartment on Znamenskaya Street where the members had separate bedrooms but shared expenses, meals, and housework. Two of the women were described by Kornei Chukovsky, who wrote a history of the commune, as genuine, militant nihilists: One, Alexandra Markelova, had been left unmarried with a baby; the second, Ekaterina Makulova, ironically called "the princess," was coarse and unattractive and wholly incapable of earning a living on her own.[26] The other two women were of a different sort. Mariya Kopteva came of good parents, had had an institute education but, because of her "turbulent imagination," had fled her parental home and come to Petersburg to support herself. Ekaterina Tsenina, later Zhukovskaya, had travelled a route typical for advanced women in the sixties: escape from her family through marriage, desertion of her husband, odd jobs in the provinces, and some translation work in Petersburg for Vernadsky's *Economic Index*. While seeking additional work, she met Sleptsov through Markelova and was invited into the commune. Though happy to cut her rental expenses, she was reluctant and suspicious from the very outset. When Sleptsov, welcoming her into the commune, tried to kiss her hand, she withdrew it angrily and said: "I must warn you that I do not subscribe to Fourier's theory of sexual relations, even in the abstract, and I also forewarn you that if any member of the commune intends to put this theory into practice, I refuse to join."[27]

The Znamenskaya Commune lasted about a year and became a well-known haunt for the Petersburg intellectuals, Lavrov, Sechenov, and Panaeva. Benni

[25] Zhozefina Sleptsova, "Vasilii Alekeevich Sleptsov v vospominaniyakh ego materi, 1836–1878," *Russkaya starina*, XLV (Jan. 1890) 233–41; Chukovsky, *Lyudi*, 166–71, 239–40; Panaeva, *Vospom.*, 328–30.

[26] Chukovsky, *Lyudi*, 171–72, 228–31; Panaeva, *Vospom.*, 436n. Zhukovskaya, *Zapiski*, 154, 156, 167.

[27] Chukovsky, *Lyudi*, 230; Zhukovskaya, *Zapiski*, 19–165 (her encounter with Sleptov, 158–65). The memoirs are biased and were written forty years after the events.

courted Kopteva; and the economist Yuly Zhukovsky won the hand of Tsenina. But friction grew up, partly because none of the women cared to help in the housework, but mostly because of the deeper hostility between the two factions: Kopteva and Tsenina on one side, all the rest on the other. The former two viewed with scorn Sleptsov's obviously sincere attempt at social experimentation. They also retained the fashionable dress habits of their upbringing, while the other two women assumed the more typical unsightly appearance of nihilists: Thus Tsenina called herself and Kopteva "aristocratic nihilists" and Markelova and the princess "sloppy nihilists." One need not go so far as Chukovsky's characterization of these women as "the Mensheviks and Bolsheviks of nihilism" in order to recognize that there were fundamental differences in outlook between them. The commune also invited gossip. Nikolai Uspensky called it the Muslim harem of Sultan Sleptsov; Saltykov-Shchedrin made the appropriate analogies with Ménilmontant and Enfantin. Leskov claimed that Sleptsov had entered Kopteva's room in a state of partial undress. But scholars as well as other contemporaries insist, no doubt correctly, that the commune was monastic. The real cause of its dissolution were the personal animosity, the marriage plans, and the familiar rumors of a police raid.[28]

Another experiment inspired by *What Is To Be Done?* was a laundry *artel* for women, organized in the spring of 1864 by a Mme. Garshina. The overenthusiastic patroness, in an obvious effort to emulate Vera Pavlovna, overpaid her women (even when they did not work) and introduced prostitutes into the establishment in order to rehabilitate them through useful labor. The results were both disastrous and comic. Her employees, suspicious of the high wages and good treatment, refused to listen to Garshina's sermons on cooperation, demanded an end to equality of wages, and began, in emulation of the prostitutes, drinking and carousing with soldiers on the premises of the *artel*. In relating her sad story, Mme. Garshina also took a swipe at the hypocritical liberals who sympathized with women's rights but who never paid their laundry bills. Similar episodes were reported in other parts of Russia.[29]

Vodovozova recalled how young people would sit around a table with a copy of *What Is To Be Done?* in front of them and laboriously plan an *artel*. One of these *artels* collapsed because of conflicting interpretations of the novel. Its organizer insisted that it be lavishly furnished and designed to make large profits; the New People, he said, were egoists, not ascetics. But when he introduced a contingent of prostitutes, citing Vera Pavlovna's love for

---

[28] *Ibid.*, 168–224 for Zhukovskaya's version; Chukovsky, *Lyudi*, 232–66 is a more balanced account. Tsenina-Zhukovskaya, though a self-styled nihilist and a friend of radicals, never became one herself but adapted nihilist practices to her personal life. Leskov, *Sob. soch.*, III, 353–54; Panaeva (*Vospom.*, 335) and Vodovozova (*Na zare zhizni*, 3d ed. II, *passim*) give favorable verdicts on Sleptsov. Saltykov-Shchedrin cited in V. Bazanov, *Iz istorii literaturnoi polemiki 60kh godov* (Petrozavodsk, 1941) 121.

[29] "Pochemu inogda plokho udayutsya zhenskiya arteli?" *Sov.*, CVII (Apr. 1865) 259–72.

Kryukova and Julie Letellier, the refined widow who acted as his manager resigned and the *artel* ran aground. Vera Zasulich, who recalled that such enterprises grew up like mushrooms after the appearance of *What Is To Be Done?*, mentioned one where the seamstresses broke away and demanded the sewing machines on the principle—which they had just learned—that "machinery belongs to labor."[30]

Communes and *artels* became a kind of a fad in the 1860's. Ilya Repin lived for a while in a commune of painters; Modest Musorgsky lived in another. But their god, as Chukovsky reminds us with gentle irony, was Flaubert and not Feuerbach. The idea received another boost in 1866 when Eduard Pfeiffer's *Zur Genossenschafttum* (1865) appeared in a Russian translation.[31] But after 1866, with the onset of reaction, the fad died and *artels* and communes became almost the exclusive preserve of radical circles.

If the important publicists of the 1860's were in favor of the New Woman, most of the literary figures were against her. Tolstoy, who nourished a warm loathing for the ideas of George Sand, wrote an anti-nihilist play, *The Infected Family*.[32] Pisemsky, Leskov, Goncharov, and Dostoevsky all wrote novels attacking nihilism and its doctrines on women. These, and a dozen other minor representatives of the genre, are discussed together in Charles Moser's *Antinihilism in the Russian Novel of the 1860s*.[33] The book demonstrates how deeply these Russian writers, who clearly voiced the sentiments of a large sector of "society," were distressed by what they took to be the immoral antics of the nihilists. But it also demonstrates, if taken together with the historical reality, how distorted and muddled was their view of nihilist behavior.

Pisemsky's *Troubled Sea* (1863), and Nikolai Akhsharumov's story "A Delicate Affair" (1864) merely documented the harmful effect of the idea of "free love" on a circle of nihilists. Klyushnikov's *Mirage* (1864) was more devastating. In it, a *nigilistka*, in whose room hang portraits of George Sand and Jenny d'Héricourt, is seduced politically by an evil Polish intriguer, and physically by a Russian radical working with the Poles. These corrupted people are contrasted with the upright, slavophiloid hero, Rusanov, who rescues the girl after her fall. Pisarev, Zaitsev, and Saltykov-Shchedrin roasted the novel in their reviews, while the conservative critic, Edelsohn of *The Readers' Library*, saw it as a healthy antidote to the toxic effects of *What Is To Be Done?* Leskov's *No Exit* of the same year, was a fictionalized treatment of the Znamenskaya Commune where Sleptsov is cast as a lecher, and "Prin-

[30] Vodovozova, *Na zare zhizni*, 3d ed. II, 199–209; Vera Zasulich, *Vospominaniya* (Moscow, 1931) 18–19. A number of similar ventures are mentioned in Kozmin, *Iz ist. rev. mysli*, 99–103.

[31] Chukovsky, *Lyudi*, 222; Pfeiffer's work translated by M. Antonovich as *Ob assotsiatsii* (SPB, 1866). Skabichevsky attested to its brief influence (*Lit. vospom.*, 226).

[32] See D. V. Grigorovich, *Literaturnye vospominaniya* (Leningrad, 1961) 148; Bazanov, *Iz ist. lit. polemiki*, 64.

[33] The Hague, 1964.

cess" Makulova—Bertholdi in the novel—is made to voice the view that "the family is the most disgusting form of what fools call civilization."[34]

The complete parody of the nihilist idea of love was Avenarius' *Disease* (1867) in whose sensational seduction scene a "progressive student" explains to his victim, a sincere but misled young girl, why she should make love with him. "Without this sympathy [between the sexes] the world would die out," he explains; "but it is instilled by nature, as an instinctive striving, into every living thing, and every four-footed animal, every stupid bird, every insect even, upon maturity searches for a sympathetic heart. Do you mean to say that man, the highest creature in the organic world, should flout the laws of nature?" The passage was a paraphrase of Gieroglifov's "Love and Nihilism," and the message was that the New People, afflicted with these contagious ideas, were "infecting" innocent girls. It was hardly a novelty in Russian intellectual or political history to compare a new idea to some raging disease, for the analogy had the advantage of invoking some kind of quarantine.[35]

But the physiological cynicism depicted by Avenarius was not a feature of the nihilist love ethos. It was, however, an accurate foreshadowing of the outlook of the "Saninists" of 1908–1914 and the Soviet "drink of water" enthusiasts of the 1920's whose brutish attitude toward sex would evoke indignant attacks from the spiritual descendants of the nihilists of the 1860's. For the nihilists, sexual morality signified a liaison with one person, based on love and lasting only as long as love lasted; it did not permit casual conquests, unfair seductions, the patronizing of prostitutes, or even adultery (in their sense of the word)—in short any of the conventional immoralities recognized as such in the bourgeois moral code.

The anti-nihilist writers were as tendentious as the nihilists themselves. Their characters were caricatures, not portraits. The anti-nihilists were not, however, necessarily hostile to women's emancipation, but rather to the nihilist men who showed them the wrong way. Leskov's *The Bypassed*, for instance, described a workshop that combined feminism, charity, and religion, and was designed to look after the welfare of young girls. It was in sharp contrast to Vera Pavlovna's wondrous arcadia of reason and self-interest. Goncharov, whose anti-nihilist novel, *The Precipice* was among the most scorching, explained his position on the matter: "Isn't it a fact," he asked, "that women disregarded their loved ones, were seduced away from respectable life, society, and family by the crude heroes of the 'new force,' the 'new

[34] Moser, *Antinihilism*, 162, 166, 192–94 (quotation, 102). Pisarev, *Soch.*, III, 218–50; V. Zaitsev, in *RS*, VI (June 1864) 43–52; Saltykov-Shchedrin in *Sov.*, CI (Mar. 1864) 46–62. E. Edelson in *Bib. chten.*, XXI (Apr. 1864) 13–25 (section on Russian literature).

[35] Moser, *Antinihilism*, 161. During the European crisis of 1848, Nesselrode's letters abounded in such terms as "contagious disease" (*zaraza*) and "pestilential" (*tletvornyi*): R. Averbukh, *Krasnyi arkhiv*, LXXXIX, XC (1938) 185. After the upheaval, he wrote:"Le renversement des idées est encore plus contagieux que la choléra." K. R. Nesselrode, *Lettres et papiers*, ed. A. de Nesselrode, 11 v. (Paris, 1904–1912), IX (1847–1850), Nesselrode-Fonton, Feb. 3, 1849.

course' and by the idea of some sort of 'great future'? Isn't it a fact that fine young girls followed them into their cellars and garrets, abandoning parents, husbands, and worse, children?" These women had been corrupted, he said. But there were others, genuinely serious women who were working to prepare themselves for an independent life by discipline and education. "In the hands of these women," said Goncharov, "lies the correct solution of the so-called woman question."[36]

Nihilist teaching on the woman question, for all its egalitarian and liberationist sweep, did not provide a very solid theoretical or social base for the further emancipation of women. The Chernyshevsky synthesis—brothers liberating sisters (the fictitious marriage), women liberating women, freedom of choice in love and marriage, cooperative work and communal life for both sexes, full development of the mind and the personality of women—was officially adopted by the revolutionary intelligentsia of the 1870's and after, though parts of it were obscured or downplayed by the imperatives of a desperate struggle for power. Indeed, much of it was absorbed into the ethos of the non-radical progressive intelligentsia. But opposition to the nihilist view of sexual equality among the conservative elements of the empire remained very potent; and revolt against the established order in this domain of human relations had to be personal, sporadic, and often traumatic. The fictitious marriage, though regularly used by later radicals to recruit women, was an individual and not always successful device outside the radical fold. Free unions and freedom of love had little relevance to economic or professional development of upper-class women; none at all to the masses of female peasants. And cooperative and communal experiments—an attempt to adapt popular forms (*artel* and *obshchina*) to the life of the repenting privileged—did not enjoy great success in the 1860's, even when employed by outright radical groups (see next chapter). They were swept away in the "white terror" of 1866 and replaced in the 1870's by underground conspirative cells.

Nihilism, as a way of life distinct from radicalism, began to dissolve at the end of the 1860's. Various historical punctuation marks have been offered: the so-called "white terror" of 1866, the shutting down of *The Russian Word* and *The Contemporary*, Pisarev's death in 1868, Lavrov's *Historical Letters* with its new ethic of populism, and so on. Those who had brandished nihilist ideas and habits in the early 1860's tended either to join the revolution—with which society identified them anyway—or pass back into the mainstream of Russian life, retaining only superficial vestiges of their non-conformist youth. But nihilism, in its isolated form, had to end in a *cul de sac* as far as the general

[36] V. Avenarius, in the then fashionable effort compulsively to explain one's stories, said that he was mainly hostile (in *Povetrie*) to the principle which allowed the girl to be seduced: *Vsemirnyi trud*, I (Apr. 1867) 231. See also: Kotlyarevsky, *Kanun*, p. 441; Bazanov, *Iz lit. polemiki*, 142; Goncharov, *Polnoe sobranie sochinenii*, 12 v. (SPB, 1899) I, 67–68; and *Kniga i revolyutsiya*, II (Jan. 1921) 16–22.

emancipation of women was concerned. Refusing to accept or to destroy the culture, the nihilists had only the alternative of disobeying it. Their active responses to the woman question, taken by themselves, could not lead to its solution. The radicals came to recognize that the superficial "nihilist" devices of *What Is To Be Done?* could have no long range effect unless its central, socialist ideas were realized in Russian life. The nihilists, however, did pass on their sexual ideas and practices to generations of revolutionaries who, after some fifty years of struggle, would attempt to translate them into public policy.

V

The Radical Response

We began a great thing. Perhaps two generations will have to be
sacrificed for it. But it must be done. . . .
—SOFYA PEROVSKAYA

1. WOMEN IN THE CIRCLES

It makes little sense to talk about "female radicalism" in Russian history before 1860. If we employ the system of pushing the origins of modern phenomena far back into the past, we could, of course, point with pride to a
Marfa Boretskaya of Novgorod, or to the mother of a rebel executed in the
1819 Chuguev Revolt, who said to her grandchildren in the presence of the
authorities: "Learn, children, that your father had to die for the sake of the
community,"[1] or to the many women who joined in agrarian disorders. But
the editors of *Figures of the Revolutionary Movement in Russia* list only three
names of women who were in any way connected with radicalism before
1860, and Soviet editors usually do not ignore examples of radicalism where
they can be found. In the one great radical effort of the early nineteenth century, the Decembrist movement, women were conspicuous by their absence.
The Union of Welfare, a part of this movement, explicitly excluded women
from its ranks, and its successors, the Northern and Southern Societies upheld
this rule. Furthermore, women would have played no more than the traditional role in the future society envisioned by the Decembrists. The Union of
Welfare looked upon their education merely as a source of national virtue; in
the constitution of the Northern Society, women were to be denied the right of
succession to the throne as well as the vote; and Pestel's *Russian Justice*, the
most radical of these projects, allowed fifteen-year-old girls the privilege of
taking an oath of allegiance to the state, but not the right to vote.[2]

The only aspect of the Decembrist movement that had even a marginal bearing on women was the fate of the wives of the convicted Decembrist rebels,

[1] Quoted in Aleksandr Amfiteatrov, *Zhenshchina v obshchestvennykh dvizheniyakh Rossii*
(Geneva, 1905) 30.
[2] *Deyateli revolyutsionnogo dvizheniya v Rossii: biobibliograficheskii slovar*, ed. Feliks Kon *et
al.*, 5 v. in 10 pts. (Moscow, 1927–1934) I/1, 160, 171. Marc Raeff, *The Decembrist Movement*
(Englewood-Cliffs, N.J., 1966) 73, 75, 115; Nechkina, *Dvizh, Dekab.*, 1, 419–20. *Russkaya
Pravda* preserves the traditional family almost intact: see *Vosstanie Dekabristov: dokumenty*, 11
v. (Moscow, 1925–1958) VIII, 192–97.

and the legend and literature that grew up around them. Princess Volkonskaya, typical of the handful of well-born ladies who followed their husbands into Siberian exile, won immortality by throwing herself at the feet of her husband and kissing his fetters. It was no small gesture to give up children, home, and comfort to trek into distant exile with little hope of returning, especially since Russian law gave a wife the right to divorce a political criminal. The selfless activities of these devoted women has earned them a deserved place in the martyrology of the revolutionary movement, as well as in literature. But were they motivated by anything more than marital devotion? Marina Nechkina, a Soviet historian of the movement, has shown that some of the Decembrist wives shared the ideological convictions of their husbands, but these were exhibited only after the movement had been crushed. From beginning to end, the Decembrist movement had been a man's affair. The same thing is true for the more innocuous intellectual circles of the thirties and forties.[3]

When we turn to the 1860's, the picture changes. For this period, *Figures of the Revolutionary Movement* lists some 65 women out of a total of 2,000 revolutionaries. The relative number is tiny—far from the two-to-eight ratio which Chernyshevsky suggested between the New Women and the New Men[4]—but impressive nonetheless, particularly since most of them were concentrated in Petersburg and Moscow. The reason for the sharp increase must be sought in the growing consciousness of women, frustration in their aspirations for education and useful social activity, and, for some, a deep-seated resentment over their declining economic status. Some of these women, no doubt, perceived at once the need to reconstruct, on a radical basis, the social system that silently mitigated against their emancipation, and the emancipation of the entire Russian people. Others, beginning as nihilists in the limited sense, were only gradually drawn into radicalism, as much by the influence of friends, brothers, or sweethearts as by personal conviction.

In the first few years female radicalism was rather formless, consisting of individual actions and adventitious participation in radical circles without any great significance either for radicalism or for the women. Its first manifestation was the student disorders at St. Petersburg University that pulled some female auditors into its vortex. Three of them signed a petition of some 700 names in protest against a new set of regulations, but were only marginally involved in the tumult that followed. One, Mariya Bykova, even tried to restrain her fellow students by warning them in an impassioned speech that if

---

[3] Nechkina, *Dvizh. Dekab.*, II, 427–54, esp. 433 and 438. The sacrifices of the Decembrist wives have been celebrated in Nekrasov's *Russkie zhenshchiny* and Alfred de Vigny's "Wanda: histoire russe, conversation au bal à Paris," *Oeuvres complètes*, 2 v. (Paris, 1948) I, 21?–19. There is a brief treatment in English: Anatole Mazour, *Women in Exile: Wives of the Decembrists* (Tallahassee, Florida, 1975).

[4] *Chto delat?*, 291.

they did not disperse they would receive a shameful beating from the police instead of dying as heroes. This may have been the first political address by a woman in modern Russian history. It was a relatively harmless affair in itself; but, since the university was an arm of the government, it was also women's matriculation into the meaning and the techniques of resistance and an opportunity to see the relationship between the quelling of student unrest and the interventions and punitive expeditions in other parts of the empire.[5]

The Sunday School movement also was used by the radicals as a means of spreading their propaganda. The arrest of two young women in May 1862 for criminal, anti-government activity was used as a reason for closing down the schools. Both women were related to male radicals. Antonina Blümmer, the sister of Leon, was placed in the custody of her father. Elizaveta Pavlova, the thirty-two-year-old sister-in-law of Pavel Evropeus, was put temporarily into a convent, a time-honored Russian method of dealing with refractory women. In most of the early conspiracies, women were recruited through male contacts: Nadezhda Suslova through her brother, Korsini through her husband Utin, Varvara Zaitseva through her brother and his friends, and so on. Most of them, after marginal involvement in the events of these years, drifted away from the circles or, like Suslova and Zaitseva, went abroad.[6]

Most of the revolutionary proclamations of this period, which radical women helped distribute, failed to mention women at all, and were thus typical of the underground literature of the next two decades. *Young Russia* (1862), was a striking exception. Unlike the others, its tone was uncompromisingly revolutionary throughout. As a part of its program, it demanded not only the complete emancipation of women, including civil and political equality with men, but also "the abolition of marriage, a phenomenon immoral in the highest degree, and unthinkable in a situation of the full equality of the sexes: and, therefore, the abolition of the family which hinders the development of mankind and without whose abolition the abolition of inheritance is unthinkable." Consistent with this, *Young Russia* also demanded "the public education of children and their support at public expense up to the completion of their schooling. . . ." The authors of the proclamation were Moscow radicals headed by the fiery twenty-year-old Peter Zaichnevsky who later admitted that his friend, the poet Holzmüller (Golts-Miller), had put in the passages on the family as an "added charge of powder" to make the program more incendiary.[7]

[5] Stackenschneider, *Dnevnik*, 295–306; Skabichevsky, *Lit. vospom.*, 338, 345. For individuals, see *Deyateli*, 1/2, 54, 316, 422.

[6] On these and other minor figures, see: E. S. Vilenskaya, *Revolyutsionnoe podpole v Rossii (60-e gody XIXv)* (Moscow, 1965) 330, 337; Kozmin, *Iz istorii*, 103; B. Bazilevsky [V. Ya. Yakolev], ed., *Materialy dlya istorii revolyutsionnago dvizheniya v Rossii v 60-kh gg.* (Paris, 1905) 158; *idem.*, ed., *Gosudarstvennyya prestupleniya v Rossii v XIX veka*, 3 v. (Stuttgart, 1903; Paris, 1903–1905) I, 231–34; *Deyateli*, 1/2, 42, 113–14, 135, 304, 443–44.

[7] Lemke, *Polit. prots.*, 521. For the quoted passages, V. Burtsev, ed., *Za sto let (1800–1896)* (London, 1897) 40.

The proclamation deserves comment, if only to put it in proper perspective. As far back as the 1840's, the Fourierist Khanykov, a member of the Petrashevsky Circle, had called the family a misery, an oppression, a monopoly, a depravity, a miasma, and an epidemic. But his friend, Chernyshevsky, had presented the issue as one of timing in *What Is To Be Done?*: the conjugal family now, children at work in the commune in the socialist future. Similarly, A. D. Putyata, a leader of Land and Liberty, the largest radical organization of the period, refuted Zaichnevsky in his *Answer to "Young Russia."* The family was to be kept intact and public institutions for child-raising would only be available for children of divorced parents who did not want to raise them and for children of unfit parents. The friends of Vodovozova divided sharply over the problem, one side claiming that marriage and children turned parents into "manacled hard-labor convicts," the other defending the immutability of maternal love. On that note, the matter pretty well rested until the twentieth century, all parties agreeing only that forced marriages and "bourgeois" marriages would disappear under the new order.[8]

The mid-1860's (1863-1866) was the age of *artel* and workshop for the radicals as well as for the non-radical nihilists. Through them, women were pulled deeper into the underground, though the process was gradual and the numbers not very large. The best known example was the extensive network of clubs, workshops, and circles centering around the ex-students N. A. Ishutin in Moscow and I. A. Khudyakov in St. Petersburg. These Rakhmetov-like ascetics wrapped themselves in a cult of Chernyshevsky and endeavored to utilize the ideas of his novel in order to get into contact with "the people," and to recruit supporters for their ambitious but vaguely conceived revolutionary plans. Out of this circle came Dmitry Karakozov, whose attempt to murder the tsar in 1866 brought about its destruction.

The first such activity in the capital to attract women was a "free school" founded in 1863 by the radical engineering officer, P. B. Mikhailov; attached to it was a dressmaking workshop led by Tkachëv's sister, Sofya, and used by her to spread revolutionary propaganda among the seamstresses. Far more interesting was the bindery *artel* and commune also formed by associates of Khudyakov in 1864. Life in the cooperative had a curious effect upon one of its members. A. A. Komarova was a graduate of an exclusive Petersburg institute who became engaged to the novelist Pomyalovsky and was drawn by him into radical circles. Aroused by the travail of the Polish rebels, she offered to go to Poland to fight on their behalf. But upon discovering that she was pregnant, she joined the bindery *artel*, composed of some twenty girls,

---

[8] A. V. Khanykhov's remarks in *Delo Petrashevtsev*, 3 v. (Moscow, Leningrad, 1937-1951) III, 19; A. D. Putyata's unpublished "Otvet 'Molodoi Rossii' " is in TsGAOR, f. 95, op. 1, delo 214, 11. 67-a/2 ob.-3 and is cited by the editors of Vodovozova, *Na zare zhizni*, 3d ed. II, 539 (note 2 to ch. XVIII). Discussions in Vodovozova's circle in *ibid.*, 121.

and lived in a commune associated with it. Under the influence of cooperative activity, Komarova renounced her recent beliefs in bloody insurrection and arrived at the conviction that associations would soon cover the earth. "It seemed to me," she wrote later, "that the great transformation would be accomplished slowly and gradually by means of the dissemination of healthy ideas among the people." Convinced of this, she went out among the poor preaching that "Christ was a great socialist whose teachings had been distorted," and reading passages from *What Is To Be Done?*, particularly Vera Pavlovna's dreams. Her radicalism died young, and in later years she became a fanatical religious zealot.[9]

In Moscow, such enterprises were even more numerous and varied. They included a "nihilist salon" held by Countess L. N. Tolstaya for her revolutionary friends from Nizhny Novgorod; another "free school" whose faculty included a half-dozen radical women; and a women's commune of compositors whose members endeavored to raise their political consciousness through reading and discussions. In these and a half-dozen others we find not only a broad spectrum of social classes and educational backgrounds, ranging from a Smolny graduate to an ex-prostitute, but also vast differences in the level of political awareness. All of the enterprises were founded, financed, supervised, or suggested by active (male) members of Ishutin's "Organization" with the express purpose of recruiting revolutionary talent; yet few of the women ever became true radicals, though nearly all of them were arrested and questioned as such during the great raids of 1866. Some, like the women of the Compositors' Commune even rejected overtures made to them to become actively "political."[10]

By far the most important and best known of the enterprises created for women by Ishutin and his associates was the so-called Dressmaking Workshop of the Ivanova Sisters. The sisters, Ekaterina and Aleksandra, were Nizhny Novgorod gentry who had come to Moscow in 1864 where their brother, D. L. Ivanov, introduced them to Ishutin. When Ishutin suggested the idea of the workshop to them and agreed to finance it, Ekaterina was at first reluctant; but her sister managed to persuade her, arguing that cooperative work was more suitable for young women than the work of teachers and governesses who were required to teach a pack of lies about life, which they themselves did not believe, and more meaningful than translating, which often meant rendering into Russian a lot of useless nonsense.[11] Here is evidence of expanded awareness, not only of the limited significance of the roles usually assigned to educated and independent women but also of the rigidity of the class system reinforced by such occupations. Hundreds of gentry women, in years to come, would make similar "social leaps" from the highest and most privileged estate to the most desperate and radical of socialist cir-

---

[9] Vilenskaya, *Rev. podpole*, 329–33, 341–50; *Devateli*, 1/2, 178.
[10] Vilenskaya, *Rev. podpole*, 216–35, 279–80.   [11] *Ibid.*, 270–71.

cles, bypassing with scorn the intellectual and professional careers that gradually opened before them.

In structure and purpose, if not in efficiency, the Ivanova Workshop resembled Vera Pavlovna's. The members included seamstresses of the lower classes as well as educated women. Among the latter, about ten, were Vera Zasulich's sisters, the young Anna Shabanova (the future leader of Russian feminism), and Mariya Krylova, a prominent revolutionary of the 1870's. Nothing is more demonstrative of the youthfulness and tentativeness of these early groups than this coterie of future radicals, anti-radicals, and non-radicals. In spite of a charter calling for election of a leader, Ekaterina Ivanova kept accounts and generally ran things. The women lived, worked, and ate together, listened to lectures by visiting males, and read the works of Chernyshevsky, Mikhailov, and Herzen to each other. The mother of one of the members, a simple midwife, later told the police that debauchery, the abolition of the family, and hatred of legitimate authority were preached in the Ivanova Workshop. Such charges were almost always attached to politically shady groups whose members included women, but there is no evidence that the Ivanova members were given over to "debauchery" either in theory or in practice. On the other hand, being advanced women of the intelligentsia, it is hardly likely that they would have avoided ventilating all aspects of the sexual questions raised by the authors they were reading.

In regard to "hatred of authority," the charge had greater weight. Three of the members were sisters of Ishutin activists; at least one other, Krylova, was taken fully into the confidence of "The Organization" whose members frequented the Workshop continuously. If it had lasted longer, the Ivanova Workshop might have become a kind of female auxiliary to the all-male organization. Furthermore, the Workshop functioned illegally, that is without the required police licence, and some of its members joined another front group, "Mutual Aid Society," and agreed to recruit new members. But suddenly the Workshop was destroyed by a police raid in May 1866. It was, like most others of its type, already in financial trouble. Relying too heavily on the good will (or rational egoism) of mankind, the Ivanovas sold their goods too cheaply and were barely able to cover the cost of rent, material, and wages.[12]

The destruction of the Ivanova Workshop and the widespread police cleanup that accompanied it marks the end of another phase of female radicalism. For most of the female participants, these groups signified an effort, however slight, to go beyond the mere personal emancipation inherent in the spirit of nihilism. The urban cooperatives described above were really the first practical experiments in socialism for the new generation, a socialism that has, incidentally, too long been overlooked by historians of the revolutionary movement who have given most of their attention to the theories, or-

[12] *Ibid.*, 269–82.

ganizational questions, and abortive plots of the period. For it was here in the growing cities that the Russian socialists first went "to the people" by endeavoring to help the dressmakers, workers, petty artisans, prostitutes, and other elements of the city poor. The urban cooperative movement anticipated the mass movement of the "populists" into the countryside. For women of radical tendencies, it was "social action" on a grander philosophical scale than the charitable activities of the feminists. And for most of them, it was little more than that.

There was considerable ambiguity in the relationship between the radical men and their female followers in these years. In theory they followed their prophets, Chernyshevsky, Robert Owen, and Saint-Simon, in teaching the equality of sexes; but their practical behavior showed otherwise. Khudyakov himself, for instance, openly recounted how he hoped that his wife, though "whole-heartedly sympathic to social needs," would become an opera singer so that she could finance *his* revolutionary activities. When his sister-in-law was tardy in delivering a promised thousand ruble endowment to the cause, he said, "In the war of life, every moment is precious, but women do not understand this." In their enterprises as well, there is more than a little deviousness and manipulation. One can appreciate the need for secrecy of course, but was it a mere coincidence that both "The Organization" and its secret inner core "Hell" contained no women? The women were limited to membership in the various *artels* and communes and in the seemingly innocent "Mutual Aid Society," the "gateway" to the illegal inner sanctums, which one of the conspirators described "as a kind of lake from which we will catch fish." Russian radicalism was still far from the time when women would sit as equals in the inner councils of its organizations.[13]

Karakozov's unsuccessful attempt on the life of the tsar brought almost all of these activities to a sudden end. A wave of arrests and searches, tendentiously called the "white terror" in radical circles, caught up large numbers of men and women, innocent and guilty alike. Though the women escaped the terrible fates of Karakozov, Ishutin, and Khudyakov, they were persecuted nonetheless. Convinced that nihilism, sexual licence, and regicide were inseparable elements of the conspiracy, the police subjected female suspects to needless harassment. When the Ivanova Workshop was raided, members were asked how many men they had slept with and how many civil marriages they had had; and they were treated to "cynical, rude, and obscene barracks language." When women were found with male suspects, the questions were: "Do you get paid? Didn't they read you *What Is To Be Done?*" or "Do you belong to the nihilist sect?" If the answer was no, then: "Why do you wear blue glasses" or "Why do you go around without a crinoline?" The Moscow

[13] *Ibid.*, 316–21, 391–93, 399–400 (quotations, 320, 391).

Chief of Gendarmes ordered that all women wearing the "nihilist" costume be banished from the city within twenty-four hours. The Governor-General of St. Petersburg issued prostitutes' yellow passports to "nihilist" girls. In Saratov two "gentlemen" knocked down a young woman who was wearing dark glasses and smashed them. And the Governor of Nizhny Novgorod Province ordered that women without crinolines and sporting short hair, blue glasses, and hoods were to be taken to the police station and given a written order to change their costume or else be banished from the province. Among the rumors circulating at the time about women suspects was that they lived in sin with their male associates and, in obedience to their own code, never washed. Prince Odoevsky wrote in his diary that "one of the rules of the nihilists was not to be clean. What filth, especially if they lived in fornication; their stench must be unbearable."[14]

In view of all this, there was a general lull in underground activities for a few years, though a number of small radical groups, which included women, attempted to maintain some semblance of organizational life. The most important of these was the so-called Smorgon Academy, a handful of Petersburg survivors of Ishutin's circles. Apparently it was the first genuinely revolutionary group to give women full membership. But its numbers were tiny and its headquarters a cluttered flat and a communal kitchen. Out of this commune arose a typical legend about "a beautiful nihilist" who allegedly sold her body for the sake of the cause. She has been identified as Evdokiya Kozlovskaya, the civil wife of one of the Ishutin conspirators.[15] Similar legends cropped up again in 1905 and during the Civil War and were, as far as we can tell, nothing more than the products of malicious wishful thinking.

The last episode of female radicalism in the 1860's centers around the figure of Sergei Nechaev, the fanatical and frightening young revolutionary who capped his career of conspiracy and cynicism by arranging the cold-blooded murder of one of his own fellow radicals. One of Nechaev's methods of spreading revolutionary consciousness was to arrange the arrest of luke-warm comrades in order to fill them with hatred for the regime. Vera Zasulich, a budding young radical in those years, gives a vivid account of her first brush with Nechaev in 1868. When she met him, she had just finished reading Dobrolyubov's famous review of Turgenev's *On the Eve*, "When Will the Real Day Dawn?" Nechaev asked her when it would dawn, and she replied that Dobrolyubov was speaking of a generation which "grows up in an atmosphere of hope and expectation." Nechaev then suggested that the day

[14] [N. A. Vorms], "Belyi terror," *Kolokol*, (Jan. 1, 1867) 1889–1895; "Dnevnik Odoevskogo," 211, 223.

[15] Venturi, *Roots*, 351; Vilenskaya, *Rev. podpole*, 327; N. I. Sveshnikov, *Vospominaniya propashchego cheloveka* (Moscow, Leningrad, 1930) 159–60. For other circles which included women, see Vilenskaya, *Rev. podpole*, 244, 337, 417.

had already dawned and he tried to enroll her as an unquestioning and obedient member of his organization. Though flattered and impressed, Zasulich displayed some skepticism. When Nechaev then tried to capture her interest through romantic overtures, she saw through the clumsy device and failed to succumb to his magnetism. Soon after this she and her associates, including Nechaev's sister, fell into the police dragnet which was undoubtedly made possible by a list of names supplied to them by Nechaev himself.[16]

Nechaev's career was spectacular but brief. Two years after this episode, eighty-one of his followers stood trial in Moscow, nine of them women. Most of these were veterans of earlier circles. Varvara Aleksandrovskaya a former associate of Young Russia, astounded her captors by announcing her pregnancy after a year and a half in solitary confinement; an accommodating guard had allowed one of her co-defendants to visit her cell. Zasulich's sister, Alexandra Uspenskaya, went into exile for ten years with her former lover whom she had married just on the chance that he might be arrested some day, for only a legal wife could accompany a prisoner into exile. Others received sentences much stiffer than those handed out in the days of the "white terror."[17]

Nechaev's cynicism toward women far surpassed that of his revolutionary predecessors. Like them he used women to infect other women with radical ideas; this was within the bounds of accepted revolutionary morality. But he also used them to spy on his own comrades. Prostitutes, pitied or admired by most men of the left, were to be enrolled by Nechaev as agents who could be easily blackmailed and forced to carry out revolutionary orders. For Nechaev, anything that served the revolution was moral. Sexual seduction for political purposes was only a minor item in the catalogue of activities that Nechaev considered admissable for the devoted revolutionary. Yet the *Catechism of a Revolutionary* that he and Bakunin composed is no more cynical toward women than it is toward men. Certain types were to be used as pawns whatever their sex; others were to be indispensable helpmates in the struggle for power. The revolutionary men and women of the succeeding decade, though recoiling in horror at Nechaev's amoral outlook, would nevertheless share his view that the woman question was clearly subsidiary to the over-riding question of the Revolution.[18]

[16] Zasulich, *Vospom.*, 21–60; René Cannac, *Aux sources de la Révolution russe: Netchaïev, du nihilisme au terrorisme* (Paris, 1961) 57.

[17] *Gos. prestup.*, I, 289–411 (the defendants are listed *passim*); Kozmin, *Iz istorii*, 236–37; Cannac, *Netchaïev*, 56, 80–81; A. I. Uspenskaya, "Vospominaniya shestidesnyanitsy," *Byloe*, No. 18 (1922) 19–45.

[18] Cannac, *Netchaïev*, 59. Zasulich, *Vospom.*, 43, 47. "Katekhizis revolyutsionera," *Borba klassov*, No. 1–2 (1924), 268–72. Nechaev, who would blackmail anyone, shocked even Bakunin, far from a purist himself in these matters: "If you introduce him to your friend [complained Bakunin], his first aim will be to sow dissension, scandal and intrigue between you and make you

By the end of the 1860's, the radicals had had their say about the woman question. When the Georgian political exile, N. Ya. Nikoladze, complained in 1866 that the government and Russian society "beat out of women any possibility for intellectual activity, dress her up like a doll, and tell her that she is made only for love," he was merely revealing how far out of date he was.[19] Other revolutionary voices from abroad spoke of what they took to be bigger issues. The influential first issue of Bakunin's *People's Cause* was a case in point. Its publication was financed by Olga Levashëva, a veteran of Ishutin's circle, and it was composed in Switzerland by Bakunin and his associate, N. Zhukovsky. Its program included sexual equality, abolition of church and civil marriage, and public education of children almost as a matter of course in the new society. But its principal and most potent message was a vigorous denunciation of the tendency toward science-worship and extreme individualism that had enthralled large numbers of the nihilist generation; and a stirring appeal to the young, of both sexes, to go out among the people and ignite the tinder of social revolution.[20]

Even more explicit in its treatment of the revolutionary imperative was the first known revolutionary manifesto addressed to women. Issuing from the shadowy "Russian Revolutionary Society" in Geneva, it was written (in late 1869 or early 1870) either by Zaitsev or Nechaev and consigned to Varvara Aleksandrovskaya for distribution inside Russia. She was arrested and the documents were confiscated. Aleksandrovskaya, earlier in the 1860's, had been close to Zaichnevsky and "Young Russia." Whether the ideas on women in the proclamation came from "Young Russia" through her or from Bakunin through Nechaev is of no great consequence, for they were already in the air, and would serve as guiding principles for the revolutionary women of the next decade. Although it never reached its intended audience, it was the first to advance publicly a "radical" response to the woman question that was distinct both from feminism and from nihilism.[21]

Its depiction of the subjected women in Russian society was, though strongly worded, fairly conventional. "All laws are written so that the most talented of you is placed lower than the stupidest of men." The lascivious male, "beginning with the debaucher, Alexander II, himself," treated women

---

quarrel. If your friend has a wife or daughter, he will do his best to seduce her and get her with child, in order to snatch her from the power of conventional morality and involve her, despite herself, in a revolutionary protest against society." Quoted in Carr, *Romantic exiles*, 353.

[19] Nikifor G*** [N. Ya. Nikoladze], *Pravitelstvo i molodoe pokolenie* (Geneva, 1866) 40.

[20] *Narodnoe delo*, No. 1 (Sept. 1869) 6–7, quoted in Burtsev, *Za sto let*, 87–89. On Levashëva, see Vilenskaya, *Rev. podpole*, 230–33 and Kozmin, *Russkaya sektsiya Pervogo Internatsionala* (Moscow, 1957) 72, 85–86.

[21] "Ot Russkogo Revolyutionnogo Obshchestva k zhenshchinam," ed. E. Kusheva in *Lit. nasled.*, XL–XLII (1941) 147–50. Kusheva names Zaitsev as the author; Venturi names Nechaev (*Roots*, 382). On Aleksandrova, see Meijer, *Knowledge*, 172, n. 60.

like a doll and a sexual object, thus robbing them of natural love and pure feelings. Without these, "you lie when you make your vows, when you stand at the altar, and throughout your life." The first step away from all this was independence and work. "Only a working man can present himself as a member of human society and thus demand human rights. In this, there is no difference between a man and a woman; the parasites of both sexes are doomed to rightlessness and ruin. Only workers, male and female, have the right to life. If a woman remains merely a daughter or a concubine, she cannot ask for her so-called emancipation." A kept wife was no better than a prostitute, and work alone would transform her into a person.

But freedom from the family was only the first step, said the proclamation. The nihilists had won this, only to be beaten senseless in the wave of police brutality. Sexual and personal liberation would never be secure in Russian society without deeper transformations. What then was the correct path?

> You will find it in social revolution [was the answer]. Only after such a revolution, which will abolish all exploitation, will you have the possibility of human existence. Your cause is intimately tied to that of the entire mass of oppressed working people. Join them. Destroy the empire of the landowners. Destroy it and its legal framework which oppressively binds the people. Only then will a free field of women's labor be open; only then will you become productive individuals in society; only then will your rights be equal to those of men. Only by abolishing private property can we abolish the juridical family.

In the future society, a network of socialist *artels* within a federative system, no one would interfere with those who wished to live outside religion and the family. The manifesto demanded, in emphatic tones, that women share in the struggle to overturn the old order, that they devote their well-known bravery and stoicism "to the cause of national liberation." It was time for them to join the movement as equal partners.

Here at last we have the full elaboration of the two principles of revolutionary emancipation of women in nineteenth-century Russia: the program—complete equality of women in conjunction with the general liberation of the Russian people; the tactic—full and equal participation of women in the revolutionary struggle to bring about these goals. The "woman question" was to be subsumed in the "human question" and special campaigns on behalf of women's rights were to be abandoned in favor of the "common cause." This was a specific rejection of feminism that was to have its echo in the Marxist "proletarian women's movement" a generation later. But it was also a rejection of the nihilist ethos as a permanent solution to women's subjection. As worried theorists like Bakunin and Lavrov had observed, too many nihilists had diverted their rebellious energies to personal improvement, intellectual development, and sexual freedom, taking from Pisarev *only* the ideas about individual liberation and from Chernyshevsky *only* the spirit of psychological egoism, ignoring the more fundamental premise of both those writers: that personal emancipation was meant to be the prelude to national emancipation. In the new revolutionary ethic of the 1870's, it was universally agreed that personal goals—whether masculine or feminine—concerning work, learning, or love would only be fully realized in the wake of the general upheaval.[22]

2. EDUCATION OR REVOLUTION?

The Russian revolutionary movement of the 1870's was unparalleled elsewhere in the nineteenth-century Western world. Thousands of young men and women streamed into the countryside to make contact with the peasants; hundreds perished in exile, prison, or on the scaffold for their efforts to destroy the administrative core of the Empire through assassination. The agonizing and immediate problems of personal and social life that had consumed the intelligentsia in the 1860's, were shunted aside and all energies were devoted to the People and to the Revolution. The "woman question," as such, was practically non-existent in the theoretical formulations of the revolutionaries. The most prominent émigré theorists of the movement, Lavrov, Bakunin, and Tkachëv, simply intoned variations of the theme exposed in the proclamation "To Women": present equality of the sexes in revolutionary obligations; future equality in the socialist society. And as socialists, they made obeisance, too, to the notion of the abolition of the family, though there was no precision, either in definition of "the family" or in timetable. Since all of them did marry, the difficulty of interpretation is intensified. Their sporadic references to the problem, in any case, occupied an insignificant place in their theories, and had even less significance for those who read their works.[1]

In Russia itself, the situation was the same. Although women played an important role in the movement and thus raised problems and possibilities shared by few other radical movements in history, the revolutionary literature of the 1870's is almost barren of any reference to the question. Within the movement, there were discussions and even clashes of opinion on the matter, but the programs of the underground groups never reflected or reported these.

[22] Shashkov, at the turn of the decade, complained of some aristocratic tendencies in the women's movement and an abuse of freedom on the part of emancipated women. He warned that this movement must not have a lordly manner but must be tied closely to that of the popular masses. *Ist. sudby*, 313, 369–70.

[1] Lavrov, as early as 1858, had voiced his belief in the ultimate disappearance of the family to Elena Stackenschneider: (*Dnevnik*, 239), though he had little to say about the matter in later years. Bakunin's strongest statement is found in the first issue of *The People's Cause*, discussed on p. 124 of the present work. Tkachëv, in spare and cautious terms, called for "the *gradual* abolition of the *existing* family," (italics added) in his description of the aims of the Revolution: "Tsel revolyutsii," cited in Burtsev, *Za sto let*, 133–34.

The women approved this silence, for most of them had been attracted to radicalism by the people's cause, not by the women's. Since the major target of revolutionary propaganda was the ignorant, superstitious, and tradition-ridden peasantry, programmatic frankness on matters of sexual equality would certainly have complicated the already enormously difficult job of communicating with the peasants—though in matters of religion, armed upris-ing, and tsar-hatred, propagandists were often willing to risk a violation of the village ethos. The program of Land and Liberty refused to treat "questions dealing with the private relations [*chastnykh form*] of the future socialist or-der," adding that the future should be left to the future. The Executive Com-mittee of the terrorist group, The People's Will, exhibited similar reticence: "Only the will of the people can sanction future social forms."[2]

If there was a single burning question which plagued women at the onset of the 1870's, it was not the woman question but the uneasy relationship be-tween education and revolution. For many women of the 1860's, the first step leftward, so to speak, had been into the realm of serious study, especially of the natural sciences. Familiarity with books like Darwin's *Origin of Species*, Vogt's *Physiologische Briefe*, and Buchner's *Kraft und Stoff* was the hallmark of an advanced woman. Peter Lavrov was one of the first to perceive that this love of pure science had often led progressive people away from the path of social concern. He conceded, in the very first of his extraordinarily influential "Historical Letters," that "natural science is the very foundation of a rational life," that without it, man is blind and deaf to life's requirements and thus cannot be called a modern, educated person. But closer to life, he continued, were the problems of politics, economics, and society. The truly learned per-son must advance from science to social science.[3] And throughout his works runs this recurrent theme: Knowledge is not to be an end in itself or a mere vocational training, but a form of self-preparation for the lofty and formidable task of liberating the people.

The memoir literature of the period bulges with references to this problem. Mikhail Popov tells how, in the third year of his medical studies, he stood on the Sampsonievsky Bridge—which, as it happens, was halfway between the Medical Academy and the Peter Paul Fortress—pondering whether to face his examination and further study or throw himself wholeheartedly into the revo-lutionary movement. Another medical student, S. I. Chudnovsky, posed the question in clear-cut terms: "knowledge or work [among the people]?" Vera Figner, Sofya Perovskaya, and countless others agonized over the same prob-lem and finally deserted the classroom to go out among the people. For all of them, men and women, had reached a point of awareness that was illustrated

[2] From the program of Land and Liberty (Zemlya i Volya) cited in Burtsev, *Za sto let*, 138; from that of the People's Will (Narodnaya Volya) in *Literatura sotsialno-revolyutsionnoi partii "Narodnoi Voli,"* (n.p., 1905) 162.

[3] Lavrov, *Izbr. soch.*, I, 172.

by the well-known words of Lavrov: "We have no right *to study at the expense of the people*."[4]

The great "movement to the people" of 1874 drew its female participants from two principle sources: the Russian colony in Zurich in the early 1870's; and the propaganda circles in Russia of the same period, chiefly the Chaikovtsy of St. Petersburg. In outward form these latter circles were not so very different from those of the 1860's—students of both sexes, based in rough-and-ready communes, spreading the word, initially at least, among the city's lower classes. But their outlook, derived from Lavrov's doctrine of willful sacrifice and humility and a clear-cut rejection of Nechaevism, was both more ethical and more democratic. The Chaikovsky Circle was the result of the merger of a male student commune with a small group of women doing preparatory work at the Alarchin Courses. Its founder was Mark Natanson, a medical student; out of it came such illustrious figures of the revolutionary movement as Kropotkin, Stepniak-Kravchinsky, Lopatin, Sinegub, and Shishko, as well as Nikolai Chaikovsky whose name it later adopted. Through his future wife, Olga Shleisner, Natanson met the other Alarchin students and suggested a merger. It may have been this proposal that prompted the males to give the "woman question" an airing during one of their interminable debates. Some speakers merely recited platitudes from Mikhailov and Chernyshevsky. Most probably agreed with the member who said that it was incorrect to isolate the woman question from the general question—the emancipation of the proletariat. On this note, no doubt, it was agreed to accept the women into the circle.[5]

These ten or so women, ranging in age from fifteen to about twenty-one, came from privileged families, gentry, or rich merchants. In the spirit of the decade, they had flocked to the Alarchin Courses in the late 1860's in order to soak up knowledge, but without any particular goal. In the spirit of those years, too, they dressed like nihilists, with short hair and the plainest of costumes, giving endless verbal attention to the niceties of women's emancipation. There was some of the shyness and veiled hostility to men that often accompanies early phases of feminist consciousness, in the broadest sense of the words, and some fear of dependence as well. This was especially marked in Sofya Perovskaya, who at first opposed joining intellectual forces with the

[4] M. R. Popov, *Zapiski zemlevoltsa*, ed. I. A. Teodorovich (Moscow, 1933) 45, 102 (in the earlier passage, Popov refers incorrectly to the Semënovsky Bridge); Zasulich, *Vospom.*, 118 (for Chudnovsky); Lavrov, *Narodniki-propagandisty, 1873–78 godov* (SPB, 1907) 185.

[5] A good picture of the propaganda circles of the period can be gotten from the following three accounts: V. Bogucharsky, *Aktivnoe Narodnichestvo semidesyatykh godov* (Moscow, 1912) 152–72; Venturi, *Roots*, 469–506; and B. S. Itenberg, *Dvizhenie revolyutsionnogo Narodnichestva: narodnicheskie kruzhki i 'khozhdenie v narod' v 70-kh godakh XIX v.* (Moscow, 1965) 129–93 and *passim*. But the best introduction to their spirit is to be found in the memoirs scattered through the following notes. For the debate on the woman question among the male Chaikovtsy, see the eyewitness account by I. E. Deniker: "Vospominaniya I. E. Denikera," *Katorga i ssylka*, No. 3 (1924) 20–44 (27).

men and later insisted on reading the sources herself rather than at the feet of radically seasoned males. At length, she relented and the merger was effected in the spring of 1871 with the women making up some 25 percent of the Chaikovsky Circle in the years to come.[6] With the Chaikovsky women, we can begin to focus more clearly on the kinds of female personalities that lent themselves to the revolutionary struggle of the coming years.

Olga Shleisner, aged nineteen, was of a Kursk gentry family and had attended an institute in St. Petersburg. Feeling a need for more learning, she enrolled in the recently opened Alarchin Courses. But her real education began when she met Natanson, who came from a cultivated Jewish family of Vilna. Despite her social and religious background, she fell in love with him and married him, and made her name in revolutionary annals as Olga Natanson. Being without the slightest trace of a pretension or pose, as one of her comrades described her, she found it as natural to marry a Jew as to clip her hair or read a book, even though at the time such mixed marriages were unheard-of in conventional society. It was an early example of a phenomenon which was to become commonplace in later years. She was easily converted to "the cause" and became the liaison between Natanson's group and her own schoolmates. She studied medicine for a while at the newly opened courses for women, but soon buried herself completely in the underground movement, becoming one of the leading spirits of Land and Liberty. She died in 1881—a bit over thirty—of an illness contracted while she was confined in the fortress prison.[7]

The four Kornilov sisters were the daughters of a wealthy porcelain manufacturer of the capital who had means enough to send them to the best schools and liberalism enough to let them come and go as they pleased. One after another they passed through institutes and gymnasiums into the Alarchin Courses. Their spacious home was the meeting place for their classmates, and their dowries were put at the disposal of the Chaikovtsy. The best known of them, Alexandra, was also the youngest, sixteen when the Alarchin Circle was formed. Known in history as Kornilova-Moroz, she followed the zig-zag path that was so typical for the politically active women of her generation: scientific study and propaganda, arrest, medical study in Vienna, "to the people," and eventual exile.[8]

From still another sort of background came Elizaveta Solntseva of Kharkov. Born the illegitimate daughter of a noble landowner and a serf woman, Solntseva was compensated by nature with great beauty, charm, and intelli-

---

[6] Itenberg, *Dvizhenie*, 142–43; Elena Segal, *Sofya Perovskaya* (Moscow, 1962) 63.

[7] O. V. Aptekman, *Obshchestvo 'Zemlya i Volya' 70-kh gg. po lichnym vospominaniyam*, 2d ed. (Petrograd, 1924) 210–14; *Deyateli*, II/2, 2042–43.

[8] *Ibid.*, II/2, 640–44; Ekaterina Breshko-Breshkovskaya, "Iz vospominanii (S. A. Leshern, N. A. Armfeldt, T. I. Lebedeva, M. K. Krylova, G. M. Gelfman)," *Golos minuvshago* (Oct.- Dec. 1918) 169–235 (209); Venturi, *Roots*, 481; S. S. Sinegub, *Zapiski Chaikovtsa* (Moscow, 1929) 6, 305; Segal, *Perovskaya*, 43–44 and *passim*.

gence; and by her repentant father with freedom, the best education, and a number of fine houses in Kharkov. A typical *intelligentka* of the 1860's, she held "advanced" ideas and was a staunch apostle of women's rights. She and her husband, Kovalsky, became the center of Kharkov's leftist intellectual life. She converted one of her properties, known as "The Pink House," into a commodious school for socialism and feminism where she taught basic skills to poor milliners and gave courses in utopian socialism and women's rights to the more advanced women. When the school was closed by the police, Solntseva-Kovalskaya, leaving her feminism behind, came to St. Petersburg and joined the Chaikovsky Circle.[9]

The best known woman in the circle, and subsequently the most famous woman revolutionary in nineteenth-century Russia, was Sofya Perovskaya. In terms of social status, she towered over her companions, for her father, though of only middling gentry origin, had climbed the table of ranks to become Governor-General of St. Petersburg Province, one of the most crucial administrative posts in the Empire. As a father, Lev Perovsky was not the total domestic tyrant that some have made him out;[10] but he certainly acted like an officer and administrator to his family, and harried his wife for not being "wordly" enough. Little Sonya, while loving her mother to distraction, feared and disliked her father, and early developed an aversion to men that lasted late into her life. Her early home life may help explain her later hostility to aristocratic society and her burning hatred of the tsarist regime. But all of this came later, with womanhood.

A bad year for the family was 1866: Perovsky was demoted from his post because of the Karakozov affair and Sonya's brother, Vasily, was involved in some student disturbances. Henceforth brother and sister were at odds with the rest of the family. He was the only male who could influence her and from him she received her matriculation into the world of the "thick journals." From Pisarev, it was a short step to the desire to "enroll" somewhere. The Alarchin Courses presented themselves in 1869 and Perovskaya began her studies; she was not yet sixteen. The Kornilova girls became her friends, and through them, Shleisner and later the Chaikovtsy men. Her father tried to retrieve his wayward daughter by means of the police, but to no avail. His will was no match for hers. At the courses, Perovskaya revealed a gift for mathematics and was a diligent student; but her conscience grew more and more uneasy at the unfolding awareness of the vast social sufferings which surrounded her. As she said later, she joined the socialist circle "in order to make

[9] Popov, *Zapiski*, 445; Itenberg, *Dvizhenie*, 157.

[10] For instance, N. Asheshov, *Sofya Perovskaya: materialy dlya biografii i kharakteristiki* (SPB [sic] 1920) 9. The judgement is somewhat softened by Segal, *Perovskaya*, 11. For some reason, major women revolutionaries like Perovskaya, Figner, and Zasulich have failed to attract serious, critical biographers. Asheshov is the standard older work for Perovskaya, but is very sketchy. Segal's book, although written in a popular vein and without documentation, is full and accurate and has a useful list of sources.

possible the development of the people," a notion as psychologically sound as it was ideologically amorphous.[11]

Perovskaya's place in the Chaikovsky Circle explains its *byt*, its inner life. She seems to have possessed all that was most admired by its members: simplicity, love of the oppressed, raw hatred of the oppressors, and stoicism—the best qualities of the revolutionary women of the 1870's. Personal relations in the circle were based upon complete equality, and a warm, informal, and comradely spirit prevailed. In matters of sex, if Perovskaya's outlook was an accurate index, puritanism and "seriousness" were the order of the day. In a culture that idolized the rigorism of Rakhmetov, Chernyshevsky's ascetic hero, Perovskaya was a rigorist of the rigorists, and as Tikhomirov once said, "the most tranquil of the tranquil." On one occasion, Perovskaya was influential in expelling a male from the group because of his "loose living"; her distaste for his company was colored by the fact that she considered him a "ladies' man."[12]

The Chaikovtsy's first venture into illegal activity was called "book work": spreading the ideas of Marx, Lassalle, Lavrov, and Bervi among the youth of the capital. This was the occasion of Perovskaya's first brush with the police: arrest, a cursory investigation, and release for lack of evidence of criminal activity. She then spent a summer as a vaccinator in the villages of the Volga—an early version of "going to the people." The experience of how Russians actually lived was a disturbing revelation. Under this impulse, reinforced by Lavrov's idea of "the repentant noble" and the asceticism of Rakhmetov, she traveled everywhere on foot, and slept on the hard floor. Back in St. Petersburg, she and her comrades conducted propaganda work in the factories, living simply and taking their water in pails from the Neva. The police soon scooped most of them up and put an end to the original Chaikovsky Circle. Perovskaya was remanded to her mother, thus closing the first phase of her revolutionary career.[13]

Smaller groups, contemporary with the Chaikovtsy, also channeled women into the revolutionary movement. But the largest and most spectacular contingent of women radicals in the early seventies was formed in Zurich. Since the time of Suslova, Russian women, unable to study at home, had been streaming abroad to continue their studies, mostly in medicine. From 1864 to 1874, some 118 Russian women (twice the number of men) had attended the University of Zurich. Most of them arrived for serious study, though medicine

---

[11] Asheshov, *Perovskaya*, 1–15; Segal, *Perovskaya*, 7–61.

[12] Asheshov, *Perovskaya*, 18–23; S. M. Stepniak-Kravchinsky, *Sofiya Perovskaya* (Berlin, 1903) 6–12, (her name is spelled both as Sofiya and Sofya); N. V. Chaikovsky, "Cherez pol stoletiya: otkrytoe pismo k druzyami," *Golos minuvshego na chuzhoi storone*, XIII (Nov. 3, 1926) 179–89 (186).

[13] Asheshov, *Perovskaya*, 28–36; Stepniak-Kravchinsky, *Perovskaya*, 15–19; Kropotkin, *Memoirs*, 211.

was more often seen as a way of serving and contacting "the people" than as a mere science or profession. The more politically minded of them also came to inspect the radical community there and to taste the sweet air of civic freedom. All certainly shared a sense of adventure, for it was no easy matter for a young Russian woman to obtain a passport to travel on her own in those days. Some daughters benefited from their mothers' fear of Nechaevist infection at home; others employed the now widely accepted device of fictitious marriage as a passport to freedom.[14]

Among the Russians who helped heat up the political atmosphere in Switzerland were the veterans of conspiratorial circles of the 1860's, members of the First International, and refugees from the Paris Commune. There were women in all of these groups, but they made very little impact outside them. At least four Russian women participated in the Commune. Of these, only Elizaveta Dmitrieva made an important contribution to the political work and the fighting during that bloody episode. Dmitrieva was an illegitimate gentry child, brought up in privileged surroundings. As a girl, she had taken piano lessons from her "poor cousin" Musorgsky, and had hatched schemes with another, Kuropotkin, to finance socialist cooperatives. She passed through nihilism to Marxism and became one of Marx's active supporters in the International. At twenty, vibrating with energy, she hastened to Paris from her Swiss base and there, with Louise Michel, founded clubs for female workers, nursing units, and finally a Woman's Batallion. Known to the Communards as Madame X, she appeared in person on the barricades clad in a blood-stained dress, with a red sash draped over her breast, like Delacroix's "Liberty at the Barricades."[15]

Tales of the Commune stirred the Russian women in Zurich, to be sure, but their influence was slight compared to the atmosphere of revolt generated by Lavrov and Bakunin. The latter, during his sojourn there in the summer of 1872, managed to infect a small but loyal following composed chiefly of women whom the Swiss students nicknamed "Cossack Ponies." But much of Bakunin's influence was personal and charismatic and it rapidly faded when he went elsewhere. Though conventionally extreme on women's emancipation, Bakunin once astounded his female followers by announcing that he could not bear to see women drink or smoke. Lavrov, less picturesque than Bakunin, nevertheless exerted more influence over the minds of the young women in Zurich. His advocacy of women's rights was expressed more in action than in theory, for he never wrote very much about it. In Switzerland,

[14] For the Zurich colony, the indispensable, if rather dense, work is Meijer, *Knowledge and Revolution*. See 131–32 for a brief comment on the non-politicals. Lavrov's brief, but intimate and psychologically perceptive, characterization is in his *Narodniki*, 62–69. See also Breshkovskaya, *Hidden Springs of the Russian Revolution: Personal Memoirs*, ed. L. Hutchison (Stanford, 1931) 335; Kropotkin, *Memoirs*, 179.

[15] Knizhnik-Vetrov, *Deyatelnitsy*, 16–134. See also Frank Jellinek, *The Paris Commune of 1871* (London, 1937) 253–54, 324, 400.

he added to the development of revolutionary consciousness in women by inviting them into his circles and putting them to work on his journals; and both there and in Russia itself, his ethical revolutionary teachings had a tremendous impact.[16]

Of the numerous circles, coteries, and reading clubs for women that mushroomed around the Oberstrasse, three have more than passing interest. The Women's Club for Logical Thought had a short and stormy life. It was conceived by Rozaliya Idelson, a Jewish medical student who had arrived in Switzerland thanks to a fictitious marriage in order to be with her non-Jewish sweetheart. She found herself in a phase of feminist consciousness shared by many nascent female radicals: wanting the intellectual companionship of men, but feeling the need to develop self-confidence in the safer company of women. Thus was founded the Women's Club (*Zhenskii Ferein*), a women-only debating club where members could polish their rhetoric and test their convictions without the threatening presence of men. Some older women incorrectly saw in this an anti-male tendency, but the younger majority embraced the club with enthusiasm. Untrained as they were, however, in the art of "reasonable debate," the club members slipped into personal abuse at the third exercise in logical thought, ending it in a scene of emotional outbursts over the recondite question of what would happen to the fruits of civilization after the Revolution. The women left the meeting, shouting "we'll destroy them" or "we'll keep them" through the sleepy streets of Zurich. The club expired some weeks later, having taught some of the women, no doubt, the foolishness of trying to emulate men's ways of posing such questions.[17]

The St. Zhebunists were a circle of five men and three women who held aloof from other political groups at the University and dedicated themselves to an intense study of the ideas of the French utopian socialists. Their name, a pun on the Zhebunev brothers who started the circle and "Saint-Simonians," arose from their penchant for exalted and febrile debates which often ended in fainting, as had happened to Enfantin's disciples at Ménilmontant. Its most remarkable member was Anna Rosenstein (Rozenshtein) who, like many of her fellow students, was the daughter of well-to-do converted Jews. Having been endowed with beauty, brains, and a happy childhood, she walked off with honors from her Simferopol high school at sixteen and went directly to Zurich to study science. There she joined the St. Zhebunists and two years later, when Lavrov met her, she was already "a fervent anarchist." When the

[16] For Bakunin in Zurich, see: Carr, *Bakunin*, 465–66; Meijer, *Knowledge*, 99; Vera Figner, "Studencheskie gody (1872–1873)," *Golos minuvshego*, X (Oct. 1922), 165–81 (173); M. P. Sazhin, "Russkie v Tsyurikhe (1870–1873 gg.)," *Katorga i ssylka*, No. 10 (1932) 37. Lavrov's avid interest in the woman question is illustrated in two of his letters: Provintsial [Lavrov], "Pismo v redaktsiyu," *Bibliograf* (Oct. 1869) 1–14 (14); and, *Izbr. soch.*, I, 63. I am indebted to Professor Philip Pomper for the former reference.

[17] The story, is told, with great economy, by Vera Figner in her memoirs: *Zapechatlënnyi trud: vospominaniya*, 2 v. (Moscow, 1964) I, 116–19. On Idelson, see Meijer, *Knowledge,* 69, and Itenberg, *Dvizhenie*, 173.

circle returned to Russia to work in the villages, all except Anna were arrested. She herself, at the ripe age of twenty, became a rebel (*buntarka*), moving among the extremist groups of Southern Russia. When these collapsed she went back to Europe where she eventually married Filippo Turati and became one of the early leaders of the Marxist movement in Italy and the editor of *Critica sociale*. She was one of a number of fascinating and cultivated Jewish women of the Russian Empire—of whom Rosa Luxemburg, Emma Goldman, and Golda Meir were only the most famous—who combined many traditions and passed through many revolutionary and intellectual currents before arriving at confident maturity. "Signora Kuliscioff," as the Italians came to know her, also managed to complete her studies and become a brilliant physician.[18]

Most famous of the Zurich female circles was the "Fritschi" so named after the boarding house of Frau Fritsch where they lived. Its best known member was Vera Figner, though she was the last to join the circle and for a long time exhibited great reluctance to give up her studies for the sake of the revolution. Her illuminating recollections afford us the best account both of the Fritsch Circle and of the emergence of an outstanding revolutionary.[19] Figner came of a prosperous Kazan gentry family. Although her father, a government official, is described in her memoirs as somewhat despotic, Vera's early years were happy and unmarred by any great internal struggle. Hints of future radicalism are minimal: contempt for an aristocratic cousin, sympathy for some Polish relatives mistreated in the 1863 disturbances, and a vague feeling of "obligation" to help other people—attitudes that might have led just as easily into liberalism, or feminism, or nothing at all. She was no born revolutionary: One of her childhood daydreams was about being selected, Muscovite fashion, to be the bride of the tsar. Her younger sisters preceded her on the path to radicalism, while her brothers carved out respectable careers for themselves.

Figner's education was "appropriate to her station": home tutoring and then the Rodionovsky Institute in Kazan. There is some evidence that the salutary reforms of the 1860's had brightened the pedagogical atmosphere at Rodionovsky; but even with this, the subjects were as devoid of life as was the teacher—"a dried-up old maid," Figner called her. Books were discouraged,

---

[18] On the Saint-Zhebunists see Figner, "Stud. gody," 168 and Lev Deutsch, "Yuzhnye buntari," *Golos minuvshago*, XX (1920–1921) 44–71 (51–52). On Rosenstein (alias Makarevich and Kuleshëva): Deutsch, *Rol Evreev*, 217–31; Lavrov, *Narodniki*, 218; Franco Venturi, "Anna Kuliscioff e la sua attività rivoluzionaria in Russia," *Movimento operaio*, new series, IV (Mar.-Apr. 1952) 277–87.

[19] Figner, whose lifetime (1852–1942) spanned the most critical years of modern Russian history, also awaits serious biographical treatment, though writings by and about her are plentiful. The fundamental work is her memoirs, cited fully in note 17 above. Volume I covers her life to 1883; volume II her twenty years in the Schlüsselberg Fortress prison. The abridged English translation, *Memoirs of a Revolutionist*, tr. C. C. Daniels *et al.* (London, n.d.), is extremely unreliable and, by its very brevity, misleading in respect to the rate of speed at which its subject achieved revolutionary consciousness. For the Zurich years, the memoirs should be supplemented by "Stud. gody," cited in full, note 16 above.

and little effort was made to teach about life or to inculcate a moral sense. Looking back on her six years at the Institute, Figner tried to describe what she got from her sojourn there: a cultivated manner, a sense of self-discipline in study, and, as in any boarding school, a thirst for comradeship. "But in regard to scientific knowledge and especially mental development," she wrote, "these years gave me precious little and even stunted my spiritual growth, to say nothing of the harm wrought by the unnatural isolation from life and from people." But like many cultivated girls of her generation, she balanced the schoolroom dullness by wide reading in the major sources of radical sensibility: the Russian classics, the "thick journals," and Western science.[20]

A turning point came in 1869, shortly after graduation, when she was feeling "a youthful, individual, exuberant mood and a desire to reach out toward some meaningful and challenging activity." She chanced upon an article on Suslova's career. Shortly after that she read an article on utilitarianism and decided that "the greatest good for the greatest number" was an appropriate goal and medicine the shortest path to it. Her plans to go to Zurich were postponed by her courtship and marriage to a Kazan lawyer, Aleksei Filippov. She and sister Lidiya studied elementary sciences with Professor Leshaft at the University. When that generous teacher was dismissed as "a bad influence on the younger generation," Vera was disturbed but, as she later wrote, made no connection between this event and the arbitrariness of the Russian government. Even in Zurich, where she, her husband, and Lidiya went in 1872, Vera at first moved among the "conservative" girls whose only interest was study, and she was rather diffident about mixing with the more politically minded friends of Lidiya. It was the latter who eventually drew her sister into the radical circle.[21]

The Fritsch group, which Lidiya joined, was composed of some twelve to fifteen girls with an average age of about twenty, largely Russian gentry, except for a couple of Jews. The differences in national and religious background were practically obliterated by other considerations: All were reasonably well off, well educated, and with a common experience in reading habits and philosophical values. Here, as with the men, Jewishness played almost no role in the relationships between members of radical circles. Outside the classroom, the Fritsch women studied socialism, attended meetings of the exile community, and did volunteer work on Lavrov's press. Equality reigned, although one of them, Sofya Bardina—whom the girls called "aunt"—was treated as kind of an elder. Serious and respected by the others, she possessed the finest qualities of that boarding-school spirit which allowed for exalted relations among adolescent girls without a hint of overt sexuality.

[20] Her childhood and school years in *Zapechat. trud*, I, 46–96 (quotation, 86).
[21] *Ibid.*, I, 99–122; "Stud. gody," 171.

Bardina exuded an air of strength and readiness for sacrifice, a readiness which was tested and proven by her terrible fate.[22]

The three Subbotina sisters, typified the background of most members of the circle. But, untypically, they had arrived in Zurich not against the wishes of their mother, but with her assistance. She was a liberal lady of the older generation who used her fortune to open schools for peasants and to send her daughters off to Switzerland where she herself became affectionately known as "the Mother of the Gracchi." Not content with launching her daughters, Evgeniya, Mariya, and Nadezhda, on the path to revolution, Mme. Subbotina herself played an active role and shared their fate.[23]

Berta Abramovna (Beti) Kaminskaya, was one of the Jewish members of the circle. Born into a family of well-to-do merchants in Militpol, she lost her mother early and her indulgent father gave her a great deal of freedom while she was growing up, a freedom that led not to indolence but to an early consciousness of the poverty which surrounded her. Reading the Russian classics sharpened Beti's sensitivity to suffering, and in her loneliness, led her to ask herself the question: "How can I help the masses?" Medicine seemed the answer, for it allowed both the cultivation of one's own mind and the chance to serve others. At eighteen she got permission to study in Zurich. Once there, Kaminskaya found in the Fritsch Circle both the companionship she had lacked as a child, and an attitude of serious and deep moral questioning.[24]

The turning point for the Fritsch Circle and for the entire community of Russian women in Zurich came in May 1873 with a tsarist decree ordering all of them to end their studies there by January of the following year. Russian police spies had been observing the colony for some time, and the decree was an attempt to disperse it by removing its most numerous members, the Russian women students. Mincing no words, the order accused the women of engaging in subversive activities in Zurich and implied that most of them were not there to study at all; beyond this it indicted "some" of the girls for studying obstetrics only in order to perform abortions—presumably upon each other since they were also charged with practicing "communist theories of free love." For many of the women, the charge of political activity was true. But there was no moral depravity; quite the reverse—many of them had come to Zurich by means of the fictitious marriage in order to enter serious and enduring, if illegal, unions with men they loved. But tsarist police could hardly be expected to appreciate such nuances. The decree announced that those women who persisted in staying on after the deadline would be forever denied employment or educational opportunity in any government institution.[25]

[22] For the Fritsch Circle: Amy Knight, "The Fritschi: a Study of Female Radicals in the Russian Populist Movement," *Canadian-American Slavic Studies* (Summer 1975) 1–17. Figner, *Zapechat. trud*, I, 119–27; *idem.*, "Stud. gody," 175–77; Meijer, *Knowledge*, 70–72. For Bardina: *Deyateli*, II/2, 81–82; Lavrov, *Narodniki*, 68–69.

[23] *Deyateli*, II/2, 1634–43; Burtsev, *Za sto let*, 120; Figner, "Stud. gody," 170.

[24] *Deyateli*, II/1, 537–38; Deutsch, *Rol Evreev*, 88–98; Lavrov, *Narodniki*, 67.

[25] The decree is printed in Bogucharsky, *Aktivnoe Narodnichestvo*, 213–15.

The tactlessness of the decree and its sweeping imputations of immorality and radicalism not only shocked the Zurich community but also revealed the group's natural divisons. A few who had married locally and had no plans to live in Russia remained at the University; a few more, lured by the decree's promise to study opportunities in Russia, went home. Most, however, merely transferred elsewhere, though only about 25 percent ever completed their degrees. These were the non-radicals who had begged the revolutionaries to leave them alone and "let the revolution remain on the shelves."[26] But for the Fritschi, the decree was an insult and an indication that it would be necessary to break with the past. They formed a "secret society" and vowed to return to Russia to enter the revolutionary movement. Their first program was replete with hackneyed phrases about exploitation of the masses and the need for socialist production and distribution, but it lacked a tactical line applicable to Russian conditions. After the diaspora to Paris and Geneva, some of the Fritsch members met some Georgian students, who were so impressed by their learning that they agreed to merge with them in a party to be called the All-Russian Socialist Revolutionary Organization. The Georgians, though willing to accept sexual equality in the future legal order, balked at the women's proposal of sexual celibacy for the entire group. When this difficulty was ironed out, in the Georgians' favor, the party was formed and its members returned to Russia to throw themselves into revolutionary work.[27]

Vera Figner remained. She was not a member of the new party. Indeed it was a long time before she could bring herself, against the wishes of her conservative husband, to join the Fritsch Circle. The decree decided her. Once a member, she began to rethink her situation and to perceive that medicine would only cure the sores and only give "temporary relief" to the maladies of Russian civilization. A fundamental change in the social and economic order was required; as a result, the medical profession, once such a lofty calling in her eyes, seemed nothing more than another craft. She recalls how the realization slowly dawned on her that nothing could remedy the evils of the "iron law of wages" short of establishing socialism; and nothing could bring about socialism except organization and propaganda among "the working class, the people." Armed with this simple amalgam of Lassalleanism and Lavrism, Figner finally made her decision to become a revolutionary.[28]

Thus the Fritsch women, and others like them in Zurich, had, by the summer of 1873, arrived at the stage of development reached by their sisters of the Chaikovsky Circle back in Russia. They had rejected study, self-improve-

---

[26] Meijer, *Knowledge*, 145–46, 155–56; Lavrov, *Narodniki*, 62. Meijer's useful tabulation (208–12) shows that 70 of the 120 girls studying at Zurich University also found their way into the biographical dictionary of revolutionaries (*Deyateli*). But this is misleading, for some of them, as is pointed out, were listed merely for being at Zurich in those years.

[27] Figner, *Zapechat. trud*, I, 124–28; I. S. Dzhabadari, "Protsess 50-ti (Vserossiisskaya Sotsialno-revolyutionnaya Organizatsiya) 1874–77 gg.," *Byloe* (Sept. 1907) 183. Bogucharsky, *Aktivnoe Narodnichestvo*, 221; Meijer, *Knowledge*, 165.

[28] Figner, *Zapechat. trud*, I, 120–24.

ment, and professionalism in their quest for identity as women and as human beings. Feminism and nihilist self-expression was left even further behind. As Figner recalled, "the students abroad, as a whole, were not proponents of the woman question and reacted with a smile to any sort of recollection of it. We had arrived, not worrying about being pioneers or about realizing the actual solution to this question; to us the woman question didn't seem to need a solution. It was *passé*: equality of men and women in principle already existed in the sixties and left to the next generation a precious heritage of democratic ideas."[29]

3. THE COMMON CAUSE

The great crusade "to the people" that began in the spring of 1874 was the first large-scale manifestation of what came to be called "populism"—the fierce longing to move out among the peasants in order to share their sufferings and toil, and to expose them to the ideas which had been germinating in the breast of the intelligentsia for a generation. Lavrov, one of its molders, caught the spirit of the movement in a few words: "People strove not only to achieve well-defined practical goals but also to satisfy deep needs of personal moral purification." For the radical women, his words were particularly applicable. Going to the people was a way to act out the visions of their exalted social consciences and to quell lingering doubts about their worth as human beings. But it was also a practical and experiential opportunity to see at first hand the objects of their pity and reverence and to inspect the human material out of which the Revolution would be forged. Violence played no role; action and movement did. Like their male comrades, they strained outward in the mood of the over-ripe student who yearns to throw down his books in order to taste life.

> Then friendly hands together link,
> Move out! and boldness show.
> Of science now we musn't think—
> But to the People go.[1]

"To the People" was not wholly spontaneous. It had a long ideological preparation and was preceded by a number of smaller propaganda excursions

[29] Figner, "Stud. gody," 181.

[1] Quoted in Itenberg, *Dvizhenie*, 308. Lavrov's quotation is from *Narodniki*, 195. The word Populism and its derivatives are here used in the misleading but commonly accepted historical sense to indicate all the revolutionary socialists of the 1870's in Russia, though they themselves and their enemies used such terms as socialists, social revolutionaries, nihilists, terrorists, rebels, anarchists, villagers or settlers, propagandists, Jacobins, even social democrats, in addition to nicknames derived from the names Bakunin, Lavrov, Tkachëv, and their journals. Prince Odoevsky, as early as 1862, had used the word Narodnik as a synonym for Herzenist, ultra-liberal, and nihilist: "Dnevnik," 148. A useful guide through this terminological confusion is Richard Pipes, *"Narodnichestvo*: a Semantic Inquiry," *Slavic Review*, XXIII/3 (Sept. 1964), 441–68.

among peasants and workers through the 1860's and early 1870's. The general contours of the 1874 movement were laid out in the preceding winter and spring in the two dozen or so circles situated in the largest cities. The circles were stoutly independent and democratic, and lacked any kind of conspiratorial center, though there was coordination and communication among some of them. The common goal of the summer crusade was to reconnoiter the countryside and to reassemble in the fall to exchange experiences and plan further action.[2] The women participants, apparently something less than a fifth of the total, were drawn into the effort largely through the circles. Recognizing that women propagandists might encounter greater difficulties in the villages, some of the circles discussed the wisdom of sending them out. Most of the young propagandists, including the women themselves, felt that the principle of sexual equality in active work, by then an established fact, ought not to be violated in this case. "Let those women who can," they said, "go to the people, just as the men do, in peasant costume; and let them avoid, as best they can, the unpleasantness which is associated with being a member of the fair sex."[3]

Hundreds of them went among the people, masquerading as itinerant artisans or migrant field hands. Their amateurish deportment and the suspicion of the peasants combined to betray them and by summer's end some 1,600 had been taken by the police. Only 770 were actually arraigned, of which 158, about 20 percent, were women. But we know little about them, since only about 40 were brought to trial. These were veterans of the Chaikovsky and other circles, returned students from Zurich, and a varied assortment of high school girls and lower-class women. Count Pahlen, in his oft-quoted report on the propagandists, noted that women played a fairly responsible role in some of the coordinating centers of the movement; and he was disturbed by the fact that so many of them came from well-connected families.[4] Typical of these was Sofiya Löschern von Herzfeldt (Leshern fon Gertsfeld) the thirty-two year old daughter of a wealthy major-general of Novgorod, whose family had impressive court connections. Having learned foreign languages at an institute, Sofiya had eagerly steeped herself in foreign progressive literature and had opened a school in one of her father's villages. When the school was closed by the authorities, she went to the capital and there was quickly taken into the radical community. She married F. N. Lermontov, an anarchist student of peasant parentage, and went with him to the people. Later she attained the distinction of being the first woman sentenced to death for revolutionary activities.[5]

[2] Itenberg, *Dvizhenie*, 278–97.

[3] Cited from the memoirs of "Starik" (Kovalik) by Bogucharsky, *Aktivnoe Narodnichestvo*, 187.

[4] "Zapiska, razoslannaya Grafom Palenom," *Vpered!*, August 15, 1875. Reprinted in Burtsev, *Za sto let*, 113–23.

[5] Breshkovskaya, "Iz vospom.," 174–92; *Deyateli*, II/1, 771–72.

Typical of those who went to the people, but much better known, was Ekaterina Breshko-Breshkovskaya (1844–1934), known to three generations of Western readers as "the little grandmother of the Russian Revolution." One could hardly conceive of a less democratic pedigree than hers: Her father was a West Russian landowner of Polish noble ancestry; her mother, an aristocratic Smolny graduate. Yet doubts about her status began stirring early, and she claimed to have always sided with the house serfs when they were punished. "From the age of eight," she recalled, "how to find justice was the question that troubled me"; and she sublimated her maternal-benevolent impulses by "feeding" a nearby shrub, which in her childish imagination, resembled a calf. Her strong feelings of otherness, which often nourishes a philanthropic personality, may have been heightened by a physical disability, a congenital crooked neck. But unlike most of her later colleagues, she gave vent to her humanitarian longings in a drawn-out phase of gentry liberalism—*zemstvo* work and peasant schools—bypassing nihilism and arriving at radicalism only at the end of her twenties.[6]

Harrassed by the authorities, she lost faith in liberal "small deeds" and asked her husband, a *zemstvo* liberal, to join her in propaganda. When he refused, she left him, cutting all family ties (except one: she was pregnant), and went off to Kiev to join the "cause." Possessing a highly volatile nature, Breshkovskaya was bored by Lavrovian abstrusities and was quickly drawn to the teachings of Bakunin, dubbing herself a "flame-seeker." In such a frame of mind, she had her baby, promptly handed it over to her brother, and began her trek along the Dnieper, sowing the ideas of equality and justice among the peasants. She and her companions were captured by the police and sent to the capital for trial.[7] Breshkovskaya's later career with the Socialist Revolutionary Party, her wide contacts in America, and her coming and goings in 1917 at a grand old age have helped contribute to the myth that she was somehow a key figure in the revolutionary movement. In fact, her activities as a female radical were entirely typical. The hard will, the resilience, and the confidence approaching arrogance all of which have made her a legend, were the standard personal equipment of most Russian revolutionary women. In prison she "dreamed dreams of freedom and of intense activity. My faith in my own capacity increased. I knew that I was ready to dare and bear everything." She became a living example of her belief that history is made by

---

[6] The two main sources for her early life are in English: *The Little Grandmother of the Russian Revolution*, ed. Alice Stone Blackwell (Boston, 1930), a translation of autobiographical notes and letters which first appeared in Yiddish; *Hidden Springs of the Russian Revolution*, ed. L. Hutchinson (Stanford, 1931). The former work covers her early years. The fact that its editor was an American feminist and the daughter of a more famous feminist (Lucy Stone), partly accounts for Breshkovskaya's fame in this country. When it appeared in 1917, its author was "a grandmother (*babushka*)"—the sense here is Grand Old Lady—of the Russian Revolution; but certainly not "the grandmother." The second work deals with her revolutionary career, but is badly edited. My remarks are drawn from *Grandmother*, 2–25 (quotation, 8) and *Hidden Springs*, 328.

[7] *Grandmother*, 26–77; *Hidden Springs*, 3–30.

"people of high mental and moral aspiration," and "persons of outstanding character."[8]

In 1874–1875, the women of the All Russian Social Revolutionary Organization—the erstwhile Fritschi from Zurich—began to disseminate propaganda in factories. "The Moscow Amazons," as they were called at their trial, literally moved into the Moscow factories "to share the sufferings of the people." Bardina worked fifteen hours a day and lived in lice-ridden quarters. Kaminskaya, posing as a soldier's wife, inhaled the dirt and paper dust of an unventilated room by day and squeezed into the cold and smelly female barracks at night. Transferring to a textile mill, she found she could make no headway with the women workers, who used what spare time they had to cavort with the men. And the men in turn tried to lure the young Kaminskaya into the tavern. In time she won the confidence and attention of the workers by the simple device of telling them clearly but eloquently about the contrast between their wretched poverty and the wealth of their masters. Such social pictures often held them spellbound even after the closing whistle. For Kaminskaya, these were the happiest days of her life. It all ended in the spring of 1875 when she and the others were arrested.[9]

Vera Figner was one of the last to confront "the people." After the breakup of her sister's Moscow organization, she was summoned to Russia by the survivors to take up the work. Conflict now raged within her; with great difficulty, she broke with her husband, abandoned her studies, and returned home bearing with her a memory of the Zurich years that had given her "learning, comrades, and a life's goal, a goal so exalted that all sacrifices paled before it." Unable to revive the shattered circle in Moscow, she finally went out to the wretched villages of Samara Province. Figner was stunned at the realization that contact with the peasants had played no role in her path to radicalism. Her consciousness had begun with a desire to avoid the "arid, dull and narrowly egoistic" life which would have enveloped her in the cramped surroundings of family and kitchen. She had chosen The People as her goal, and study as the means. Now at twenty-five, after years of escape from reality among her books, she stood before them—diseased, undernourished, dirty, and poor—and she felt like an inexperienced child.[10] After a year and a half of work among them, she was ready to return to the revolutionary centers. By this time their character and hers had undergone a decisive change.

The great political trials mounted by the tsarist government in 1877–1878 were part of an effort to demonstrate to the "moderate" intelligentsia that the revolutionaries were an extremist fringe of evil people. The effort was a dismal failure, and not least because of the women prisoners in the dock, who

[8] Quotations from *ibid.*, 177, 120.

[9] For the makeup and activities of the Moscow Organization, see: Lavrov, *Narodniki*, 257; Figner, *Zapech. trud*, I, 131: Venturi, *Roots*, 531–33; *Gos. prestup.*, II, 399–401: Dzhabadari, "Protsess," 169–73. On Kaminskaya: Deutsch, *Rol Evreev*, 90–93; Stepniak, *Russia*, 92.

[10] Figner, *Zapech., trud*, I, 132–36, 153–75 (quotation, 132).

gave impassioned speeches, bore themselves with dignity, and received gratuitously harsh sentences. The first was the Trial of the Fifty that dealt with the members of the All Russian Social Revolutionary Organization. Among the defendants were sixteen women, mostly from the Fritsch Circle, who were given various terms of hard labor or exile. Though charged with plotting to overthrow the government and inciting to revolution, the women made a favorable impression upon the public. Sofya Bardina, the twenty-three year old "aunt" gave a well-rehearsed speech that became a classic in the revolutionary literature. Stepniak, Figner, and others have testified to the vivid impression it made. One young school girl was steered toward revolution by the spectacle of privileged ladies who had "gone to the factories in order to bring light into the realm of darkness." The Serbian publishers of Turgenev's *Virgin Soil* (1877)—likening the author's heroine to Bardina—included a copy of her speech as an appendix to the novel.[11]

Bardina's address—aside from its value as an explanation of what the revolutionaries were about and of their moral justification of their behavior—is important on another count. It is one of the rare instances of a female "populist" publicly voicing her views on the woman question; and it provides illuminating testimony as to how deeply the simplistic economic interpretation of the problem had penetrated into the rank and file of the movement. To the prosecutor's accusation that she was trying to undermine the family (as well as property and religion), she answered as follows:

> As far as the family is concerned, isn't it really being undermined by that social system which forces woman to leave her family and go to work in a factory for a miserable pittance, a subsistance wage, there to be debauched along with her children? Isn't it being destroyed by a social system which forces an impoverished woman to abandon herself to prostitution, and which even sanctifies this prostitution as a legal and necessary element of every civilized state? Or is it we who are destroying the family? we who are trying to root out this poverty—the major cause of all society's ill, including the erosion of the family?

After warning her judges that "even our sleepy and lazy society" would some day rise up and avenge the wrongs done to it, Bardina was sentenced to exile in Siberia. She managed to escape; but, profoundly shaken by her experiences, she committed suicide in 1883.[12]

[11] For the trial: *Gos. prestup.*, II, 399–401. For the impact of Bardina's speech, see: Stepniak, *Russia*, 108–109; Figner, *Zapech. trud*, I, 146. The schoolgirl's reminiscence, with quotation, is given in Fanina Halle, *Woman in Soviet Russia*, tr. M. Green (New York, 1933) 54–55. The speech was transcribed and read at student meetings that year (*Revol. narod.*, II, 128). The International Institute of Social History in Amsterdam has at least three reprints of it (two in Russian, one in French) printed in Geneva between 1893 and 1903. The information on the Serbian edition of *Nov* is from Amfitreatrov, *Zhenshchina*, 37. Mariyanna, the heroine of the novel, has variously been taken as a copy of Bardina and an anticipation of Zasulich. In view of Turgenev's colorless portrayal of this character, it hardly seems worth arguing about.

[12] Burtsev, *Za sto let*, 124–27.

The Great Trial, or "Trial of the 193" (October 1877–January 1878), meted out justice to the propagandists who had been languishing in jail for three years or more. Their abode was the Petersburg House of Preliminary Detention, a harmless looking edifice which can still be seen sprawling along Chaikovsky Street in Leningrad. A special women's section had been constructed to house the growing number of radical women; it was staffed by a female warden and a handful of volunteer princesses and officers' widows. Breshkovskaya tells us that they treated her with open contempt until they learned that she was highborn and educated. She also recalls that the prison atmosphere, not very oppressive, was lightened by visits from the "political Red Cross," radical volunteers who eased the lot of the prisoners. But the narrow cells and the inactivity drove some of them to suicide or an early death and the rest of them to an intense hatred of the government. Of the 193, 37 were women; about half the total were acquitted. Of the convicted women, a few were released because of their court connections; others escaped from penal settlements and emerged as hardened revolutionaries.[13]

The most celebrated trial of the decade was that of Vera Zasulich, would-be assassin of the Governor of St. Petersburg, and unwitting initiator of an age of terror. Zasulich's personality was a study in contradictions. Retiring, passive, and introverted, she once dreamed of leading a partisan horse brigade to liberate the peasants. Abjuring personal violence throughout most of her life, she was the first woman to raise the weapon in the revolutionary struggle. She became one of the best known Russian women revolutionaries; yet compared with Perovskaya and Figner, her political work within the movement was of minor importance. Her fatal shot was a grim illustration of the truth of Mariya Vernadskaya's assertion that a woman with a revolver could kill a man with an axe.[14]

Zasulich endured a smoulderingly unhappy childhood as an orphan; her father, a retired captain of the poorer Smolensk gentry died when she was a baby, leaving her mother with five children. Little Vera was raised by her cousins, the Mikulins. She was painfully aware of her status as an outsider and would fly into a rage when anyone called her "Vera Zasulich," screaming "It's not true. Mikulich! Mikulich!"—a pitiful effort to transform herself into one of the family. Like many children in like situations, she sought a soulmate for her pain and found it in Christ. For weeks she would pore over the Passion story and wallow in the details of Jesus' torment and death. But by the time she was fifteen, her early sympathy for Christ was directed toward "humanity" through her reading of Schiller, Ryleev, Lermontov, and Nekrasov whose works sent her into transports of "social daydreaming" and urgent longings

[13] The trial: *Gos. prestup.*, II, 262–65. Breshkovskaya's prison and courtroom experiences are in *Hidden Springs*, 105–11; 135–36 and "Iz vospom.," 179. A personal testimony of the radicalizing effect of the trial is given by Popov in *Zapiski*, 119–23.

[14] See Vernadskaya's remark and its context on p. 36 of the present study. Zasulich's sketchy memoirs, *Vospom.*, may be supplemented by the even sketchier essay by R. A. Kovnator in Zasulich, *Stati o russkoi literature* (Moscow, 1960) 3–40.

"to struggle" and perform great social deeds. She was particularly captivated by a line from Ryleev: "There are times, indeed whole epochs, when there can be nothing as beautiful and desirable as a crown of thorns."[15]

All this, revealing as it may be, is not sufficient to explain Zasulich's conversion to radicalism. At sixteen, she went to Moscow to attend one of those private boarding schools run by German women where the discipline and snobbishness surpassed those of the institutes they were trying to emulate. "At the age of seventeen," Zasulich tells us, "I considered myself a socialist." But this was hardly more than an emotional commitment, reinforced by her new reading habits and perhaps by the ideas of her two sisters who had preceded her to Moscow and had joined the Ivanova Workshop. Zasulich herself mentions no direct radical contacts until her journey to St. Petersburg in 1868 where, as we have seen, she fell in with Nechaev's followers. Four years of freedom (1869–1872) were thus snatched away from her. Upon her release, she quickly acquired a "ticket to the people,"a midwifery licence, and made her way into one of the most desperate groups, "the Kiev Rebels." Here in a two-room flat, Lev Deutsch recalled "Marfusha" Zasulich, arrayed in the careless manner of the 1860's, always with her nose in a book, shy and retiring, but healthy and happy and without a trace of morbidity. Her closest friend was the rhapsodic and rather asexual Kolenkina, a moody, nervous, and poorly educated young girl. It was she, according to Deutsch, who conceived the idea of assassinating the governor and the chief prosecutor of the Great Trial.[16]

Figner once said that educated revolutionaries looked on corporal punishment as the greatest kind of shame.[17] When the governor had a young revolutionary flogged for a minuscule offense, these two women resolved to kill. The gesture was designed to show the world that Russian officials used "Turkish bestiality" on their own people while pretending to rescue the Bulgars from it. "It is a hard thing to lay a hand on another human being," Zasulich said later, and she was plagued by nightmares and anxiety lest her comrades disapprove her act. Kolenkina failed to meet her victim; Zasulich shot hers point blank and almost killed him. But at her trial, which the authorities foolishly mounted as a common criminal case in order to discredit her act, she was received as a heroine since she had done the deed without any intention of escaping. She was acquitted and spirited off to Western Europe where, to her disgust, she became a momentary celebrity.[18] In later years she came to look upon individual terror as an aberration and became a staunch pillar of the

[15] The early years: *Vospom.*, 1–16. The Ryleev line is from "Nalivaiko's Confession": see M. G. Sedov, *Geroicheskii period revolyutsionnogo Narodnichestva* (Moscow, 1966) 69.

[16] The Zasulich quotation given by Kovnator in Zasulich, *Stati*, p. 5; *Vospom.*, 114, n. 13 and 115, n. 15; Deutsch, "Yuzhnye Buntari," 54–58.

[17] Figner, *Les prisons russes* (Lausanne, 1911) 10.

[18] Zasulich's motives and doubts: *Vospom.*, 65–70; Breshkovskaya, *Hidden Springs*, 155. Her quoted words, uttered at the trial, are given in one of Mikhailovsky's pamphlets (reproduced in *Revol. Narod.*, II, 56). Plekhanov's wife Rozaliya, then a medical student, recalled the great

non-terrorist groups, Black Repartition and Liberation of Labor. But her act of violence, which electrified society, and her acquittal, which sickened the conservatives, served to sharpen even further the brutal struggle waged between the government and the revolutionaries.

Most of the groups and individuals still at large in 1876–1878 gradually combined to form the organization later known as Land and Liberty (*Zemlya i Volya*), though its members were at first known simply as Narodniks. Bigger and better organized than its predecessors, the new party stressed immediate agitation for the peasants' needs and wants —"land and liberty"—in contrast to the rather leisurely style of the older propagandists. But Land and Liberty was weakened at the outset by a deep internal division over the question of terror as a prime revolutionary device. Among the women who voiced bitter complaints against the emphasis on "disorganization" and violence were Zasulich, Kolenkina, and Mariya Krylova. The latter, whom we have met in the Ivanova Workshop, was described by Breshkovskaya as "a typical person of the 1860's" who had fled from her domestic realm of darkness. Krylova's background and career closely paralleled those of Zasulich; but her ample conspiratorial and technical skills as custodian of the party's press made her one of the most crucial figures in Land and Liberty. She polemicized vigorously with her colleagues and refused to allow them to transform the party newspaper into the mouthpiece of the terrorist tendency. When the party finally split over the issue, she joined the non-terrorist wing which called itself Black Repartition.[19]

The terrorists took shape as The People's Will (*Narodnaya Volya*), whose twenty-eight member Executive Committee dedicated itself to assassinating Alexander II and any of his officials who stood in their way. Ten of these, over a third, were women: Vera Figner, Sofiya Ivanova (no relation to the Ivanovas of the 1860's), Anna Korba, Tatyana Lebedeva, Olga Lyubatovich, Nataliya Olennikova, Mariya Oshanina (sister of the preceding), Sofiya Perovskaya, Elizaveta Sergeeva, and Anna Yakimova. They were all Russians, ranging in age (as of 1879) from twenty-three to thirty. All but one, the priest's daughter Yakimova, came of gentry-officer families, mostly provincial; all were well educated. Most of them had begun their illegal activities in one of the circles of the early seventies. In the Committee they were regarded as equals to the men, but their abilities and performances varied widely. All but three ended their revolutionary careers in captivity or on the scaffold.[20]

Figner's path to terrorism was characteristically slow and painful. After a

---

impact Zasulich's deed made upon her circle in "Stranitsy iz vospominanii o V.I. Zasulich," *Gruppa "Osvobozhdenie Truda": iz arkhivov G. V. Plekhanova, V. I. Zasulicha i L. G. Deicha,* 6 v. (Moscow, 1923–1928) III, 82–87 (86).

[19] Breshkovskaya, "Iz vospom.," 219–30; Figner, *Zapech. trud*, I, 192: *Deyateli*, II/2, 697–98. An example of her invective may be found in Valk, *Arkhiv*, 104–105.

[20] The list is given in Figner, *Zapech. trud*, I, 302. Thumbnail sketches may be found in Stites, "The Question of Woman in Nineteenth Century Russia" (Ph.D., Harvard, 1967) 393–406.

long spell in the provinces, she had returned to Petersburg disheartened and persuaded of the uselessness of propaganda. "Show me any way," she said to Lev Deutsch; "show me how, under the present circumstances, I can serve the peasants and I am ready to go back to the villages at once." She resisted the pull of the terrorists within Land and Liberty for some time and attempted to hold the two factions together. After the break she joined The People's Will. For the next five years she served the organization with great vigor and intelligence, helping to prepare several assassination attempts, maintaining conspiratorial apartments, and conducting propaganda among the legal elements of society. Her greatest moment came after the assassination of the Tsar when, for two years, she tried to hold the decimated party together almost singlehandedly against the depradations of the police and their informers. Her commitment to terror was still deep enough for her to order and coordinate one more assassination of a hated police official. When she was finally taken in 1883, the new Tsar, Alexander III is supposed to have said "Glory to God, that horrid woman has been arrested." Tsarist vengeance was achieved: She was sentenced to life imprisonment and served twenty-two years of solitary confinement in Schlüsselburg Fortress.[21]

But Figner's views on political murder did not survive her revolutionary career. On hearing the news of the assassination of Alexander II, she had wept profuse tears of relief, happy that "the dreadful nightmare which had suffocated young Russia before our very eyes for a whole decade was at last ended." But in later years, she looked back with regret upon certain aspects of the struggle which she and her comrades had chosen to pursue.

> The violence engendered by the struggle arouses ferocity, brings out the beast, awakens evil impulses, and leads to acts of disloyalty. Humanitarianism and greatness of soul are incompatible with it. And in this sense, both the government and the party, joining so to speak in hand-to-hand combat, competed with one another in the process of corrupting everything around them. On its side, the party proclaimed that all methods were permissible in the struggle against the enemy, and that the end justified the means. It also established a cult of the bomb and the revolver, and cannonized the terrorist. Murder and the gibbet captivated the imagination of our young people; and the weaker their nerves and the more oppressive their surroundings, the greater was their sense of exaltation at the thought of revolutionary terror.[22]

Sofiya Perovskaya's view of terror was more complex. Her fierce hatred of the government was a suitable obverse to her love of the common people. The

---

[21] Figner, *Zapech. trud*, I, 175–360. Her remark to Deutsch in his *Sixteen Years in Siberia*, tr. H. Chisolm (New York, 1905) 117. The Tsar's words are reported in A. M. Bikhter, ed., *Poety-demokraty 1870-1880-kh godov*, 3d ed. (Moscow, Leningrad, 1962) 468.

[22] Figner, *Zapech. trud*, I. 268, 285.

hatred deepened with the arrest of her comrades. Like Figner, she was long opposed to terror and tried to patch up the schism in Land and Liberty. But she eventually joined The People's Will and not only justified the use of terror but also practiced it with a vengeance. The word vengeance is not idly used here, though she herself once denied that it ever played a role in the motivation of her party:

> Vengeance [*mest*] is a personal affair, something that might, by stretching a point, explain those acts of terror carried out by the personal will and initiative of separate individuals—but not those of an organized party. But such acts, except those done in self-defense, are almost unknown in our revolutionary history. A political party cannot be formed around the banner of revenge, especially if it attracts the public sympathy that ours undoubtedly enjoys. The first shot—Zasulich's—was fired not in revenge, but as retribution for an insult to human dignity.

Even the notion of retribution (*vozmezdie*), she explained, was insufficient to account for the terror, for it served mainly to frighten and disorganize a government which left the revolutionaries no other means of expression. All this was said shortly before the assassination of the Tsar. Yet she told her brother before her execution that to her the terror "was simply a matter of revenge for the death of those near and dear to her."[23]

Perovskaya's personality is fascinating and cryptic. A hostile source pictured her as aloof, secretive, stubborn, rude, scornful of men, heartless, evil and cruel.[24] Figner, Stepniak, and others have contrasted her maternal tenderness for "the people" with her judgmental sternness toward her colleagues and her merciless and lethal enmity toward her political foes.[25] About the last there can be no doubt. Of all the leaders of her party still at large in late February 1881, she was the coolest and best fitted to oversee and carry to completion the long-sought murder of the Tsar. On March 1 she arranged her lookouts and bomb-throwers in their proper places and, from her post on the canal, gave the final signal for the fatal bombs to be hurled. But after the successful assassination, the narcotic of her hyper-active tension wore off; she wandered as in a dream—becoming, as her biographer put it, a "woman" once again.

Arrest followed quickly: To her first questioner, the famous Plehve, she

[23] Asheshov, *Perovskaya*, 88–89. "Iz vospominanii brata S. L. Perovskoi," *Na chuzhoi storone*, X (1925) 204–209 (207).

[24] *Khronika sotsialisticheskago dvizheniya v Rossii, 1878–1887: offitsialnyi otchët* (Moscow, 1906) 169–71. This is a vivid, detailed, officially inspired anti-revolutionary account of the movement, originally published in French (apparently for foreign consumption). It seems probable that the writer who describes Perovskaya either knew her or drew on persons who did; but any semblance of objectivity that he might have wished to convey is damaged by his crude remarks about her personal appearance and his anti-semitic description of Gesya Gelfman.

[25] Figner, *Zapech. trud*, 1, 276–77; Stepniak, *Perovskaya, passim*. Like so many of her colleagues, Perovskaya, between revolutionary episodes, had studied to be a *feldsher* (Medic) and had performed medical work in the Crimea.

freely confessed her guilt; but at the trial of the six assassins—two women, four men—she challenged the interpretation of her crime offered by the prosecutor, N. V. Muraviev, a man who had been, ironically enough, her childhood playmate.

> Much, very much blame has been heaped upon us by the prosecutor. I have nothing more to say about the factual side of these [charges], for I have admitted to all of them in my deposition. But when it comes to charges against me and the others of immorality, brutality, and disregard for public opinion, I should like to object and to point to the fact that anyone familiar with our life and the conditions under which we had to work would not hurl charges of immorality and brutality at us.[26]

All were sentenced to death; but Perovskaya's female co-defendant, Gesya Gelfman was reprieved because she was pregnant. Thus Perovskaya became the first woman political to mount the scaffold. Pleas for mercy from prominent members of society were ignored. Perovskaya's last days were occupied with attempts to console her grieving mother. Her demeanor on the scaffold was cool and dignified. Displaying to the end her emotional discrimination, she refused to render farewell to the informer Rysakov who was about to share her fate, but embraced the others warmly. Her stoicism held sway over instinct almost to the last moment. Though she retained her haughty smile as the noose was fixed upon her neck, some force deep within her took over: she fastened her feet firmly to a protuberance on the platform and it took the violent exertions of two men to dislodge her feet and hang her.[27]

How many women were engaged in this appalling yet, in its way, elevating struggle? It is still difficult to say, both because of the paucity of statistical analyses and the relative lack of attention given to all but the most prominent women revolutionaries by the scholars who have the data at their disposal. At best we can offer only a few crude observations based on the figures available. Of the 5,664 revolutionaries of the 1870's listed in *Figures*, about one-eighth were women, an impressive increase over the 1860's where the female radical contingent accounted for only 3 percent of the total. These bare percentages tell us little, however, for the brief entries in that biographical compendium are often little more than catalogues of arrests, surveillances, and vital statistics. But we do have other samples which, when combined, exhibit a certain pattern. If we put them in a scale,[28]

[26] Burtsev, *Za sto let*, 191.

[27] Asheshov, *Perovskaya*, 137–40; L. Planson, "Kazn tsareubiits (iz lichnykh vospominanii)," *Ist. vest.*, XXXIV (Feb. 1913) 20–35.

[28] Sources for the samples in the table: (1) Itenberg, *Dvizhenie*, 375, n. 35; (2) *Literatura "Narodnoi Voli,"* 348; others referenced elsewhere. See the interesting remarks of Robert McNeal in "Women in the Russian Radical Movement," *Journal of Social History*, V, 2 (Winter 1971–1972) 143–61.

Sample	Percentage of Women
5,664 revolutionaries of the 1870's	c. 12.5
1,611 arrested 1873–1877	15
770 arrested and indicted 1874	20
193 tried in the Great Trial of 1877–1878	18
50 tried in the Trial of the Fifty 1877	32
28 members, Executive Committee of People's Will	33

they tend to show that, while the proportion of women in the movement is rather low, it increases in those samples that reveal greater involvement or extremism. Such limited and tiny samples can be taken as no more than tentative and suggestive; men always outnumbered the women at every level from the first propaganda circles to The People's Will, held the most responsible posts, and performed most of the rigorous, dangerous, and criminal work. But having said this, we must also accept the fact that, individual for individual, women were more deeply involved than the men: "better fewer, but better," as Lenin would have put it. This does not prove that women were on the whole "better" revolutionaries than men, but only that it was easier for the latter to come in and out of the movement in large numbers and have relatively little impact on it. Women found it harder to resume a normal life after a radical sojourn; and their initial impulse to commit themselves was probably much stronger than that of their brothers for whom radicalism was a more natural vocation.

Age level, class background, and education are easier to document. Like the men, the women in the movement were almost all between twenty and thirty. To a much greater extent than the men, they were of gentry origins— some 67 percent of those most deeply implicated in the years 1873 to 1877— and at least four of them were daughters of generals. All but a handful had been given good to excellent educations, many of them in European and, after 1876, Russian universities.[29] This is hardly cause for wonder: Russian radicalism, even in its simplest forms, was not likely to appeal to women of primitive education. On the other hand, a good education in and of itself was not the final determinant of Russian women's drift to revolution. Modern scholars have tentatively concluded that the only sure relationship between educational level and politics is that the former helps create a high political awareness. But higher learning "may reinforce or weaken prejudice; it may lead to either radicalism or conservatism, and it certainly does not ensure rationality in political orientation or behavior."[30] A superior academic experience and broad reading habits disclosed to many women the specter of social injustice, but it was not sufficient to draw them into the fight against it.

[29] The figure on class origin is from N. N. Sidorov, "Staticheskie svedeniya o propagandistakh 70-kh godov v obrabotke III Otdeleniya," *Katorga i ssylka* (No. 1, 1928) 30; Perovskaya, Löschern, Armfeldt, and Batyushkova were the generals' daughters. S. I. Strievskaya mentions eight *Bestuzhevki* in Valk, ed. *Kursy*, 32.

[30] James S. Coleman, ed., *Education and Political Development* (Princeton, 1965) 19–20.

Of all the non-Russian females in the movement, only the Jews enjoyed an impressive representation. The traditional Jewish family was, if anything, more despotic for girls than the Russian, practicing as it did the arranged marriage through a matchmaker and tying its daughters securely to the home. The new girls' high schools of the early 1860's afforded previously unheard of opportunities for the cloistered Jewish girl; by the end of the decade the Jewish *nigilistka* had made her appearance both in the Russian cities and in the *shtetls* of the Pale, complete with bobbed hair, a plain dress, a sincere manner, and a feverish desire for "goyish" learning. Once in the movement of the 1870's, these women quickly assimilated, inter-marrying with Russians at a higher rate than did Jewish men. Typical was Anna Epstein, daughter of a smuggler, who attached herself to a band of ex-rabbinical students who helped smuggle revolutionaries across the frontier. She was drawn to radicalism not through study or worship of the plain folk, but by her veneration of the hounded revolutionaries, one of whom, Dmitry Klements, she married. Gesya Gelfman was another woman of Jewish background. Though of wealthy Orthodox parents, she received no schooling and was mistreated by her stepmother. After many misadventures she joined The People's Will and shared a conspiratorial flat with Sablin, by whom she became pregnant. Her condition saved her from the gallows in 1881, though both she and her child died not long after the executions.[31]

The backgrounds and psychological types of radical women were so varied that it is impossible to generalize about their motivation in terms of emotional frustration, sex-need, father-hatred and the like. It is true that many had an unhappy childhood; but so did many non-radical women. Most of them, like Madame Roland, possessed "religious feelings without religious faith."[32] Sofiya Kovalevskaya managed to capture this spirit fictionally in her character Vera Vorontsova who as a young girl revelled in the Book of Martyrs and longed to go to China as a gesture of sacrifice in the struggle for the salvation of mankind. After reading Dobrolyubov, she replaced the heathen of China with the masses of Russia; but her secular dreams were still couched in a religious apostrophe: "O Lord! I know that there is much woe in the world, much injustice, and many who are needy. I want to serve the people. I am ready to give my life for them."[33] The classic pattern seems to have been a high degree of religious sensitivity, reinforced by literature and transformed into "social

[31] Deutsch, *Rol Evreev*, 18-28; Louis Greenberg, *The Jews in Russia*, 2 v. (New Haven, 1944-1951) I, 158. On Epstein: *ibid.*, I, 153 and Zasulich, *Vospom.*, 80-81. On Gelfman: Breshkovskaya, "Iz vospom.," 230-35 and Alphonse Thun, *Geschichte der revolutionären Bewegung in Russland* (Leipzig, 1883) 264-66. The law prohibiting the execution of a pregnant woman until forty days after childbirth is from the *Ulozhenie* of 1649: P. Mullov, "Zhenshchina po russkomu zakonodatelstvu," *Zhurnal Ministerstva Yustitsii*, VII (Mar. 1861) 540-86 (559).

[32] J. M. Thompson, *The French Revolution* (New York, 1966) 292.

[33] From her story "Nigilistka" (1889-1890) in *Vospominaniya detstva; Nigilistka* (Moscow, 1960) 177-78. This tale, though not of a high literary order, offers a strikingly faithful portrayal of a Russian female radical.

daydreaming"—fantasies in which observed injustices to self or others were obliterated by a future realm of Total Justice.

Altruism, whether radical or philanthropic, is much more the result of the consciousness of social injustice than it is of the "objective" conditions of exploitation, though one can hardly deny that such conditions abounded in nineteenth-century Russia. The heavy strain of altruism, so prominent in both sexes of the Russian intelligentsia, divided into the abstract and the concrete. Those who could satisfy themselves with direct, immediate, and "small" manifestations of such altruism could express it in teaching, medicine, or charity. Those who tended to make "humanity" the object of their unselfish love looked at medicine as a mere craft. Vera Figner was the clearest example of a female radical who tried desperately to hold to her view of medicine as an adequate means of serving mankind, but who drifted into abstraction and thus revolution. How and why Figner crossed this line into the realm of abstract altruism is a question whose answer would give us a key to the problem of revolutionary consciousness.

According to the bylaws of the Executive Committee of The People's Will, members were to donate all their spiritual power to the cause of revolution, and to renounce all family ties, friendship, sympathy, and love that interfered with that cause. Love within the movement was allowed if it did not distract the revolutionary's attention from the main business. Frivolous or loose sexual behavior was forbidden. But beyond these general rules, there was scope for some variety in sexual behavior: Figner had been married, Perovskaya had a lover, and Zasulich seems to have had neither. Some, like Alexander Mikhailov preferred celibacy for themselves. Zasulich's friend, Kolenkina, paraded her indifference to men. "I love the movement," she said. Olga Lyubatovich tried for a while to persuade her comrades that love interfered with revolutionary activity, and she and her beloved Morozov agreed to postpone sexual relations. But the flesh asserted itself and she bore his child and later married another revolutionary. For the most part, "nihilist" attitudes toward sex prevailed. Fictitious marriages were widely used to free the energies of domestically incarcerated daughters. If we can take Stepniak's novel, *Career of a Nihilist*, as an authentic picture of life in the movement, love-triangles were quietly resolved in the manner of *What Is To Be Done?* In general, marriages or free-unions, based on attraction and incubated in the intimacy of conspiratorial apartments, were the norm. The most celebrated of these was the revolutionary romance of Perovskaya and Zhelyabov. The governor's daughter, at first wooed by Tikhomirov, finally overcame her aversion to men and found brief happiness with the peasant-revolutionary, Andrei Zhelyabov. Their love, which ended on the gallows, is commemorated by the two adjoining Leningrad streets that bear their names.[34]

[34] Bylaws: *Revol. Narod.*, II, 200; Kolenkina: Deutsch, "Yuzhnye Buntari," 56–58; Lyubatovich: *Byloe* (May 1906), 208–48 and (June 1906) 108–54; N. Morozov, *Povesti moei*

The functions of women in the movement varied widely, ranging from clean-up duties performed by the illiterate Gryaznova[35] to leadership roles assumed by women like Figner and Perovskaya. There were no women theorists except Mariya Oshanina, called Madame Jacobson by some in droll reference to her Jacobin tendencies. But she was unable to impose her views upon the Executive Committee, and she was opposed by Perovskaya and others.[36] Fourier had once voiced the belief that "the cabalist passion is the favorite passion of women; they are excessively fond of intrigue, rivalries, and all of the greater and lesser flights of cabal."[37] This certainly did not apply within The People's Will; if anything, the women were less devious than the men, especially at the time of the schism. They performed their jobs quietly and efficiently, whether acting as "wives" in conspiratorial flats, masquerading as the fiancées of prisoners, or performing technical jobs with dynamite or printing presses. In the decision-making process, the women members of the Executive Committee spoke as equals. In the literature of the revolutionary movement which I have read, I have encountered only one minor instance of a radical opposing women's holding of responsible posts: this was an 1880 letter of the eighteen-year old I. G. Shiryaev complaining of the large number of women police spies recruited from among arrested women.[38]

Formally equals in the revolutionary movement, women were increasingly so treated by the police and the courts. They paid heavily for their actions during the 1870's and 1880's. Up to Perovskaya's conviction, death sentences for women had all been commuted. After that, many women revolutionaries marched to the gallows or fell before the firing squad. Particularly during the 1880's large numbers of women came to know the inner walls of The Crosses, the Peter-Paul Fortress, the Kharkov "house of terror," and Moscow's grim Lubyanka and Butyrki prisons; many more experienced hard labor at Kara and the desolate settlements of Siberia. Figner languished for twenty years in a Schlüsselburg cell which gave this writer claustrophobia after being in it for five minutes. The treatment of women prisoners, though generally mild, occa-

---

zhizni, 3 v. (Leningrad, 1947) II, 417–19 and III, 281; Stepniak, A Female Nihilist, 3d ed. (Boston, 1886) 16–25. Fictitious marriages: Sinegub, Zapiski, 18–84; Popov, Zapiski, 249–50. Triangles: Stepniak, The Career of a Nihilist: a Novel (New York, n.d.), a fictitious but accurate gallery of revolutionary types.

[35] Figner, Zapech. trud, I, 192. It ought to be noted that even the major women figures, like Perovskaya, were not above running "to the market after some milk." Segal, Perovskaya, 286.

[36] The Jacobin clique got their ideas from Zaichnevsky who was exiled in their native province, Orël; later they became the admirers of Tkachëv. See: Kozmin, Iz istorii, 307–11, 327; Popov, Zapiski, 87–88; Figner, Zapech. trud, I, 200–201; Segal, Perovskaya, 219. Oshanina's political views may be inspected in Byloe (June 1907) 1–10; Perovskaya's in Asheshov, Perovskaya, 86–90.

[37] Fourier, Oeuvres complètes, 3d ed., 6 v. (Paris, 1846–1848) IV, 406.

[38] Shiryaev's opinions alluded to in a letter to him from V. A. Bronevsky (Revol. Narod., II, 96). Bronevsky dismissed Shiryaev's suggestion that women be confined to giving "moral support" to the Party; he alluded to the large number of male police informers and to the doctrine of equality which was lodged in the charter of the People's Will (of which Shiryaev's brother was a leader).

sionally descended to brutality: Stories of rape, forcible stripping, physical violence, and verbal abuse have all found their way into the enormous prison literature. Nadezhda Segida, for example, a *narodovolka* of Greek extraction, was given 100 blows for having slapped the warden; she died two days later. Many of the women prisoners, lacking the stoicism of a Figner, went insane; others committed suicide—something like a third of the number of male suicides.[39]

In all of this, Russia distinguished itself from the rest of Europe in a grimly dramatic way. The women's struggle there was hardly a generation old, when numerous Russian women, bypassing it, were marching in the ranks of a violent, determined, and historically significant revolutionary movement. The last flame of French female radicalism, born in 1789, had flickered out in the Paris Commune. Britain saw no violent women until the present century and then only in the fight for specifically women's causes. Other countries knew even less of such a development. Perovskaya and her comrades represent a unique phenomenon in nineteenth-century European social history. More important, they set a precedent for the large numbers of women who joined the revolution in 1905 and in 1917. "From the experience of all liberation movements," wrote Lenin in 1918, "it can be noted that the success of revolution can be measured by the extent of the involvement of women in it."[40] The significance of this pronouncement is not its author, but the fact that it was shared by all Russian revolutionaries. Their faith was more than justified by events.

The relevance of female radicalism to the history of women's emancipation in Russia is enormous, in spite of the paradoxical fact that the women revolutionaries rejected any outright activity on its behalf. First, it was the rapid assimilation among the Russian intelligentsia of the idea of sexual equality that allowed women to enter the movement as equals, and it was the self-confidence that women silently absorbed from the literature on the woman question which acted as their psychological armament in the revolutionary struggle. In the 1870's, the vocation of revolutionary was the only one open to women which would greet her as an equal, allow her talents fully to unfold, and permit her to rise to the top; there her energies, character, and skills were unlocked and put to use. At the very least, the revolutionaries proved that woman was capable of things undreamed of in the traditional view. An ironic measure of this is the fact that in the very year of Perovskaya's birth, a Rus-

[39] On Sigida: Stepniak, *King Stork and King Log: a Study of Modern Russia*, 2 v. (London, 1895) II, 88–93. Since the appearance of Linguet's memoirs of the Bastille and Silvio Pellico's *My Prisons* (1832), tales of incarceration have played an interesting role in the political literature of Europe. The volume of such literature in Russia is enormous, but the two standard works are: M. N. Gernet, *Istoriya tsarskoi tyurmy*, 3d ed. 5 v. (Moscow, 1960–1963) and George Kennan, *Siberia and the Exile System*, 2 v. (New York, 1891). As a tiny sampling see: *Galleriya shlisselburgskykh uznikov* (SPB, 1907), 222–223; Stepniak, *Russia*, 63, 110, 147–58, 173–74; Kropotkin, *Memoirs*, 270–71; Deutsch, *Sixteen Years*, 193; and, most illuminating of all, Figner's account of her years in the fortress (*Zapech. trud*, II).

[40] V. I. Lenin, *Polnoe sobranie sochinenii*, 5th ed., 55 v. (Moscow, 1960–1965) XXXVI, 186.

sian physician had written that "naturally, modes of activity involving heroism or deeds of violence could not be open to women."[41] Like the Salvation Army, the Russian revolutionary movement discovered early that sexual equality was not incompatible with either discipline or ideological purity.[42] This notion, buttressed by a lengthy martyrology of fallen revolutionary women, constituted a legacy for twentieth-century Russian women of a broad spectrum of political views. To the female Left, it bequeathed two additional things: revolutionary anti-feminism—the idea that the common cause superseded and contradicted any special women's cause; and revolutionary sublimation, whose substance has never found clearer expression than in Alexandra Kollontai's tribute to Sofiya Perovskaya: "a daring 'man's mind' and an ability to subordinate her woman's 'ego' and her loving, passionate heart to the cause of the revolution."[43]

On the other hand, if the feminists can be faulted for ignoring the revolution and focusing on women, the radical women were guilty of the opposite sin. They repudiated feminism for themselves (though a few had passed into radicalism via a feminist stage of consciousness), and perceived themselves as revolutionaries equal to men. But they also ignored the enormous mass of peasant women who would one day have to be led into the light of civilization if the revolution were to have any meaning. Female propagandists who made contact with peasant women in the factories and in the villages apparently did not mount a "special effort" for peasant women or utilize any women-oriented arguments or messages in their propaganda work. The result was a virtually total absence of contact between educated women propagandists (except through medical activity) and the Russian peasant women—a crucial weakness that the successors of the populists, the Socialist Revolutionaries, would make little effort to correct. There would be no village equivalent of the Marxist "proletarian women's movement" in prerevolutionary times; and radical contact with women-as-women in the Russian countryside would have to wait until the 1920's.

[41] V. V. Deriker, *Fiziologiya zhenshchiny* (SPB, 1854) 120.

[42] Cf. Strachey, *Struggle*, 215.

[43] Kollontai, *Polozhenie zhenshchiny v evolyutsii khozyaistva* (Moscow, 1922) 126. An excellent collection of translations of the works of some of the women discussed in this chapter is *Five Sisters: Women Against the Tsar*, ed. and tr. Barbara Engel and Clifford Rosenthal (New York, 1975).

Voices of the 1860's

N.G. Chernyshevsky
E.N. Vodovozova, *Na zare Zhizni*.
3d ed, 2 v. Moscow, 1964.

E.N. Vodovozova
E.N. Vodovozova, *Na zare Zhizni*.
3d ed. 2 v. Moscow, 1964.

Conflicting Views of Women's Work
In the Print Shop

Manager: . . . and they [the women] are excellent workers.

Visitor: But what social class are they from?

Manager: Primarily from the educated—former governesses and ladies' companions.

Visitor: What immorality! To give up life in a wellborn family for unclean work.

Manager: Apparently life in such a family is very unpleasant, whereas here no one injures their self-esteem or insults their honor.

Visitor: Honor, my dear fellow, is a luxury for the poor.

(Source: "V tipografii," graviura P. Kurenkova po risunku N. Stepanova v No. 22 zhurnala "Iskra" za 1864 god.) From Vodovozova, *Na zare zhizni*, II, 304.

Heroines of Terror

Sofya Perovskaya
E. Segal, *Sofya Perovskaya*. Moscow, 1962.

Vera Figner
(Soviet Postcard)

Vera Zasulich
V.I. Zasulich. SPB, 1906.

Feminist Leaders

Anna Filosofova
Sbornik pamyati Anny Pavlovny Filosofovoi. 2 v. Petrograd,
1915, I.

Organizers of the Women's Congress of 1908
Trudy Pervago Vserossiskago Zhenskago S"ezda . . . 1908. SPB, 1909.

Competing Issues of Feminism:
Prostitution and Politics

Типъ малолѣтней проститутки. Снимокъ сдѣланъ въ Кіевѣ въ 1904 году.

A Nine-Year-Old Prostitute of Kiev (1904).
M.K. Mukalov, *Deti ulitsy*. SPB, 1906.

Competing Issues of Feminism:
Prostitution and Politics

Suffragist Cartoon.

Top Caption: Concerning the Question of National Representation in Russia without Distinction of Sex.

Gallows Caption: (above) Hanged for Political Convictions; (below) The Political Trial of 1881. The Execution of Sofya Perovskaya.

Bottom Caption: "If woman is eligible to mount the scaffold, she is worthy of entering parliament" (from Olympe de Gouge, 1792).

PZhK, VIII (1906) 335–43.

Prophets and Organizers
of Bolshevik Liberation

Inessa Armand
Kommunistka, 8–9 (Jan.–Feb. 1921).

A.V. Artyukhina
Svetlyi put. Moscow, 1967.

Nadezhda Krupskaya

Prophets and Organizers
of Bolshevik Liberation

Sofya Smidovich
Svetlyi put. Moscow, 1967.

K.I. Nikolaeva
Svetlyi put. Moscow, 1967.

Alexandra Kollontai
Kommunistka, 8–9 (Jan.–Feb. 1921).

PART THREE

The Women's Movement 1881–1917

VI

The New Generation

Irina: It would even be better to be an ox or a common horse—if only to work—than to be a young woman who rises at noon, has her coffee in bed, then takes two hours to dress. . . . How horrible that is! . . .

Tusenbach: . . . The time has come; something enormous is headed this way; a storm is brewing, mighty and freshening, and it will soon reach us and blow away with its cleansing blasts all the laziness, unconcern, contempt for work, and rotten boredom of our society. I will work—and in some 25 or 30 years everyone will work. Everyone!

—CHEKHOV, *Three Sisters* (1900)

1. FACTORY AND SCHOOL

"Russia is now in the grip of a quiet, slow decay," wrote Konstantin Leontiev in 1880; "one of those Great Russian processes is taking place, which with us always precedes a profound historic upheaval—the baptism of the Kiev people in the Dnieper, Peter's destruction of national traditions, and finally the present state of affairs, essentially a transition towards something different." Alexander II's reign had opened with the breath of change and had ended in retrenchment and his own destruction. His son's opened with a "darkening of social and intellectual life," in Ariadna Tyrkova's phrase, and ended as Russia began that great economic upsurge which would enrich the political and revolutionary movements of the succeeding generation. To the progressive spirits who lived through the "obscure eighties"—Kerensky's words—the upsurge seemed remote, and the darkness real. The critic, Semën Vengerov, called its outer form the *pobedonostsevshchina* (after K. P. Pobedonostsev—the bureaucratic contempt for human worth; and its inner form the *chekhovshchina*—the quietism and resignation of Russian society that was mirrored so faithfully in Chekhov's writings. Not only were the overt forms of radicalism crushed, but the very belief in the possibility of a major amelioration of Russian life seemed, on the surface at least, to have dissipated among the intelligentsia.[1]

[1] Quotations: Leontiev cited in Richard Hare, *Pioneers of Russian Social Thought*, 2d ed. (New York, 1964) 344; Ariadna Tyrkova-Vilyams, *To, chego bolshe ne budet* (Paris, 1954) 251;

One of the few exceptions to the mood of cultural despair was the brave and futile gesture of Mariya Tsebrikova, an active feminist of the 1870's, who wrote a lengthy and impassioned letter to Alexander III in 1890. Avoiding all criticism of the Tsar himself or of autocracy, she frankly excoriated the "bureaucratic anarchism" of his reign and asked that the wall of arbitrary officials which stood between him and Russia be dismantled. Only then, she wrote, could society rid itself of the stupid, inhumane, and corrupt practices that prevailed in it. She implored the Tsar to stop the senseless waste of public funds and to spend money on expunging poverty, hunger, ignorance, dirt, and disease from the groaning villages. In reply, the uncomprehending autocrat could only exclaim "What business is it of hers?" and banish Tsebrikova to a village in Vologda Province. Her letter, published as a brochure, circulated in the underground for years.[2]

Like all other "liberal" causes in this epoch, the cause of women's rights suffered retardation and reaction. Alexander III himself was a conventional family man (married to a prim Danish wife) who had looked with disapproval upon his own father's private life. He harbored no sympathy whatsoever for the idea of advancing the frontiers of women's opportunities, and he sided readily with those in his government who opposed women's education. The most powerful of these was Pobedonostsev, the man who has earned his place in nineteenth-century European history as the archetype of reaction. He openly menaced those who were trying to undermine the sacred institutions of Holy Russia—the Church, the State, property, and the family. His distaste for any movement toward sexual emancipation—or indeed any form of self-initiated emancipation—found expression in his exhortation to the Russian people "not to dissipate our strength on a multitude of generalities and aspirations, but to choose a work and a field *according to our measure*." Medicine, the professions, and especially politics did not, in his view, accord with the measure of women. As we shall see presently, his actions spoke even more eloquently than his words.[3]

None of this was supported by any firm body of native anti-feminism. Only matters related to sex or suffrage were likely to evoke storms of controversy, and then only after 1905. In regard to the "woman question" as a general philosophical issue, conservatives had to feed themselves largely from reprints and translations of European works.[4] The main exception was

Alexander Kerensky, *The Crucifixion of Liberty* (London, 1934) 7. Vengerov's comments are in his introduction to M. K. Tsebrikova, *Pismo k Aleksandru III (1890)* (SPB, 1906) 4–5. For further evidence of the psychological subsidence of revolutionary enthusiasm among women, see V. I. Vakhovskaya, *Zhizn revolyutsionerki* (Mosow, 1928) 15.

[2] Tsebrikova, *Pismo*.

[3] K. P. Pobedonostsev, *Reflections of a Russian Statesman* (1896) tr. R. Long (Ann Arbor, Mich., 1965) 121. For other cogent remarks see 117, 134.

[4] Some samples of these translations: Prof. Fehling, *Zhenshchina*, 3d ed. (Kiev 1894); J. Michelet, *Lyubov i zhenshchina* (SPB, 1900); P. Mobius, *Fiziologicheskoe slaboumie zhenshchiny* (Moscow, 1909).

Tolstoyan anti-feminism. Aside from the lugubrious asceticism that Tolstoy preached in tales like *The Kreutzer Sonata*, he made his general views on women abundantly clear in an interview given to Repin's wife a few years before his death. He said nothing new, but contented himself with pontification on the weakness and the general inferiority of women. Granting the desirability of an improved legal status for woman, Tolstoy insisted on her moral subordination to man, and rounded off his remarks with the homely advice that wives ought to do the washing themselves if their husbands refused to hire a laundress. Thus it had been for 6,000 years.[5] These comments of Tolstoy would hardly be worth citing if it were not for the enormous moral influence that he wielded in Russian society in the last two pre-revolutionary decades. It is to the credit of the feminists (who published this interview) that their admiration for the man never diminished in the face of the quaint views he held about them.

The pro-feminists were also unable to add anything significant to the classic arguments of the nineteenth century. Liberal academics and pedagogues continued to adduce medical and anthropological "proof" of women's capacity for work and professional activity; but these served no great purpose except to provide feminists with the necessary arguments to refute the more extravagant ones of the traditionalists. The only striking idea to emerge from this tedious array of clichés was V. M. Khvostov's persuasive answer to Michelet's doctrine of the "eternal malady" of women. Khvostov, professor of law and moral philosophy at Moscow University, advanced the simple and eminently reasonable idea that although woman was conditioned to habitual "illnesses"—menstruation and pregnancy—she was also conditioned to habitual recovery; and the habit of recovery made her stronger and more resilient than man. But alas by the time this was written (1914) virtually no one in Russian society was greatly interested in it. One had only to look around for evidence of the strength and capacity of Russian women.[6]

In a sense, the age of the "woman question" was over; it had received so much publicity during the 1860's and 1870's that there was nothing more to say about it as a general problem.[7] The results wrought by all this publicity had been impressive indeed: a gratifying reform of women's education, a bright galaxy of female revolutionaries, and a widespread acceptance of women's equality among the intelligentsia. Now the "women's movement" was about to begin, or better to say the women's movements, for there will be two of them: one feminist and one socialist. Both began haltingly in the mid-

[5] *Zhenskoe delo* (to be cited as *ZhD*) (June 25, 1910) 21–22.

[6] V. M. Khvostov, *Zhenshchina i chelovecheskoe dostoinstvo* (Moscow, 1914), 272. For more profeminist arguments: *idem, Zhenshchina nakanune novoi epokhi* (Moscow 1905); S. D. Mikhnov, *O zhenshcine s biologicheskoi tochki zreniya* (Yurev, 1904); P. G. Mizhuev, *Zhenskii vopros i zhenskoe dvizhenie* (SPB, 1906).

[7] The practice of making irrelevant and half-ironic references to the "woman question" which we find in the novels of the 1870's (for instance *Devils*, *Karamazov*, and *Karenina*) seems to have been abandoned by the writers of this epoch.

1890's and then leaped forward vigorously in 1905. Both drew their leadership largely from the female intelligentsia; and both attempted to win the allegiance of the women "toilers"—workers, servants, and even peasants.

"Can harder lot be found than that of Russian woman?" wrote Nekrasov in his perennially popular *Who Can Live Well in Russia?* He was speaking of the women of the peasantry who as a class accounted for more than three-quarters of the population in 1897. Among them the birth of a son was greeted with joy and pride; that of a daughter with woe or at best indifference. The chief concern of the parents was to marry her off as soon as she came of age, usually sixteen. In marriage the woman was ideally to be the unquestioning co-worker, servant, and bed-partner of her husband, a relationship symbolized in some regions by the wedding custom of the bride presenting bedding and a whip to her new master. If she lived in an extended family, the young wife sometimes had to suffer the indignity of sexual intercourse with her father-in-law, a practice—known as *snokhachestvo*—resulting from the long absences of husbands from the villages. Much more common was mistreatment at the hands of her mother-in-law. Village girls were often victims of a special kind of hysteria, and they aged rapidly under the burden of heavy field work and regular pregnancies. Since birth control devices were unheard of in the villages, and since girls married young, a wife at age twenty-five had already been pregnant about five or six times; at forty-five, about nine times. According to data gathered in 1908, 25 percent of forty-five-year-old peasant wives had had more than ten pregnancies, one-fourth of which had ended in miscarriages. A not atypical example is that of a fifty-five-year-old woman who had been married for thirty-five years and had been pregnant twenty-four times. Two children had lived. Miscarriage, child mortality, and post-natal complications were so widespread among the peasants that they were hardly noticed.[8]

Nothing can soften or modify this picture the details of which were blurred in the public consciousness by stock phrases about the backwardness of village life. But there is another side to it. The peasant woman was entitled to her dowry and to her own earnings, the well known "women's box." After various rulings of the 1880's and 1890's household property was defined as family property and the male head of household could not claim sole ownership; and a woman could be recognized as the legal head of household if that conformed to local custom. "Women without a lord"—widowed or abandoned heads of household—not only participated in the village meetings but also in some lo-

[8] Alfa (pseud.), "Babii vopros," *Zhenskii vestnik* (to be cited as *ZhV*) (Aug. 1905) 225–27; L. Tikhomirov, *Russia, Political and Social*, tr. E. Aveling, 2 v. (London, 1888) I, 185–87; Bernhard Stern, *Geschichte der offentlichen Sittlichkeit in Russland*. 2 v. (n. p., 1907), II (2d ed., 1920) 511–18; John Maynard, *Russia in Flux* (New York, 1962) 54–56; E. Shchepkina, "Trud i zdorove krestyanki," *Soyuz zhenshchin* (to be cited as *SZh*) (Jan. 1909) 12–15.

cales actually ran them because of the absence of men.[9] Nor was the "extended family" (*rodovaya semya*) much of a barrier to the emergence of freer conjugal households. They had rarely been fully communal, and students of the village had observed several wives cooking their kasha separately on the same stove, feeding their children, and wiping off "their" sector of the table. Young wives, chafing under the autocratic regimen of the in-laws, hastened to take this familial atomism to its logical conclusion and set up a separate household where "her own housekeeping" (*se babskoe khozyaistva*) would augment her motivation and her satisfaction. Wives took the initiative in this, and they often displayed greater entrepreneurial spirit (and more egoism) than their husbands. A Petersburg agronomical society voiced the belief that village women would play a major role in the renovation of Russian agriculture.[10] By 1905 the female population of the villages was attracting the attention of the political parties as much by its progressive potential as by its pitiful backwardness.

But by that time also many had left the countryside. The main reason was the economic bite that affected most peasants at the end of the nineteenth century. Too little research has been done on the subject for us to be able to plot the numbers, the pattern, the motivations, and the techniques of the village-to-city migration the magnitude of which increased steadily during these years. One thing is certain: No "social daydreams" or prickings of moral conscience were involved. The peasant girl was as apolitical as she was unromantic and was concerned almost solely with questions of bread and butter. A very small number escaped village life through the venerable custom of entering a convent: The increase in nuns from 1855 to 1911 was from 7,000 to only 47,000, in spite of the spectacular example set by the Tsarina's sister Ella, widow of the murdered Grand Duke Sergei. Others tried seasonal work that, alas, sometimes included an annual prostitution tour at some nearby city or fair. The money economy transformed many rural women into hired field-hands (about 25 percent of all women wage-earners in 1897). From the agrarian labor market to the urban one was not a very big step and soon female peasants began arriving at the railway stations of Russia's major cities.[11]

There most of them became not workers but servants, the largest group of female wage-earners in Russia and probably the most exploited. Children and

[9] W. T. Shinn, "The Law of the Russian Peasant Household," *Slavic Review*, XX, 4 (Dec. 1961) 600–21; *SZh* (Nov. 1908) 2–4; Tikhomirov, *Russia*, I, 119–20.

[10] A. M. Kollontai, *Sotsialynyya osnovy zhenskago voprosa* (SPB, 1909), 124–26; V. N. Shishkin, *Tak skladyvalas revolyutsionnaya moral: istoricheskii ocherk* (Moscow, 1967) 28 (citing A. N. Engelgardt); Tikhomirov, *Russia*, I, 198; Roger Portal, ed., *Le statut des paysans liberés du servage, 1861–1961* (Paris, 1963) 297 (also citing Engelgardt); I. Klingen, *Rol zhen-shchiny kak obrazovannoi selskoi khozyaiki v obnovlenii russkoi derevni* (SPB, 1903), *passim*.

[11] The figures on nuns are from Kollontai, *Sots. osnovy*, p. 127 and *ZhD* (Mar. 1, 1911) 28. According to the 1897 census there were about 600,000 women agricultural wage-earners. A. G. Rashin's population estimates show a steady growth in the female urban population in relation to the male: *Naselenie Rossii za 100 let (1811–1913 gg.)* (Moscow 1956) 258–79.

grandchildren of serfs, they had deeply internalized the notion of respect for their "betters" at an early age, and, long after the abolition of serfdom, exhibited a fierce loyalty and dog-like devotion to their masters. Princess Dolgorukaya, in one of her candid moments, confessed that members of her class all too often rewarded the loyalty of their servants with tyrannical abuse, long hours, and low wages. Three or four rubles a month, food, and a corner to sleep in was the normal income for a domestic servant. The low status and level of education and the extreme naïveté of the village girls who came to the city to become maids and cooks made them easy prey to seduction by their masters—or more commonly the master's sons—or their fellow male servants. Pregnancies, expulsions, and illegitimate births of the kind that gave Tolstoy the material for *Resurrection* were common events in upper-class Russian households. Female service personnel in tea rooms, restaurants, and inns fared no better and were frequently confounded in the public mind with ordinary prostitutes. As a group, female servants were among the most rightless people in the Russian empire.[12]

The urban lower-class females who gave the most promise of increasing their consciousness were the women factory workers. The "female proletariat" was to become a major object of attention for both the feminists and the socialists after 1905. There was nothing new about women in the labor force but their numbers began growing steadily in the 1890's. A notable spurt occurred in 1904–1906 when women replaced men mobilized for the war with Japan and when the employers found them both cheaper and more manageable than the male workers of the turbulent revolutionary years. The same phenomenon was repeated on a much larger scale during World War I. Numbers of factory women rose from 192,000 in 1887 to 723,000 in 1914, reaching over a million during the war; and these figures refer only to the women in the so-called inspected industries. In terms of percentages, women accounted for about 25 percent of the labor force in the 1880's and 40 percent in 1914. The greatest concentration of women was in the textile industry and by 1912 they accounted for over half its workers. Tobacco, leather, and other light industries also employed large numbers of women.[13]

Getting paid a wage lower than men for the same work was not peculiar to Russian working women, but it hurt nonetheless. A Soviet writer has estimated that before the Revolution the average daily wage for a male industrial laborer was 1.20 rubles and for a female 45 to 85 kopecks. A contemporary

[12] Stephanie Dolgorouky [Dolgorukaya], *La Russie avant le debâcle* (Paris, 1926) 165; Berenice Madison, "Russia's Illegitimate Children Before and After the Revolution," *Slavic Review*, XXII, 1 (Mar. 1963) 83; *ZhD*, (Mar. 14, 1910) 4 and (Apr. 1–15, 1911) 30. Tolstoy's theme was given to him by the jurist A. F. Koni from a real-life case.

[13] G. Goldberg, "Zhenskii trud v russkoi promyshlennosti," *Russkiya vedomosti*, 285 (Nov. 17, 1910) 4; A. G. Rashin, *Formirovanie promyshelennogo proletariata v Rossii* (Moscow, 1940) 185–94. The best treatment of the subject is Rose Glickman, "The Russian Factory Woman, 1880–1914," to appear in Atkinson *et al.*, eds., *Women in Russia*.

foreign visitor claimed that women's wages were as a rule two-thirds those of men; in the textile trade, women and children earned 30 to 50 as opposed to a man's 70 kopecks to one ruble a day.[14] This situation encouraged a few factory women to pose as men in order to enjoy the better wages. "When I get hungry," complained a woman at a 1905 workers' meeting, "and go buy myself a pickle, they don't charge me a half a kopeck for it do they? No I pay the same kopeck a man does."[15]

Socialist and feminist writers both believed that women's real wages were too low for a normal human existence. A 1909 sample budget for a woman textile worker allowed for the minimal needs: a tiny room or "corner," some clothing, and a simple diet of tea, sugar, bread, herring, and soup (a hot meal was a rarity). This regimen consumed all her twenty ruble monthly pay and left not a kopeck either for cultural pursuits or the dreaded fines imposed for lateness. In factories such as the Ottoman Tobacco Plant in St. Petersburg, being fifteen or twenty minutes late could cost the worker a half-day's wages. Mothers were not even permitted to leave ten minutes early to pick up their infants. Wage cuts were feared like the cholera: At the end of the 1890's, the women of another Petersburg cigarette factory begged the owners not to impose one. Those gentlemen, in the best spirit of nineteenth-century capitalism, replied that they would rather be closed down than reverse their decision.[16]

If wages were unequal for the two sexes, hours and conditions of labor seldom were. Before the factory law of 1885, they were practically unregulated. Women shared the twenty-four hour shift with men; in one leather tannery they worked eighteen hours a day with two breaks of two and four hours each. The new law forbade night work for women (and children) in the textile trade and its provisions were gradually extended to other "women's" industries. But its effects were partially nullified by other legislation that allowed exceptions and by the fact that many women were employed in firms too small to come under the laws. These were the sweatshops, mostly in the needle trades, where, as one female revolutionary recalled, a twelve hour day was a luxury which had to be fought for. Safety devices were rarely in evidence, and the

[14] V. A. Bilshai, *Sovetskaya demokratiya i ravnopravie zhenshchin v SSSR* (Moscow, 1948) 20; Francis Palmer, *Russian Life in Town and Country (1901)* (New York, 1903) 277; the textile industry wage figures, referring to the 1890's, are from P. I. Lyashchenko, *History of the National Economy in Russia to the 1917 Revolution*, tr. L. M. Herman (New York, 1949) 546. By 1911–1914, the ratio had not changed, according to the British engineer, Allan Monkhouse, *Moscow: 1911–1933* (London, 1933) 40. Glickman, (see note 13 above) estimates that women's wages were one third to one half those of men throughout Russian industry.

[15] In 1902 there were five cases of women posing as men in order to receive higher wages: Amfitreatrov, *Zhenshchina*, 53. The complaint of the woman worker is from Tsetsiliya Bobrovskaya, *Zapiski podpolshchika, 1894–1917* (Moscow, 1957) 69.

[16] The worker's budget is given in Kollontai, *Sots. osnovy*, 155–56; a similar one is cited by Tyrkova in *Russkaya mysl* (June 1910) 133. On fines, see *SZh* (Nov. 1907) 7–10. On the wage slash: *Rabochee dvizhenie v Rossii v XIX veke: sbornik dokumentov i materialov*, 5 v. in 7 (Moscow, 1951–1963) IV, 2, 29–30.

long hours of standing in cramped quarters damaged women's lungs and kid-
neys. Girls fainted after more than fifteen minutes in the drying room of a
Kharkov cigarette factory; and tobacco processors everywhere suffered dis-
tending of pupils, heart ailments, asthma, migraines, and acute cramps. The
liberal journalist, Tyrkova, described a small cloth mill in Byalostok as a
dark, damp cellar packed with emaciated consumptive girls—"not a factory
but a regular Dante's Inferno." This was in 1909, after the great bulk of factory legislation had been passed. In the main, there was little distinction made
between men and women by employers when it came to exploiting their labor.
Can we be very surprised when Sir John Maynard tells us, in subtly indignant
tones, that in Moscow a woman's body was used to sweep a chimney?[17]

Even more dismaying were the workers' living conditions. Some simply
slept on the premises beside their machines; others, if in a town, managed to
get a room. But the growing tendency was for workers of all ages and sexes to
live in barracks provided them by the owners. Gvozdëv, a factory inspector of
the period, has left a vivid description of these in a typical factory center in
Central Russia set in the middle of a barren landscape dissected by a stinking,
polluted river. Here, in contrast to the stately homes of the owners, stood ugly
barracks—fetid and foul from the stench of human bodies—that had no washing facilities at their disposal. Here where 44 percent of the district's workers
lived, three or four families shared one room, and two or three workers shared
the limited number of beds that were used in shifts. Numerous sources remind
us that such conditions were not confined to the textile belt but were widespread and commonplace. In the capital, in Peterhof, in Kiev some workers
occupied an average living space the size of a telephone booth; men, women,
and children slept wall-to-wall on the floor, too exhausted even to undress.
Indeed, all the wretchedness of the workers' everyday life (*byt*) conveyed to
us by the tales of Gorky and Kuprin and other writers are amply documented
in the dry reports of the factory inspectors.[18]

As in the England of an earlier generation, conventional sexual morality
was a casualty of this system. One source of the change was the seigneurial
sexual code of some of the foremen and managers. As early as the 1870's,
factory "sultans" used economic pressure to elicit carnal favors from their
female employees. From the 1890's onward, labor newspapers and under-

---

[17] For pre-reform conditions and a chronology of the major legislation, see: M. Tugan-
Baranovsky, *Russkaya fabrika* (1898) 6th ed. (Moscow, 1934) 313–20; S. Gvozdëv, *Zapiski fab-
richnago inspektora* (Moscow, 1911) 58–60; M. Florinsky, *Russia*, 2 v. (New York, 1947–1953)
II, 1105–1106. For the examples cited, see: M. N. Sobolev, *Zhenskii trud v narodnom
khozyaistve XIX v.* (SPB, 1901) 84–86; the memoir of the Kiev Social Democrat, V. G.
Kryzhanovskaya-Tuchapskaya, "Iz moikh vospominanii," *KS*, VI, 67 (1930) 24–25; Tyrkova,
"Zhenskii trud i prostitutsiya," *Russkaya mysl* (June 1910) 131; Maynard, *Russia in Flux*, 68.

[18] Gvozdëv's description in his *Zapiski*, 149–51. For further evidence, see: Sobolev, *Zhen.
trud*, 85; Bobrovskaya, *Zapiski*, 87; K. A. Pazhitnov, *Polozhenie rabochago klassa v Rossii*, 2d
ed. (SPB, 1908), 216–32. A model of a workers' barracks is on display at the Leningrad Museum
of Ethnography.

ground leaflets regularly printed complaints of sexual exploitation and mistreatment of women; and some factories were used as recruitment pools by
white slavers and pimps. Only rarely could a girl, like the thread-piecer who
married Savva Morozov, escape this morass through her charm and beauty.[19]
Marriage—to other workers—continued to be the norm for the factory girl;
though here, as communists have proudly pointed out, she enjoyed more sexual freedom before and equality after the marriage (which was often unregistered) than did her sisters in the villages. The considerable divergence in sexual matters between the country and the city that was to become a great social
controversy in the 1920's was already in evidence in the 1890's.

But her relative freedom and equality afforded the working woman no
guarantee of family security or happiness. Children were an economic burden
to the toiling couple, particularly to the mother who enjoyed no adequate
maternity protection until 1912. Unwanted children were often aborted or sold
after birth, and sometimes abandoned or killed. Since there were almost no
nurseries, working women had to entrust their children to old women or in-
competent older children—like the girl in Chekhov's "Sleepy" who strangled
her charge. The street, as Kollontai put it, was the elementary school for most
proletarian children. The working mother, buffeted between the factory
bench, neglected children, and an all too often drunken husband found little
consolation in "proletarian" moral equality; and marriage, to invoke Kollontai again, was little more than a series of intervals between drinking bouts.[20]

The government, notwithstanding its imposing fiscal and political powers,
did little enough to alleviate the general conditions of the working population.
It considered the central issues to be limitation of night work for women and
children and enforcement by inspection, both of which encountered angry opposition by Russian businessmen. As far back as 1859, when the idea of inspection was first broached, the Khludov brothers, owners of a large textile
mill, offered the blunt opinion that "factory inspection ought to be the business of the factory owners." The standard argument against curtailing hours
was the low productivity of the labor force. When women's night work was
eliminated, it was at the behest of St. Petersburg manufacturers who wished to
undercut the cheap labor advantages of their Moscow competitors, and was
done so over the enraged thunderings of the Muscovites and their spokesman,
Mikhail Katkov. After 1905, aside from insurance, the reformers focused on
the introduction of female factory inspectors. Opponents of this measure

[19] On this practice, see: Shishkin, *Revol. moral*, 63; *Rabochaya mysl*. 4 (Oct. 1898), 2–3 cited
in Allan Wildman, *The Making of a Workers' Revolution: Russian Social Democracy, 1891–1903*
(Chicago, 1967) 33: *Listovki peterburgskikh Bolshevikov, 1902–1917*, 2 v. (Moscow, 1939) I,
38; Bochkarëva, *Svetlyi put*, 3–4. The reference to Morozov's wife is from Buryshkin, *Moskva
kupecheskaya*, 115.

[20] This aspect of workers' *byt* is described in I. Bezdomnyi, "Zhenskii proletariat," in
Zhenskoe dvizhenie poslednykh dnei (Odessa, 1905) 11–13 and Kollontai, *Sots. osnovy*, 128–30.
The question of "proletarian" sexual morality and its sources will be discussed in Chapter VIII.

claimed either that they were unnecessary or that women were incapable of handling such a job. A male factory inspector who knew the problem well, argued convincingly that the mass of women in the factories had special needs and problems which they could effectively communicate only to another female. At the time of his writing, there were some 700,000 working in the inspected enterprises without the benefit of female inspectors.[21]

In spite of fearful working and living conditions, the proletarian women were generally quiescent and were valued by the factory owners as "the peaceful element" (*spokoinyi element*) in the labor force. Like their peasant counterparts, most women workers accepted their harsh lot as the judgment of fate or the will of God, and under normal conditions they were difficult to organize politically. Only when subjected to unbearable rudeness, wage cuts, or heavy fines did they engage in industrial violence. As time went on, their level of tolerance gradually dropped and they began to reveal more frequently their potential hostility toward the unfair employer. But they also showed, with less vehemence, a grudging resentment against male fellow workers who took their jobs, froze them out of extra work, and sometimes abused them. One of the delicate problems of the reform of women's labor, and one not unique to Russia by any means, was the embarrassing fact that very often women themselves did not wish limitations on either the hours or the nature of their work; it was another issue that would cause consternation in the Russian labor movement after the Revolution. The whole question of women's potential dual hostility toward the capitalist who exploited them and the male worker who competed with them was to be of burning interest to the leaders of the socialist and the feminist women's movements.

In shifting attention from the working classes to the educated stratum of the female population, the focus is narrowed to a very tiny group of people. Russia was still a traditional society, and it was very difficult for a girl from the lower orders to make her way through the maze of Russia's educational system. No fewer than seven different bureaucracies were involved in education; but the results were much less impressive than the table of organization. In 1894, to begin with the gloomiest of figures, only 1 percent of all females were in school (as opposed to 3.9 percent of boys). The numbers and percentages increased steadily up to the Revolution, but the ratio between girls and boys in attendance remained around 1:3 throughout the period. Figures for the years 1903–1905 revealed that 13.7 percent of the women were literate as compared to 32.6 percent for men. The quality of education varied greatly in

[21] The Khludov Brothers are quoted in Tugan-Baranovsky, *Russ. fabrika*, 300. The Moscow, Petersburg wages rivalry in *ibid.*, 310 and in F. G. Giffin, "The Prohibition of Night Work for Women and Young Persons: the Russian Factory Law of June 3, 1885," *Canadian Slavic Studies*, II, 2 (Summer 1968) 208–18. See *ZhD* (Feb. 15, 1913) 1–2 and B. D. Belikov (a factory inspector), *Zhenshchina v promyshlennoi inspektsii zapada: k voprosu vvedenii zhenskoi fabrichnoi inspektsii v Rossi* (Tver, 1914), 51, and *passim*.

the primary schools, though most of them were built on a core of the four R's: reading, writing, arithmetic, and religion. In the country, the *zemstvo* schools were invariably better than the church schools; in the cities schooling was much more accessible to children of the poor. Certain groups like the Old Believers, the Jews, and the gentry possessed advantages of home education that were based on wealth or on cultural traditions; whereas the peasants remained reluctant to lose the labor of a daughter for the sake of an education the purpose of which they could but dimly perceive.[22]

As a result, only about 120,000 girls were enrolled in secondary schools in 1907. The worst of these were the Parish schools, whose principal mission was to transform daughters of priests into future brides of priests. As late as 1915, the Imperial Princess Mariya sadly observed the training of these strictly disciplined, heavily uniformed, undernourished girls who learned embroidery, liturgical singing, and religion to the exclusion of almost everything else. The institutes, which were still reserved for well born ladies, had hardly progressed beyond what had been achieved by the reforms of the 1860's. For Smolny, the only requirements for admission, beyond birth, were knowledge of Russian and French, the ability to count to a thousand and to memorize certain prayers, and absence of communicable disease. According to an institute graduate writing in 1904, it was still "a hothouse for cultivating femininity" a kind of barracks where the spirit was smothered and dependent fantasies nourished. During the turbulent days of 1905, girls from some of these aristocratic establishments actually petitioned their administrations to stop treating them like "muslin misses" who dreamt of balls and officers and to give them a serious education. The Parish and the institute pupils accounted for one-third of all high school girls.[23]

The other two-thirds were enrolled in the open day schools founded in the 1860's for girls of all social classes. These were superior to the institutes and Parish schools, and they formed the backbone of secondary education for women in pre-revolutionary Russia. From them came the bulk of university

[22] The source for most later estimates on school population before the Revolution is N. Kibardin's statistical report in *Zhurnal Ministerstva Narodnago Prosveshcheniya*, n.s., LXIX (May 1917) 24–38. Data in L. D. Filippova, "Iz istorii zhenskogo obrazovaniya v Rossii," *Voprosy istorii* (Feb. 1963) 209–18 show that one out of thirty-five of all *city* girls *of school age* (as opposed to one out of sixty-nine of rural girls) were in school in 1898 (212). See also Norton Dodge, *Women in the Soviet Economy* (Baltimore, 1966), 101. The literacy figure is from *Russkaya mysl* (June 1910) 130 and is roughly in accord with the figure usually cited from the 1897 census (13.1 percent).

[23] The figures and percentages cited are from Mizhuev, *Zhenskii vopros*, 31–32. Princess Mariya's comment on the Parish schools (Grand Duchess Marie, *Education of a Princess: a Memoir* [New York, 1931] 208–10) must be set against the observation of a Duma deputy in the same year on the restlessness of their inmates: J. S. Curtiss, *Church and State in Russia: The Last Years of the Empire* (New York, 1940) 359. On the institutes, see: V. Mravitsky, *Pravila i programmy zhenskikh uchebnykh zavedenii . . . na 1909–1910 g.* (Moscow, 1909) 107; N. A. Lukhmanova, *Nedochety zhizni somvremennoi zhenshchiny* (Moscow, 1904) 6–19. See *ZhV* (July-Aug. 1906) 207–10 on the petitions.

entrants. Because of this they became the targets for reactionary forces in the country on a number of occasions. In the 1880's when the Ministry of Education became known among some people as the Ministry of Public Ignorance, these forces launched an attack on all institutions that catered to "children of cooks" and other menials unworthy of education, and female applicants from non-gentry classes were often excluded. A more vicious, but little-known, assault on female education was directed by the Minister A. M. Shvarts (1908–1910) who wished to dismantle the provincial network of girls' high schools and replace them with local centers for home economics training. The schools survived all these efforts to demolish them and continued to grow impressively in quantity and in quality.[24]

The history of university education for women in this epoch was even stormier and more erratic. Of the four "women's higher courses" established in the 1870's—Moscow, Kazan, Kiev, and St. Petersburg—only the last managed to survive, and barely so, to the Revolution. The imperial couple were not sympathetic to university education for girls. The Tsar refused to allow his wife's image to be used on the diploma of women's courses. The Empress did not think it was proper for a woman to study the natural sciences, and she once told a deputation of women that they ought to stay home and knit. The new Minister of Education (1882), I. D. Delyanov, needed little encouragement to close the women's universities; when he was informed by the police and by the reactionary journalist, Prince Meshchersky, that the courses were "a veritable sewer of anarchist disease" he promptly agreed. In 1886 a committee of the Ministries of Education and the Interior concluded that they had to prevent the further concentration of young girls in the university towns, for such girls came there not for learning but for "freedom as they in their twisted fashion perceived it." All courses were ordered to stop admitting new students as of that year. Those in Moscow, Kiev, and Kazan closed their doors at the end of the decade. The St. Petersburg Bestuzhev Courses were more fortunate. Their board, staffed by the older feminists, argued that if the school were closed, Russian girls would go abroad again, and so the government reluctantly allowed the courses to reopen under new regulations. Some of the directors were removed, including Nadezhda Stasova, and supervision was tightened up; but the courses were saved. In 1900 new women's courses in Moscow managed to open under similar conditions. There were no others until 1905.[25]

---

[24] The pedagogical reaction of the 1880's has been amply documented elsewhere; for Shvarts' démarche, see *ZhD* (Sep. 10, 1910) 1–2.

[25] The attitude of Alexander III and his Empress are reported in Amfitreatrov, *Zhenshchina*, 50; Tyrkova, *To, chego*, 252; and Georg Brandes, *Impressions of Russia* (1889), tr. S. Eastman (New York, 1966), 106. The most recent account of Delyanov's policies is in P. G. Zaionchkovsky, *Rossiiskoe samoderzhavie v konste XIX stoletiya* (Moscow, 1970) 340–42 (whence the two quotations). Additional details in Valk, *Kursy*, 11–19; *Vysshie zhenskie (bestuzhevskie) kursy: bibliograficheskii ukazatel* (Moscow, 1966) 11–17; Satina. *Education*, 101–109, 114–15.

During the frantic revolutionary years 1905 and 1906, the pendulum swung far in the other direction. Advanced courses for women opened in all the university towns including the new one, Tomsk; all were granted autonomy, thus becoming, in everything but name, genuine women's universities. New faculties were added and women instructors hired to teach some of the courses; and a large number of women began attending the men's universities as they had done in the early 1860's. All this was accomplished in the heat of the revolutionary uproar and under the fairly liberal Minister of Education, P. M. Kaufmann (1906–1908). But under the reactionary ministers who succeeded him, Shvarts and Kasso, women students were again subjected to official harrassment: Female auditors at the universities were expelled in large numbers and new matriculations prohibited, and the autonomy of the purely women's higher courses sharply diminished. Yet none of this was able to halt the advance of women's university education. By 1914, there were some 25,000 enrolled in the women's university courses of ten cities. When the War of 1914 began, the new liberal Minister of Education, Ignatiev, began to allow them in limited numbers into the regular universities.[26]

The best known of the women's higher courses were the Bestuzhev Courses. Their two faculties, History-Philology and Physics-Mathematics, were housed in a spacious building on one of the quiet streets of Vasilevsky Island. Today its wide halls and auditoriums constitute the Mathematics-Mechanics Faculty of Leningrad University. In the years before the Revolution, the high standards of the Bestuzhev Courses and the superior caliber of its professors (drawn mostly from the University) made it a prime objective of hundreds of young women from all over the Empire. But there were severe obstacles, even in the twentieth century. Large numbers of parents, especially provincial ones, still held the belief that it was "unfeminine" to study, a belief nimbly described by Mikhail Chekhov in his novella *The Bluestocking* (1904). A girl had to be seventeen and armed with parental permission before facing the difficult and competitive admissions hurdles. Jewish girls had the additional handicap of the quota system (3 percent) and the various measures confining them to the Pale of Settlement. When bribery of janitors or fictitious marriages did not work, a Jewish woman would sometimes enroll with the police as a prostitute in order to receive the shaming yellow ticket that gave her the right to residence. In spite of the formidable difficulties, knowledge-hungry girls of all classes continued to crowd the university towns and the

---

[26] The topic of women university students in Russia is so vast and the sources for it so rich that it would require a monograph itself to do justice to it. In addition to the last three cited sources, see brief accounts in *ZhD* (Aug. 1, 1915) 17 and (May 25, 1910) 16; and in *Trudy I-go Vserossiiskago S" ezda po obrazovaniyu zhenshchin* (SPB, 1914) I, 2–32. My estimate of the number of women students is a simple extrapolation of the figures given by William H. E. Johnson (20,000 for 1910; 30,000 for 1916) in his *Russia's Educational Heritage* (Pittsburgh, 1950) 196. For a detailed account of the pre-1905 years, see Ruth Dudgeon, "Women Students in Russia, 1860–1905" (Ph.D., George Washington University, 1975).

social composition of the Bestuzhev student body, like the others, became gradually more democratic.[27]

Most of the students admitted to the Bestuzhev Courses could not afford the tuition fees, even though some 40 percent of them were gentry (in 1909). The Society for Providing Means to Needy Students, founded and managed by the feminists since the 1870's, offered the necessary financial assistance. In her everyday existence, the *bestuzhevka* did not lead the life of a Petersburg lady. In the early 1880's, we hear of three or four girls sharing a damp and dirty cubicle, alternating the use of a single bed, and huddling together in their overcoats over a cup of tea and a slice of salami. In 1901, Ariadna Trykova, observing the female students among her fellow prisoners jailed for a demonstration, noted wryly how they relished the modest prison meal. But conditions improved very quickly. By 1905 single and double rooms in a dormitory were available for girls at a reasonable fee and regular meals were served. A questionnaire of 1909 reveals that almost all women students had an income in excess of 20 rubles per month and 34.9 percent of them an income of 26-35 rubles—impressive when compared to that of a factory woman. Only 1/5 of them worked, mostly as tutors. Almost half of them occupied private rooms. Rent averaged 11.5 rubles per month. Other figures seem to indicate beyond question that female students were better fed and better housed than males.[28]

From the evidence, or lack of it, it would seem that the sexual ethos of the woman student was still pretty much that of "the woman of the 1860's" (*shestidesyatnitsa*). Eroticism detached from the intimate act of love held no fascination for her. At the very peak of the decadent moment in Russian literature (1909) a large percentage of female students registered their lack of interest in this theme. Some eschewed marriage, family, and children but did so in the spirit not of *Sanin* but of *The Kreutzer Sonata*, ascetically storing their energies for a life of independence and work. Others entered into a "Platonic" or "Tolstoyan" marriage—a latter-day version of the Chernyshevskian arrangements of the 1860's—where the partners gave each other comradeship and assistance unaccompanied by the ground base of sexual relations. But most women students, succumbing to nature and to the stretches of loneliness in their student lives, married in the usual way. A memoirist of the 1890's,

---

[27] Memoirs on the intellectual life, the faculty, and the instructors make up a large part of Valk, *Kursy*. Requirements for admission listed in Kage's 1905 school guide: *Svedeniya dlya zhenshchin poluchivshikh srednee obrazovanie o vysshikh i professionalnykh uchebnykh zavedeniyakh i kursakh* (SPB) 3–5. On Jewish disabilities: *ZhD* (Sept. 10, 1910) and Fanni Shvartsman, *Moya sudba: vospominaniya*, 2 v. (Paris, 1964) I, 169–77. Gentry girls made up 39.7 percent of those who answered a 1909 questionnaire given to Bestuzhev Students: *Slushatelnitsy S-Peterburgskikh vysshikh zhenskikh (bestuzhevskikh) kursov* (SPB, 1912) 4; M. P. Chekhov's novella is *Sinii chulok: povest* (SPB, 1904). The word "bluestocking," though present in literature at least as early as 1860 in Pomyalovsky's *Molotov* (185), never caught on as an antifeminist term in Russia.

[28] Valk, *Kursy*, 10–11; Tyrkova, *Na putyakh k svobode* (New York, 1952) 80; Kage, *Svedenie*, 5; *Slushatelnitsy*, 19–52; K. A. Kablukov, *Studencheskii kvartirnyi vopros v Moskve* (Moscow, 1908) 24, 31.

Elizaveta Dyakonova, recorded in scorn how the engagement rings flashed from the fingers of her comrades on examination day. If student marriages differed from those of "established" society, it was in their greater spirit of equality. A 1901 cartoon, showing a student husband rocking the children to sleep while the student wife—cigarette in mouth and feet on desk—reads Büchner and Moleschott, depicted a situation which was, if not universal, at least common.[29]

Conservative anti-feminists continued to equate female students with prostitutes. Vladimir Purishkevich, the champion of all reactionary causes in the Duma, insisted that the universities were honeycombed with "street girls," libertine-radicals, and depraved Jewesses "defiling our youth." He was seconded by the deputy Obraztsov who announced in the Duma that women students not only had immoral relations with the professors but also "by the hundreds gave themselves to drunken sailors." In the Russia of 1910 such archaic hysteria had little influence.[30]

Since Russian male students as a whole were far more radical than their counterparts elsewhere in Europe, the authorities warned their female charges to stay away from them. V. I. Guerrier, rector of the Moscow Courses and a pioneer of higher education for women, was primarily concerned with training good conversationalists, mothers, and teachers, and patronizingly advised an incoming class to avoid politics and men. Baroness Lyudmila Vrangel, a *bestuzhevka*, was made to vow by a senator friend not to involve herself in political activity. Dyakonova, Tyrkova, and others relate similar episodes. Over this question, the female student body usually split into "politicals" and "academics." The latter expressed their point of view in the simple words "we came here to study." Their main concern was to avoid giving the government an excuse to close their courses. Sofiya Satina, sharing this view, would often attend political meetings in order to protect her friends from the dangerous influence of radical speakers. Dyakonova was an even clearer example of the intelligent and socially conscious student who nevertheless was appalled at the dogmatic radicalism of her comrades and shunned the wordy debates between the Marxists and Populists who threatened "to drown each other in a flood of evidence." When a fellow student once proclaimed that "there is a good higher than learning," she replied: "Oh yes, dear comrades, but we women, in order to reach such things have to have an

---

[29] Sexual attitudes will be examined more fully in the following section, but see *Slushatelnitsy*, 122 for the unpopularity of "the decadents" among female students. On marriage attitudes, see *ibid.*, 134 and Elizaveta Dyakonova, *Dnevnik Elizavety Dyakonovoi na vysshikh zhenskikh kursakh (1896–1899* g.), 2d ed. (SPB, 1905) 122, 283. The student marriages are described, on the basis of conversations among Moscow students, in P. Ivanov, *Studenty v Moskve: byt, nravy, tipy*, 2d ed. (Moscow, 1903) 99–102. The cartoon is on p. 121 of N. Melnikow, *Die gesellschaftliche Stellung des russischer Frau* (Berlin, 1901).
[30] V. Purishkevich, *Materialy po voprosu o razlozhenii sovremennogo russkogo universiteta* (SPB, 1914) 35–36, 190, 261–64; *ZhD* (Mar. 15, 1911) 2 (on Obraztsov).

education." Yet Satina, Dyakonova and many like them would often march in honorable solidarity with their comrades during a conflict with the administration.[31]

The radical women could not comprehend such an outlook. One of them once asked Dyakonova: "Why did you come to St. Petersburg anyway?"[32] Furthermore the radicals denied the charges of anti-intellectualism. "They say we do not value learning," ran a Bestuzhev proclamation of 1904, "and do not appreciate our school. This is not true; science is precious to us all, but we have found that learning and life ought to go hand in hand." The atmosphere of mild poverty and free and easy equality among the women doubtless helped to nourish dreams of social justice. They frequented tea rooms and tiny cafés, called each other comrade and rubbed shoulders with male radicals everywhere on Vasilevsky Island in Petersburg. Meetings and social gatherings were scenes of noisy debates between Marxists and Narodniks. Corporate student bodies, aid funds, "sororities of girls from the same locale" (*zemlyachestva*), and strike committees gave the *bestuzhevki* a taste of organization and political activity. Indeed it required either an act of will or supreme aloofness not to be affected in some way by the political scene. One *bestuzhevka* tells how she arrived fresh from the provinces and on the first day was stunned by a matter-of-fact request to give a few kopecks for the mother of a fellow Bestuzhev student recently hanged. The girls who chose the radical curriculum, always fewer than the academics and the uncommitted, took their mission with great seriousness, assumed the severe dress of their nihilist precursors, and often paraded the most extreme of the then current revolutionary doctrines.[33]

During the 1880's, only a handful of Bestuzhev girls were involved in radical activities, chiefly in tiny Social Democratic Circles. Through the 1890's, with the growth of the labor movement, the number steadily increased, with future Bolshevik luminaries such as Nadezhda Krupskaya, Samoilova, and Kudelli dividing their time between study and political work. The first real manifestation of unrest was the Vetrova Affair of 1897, a demonstration triggered by prison suicide of the *bestuzhevka*, Mariya Vetrova, who had burned herself to death inside her cell in the Peter Paul Fortress in protest against her treatment there. Since her only crime had been the possession of an illegal printing press, her classmates were outraged; and their demonstration, whose participants were arrested and then released, was the first defiant episode in a series which would run for the next twenty years. During the major disturbance of 1901 at Kazan Cathedral, women appeared in large numbers, were beaten, and jailed. Male radicals praised them and published a

[31] Lyudmila Vrangel, *Vospominaniya i starodavnie vremena* (Washington, 1966) 33; Valk, *Kursy*, 273; Satina, *Education*, 109–32; Dyakonova, *Dnevnik*, 14, 20, 65, 121, 145, 214, 252.
[32] *Ibid.*, 21.
[33] Proclamation quoted in Valk, *Kursy*, 67. Student life and the radical atmosphere is evoked by a number of memoirists in *ibid* and in other memoirs previously cited.

demand for sex equality in one of their bulletins. Henceforth the rhythm of female student radicalism was synchronized with that of the country at large. In 1905–1906 and to a lesser degree in 1913–1917, it assumed impressive dimensions which we shall attempt to measure elsewhere.[34]

Most of the women enrolled in the various courses—whether academics, politicals, or neither—had to think about some kind of job or profession after graduation if they wished to escape the dependent lot of a "bourgeois" wife. But educated women seeking employment continued to meet rudeness and hostility, inequality, and insecurity. And in 1904, more than forty years after Mariya Vernadskaya had uttered it, a feminist writer had to proclaim again the importance of self-respect and skilled training: "With a trade, you'll never go wrong."[35] The educational ladder for women was all but completed by 1905; but there was still a wide gap between the degree-holding woman and opportunities for employment commensurate with their education. Russian women at the highest levels were in fact notoriously over-educated in relation to the social uses made of them. Chekhov, a perceptive social observer, caught this in his portrayal of three sisters, endowed with linguistic gifts and poetic imaginations, wasting away in a provincial town.

The majority of women graduates went into teaching but only because of the barriers standing before the other professions. Schoolteachers were beset by all sorts of disabilities—social, economic, and intellectual. Until 1911, women were consigned to the lower grades or to girls' schools, a situation evoking the comment from *New Times* that "giving higher education without corresponding rights is like teaching shipbuilding to hundreds of people and then assigning them to the Sahara to apply their learning." Female teachers' wages in 1900 were about 8–20 rubles a month, lower than those of a skilled woman worker. And the teacher could rarely depend on a husband's income because in most places there was a prohibition against married teachers. In one provincial town the City Duma ordered married females to resign "so that the morals of the girl pupils are not spoiled; for pregnant women are irritable and bad-tempered." Someone replied that "old maids are even more irritable and bad-tempered" and the ruling was reversed. In Petersburg, even the conservative Peter Durnovo conceded that marriage was a private matter and preferable to illicit liaisons by women teachers, and the rule was abolished there in 1913. In other towns, authorities took special pains to regulate the private sexual life of the unmarried teacher by placing restrictions on her dress, her social behavior, and even her place of residence—to be no closer than two blocks from that of a male teacher. One provincial schoolmistress, driven to despair over a forbidden love affair with a peasant, joined him in a double suicide (1911). No wonder that young women like Dyakonova, when contemplating the future, regarded schoolteachers as no better than governesses

---

[34] A brief chronicle of these events, as they affected the Bestuzhev Courses, is Strievskaya's previously cited article in Valk, *Kursy*, 30–73.

[35] Lukhmanova, *Nedochety*, 24–39.

or kept wives; no wonder also that so many women village teachers had strong socialist leanings.[36]

To become a university instructor was much more difficult. The Russian academic establishment had recognized female ability in the highest realms of scientific work by honoring Sofiya Kovalevskaya in 1890; but she had won her academic distinctions abroad, in Germany and Sweden. At home the faculty chairs and the seats in the academies remained *Frauenrein*, even though, ironically enough, a woman had been the first president of the Russian Academy. During the Third Duma (1907–1912) masters' and doctors' degrees and membership in the Academy of Science were made available to female recipients. After 1905, women began to teach in the women's courses. In 1910 the historian Alexandra Yakovlevna Efimenko became the first woman to receive a Russian doctor's degree. She taught at the Bestuzhev Courses and produced a number of works on history and ethnography.[37]

At the beginning of the present century, non-radical women still tended to regard medicine as the most suitable and satisfying profession. This, in spite of the heavy blows that women's medical education had suffered in the recent past. When the reactionary Vannovsky replaced Miluytin as Minister of War in 1881, he ordered the women's medical courses to be transferred from the army hospital. The other ministries refused to touch them. Dmitry Tolstoy, the Minister of Education, wanted to rename all woman doctors "learned midwives" and install them in girls' schools and convents, but this proposal evoked so many coarse jokes that it was abandoned. When asked to support the opening of new courses, his answer was unequivocal: "All these suggestions about the practical significance and need for the proposed courses are based not on the actual demands of the state for such an institution, but only on the theoretical concepts and aspirations of individuals towards the so-called emancipation of women." Girls just finishing school and planning to become doctors, like the young Tyrkova, had found the doors to a medical career closed to them. As had happened with the Bestuzhev Courses, alumnae, feminists, and friends began agitating for the reopening of the courses on a new basis. A proposal presented to the State Council in 1891 was approved after four years scrutiny, with only Pobedonostsev dissenting. Finally, in 1897 the new Women's Medical Institute, located on the Petrograd Side (on the present site of the Pavlov Medical Institute), was able to open its doors. In the following decade, similar schools were established in other university towns.[38]

[36] Valk, *Kursy*, 12 (quotation), 16, 20. Numbers and wages of teachers: Johnson, *Russ. Educ. Herit.*, 195, 209. Materials on teachers' social disabilities: *ZhD* (Feb. 15, 1911) 29; (Mar. 15, 1911) 27; and (Dec. 15, 1913) 21. Dyakonova's musings: *Dnevnik*, 51–52.

[37] On Kovalevskaya: *ZhD* (June 10, 1910) 3–4. Anna Shabanova, *Ocherk zhenskago dvizheniya v Rossii* (SPB, 1912) 24, 30. On Efimenko as a teacher, see Valk, *Kursy*, 185–87.

[38] Satina, *Education*, 88–92; Zaionchkovsky, *Ross. samoderzh.*, 341, n. 16 (the quotation from Tolstoy); Shabanova, *Ocherk*, 11–13; and *idem* in *Trudy I-ogo . . . s"ezda po obraz. zhen.*, I, 81–90.

Graduates of the women's medical schools, whether Russian or foreign, were given a fairly wide scope of activity. On paper their status was almost identical to that of their male colleagues. In private practice they had the same rights of consultation, prescription, and referral to hospital; and they could work as civil servants but without rank or military obligation. In practice, the public work of women doctors was confined to pediatric, gynecological, and maternity hospitals, to girls' schools, and to the police-medical inspection apparatus that examined prostitutes. In the countryside, their roles were much broader, and the woman physician soon became a familiar type among the salaried *zemstvo* employees. Restrictions and discrimination persisted, of course, but the fact remains that Russia, with its almost 1,500 women doctors in 1910 was impressively ahead of countries like Britain, Germany, and France with only one-third that number in 1911, 1914, and 1928 respectively. What most disturbed Russia's women doctors was not that they constituted only 10 percent of the nation's doctors, but that Russia, with its 90 millions in the 1880's, possessed only 14,000 doctors, and yet the highest officials smugly claimed that the Empire had no need of additional medical personnel. This situation helps to explain why three of the four women's suffrage organizations in the years 1905–1917 were headed by women doctors.[39]

Other "free" professions like pharmacy, dentistry, and law were stormed by women in these years also, but not without the usual struggle. The very persistent aspiring druggist, A. Lesnevskaya, has left us a depressing account of her wanderings and her efforts to study and to practice pharmacy in the face of every sort of unpleasant obstacle. Fanni Shvartsman, in a highly personal memoir, *My Fate*, offers a familiar account of the young Jewish female student in pre-revolutionary Russia, making her way from the Pale to the university, and then to the dentistry courses in St. Petersburg, where she won her degree after numerous misadventures. Yet, once established in practice, Shvartsman, and others like her, were able to pursue a normal professional life until buffeted by war, revolution, and love. After 1906, with the inauguration of women's law faculties, female lawyers made their appearance in modest numbers. But there was no work for them except legal consultation, which was hard to find; one woman worked as a maid until she found a position with a railroad office. The problem was that the rules of court procedure, by omission, did not allow women to plead cases in court, though they could work behind the scenes. When the woman lawyer, E. A. Fleishits, challenged the rule, she was defeated and the Senate ruled against women, minors, and the insane as advocates in court. A bill, passed by the Duma in 1913 to rectify this situation, lingered in the State Council until 1916, when it was defeated. On

[39] A. Polyansky, ed., *Russkaya zhenshchina po gosudarstvennoi i obshchestvennoi sluzhbe* (Moscow, 1901) 1–9; Vera Mikhailova, *Russkie zakony o zhenshchine* (Moscow, 1913) 10–11. The comparative figures on women doctors are from Melina Lipinska, *Les femmes et le progrès des sciences médicales* (Paris, 1930) 153, 175, 182, 198.

the eve of the decision, according to the recollections of a Soviet woman lawyer, she and another woman lawyer visited Akimov, the chairman of the State Council, who told them that the Empress was opposed to women practising law and that he had given his word to kill the measure in the Council.[40]

A phenomenon peculiar to Russia in these years was the quickened development of women's technical education. Opposition to it ranged from quaint conservative warnings that women could not mount ladders with their long skirts to the more thoughtful notion of the liberal nationalist Peter Struve that students, women included, were becoming too specialized and vocational. The mainspring of the movement was an enterprising feminist journalist, Praskoviya Ariyan, a science graduate of the Bestuzhev Courses. With wide contacts among technical teachers and feminist fund raisers (the same familiar faces: Filosofova, Konradi, and the rest), she formed a society to raise money in 1904 and within two years had received permission to open the new school. The St. Petersburg Women's Technical Institute (1906-1924) was the first of its kind anywhere and in its first decade it graduated some fifty women architects, designers, and engineers of all sorts. The wide-eyed disbelief, the physical hazards, and the gratifying successes met by these women are the ingredients of some of the most entertaining memoirs in the history of the women's movement.[41]

Our picture of the limitations and opportunities for women in professional life would be incomplete if we did not mention journalism. In the tradition of Vernadskaya, Konradi, Likhachëva, and Evreinova, Russian women of high mettle and public spirit edited, published, and contributed to journals and newspapers in ever increasing numbers. As an occupation it required no special schooling and yet offered immense intellectual satisfaction. Of the growing number of women editors-publicists, Lyubov Gurevich, a graduate of the Bestuzhev Courses and a member of an established family of pedagogues, may be singled out. In the 1890's she became the editor and publisher of *The Northerner Messenger*. Working with Leskov, Tolstoy (who was once accused by his wife of having an affair with Gurevich) and Chekhov, she was drawn into literary criticism and into an interest in social questions. After 1905 she became an active feminist.[42]

The rapid industrialization of Russia and the increasing complexity of its society opened myriads of new opportunities for women. In St. Petersburg alone, in 1905, there were over fifty different institutions of higher learning

---

[40] A. Lesnevskaya, *Po neprotorënnoi doroge* (1901) (SPB, 1914). Shvartsman, *Moya sudba*, I. Material on women lawyers from Shabanova, *Ocherk*, 14 and Valk, *Kursy*, 148–55, 249–55.

[41] *Pervye zhenshchiny-inzhenery* (Leningrad, 1967), memoirs and historical introduction, 7–28; *Ustav S-Peterburskago Obshchestva isyskaniya sredstv tekhnicheskago obrazovaniya zhenshchin* (SPB, 1905). For other technical opportunities, see Valk, *Kursy*, 20 Filippova, "Iz istorii," 217; and E. K. Stolitsa's memoirs on agronomical training in *Bestuzhevki v ryadakh stroitelei sotsializma* (Moscow, 1969) 54–60. Struve's remarks are in *Trudy I-ogo . . . s''ezda po obraz, zhen.*, I, 76–79.

[42] *Bestuzhevki*, 187–90.

for women, offering a wide variety of courses in arts, sciences, and commerce. Even the lethargic and hostile bureaucracy recognized the usefulness of women and in 1900 the academic council of the Ministry of Education established a "section for women's professional education." By the time of the World War, a broad range of civil service posts were open to women in offices, prisons, railways, schools, and laboratories. The major difficulty remaining was that the government would often hire women in the central administration of its agencies but ban them from the provincial branches. One of the byproducts of this policy was the concentration of educated women in the two capitals, which in turn reduced the organizational problems of the women's movements which sprung up after 1905.[43]

Was there a female intelligentsia in Russia? If so, it was certainly not coterminous with the entire corps of educated and professional women whose main features we have just sketched. Aside from the apathetic and the anti-intellectual who will always be found in so large a group, it is also necessary to subtract from it the pure intellectuals and the aesthetes, whose dedication to art or knowledge left them with no inclination to contemplate the social scene or to act upon any civic impulses. A talented writer like Zinaida Gippius, except for brief voyeuristic excursions into the social realm, remained altogether alien to such concerns and, incidentally, a hostile critic of any sort of women's emancipatory movement. And Anna Pavlova—the illegitimate, half-Jewish daughter of a laundress and a soldier—gained no democratic insights from the contrast between her lowly background and the brilliant entourage that surrounded her at the peak of her dancing career. The spirit of Russian art at the turn of the century was so infused with the passion for personal expression and often with a Nietzschean contempt for the masses that it was exceedingly difficult for individuals to master the tension which might arise between social conscience and artistic self-expression. Sofya Dubnova, a socialist intellectual of the period and later a prominent Menshevik, illuminates this problem in her memoirs where she relates that the most painful dilemma for the young people of her circle was resolving the conflict between their two main intellectual interests: politics (which to them meant socialism) and the culture of the Silver Age. The two seemed to be at philosophical loggerheads on every major issue of life.[44]

The female intelligentsia was not necessarily socialist or even political; it was social (*obshchestvennaya*), outward-looking, and public spirited. Indeed it was Tolstoyan in the broadest sense of the word—personally religious,

[43] Kage, *Svedeniya*; N. P. Eroshkin, *Istoriya gosudarstvennykh uchrezhdenii dorevolyutsionnoi Rossii* (Moscow, 1968) 226. Polyansky, *Russkaya zhenshchina; Pervyi zhenskii kalendar* (to be cited a PZhK) (SPB, 1899–1916) (annual), VIII (1906) 396–98.

[44] On Gippius: Temira Pachmuss, *Zinaida Hippius* (Carbondale, Illinois, 1971). On Pavlova's origins see: R. Buckle, *Nijinsky* (London, 1971) 26–27. S. Dubnova-Erlikh, *Obshchestvennyi oblik zhurnali "Letopis"* (New York: Interuniversity Project for the History of the Menshevik Movement, 1963) 2–3.

populist, and non-violent. Its moral code and world outlook had changed little since the 1860's; it was optimistic, enthusiastic, and progressive. Turgenev, Dostoevsky, and especially Tolstoy were the favorite writers of women students, leaving Marx and Nietzsche far behind; and in the classroom, philosophy and intellectual history, having at last dethroned the natural sciences, now fed their hungry minds and nourished their burgeoning spirits.[45] The stratum of educated and socially conscious women, though tiny, was, like society itself, far too complex for any more precise generalizations. Within its breast lay deep economic and philosophical contradictions which would eventually break forth into conflicting ideologies, though long after this has occurred, the careful observer can still detect traces of a kind of moral solidarity which characterized the female intelligentsia.

2. THE SEXUAL QUESTION

Right up to the day of the Revolution, the Russian intelligentsia was always adequately supplied with "questions" or "problems" (voprosy)—philosophical issues having immediate social implications—which could lay claim to its intellectual energies and its moral concern. Early in the twentieth century, the sexual question took its place among these. Not only was there a broad range of inequities in the realm of sexual relations, both in and out of marriage, but, more important, there was widespread recognition of them. Public awareness of the problem in the 1880's and 1890's took the form of limited and discrete probings into moral irregularities and institutional inadequacies; by 1908 it had swelled to a crescendo of agonized collective criticism. In this Russia was not unique, though its approach to the problem sometimes took forms peculiar to the Russian intellectual tradition. Russia's odyssey through this most treacherous region of mankind's moral labyrinth—an odyssey the chronological limits of which are not 1900 to 1914 but c. 1890 to the mid-1930's—ought to be viewed as part of a general movement to re-examine the so-called double standard that concerned a large segment of the North European intellectual community (Germany, Scandinavia; to a lesser extent England and America) in the same period. The solutions found at the end of this odyssey would have a decisive influence on the nature of the women's liberation in Russia.

Until 1917, only two sexual institutions were recognized by Russian officialdom: marriage and prostitution. But between these two, every kind of illegal liaison flourished in all ranks of society. The privileged classes traditionally displayed a fairly tolerant attitude toward sexual vagrancy among their members, especially the males. Chekhov's "Papasha," who manages to

---

[45] On reading preferences of selected women students, see *Slushatelnitsy*, 114–18; and *Perv. zhen,-inzhen.*, 19. Figures on subject enrollments in Kage, *Svedeniya*, 8–13; and Melnikow, *Gesell. Stellung*, 126 (for Petersburg); and *Studencheskaya zhizn*, I (Jan. 17, 1910) 20 (for Moscow).

satisfy wife, maid, son, and tutor with a bit of infidelity and corruption, was a good-natured depiction of the live-and-let-live morality that prevailed in Russian society. But with the growth of cities and the burgeoning complexity of economic life, immorality became a "problem." In 1886 Vladimir Mikhnevich published a lengthy study of urban poverty, crime, and vice entitled *The Running Sores of St. Petersburg*, one of the earliest of a long line of indignant descriptions of sin in the cities. In a section devoted to "secret vice," Mikhnevich attempts, somewhat artificially, to classify the various types of women engaged in illicit relations. The author observed that among the educated classes, the good old "mistress" relationship—illegal but associated with love—had given way to the growing practice of maintaining a "kept woman" (*soderzhanka*), a genteel economic nexus hardly better than prostitution. Among the urban lower classes, free sex—symbolized by the *dushenka* or girl of easy virtue—was a way of life, though less economically motivated. By the 1890's, illegal cohabitation had become so common in the capital that parish priests were discussing measures "to combat this evil."[1]

Most people, however, were bothered not so much by the fact of fornication as by the results of it: swarms of illegitimate children. According to a study by Bernice Madison, the number averaged 111,414 between 1884 and 1892, or 268 per 10,000 births in European Russia. This was a lower rate than Europe's, but serious enough, especially in the cities where the concentration was much heavier—another sign of the coming tension between urban and rural sexual codes. Until the 1902 law on illegitimacy, there was no protection for unmarried mothers, most of whom were workers fresh from the village, or servant girls—reported as the favorite sexual partners (except for prostitutes) of a group of male students. Economic and psychological hardships imposed by society on unwed mothers led many of them to infanticide or abandonment and also helped to swell the statistics on suicides and prostitution. The unwanted children suffered even more. The network of homes and foster families built up over the years and adorned with the names of exalted patrons was so hopelessly inadequate that, according to Madison, an almost permanent death rate of 75 percent prevailed for such children! Groups of women baby-farmers—known as "angel factories"—would bring baskets full of dead and half-dead infants, choking in their own excrement, to the official shelters in order to collect the fee of two rubles per head.[2] The vicious conjunction of extra-marital love, male irresponsibility, and massive desertion of children was yet another social puzzle that the Bolsheviks would have to unravel after their accession to power.

[1] V. Mikhnevich, *Yazvy Peterburga: opyt istorikostatisticheskago isledovaniya nravstvennosti stolichnago naseleniya* (SPB, 1886) 423–30; V. V. Rozanov, *Semeinyi vopros v Rossii*, 2 v. (SPB, 1903) I, 274–86.

[2] Berenice Madison, "Russia's Illegitimate Children Before and After the Revolution;" the illegitimacy law is in *Svod zakonov*, X, 10. On student sex partners, see *Stud. zhizn*, 12 (April 1910) 11.

Birth control, both as a response to this problem and to the one of population (thus its European designation "Malthusianism") met with little success in Russia. Building on the work of Francis Place, Bentham, and the Mills, bolder spirits such as Charles Bradlaugh, Annie Besant, and George Drysdale in England and Margeret Sanger in America had transformed the idea into an international—if not quite respectable—movement, but only against bitter opposition from religious, political, and judicial forces. The topic appeared in the Russian press only after 1905 and, if we may credit a reporter from *Russian Wealth*, was a popular theme of conversation in provincial towns and among railroad passengers by 1907. In 1910 a Petersburg doctor, Karl Drexler, published an illustrated catalog of the methods known at the time, with commentary on each. Biological methods such as restraint, rhythm, and *coitus interruptus*, he dismissed as unrealistic, unreliable, and unsatisfying respectively. Instead he promoted a wide variety of mechanical and chemical means—condoms, pessaries, diaphragms, vaginal douches, and suppositories. Although the book was officially titled *How to Prevent Pregnancy in Sick and Weak Women*, the author left no doubt that he also favored birth control as a means to relieve the lot of the poor, and he reminded his readers that this was "a matter of individual conscience which permitted no outside interference."[3]

Of the various endorsements of this notion which reached the public, certainly the most far-reaching was that of Sofiya Zarechnaya, a feminist journalist, who was the first to tie it to the "woman question." Not only, she wrote, would birth control reduce the incidence of child mortality—a favorite argument among doctors—it would also free woman, if she so chose, to become the equal of man in the state. This in turn could reduce the dangers of war in two ways: First, it would pit woman's ethic of justice and love against man's ethic of violence and cruelty at the highest levels of political life; second, curtailing the number of births would make lives more precious and reduce the store of cannon-fodder (the Russian term, so much more vivid, is "cannon meat") available to the war-makers. Thus, reversing the old feminist equation of the risk of birth with the risk of battle, Zarechnaya suggested that the diminution of one would help diminish the other. She also insisted that only the woman had the right to decide about the uses of her own body and criticized the social, religious, and legal pressures that forbade the unmarried girl to have a child and constrained the married one to do so even against her will. Zarechnaya's forceful posing of the issue evoked a few murmurs in the same feminist journal, though only one (which warned that "chilling birth

[3] For a brief history of the subject, see Peter Fryer's *The Birth Controllers* (London, 1965) and an article in *Russkaya mysl*, XXXI, 7 (July 1910) 40–65. The *Russkoe bogatstvo* report is in No. 9 (Sept. 1907) 121. The sixth edition of the Drexler book is cited (the first edition has not been traced): K. Dreksler, *Kak predupredit beremennost u bolnykh i slabykh zhenshchin* (SPB, 1910) (quotation, 49). The front cover bears the somewhat more marketable title, *How to Prevent Pregnancy*. According to a clipping found inside the book, it was on sale in nine cities of the Empire.

control measures" might alienate husbands) had much point. On the other hand, Malthusianism, which had frightened many a feminist in other lands, found little intellectual support in Russia among feminists, socialists, and the public at large; and its cool reception at this time portended the very mixed welcome it would have under Soviet power.[4]

Unlike birth control, abortion was illegal in Russia. But illegal or "black market" abortions flourished nonetheless: In Moscow the number increased two-and-a-half times in the years 1909–1914; in St. Petersburg the increase was tenfold from 1897 to 1912. By that year, the medical profession became alarmed and a congress of gynecologists (one of the first in a series that would examine this problem over the next twenty-five years) heard a proposal for legalizing abortion for medical reasons. Two years later a St. Petersburg congress of criminologists, lawyers, and police officers voted three to one in favor of changing the law. Their reasons? It was medically imperative for some women; only a tiny fraction of illegal practitioners could be caught and punished; and the present law was unfair to poor, unmarried women who were often pushed into prostitution out of shame and economic hardship. The government resisted on moral grounds. The most imaginative counter-measure it could offer was a Ministry of Justice proposal to increase the punishment of both mother and abortionist to three years imprisonment.[5]

To all sexual problems the standard answer of official Russia was: marry, have children, keep a family. Indeed, marriage and the family remained the dream of most women in pre-revolutionary Russia. In a student questionnaire of 1912, only 25.1 percent of the female respondents registered their hostility toward marriage. Indifferent were 3.2 percent, most of them opposing its narrowness, egoism, "petty-bourgeois" (*meshchanskii*) character, and its subjugation of women. The great majority of young women—and a slightly larger percentage of men, incidentally—looked forward to marriage and motherhood as the natural life, some of them declaring their aversion to divorce and birth control as well. The strongest opinion voiced may have enjoyed wider support than is ordinarily imagined: "I passionately want to be a woman and a mother—both these feelings are equal in me. I will marry, even if love is not present in full measure. If the husband and wife are temperamentally compatible and understand each other, all the better. If not, they have got to get along without that. The main purpose, after all, is the satisfaction of sexual and maternal instincts and not to be completely alike."[6]

But marriage in practice, particularly when there is almost no possibility of

[4] Zarechnaya's article and responses to it in *ZhD* (Aug. 10, 1910) 10–12; (Oct. 25, 1910) 6–7; and (Nov. 25, 1910) 7–8. On the British feminists' suspicion of Malthusianism, see J. A. and Olive Banks, *Feminism and Family Planning in Victorian England* (Liverpool, 1964) 104–11.

[5] The abortion figure for Moscow is from *L'égalité de la femme en U.R.S.S.* (Moscow, 1957) 220. All other data are from *ZhD* (Jan. 15, 1912) 24; (June 1, 1913) 21; and (Apr. 1, 1914) 3–4.

[6] G. Gordon, "Brak i prostitutsiya v suzhdeniyakh sovremennoi molodëzhi," *Novaya zhizn*, (Feb. 1913) 190–205. The sample, 200, is rather small.

divorce, can be quite a different thing from the "natural" mode of life postulated by young men and women at the most idealistic time of their lives. In the villages where "the right to abuse given to the husband in marriage" prevailed, despotism, premature marriages, and infidelity on the husband's part sometimes provoked a peasant woman to murder her husband. In the cities, the causes of marital friction were diverse, though observers seemed to trace most of them to drink at least among the working classes. An endless series of pamphlets, articles, and resolutions dwelt upon vodka as the destroyer of the family. Among the intelligentsia there were both more sobriety and more equality—but by no means ideal harmony. Observers at the turn of the century tell us of problems raised by discrepancy in education between spouses, of lapses in marital communication, and of sexual ignorance and frigidity among women of the educated classes. Though the evidence is far too thin to permit anything more than speculation, it seems reasonable to suppose that the widespread agitation for divorce reform reflected an equally widespread malaise with the institution of matrimony as it was then understood.[7]

By the early twentieth century, the divorce laws had not been significantly altered. Adultery remained the only admissible ground for most Russian spouses, and it was admissible (as a crime) only with eye-witness testimony. No wonder Tolstoy's Aleksei Karenin shuddered with horror at the thought of publicly using such evidence. There were, however, ways for well-off people to produce "witnesses" and "correspondents"—a possibility hinted at by Karenin's attorney. A reform-minded writer of the period (1904) relates that it was not uncommon for clients to hire maids and manservants to serve in this capacity, thus making the divorce court "a perpetual and shameful comedy." The tortuous proceedings, involving no less than nine separate stages, well spaced by bureaucratic delays, the various liabilities devolving upon a confessed adulterer, and the expensive fees all combined to put divorce well beyond the reach of most people. And for a female defendant, the humiliating court interrogation about her intimate life was an added deterrent. Little wonder that so few divorces per year were processed.[8]

Prostitution, which had not been much of a visible issue since the 1870's, now re-emerged as a social problem. Its twin impulses were the shortcomings of the marital culture that provided the clients; and industrialization that

[7] The village expression is quoted by V. M. Khvostov in *Zhenshchina*, 465. On alcoholism and the family, see: S. Argamakova, *K voprosam etiki v sovremennom brake* (Polotsk, 1895); and *ZhD*, (Jan. 17, 1910) 3. On marriage among the educated—where the sources are very thin—see: Davydov, *Zhenshchina pered ugolovnym sudom* 25 (on inequality); Amfitreatrov, *Nestroenie*, 122–27 (on the education gap); P. V. Bezobrazov, *O sovremennom razvrate* (Moscow, 1900) 53–57 (on frigidity).

[8] The most detailed description of the stages of divorce proceedings is in Mikhailova, *Russkie zakony*, 97–103. On abuses and absurdities, see Rozanov, *Semeinyi vopros*, I, 140 and Lukhamanova, *Nedochetie*, 57–64 (quotation, 57). For more on Church law and the background of the divorce problem, see: Sposobin, *O razvode*; Filippov, "Vglyad;" and Zagursky, *Rechi*, 159–204.

brought urban migration of women and a consequent increase in the number of prostitutes. A dry medical report released in 1896 demonstrated that after fifty years of the state medical quarantine, venereal disease was spreading luxuriantly among the urban population: For the next twenty years, doctors, novelists, and publicists would flood the country with writings on the alarming spread of public vice, child prostitution, white slavery, pathological sex crimes, and venereal disease. The most obvious and measurable manifestation of the problem was the absolute growth in the numbers of prostitutes. Petersburg had between 30,000 and 50,000 prostitutes, registered and unregistered, out of a population of 1,400,000—a ratio comparable to those of London, Paris, Berlin, and Vienna. Other centers were Moscow and its satellite factory towns, the Baltic, the mining regions of the Ukraine, and the maritime cities on the Black Sea. Most of the newcomers to the occupation were peasant migrants. Greeted at railroad stations by brothel agents, young wide-eyed rustic women were easy targets for recruiters who lodged them in nearby "hotels" and promised them good jobs. The main motive pushing such women into prostitution was economic hardship or the fear of it. The arithmetic of Russian wages meant that servants and women workers could hope for 15–20 rubles a month; while even the lowest-paid whore could earn 40 rubles and a very attractive one as much as 500–700 rubles.[9]

The inner life of a Russian brothel was made public knowledge by Kuprin's sensational novel *Yama* which began appearing in 1909. Based on medical reports and firsthand accounts, Kuprin was clinically authentic in his vivid description of the devastation of human souls and bodies conducted nightly in the state-licensed houses. The alcoholism, the perversions, the beatings, the police collusion and the degradation of both client and prostitute all had their counterparts in a well-documented reality. The official image of a Russian "public house"—one of a clean, well-supervised social prophylaxis—now gave way to a far more realistic picture of a festering disease center, a nest of crime, and a prison house for sexual slaves. Beyond the licensed houses, loners struck bargains in theaters, clubs, Cafés Chantants, and in the alcoves of plush restaurants, and consummated them in bathhouses, gardens, streets, and dance studios. Most hotels, according to an observer, were "anthills of vice, swarming with secret prostitutes." The Nevsky became a fashionable haunt for wealthy men in search of women of the night. The trade became so lucrative that it attracted not only café singers, tearoom waitresses, and flower girls, but also well-bred, even titled, ladies and modestly dressed matrons who frequented the saloon cars of railway trains. A post-revolutionary investigator estimated that some 70 percent of urban men patronized prostitutes in one way or another.[10]

[9] For a detailed description of prostitution in Russia before the Revolution, and fuller documentation, see R. Stites, "The Prostitute" to appear in Rose Glickman and Richard Stites, eds., *Women in Nineteenth Century Russia*.
[10] *Ibid*.

What aroused the greatest social concern was child prostitution and white slavery, both of which grew alarmingly in the last years of the monarchy. A 1906 report entitled *Children of the Streets* was filled with sickening descriptions of tiny prostitutes and their clients. The English newspaper crusader, W. T. Stead, had once been made ill by the sight of small children chloroformed before being sexually molested by old men. Similar things were happening in Russia. In 1913, we hear of a rendezvous in Lodz where prominent manufacturers gathered to enjoy the favors of young girls; and of a Petersburg theatrical school for children used for the same purpose. Files of charity organizations bulge with cases of small girls who began a life of vice by performing "unnatural acts" upon men who paid them and gave them wine. Child seduction and recruitment helped feed the insatiable maws of the white slavers who operated almost unhindered throughout West and South Russia in a highly organized network of agents and middlemen who combed the towns, seducing and enticing girls and young women from shops, inns, factories, and railroad stations. Once recruited and given the yellow ticket, it was enormously difficult for a girl, however she protested, to escape her new profession. White slave rings (such as the one described in *Yama* which operated "from Kursk to Odessa and from Warsaw to Samara") drained the cities of the Pale of children and girls, Jews and Gentiles, who were gathered at assembly points such as Berdichev or Odessa and shipped off via Rumania to Istanbul and points east or to Argentina.[11]

In Imperial Russia, the Ministry of Interior was responsible for the control of vice and venereal disease as well as for the prevention and detection of crime. In its attitude toward prostitution, the ministry seems to have embraced the view that the prostitute herself, though an essential member of the moral community, possessed no civil rights whatsoever and certainly no right to police protection. The police not only allowed her to be abused, exploited, robbed and beaten but also through its passport system helped recruit new prostitutes and erected barriers to their escape and reform. But if we wish to judge the effectiveness of the ministry in these matters, it must be on the basis of its established goals. These were the containment of venereal diseases and the prevention of criminal activity allied to prostitution. On both counts, its record was one of dismal failure and cynical lack of concern. Shortage of doctors, abysmal organization, and corruption in the police-medical inspection apparatus (a subdivision of the Interior Ministry) all combined to insure superficial and inadequate examinations of prostitutes. Since the clients were never examined, syphillis spread. And the general malfeasance and corruptibility of the police accounted for the regime's failure to stop the growth of organized kidnapping, molestation of minors, and white slavery. It would be

[11] *Ibid.*

difficult to find a better example of institutionalized impotence of the Imperial bureaucracy in the pre-revolutionary years.[12]

Equally disquieting to educated society was the cultural and social phenomenon known as decadence. Appearing after 1905 and growing to alarming proportions in the years up to the War, it became one of the major—and to this day the least studied—preoccupations of the Russian intelligentsia. As an erotic trend in literature, decadence was part of a general reorientation in Russian thought that also witnessed the rejection of the simplistic materialism, the critical utilitarianism, and the dry atheism of the preceding generations in favor of Neo-Kantianism, art for art's sake, and a sincere if frenetic sort of mysticism. In life-styles, "decadence" meant the display of pagan, amoral, or cynical sexual views and habits. For the more conventional intelligentsia, it was a serious challenge to the ethos of nihilism that it had worked out in the 1860's. The collective pain of the intelligentsia was sharpened by the fact that decadence made its appearance at a moment of profound cultural despair among the young. After sixteen years of gradually increasing social activity and ferment, beginning with the famine of 1891 and reaching its climax in the stormy years 1905–1907, there had been a sudden collapse followed by political reaction and social immobility. It was as though the inflated spirit of the nation had been pricked like a balloon. To the dismay of the majority of the intelligentsia, literature turned inward, often indulging its private themes of sexual inversion, sadism, incest, and perversion, oblivious to the noise of public violence, murders and executions, mutinies and punitive raids that echoed across the countryside. To the sensitive social critic, such preoccupation with refined and unnatural pleasures was a feast in time of plague.[13]

The primary focus for critics of social decadence was Mikhail Artsybashev's 1907 novel, *Sanin*, a distinctly second-rate tale of lust, incest, and suicide. Some of the great literary talents of the time—Ivanov, Zinoveva-Anibal, Kuzmin, Gippius, Sollogub—also addressed themselves to these themes, often with great delicacy and taste and always with intelligence; but their efforts were buried beneath the heap of abuse that was piled on *Sanin*. Its hero exhibits many of the new values that were being set against the rather brittle morality of the older intelligentsia. By no means the sick pervert that critics of almost every persuasion proclaimed him to be, Sanin is an amoral and carnal animal, displaying not only a healthy scorn for convention and religion à la Nietzsche but also a scorn for any idea of progress or histori-

[12] For a detailed critique of official mishandling of the problem written by a Soviet doctor, see V. M. Bronner, *La lutte contre la prostitution en URSS* (Moscow, 1936) 5–13.

[13] For the flowering in Russian literature of erotic themes, see G. S. Novopolin, *Pornograficheskii element v russkoi literature (1907–1908)* (SPB, 1909), esp. chs. vii–ix.

185

cal morality. Bored as easily by Social Democrats as by Christians, he be-
friends a Jew, but encourages him to end his self-doubts in suicide. He de-
flowers an innocent but willing virgin and lusts after his own sister; but he
defends the latter when she is betrayed and dishonored by an arrogant officer.
Attractive, clever, manly, and life-loving, Sanin is the quintessential adver-
sary of hypocrisy. But the "theory" bequeathed by the novel turns out to be
no more than a thinly clad hedonism.[14]

Critics of all persuasions greeted *Sanin* with hostility. Kornei Chukovsky
called Sanin a coarse and colorless figure; and Ariadna Tyrkova complained
that his cock's crow drowned the voice of love. The Populist critic, Petrishchev, contrasted the love codes of three generations: the fathers of the
1840's who had accepted conventional marriage; the sons of the 1860's who
had taught a view of sex based solely upon love and mutual attraction; and the
Saninist grandsons who were preaching a degrading loveless sensuality.
Another Populist reviewer speculated that if a Sanin were to meet Chernyshevsky's Vera Pavlovna he would be utterly repelled by her integrity and
her impulses to liberate mankind. Gorky, Lunacharsky, and Plekhanov all
found *Sanin* repugnant, the last calling it "erotic madness." The Marxist
critic, Vatslav Vorovsky, characteristically contrasted Sanin's anti-social
nihilism with the "progressive" nihilism of Turgenev's Bazarov. An Orthodox priest expressed a concern by no means limited to the conservative
clergy when he bemoaned the dehumanizing and despiritualizing of the sex
act in *Sanin* and its hedonistic "cult of the moment." The Saninist phenomenon among other things revealed a kind of moral alliance of the "old"
nihilism against the new. Nothing shows better how potent the moral and intellectual currents of the 1860's still were; and nothing shows better the ethical solidarity on matters of sex which characterized the intelligentsia as a
whole and which transcended political differences.[15]

"Saninism" was not confined to the realm of literary polemics. It became a
style of behavior among the young in the twilight years of the monarchy as it
would again, in a different guise, among the pessimistic Soviet youth of the
1920's. In both instances, a major cause was acute *Weltschmerz* following in
the wake of intense political and social activity. During the post-1905 reaction, young people vented their blocked energies in sexual adventures and
carnal excesses, covering their compulsive behavior with the vulgar Saninist

---

[14] The novel must be read as in its entirety in order to understand its popularity at the time; but
see 15, 111, and 154 of the Berlin Russian edition (1911) for typical passages. An English edition
is *Sanine*, tr. P. Pinkerton (New York, 1932).

[15] K. Chukovsky, "Geometricheskii roman," *Rech* (May 27, 1907) 2; A. Verzhetsky [A. Tyr-
kova], "Krasnyi petukh," *Rech* (May 13, 1907) 2. The Marxist opinions are all from B. P.
Gorodetskii, *et al.*, eds., *Istoriya russkoi kritiki*, 2 v. (Moscow, 1958) II, 575–76, 595, 686. A
Soviet historian has recently dubbed *Sanin* "an offensive of The Reaction in the realm of morals":
Shishkin, *Moral*, 326–27; (Archimandrite) Mikhail, "Problema Sanina," in *Zakonnyi brak* (SPB,
1908) 1–11. A. Petrishchev's article in *Russkoe Bogatsvo*, 9 (Sept. 1907) 95–126; Peshekhonov,
"Sanin," *RB* (June 1908) 159–68.

notion of pleasure for its own sake. Saninist sex clubs sprang up in Russian cities bearing such names as The Burned-Down Candles, The Union of Beer and Freedom, The League of Free Love, and The Minute. *The Sex Market* (1908) told of a family house or love shop where people could meet casual sex partners, of sadists who roamed the Nevsky in the pre-dawn hours in search of young girls to be whipped, and of an opulent apartment, The Temple of Eros, whose orgies included men, women, and children. The saturnalia of self-gratification was accompanied by an even more depressing wave of self-destruction among the young. Suicide and sensualism, said a Kiev critic, were both "flights from life" forms of escape, and desperate responses to the apparently insoluble problems that Russian society faced as it stood amid the rubble of an unsuccessful revolution. *Sanin* was no more the cause of Saninism than *What Is To Be Done?* had been of nihilism; it merely reflected the spirit of social and psychological despair that had engulfed youth and was driving it either to self-immolation or to sexual self-oblivion.[16]

Popular fiction of the period took up the themes of the "personal" and "psychological" character of sexual relations, foreshadowing what came to be called the "glass of water" theory in Soviet times. The author of *A Base Condition* (1906) tells us of intelligent women "who find nothing more worth remembering about where, under what circumstances, and with whom they satisfied a natural function than they would about a chance dinner companion and the menu in the restaurant where they happened to dine." *Honesty with Oneself* (1912): "If you think that spiritual and physical love combined are better than merely physical love, fine. But if I find pears tastier than cherries, does that mean I should give up cherries altogether? On the contrary: the more I taste cherries, the better I shall appreciate pears." *Yama* (part II, 1914): "The desire to make love is the same as the desire to eat, drink, and breathe. . . . A physiological pleasure, perhaps stronger, perhaps keener than any of the others—but that's all." Leda, in Kamensky's 1906 tale of that name, proclaims that a woman must have the same right as a man to pursue and conquer a member of the opposite sex. In Verbitskaya's *Keys to Happiness* (1910), the heroine loves two men and sleeps with both. And Vinnichenko's heroine carries this brand of self-assertion to the limit by having her visiting cards engraved with the device: "Olga Matveevna Shcherbina-Prostitute." And yet, in the literature, as well as in real life, it is mainly the man who exalts free, physiological sex, unencumbered by tenderness or commitment; and mainly

[16] *RB*, 5 (May 1908) 104–30 and 6 (Jun. 1908) 146–75; A. I. Matyushevsky, *Polovoi rynok i polovyya otnosheniya* (SPB, 1908) 35–38, 119–29, and *passim*. Similar reports of "Free Love" leagues may be found in A. M. Bogdan-Sokolsky, *Pod maskoe* (Kiev, 1911) 63ff. Hard pornography and smutty boulevard novelettes also made their appearance at about this time: Novopolin, *Porn. element*, 226. On suicide see: N. K. Krupskaya, "Samoubiistovo sredi uchashchikhsya i svobodnaya trudovaya shkola," in *Voprosy narodnago obrazovaniya* (Moscow, 1918) 171–81 (see 171); and *ZhV*, (Nov. 1910) 219–22; "Begstvo ot zhizni," in *Zhenskaya mysl* (*ZhM*), 4 (Jan. 1, 1910) 10–15.

the man who makes the greatest gains on the pleasure market—a situation which throws glaring light on the relation between sexual freedom and women's rights. The implications of that relation would not become fully clear until the Revolution had proclaimed them both.[17]

The fullest responses to the "sexual question" were offered by the feminists and the socialists. But the range of opinions between them was sufficiently wide to warrant comment. Some conservatives simply affirmed the traditional family as the only path to contentment and salvation. "In these times of skepticism and disillusionment," said an 1888 guide to family life, "let this book teach you that there is still happiness in the world, and that family life is the most natural life for man—and an abundant source of joy." Priests ground out sermons on women and the family "from the Christian point of view." Others addressed themselves to the noxious effects of unchecked passion. In a marriage manual of the age, a doctor admonished his readers that "one must not give in to immoderate desires for pleasure; one must carefully avoid allowing one's sexual relations to fall under the sway of the ruinous force of voluptuousness and not let it become a habit." In 1907, a woman published a sustained assault on the male libido, alleging that man's passion was responsible for all sexual miscreance, including women's. Tolstoy's enormously influential story, *The Kreutzer Sonata* (1889) popularized the conviction that lust was the root of all evil. The idea was endorsed by swarms of conservative moralists.[18]

Liberals and moderate reformers felt that more than Biblical platitudes and outraged moralism was needed, and that greater equality in the family was the proper solution to the problem. A woman writer in 1904 called for marriages in which "love would be accompanied by comradely relations and would develop into worthwhile, enduring relationships." A religious writer wished to graft onto the Biblical ethos the notion of a "family composed of equals, enjoying similar education, mutual respect, and comradely relations." And pro-

---

[17] Discussion of *Base Condition* in Kuzmin, *Zhenshchina*, 29–35 (quotation, 34–35); V. Vinnichenko, *Chestnost s soboi (povest)*, Munich, 1914, 133; *Yama* (Kuprin, *Sob. soch.*, V) 234. The purely sensual view of sex was also nothing new to Russian literature: e.g., "Vodka is for drinking, sturgeon—for eating, women—to be with, snow—to walk in" (Chekhov, *Sob. soch*, VI, 219; "Pripadok")—but appeared with greater frequency and audacity in post-1905 writings. "Leda" reviewed in Kuzmin, *Zhenshchina*, 8–13; Verbitskaya's story reviewed in *ZhV* (Dec. 1910) 266–68; *Chestnost*, 84.

[18] *Semeinaya zhizn v eya radostyakh i pechalyakh: pravila zhiteiskoi mudrosti dlya muzhei i zhën* (SPB, 1888), dedication; similar views were voiced in a translation of the writings of George Peadbody, a Harvard professor of Christian ethics: *Iisus Khristos i sotsialnyi vopros* (Moscow, 1907) 104–54; Nikanor (Bishop of Ufa), "Ideal zhenshchiny-khristianki," *Pravoslavnoe obozrenie*, III, 11 (Nov. 1882) 578–93 and M. Galakhov, "Zhenskii vopros, ego prichiny i otsenka s khristianskoi tochki zreniya," *Khristianskoe chtenie*, 215 (1903) 94–107, and 216 (1903) 217–34; V. Silov, *Zhenshchina zamuzhem*, 2d ed. (Moscow, 1897) 54–58 (quotation, 54); M. N. Anzimirova, *Prichiny nravstvennoi fizionomii zhenshchiny* (SPB, 1901); M. G. Bolkvadze, *Ne razvrashchaite zhenshchin! ili "vragi chelovechestva"* (SPB, 1908); A. Kh. Sabin, *Prostitutsiya* (SPB, 1903) 213–29.

fessor Khvostov, while clinging to a juridical monogamy, warned that the preservation of the family would require at the least a reduction in the husband's power, an end to the double standard, respect for the wife's individuality, and—most critical—an easing of the divorce laws. But these ideas, reasonable as they were, were only minor variations on the themes first enunciated by Mikhailov back in 1860 and were considered truisms by most of the intelligentsia.[19]

The religious thinker, V. V. Rozanov, rejected both the ostrich-like piety of the conservatives and the pallid liberalism of the reformers and attempted to refashion the family through the affirmation of religious sensuality. As George Kline has pointed out, Rozanov challenged the asceticism of the New Testament and its most powerful defender, Tolstoy, and sought to revive what he believed to be the intimate connection between sexuality and godliness as contained in the Old Testament. Marriage, he wrote, was a sacrament; but unlike Eucharist, confession, and the others, where the receiver stands passively before the Church, marriage makes the receivers the active agents who consummate the sacrament. Thus carnal intimacy in marriage is really beyond Church and law, and is solely the affair of the partners and of their God. When the sanctity of marriage, he said, was broken by infidelity, the marriage ceased to exist whatever the Church and courts may say. "From the first transgression, the marriage is a corpse" and divorce proceedings merely its funeral rites. In his long, rambling, and beautifully written *Family Question in Russia* (1903), Rozanov shows a deep concern with replacing the empty forms of marital stability—outward, dry, and negative—with a positive loving relation built on the twin foundations of the Orthodox faith and the natural sensuality of human beings.[20]

The sexual left, which in principle included most of the intelligentsia, went beyond efforts to preserve the juridical family under God and continued to insist upon the kind of free love that was taught in the 1860's. The historian of Russian pornography, Novopolin, remarked in 1909 that "to enter Russian society propagating the theory of freedom of feelings, freedom of love, freedom of motherhood is like knocking at an open door." But since these ideas were under debate in Europe, they became suitable public issues in Russia too in the last years before the Revolution. By around 1900, the Swedish feminist, Ellen Key, had elaborated a program of abolishing the double stand-

[19] Lukhmanova, *Nedochety*, 37; A. V. Govorov, *Zhenskii vopros v svyazi s istoricheskimi sudbami zhenshchiny* (Kazan, 1907) 73; Khvostov, *Zhenshchina*, 447–56, 465–76.

[20] Rozanov's liberal views of women's education (*Sem. vop.*, II, 431–39, 456–58) won him the ironic sobriquet "the Alexander the Great of the Woman Question" from the corrupt reactionary, Prince Meshchersky. On Rozanov and prostitutes, see the interesting memoir by D. Lutokhin in *Vestnik literatury*, 4–5 (1926) 5–7; George Kline, *Religious and Antireligious Thought in Russia* (Chicago, 1968) 36, 64–68. For Rozanov on marriage: *Sem. vop.*, I, 72–81 and *V mire neyasnago i ne reshennago*, 2d ed. (SPB, 1904), 97–136. The quotation on divorce: *Sem. vop.*, I, 781. A valuable commentary on Rozanov's place in the intellectual currents of the time is D. V. Filosofov, "V. V. Rozanov," in *Slovo i zhizn* (SPB, 1909) 139–61.

ard by granting to unmarried women the right to love, to sexual experience, and to children in or out of marriage—a right not only tolerated but also supported by society. Key became the major voice for sexual emancipation in Scandinavia and her formulation of the "right to motherhood" also was received sympathetically in Germany where Ruth Bré, leader of the Motherhood Movement, demanded the unconditional right and the material means for every woman to become a mother, claiming this to be the only means of abolishing prostitution, venereal disease, and the horrors of old maid life. All this was faithfully covered in the Russian press, even though the essential points had been fixed long ago in the public mind. As "decadent" behavior began to spread, advocates of "free love" took pains to distinguish it from petting, flirting, cynicism, and promiscuity, stressing the lofty ideals of nineteenth-century free love.[21]

Conservative opponents of free love were rarely able to detect these nuances and continued to call it destructive and criminal or to liken it to the mating of dogs in the street. But even some liberals felt that a full acceptance of free love by society would be harmful. Anna Milyukova, the feminist, announced in 1908 that "the propagation of the idea of free marriages in a broad sense can only lead to seduction . . . in a society where neither the children nor the mothers are protected by law." Another feminist observed that many morally retarded men supported the idea of free unions only to turn them into casual liaisons. Liberal society was still groping for the "correct" solution to the sexual problem but had reached no clear consensus. Only the far right and the far left had definitive answers. The conservatives had certainly failed to face the problem realistically much less to solve it. The Marxists would have their chance after 1917. History would show, in those stormy years of revolution and civil war, that some of the doubts of the liberal intelligentsia about free love as the obvious solution to women's sexual emancipation were well founded.[22]

[21] The fullest outline of Ellen Key's ideas is in *Kaerlighed og aegteskab*, Danish tr. Z. Petersen (Copenhagen, 1905), esp. chs. iii, v–ix. The Russian translation is *Lyubov i brak* (Moscow, 1907). Ruth Bré's program is found in her *Das Recht auf die Mutterschaft* (Leipzig, 1903). Russian commentaries: E. Lozinsky, *O nastoyashchem i budushchem zhenskago dvizheniya v svyazi s problemoi tselomudriya i zadachami materinstva* (N.p. 1903 or 1904); *ZhV* (Oct. 1905) 296–300; M. Eletsky, *Svobodnaya lyubov* (SPB, 1908); Kollontai, *Sots. osnovy*, 202–208; *ZhD* (Sept. 15, 1911) 1. M. Volokov, *Emansipatsiya zhenshchin i svobodnaya lyubov* (SPB, 1906); *ZhD* (Aug. 1, 1914) 10–12, (June 1, 1915) 12–14, and (Nov. 1, 1914) 1–3.

[22] E. de Cyon [Tsion], an émigré conservative publicist, *Nihilisme et anarchisme* (Paris, 1892) 92–93; E. M., *Golos russkoi zhenshchiny* (SPB, 1906) 57; *ZhM*, 4 (Jan. 1, 1910) 8–9.

VII

The Feminist Movement

La femme a la droit de monter sur l'échafauld; elle doit avoir
également celui de monter a la tribune.
—OLYMPE DE GOUGES, *guillotined November 3, 1793*

1. THE OLD FEMINISTS

Although the issue of women's emancipation had occupied the attention of
the Russian public for some fifty years before 1905, there was no genuine
women's movement until that year. And then, true to the ways of Russian
social history, two separate movements for women appeared almost at once: a
feminist women's suffrage movement, and a socialist one opposed to it. Both
had a pre-history beginning in the 1890's, but were largely unknown to each
other until 1905. The feminists, before 1905 continued and expanded the traditions of social activity laid down in the 1860's and 1870's. After 1905,
when the women's suffrage movement arose, the older feminists persisted in
their stress upon the non-political aspects of the women's struggle and either
rejected the political movement altogether or made up its conservative wing.
The difference in outlook and behavior between them and the new generation
of 1905 was certainly great; and many in both groups would have spurned the
use of the word "feminist" either for themselves or for the movement as a
whole. But, while allowing these differences, we must not permit ourselves to
violate the useful conventions of comparative history by stressing only the
unique. And there is sufficient unity in the efforts of the non-socialist women's
rights activists for us to speak unhesitatingly of a feminist tradition running
from 1860 up to the Revolution of 1917.[1]

A very proper women's manual of 1901, *Woman in Family and Social Life*,
offered charity and education as the only appropriate public activities for the
lady outside the home. These remained, indeed, the principal concerns of the
older feminists. There were of course "charity ladies" of the purer sort, quite
alien to feminism, who pursued philanthropic activities either out of a genuine
concern for the poor, a desire for social prominence, or both. They could be
found on the council of the very undemocratic Union of Charitable Organizations and Leaders, hobnobbing with the Dowager Empress and other promi-

---

[1] On the currency of the word *feministka* as of 1911, see *ZhD* (Jan. 1, 1911) 17–18.

nent figures, and "promoting charity as a way of life." But some charity enterprises catered particularly to women. In 1896 a *Dom Trudolyubiya* (best rendered as "Center to Promote Diligence") for "educated women" was added to the seven others that served as workhouses for orphans and the poor in Petersburg. Founded on the principle that "the only rational form of charity is to provide the needy with *paid employment*," the Center was located in a fairly well-to-do quarter and catered to middle-class high school or institute graduates unable to make a decent living. The Society for Assisting Young Girls, by contrast, was designed specifically for servants, shopgirls, and working women, with the aim of protecting them from the harmful moral atmosphere of their natural milieu. By 1906, some 2,000 women and girls were regularly visiting the nine Petersburg chapters of the Society to receive lessons in reading, stitching, and religion.[2]

The most important of the strictly charitable enterprises for women was the Russian Society for the Protection of Women founded in 1900. Headed alternately by two princesses, Evgeniya Oldenburgskaya and Elena Saksen-Altenburgskaya, it was well staffed by titled patricians and by wealthy philanthropists like Baron Gintsburg, Countess Panina, and the Tereshchenkos of Kiev, as well as representatives of the intelligentsia, the world of culture, the professions, and a number of feminists. The Society's headquarters on Nadezhdinskaya Street, as well as the homes of many of its members, lay in that enchanted triangle of Petersburg north of Nevsky Prospect. The central budget, which was strictly managed, drew the bulk of its income from church and personal contributions and disbursed various sums to its branches in the capital and eight other cities. Like most such organizations, the Society was designed to be run efficiently rather than democratically, and though a general meeting of its 250 members was to take place twice a year, it was usually faced with a fixed and concise agenda.

After 1905 the Society became one of the chief lobbyists against prostitution. But its political tactics, not to mention the substance of its reform program, remained exceedingly cautious. For instance in 1913 the Society agreed that when a project was being considered by the State Council, it ought not to bother itself with independent and parallel deliberation of the project.[3]

---

[2] *Zhenshchina v semeinoi i sotsialnoi zhizni*, ed. I. P. Goldberg (SPB, 1901) 1–20, 447–80. The charter of the *Vserossiiskii Soyuz Uchrezhdenii Obshchestv i Deyatelei po Obshchestvennomu i Chastnomu Prizreniyu* is in TsGIAL, f. 1075, op. 2, d. 25 (quotation, 3). Description and location of archival items will be found in the bibliographical section at the end of the book. For the Dom Trudolyubiya, see *ZhD* (Aug. 1899) 116–20 (quotation, 16) and *Zhenskii almanakh*, 142–63. The *Obshchestvo Popecheniya o Molodykh Devitsakh* is described in *ZhD* (Apr. 1899) 152–56 and by Kollontai (who substitutes the word *Rabotnitsakh* for *Devitsakh*) in *Sots. osnovy*, 177–79.

[3] Information on this society is drawn from its program, rules, financial reports, and other documents in TsGIAL, f. 1335, op. 1, d. 5 (1900), d. 7 (1900–1901), and d. 10 (1905) and from *Rossiiskoe Obshchestvo Zashchity Zhenshchin v 1913 godu* (Petrograd, 1914). Commentary by Kollontai in *Sots. osnovy*, 179.

Opportunities for women in philanthropy abounded in pre-revolutionary Russia. Charities, public and private, mutual aid societies, funds and scholarship committees sprang up at the beginning of the century as educational and professional opportunities for women expanded. All provided a modicum of training in organization and finance. But the energetic flurry of women so engaged by no means attracted universal approval.

> We watch the meetings of boards, where speeches are delivered, and the committees where men and women sit wearied and indifferent, ignorant of affairs, discussing regulations and paragraphs; we read reports prepared by paid officials, we hear the magniloquent verdicts of self-appointed pedagogues on systems of instruction; we attend, O height of hypocrisy! the charity bazaar, where the lady stall-keepers, who sacrificed not a penny, are dressed in costumes costing double the profit of their sales. And these we call the works of Christian charity!

These are the words not of some sardonic Social Democrat, but of Pobedonostsev, a powerful government official and the patron of a number of charities; and his nebulous but decidedly negative view of "charity ladies" was certainly shared by many in all ranks of society. That many women held it as well was to become apparent within a few years of Pobedonostsev's remark.[4]

By 1900 almost all of the original feminists of the 1860's had left the scene. Trubnikova, beset by illness and economic difficulties, had withdrawn from feminist activities after 1881, spent some time in a mental hospital, and died in 1897. Nadezhda Stasova busied herself helping women students up to the day she died in 1897. Engelhardt had also withdrawn from active work and Mariya Tsebrikova was in exile for her brash letter to the Tsar.[5] Only Anna Filosofova remained to greet the new century. Like most of her generation, she had given up civic pursuits in the 1880's. But with the death of her husband and the revival of women's education in the 1890's, she became active again in the last of the pre-1905 feminist organizations, the Mutual Philanthropic Society. Filosofova devoted her remaining years to uniting all women's clubs in Russia and affiliating them to a feminist international organization. As a result, the political struggle largely bypassed her (she was out of the country in the crucial years 1905–1906) and her last major act was the decorative one of presiding over Russia's own Women's Congress of 1908. When she died in 1912, she was widely honored.

[4] The Pobedonostsev quotation is from *Reflexions*, 107 (and see 335–36 for a similar comment). For descriptions of smaller charities and their leaders: Polyansky, *Russkaya zhenshchina*, 291–331; *Pervyi zhenskii kalendar* (to be cited as *PZhK*), XIII (1911) 104–18; and *Zhenskii almanakh*, 144–47.

[5] *ZhD* (Dec. 1899) 35–37; *ZhD* (Apr. 1–15, 1912) 1–2.

Vladimir Solovëv, in his seminal article "The Idea of Superman" (1899), divided contemporary Russian thought into three streams: economic materialism, daemonic "supermanism," and passive moralism. Marx, Nietzsche, and Tolstoy. Anna Filosofova was, like many of her feminist colleagues, essentially a "woman of the 1860's" and had no understanding either of Marx or of Nietzsche. Upon symbolism, decadence, and Saninism—indeed upon the whole new world of ethical and aesthetic values being shaped before her very eyes by Dmitry Filosofov and Sergei Diaghilev (her son and nephew)— she gazed with embarrassed incomprehension. Hers were the simple and vibrant moral ideals of the 1860's; and to her, Tolstoyanism, with all its vagueness and contradictions, appeared to be the only intellectual system that contained them. For Marxism she had no use, and in fact looked upon all political parties as "a herd of bison" almost indistinguishable from one another. Although she joined the Kadets as a concession to modernity, she left politics wholly to her closest associate Anna Shabanova, expending her own energy on good works and the job of unifying Russian women. In her last years, at odds with the times, she sought further spiritual solace in Theosophy.[6]

Filosofova's chief collaborator in the Philanthropic Society and a myriad of other activities was Anna Nikitichna Shabanova (1848–1932), a somewhat older contemporary of Figner, Perovskaya, and Zasulich. Like them she was gentry, well educated, and possessed a police record for political activities— in her case as a member of the Ivanova Dressmaking Workshop (chapter V, 1). But unlike them Shabanova walked a path from radicalism through medicine to charity and feminism. After six months in prison she was cured of radicalism forever and pursued medical studies in Helsinki and then at the new Women's Medical Academy from which she graduated as one of the first class. Her teaching, writing, and clinical work on children's diseases put her into contact with the philanthropist, Princess Oldenburgskaya, and thus into the world of the feminists. In 1895 she helped to found the Mutual Philanthropic Society and became its real leader, though always tactfully sharing the honors with Filosofova. In 1905, she established the Society's Electoral Department that addressed itself to women's suffrage. After Filosofova's death, Shabanova became the sole leader of the Society until its demise after the October Revolution. She was the first of a number of women doctors to take up a commanding post in the feminist movement, showing, if nothing else, that medicine could lead as naturally to feminism as it could to radicalism.[7]

[6] Tyrkova, *Filosofova*, 259–429. For more on her views on Diaghilev and her son, see Sergei Lifar, *Serge de Diaghilev: sa vie, son oeuvre, sa légende* (Monaco, 1954) 42–43 and Arnold Haskell, *Diaghileff* (London, 1935) 31–44. Appreciations and obituaries: *ZhD* (Apr. 1, 1913) 22; *Otchët o deyatelnosti Rossiiskoi Ligi Ravnopraviya Zhenshchin za 1913 god* (SPB, 1914) 33–34; all of *Sbornik: Filosofova*, II.

[7] The only reliable biographical sketch of Shabanova seems to be E. D. Zabludovskaya, "Odna iz pervykh zhenshchin vrachei-pediatrov v Rossii: A. N. Shabanova," *Pediatriya* 6 (1957) 71–78. Those in *Sovremenniki: albom biografii*, 2 v. (N.p., 1909–1910) II, 456–57 and *ES* (Granat), XL (7th ed., 1938), 31 contain minor errors. See also *ZhD* (Jan. 14, 1910) 5.

The Mutual Philanthropic Society was by far the most important feminist institution prior to 1905 and marked the transition between the older feminism of the nineteenth century and the suffrage movement of the twentieth. It was to be modelled on the American club "for the intellectual and moral improvement of women" and unencumbered by the presence of men. But a women's club, properly speaking, was not acceptable to the Ministry of Interior that licensed all private organizations and could close them at will, so the founders had to content themselves with the clumsy title of Russian Women's Mutual Philanthropic Society. Difficulties plagued the early years of the Society. At its birth, cartoons, anonymous letters, and dirty stories circulated about its members, while its first headquarters on Pushkinskaya—a block away from the notorious Ligovka—was nicknamed The Terem and Bald Mountain (the witch's haunt of Russian legend). Then its first years were marked by internal strife, petty squabbles, and "egoism" as Shabanova herself called it. The main cause of this, we know from other sources, was the resentment of certain "democratic feminists" toward what they took to be the autocratic manner of the leadership.[8]

In spite of its limiting title and government strictures, the Society managed to function as a genuine women's club, concerned at first with charity, organization of women, education, and culture, then later with a broad spectrum of political and social problems. Its organization was standard for the time: a General Meeting elected by the members at large; a Council (*sovet*) chosen by it with regular and candidate members; and various special commissions for charter revision, budget, and so on. And its actual functioning, undescribed in any charter, was also standard: self-perpetuating leadership, cooptation, flow of initiative and control mostly from the top. Assisting Shabanova and Filosofova were gentry women (though no titled ones), widows of medium-high officials, *intelligentki*, and professionals. The Charity Division maintained a network of day nurseries, shelters, dormitories, and cheap eating places for educated and professional women tied down by children or in financial doldrums. Such eminently practical activity must account for some of the prestige which the Society, in spite of its political conservatism, continued to enjoy among the female intelligentsia.[9]

Much of Shabanova's, and all of Filosofova's, attention came to be riveted

[8] A brief sketch of the Society's history is in "Rossiiskoe Zhenskoe Vzaimno-Blagotvoritelnoe Obshchestvo (osnovano 25 maya 1895 g.)," a 1915 speech in TsGIAL, f. 1075, op. 2, d. 53. Comments on its birth by Ida Posnansky (Ida Poznanskaya, a doctor and a member) on 89–90 of Ishbel Aberdeen, *Women in Social Life* (London, 1900)—a speech at the 1899 International Women's Congress; and by Dyakonova, *Dnevnik*, 52–53.

[9] Details of the administration are from the following documents: "Polozhenie o detskikh ochagakh" (1901); "Ustav RZhV-BO v S. Peterburge" (1902); "Instruktsii dlya soveta RZhV-BO v S. Peterburge" (1903); "Instruktsiya Blagotvoritelnago Otdela RZhV-BO v S. Peterburge" (1908); "Proekt ustava RZhV-BO" (1913). They reside in TsGIAL, f. 1075, op. 2, d. 3, 14, 16, 22, 40 respectively. Kollontai's critique in *Sots. osnovy*, 175–77. For the (hardly surprising) organizational similarity among women's associations, see Polyansky, *Russ. Zhen.*, *passim*.

on the growth of a conservative world feminist organization, the International Council of Women (ICW). Founded in Chicago in 1893, the ICW held congresses every few years in the major cities of Europe. It was largely based on the Anglo-American idea that women's charity and benevolent groups throughout the world ought to organize and communicate with each other. Political and economic issues were ignored. When Lili Braun of the German Socialist Party challenged this narrow focus and raised the problem of protection of women's labor, the ICW leaders countered with a resolution on "complete freedom of work" and neglected to invite socialist delegates to their next congress. In fact the program of the ICW became so laden with trivia (the joys of gardening, pocket money, and luxurious breakfasts at Windsor Castle) that by 1904 the more political non-socialist women formed their own International Women's Suffrage Association (IWSA). These two groups plus the women's division of the Second (socialist) International constituted the three women's internationals of the pre-war period. Russian women were to affiliate with all three and their choice of affiliation is a key to their position on the ideological spectrum of Russian feminism.[10]

When the Mutual Philanthropic Society leaders began displaying an interest in international affiliation, the ICW was the only important world-wide women's group in existence. Shabanova and others attended the early congresses as guests and their glowing description of Filosofova's great pioneering work over the past generation led the ICW to appoint her Honorary Vice President and to invite her to form a National Women's Council in Russia. Such a council could only be recognized if it was elected by all the women's groups in the country. Typical of a national council in a small European state was the Danske Kvinders Nationalraad formed in 1899 of fifty-five women's organization with some 80,000 members. By 1908, there were twenty-three such councils, including ones from tiny new nations like Bulgaria, sending delegates regularly to the ICW congresses. Filosofova maintained a constant stream of petitions to the Ministry of Interior for permission to form a national council. Personal vanity was probably at stake here too; one guesses from her correspondence that the old lady's dream was to host a congress of the ICW in Petersburg and take Lady Aberdeen (its President) to a reception at the Winter Palace. The government consistently refused. A national network of women formed "without distinction of religion or nationality" and with foreign connections was not the kind of idea that tsarist bureaucrats could swallow. When

[10] Aberdeen, *Women in Society*; *Novoe slovo*, II (Feb. 1896) 90–91; and see the next note. Kollontai's criticism of the ICW, though heavy-handed, is on the mark (*Sots. osnovy*, 90–95, 236–52).

[11] A. Shabanova, "Vospominaniya o zhenskom mezhdunarodnom kongresse v Berline," *Novoe slovo* II (Nov. 1896) 82–93; *ZhD* (Jan. 1, 1913) 28 and (May 15, 1913) 22. Samplings of Filosofova's efforts may be found in TsGIAL, f. 1075, op. 2, ed. khr. 2, 24, 1, 3, a report on the 1908 Geneva Congress of the ICW, a draft charter for a Russian National Council of April 26, 1908, a brochure *O natsionalnykh sovetakh zhenshchin* (1910), and a letter to the Gradonachalnik

Filosofova died, Shabanova continued the fruitless campaign. But Russia remained formally outside the ICW, though bound closely by mutual sympathy and regular communication.[11]

Other public causes that attracted the feminist-minded woman may be summed up quickly. First among them was Temperance. An uneasy combination of hostility to alcoholism (Alexander III) and a thirst for more state revenue (Witte) led to the gradual imposition of a government vodka monopoly in the years 1890–1901. But drunkenness did not slacken and its growth alarmed every element of society from the socialist to the priest. Government and Church responded with a network of tearooms and lecturers called Guardians of Public Sobriety. Feminists followed this pattern with their own temperance societies. Mme. Chebysheva-Dmitrieva, a colleague of Shabanova's in the Mutual Philanthropic Society, established a Society for the Struggle Against Alcohol, and proclaimed that alcohol was the chief obstacle to women's emancipation and happiness. Mme. Baudouin de Courtenay, a Polish resident of St. Petersburg, founded her own temperance organization as a part of the Ethical-Social Movement. Her circle of 170 men and women maintained a tearoom, but when soldiers began invading the premises and insulting the teetotalers, the government closed the circle on a formal pretext. By 1913 half the state budget was generated from vodka sales and the problem was only solved (temporarily) by the Tsar's 1914 prohibition decree.[12]

Health and dress reform had less attraction for Russian women than it seemed to for those of the West, though physical culture clubs like the Women's Health Preservation Society did appear occasionally. Dress reform programs, like the assault on the bone corset, aroused no enthusiasm; nor did the bicycle. In any case, nihilist austerity had been the fashion for decades among the female intelligentsia.[13] On the more serious side, each new year saw the birth of societies for winning and protecting the rights of women in the various professions. Scholarship committees appeared in the wake of each newly opened women's educational institution, the oldest of these celebrating its twenty-fifth anniversary in 1903. Thus in every major city and in many towns, women's committees, *ad hoc* groups, and charities sprang up to serve as schools of organization, finance, and communication. No central body and no journal served as a hub for these. The only common reading matter for

---

of St. Petersburg, April 13, 1910, asking for approval—all authored by Filosofova. The Danske Kvinders Nationalraad is described in *Raunkjaers Konversations Leksikon*, 13 v. (Copenhagen, 1948–1957) VII, 383.

[12] Theodore Von Laue, *Sergei Witte and the Industrialization of Russia* (New York, 1903) 102–103; V. B-t [Bat] "Alkogolizm i borba s nim," *Mir Bozhii*, VI (June 1897) 49–78; E. A. Chebysheva-Dmitrieva, *Rol zhenshchin v borbe s alkogolizmom* (SPB, 1901); Rom. Boduende-Kurtene [Baudouin de Courtenay], "Iz oblasti sovremennago etiko-sotsialnago dvizheniya," *SZh* (May-June 1908) 20–25.

[13] *Ustav Obshchestva Okhraneniya Zdorovya Zhenshchiny v g. S.-Peterburge* (SPB, 1898); *ZhD* (Aug. 1899) 208–25; *ZhV* (Jan. 1905) 15–17. Kechedzhi-Shapovalov, *Zhen. dvizh.*, 190–203.

feminist minded people was the annual *First Women's Calendar* (1899–1915?), a mish-mash of useful information edited by Praskoviya Ariyan, the energetic organizer of women's engineering courses.[14]

The young, sensitive, intelligent—and basically man-hating—student Dyakonova, who gave freely to narrow feminist causes, perceived that this impressive looking array of organization was hardly sufficient to free woman as long as she lacked political power. She despised "the official barracks atmosphere which men with such needless artificiality introduce everywhere" and recognized that power, connections, and the chance for a brilliant future belonged only to them. Without political power, she wrote, women must remain hopelessly shunted along fenced roads, slaves, squirrels on a treadmill.[15] It was precisely this feeling of inadequacy and frustration that would push women of the younger generation into a struggle for political rights within a few years.

2. THE SUFFRAGE STRUGGLE: 1905-1907

In 1904, on the eve of a revolution, Alexander Amfiteatrov observed that ten years earlier only a few hundred Russian women dreamed of equality, while at the time of his writing there were tens of thousands. If the first part of his statement was an understatement, events were soon to bear out the truth of the second. The Russian women's movement synchronized closely with the rhythm of the nation's social history. In times of general apathy, the feminists languished in charity work and internal dialogues; in times of stress they were galvanized into political activity. In the winter of 1904–1905, the ingredients for such a burst of activity were present: the organizational skills and self-confidence developed over the years by the old feminists; and the dissatisfaction of the new generation of feminists with mere organization and philanthropy. Close at hand was a stirring example—the suffrage movement in Finland. There the history of women's emancipation had followed the general continental pattern: philosophical probing in the literature of the 1840's, educational victories in the 1870's, "social work" at the end of the century. The conservative Finnish Women's Association (from 1884) and the more militant Women's Rights Union (from 1892) differed in their stress on votes for women but, because of the unusual turbulence of the Finnish nationalist movement in 1898–1906, a large degree of unanimity among women was achieved. Their solidarity was expressed in a resolution on women's suffrage adopted by a congress of women on November 8, 1904, and their continued agitation led to their enfranchisement in a year and a half.

---

[14] *PZhK*, 16 v. (SPB, 1899–1915). Two other publications merit brief mention: *Zhenskoe delo* (not to be confused with the journal of the same name published 1910-1917) (SPB, 1899–1901); and *Zhenskii almanakh* (Odessa, 1901).

[15] Dyakonova, *Dnevnik*, 285–97 (quotation, 295).

This display of solidarity and agitational skill was not lost on the Russian feminists who awaited only an opportunity. It came in January 1905.[1]

During the winter, the Union of Liberation and other liberal groups invited women to their political banquets, though sometimes only as decoration. A month after Bloody Sunday, a large group of women, 468 members of "Moscow society" published in *Russian News* a lament for the violence in St. Petersburg and for the bloodshed in the Far East. At the end of the same month, some 30 women liberals of Moscow declared the formation of a national women's political organization, The All-Russian Union for Women's Equality (*Vserossiiskii Soyuz Ravnopraviya Zhenshchin*) whose general aim was "freedom and equality before the law without regard to sex." Its first act was to petition the City Duma and the local *zemstvo* for voting rights in those bodies. Next it formed branches all over Russia and within a month a solid organization had arisen in Petersburg that then became its center. The leaders lived in both capitals and were mostly women journalists, notably Zinaida Mirovich-Ivanova and Anna Kalmanovich from Moscow, Lyubov Gurevich and Mariya Chekhova from St. Petersburg. Their ranks were strengthened by the presence of two female members of the circles that became the Kadet Party—Anna Milyukova and Ariadna Tyrkova. Perceiving that "the old order was in disarray," the Union called the first political meeting for women in Russian history on April 10 in the capital. It attracted about 1,000 visitors, including some hostile socialists and workers, and laid the groundwork for the Union's first congress.[2]

By May, twenty-six local chapters had sent 70 delegates to the congress which was held in Moscow, May 7-10. Milyukova presided over the 300 recognized delegates who included some of the older feminists from the Mutual Philanthropic Society as well as some who would later break away to establish their own group. The charter adopted by the congress provided for an elected central bureau, autonomous local chapters, and special committees for politics, education, labor, and organization. The program of the Union, specific and far-reaching, demanded: immediate convocation of a constituent assembly elected by the so-called seven-tailed suffrage (equal, direct, secret, and universal, without distinction of nationality, religion, or sex); national au-

[1] Amfiteatrov, *Nestroenie*, 78. On Finland, see N. Mirovich (this and Z. Mirovich are pseudonyms for Zinaida Ivanova, one of the leaders of the Women's Union), *Pobeda zhenskago dvizheniya v Finlyandii* (Moscow, 1907).

[2] The best history of these events is the brief but indispensable account by N. Mirovich: *Iz istorii zhenskago dvizheniya v Rossii* (Moscow, 1908) (see 1-5). An even shorter, but still useful, report was written by Vera Figner, who followed the campaign from abroad, in International Institute of Social History, Amsterdam (IISHA) Brupbacher Archive, folder "Wera Figner," mss. letter in French from Figner to Brupbacher (n.d.), 7 (to be cited as Figner Letter). The Moscow letter is from *Russkiya vedomosti* (Feb. 4, 1905) 3. The meeting is described in *PZhK*, VIII (1906) 332 and in S. Serditova, *Bolsheviki v borbe za zhenskie proletarskie massy (1903-fevral 1917 g.)* (Moscow, 1959) 54-55. The most exhaustive treatment of the suffrage movement in English is by Rochelle Ruthchild, "The Russian Feminists, 1905-1917" (Ph.D., University of Rochester, 1976).

199

tonomy; equality of the sexes before the law; equal rights of peasant women in any land reforms; laws for the welfare, insurance, and protection of women workers; equal opportunity for women; co-education at every level; reform of laws relating to prostitution; abolition of the death penalty. The crucial question of whether to adhere to the narrow struggle for female suffrage exclusively or to join in the liberation movement was thus resolved emphatically by this program and by the Union's official declaration: "a change in women's status is impossible without the general political liberation of our country."[3]

The Women's Union now set out energetically to win support from the professional and trade unions which were then joining forces in the Union of Unions. The women were invited to join the Union on the basis of their program, but when they appeared at one of its meetings, members of its central bureau exclaimed in surprise: "But there must be some misunderstanding." The women continued to attend meetings and to bombard the members with their propaganda until at last in July 1905, the Union of Unions agreed to endorse the Women's Union as one of its own. One of the few who voted against the proposal was the future Kadet leader, Paul Milyukov. The Women's Union also asked the City Duma and *zemstvo* organizations to be allowed to vote in local elections and later, when the word "parliament" was in the air, sought their support on the national suffrage issue. In at least three dozen cities women organized meetings, signed petitions, and presented them to various political and public bodies throughout the spring and summer. In response to all this—often sincerely and spontaneously—local ruling bodies (especially urban ones) passed resolutions endorsing women's suffrage. But the usually liberal congresses of *zemstvo* and city leaders resisted. In April they simply received the petition without comment or action, though some delegates privately voiced hostility or amused contempt. The next congress in July was more polite: its bureau replied to inquiries from the Women's Union that it supported the *principle* of women's suffrage but not as a practical issue at the moment. This was an opinion widely shared by Russian liberals and it came to be their favorite argument against putting women's suffrage in their programs.[4]

The word "inopportune" became a hated one among the feminists, and some of them were never able to forgive the liberals for what they took to be paternalistic cant. The notion of tactal timing in the emancipation of this or that rightless segment of the population was hardly unique to Russian

[3] Mirovich, *Iz istorii*, 6–10; *ZhV*, I (Nov. 1905) 342–43; *PZhK*, VIII (1906) 332, 386–89.

[4] Mirovich, *Iz istorii*, 11; Figner Letter, 9; Kollontai, *Sots. osnovy*, 348–50. For the programs of the Unions: L. [Yu.] Martov, P. Maslov, A. Potresov, *Obshchestvennoe dvizhenie v nachale XX-go veka*, 4 vols. (SPB, 1909) II, 171–79. For agitation among the provincial town councils and *zemstva*, see: *ZhV* (May 1905) 143–48; *PZhK*, VIII (1906) 316–35; Kollontai, *Sots. osnovy*, 305–309, 343–44. And at the congresses: Mirovich, *Iz istorii*, 11–16; Figner Letter, 9; Kollontai, *Sots. osnovy*, 344–46; *ZhD* (Oct. 1910) 2 (obit. of Muromtsev); and Nathan Smith, "The Constitutional-Democratic Movement in Russia, 1902-1906" (Ph.D., University of Illinois), 382–94.

liberals—or to liberals in general. In Europe one could always find figures even on the far left offering the same argument against enfranchisement campaigns for women until after "bigger" things were settled. This infuriated the Women's Union, which asked, in a stiffly worded note, what guarantees women had that the urban-*zemstvo* leaders would ever try to realize such a principle as women's rights. Monarchs and privileged orders, they said, always urged the underprivileged to be patient. But if the next congress did not support women's suffrage, the letter warned in angry cadences, the Union would have to look for support among the extreme parties of the working class. The Women's Union soon learned through a questionnaire that other fears were at work: fear of peasant women voters, of female conservatism, and of the unnerving effects of politics upon the gentle sex. But the delegates to the next congress of City and *zemstvo* government, unnerved perhaps themselves by the unrelenting barrage from women lobbyists, finally gave in and approved a project giving both sexes the right to vote and hold office. In the end, the Union and most other feminists found themselves in the liberal camp even though many disliked the sour taste of male liberalism in action.[5]

The Union for Women's Equality, though unquestionably the largest and most vigorous feminist group operating in 1905, was not the only one. In April 1905, Anna Shabanova steered the Mutual Philanthropic Society into Russian politics. She called on the membership to work for women's participation in any national assembly that might be convoked by the government, explaining that men could not be trusted to look after the rights of women in the future political order. Throughout the year she and her colleagues unleashed a blizzard of paper upon official Russia, ignoring the parties, the unions, and the liberation groups, and concentrating their persuasive techniques upon those in power. Before the year was out Shabanova's words had reached the Premier (Witte), the State Council, all the Ministers, fifty-one Governors, forty-six Marshals of the Nobility, scores of other officials, hundreds of *zemstva* and City Dumas, and thousands of private and public organizations. Her requests and questionnaires all dealt with the possibility of women receiving the vote. But her efforts were futile, and the Society, though caught in the spirit of the times, remained pretty much on the margin of the active suffrage struggle for the next two years.[6]

[5] Mirovich, *Iz istorii*, 12–18; Figner Letter, p. 9; Kollontai, *Sots. osnovy*, 346. In rejecting the idea that women were more conservative than men, some feminists appropriately alluded to the great revolutionary tradition among Russian women and—less appropriately—tied their suffrage cause to that of the Figners, the Bardinas, and the Perovskayas. A cartoon of the period linked the scaffold to the ballot box by showing Sofya Perovskaya dangling from a rope while a suffragist spoke from the tribune of parliament, and was captioned by the words of Olympe de Gouges in 1792: "If woman has the right to mount the scaffold, she has the equal right to mount the tribune." The cartoon is reproduced in the illustration section of this book. See it and the accompanying article in *PZhK*, VIII (1906) 335–46.

[6] Anna Shabanova, *Ocherk zhenskago dvizheniya v Rossii* (SPB, 1912)—the standard history of the Mutual Philanthropic Society—16; *PZhK*, VIII (1906) 326–27, 389; Kollontai, *Sots. osnovy*, 303. An example of one of Shabanova's letters (among many others) is in TsGIAL, f.

In December the third and last of the feminist groups of 1905–1907 was born under the leadership of Dr. Mariya Ivanovna Pokrovskaya (1852–?) of St. Petersburg. An 1882 graduate of the women's medical courses, Pokrovskaya, like many of her colleagues, had been drawn to the problem of women's inequality through her social-medical work with children, the poor, and prostitutes. In 1904 she had founded a journal, *The Women's Messenger*, which devoted itself to these problems. As a member of the Mutual Philanthropic Society, Pokrovskaya found the tactics of the Women's Union too militant and those of the Society too apolitical, so at the December 15 meeting of the latter body she introduced the idea of a women's political party. Finding no support among the leaders there, she and a handful of supporters established a Women's Progressive Party (*Zhenskaya Progressivnaya Partiya*) that held its first meeting early in the following year and adopted a broad political platform: a "democratic constitutional monarchy" with the usual civil rights; family equality in financial and parental matters; liberalization of divorce and legitimacy laws; abolition of state-licensed prostitution; labor reforms; equal rights to land for peasant women; co-education; and an end to militarism.[7]

The broad sweep of this program was opposed by some of the "purer" feminists whose views had been voiced earlier by Praskoviya Ariyan in *Women's Messenger*: "Many people think that women's interests are too narrow," she wrote, "and so would like to see women in the ranks of those who fight for the general [*obshchechelovecheskiya*] interests. But such people fail to see that the private struggle of small groups with their own demands, aspirations, and ideals of society and humanity really contribute to the realization of common ideals." But Pokrovskaya's wider view prevailed and the Progressive Party, like the Women's Union, subscribed to the "liberation" movement—at least in theory. Unlike the Union, however, which admitted and cooperated with men, Pokrovskaya's party excluded them. "Supporters of united action with men in the struggle for women's rights lose sight of the fact that in many resolutions and projects of the future political order, women's rights are completely omitted," wrote one of Pokrovskaya's adherents. And she herself warned members of the new party that cooperation with men would mean advantages for men alone. The question of a united front of the sexes was to become one of the major issues of Russian feminism.[8]

Politically, the Women's Progressive Party stood about midway between the effervescent militance of the Union for Women's Equality and the cautious conservatism of the Mutual Philanthropic Society. Always impeccably legal in its activities, the Party repudiated revolution and violence and adhered to

1075, op. 2, N. 17. M. Bubnova of the Society claimed that it and not the Union was the first into the field in 1905, a claim easily demolished by Olga Volkenstein: *SZh* (Jan. 1909) 22–24.

[7] Pokrovskaya's birth date provided by the bibliographer of the Saltykov-Shchedrin Library in Leningrad. On the Party: *ZhV* (Jan. 1906) 26–29 and (March 1906) 90–91.

[8] Ariyan: *ZhV*, (Aug. 1905) 239–41; Gorizontova, supporting Pokrovskaya, *ibid.* (July 1905) 194–97; Pokrovskaya: *ibid.* (Mar. 1906) 65–69.

the tactic of rapid, but peaceful, improvement through lawful means. But it boasted a social dimension as well. Dr. Pokrovskaya herself believed in a vague kind of socialism compounded of the European principles of 1789 and the Russian traditions of the 1860's, though she wore this "socialism" as lightly as did the Western feminists their Christianity, and in practice was opposed to strikes. Yet the Party differed from its "bourgeois" counterparts in the West by the detailed attention that it gave to women workers, calling not only for general factory reform but specifically for women factory inspectors, a ten-month fully paid pregnancy leave, nursing facilities in the factories, and equal wages for equal work. The Women's Progressive Party was one of those Russian liberal groups whose outlook was far more social than their presumed opposite numbers in Europe.[9]

In the Manifesto of October 17, the Tsar had made a qualified promise to give the vote to those previously deprived of it, and many women had hoped that they would be among the favored. The mood of disappointment was deep when, on December 11, 1905, the government announced that the electorate for the new parliament (the Duma) would not include "persons of the female sex." But since the Manifesto had also suggested that the new Duma would take up the question of broadening the suffrage, the feminists now set to work to find out where the new political parties stood on the issue. These ranged from Tolstoyans and anarchists on one side to the extreme monarchist groups on the other. Of them, only three of the major parties mentioned women's suffrage: the Social Democrats (Bolshevik and Menshevik), the Socialist Revolutionaries, and the Constitutional Democrats. The Marxist parties endorsed women's suffrage as a matter of principle along with universal suffrage, and never as a separate issue. But both the Socialist Revolutionaries and the Kadets had some initial problems over the issue.[10]

The Socialist Revolutionary Party, established some five years earlier by Dr. Gershuni, Viktor Chernov, Breshkovskaya, and others, saw itself as the heir of the *narodnik* traditions, and it looked with hostility upon sexual discrimination. When Chernov finally set down the first draft of the Socialist Revolutionary program in 1904, he included a clause on universal suffrage "without distinction of sex" as a matter of socialist principle. However at the congresses of the Peasant Unions—upon whose constituency the Socialist Revolutionaries heavily relied—some voices of opposition were heard. A few insisted on giving village women only "active" rights (i.e., the right to vote and *not* to be elected). Proponents of full equality for women exhibited an impressive array of evidence that village women were competent members of the village community. At one of the congresses, several peasant women appeared as delegates, decked out colorfully in national costumes. In the end,

[9] In addition to references in the two preceding notes, see: *ZhV* (June 1906) 175–79; Kollontai, *Sots. osnovy*, 100–101, 333–35.

[10] *ZhV* (Jan. 1906) 1; L. Velikhov, *Sravnitelnaya tablitsa russkikh politicheskikh partii, 3d* ed. (SPB, 1906).

the Peasant Union joined the intellectual-led Socialist Revolutionary Party in endorsing political equality for women. This explains the fact that the Trudoviks, independent Socialist Revolutionaries or non-party socialists in the Duma who held Socialist Revolutionary views, became the first champions for women's rights in that body.[11]

The Kadets were more deeply divided and owed their eventual adoption of a women's suffrage clause largely to the efforts of two women, Anna Milyukova and Ariadna Tyrkova. Milyukova (née Smirnova, 1861–1935), was the daughter of the rector of the Moscow Theological Academy. Her struggle to study and to escape the life of a priest's wife led to a family drama reminiscent of the 1860's. She studied history at the Guerrier Courses and there met Milyukov whom she married. Milyukova acquired her interest in the woman question from a circle of Bulgarian feminists whom she met when her husband was teaching in Sofia. At the first congress of the Kadet Party— much to the chagrin of her husband and the amusement of the delegates—she led the forces favoring women's suffrage. Milyukov was strongly opposed on the grounds that it would alienate peasant voters. According to Kollontai, Struve also opposed the measure, employing the curious argument that it would be unjust to enfranchise Russian women since Muslim law denied the same right to women of the East. Milyukova's resolution to include the words "regardless of sex" in the appropriate place in the platform won by two votes. Her husband won approval for a footnote which explained that support of women's suffrage was not binding on members.[12]

Tyrkova came late to the cause of women's emancipation. She was born in Petersburg in 1869 to an old Novgorod landowning family and was a cousin of the revolutionary, Sofiya Löschern von Herzfeldt. But her childhood, though filled with heroic "daydreams" and admiration for the Girondistes, betrayed no deep radical commitment. Frustrated in her plans to become a doctor by the closing of the women's medical courses, she enrolled in the Bestuzhev Courses. At the same time, she married and divorced soon afterward; she subsequently married the English journalist, Harold Williams. Tyrkova always remained cold to Marxism, though as she tells us, all her closest school friends were married to sometime Marxists: Lida Davydova to Tugan;

---

[11] *SZh* (June-July 1907) 9–11 and (Feb. 1908) 13; *RM*, XXVII (Nov. 1906) 144 note; *PZhK* VIII (1906), 392; Mirovich, *Iz istorii*, 29–30. The Socialist Revolutionary program is in *Polnoe sobranie podrobnykh programm russkikh i polskikh politicheskikh partii*—hereafter cited as *Programmy*—(Vilna, 1906) 105–12. The semiofficial Socialist Revolutionary view on women's rights was composed by Chernov's colleague and coeditor, Rusanov [N. Kudrin], *O ravnopravnosti zhenshchin* (SPB, 1905).

[12] A. Zhikharëva, "Anna Sergeevna Milyukova," *Poslednye novosti*, April 5, 1935 and the following Sunday; Smith, "Constitutional-Democratic Movement," 466–68; Kollontai, *Sots. osnovy*, 351; *Programmy*, 68–76. Gessen and Nabokov, supporters of Milyukov on this issue, walked out during the vote thus causing their colleague's defeat: I. V. Gessen, "V dvukh vekakh: zhiznennyi otchët," *Arkhiv russkoi revolyutsii*, XXII, 205.

Nina Gerd to Struve, and Nadya Krupskaya to Lenin. Through Williams, Struve, and Prince Shakhovskoi, she was drawn eventually to liberalism and had several brushes with the police for appearing in demonstrations and smuggling in *Liberation* from Europe. But up to 1906, Tyrkova showed no sympathy for the women's cause as such because, as she tells us, she considered herself equal to men already. A meeting of the Women's Union left her unimpressed, and when practically commanded by her acquaintance Olga Volkenstein to join, she refused.[13]

Tyrkova's view of things quickly changed, however, when at the second (first legal) Kadet congress in January 1906 she learned that she and other women were not considered equals by their political colleagues. Milyukov, in a serious effort to erase the offending clause inserted by his wife at the last congress, made another speech, this time alluding to the low cultural level of peasant women. He was strongly seconded by a Kazan Tatar who informed the delegates that Muslim women did not want the vote. Tyrkova, who had never read a thing on the woman question, rose to her feet and instinctively presented the standard counter-arguments. She was followed by Milyukova and then by the gentle and esteemed Professor Petrazhitsky whose support of the women's suffrage clause won the day for the feminists. But the Kadet Party remained divided on the issue until after the First Duma. The four other tiny liberal parties, while evincing an interest in legal and educational equality, made no mention of female suffrage in their programs. Tyrkova now joined Milyukova in her work, both as voice for the feminists among the Kadets and as an agent for the Kadets among the feminists. It was at least partly due to them that the women's suffrage movement became largely Kadet in its sympathies.[14]

The Octobrists clearly opposed women's equality, though their program was silent on the issue. When Zinaida Mirovich, a pro-Kadet member of the Women's Union, asked permission to speak on women's suffrage at one of their meetings, the Octobrists flatly refused. The party also circulated an anti-Kadet brochure accusing liberals of Jesuitical manipulation of women for political purposes. The brochure also spoke of the deep psychological gulf between sexes, and of the special female capacity for great love and for great cruelty. When confronted with the issue individually, according to Mirovich, Octobrists usually offered the more chivalrous explanation: "Europe does not have it yet." Of the seven other moderate conservative parties clustered around the Octobrists, only one, The Union of Peaceful Reconstruction, demanded equality of sexes before the law. Three mentioned improvement of

[13] Ariadna Tyrkova-Vilyams, *To, chego bolshe ne budet* (Paris, 1954) for her early years and *Na putyakh k svobode* (New York, 1952) for the years up to 1914. See 1–233 *passim* and especially 216–17 for her first encounter with the feminists.

[14] *Ibid.*, 234–43 and the author's perceptive comments on Milyukov's attitude to women, 240, 410. Programs of the smaller liberal parties in *Programmy*, 50–60, 76–79.

working conditions for women; the other three said nothing at all. None mentioned the suffrage question. These parties and all those to the right of them had no female members.[15]

The program of the ultra right Russian Assembly whose motto was "For Faith, Tsar, and Fatherland," was too cluttered with praise for autocracy, church, and gentry and with attacks upon the Jews to leave any space for comments on women. The same thing held for the Russian Narodnik Non-Class Union. The Monarchist-Constitutionalists (Tsarists) opposed the four-tailed suffrage as "absolutely impossible" for Russia. The Fatherland Union refused to believe that all Russians, even males, possessed any understanding of politics, and for good measure added that the schools should teach respect for the family as well as for church, country, and law. Thus stood the Russian parties on the eve of the election to the Duma.[16]

The suffragists were not happy with the small base of party support for their program. The Union soon found itself torn between the socialists and the Kadets. In the heat of the revolutionary upsurge of spring and summer, it had wooed the "liberation movement" and all opposition parties. But the autumn shattering of the nation-wide united front of public opinion affected the feminists as well. A schism arose in early October. The question of whether or not to support the so-called Bulygin Duma with its narrowly restricted suffrage divided the assembly into "boycotters" and "burrowers," the latter hoping to use any kind of parliament as a means for further extension of the suffrage. After the October Manifesto widened the suffrage for the new Duma, the two wings revealed a deeper difference and became transmuted into pro-socialists and pro-liberals. "If our Union wishes to remain close to life and to the struggle, and if it wishes to be a women's rather than a ladies' organization, it must learn how to broaden its efforts and it must encounter the woman worker directly," proclaimed the new program hammered out by the pro-socialist wing. It also passed a resolution forbidding Union members to join any party that did not demand women's suffrage. Until January 1906, with the revision of the Kadet program, this meant only the Socialist Revolutionaries and the Marxist groups. After the Kadets made the support of women's suffrage binding on their membership, many Unionists turned to them in relief, while the left wing of the Union chose the Trudoviks as their champions in the Duma. Pokrovskaya and Shabanova were even less inclined to support the socialists, and their groups endorsed the Kadets as the least radical of the pro-feminist parties.[17]

The troublesome issue decided, the suffragists threw themselves energeti-

[15] Two articles by Mirovich in *RM*, XXVII, 3 (Mar. 1906) 100–104 and XXVII, 4 (Mar. 1906) 206–10. The other parties: *Programmy*, 19–50.

[16] *Programmy*, 3–19.

[17] Mirovich, *Iz istorii*, 18–21, 30–31; Figner Letter, 9; Kollontai, *Sots. osnovy*, 96 (the quotation from the new program), 309–11, 336–40; Kollontai, *Iz istorii dvizheniya rabotnits v Rossii* (Kharkov, 1920) 13; Serditova, *Bolsheviki*, 22.

cally into the election campaign and deluged Russia with books and brochures on the woman question. Female volunteers supported candidates and agitated alongside them in the hustings. They organized meetings, raised money, and helped count returns. The suffragists and their allies regained the verbal militance that had been theirs in the previous summer. Some factory women, having caught the spirit, appeared at the polls and demanded the right to vote and interfered with the voting. In the provinces, some enterprising women even managed to vote in place of men.[18]

On election day, March 16, 1906, the Moscow branch of the Women's Union issued the following statement:

> Citizens! We the women of Russia, who chance to be living in this great epoch of Russia's renewal, and who have more than once demonstrated our undying love for the Fatherland, feel at this moment with special intensity the bitterness of being without rights, and we warmly protest being excluded from taking part in decisions which concern us. Though bearing full responsibility and liability before the law for our actions, we are deprived of our rights. Therefore we appeal to your conscience and honor and demand—not request—recognition of civil and political rights equal to yours.[19]

The quotation is revealing in a number of ways. It repeats, in a more frenetic and expectant context, what Mme. Destunis and other Russian women had said on the eve of serf emancipation five decades earlier. Indeed it voices the very feeling that had given the first vigorous impulses to feminists almost everywhere in Europe two or three generations before: a fear of being left behind, floating in the wake of "great events"; and the urgent desire to "play a role" in society and to be taken aboard the swiftly moving ship of state. Less obvious, but audible enough behind the sharply imperious tones of the demand, is also the theme of loyalty in return-for-rights that would become the dominant theme—played fortissimo—in the feminist patriotism of World War I.

After the election the feminists kept the pressure on through the work of the Agitational Commission of the Women's Union, which, in techniques of propaganda if not in aims, showed marked similarity to the more famous Zhenotdel of post-revolutionary Russia. It drafted appeals to public leaders, Duma deputies, and party officials; it secured endorsements from literary and cultural leaders; and in general it endeavored to give the impression to all who could read that women's suffrage was one of the foremost issues of the times. But the Union went beyond the limited appeal of the printed word. In the capital it established four women's political clubs, one of which became a meeting place for feminists, workers, trade union people, and socialist politicians.

[18] *SZh* (June-July 1907) 5–7; Tyrkova, *Na putyakh*, 257: Kollontai, *Sots. osnovy*, 314–15.
[19] Mirovich, *Iz istorii*, 25–27.

Even more impressive was the sending of agents into the villages to agitate among peasant women. Neither the Populists nor the famine volunteers and other village social workers of recent years had been able to make much contact with peasant women. Now feminists from the city arrived to agitate among them and to persuade their husbands to support equality for their wives. And they met with a surprisingly successful response. From the provinces of Tambov, Tula, Yaroslavl and Tver came reports of village women insisting on equal political representation.[20]

Some feminists invaded the cloakroom of the Duma itself, adding a festive air to the scene, and acting as though they owned the Tauride Palace—at least according to Tyrkova who, as a Duma reporter, felt perhaps somewhat superior. Bernard Pares, who was transparently hostile to them, recalled how one day the lobby was "raided by suffragettes, short-haired young ladies in spectacles, most of them very puny looking." One of them cornered a peasant deputy from Tambov and queried him about women's suffrage. " 'Give us a little time,' he answered, 'we have only just got here ourselves, and when we have had time to find our feet, we'll give you some rights.' 'Give?' said the young lady indignantly: 'we mean to take them.' " The peasant then disclosed his deeper sentiments and replied ("kindly" according to Pares): " 'Look here, let me give you a piece of advice. You get married: then you'll have a husband and he'll look after you altogether.' The lady was furious but speechless."[21]

As hopes for a women's suffrage bill from the Duma began to fade, the feminists strove for unity at a meeting of members of the Union, the Women's Progressive Party, and the Mutual Philanthropic Society. But this meeting (May 1906) was punctuated by quarrels. Pokrovskaya advised the feminists to punish the Kadets by withdrawing from the party if it did not mount a suffrage bill. Von Rutzen, titular head of the Union, vigorously supported the Kadets. The socialist women present heaped ridicule on the entire issue, yelling "We don't need paper resolutions." Feminists with socialist sympathies had to defend feminism itself against "the smirks and guffaws" of the Social Democrats and at the same time had to ward off the proposals of the "narrow feminists" who wanted to abandon the general struggle in favor of a purely women's effort.[22]

What was happening in the Duma? The first item of business of the new body was to draft a response to the Address from the Throne. Drafted in committee by Kadet deputies, it dealt with the abolition of archaic privileges and the establishment of equality before the law. When it was reported out on May 2, the Trudovik, Ryzhkov, moved to amend by including a demand for

---

[20] Mirovich, *Iz istorii*, 27–54 (especially the documents); Kollontai, *Sots. osnovy*, 23–24.

[21] Tyrkova, *Na putyakh*, 287; Bernard Pares, *My Russian Memoirs* (London, 1931), 113.

[22] *ZhV* (May 1906) 153–55; Kollontai, *Sopts. osnovy*, 311–14.

women's suffrage in the Response. "We have forgotten," he said, "that a son of a slave-woman cannot be a citizen." In this he was echoed by a half-dozen more Trudoviks and one Kadet. But three other Kadets opposed, one on the grounds that the Duma could not know whether or not all Russia really wanted women's suffrage. The non-party peasant Kruglikov put it more bluntly: "Our women are not concerned with universal suffrage; our women look after the household, the children, and the cooking." The motion was defeated. The Response was amended in committee, however by adding the words italicized in the following clause: "Abolition of all disabilities and privileges occasioned by class, nationality, religion, *and sex.*" Even this was challenged by a Kadet deputy from Minsk, but the revised passage and the Response passed.[23]

On May 15 a group of 111 deputies signed a declaration concerning the equalization of rights of peasants, nationalities, underprivileged classes, and women. The eminent Polish jurist, Lev Petrazhitsky, an ardent adherent of sexual equality, headed a subcommittee on women's rights that was eagerly assisted by lobbyists from the Women's Union and the Mutual Philanthropic Society. During the June debates on this issue, Petrazhitsky gave the main report, speaking eloquently in support of civil, economic, educational, and political equality for women. His main opponents, aside from the silent, sneering deputies on the right benches, were Count Geiden of the Octobrists, who opposed the project on "practical" grounds, and Maksim Kovalevsky, a brilliant scholar, who could find no better argument than the suggestion that Russia would have to draft women into the army if they insisted on equality. The droll Kruglikov, whose previous remarks had evoked a sharp letter to the Duma from Samara peasant women, amused the deputies with his homespun wit. "The peasant lives, ye see, by God's law," he said. "And the Lord made Eve to be Adam's helper and not his equal. And Paul said 'Let the wife fear her husband' (Laughter and applause)." Petrazhitsky's project was referred back to committee for more work. A month later, the Women's Union presented him with an elaborately worked out legislative project. But the Duma was dissolved two days later.[24]

The suffragists largely marked time for the next seven months and then re-

[23] All the speeches on the woman question were excerpted from the records and published as *Zhenskii vopros v Gosudarstvennoi Dume* (SPB, 1906). See 5–21 (Ryzhkov's speech, 7; Kruglikov's, 17).

[24] *Ibid.*, 22–58 (Kruglikov's remarks, 42–44). Petrazhitsky's speeches were also published separately: *Rech Petrazhitskago* (SPB, 1907). Scholars who have no access to these should see *Gosudarstvennyaya Duma: stenograficheskii otchët* (SPB, 1906), cols. 1006–10, 1117–21, 1058–65. The Samara letter is printed in *Gosudarstvennaya Duma v Rossii v dokumentakh i materialakh* (Moscow, 1957) 180–81. Both its substance (a vigorous denial of Kruglikov's opinion that peasant women did not want the vote) as well as its style make it almost a certainty that it was composed by a feminist. For reactions of the suffragists to the Duma: Mirovich, *Iz istorii*, 33–34; Figner Letter, 10–11; Shabanova, *Ocherk*, 17–18; Pokrovskaya, *Zashchitniki i protivniki ravnopraviya zhenshchin v Pervoi Gosudarstvennoi Dume* (SPB, 1907); *SZh* (June-July, 1907) 3–4; and Kollontai, *Sots. osnovy*, 357–61.

peated their efforts of the previous year. After the election of the Second Duma in February 1907, the Women's Union mounted an intensive lobbying campaign among Kadets, Trudoviks, Social Democrats, Socialist Revolutionaries, and even Muslims whose Duma fractions were lobbied by teams of Unionists. The Kadets promised to support "the sacred cause"; so did the Trudoviks, the Socialist Revolutionaries (who had boycotted the first Duma), and some Muslims who favored votes for non-Muslim women. The Social Democrats, however, were indifferent. "The woman question," said the Bolshevik deputy Aleksinsky, "will be resolved only with the final victory of the proletariat."

The Russian feminists, like their counterparts elsewhere, had an inordinate faith in the power of petition and spent much of their energies in gathering signatures. In this they were extremely successful, both in numbers and in variety of signatories. Petition forms were mass-mailed, placed in journals, and passed out to thousands of women and men. Young peasant women gathered names in their villages; a Petersburg carter filled a large sheet with Avdotiyas, Lukas, and Trofims from his own courtyard; another worker obtained the signatures of eighty-four laundresses. In all, the monster petition presented to the Trudoviks contained over 26,000 names. But once again, the Duma was dismissed before the substance of the petition could reach the floor.[25]

In terms of concrete results, the Revolution of 1905–1907 had brought precious little to Russian women, except consciousness and organizational activity. "Her legal position had not changed one iota," observed Anna Shabanova. "She was neither recognized as a citizen nor granted a human right, but remained as of old at the washtub while the golden fish concealed herself in the depths of the blue sea."[26] The reference to Pushkin's wonder-granting golden fish was not merely poetic. The friends of feminism were to be largely absent from the next Duma; and many enthusiasts for women's suffrage lost interest after the curtain of political reaction descended upon Russia. Nothing fails like failure, and the suffragists themselves retreated glumly into rhetoric. Not until 1917, when it was far too late, would the suffrage movement reach such a level of activity as it had reached in these years.

3. THE SUFFRAGE STRUGGLE: 1908–1914

When the women's suffrage movement entered the doldrums at the end of 1907, its three main branches were still in existence. But the largest and most important of them, the Women's Union, collapsed the following year and brought the whole movement into a serious state of decline. This was partly

[25] Figner Letter, 11; *SZh*, (June-July, 1907) 8–9; Shabanova, *Ocherk*, 18; Kollontai, *Sots. osnovy*, 318–19.
[26] Shabanova, *Ocherk*, 18.

because of official persecution and assaults by the Social Democrats, as well as a lack of leadership and lack of unity. These latter factors had been at work from the very beginning, but were partially obscured by the euphoria of the Revolution and were never seriously analyzed by the leaders themselves. At least six different approaches to women's emancipation in the movement at large, including two conflicting socialist views which will engage our attention a bit later, may be detected. The four that divided the Women's Union lay upon two continua: one measuring class cooperation and the other, for want of an adequate term, cooperation between the sexes.

Kadet women like Milyukova and Tyrkova, who applauded cooperation in both areas, devoted their main efforts to their party, the former through Kadet clubs and the latter as a member of the central committee and head of its press bureau. Though they donated time and energy to women's affairs as well, they believed that the problem could only find a solution in a liberal Russia led by Kadet forces, men and women. Another woman close to Kadet circles held a view essentially identical to theirs. This was Ekaterina Kuskova, whose precise position in Russian politics is impossible to define, unless one employs the rather unsatisfying term "democrat." She had been a Populist, a volunteer to fight famine, a Marxist (infamous in Bolshevik annals as the author of the well known "Credo"), a liberationist, and a Kadet (and has been identified as a Freemason as well). The revolutionary years drew her to feminism, though her remarks on the subject disclose neither originality nor excessive excitement. Being, in her Russian way, both a socialist and a liberal, Kuskova found more satisfaction in the men-and-women led Cooperative Movement than in the women's movement *per se*. And so three politically talented and influential women remained on the fringe of the suffrage movement.[1]

Within the Union itself, the liberal or non-socialist tendency came to prevail, though its leaders insisted on a more specifically feminist approach than that offered by the Kadets. A founder and President, L. N. von Rutzen (fon Ruttsen)—wife of a high Petersburg official—was a staunch Kadet, but lent her energies to the Union and to a kind of consciousness-raising club for men and women. Mariya Chekhova, teacher and editor of the Union's journal, *Union of Women*, voiced both sides of the liberal feminist view in her first editorial: "This journal will be devoted to problems related to the struggle for women's equality and chiefly for her electoral rights as the first requirement for her emancipation." Most outspoken of the purer suffragists was Zinaida Mirovich (1869–1913), a Moscow translator and critic of European letters, who led the Union into the International Women's Suffrage Alliance. That body, skillfully directed by the cautious Anglo-Saxons, Carrie Chapman Catt

---

[1] Tyrkova, *Na putyakh*, 290–407. Tyrkova's feminist activities play a minimal part in her memoirs. An example of Kuskova's feminist writing is "Zhenshchiny i ravnopravie," in *SZh* (Dec. 1908) 1–3. See George Katkov's brief comments on her role in the Revolution in his *Russia: 1917* (New York, 1969) 168, n. 2, 169.

of the United States and Millicent Fawcett of England, had been founded in America in 1902 on the principle "that the ballot is the only legal and permanent means of defending the rights to 'life, liberty, and the pursuit of happiness' pronounced inalienable by the American Declaration of Independence and accepted as inalienable by all civilized nations." In 1904, the IWSA held its first congress (in Berlin); in 1905, the Russian Union was invited to join; and in 1906, a Russian delegation made its first appearance at the third (Copenhagen) congress. Mirovich headed the delegation and held the congress spellbound as she related the recent events of the Russian revolution. Though far bolder than the old ICW, the IWSA was in fact the right wing of women's suffrage by 1906 and remained aloof from universal suffrage movements, from the militant "suffragettes," and from the organized working class. Mirovich and her followers in the Union upheld these views within the Russian feminist movement.[2]

A more interesting, though far less typical, feminist view was that of Anna Kalmanovich, one of the most active publicists of the Union. Unlike her colleagues, who usually toned down their distaste for the Social Democrats, Kalmanovich was openly and stridently anti-socialist, lashing out at the double standard and lack of clarity within that movement at home as well as abroad. She was also more sharply hostile to men and thereby invited the facile charge of amazonism from some quarters, a charge that she regularly denied. But she was one of the few women in the movement who bore the label "feminist" consciously and proudly, pointing to women as the historic bearers of "peace, humanism, and culture." She had no patience with those male politicians and their female followers who urged women to wait or to join some "larger" cause. When the English Suffragettes, led by the Pankhursts, began employing forms of violence unknown to the earlier women's movement in Europe, Kalmanovich was one of the few Russian feminists who displayed sympathy for them. She distinguished herself from her colleagues by her militance and by her belief that cooperation between sexes often meant only cooptation in practice.[3]

[2] For Von Rutzen's club, see *Ustav S.-Peterburgskago zhenskago kluba* (SPB, 1908); Chekhova's editorial: *SZh* (June-July 1907) 1-2. Mirovich's dates are from the bibliographer of the Saltykov-Shchedrin Library in Leningrad. See her *Genrikh Ibsen* (SPB, 1892) for a sample of her (rather slight) literary writings. Data on the IWSA in Adele Schreiber and Margaret Mathieson, *Journey Toward Freedom* (Copenhagen, 1955), 3, 6, 78. Mirovich's appearance: Mirovich, *Zhenskoe dvizhenie v Evrope i Amerike* (Moscow, 1907) 36-41; and her reports in *RM*, XXVII (Aug. 1906) 140-49, (Sept. 1906) 169-74, and (Nov. 1906) 125-49. She continued to attend IWSA congresses until her death in 1913.

[3] No personal or biographical information on Kalmanovich has been found. For her views, see the following works by her: *Otchët o zhenskom Mezhdunarodnom Kongresse 1904 g.*, 2d ed. (Saratov, 1905); *Zhenskoe dvizhenie*, 35-39; an article on Israel Zangwill in *Zhenskaya mysl*, 4 (Jan. 1, 1910) 1-3; *Pretenzii k zhenskomu dvizheniyu voobshche i k l-mu Vserossiiskomu Zhenskomu S"ezdu v chastnosti* (SPB, 1910) 7-9 and *passim* (a rebuttal of Kollontai); *Suffrazhistki i suffrazhetki* (SPB, 1911) and a translation from Christabel Pankhurst (the Suffragette), *Strashnyi bich i sredstvo ego unichtozhit* (SPB, 1914).

The left wing of the Women's Union was composed of what we might call—but not in the ironic, Leninist sense—"social feminists" to distinguish them from their colleagues in the Union and from the Social Democrats outside it. Typical of them were Lyubov Gurevich and the ubiquitous Socialist Revolutionary publicist, Olga Volkenstein. The latter, an ardent feminist, was highly critical of the "more or less well-to-do ladies" of the Mutual Philanthropic Society; but she also lamented, as a delegate to the IWSA congress in 1906, the excessively "bourgeois" character of the Union itself. Her writings betray a strong pro-labor tendency and a commitment to universal suffrage rather than to a limited female suffrage. Gurevich was an outright Marxist, though apparently not a party activist. She lobbied among the left parties, compiled women's book lists, bristling with the works of Bebel, Kautsky, Zetkin, and Krupskaya, and endeavored to organize women workers. But, like Volkenstein and others, she tried to do this within the context of the women's movement.[4]

Ironically, it was the social feminists in the Union who evoked the most vigorous attacks by the Social Democrats. Kollontai and others campaigned fiercely against any effort, however well-intended, to entice female workers into an all-women's movement and away from their "natural" place in the Social Democratic trade unions and parties. From the very beginning of the suffrage movement in 1905, Social Democratic women agitators appeared at feminist meetings to harass the leaders. Kollontai's hostile remarks at the founding session of the Women's Union evoked the cry "Strangling is too good for you" from an irate feminist. The Union was beset by this kind of harassment right up to the Women's Congress in 1908, after which there was no longer any need for it. The assault from the left embarrassed the social feminists who wished to maintain friendly relations with the socialist parties, and it also dramatized the political differences between them and the non-socialist members in the Union. But worst of all, it diminished their chances of extending their influence among the female working class.[5]

The assault from the right was even more devastating. The wave of reaction brought to the surface the most reactionary sentiments on women's suffrage. Tolstoy, whose animosity toward government was complete, was merely being consistent when he lamented the current effort (1906) to subject women also to the evils and deceits of parliamentary government. The anti-socialist

[4] Volkenshtein, *Komu i zachem nuzhno vseobshchee izbiratelnoe pravo* (SPB, 1906); *Osvobozhdenie zhenshchiny* (Petrograd, 1917); and *SZh* (Dec. 1908) 3–8. Gurevich, *Pochemu nuzhno dat zhenshchinam vse prava i svobodu* (SPB, 1906); *PZhK*, IX (1907), book list.

[5] Bochkarëva and Lyubimova, *Svetlyi put*, 26. Documentation of these activities will be found in Chapter VIII.

[6] Tolstoy, "The Meaning of the Russian Revolution," tr. Aylmer Maude, excerpted in Marc Raeff, ed., *Russian Intellectual History* (New York, 1966) 331; Kuzmin, *Zhenshchina*, 14–15; *Golos Moskvy* quoted in *SZh* (May-June 1908), 27; activities of the Union of Russian people reported in *ibid*. (Feb. 1908) 17–18; Bolkvadze, *Ne razvrashchaite zhenshchin*, 57. Evidence of police harassment in *SZh* (Aug.-Sept. 1907) 16.

Kuzmin, employing an old device of the 1860's, linked the women's rights movement to the spread of vice. The Octobrist paper, *Voice of Moscow*, indicted the suffragists for useless chatter and waste of energy. And women auxiliaries of the Union of the Russian People campaigned actively in the provinces against equality for women. To sharpen the attack, one indignant writer claimed that all the Duma deputies were in accord on one aspect of the woman question: running after the female stenographers in the Duma chancery. But government actions hurt far more than verbal abuse: in 1907 police forbade Mirovich from reading a lecture about English feminists for fear that it might excite her listeners; another speech was cancelled by the authorities on the grounds that it contained inflammatory words like "propaganda"; on one occasion a man was actually dismissed from his job because his wife was a member of the Women's Union. By 1908, it was virtually impossible for suffragists to hold a legal meeting or to reach an audience.[6]

With its larynx cut, the Women's Union soon perished. The combination of poor organization, differences among the leaders, competition from the Social Democrats, and government persecution was too much for this earliest and largest of Russian suffragist groups. Already by 1906 its membership had declined from its peak of 8,000 to about 800; the St. Petersburg core was reduced to a handful of cadres. By the time Chekhova founded its journal in 1907, most of the old members had quit; and the demise of that journal in 1909 occurred long after the Union itself had withered away. All the provincial branches folded up—or were closed by the police—in 1908, and in the course of that year the organization simply ceased to exist, though its name was occasionally invoked for some time afterward.[7]

The other two women's suffrage organizations survived the storms of reaction. The Women's Progressive Party was largely a one-woman show of Pokrovskaya, who lived modestly by her medical practice in a two-room flat where she produced her journal, *The Women's Messenger*. The functioning body of the Party was its Women's Club, a smallish affair that featured reports and discussions of various women's topics. Kollontai addressed it once and carried away the impression that it was pre-eminently bourgeois. Yet Pokrovskaya maintained her distant adulation of the working class; her little tale, "Proletarian Girl," for example, could hardly be distinguished in tone from the vignettes of Krupskaya and Kollontai. Pokrovskaya, like her friend Ariyan (who once called Milyukov and his associates "little Robespierres, Dantons, and Mirabeaus" for opposing women's suffrage), also continued to nourish a strong distaste for the Kadets in these years, and took the trouble to display it in a didactic short story entitled "Kadetka." But her main thrust, though gentler than Kalmanovich's, was anti-male, arising out of years of struggle against prostitution and its male clients and protectors. Thus *her*

[7] *PZhK*, VII (1908) 149; *ZhV* (June 1906) 187–88; Schreiber and Mathieson, *Journey*, 12; Chekhova's farewell editorial in *SZh* (Dec. 1909) 1–2; Kollontai, *K istoriyu*, 13.

"feminism" was more sexual than political and allowed her no sympathy for class struggle. "Every woman aspiring to equality," she wrote, "ought to be called a feminist—be she landowner or peasant, wife of the factory owner or working woman, privileged or not. For feminism there are no classes, legal castes, or educational levels. It is an idea which equalizes all." In harmony with this, the Party, after the recession of the revolutionary wave, narrowed its original scope and focused its attention on specifically female issues; and though it remained on the scene until 1917, it added little to the cause of women's suffrage.[8]

The suffrage work of the Mutual Philanthropic Society had been somewhat over-shadowed by the energetic campaigns of the Women's Union in 1905–1907. But its own lobbying went on steadily, if undramatically. One sample of its non-revolutionary rhetoric may suffice: "We work as equals in the fields and factories," ran its petition to the First Duma; "in science, literature, and art; in government, public and private organizations, as doctors and teachers, as rearers of the future generation. As taxpayers, workers, and obeyers of the law in the same measure as men, we need the right to make those laws." Similar sentiments were communicated to subsequent Dumas. But, like the other groups, the Society by 1908 had suffered a decline and was forced to restrict its activities. Ironically enough, however, at the end of the same year, when the suffrage movement was in a shambles, the Mutual Philanthropic Society emerged as the organizing force of what promised to be a national revival and a unification of the entire women's movement in Russia: The First All-Russian Women's Congress of 1908.[9]

Efforts to organize a women's congress in Russia pre-dated the suffrage movement by three years. Shabanova, wishing to unify the work of the various feminist groups, actually received permission in 1902 from Minister of the Interior Plehve. Bureaucratic delays and the frequent succession of ministers helped defer the meeting time for the Congress until June 1905. But by then the new Minister Trepov, beset by nation-wide upheaval, cancelled it. Shabanova and the Society—the only group, according to Kalmanovich, with sufficient government connections—resumed their plans after the Revolution had subsided. There was some difference of opinion over the scope of the Congress and its program. Some of the leaders wished to avoid "agitational matters" and confine themselves to "concrete problems" such as alcoholism

[8] For a fair sampling of Pokrovskaya's views, see: *ZhV* (Sept. 1904) 1 (inaugural editorial); "Feminizm," *ibid.* (May 1905) 129–33; "Edinie zhenshchin i klassovaya borba," *ibid.* (Mar. 1908) 65–69; "Kadetka," *ibid.* (Feb. 1908) 74–78 and (Mar. 1908) 37–42; "Proletarka," *ibid.* (Apr. 1909) 93–97; the quotation cited in the text from *ibid.* (Sept. 1909) 164; and a refutation of Kollontai's critique in *ibid.* (Mar. 1911) 78–82. Ariyan's comment in *PZhK*, VIII (1906) 399. For a Soviet assessment of *Zhenskii vestnik*, see *Russkaya periodicheskaya pechat (1895-oktyabr 1917); spravochnik* (Moscow, 1957) 58.

[9] Letter to the Duma: Shabanova, *Ocherk*, 16–17. Evidence of decline in *PZhK*, VII (1908) 149.

and other broader social issues; others were willing to face the hotter topic of women's political rights. The final format of the Congress provided for the usual machinery of communication: committees, reports, debates, and resolutions on a wide range of issues relating to women. Preparations and publicity were elaborate; even the Petersburg coachmen and servants gossiped about the coming Congress. The 1,053 ticket-holding guests included, in addition to all the major feminists, a number of male officials, professors, and politicians sympathetic to women's emancipation. On December 10, 1908, the First All-Russian Women's Congress was formally opened by Shabanova, amid flourishes and flowers, in the ornate Alexandrovsky Hall of the St. Petersburg City Duma.[10]

We are fortunate in having the first-hand and reasonably detached observations of a reporter from *The Contemporary World*, A. Ermansky. At first glance, the large crowd of women in the hall appeared rather homogeneous; but closer inspection revealed three clearly distinct strata: the organizers, the labor group, and all the rest. The organizers, comfortably arrayed on the dais, formed "a brilliant retinue," in his words, and were headed by Shabanova, Filosofova, and other solid, well-dressed ladies, or "lady-patronesses." An extant photograph of the organization committee of the congress confirms Ermansky's somewhat ironic description. The organizers dwelt upon the theme of women's solidarity and upon peaceful, legal work. Assisting them were the leaders of the now defunct Women's Union, Mirovich, Kalmanovich, and von Rutzen, who had helped organize the Congress and emphatically echoed the conservative views of the organizers.[11]

At the far end of the hall, some forty or so thin, poorly dressed factory women gazed in awe at the unfamiliar surroundings and whispered timidly to one another. These were the women of the "labor delegation."[12] Between these two contrasting groups sat the main body of the Congress, some 600 women of the intelligentsia, including a large number who were doctors. They were set off from the workers, Ermansky noted, by their professional mien; and from the organizers by their somewhat severer costumes. But we have more than this visual impression. According to a questionnaire returned by about a third of those present, the typical delegate to the Congress was from St. Petersburg (58 percent), middle-aged (60 percent between 30 and 50), married, and educated at least through high school (84 percent, including

[10] Shabanova, *Ocherk*, 19–20; *Trudy I-go Vserossiiskago S"ezda pri Russkim Zhenskom Obshchestve v S-Petersburge, 10-16 Dekabrya, 1908 goda* (SPB, 1909), to be cited as *Trudy Zhen. S"ezda*, i–ix and 1–11; Kalmanovich's report in *International Women's Suffrage Alliance: Report of the Fifth Conference and the First Quinquennial* (London, 1909) 116–17; Kollontai, *Sots. osnovy*, 2–3. The best account of the congress is Linda Edmondson, "Russian Feminists and the Women's Congress of 1908" to appear in *Russian History*.

[11] Ermansky's report is in *Sovremennyi mir* (Jan. 1909), pt. 2, 103–12 (see 103–108). The photograph is from TsGIAL, f. 1075, op. 2, d. 23, p. 9.

[12] See Ermansky, 109–10.

30 percent with university degrees). Of those employed (58 percent), 75 percent were professionals; and 63 percent of the non-employed were wives of professionals (the rest being wives of officers, landowners, and a few other types).

No refined judgments can be drawn from these few data, of course, but the indication is that rank-and-file feminists in Russia were "middle-class" and overwhelmingly professional. On the world outlook and political aspirations of Congress delegates we are even less informed, but it is not unreasonable to infer that the person they elected to represent themselves on the platform, Vera Belokonskaya, embodied the general social outlook of the middle stratum of the Congress. A former *narodnitsa* and a veteran of Siberian exile, she had married the well-known *zemstvo* publicist I. P. Belokonsky and had thrown herself into the "civic work" so popular in the 1890's: education, relief, charity, and aid to women. By the time of the Congress, Belokonskaya had attained a national reputation as a feminist, and was a living illustration of how deeply the small-deeds activity of the 1890's and the feminism at the local level were indebted to the moral impulses of the "To the People" movement. To one observer, Belokonskaya was the spirit of the "democratic feminists" who were half-way between the genteel leaders and the rough hewn factory girls.[13]

Most of the committee reports were competent and were delivered without incident. But whenever the labor delegates and their opponents from the organizing group shared the podium, friction erupted. The workers dwelt upon economic problems and class interests and rejected feminism as useless; Mirovich, von Rutzen, and others contradicted them and sought a resolution for voting rights equal to those of men. Both sides resorted to grimacing, foot-stamping, and interruptions. The strongest anti-socialist position was taken by Kalmanovich, who lashed out at parties and leaders in the Second International for failing to support votes for women. Citing Bebel, she maintained that the struggle for socialism did not rule out a special movement for women's rights (though she herself personally believed that it had to be led by bourgeois women who possessed the leisure and the means). The stinging tone of her speech as well as its uncompromising thesis evoked interruptions from the floor and was criticized not only by the worker's delegates but also by Tyrkova who accused Kalmanovich of wishing to divide the world into opposing camps of men and women.[14]

Alexandra Kollontai, one of the leaders of the working women's delega-

---

[13] Statistical data from Ermansky, 104–105. On Belokonskaya (née Levandovskaya or Lewandowska), see Kennan, *Siberia*, I, 259 and the obituary in *ZhD* (Jan. 10, 1910) 15–16.

[14] For instances of friction, see *Trudy Zhen. S"ezda*, 456–57, 494–95, 744; Ermansky, 106–108. Kalmanovich was well prepared, having already dealt with the same topic before the Amsterdam congress of the IWSA the previous summer (*SZh*, [Sept. 1908] 2–7). Her speech at the Petersburg congress is in *Trudy Zhen. S"ezda*, 779–91 (see also 744, 765–66, and *SZh*, [Oct. 1909] 13).

tion, delivered a number of verbal assaults against the "bourgeois" feminists. Her main report, presented *in absentia* by the worker Volkova, was the antithesis of Kalmanovich's. There could be no separate woman question while the "general social problem" loomed so large on the nation's horizon. Since sharp class differences existed among women, there could be no all-women's movement. Working women had nothing in common with bourgeois feminists and their proper place was in the party of the proletarians. Prostitution grew apace while the feminists built shelters. And so on. The report concluded with a presentation of the main points of the Social Democratic Party program that related to women. According to a Soviet account, the report was received with applause by the labor delegates and by foot-stamping and shouts of "We don't want to listen! Go away!" from the so-called bourgeois delegates. The Petersburg police official whose presence was required by law was quite at a loss at this eruption among women of good society.[15]

The labor group moved for a resolution affirming the senselessness of the single all-women's movement that Filosofova and her adherents dreamed of. The majority on the political committee agreed with the labor position and supported its motion. But the organizing committee, insisting on its prerogative of drafting the political resolution for the Congress, and concerned about police presence, sent Tyrkova back to committee with a substitute resolution which she, by means of what Ermansky called a "Kadet cavalry charge," imposed upon it. At this, the angry delegation of working women walked out. Some of the feminists, Pokrovskaya among them, were also distressed by the un-democratic tactics of the organizers. The final political resolution adopted by the Congress (without debate) called for equality for women in culture, life, and politics and declared that the *final* access to such equality would come only with democracy and universal suffrage. Other resolutions dealt with expanding rights and opportunities for women in social and economic activity, education, and the like; called for the abolition of state-protected prostitution and for prohibition of the sale of alcohol; and suggested a program for easing divorce laws. The organizers had triumphed over the socialists through parliamentary tactics. But the victory was a hollow one indeed; for after the bitter verbal strife of the Congress, unity among Russian women, or even Russian feminists, was as remote as it had ever been.[16]

There were some repercussions after the Congress. The right-wing deputy Purishkevich drove old Filosofova to tears by his letter to her in which he likened her Congress to an assembly of whores. Society was shocked when she published the letter, and a minor scandal ensued. Octobrists censured him, Trudoviks suggested a mental examination, and a Mariupol woman tried to challenge him to a duel. He was tried and fined for his slandering remarks.

[15] The report: *Trudy Zhen. S" ezda*, 792–801. Reaction to it: *Svetlyi put*, 30.

[16] On the juggling of resolutions: *Trudy Zhen. S" ezda*, 818–19; Ermansky, 110–11; *SZh* (Dec. 1908) 3–8. The final list of resolutions is on 820–25 of *Trudy Zhen. S" ezda*.

But if the press sided with Filosofova on this personal issue, the Congress was frequently denounced. A peasant Duma deputy criticized it for almost ignoring the village woman and for too much self-congratulatory banqueting after the Congress. Kuskova thought the Congress had been too general, too abstract, too trivial, and catered too much to financially independent women. Prostitution had received little attention, though the Congress found time to hear a report on the beauties of Esperanto, as the proceedings confirm. As Ermansky suggested, women showed themselves the equals of men in organizational and scholarly preparation of a congress, but not in political maturity—though it is hard to imagine men achieving any greater measure of unity in such a politically variegated assembly as this Congress. In any case, it was certainly not the harbinger of a political spring for the women's movement some thought it to be, but rather the last and unsuccessful effort toward a unified women's movement whose possibility had been suggested by the democratic ferment of 1905–1907.[17]

The impressive display of organization provided by the Women's Congress of 1908 could not check the decline of the feminist movement. Some delegates, to be sure, returned home from St. Petersburg burning with enthusiasm for fresh achievements; and speakers like Tyrkova roamed the provinces in an attempt to spread the message of strength and solidarity. But many governors hindered local women from organizing meetings and even forbade feminist emissaries from the capital to appear in public. Tyrkova found evidence of sympathy and interest in those places where she was allowed to speak but was often harassed by masculine hecklers. In Simferopol, upper-class ladies formed a group dedicated to fighting feminist propaganda; and the Union of Russian Women, sponsored by the Empress, sought permission for a congress of "purely Russian Women" to offset the efforts of the feminist congress. By the spring of 1909, a large-scale reaction against the women's movement was in evidence at the grass-roots level and minor officials, *zemstvo* people, and the husbands of feminists were harassed for evincing sympathy for the women's cause. Timidity verging on fear among women resulted in a diminution of organizational activities. In the fortunes of Russian feminism 1909 proved to be the nadir.[18]

The next two years saw a renewal of feminist activity in the form of a new journal and a new organization. The journal, *The Women's Cause*, was a frankly popular illustrated weekly, but it helped fill the gap left by the disap-

[17] The Purishkevich affair: *SZh* (Feb. 1909) 13–17 (Mar. 1909) 15–17, and (Apr. 1909) 17. Kuskova's comments on the congress in *Obrazovanie* (Jan.-Feb. 1909) 74–99, 33–43. Kalmanovich's reply in *Pretenzii*, 9–11. Ermansky's final comments, 111–12.

[18] Report of Kalmanovich in *International Women's Suffrage Association: Report of the Fifth Conference*, 117; Tyrkova in *SZh* (May-June 1909) 20–21; *ibid.* (Oct. 1909) 21 (on Simferopol); *ibid.* (Mar. 1909) 17 (for the activities of the Union of Russian Women [*Soyuz russkikh zhenshchin*]); *ZhV* (Jan 1907) 29 and (Apr. 1909) 92–93; and Orlovskaya, *O zhen. dvizh.*, 4–7 for the general reaction.

pearance of *Union of Women*.[19] The new group, the Russian League for Women's Equality had had a brief and undistinguished pre-history. It was registered as early as 1907 but had remained dormant. In 1910, it emerged as a regrouping of the right wing of the defunct Union and doubtless owed its origin to the dissatisfaction of the more conservative Unionists with the militance and the socialist leanings of its left wing. In announcing the League's revival, its secretary, Mariya Chekhova, explained that the recent Women's Congress had perceived two main tasks for the Russian women's movement: The first was unifying women's charity, educational, and cultural organizations into a National Council, and it was assigned to the Mutual Philanthropic Society; the second was winning political rights for women, the primary function of the new League. By the end of 1909, the League was functioning. Its president, right up to the Revolution of 1917, was an energetic, thirty-five year old St. Petersburg doctor, Poliksena Shishkina-Yavein.[20]

The League for Women's Equality, though the largest feminist organization in Russia, could not (at least before 1917) claim more than a thousand members, about one-tenth the size of the old Union, even if we accept the more optimistic estimates. Its membership interlocked with other feminist organizations and included the former Unionists Mirovich, Kalmanovich, Chekhova, von Rutzen, Volkenstein, Tyrkova, and Milyukova. But the leadership was new, consisting for the most part of otherwise unknown wives, widows, or daughters of high-ranking government men, officers, and landowners. Tactics had also changed. The mammoth rallies, monster petitions, and the vast network of branches of which the Union could boast during its successful years were unknown to the League, which limited itself to orderly meetings and quiet and persistent lobbying in the Duma. Although modest in size and moderate in tone, the League was organizationally stronger than the Union. Its first charter (1911) stipulated that at least four of its founding members should continue to sit on successive executive councils. Though this provision was later abolished as undemocratic, it afforded the League some administrative continuity in its early years. Financing was also more refined: In addition to the yearly ruble dues there was a ten ruble membership fee, and additional revenue was obtained from life memberships, gifts, benefit performances, and real estate investments. Local chapters had no fiscal autonomy.[21]

[19] *Zhenskoe delo* (*ZhD*), weekly (SPB, 1910–1917) see also *Zhenskaya mysl*, semi-weekly (Kiev, 1909–) (the Helsinki University Library has a set that ends in June 1910).

[20] *PZhK*, VII (1908) 149; *International Women's Suffrage Alliance: Report of the Fifth Conference*, 117; Chekhova's account in *SZh* (Feb. 1909) 17–19; Mirovich's in *ZhD* (Jan. 10, 1910) 5. On Shishkina-Yavein, see *Rossiiskii meditsinskii spisok: 1914* (SPB, 1914) 624.

[21] Organization, membership, and numbers described in *Ustav Obshchestva pod nazvaniem "Rossiiskaya Liga Ravnopraviya Zhenshchin"* (SPB, 1911) and *Otchët o deyatelnosti Rossiiskoi Ligi Ravnopraviya Zhenshchin za 1913 god* (SPB, 1914). An estimate made by the 1911 Congress of the IWSA puts the total membership of the League at about 1,000 for that year: *Report of the Sixth Congress of the International Women's Suffrage Alliance . . . Stockholm . . . 1911* (London, 1911). Variant versions of the League's title use the words *Vserossiiskaya* and *Ravnopravnost* in place of the equivalent words in the official name.

Another feminist group of more or less national importance appeared in 1910; the Moscow Branch of the League for Women's Equality that, in spite of its name, was independent of the St. Petersburg group. Like the main League, the Moscow Branch included some former Union members, and it was led by women doctors. Like the St. Petersburg branch, it sometimes allowed itself to be unduly attracted to such trivial matters as commemorating the death of Sergei Muromtsev or Tolstoy and celebrating the fiftieth anniversary of women's higher education in Russia. Such antiquarian introspection, though harmless in itself, was perhaps evidence of a lack of élan. The Moscow group was somewhat weakened also by an unpleasant schism that erupted in 1911 over a largely personal feud between the veteran Mirovich (a member of both Leagues) and the sometime president of the Moscow Branch, Dr. Mariya Raikh at the Stockhom Congress of the IWSA. Raikh was upheld by the Moscow leadership and Mirovich and her supporters withdrew from the organization. She died two years later. Though trivial, the incident was enlarged by the press and helped to discredit some of the feminists and also created hostility between Moscow and St. Petersburg, which had supported Mirovich.[22]

The St. Petersburg League became the leading suffrage group in prerevolutionary Russia, attracting by its moderation the support of the Mutual Philanthropic Society, and by its tact the cooperation of the Women's Progressive Party. Under the League's auspices joint meetings were held. The central concern of the League was extracting favorable legislation from the Duma. Its leaders lobbied among those deputies who were sympathetic, decorated its headquarters with their portraits, and invited them to speak at their meetings.[23]

Among the many legislative projects dealing with women's rights for which the League lobbied, suffrage was central. In 1912, the League presented the Third Duma with a petition to revise the electoral law by adding the following words: "Persons of the female sex enjoy the right to elect and to be elected in the same way as men to the State Duma." The arguments supporting it were familiar: Women voters had shown their fitness elsewhere; certain social problems (alcoholism, prostitution, the protection of children, for example) might be more amenable to solution at the hands of sympathetic and talented women; and women would oppose militarism and ease relations with other states. It was presented to the Trudovik, A. A. Bulat, who shaped it into a floor bill signed by forty deputies (18 Kadets, 11 Trudoviks, 4 Progressives, 4 non-party deputies, 2 Octobrists, and 1 Social Democrat—the Bolshevik, Petrovsky). On first reading, the conservative deputies showed their

[22] Description of the Moscow League in *Otchët . . . za 1913*, 89–91; of its origin in *SZh* (Dec. 1909) 15–18 and *ZhD* (Apr. 18, 1910) 8; of its activities in *ibid.* (Jan. 1, 1911) 18–21 and (June 15, 1911) 19–20; and of the schism in *ibid.* (Dec. 1, 1911) 17–20.

[23] On cooperation see *ZhD* (Dec. 1, 1912) 20 and (Jan. 1, 1913) 28. On relations with the Duma deputies, *Otchët . . . za 1913*, 29–50.

opposition. The bill was then consigned to a committee where it still lay when the Third Duma came to an end a few months later.[24]

But before this occurred, Bulat's project was the subject of some interesting commentary by the Premier, the Minister of the Interior, and the Minister of Justice. Maklakov of the Interior submitted to Premier Kokovtsev the simple opinion that giving political rights to women was "not in accord with the tenor of life in our country." Shcheglovitov, in a more scholarly letter (supported by an impressive legal bibliography), arrived at the same conclusion. But he added, in addition to the conventional objections, his fear that—contrary to the beliefs of some liberals that women voters would strengthen conservative and clerical forces—Russian women, if drawn too closely into political life would be tempted by the attractions of revolutionary ideas. Since the premier and the other ministers agreed with these recommendations, there could have been no hope for the Bulat Bill, even if it had passed the Duma. Milyukov's universal suffrage bill of the following year in the Fourth Duma was an anticlimax. When speaking to the provision that would have enfranchised all Russian women, he was greeted by the customary laughter and derision from the right which easily defeated the whole bill by 206 to 106. The struggle for women's suffrage in the Duma had ended.[25]

4. THE BALANCE SHEET

To judge the success of the Russian feminist movement exclusively by its efforts to secure the vote, would be unfair. All four suffrage organizations addressed themselves to a wide range of social problems relating to women outside the domain of electoral rights. The Society and the League used their connections in the Duma, built up carefully in the suffrage campaign, to secure desired legislation on matters far removed from the enfranchisement issue. And the Women's Progressive Party, always somewhat distrustful of the Duma and the parties, was in the vanguard of a vigorous assault upon regulated prostitution. To the list of feminist achievements must also be added those narrower rights won by women's interest groups, particularly student and professional ones, by means of local or direct agitation.

Most feminists, especially after 1908, never claimed to be socialists. It is hardly cause for surprise, then, that they did not dedicate the bulk of their energy to the masses. Shabanova once stated that those who engage in legal struggle—not revolutionary—must confine themselves to removing the visible marks of inequality between the sexes and the blatant privileges of men. But then, some inequalities are more visible than others, depending upon

[24] For the Bulat Bill: *ZhD* (Mar. 1, 1912) 1–3; *International Women's Suffrage Association: Report of the Seventh Congress, Budapest* (Manchester, 1913) 149.
[25] The correspondence, in full, is to be found in TsGIAL, f. 1405 (1912), op. 452, d. 321. But some of it has been published (see a citation in Bilshai, *Sov. demok. i ravnopravie*, p. 16). The Milyukov Bill is covered in *ZhD* (Apr. 1, 1913) 1–2.

where one stands. The feminists devoted little attention to the general plight of peasant women, for example, although they were quick to use their names on the suffrage petitions of 1906–1907. Their one legislative victory was a bill giving village women the right to vote in the *skhodka* on the use of alcohol. A similar blind spot for feminists was the servant question. Some appeared to be more interested in tranquilizing their domestic servants than in bettering their lot; others saw the labor of servants as a device for freeing educated women for professional work. Too few were concerned about liberating the female servants themselves.[1]

In labor reform, the feminists' record was better—but not much. This was not wholly their fault. In earlier years, the Union had its social feminist wing, and the Union's program reflected its concern for women workers. Its organ, *Union of Women*, for example, proclaimed in the ritualistic jargon of the intelligentsia, that the philanthropic approach to maternity protection for working women was "like putting a small bandage on a gaping wound" and that the workers, in collaboration with the Union, would have to organize to secure their own rights. When the desired alliance of feminists and women workers did not materialize, the feminists were constrained to approach the latter's problems by way of political reform. Unable to work *with* factory women, the feminists did not cease to work *for* them. The League's vice-president, for example, Olga Klirikova—a factory physician—acted as secretary to the Second All-Russian Congress of Factory Physicians (1911) and helped push through it a resolution on maternity protection which was similar to that of the Social Democrats. The campaign to introduce female factory inspectors was taken up with enthusiasm by the League in both Petersburg and Moscow. But far more time and energy was expended upon other matters—matters that most concerned the feminists. This explains why the League, in choosing a motto expressing its view on the economics of the woman question, settled on a formula as innocuous as "The Right of Women to Work at a Fair Wage!"[2]

The main objective of the feminists was, of course, to further the interests of the women of the intelligentsia—though, given the pious canons of Russian social reform, this was seldom admitted. The *kursistki* and their scholarship committees broadened the pathways to higher education. New courses and schools were opened through individual efforts (the Women's Technical Courses) or by the Duma (a Women's Theological Academy). By 1911, the battle for degrees and state examinations was won. In the following year, the League organized an All-Russian Congress on Women's Education. But for

[1] Shabanova, *Ocherk*, 15; Kollontai, *Sots. osnovy*, 104–106. A brief discussion of feminists and servants may be found in Ruthchild's unpublished paper, "Russian Feminism from 1905 to 1917," 25–26.

[2] *SZh* (May-June 1908) 19–20. Klirikova's efforts described in *ZhD* (May 1, 1911) 7; the final insurance bill is described in B. G. Dansky, *Dorevolyutionnaya strakhovaya kampaniya* (Moscow, 1925) 23, 40 and Bernice Madison, *Social Welfare in the Soviet Union* (Stanford, 1968) 20. The motto: *ZhD*, (Mar. 15, 1913) 20.

all its impressive apparatus and its 1,000 delegates, the Congress could say nothing new about the problem. Indeed one suspects that it was merely an excuse to assemble another women's congress unafflicted by the harassments of labor agitators. In the Duma, expansion of the rights of women teachers, doctors, and lawyers was the motif of many bills, much debated and often drafted outside its walls by special interest groups or by committees of the League or the Society.[3]

Even the laws improving the legal and family status of women aided those of higher income or education more than others. The right to inherit moveable and urban real property was equalized for sons and daughters by a law of 1912, initiated by the Mutual Philanthropic Society. But females in the country continued to receive only one-seventh, as opposed to one-fourth for the son, of a landed bequest. This did not affect the always changing customary law of the peasants; and it had little interest for the penniless factory woman. The same was true of the 1914 law, sponsored by the Society, removing Russian wives' names from their husbands' passports, thus ending one of the most onerous provisions of the Russian family code. It was now a great source of pride and security to otherwise independent women, especially professionals, that they could henceforth live apart from their husbands, seek employment without their permission, and even sign credit agreements, all under the aegis of their very own "personal passport" (vid na zhitelstvo). Again, most working women, enjoying a somewhat more fluid marital system and unencumbered by litigious spouses, were probably less likely to benefit from the new law than were the women of the upper classes.[4]

The feminist war on prostitution, though a losing one, took a variety of forms. The authorities maintained the official position that the system in force was the only workable one, though they knew full well that it was inefficient. At the other end of the spectrum, the socialists believed that prostitution could only be abolished along with the abolition of capitalism and wage-labor. Between these extremes the feminists managed to muster three different responses: charity, abolition of state regulation of vice, and women's suffrage. It is only against the variety and the futility of these feminist efforts that the theories of the socialists before the Revolution as well as the actions of the Soviet regime after it can adequately be appraised.

The charity approach was the old tradition of sheltering fallen girls in Magdalen homes and weaning them away from their profession. This was chiefly the domain of the Russian Society for the Protection of Women, an august

[3] For summaries of the major legislation, see ZhD (Sept. 15, 1912) 1–2 and Shabanova's report to the 1914 International Women's Congress in TsGIAL, f. 1075, op. 2, d. 43, pp. 12–13. For the Congress, see its Trudy I-go Vserossiiskago S"ezda po Obrazovaniyu Zhenshchin (SPB, 1914) vii–xii for its origins and organization.

[4] The inheritance law: Shabanova, Ocherk, 29 and Mikhailova, Russkie zakony, ii. The passport law: ZhD (Apr. 15, 1914) 2 and TsGIAL, f. 1075, op. 2, d. 43, 6.

body that clung to its conservative, apolitical mode of action long after other feminist groups had found other outlets. The Society maintained liaison with international conferences on white slavery and with the Imperial ministries. The principal result of the latter was the assurance by the Minister of the Interior that there would be no decisive resolution of the problem in the near future, due to the complexity of its "sanitary and administrative aspects." The Society also managed to develop a few new techniques. By 1909 it had caused the legal age for brothel girls to be raised from 18 to 21, and had received permission to interview prospective prostitutes before they were registered in order to dissuade them from doing so. The Society also stationed police and its own hired women at the railway stations to greet incoming women, give them information and assistance, and rescue them from the clutches of the brothel agents who infested these places. But during the entire year of 1913, only a bit more than one person a day was received in this way. Rescue work in the provinces was even less impressive. In all there is little cause to wonder at the caustic words of Dmitry Filosofov (son of the feminist) who likened the approaches of charity-ladies toward prostitution to a home-remedy: "psychologically soothing to the patient but in no way curing him."[5]

The more aggressive feminists sought the abolition of the system of state-licensed brothels. In England this had been accomplished as early as 1880 (over the protests of the armed forces); but elsewhere in Europe it remained. After 1900, American feminists successfully opposed the government's plan to introduce it in Hawaii and the Philippines (again as a prophylactic for the military). The main arguments adduced by feminists everywhere were that the system failed to curb disease, was one-sided, encouraged the double-standard, and made vice respectable. In Russia, the principal advocate of abolition was Dr. Pokrovskaya, who launched her campaign in 1902 with the book, *The Medical-Police Supervision of Prostitution Contributes to the Degeneration of the Nation*. In this and in countless speeches and articles, she argued that the brothels were instruments of white slavery. It was she or those like her who evoked Kuprin's sarcastic reference in *Yama* to the women doctors who exclaim in print "Ach, regulation! Ach, abolition! Ach, living merchandise! Slavery!" Pokrovskaya replied in kind in a bitter review, criticizing the author for viewing prostitutes as "lazy, stupid, mechanical-sewers for the passions of the city." Behind Pokrovskaya's concern with abolishing the inspection system was the deeper conviction that man's wanton lust was the cause of prostitution, a fact that explains her summons (1908) to all women to boycott men who patronized prostitutes.[6]

[5] The Society's activities: TsGIAL, f. 1335, op. 1, d. 5 (1902) 5–14 (the quotation from the Ministry, 13–14), and d. 4 (1910) 6–25; and *Ross. Obshch. Zashch. Zhen v 1913* (Petrograd, 1914) 86–91. A valuable account of prostitution in Kazan and the futile efforts to combat it is to be found in A. Baranov, *V zashchite neschastnykh zhenshchin* (Moscow, 1902) 5–28. D. V. Filosofov's remark in his *Slovo i zhizn* (SPB, 1909) 152.

[6] For the American arguments against state regulation, see Aileen Kraditor, *The Ideas of the*

Other feminists who opposed state regulation of vice had an opportunity to display their views at the First Congress on Prostitution, organized by the Russian Society for the Protection of Women in 1910. Here apologists for the system, representing the Ministry of Interior, agreed that the present operation was "a parody of regulation" but were unable to imagine anything to replace it. The futility of this position was complemented by a resolution declaring that "among other means of struggle against prostitution, the Congress recognizes the teaching of Christianity as a source of strength for those who have wandered down the path of immorality." At the opposite pole, a workers' delegation linked prostitution with capitalism in the conventional Marxist manner. The indomitable Kalmanovich answered them both, suggesting to the official spokesman that if medical inspection were applied to male clients of prostitutes, feminists might be inclined to endorse the system; and telling the socialists to stop trying to leap from yesterday into tomorrow without worrying about today. The principle of abolition won the support of most of the feminists. But the most practical suggestion—like all the others a European import—was Milyukova's idea of a network of free venereal clinics; an idea not to be realized until Soviet times when a system of prophylacteries was established.[7]

Aside from Pokrovskaya's Party, the most energetic champion of abolition was the League for Women's Equality. Shishkina-Yavein herself presented a project to the Pirogov Medical Congress, Imperial Russia's medical establishment. She then revised it in collaboration with Andrei Shingarëv, a physician and a well-known Kadet deputy to the Duma. Headed by an elaborate and well-reasoned preamble, the bill provided for a medical campaign against venereal disease, combined with the dismantling of the inspection apparatus and the closing of all houses of vice, with prison penalties for violators. Although accompanied by an unusually vigorous propaganda and lobbying campaign by the League, the bill failed to become law and the system continued up to the Revolution.[8]

Could abolition have diminished the incidence of either vice or disease to any considerable degree? Under the broad conditions of Russian society, of which the feminists showed a reasonable awareness, probably not. On the other hand, it is hardly likely that it would have led to any increase either.

Women Suffrage Movement 1890–1920 (New York, 1965) 60, 113. Pokrovskaya's main work on the subject is *Vrachebno-politseiskii nadzor za prostitutsiya sposobtsvuet vyrozhdeniyu naroda* (SPB, 1902), see esp. 82–96. Of her other writings, too numerous to list, only her review of *Yama* is cited; *ZhV* (Feb. 1910) 37–40. The passage from the novel is from Kurpin, *Sob. soch.*, V, 67. Pokrovskaya's variation on the Lysistrata theme is reported in *SZh* (Feb. 1908) 18.

[7] The Ministry official's remark is reported by Tyrkova in *Zaprosy zhizni*, 17 (Apr. 1910) 7. All others are from *Trudy pervago Vserossiiskago S"ezda po Borbe s Torgom Zhenshchininami . . . 1910 goda*, 2 v. (SPB, 1911–1912) I, 47–55, 231–233 and II, 533, 612–18 (the list of resolutions).

[8] The League's *Otchët . . . za 1913*, 5–19, 62.

And if accompanied by adequate police enforcement (using energies and skills virtually squandered under the prevailing order), it certainly would, at the very least, have lowered the rate of seduction into prostitution, of white slavery, and of the corruption of children. And it would also—for good or evil—have liberated many an unwilling prisoner of the yellow ticket. The feminists are not to be scorned for having labored toward this goal.

In comparison with the feminist movement of the West, the sharpest difference is in size. A tiny European state like Denmark, had some 80,000 members in its National Women's Council as early as 1899. In the United States, the major (but not the only) women's suffrage organization, The National American Women's Suffrage Association, grew from 17,000 in 1905 to 100,000 in 1915. The Russians possessed neither a National Women's Council nor any other body that spoke for all women's organizations. The Union for Women's Equality, by far the largest suffrage association of the whole period, reached its peak in 1905 with some eighty branches claiming, at the most generous estimate, only a membership of 8,000; and these numbers diminished drastically and rapidly after 1905. The Moscow Branch of the League had less than 500 members in 1911; the League itself numbered about 1,000, with its branches hardly able to claim that many in total. The Mutual Philanthropic Society and the Women's Progressive Party were even smaller. On the other hand, local independent groups, like the Ukrainian women's organization (*Zhinocha Gromada*) with its eighteen branches, continued to multiply right up to the Revolution, making it difficult to estimate total numbers of "organized" women who might be called feminists.[9]

The smaller scale of Russian feminism can hardly be a surprise, given the relative per capita number of cities, businesses, and schools in Russia and the West. But in other respects, the Russian feminists resembled those in the West, particularly in organization and communication. Organization was standard: the general meeting, the central or executive council, the specialized committees, providing the framework wherein the leaders made the decisions, perpetuated themselves in authority, and co-opted their friends—all of this only occasionally enlivened by democratic ferment. All the accepted methods of agitation and propaganda (except that of the deed) were employed. Russian feminists courted the bureaucrats, lobbied the Duma, and flooded the country with printed propaganda. They blackened reams of paper with signatures by petitioners, frankly emulating "the English manner," and arranged for "spontaneous" letters from oppressed women. In short, they matched the hustle and bustle of the West, and also anticipated some of the methods of the Bolshevik women's movement after the Revolution.

In social composition, Russian feminism was, like its counterparts abroad,

[9] The American figures are from Kraditor, *Ideas*, 7. *Zhinocha Gromada* is described in *ZhD*, (Sept. 15, 1916) 16; other local and national groups in *SZh* (Aug.-Sept. 1907) 17.

urban and roughly "middle-class" with an "upper-class" frosting. The older feminist leaders were more likely to be from the realm of gentry and high officialdom; the younger ones of lower and more varied backgrounds—clerical, officer, professional families, Jews, and so on. Their social and economic position distinguished them clearly and visibly from workers or peasants. The movement was filled with and led by university graduates and professionals, especially doctors. Two differences with Anglo-Saxon, particularly American, feminist leadership suggest themselves. In scanning the list of major American feminist leaders from 1890 to 1920 (including Fawcett and Pankhurst from England), it appears that they tend to be the wives and daughters of professional families rather than self-employed, trained professionals themselves, a fact illustrating the different attitude toward women's work in the two cultures. Second, leadership of Russian feminism devolved steadily from the hands of gentry-ladies to gentry-professionals, and then to the socially more democratic intelligentsia, whereas in America a contrary tendency was asserting itself, as the small-town teacher or minister's daughter was superseded by women of great wealth and influence.[10]

"Between the emancipated woman of the intelligentsia," wrote Kollontai in 1908, "and the toiling woman with calloused hands, there was such an unbridgeable gulf, that there could be no question of any sort of point of agreement between them." Aside from the sweeping exaggeration of the last words, disproved in the preceding pages, the notion of an "unbridgeable gulf" requires comment. To the extent that the gulf existed, it was not the unavoidable result of class and educational differences; for if this were so, how did Kollontai and others bridge the gulf between themselves and women workers? But there *was* a gulf between feminism and lower-class women of Russia, a gulf implicit in the limited outlook of all feminist movements of that age. By placing sexual equality before economic equality, by seeking a vertical combination of all females, by exalting the primacy of the ballot, and by sometimes focusing on a limited female franchise equal to men's rather than on universal adult suffrage, the feminists could not help but create this gulf. But it was not simply a matter of following, as a Soviet historian has put it, "the narrow class interests of the propertied classes." There was some of this to be sure; but in the movement as a whole the "bourgeois feminist" tendencies owed much more to the *feminist* than to the *bourgeois* impulse. The Russian suffragists may have been indifferent to universal suffrage; but few of them opposed it on principle, as did many of their American and British counterparts. And nowhere among them can be heard anything equivalent to the strident hostility which Americans like Catt, Stone, and Stanton lavished upon labor, the Negro, and "the steerage."[11]

[10] Data on American leaders in Kraditor, *Ideas,* 265–83. On Fawcett and Pankhurst (both daughters of wealthy businessmen), see *Dictionary of National Biography:1922-1930* (London, 1937), 297–99 and 652–54.

[11] The Kollontai judgment is from *Sots. osnovy,* 19; that of the Soviet historian, Bilshai, is

Russian feminists differed also in their unique relationship to the tradition of female radicalism. Some, like Belokonskaya, had been out-and-out radicals themselves; others, like Shabanova and Filosofova, had experienced unpleasantness because of political activity. Still others had worked alongside women revolutionaries in the charity and educational efforts of the 1890's. It is surely no exaggeration to say that most Russian feminists revered the women of the Revolution, especially those of earlier eras. Russia may not have had world-famous feminist figures like Carrie Chapman-Catt, as one journalist explained, but it had instead its Figners, Zasulich's, and Lyudmilla Volkensteins who were "greatly esteemed by the intellectual and conscious elements of Russia."[12] The very presence of a continuous large-scale revolutionary movement that included women in prominent places inhibited the feminist movement from splitting into "suffragettes" and "suffragists" as it did in England, and to a lesser degree in America. While the suffragettes or militants smashed windows, caned politicians, and provoked arrest, Russian revolutionary women fired at generals, plotted uprisings, and dangled from gallows. Although there were Russian feminists who admired the grit of the suffragettes, no similar movement ever arose in their country; and women of politically militant temperaments usually joined one of the revolutionary parties.

Most feminists were tolerant of "free love." Yet on all important sexual issues their views were the same as the more puritanical English and American feminists. Like them, Russians did not occupy themselves with the subject unduly. "The more developed a person," wrote Lukhmanova in 1904, "the less important, in general, looms his sexual life: the more futile and poor a person's spirit, the more pre-occupied he is with sex." Quite apart from the validity of this thesis, it was shared by the intelligentsia at large, including the most powerful Bolsheviks who came to rule Russia after 1917. When *Sanin* appeared in 1908, Filosofova was so fearful of its harmful influence on youth, that she devoted an "evening" to a discussion of it. Pokrovskaya, in advocating the liquidation of the double standard, desired to raise men's moral standard up to that of women's and not the reverse. She praised *The Kreutzer Sonata* and preached celibacy before marriage and fidelity during it, in cadences that would reverberate throughout party debates in the mid-1920's. Though most feminists, cared not a whit whether or not a marriage was registered, they never repudiated the family. Dr. Mariya Raikh, President of the Moscow Branch of the League, proclaimed that the goal of feminism was not to lure the woman away from the home but rather to strengthen and illuminate it. Some, copied the socialists in suggesting public care of children and communal household services, "freeing woman from the boring, tiresome con-

---

from *Sov. dem. i ravno. zhen.*, 11. Conservative attitudes of American feminists are described in Kraditor, *Ideas*, 133–34 and 153–58.
[12] M. Novikova, "Sushchestvuet li 'zhenskii vopros'?" *ZhD* (Apr. 18, 1910) 8–13 (10).

cerns of the kitchen and small-scale housework." (Lenin would voice this idea in almost identical terms a dozen years later.) These formulas, in essentially the same form, are to be found in the writings of the American feminists who also wanted to streamline the family and preserve it—not destroy it. As Alice Stone Blackwell declared in a well-known article of 1891, "The revolt of matrimony" was no revolt at all.[13]

A peculiarity of feminist movements observed—and used by their enemies—in the western world at this time was the apparent "defeminization" of some of its members. Kollontai, herself petite and feminine, complained of feminists cutting off their hair, striding along the street like men and exulting when women porters outdid men in feats of lifting. Nikolai Berdyaev, in *The Metaphysics of Love* (1907), while accepting women's rights, voiced the fear that it was leading to mannishness. "All these girls from dentistry courses," he wrote, "having lost the appearance of their sex, hasten hysterically to every meeting and gathering and create an impression of aggressiveness, and of being ego-deprived creatures who are trying to emulate third-rate men." Viewing the phenomenon of masculization with more sympathy, the psychologist V. Agafonov saw it as an unavoidable by-product of "social progress" and voiced the hope that men of the future "will stop looking for 'the eternal feminine' in their love-objects." And Tyrkova, in the same key, spoke of the "broadening" not the loss of feminity as the final outcome of emancipation.[14]

In making final judgment on Russian feminism, one must allow for the unusually powerful enemies it faced on the right and on the left. No other movement of the time was menaced by such hostile pincers. The threat from the right was at least familiar; conservative arguments against emancipation were absolutely standard and were repeated with regularity. Wilhelm II of Germany became the popular embodiment of such opinions when he delivered his oft-quoted comment that women lacked the cold objectivity required by politics and the outer world, and ought to confine themselves to church, children, and kitchen. The massing of forces on the left, as Shabanova observed, was something new and unfamiliar, imported from abroad—though not, like feminism, from the Anglo-Saxon world, but from Continental Europe. The feminists had difficulty comprehending it and coping with it. They saw their mission in winning the franchise, not in proletarian revolution. It is possible that they would have enriched the democratic process in Russia if they had won the vote; though the records of other countries give little

[13] Lukhmanova, *Nedochety*, 47; *Sbornik: Filosofova*, 11, 32; Pokrovskaya in *ZhV* (Sept. 1908) 193–96 and (Apr. 1910) 89–92; Mariya Raikh in *ZhD* (Apr. 8, 1910) 15–16. The quotation on housework is from *ZhV* (Feb. 1906) 39; see related remarks by Mirovich in *Iz istorii*, 43–44. For a digest of the American feminists' views on sex, see Kraditor, *Ideas*, 96–100, 115–16.
[14] Kollontai, *Polozhenie zhenshchiny v evolyutsii khozyaistva* (Moscow, 1922) 111; N. Berdyaev, *Novoe religioznoe soznanie i obshchestvennost* (SPB, 1907), 156–92 (176); V. Agafonov, "Polovoi vopros," *Sov. mir* (Apr. 1908) 21–22; Tyrkova's comment is from a speech at the Congress on Women's Education (*Trudy*, 1–2).

enough reason to believe this. The feminist Shchepkina, in rejecting Kollontai's summons to bourgeois women to join the proletarian cause, summed up their differences with transparent honesty. The two principal modes of human activity, she wrote, are individual and collective. People like feminists, possessing greater scope, time, and means to express themselves in individual action, do so, hoping to leave their personal stamp upon the activity they have engaged in. This, at bottom, was the underlying impulse of feminism.[15]

Finally, most women, even of the urban educated sector, never were drawn either to the feminist or the socialist women's movement. Simple indifference or aloofness accounted for most of this. Alongside the creative figures of art and literature mentioned earlier were the women of the old aristocratic background and mentality who survived well into the 1920's. The countesses and the princesses graced the charity enterprises with their presence, but the most consciously aristocratic of them considered an overdose of philanthropic zeal unlady-like and obeyed the injunction of Tolstoy's Princess Shcherbatskaya who told her overly charitable daughter "il ne faut jamais rien outrer." But there was outright hostility to feminism as well, stemming from a desire to preserve woman's traditional role in the family and thus uphold the very nucleus of the Russian state. This was the view of the Empress and of the Union of Russian Women.[16] An interesting variation on it was provided by the utopian society described in the anonymous book, *The Voice of a Russian Woman* (1906). The new Russian state was to be a family composed of Russian speaking and religiously Orthodox people, cemented together by Biblical law. To assist the tsar-father would be a Duma, a tenth of whose members would be women who were over thirty and property owners. In the Duma, women deputies would concern themselves solely with "women's" affairs: education, health, social welfare, the arts, and "the amenities of life."[17]

If women's aloofness and anti-feminism were the most obvious foes of the women's movement, a kind of female Oblomovism may have been the most insidious. Apathy, impotence, and moral immobility continued to beset the intelligentsia long after Oblomovism had ceased to be a central theme of Russian life and literature. Women were not immune. This mood is illustrated in the diary of a "superfluous woman"—educated, unmarried, and only twenty-five, who looks bleakly ahead into the void:

I do not have the preparation, the zeal, or the perseverance for serious

[15] See the American antifeminist arguments in Kraditor, *Ideas*, 14–42. Shabanova's remark in *Ocherk*, 27. Shchepkina's are to be found in *SZh* (Apr. 1909) 11–14.

[16] The mission of the Union of Russian Women was to unify *Russian* women of all classes for the purpose of "elevating the well-being of the Russian people and preserving its peculiar creative character by practicing, studying, and upholding the Russian past, Russian art, and in general the immemorial creative foundations and national customs of the Russian people:" *Ves Petrograd na 1917* (Petrograd, 1917) 1118.

[17] E. M., *Golos russkoi zhenshchiny; po povodu gosudarstvennago i dukhovno-religiozno-nravstvennago vozrozhdeniya Rossii* (SPB, 1906).

study. And now I am old; it is too late. You do not begin studying at twenty-five. I have neither the talent nor the calling for independent artistic creation. I am unmusical and understand nothing about it. As for painting, I have done no more than study for a few years as a schoolgirl. And literature? I have never written a thing except this diary. So only civic activity remains. But what kind? Fashionable philanthropy which is held up to ridicule in all the satirical journals? Establishing cheap dining rooms? That's like trying to patch up a piece of crumbling, rotting flesh. Opening literacy schools when it is universities that we need? I myself have jeered at these attempts to empty the sea with a teaspoon. Or perhaps I should turn to revolution? But to do that, one has to believe. But I have no faith, no direction, no spiritual energy. What then is left for me to do?[18]

[18] The diary is quoted at length in Elets, *Povalnoe bezumie*, 33–38.

VIII

The Socialist Women's Movement

Radical Feminists	*Abstract Socialists*
We want to liberate women from male oppression.	All people are alienated under capitalism, we want to liberate everybody to become "whole people."

—JULIET MITCHELL, *Woman's Estate* (1966)

1. MARXISM AND THE WOMAN QUESTION

The Russian feminists, taken as a whole, did not possess a binding comprehensive ideology. Aside from a widely shared belief in the solidarity of all women, their ideas about emancipation were molded out of varied, often *ad hoc*, and sometimes even conflicting responses to discrete aspects of the woman question. In spite of some "imported" and international features, Russian feminism never achieved a high degree of homogeneity. The Marxists, on the other hand, inherited a more or less complete theoretical framework for the problem as well as a sharply defined solution to it—the abolition of capitalism. If one must study the feminist movement in order to discover its "theory," for the Marxists the reverse is true. Any investigation of the Marxist theory of the woman question must begin with August Bebel's *Woman and Socialism* (1879). Marx and Engels both wrote about the subject, to be sure; but as Clara Zetkin pointed out, it was Marx's philosophy rather than any specific guidelines that was his main contribution. "The materialist view of history did not, it is true, give us ready-made answers to the woman question," she wrote, "but it gave us something better: the correct and precise method of studying and understanding the question."[1] The best remembered commentaries on the woman question by the two masters were *The Communist Manifesto* of 1848 and Engels' *Origin of the Family, Private Property, and the State* (1884). Both of them relate to our discussion of the family which follows below.

Bebel (1840–1913), "the carpenter-genius" of German Social Democracy and its leader for two generations, was the first Marxist to fit the woman question into the larger framework of Marxian theory. As early as 1869, he had

[1] Quoted by N. K. Krupskaya in *Klara Tsetkin* (Moscow, 1933) 10.

233

displayed his sympathy for the working women of Germany by being the first Socialist to introduce female labor legislation into the Reichstag. In prison Bebel began a systematic study of the problem. Two years after his release, he addressed a women's meeting, the first ever held by the German Social Democrats, and summoned his listeners to support the Social Democratic movement. In 1879 he published *Woman and Socialism*. In spite of the harassments of the anti-socialist laws, the book went through eight editions in eleven years; thereafter, the growth of its circulation was phenomenal. By 1909 there had been fifty editions and numerous translations. Because of its wide scope, far transcending the implications of its title, this book became the unofficial Bible of the European Marxist movement.[2]

The chronological "tenses" into which Bebel's book falls deserve a comment, if only because they were so often the source of distortion, deliberate or otherwise, of his positions. Broadly speaking these are the past, the present, the immediate future, and the distant future, corresponding roughly to "feudalism," capitalism, the Revolution, and socialism. The first part, historical and anthropological, is least interesting, both because of its subject matter and because of the more serious treatment accorded to it later by Engels. The section on the present (including the preceding half century) is an analysis of the economic and sexual condition of the woman worker under capitalism. It echoes Engels' *Condition of the Working Class in England* and Marx's *Capital*, but is based also on German factory conditions and provides vivid descriptions of unequal wages, deterioration of health, the lack of maternity benefits, and the intrusion of "vice, demoralization, degeneration, and illness" into the worker's home.[3]

The last part of *Woman and Socialism*, dealing with the future, contains the earliest Marxian description of the organization of life under socialism, including a prognostication of woman's equal role in the economic, familial, and cultural life of the new society. Bebel's remarks on the immediate future—the appropriate strategy and tactics of a women's movement—are, by contrast, unsystematic, ambiguous, and scattered throughout the work. But it is precisely feminism, suffrage, and the proletarian women's movement, which formed the core of the controversy raging in Europe and in Russia between the feminists and the socialists and among the socialists themselves.

If Bebel showed ambivalence on these issues, it was not because of any lack of confidence in women as equals. Marx himself, echoing Fourier, had

[2] The first edition is *Die Frau und der Sozialismus* (Zurich, 1879). For the references given here, a Russian translation of the 55th German ed. (Berlin, 1946) has been used: *Zhenshchina i sotsializm* (Moscow, 1959); it contains all the revisions made by Bebel up to his death in 1913. A useful English edition is *Woman and Socialism*, tr. M. L. Stern (New York, 1910), the Jubilee Edition. Data on Bebel and the background of his book are from the preface to Bebel, *Zhenshchina*, 3–4 and *Biographisches Lexikon zur deutschen Geschichte* (E. Berlin, 1970) 43–45. For deeper analysis of the German Marxists' views on the woman question, see Alfred G. Meyer, "Marxism and the Woman's Movement," in Atkinson *et al.*, *Women in Russia*.

[3] Bebel, *Zhenshchina*, 286.

written (1868) that "major social transformations were impossible without ferment among women." Bebel merely embellished this comment by saying that "right up to the present time, there has not been one important movement in the world in which women have not been present as fighters and martyrs." He referred unceasingly in his book to women fighting "side by side" with men, as comrades and equals, and his assessment of women's potential abilities could hardly be distinguished from that of Mill. Furthermore, conceding that women's rightlessness was partly due to men (and not just capitalism), he dwelt at length on the purely "feminist" efforts to win legal rights, professional opportunities, and even political equality. "What is right for the working class," he wrote, "cannot be wrong for women." Recognizing that women's parties had more in common than those of men which were divided only by class, he concluded that all women "can join the battle, marching in separate columns, but fighting together." Though Bebel was in practice capable of exhibiting caustic hostility to particular feminist groups, especially in Germany, he never removed those passages quoted above, so flattering to the feminists and so often cited by them out of context.[4]

On the other hand, Bebel declared unambiguously that the achievement of feminist goals in itself could never "solve" the woman question; he urged working women and their sympathizers to join the proletarian movement. The constant improvement of the juridical and educational status of women "does not change the general position of their sex." Though women suffered under the double yoke of "dependence on man" and "economic dependence," only the removal of the second will allow the removal of the first. Since "the woman question is for us only one aspect of the general social question," he wrote, women workers have a special duty to battle side by side with working men for the protection of labor and "for a root and branch reorganization of society," a notion, incidentally, which had often been previously expressed in the Russian revolutionary movement. "The woman," wrote Bebel again, "must seek allies, and she will find them naturally in the proletarian movement. The conscious proletariat began a long time ago its storming of the fortress of the class state which shelters within its bastions the system of the dominion of one sex over another." Both here and in more specific comments on feminist efforts to join all women in a single movement, Bebel showed his unremitting hostility to that goal and his firm committment to the idea of "the female half of the labor movement."[5]

But what—to anticipate two controversies within the socialist camp—was

---

[4] Marx's words are from a letter to Kugelman, Dec. 12, 1868 cited in *K. Marks, F. Engels, and V. I. Lenin, o zhenskom voprose*, ed. V. Bilshai (Moscow, 1971)—hereafter given as Bilshai, *O zhen. vop.*—64. Bebel's coverage of the feminists, in *Zhenshchina*, 289–365. Quotations are from, in order, 97, 338, and 43. Evidence of Bebel's practical distaste for feminists in Bilshai, *O zhen. vop.*, 70 (Engels-Laura Lafargue, Oct. 2, 1891).

[5] Quotations, in order from Bebel, *Zhenshchina*, 43, 39, 44, 364. For Engels' endorsement of this general view, see Bilshai, *O zhen. vop.*, 70 (Engels-Bebel, Sept. 21, 1891).

to be the exact role of women within the proletarian movement? And what about such questions as women's suffrage? On the first point, Bebel offered almost nothing. "We need to pay special attention to the woman question," he admitted; but the "measures and special institutions" required to bring about liberation of women were purely a matter of tactics upon which he declined to elaborate. This problem would have to be fought out by the leaders of the women's movement: by Zetkin in Germany, and by Kollontai in Russia. As to suffrage, Bebel devoted an entire chapter of *Woman and Socialism* to a history and a rather flattering description of the women's suffrage movement in Europe and America—additional material for the devotees of the myth of Bebel's sympathy with feminism. On the issue, raised by socialists as well as liberals, of the alleged "conservative-clerical" danger in giving females the vote, Bebel was unequivocal: "this can in no case be seen as a reason for denying electoral rights to women." For in so doing, he explained, socialists would logically have to deny it to potentially conservative elements among the men, of which there were sufficiently large numbers.[6]

Marxist ideas on women were put into practice, and to some extent reinterpreted, for the European socialist movement by Clara Zetkin (1857–1933). Born Clara Eisner into the family of a middle-class Saxon schoolteacher, she spent her student years in Leipzig preparing to follow her father in a teaching career. She was deflected from this by her contacts with a group of Russian students enrolled at the university there; one of these, a young Russian radical named Osip Tsetkin (Zetkin), attracted her and became her tutor in the study of Marx and Lassalle. When he was deported in 1878 under the anti-socialist laws, Clara followed him and they were married. During the ensuing twelve years of expatriation, chiefly in Zurich and Paris, her days were filled with Party work, the bearing and raising of two children, and the nursing of her sick husband. By the time of his death in 1890, Clara Zetkin had developed into a sturdy and self-sufficient socialist woman. Because of her linguistic and organizational abilities, she was commissioned by the Party to assist in the arrangements for the founding congress of the Second International in Paris in 1889. At this Congress, she delivered a major address on the woman question, unfolding the main themes that were to dominate her political work for the next thirty years. These were: the liberating character of work, public life, and political activity for women; the inability of women's rights movements to bring about full emancipation; and the need for special organization of political work among women within the socialist movement.[7]

Zetkin's open hostility to the feminists was, as many of them pointed out

[6] Bebel, *Zhenshchina*, 39, 44, 359.

[7] Zetkin's early life: Luise Dornemann, *Clara Zetkin: Leben und Wirken* (Berlin, 1973), pts. II, III; Ganna Ilberg (Hannah Ihlberg), *Klara Tsetkin*, trans. from German by A. Shtekli (Moscow, 1968) 7–52; and Krupskaya, *Tsetkin*, 7–12. The best summary of her ideas on the subject as of 1889 may be found in her *Arbeiterinnen- und Frauenfrage der Gegenwart* (Berlin, 1889).

and as she herself admitted, a clear rejection of the sympathetic treatment given them in Bebel's *Woman and Socialism*. To Zetkin, Bebel's book was "not just a book, but an event." But on the question of the feminists, she maintained, he was in error. Indeed, up to the 1890's, there was a more or less tolerant attitude toward them among the leaders of Social Democracy. Zetkin and her colleagues changed this. In 1892 she made her first speech attacking feminists before a meeting of Berlin women. Three years later, Germany's largest "bourgeois" women's organization invited working women to sign a petition calling for freedom of assembly. Zetkin replied sharply, instructing socialist women to avoid cooperating with feminist groups. When the women's suffrage movement attained an international dimension in 1904 with the founding of the International Women's Suffrage Alliance, Zetkin again took the offensive, covering it with scorn as a "ladies' rights" movement, and calling for "a class war" instead of "a battle of the sexes." She never lost her extreme animosity toward what she called the myth of "the great sisterhood" of all women. Against it she posed the unequivocal demand for universal suffrage.[8]

But this demand, much to the delight of many feminists, did not find immediate and uncompromising support within Social Democracy. Before 1907, there were countless instances of "opportunism" and caution on women's suffrage. In Belgium, Holland, and France, it arose from a fear of conservative "clericalism" among future women voters; in Austria it was a matter of "timeliness." There was much foot-dragging and even opposition to women's suffrage campaigns—or more properly universal suffrage without regard to sex—among some of the socialist parties. In 1906, the major leaders of the European socialist movement were polled on their views of women's suffrage. Although all of them voiced approval of political equality for women, the very fact that the poll was taken, and the somewhat grudging replies of some of them, was evidence enough that no unanimity existed on the matter. The issue found a kind of resolution the following year at the Stuttgart Congress of the Second International and its auxiliary International Conference of Socialist Women. The "orthodox" position, worked out by Zetkin and endorsed by the Germans, declared that all member parties must work openly and simultaneously for the enfranchisement of men and women. Two heresies then arose: a lone Englishwoman of the Fabian Society moved for the allowance of a property franchise for women; the Austrian delegation wished to make "the moment and the method" of working for women's suffrage the business of individual parties. The English heresy received no support; the Austrian amendment was defeated first at the Women's Conference and again

[8] Ilberg, *Tsetkin*, 60–62; Bilshai, *O zhen. vop.*, 74, 213 (Engels-Viktor Adler, Jan. 28, 1895); Zetkin, *Woman Suffrage*, tr. J. B. Askew (London, 1906) 1–9 (on the IWSA). For Zetkin's lingering antifeminism, see her 1923 comment quoted in Krupskaya, *Tsetkin*, 10.

at the general Congress. Lenin and Kollontai, the latter present at both meetings, were shocked at the opportunism of Viktor Adler and the Austrians on this issue. But Zetkin's efforts were at last successful.[9]

Two other victories attended this success: the formal acceptance by socialists of the principle of women's right to work; and the approval of special organs for women's political education within the socialist parties. Socialist opposition to women in the labor force had first emerged in the 1860's, when Proudhonist elements in the First International sought to preserve "the hearth" by chaining women to it. A French delegate to the 1866 Geneva Congress proposed that women be allowed to work only when they had reached their forties and had borne and raised their children. Similar ideas were heard in other countries as late as 1906. But by then both the facts of economic life and socialism's committment to equality for women made it a cry in the wilderness.

The second question was more vexed. In 1889, Zetkin had told the delegates of the Second International that "the organization and the political tutelage of women industrial workers is not only an important step toward bettering the position of women but also an important determinant of a more vigorous and speedy advance of the labor movement as a whole and a profound influence on the rapid transformation of present-day social relations." Building on this, Zetkin took over the direction of *Die Gleichheit*, the women's journal of the Social Democratic Party, and turned it into a major voice of Social Democracy as well as the central organ of the socialist women's movement in Europe, adding a staff of regular women correspondents from the factories. In the 1890's she won the right to conduct special political work for the Party among women and to hold special conferences of socialist women in conjunction with the Party congresses. Her efforts were capped in 1907 by the summoning of the first International Conference of Socialist Women (there were two more in 1910 and 1914) and the establishment of a permanent International Women's Secretariat, with Zetkin herself as Secretary. All these efforts were opposed by certain socialists, men and women, who saw in them an excessive tendency toward building a "feminist" enclave within the labor movement. But since those who scoffed at special educational work among women workers were often those who also were lukewarm about women's suffrage on the ground the women were politically retarded, their arguments were not especially convincing.[10]

[9] Zetkin, *Woman Suffrage*, 10–23. The results of the opinion poll may be examined in "Le droit de suffrage pour les femmes," *La Revue socialiste*, XLIV (Aug. 1906) 145–66 (see especially the "correct" but revealing replies of Ramsay MacDonald and Bernstein, 151–52). The Stuttgart events are described by Kollontai in *Mezhdunarodnye sotsialisticheskie soveshchaniya rabotnits* (Moscow, 1918) 1–24 and by Lenin in a 1907 article reprinted in Bilshai, *O zhen. vop.* 76–77.

[10] On the curious history of socialist opposition to women's work, see [Vera Zasulich], *Ocherk istorii mezhdunarodnago obshchestva rabochykh* (1889) 29–30 and Kollontai, *Sots. osnovy*, 210–15. *Die Gleichheit* (1890–1925), in a rather parlous state during its first two years, was taken

Thus by the years 1905–1907, which coincided with the emergence of the women's movement in Russia, Clara Zetkin had already succeeded in splitting the women's movement in Germany into what came to be called the *Frauenbewegung* and the *Arbeiterinnen-Bewegung*. And she was well on the way to winning endorsement from European Social Democracy of votes for women as an immediate agitational concern, as well as the creation of political machinery necessary to render working women worthy of that vote. All of this was to have a decisive influence on the Russian women's movement both in the era of struggle between socialism and feminism (1905–1908) and in the post-revolutionary Bolshevik women's movement.

By the year 1900, the ideas of Bebel and Zetkin on women were widely known in Social Democratic circles in Russia. An abridged Russian edition of *Woman and Socialism*, published in London in 1895, carried claims of sole authenticity, indicating that others had preceded it. A complete translation of the thirty-fourth edition made its appearance in Odessa in 1905. Others followed. The more educated Social Democratic leaders had made it their own years earlier by reading the original. Bebel's book was the last word on the woman question in Russia and had an enormous influence on women activists, feminists as well as socialists. As Plekhanov remarked in 1913 after Bebel's death, "Who has not read Bebel's *Woman*; or at least who has not heard of it?" The German ambassador Count Mirbach, during a visit to Lenin in 1918, was astonished to see it in the hands of a Red Army man. But, although a number of Russian writers had applied Marxist categories to the problem of female labor as far back as the 1860's, no Russian had given the woman question itself the full Marxian treatment until Lenin's wife, Nadezhda Krupskaya, wrote *The Woman Worker* in 1900.[11]

Krupskaya, like Tyrkova and Milyukova, was born in 1869, one year before Lenin. Konstantin Krupsky, her father, was one of those innumerable artillery officers of a radical persuasion. He had had "contacts" with the first

---

over by Zetkin in 1892; she was removed from the editorship in 1917 as a result of schism in the Social Democratic Party. For her efforts to build up machinery for special political work among women, and socialist opposition to it, see: Ilberg, *Tsetkin*, 55–82; *SZh* (Nov. 1907) 12–13; and Kollontai's report on the Stuttgart Conference cited in note 9 above. The quotation is from Vilgelm Pik (Wilhelm Pieck), *Klara Tsetkin: zhizn i borba* (Moscow, 1957) 14.

[11] Avgust Bebel, *Zhenshchina nastoyashchago, proshedshago, i budushchego vremeni* (London, 1895); *idem., Zhenshchina i sotsializm* tr. from 34th ed. (Odessa, 1905); *idem., Gosudarstvo budushchago: sotsialisticheskoe obshchestvo* (an excerpt from the 17th ed.) Rostov-na-Donu (1906). Related materials: Bebel, *Nashi tseli*, tr. L. Bri (Odessa, 1905) 14; *Spravochnaya kniga sotsialista*, tr. from German V. Ya. Bogucharsky, 2 v. (SPB, 1906) I, 234–55 and I. Sheikman, *Katalog sotsialista* (Moscow, 1906). Arch-priest Michael, *Zhenshchina-Rabotnitsa* (SPB, 1906).

For tributes from the feminist press, see for example *ZhD* (Feb. 21, 1910) 8–9 and (Aug. 15, 1913) 2–3. Plekhanov's appreciation of Bebel in his *Sochineniya*, ed. D. Ryazanov, 3d ed., 24 v. (Moscow, 1922–1927) XVI, 247–64. The anecdote about Mirbach is given by Krupskaya in her preface to V. I. Lenin, *Women and Society* (New York, 1938) 6. For Marxian writings from the 1860's by Russians, see Chapter II, 3 above.

Land and Liberty Group of the 1860's and with the First International; his overt sympathy with Polish rebels got him cashiered from the army and he was forced to earn his living as a factory auditor. From him, the young Nadya heard tales of revolutionary heroism; and his description of factory conditions once induced the child to throw snowballs at the manager. In spite of the continuous peregrinations of the family, Krupskaya managed to get reasonably good schooling, first at the uninspiring government high school, later at a more stimulating private school, headed by Peter Struve's father-in-law. Her initial ambition was to become a teacher, but since there were no jobs available, she enrolled for two months in the Bestuzhev Courses, leaving because she thought them too far removed from real life (1889). In the following years she found real life in the form of a small St. Petersburg Marxist circle led by students from the Technological Institute, and in the classes of the Smolenskaya Evening and Sunday School, where she began teaching workers. From 1891 to 1896, Krupskaya deployed her considerable pedagogical talents in teaching Marxism to the workers of the heavily industrial district of the capital known as "Beyond Nevsky Gate."[12]

While thus following in the footsteps of Perovskaya and Bardina, Krupskaya met Lenin (in January 1894) and he commissioned her to gather materials on the everyday life of the workers, men and women, of the factory districts. Donning kerchiefs, she and her comrades would visit factories and report back to the organization what they were able to observe about the life and work of the factory population. This material became the substance of her first book. In 1896, the organization was shattered by police raids: Lenin was sent to Siberia; after a spell in prison, Krupskaya followed him and they were married in Shushenskoe. Tyrkova, by no means a friendly witness, recalled that as a schoolgirl Krupskaya remained fairly aloof from boys, avoided the skating, dancing, and sailing parties of both sexes, and kept pretty much to her girlfriends. As Lenin's wife, though certainly possessing her own personality, she submerged it in that of her husband. The latter opinion is supported by Krupskaya's own explanation of their relationship throughout life. Her willingness to act as Lenin's revolutionary helpmate and comrade was no doubt fortified by her confessed distaste for housework. In Shuskenskoe, Krupskaya assisted Lenin in preparing his first major book, *The Development of Capitalism in Russia*; and he in turn encouraged her and helped her to write her first work, *The Woman Worker*.[13]

[12] S. M. Levidova and S. A. Pavlotskaya, *Nadezhda Konstantinovna Krupskaya* (Leningrad, 1962) 6–38; the livelier but less scholarly Vera Dridzo's *Nadezhda Konstantinovna*, 2d ed. (Moscow, 1966) 3–56; N. K. Krupskaya, *Memories of Lenin*, tr. E. Verney (London, 1930) vi–16; C. (Tsetsiliya) Bobrovskaya, *Lenin and Krupskaya* (New York, 1940) 3–16; L. Kunetskaya and K. Mashtakova, *Stranitsy prekrasnoi zhizni* (Moscow, 1969) 69; M. Rozanov, *Vasilii Andreevich Shelgunov* (Leningrad, 1966) 116–17 (on Krupskaya as teacher). There is a good biography in English: Robert H. McNeal, *Bride of the Revolution* (Ann Arbor, 1972).

[13] Tyrkova's appraisals in *To, chego bolshe ne budet*, 141–43 and *Na putyakh*, 188. Krupskaya's in *Memories*, 30.

This work was a minuscule brochure—some twenty-four pages of closely printed words run off on the tiny type sets of *Iskra*. Though indebted to Bebel and especially Zetkin (whom Krupskaya cites with enthusiasm), *The Woman Worker* is a genuinely Russian production, as evidenced by the attention given to the peasant woman. It was also partly inspired by Lenin's current research into the economic life of the villages. Krupskaya presents a grim tableau; the village woman, overworked and undernourished, and wracked by the village usurer; the peasant mother, unable to devote any time to her children; and the children themselves who, if they live, grow up without the blessings of education and perpetuate the age-old darkness of rural Russia. The factory woman had it no better, for the low and unequal wages made prostitution a constant temptation for her. Her children, devoid even of that inadequate care given to the village young by a *babushka*, are thrown into the corrupting maelstrom of the streets. Hardest of all, writes Krupskaya, was the lot of the pregnant woman worker who enjoyed neither job security nor maternity benefits. Krupskaya's dismal but by no means exaggerated panorama of the Russian depths, couched in familiar language, was the twentieth century version of Nekrasov's *Who Can Live Well in Russia?*.[14]

But labor, she wrote, echoing Bebel and Zetkin again, was a liberating force for women; and she warned working men that taking women out of the labor force would not end exploitation. Nor could women expect help from on high; "neither God nor Tsar" would bring them comfort, for the state always sided with the "upper crust" (*znatykh*). Only the working class itself, men and women, could effect its own liberation. Conceding that many women were indifferent or hostile to the labor movement, she criticized men who claimed that women could have no place in the movement. The task of conscious men and women was to erase the ancient prejudices and to assist women in sharing in the common struggle. The bright goal of all this was a socialist future when exploitation and inequality will have vanished; when people would work in clean, well-ventilated, spacious factories; when society would care for the old, the weak, and the sick; when no one would have to die alone or be fed by charity; when mothers would be assured that their children would be fed, clothed, and cared for in decent public institutions, and not left to the mercy of ignorant village *babas*, "angel factories," or the infested streets of the factory towns.[15]

It may be difficult now, with sensibilities jaded by seventy years of political and social rhetoric, for the reader to be impressed by the visions raised in this work. But the work must be judged from its contemporary vantage point. If so, why Krupskaya's little book played such a crucial role in the history of the socialist women's movement will be appreciated. In Europe, it would have

---

[14] [Krupskaya], *Zhenshchina-rabotnitsa* (N.p., "Iskra", 1901) 2–7, 15–18. A mutilated copy of the original resides in the International Institute of Social History in Amsterdam.

[15] *Ibid.*, 7–10, 19–20.

taken its place on a lengthy shelf of such works; in Russia it was a solitary achievement. After being printed abroad on the *Iskra* presses, it was smuggled back into Russia and was widely used as propaganda material among the factory workers, and was illegally circulated for years (except for a brief legal appearance in 1905) under the pseudonymous authorship of "Sablin." Until 1909, indeed, when Kollontai's *Social Bases* appeared, it was the only Russian Marxian statement on the woman question. And it was one of the few popular works on the subject—that is, manageable in size and format and easy to read—until the appearance of the first Russian Marxist journal devoted to women in 1914. In larger perspective, it was apparently the first revolutionary summons to women penned by a Russian (and the first ever by a Russian woman) since the 1870's.

More immediately, Krupskaya's *The Woman Worker* helped focus the attention of the Russian Social Democrats more closely on the problem. The founding fathers of Russian Marxism had given it little enough space in their writings. The program of the Liberation of Labor Group (1884) spoke of equal voting rights of all citizens without regard to religion or nationality; there was no mention of sex. One may ransack the works of Plekhanov, as well as Deutsch, Axelrod, and Zasulich, without finding anything of importance about women. Part of this was, to be sure, due to an unspoken feeling among Russian revolutionaries that the issue was "solved" and that it was beneath them even to repeat that they favored women's rights. But by the turn of the century, it was clearly time to sketch in a few more details. In 1899, while Krupskaya was writing her brochure, Lenin suggested adding to a draft program of the Party which had just come into his hands the words "establishment of full equality of rights of men and women." This was done at the Second Congress in 1903, and the completed program now called for equality of the sexes in civil and political rights and in education. It also required exclusion of women workers from "harmful" industries, ten-weeks of maternity leave, factory nursery facilities, and women inspectors.

When the party split into the Bolsheviks and the Mensheviks, leaders like Lenin, Martov, and Dan continued to espouse the principle of equality of women within the labor movement. Dan, dressing up the old "citizen-mother" concept in Marxist clothes, insisted that the working mother had to possess "proletarian consciousness" so that she could pass it on to her sons. Lenin, in his reaction to the 1907 Stuttgart Congress, revealed an uncompromising adherence to political equality for women, and an equally uncompromising hostility to any feminist solution to the problem of women's rights.[16]

---

[16] The Liberation of Labor program is in Plekhanov, *Soch.*, II, 357–62. Lenin's 1899 contribution to the draft program is reported in Krupskaya, *Zhenshchina: ravnopravnyi grazhdanin SSSR* (Moscow, 1937) 4; the program of 1903 itself is in *Programmy*, 99–105. Fëdor Dan's views are in his *Vsenarodnoe Uchreditelnoe Sobranie* (Geneva, 1905) 20–21; see also a terse comment on the subject by Yu. Martov in *Chto delat Gosudarstvennoi Dume* (SPB, 1906) 3. Lenin's comments are referenced in note 9 above.

Thus in the emigration, Bolshevik and Menshevik leaders displayed no essential differences of opinion over this issue; and the view of Clara Zetkin (who met Krupskaya in 1902 and Lenin in 1907) appeared to have triumphed in Russia. But it was not quite so simple. In the first place, the leaders paid almost no attention to the practical implications of a socialist women's movement for Russia until about 1912–1913. During the revolutionary years 1905–1907, when feminism showed its greatest strengths, the emigration had little day-to-day control over the rank-and-file party people at home; and the Party as yet did not have a clear operating principle to deal with the exact nature of political work among working women. The "proletarian women's movement" in Russia emerged in two district stages. The first of these (1905–1908) was led chiefly by Alexandra Kollontai and was characterized by more-or-less spontaneous responses to the efforts of the feminists and by sharp disagreement within the party itself about the value of political work among socialist women. The second (1913–1914) supervised from abroad by Inessa Armand, Krupskaya and others, was an official enterprise of the Bolshevik Party central itself. The communist women's movement in Soviet Russia (1917–1930) was to be built on the foundations laid by these two pre-revolutionary ventures.

2. TOWARD A PROLETARIAN WOMEN'S MOVEMENT

The path of the professional revolutionary woman ran naturally from theory to practice; to put it in another way, from politics to economics. Beginning with the mastery of the literature of Marxism, she then made her way to the factory courtyard, the barracks, or labor circle. For the working woman this was all reversed, and her horizons widened very slowly as she moved from the simple to the complex. On the right of the female proletariat were the passive and the fearful; the "peaceful element" so dear to the hearts of the industrialists and so frustrating to the revolutionaries who attempted to organize them. From 1890, new categories, ever increasing in numbers, appear on the left. First come the strikers with purely bread-and-butter demands relating to their work and their personal dignity. A bit later, a few make the rather difficult intellectual leap from narrowly economic conditions to the concept of tsar, police, and manager working hand-in-hand to exploit "the people." Some turn to spontaneous violence; others to performing minor tasks for "their" party, the Social Democrats. A small number filter into the party itself as full members, though this occurs after a much longer apprenticeship that usually served by an *intelligentka*. Once in the party, or serving it as a non-party revolutionary worker—a term frequently met—the female factory hand, weaver, or trolleycar conductor would carry out whatever political tasks she could while on the job. The very nature of her *byt*, her education, and her economic situation prevented her from emulating the professional who was mobile and usually independent. The exceptions to this, Nikolaeva and others, who graduated into the ranks of the professionals, usually became out-standing revolutionaries and then administrators after the Revolution.

Konstantin Takhtarëv has left a vivid description of the wave of strikes in Petersburg in the mid-1890's that swept like a summer storm through the mills lining the banks of the Obvodny Canal and the Neva. But preceding it by half a year was a women's strike at the Laferme Cigarette Factory on Vasilevsky Island in November 1895. Among the grievances were the coarse behavior of the bosses, new piece rates, and a mandatory fee for checking one's coat. The cigarette girls began breaking windows, smashing equipment, and making a general disturbance. The male factory inspector responded to their demands by calling the police who surrounded the factory and drenched them with fire hoses. According to Martov, the Petersburg police chief advised the striking women to balance their wage-cut by "picking up some extra money on the street." Some 800 to 1,500 women were involved in this disorder. In the end, some thirty of the ringleaders were banished from the city, and the demands of the others were met.[1]

The Laferme incident was only a beginning; the Social Democrats were de-lighted and used it as material for propaganda pamphlets. In 1898, the women of another tobacco works, Saatch and Mangub, repeated the performance, this time resisting the arriving policemen by throwing tobacco in their eyes. In the meantime the strike had been taken up by women in some half dozen cities of the empire. Krupskaya's *The Woman Worker* appeared in 1900 and *Iskra* began printing articles on female working conditions in an effort to transform these strikes from economic into political ones. In 1901, an otherwise minor incident occurred that betokened a mounting solidarity between women and men workers. During the famous Obukhov Defence, a big strike in the Nevsky District that grew into an armed action with the police, an eighteen-year-old working girl from a nearby factory rushed to the scene of the skir-mishing, handed cobblestones to the embattled male workers, and bound their wounds. The young woman, Marfa Yakovleva, was heard to say, "We stand behind our brothers." She became in a way the first female street fighter and nurse of the proletarian revolution. Other political manifestations of much greater seriousness soon followed in a number of southern cities where women massed and were shot down. In spite of this upsurge of female pro-letarian activity, most Party organizations gave women workers no attention whatsoever. During the years 1900–1905, only a few women participated in Marxist labor circles and there was a sharp decline in all activity on the part of working women. On the eve of the revolution of 1905, a female Bolshevik

---

[1] Peterburzhets [K. Takhtarëv], *Ocherk peterburgskago rabochego dvizheniya 90-kh godov* (London, 1902) 26–48; *Rabochee dvizhenie v Rossii v XIX veke: sbornik dokumentov i mate-rialov*, 5 v. in 7 (Moscow, 1951–1953) IV/1, 18–21; Yu. Martov, *Zapiski sotsial-demokrata* (Berlin, 1922) I, 276.

professional complained to Lenin of the apathy and hostility to politics that reigned among working women and the wives of workers.[2]

As the year 1905 opened, Father Gapon's Union of Russian Factory Hands counted some 200 to 500 members in its "women's section," despite the fact that the Union believed in unequal wages. A few Bolshevik women workers tried to oppose Gaponovism from within this section and to deter the workers from their fateful march, but to no avail. A few others chose to march with the procession and they witnessed the carnage of January 9. Bloody Sunday, one of the most colossal stupidities ever committed by a government, helped enormously in quickening the political consciousness of many workers. It was a moral signal that shone brighter than all the words on the agitational flysheets. Soon afterward, a number of working women were elected by their factories to the commission appointed to investigate the tragedy; when the government refused to seat them, a group of women protested angrily in the name of all the working women of the capital. Ensuing strikes, demonstrations, and elections to the St. Petersburg Soviet drew more working women into the political vortex. Even cooks tried to hold meetings on the streets; when the police pursued them, they retired to a women's bath-house to continue the deliberations under the protection of their nudity. In Ivanovo-Voznesensk, some 11,000 female textile workers took part in one of the largest strikes ever seen up to that time. And in the Moscow uprising, women workers served beside the women from the intelligentsia as scouts, medics, barricade builders, and combatants.[3]

At the height of the strike movement, the Social Democrats issued a popular sixteen-page pamphlet entitled *The Woman's Lot*, a fair sample of how they thought the transformation of an ignorant factory girl into a conscious revolutionary took place. The heroine, Mitrevna, is a pitiful creature, huddled in a cellar with four children when not working at the factory where women have to restrain themselves from spitting in the face of the fat boss who paws at them. War erupts, the revolution; when her husband returns from these upheavals, he explains to her the relationship between their grim life and the larger world of politics and revolution. The pamphlet urges working women to spread the word ("you women understand each other better") and ends

[2] *Rabochee dvizhenie*, IV/1, 194–97; Krupskaya, "Pyat let raboty v vechernykh smolenskikh klassakh," *Leninskie ustanovki v oblasti kultury* (Moscow, 1934) 222–39. *Svetlyi put*, 6–7; Ida [Lyubov?] Akselrod, *Russkiya revolyutsionnyya partii s 1898 po 1903 god*, tr. [from Yiddish?] S. Lamov (Moscow, 1906), pp. 23–29, 52, 55; *Obukhovtsy* (Geneva, 1901) 23–27. The continuing weakness of propaganda among women workers is attested to by Serditova in *Bolsheviki*, 18–19 and by the contemporary Bolshevik agent, Lazurkina, in *Zhen. goroda*, 25.

[3] Women in the Gaponovshchina: Serditova, *Bolsheviki*, 35; *Svetlyi put*, 12–13; *SZh* (Jun.-Jul., 1907) 11; and the wage demands in Harcave, *First Blood*, 72. The Shidlovsky Commission episode: Schwarz, *Revolution*, 94, 107 and *PZhK*, VIII (1906), 392. The story of the cooks is repeated in Shiskin, *Moral*, p. 282. For evidence of the sharp upsurge in militance, see Lazurkina again (*Zhen. goroda*, 33) and a brief geography of women in the strike movement in *Svetlyi put*, 14–23.

with the familiar call to "struggle at the side of husbands and brothers." It is difficult to estimate how many women were recruited into strikes or party work by this kind of summons, especially since many of them were illiterate. We have the word of one simple working girl that she was converted by reading Gorky's *Mother*; of another that she was attracted by the comradely egalitarian atmosphere of a workers' club. But as time went on, more and more of these workers tell of how they were captivated by a Slutskaya, a Stal, a Kollontai, indicating perhaps that women did "understand each other better."[4]

All this may give us a clearer understanding of why women like Kollontai, after 1905, put such store in launching a special movement for attracting working women into the Party or at least in support of its aims. The potential value of a contingent of active proletarian women was enormous. But the methods of recruiting them were haphazard; and the power of feminist propaganda all too obvious.

Because of the dominant role played by Alexandra Kollontai in the subsequent events chronicled in this book, a more than cursory examination of her early life is required here. She was born in St. Petersburg in 1872. Her father, Mikhail Domantovich, was a steadily rising officer in the army; her mother was the half-Russian daughter of a Finnish lumber dealer of some wealth. The Domantovich houses were always ample, and full of books and servants. Mikhail Domantovich served with distinction in the Russo-Turkish War of 1877 and was then appointed to the Russian staff in Sofia where the family moved in 1878. "There," Kollontai wrote years later, "I began to observe and think; there my character began to take shape." After watching a group of Bulgarian partisans being led to execution, she is said to have uttered the rather precocious words: "When I and all the other children grow up to be partisans, we will eliminate the cruelties and stupidities of grownups."[5]

---

[4] *Zhenskaya dolya* (Geneva, 1905?) 1–16 (quotations, 14, 16); the memoirs of the working women, A. N. Sedugina in *Zhen. v rev.*, 122–26 and A. D. Sokolova-Sarafannikova in *Zhen. goroda*, 49–57.

[5] A. M. Itkina, *Revolyutsioner, tribun, diplomat: ocherk zhizni Aleksandry Mikhailovny Kollontai* (Moscow, 1964), hereafter as Itkina, *Kollontai* (8–9 for quotations).

Kollontai's most useful autobiographical sketches are: *Den första etappen* (1941), tr. T. Nordström-Bonnier (Stockholm, 1945), childhood memories (the English original has not been traced); "Avtobiografiya," in *ES* (Granat), XLI/1, 194–201 (sketchy and trailing off after 1917); and "Avtobiograficheskii ocherk," *Proletarskaya revolyutsiya* No. 3 (1921) 261–302; *Iz moei zhizni i raboty* (Odessa, 1921), is a reprint of the preceding. These have recently been anthologized, together with other autobiographical fragments (some in excerpt form) in: Kollontai, *Iz moei zhizni i raboty* (Moscow, 1974). Like most revolutionaries, Kollontai has a tendency to push the origins of her political consciousness rather far back into childhood. I have tried to balance this by choosing only a few of the most plausible examples.

There are two Soviet biographies: Itkina, *Kollontai*, cited above and E. Mindlin, *Ne dom, no mir* (Moscow, 1969). The first is thin and pious but rests on valuable archival sources; the second is frankly fictionalized, but none the less useful. Of the two lives by Western Communists, Isabel de Palencia and Carsten Halvorsen, the first is almost useless save for a few personal recollec-

In one of her earliest autobiographical sketches, Kollontai tells us that "from childhood I brought my mother a good deal of trouble and woe by my determination 'not to live like others'." Cherishing her nonconformity, the little girl "dwelt in [her] own special inner world, closed off from that of the adults."[6] A favorite fantasy was that her white poodle was a little girl bewitched by an evil fairy; she read to "her" in anticipation of the day when she would resume her human form. Her loneliness and dreams of The Good found expression in her affection for the servants and for the street urchins of Sofia whom she befriended. The young Shura once shocked her parents by refusing to pass cigarettes to a guest of known "conservative" views. Enveloped in social daydreams, she became a heroine who saved children from blazing buildings, a warrior who humbled despots, a writer who lighted the way for "the People." During her school years, the youthful Kollontai's nebulous moral yearnings matured into the then fashionable Populist outlook under the skillful direction of her tutor, the austere Mariya Strakhova, the "nihilist" of the household. By the age of fourteen, Kollontai had read Buckle, Turgenev's *On the Eve*, Hugo's *Les Miserables*, George Sand, the Russian radical publicists, and Ibsen. Two years later, in 1888, she passed her examinations and received a license to teach.

Alexandra wanted to attend the Bestuzhev Courses, but her mother, fearing its radical environment, would not permit it. Instead she attended some private courses until 1891 when she met Vladimir Kollontai, a student officer and the son of a Polish political exile. Alexandra had already passed through an adolescent love affair cut short by the suicide of her admirer.[7] Now, attracted by Kollontai's sunny nature and by the aura of political martyrdom that surrounded his family, she was ready for marriage. Her parents demured and— employing a time-honored cure for love-struck girls—sent her abroad. In Berlin, while rummaging through a book-store, Alexandra chanced upon a copy of *The Communist Manifesto* which, she recalled, pulled together all her previous ideas. She also read Engels and, in Paris, the literature of the French Revolution and the Utopian socialists. Upon her return to Russia, her parents became alarmed at her recent intellectual discoveries and decided that mar-

tions. It is: *Alexandra Kollontay* (New York, 1947). Halvorsen's, though tendentious, is the best study to date for her life up to 1917. I have used the Danish translation: *Revolutionens Ambassadør: Alexandra Kollontays Liv og Gerning (1872–1917 aarene)*, tr. from Swedish by Gudren Thomsen (Copenhagen, 1946). In general, Kollontai is more reliable than her biographers; and the Soviet biographies more reliable for the Russian setting than the Western ones. Until a serious, critical study has been made, students of Kollontai must lean on these as the principle sources for her life. These works have been used to construct this brief sketch, but explicit citations have been made only for quotations or important factual statements. Biographical materials for specific periods of Kollontai's life will be cited in the appropriate places later in these pages. For some comments on the literature, see Stites, "Kollontai, Inessa, Krupskaya: A Review of Recent Literature," in *Canadian-American Slavic Studies*, IX, 1 (Spring 1975) 84–92.

[6] Kollontai, "Avtobiog. ocherk," 261.

[7] The cause of the suicide was only partially related to the victim's affair with Kollontai (*Första etappen*, 209; Halvorsen, *Kollontai*, 42–43).

riage to Kollontai was the lesser of two evils. It took place in 1893; Alexandra was twenty-one.

The Kollontais lived in Tiflis for a time where a son was born to them and they returned to St. Petersburg. Quickly bored by household concerns, the young mother found an outlet in volunteer work for the Mobile Museum of Pedagogical Aids to which she was introduced by Strakhova. This curious enterprise, staffed by Sunday school teachers, and decked out with magic lanterns and other gadgets designed to excite the wonder of the Petersburg proletariat, was the very archetype of the urban "small deeds" activities of the philanthropic and pseudo-radical women of the 1890's. It was the springboard into public activity for well-born women like Elena Stasova, whom she met there. She then began working for the Political Red Cross that specialized in helping political prisoners and exiles. Friendships made here pointed her for a time in the direction of Populism and even "terrorism," she later recalled. In 1895 her husband was appointed an engineer at the Kronholm Works in Narva; there from her hotel window Alexandra Kollontai witnessed scenes of industrial life that sickened her. When her husband once returned home from the factory with two tickets for an operetta, she realized how far their intellectual paths had diverged. Her sympathies for the workers were reinforced by the great strikes of 1896 and her reading of Marxian journals. She threw herself vigorously into strikers' benefit activities. All this pulled her further away from home and husband. In 1897–1898, she left him.

At the root of her decision was above all a fierce desire for independence. "At an early age," she wrote, "I was already convinced that I was quite unable to allow my life to take the usual course, and that I had to grow beyond my own ego in order to arrive at that which was to be my life's particular path."[8] The marriage rested on weak foundations anyway, since she had entered it partly as a protest against her parents. There was, it seems certain, no other man. Her own mother had left husband and children years before in order to marry Domantovich. But Kollontai needed no such precedent. She simply wanted to be free in order to pursue political issues; she did not wish to ensnare herself in another affair. There is some evidence that her decision may have been influenced by the fictional heroines of Ibsen's *Doll's House* and Bjørnson's *Glove*.[9] But Ibsen's Nora had left her husband without any clear alternative in mind. Kollontai was much more like Agnessa Petrovna, the heroine of *One of Those*, written by her friend Tatyana Kupernik-Shchepkina; for this story deals with a woman writer who leaves her beloved husband because the marriage interferes with her ego and her work. In any case, there is hardly any need to go beyond the Russian nihilist tradition of the 1860's for precedent and model. Neither Kollontai's gesture nor the apologia for it added a morsel of novelty to the intellectual history of the woman question in Rus-

---

[8] Quoted in *ibid.*, 52.
[9] For instance Halvorsen, *Kollontai*, 75 and Palencia, *Kollontay*, 31.

sia. It did, however, serve as the recurring *leitmotif* of her later writings on women's emancipation.

The next three years were spent mostly in Europe. Kollontai enrolled at Zurich University in order to study economics. But, to her disappointment, her professor was moving steadily and perceptibly to the right while her own contacts and inclinations were in the opposite direction. By 1899, Kollontai was sufficiently dedicated to Marxism to be negatively impressed by the Webbs during a brief London visit. And her Marxism was sufficiently orthodox to induce her to challenge the formidable Peter Struve, then a revisionist, in an evening discussion at the Stastov's in Petersburg. In 1901, she met Rosa Luxemburg, Plekhanov, and Kautsky all of whom impressed her. Having published an article on Dobrolyubov, she now turned her economic learning and her Marxist theoretical equipment to the study of Finland. In 1903, having resettled in St. Petersburg, she published the fruits of her researches as *The Life of the Finnish Workers*, a typically Marxist study of a "backward" society rapidly undergoing capitalist development.

By then Kollontai had parted company with most of her old liberal friends, and was engaged in illegal socialist propaganda work in Nevsky District. For the time being she remained non-Party. In spirit, she later claimed, she was with the Bolsheviks; but, under the spell of Plekhanov, she could not repudiate the Mensheviks. During one of the countless debates then raging between Marxists and Nietzscheans, Kollontai made her first speech on a theme that was to permeate much of her writing in later years: the subordination of individual interests to those of the collective. "Our slogan," she concluded, "is not the triumph of individualism, but the victory of sociality" (*obshchestvennost*).[10] By the end of 1904, Kollontai was being drawn into radicalism; but as yet there was little in her career to indicate that the major pre-occupation of her life as a revolutionary was to be the emancipation of women.

The Revolution of 1905 converted Kollontai into a full-time revolutionary. Bloody Sunday, she relates with distressing brevity, found her "in the streets" with the demonstrators. But the vivid description of the martyred victims contrasts curiously with the absence of any detail about her role in the demonstration other than that she had marched with the workers in defiance of the stated line of the Petersburg Committee of the Social Democratic Party. This peccadillo was quickly erased by her services to that Committee in the ensuing months. She distributed literature, maintained liaison with the Finnish Social Democrats, composed popular brochures, and acted as treasurer of the Committee. She raised money through her contacts in society. Her attractive and immaculately groomed figure graced factory meetings in the workers'

[10] Quoted in Itkina, *Kollontai*, 25.

quarters of the capital where she repeated Marxian slogans in a wonderfully musical voice. It was her first performance in a role she was to repeat on a grand scale in 1917. An old Party member recalled that he had signed up after hearing her speak at a university meeting. She worked chiefly with the Bolsheviks and first met Lenin, briefly, in the Fall of 1905. But her disagreement with the Committee on the role of the Soviets, which she thought should be independent of the Party, won her an assignment in the provinces. An impetuous radical speech in a provincial meeting forced her to flee back to Petersburg early in 1906.[11]

"Women, and their fate have occupied my whole life," Kollontai wrote in later years. "It was their lot which pushed me into socialism." There is no evidence in Kollontai's early life to support this assertion. It is only in 1905–1906 that we see the first glimmerings of her interest in the organization of women workers. The first impetus seems to have been the inaugural meeting of the Union for Women's Equality in April 1905 that she attended. Appalled at the support given to a "Kadet" all-women's effort by various Social Democratic and Socialist Revolutionary women acquantainces, Kollontai, encouraged by the "proletarian sea" that she heard churning beneath the platform, spoke sharply against classless feminism. She was attacked not only by angry feminists but also by some of her own colleagues. After that, Kollontai decided that working women ought to be drafted into the proletarian organizations and that special machinery was needed for this task. Thus the idea of a special proletarian women's movement as a bulwark against feminist recruitment of factory women arose in her mind out of practical experience. But as yet she had no plan and the events of 1905 kept her much too busy in Party work for her to give any further attention to the matter. Early in the following year she broke with the Bolsheviks over the issue of Duma elections and then turned her efforts to organizing women.[12]

The task was very difficult at first. The influence of the feminists grew daily. "Public opinion was on its side," Kollontai later lamented, "and the intelligentsia, not the workers, made public opinion." Ignoring the mixed feminist-socialist clubs, Kollontai began her political propaganda work by making direct contact with a handful of servant women, artisans, and textile workers. There was no literature to give them except Krupskaya's *Woman Worker*. Kollontai composed original lectures on various aspects of the woman question from the Marxist viewpoint. During a visit to Finland in the fall of 1906, she chanced upon Rosa Luxemburg who advised her to visit Zetkin. Kollontai arrived in Germany just in time for a conference of German socialist women in Mannheim. Her observations there and her talks with Zet-

[11] Kollontai, "Avtobiog. ocherk," 267–70; Itkina, *Kollontai*, 28. According to Tyrkova, who offers a flattering description of her political enemy's physical appearance, Kollontai was rivaled as a fashion plate only by Gippius: *Na putyakh*, 402.

[12] Kollontai, "Avtobiog. ocherk," p. 268; *idem.*, *Sots. osnovy*, 95, 301. The quotation is from Itkina, *Kollontai*, 31.

kin reinforced her conviction that a special effort among women workers was needed. Returning home, she encountered indifference and hostility among the male Social Democrats and also among the older women revolutionaries who saw in it a "harmful tendency towards feminism"—a woefully inaccurate but damaging charge that was to haunt socialist women organizers right up to 1930. The Petersburg Committee grudgingly agreed to provide a meeting room for Kollontai; but when she arrived, she found the premises locked and adorned by a sign that read: "Meeting for Women Only—Cancelled/ Tomorrow, Meeting for Men Only."[13]

In the spring of 1907, Kollontai found a broader constituency in the Union of Textile Workers, made up largely of women. Under its auspices, she organized a series of public meetings, often in response to Kadet or feminist meetings, masked as lectures on maternity hygiene, English women's clubs, and the like. There, under the watch of the police, she would quickly develop the themes of social exploitation and liberation. When she went too far, the police would disband the gathering. In the fall she attended the international socialist gatherings at Stuttgart where her ideas on women's organization were further reinforced. But returning to Russia, Kollontai found the reaction in full swing. Large-scale meetings were now out of the question; so, stealing a page from the feminist book, she helped to organize a legal club under the name of a Mutual Aid Society for Women Workers. One of Kollontai's co-workers in the club was the fifteen year old typesetter, Klavidya Nikolaeva, who would succeed Kollontai as the head of Soviet Russia's women's organization. Membership reached 300, but by the following spring solidarity between the intelligentsia and the workers had eroded. The *intelligentki* were the organizers and cadres of the club and served as its librarians and lecturers. A small group of women workers demanded that they be expelled. To avoid friction, Kollontai resigned, though she has not left us an account of the issues. Toward the entire enterprise, which was non-Party, the Petersburg Committee showed nothing but scorn. By the end of the Revolution of 1905–1907, this was as far as Social Democrats had gone in building up a women's movement.[14]

The epilogue to these events was played out in 1908. Hearing of feminist plans for the All-Russian Women's Congress, the Petersburg Committee fi-

[13] Kollontai, "Avtobiog. ocherk," 272–75 (quotations, 270 and 272); *idem.*, *K ist. dvizh.*, 15–16.

[14] Kollontai, "Avtobiog. ocherk," 270–72, 272–75; *idem.*, *Sots. osnovy*, 426; *idem.*, *Tri goda diktatury proletariata* (Moscow, 1921) 13–14; Serditova, *Bolsheviki*, 56. For Kollontai and the Stuttgart Conference, see the preceding subchapter. Nikolaeva's memoir is L. P. Zhak and A. M. Itkina, eds., *Zhenshchiny russkoi revolyutsii* (Moscow, 1968), hereafter *Zhen. russ. rev.* (290–303, 566).

There can be little doubt that socialist neglect of this aspect of agitation (at least among the Bolsheviks) was as apparent in the provinces as in the capital. Of the hundreds of flysheets and pamphlets printed by thirty-five or so Bolshevik committees in 1905–1907, none is addressed to women workers *per se* or deals with the woman question in anything but a perfunctory way: *Listovki bolshevistkikh organizatsii v Pervoi Russkoi Revolyutsii, 1905-1907*, 3 v. (Moscow, 1956).

nally acted and appointed a number of its members to prepare a delegation for the Congress. To lead the delegation, Kollontai was passed over in favor of the Bolshevik, Praskoviya Kudelli, an ex-*Narodnitsa* and Bestuzhev student. But Kollontai played the dominant role. To arm her followers, she spent the next months on a major theoretical work, *The Social Bases of the Woman Question*, which was not printed, however, until after the Congress. In the autumn of 1908, having finished the book, she assumed a leading role in preparing the labor delegates who had been elected from the factories through the trade union apparatus. To avoid police harassment, Kollontai disguised her meetings as name days, sewing circles, and health talks on the harmfulness of corsets. In two months she spoke at fifty-two such gatherings. She also disrupted the ranks of the feminists by attending their organizational sessions. After a visit to Filosofova's home, that poor woman had to make the sign of the cross in order to exorcise Kollontai's revolutionary spirit. By the time of the Congress, she was passionately hated by many feminists, one of whom referred to her as "that horrible Kollontai."[15]

But the Congress in December was as much an anti-climax for the socialists as for the feminists. The labor delegation had been instructed by the Party to demand a separate "proletarian section" (the exact meaning of this is not clear) and to state openly its hostility to the chief aims of the Congress: an all-women's feminist movement. There was no possibility for communication or partial collaboration with the broad stratum of women of the intelligentsia. The delegates themselves, though well prepared, were young and unseasoned and made a poor impression; and their speeches were too abstract. Kollontai, however, who wrote the major resolution for the delgation, explicitly demanded universal suffrage and the various measures of the Social Democrats that related to women. If the feminist leaders had wished to demonstrate genuine sympathy for a broad democratic program, they could easily have supported these demands, in spite of the antics of the labor delegates. That they refused to do so understandably resulted in a labor walkout. But the moral victory of the labor delegation was tarnished by friction between its Bolshevik and Menshevik members. The latter chose to stay; most of the non-Party women workers followed the Bolsheviks out of the Congress. Kollontai had been forced to leave the Congress a few days earlier in order to evade the police. She crossed the frontier at the end of December and spent the next years in emigration. Other labor veterans of the Congress were harassed or arrested by the police and the tiny nucleus of the St. Petersburg women's socialist movement vanished almost without a trace.[16]

[15] P. F. Kudelli, "Peterskie rabotnitsy v 1905 godu," *Kommunistka* (Nov. 1925) 15–22. On Kudelli: Z. B. Nikandrova, "Nash drug," in *Leningradki: vospominaniya, ocherki, dokumenty* (Leningrad, 1968) 52–60 and L. Batalova, "Tëtenka (P. F. Kudelli)," *Zhen. russ. rev.*, 226–35. For the delegation and Kollontai's role; *BSE* (1st ed.), XXV, 232; Kollontai, "Avtobiog. ocherk," 267–68; Itkina, *Kollontai*, 34–35. For *Social Bases*, see the appendix.

[16] For the congress, see chapter VII, 3 above and its notes. Accounts of the labor delegation: Ermansky in *Sov. mir* (Jan. 1909), pt. II, 109–10; Kuskova in *Obrazovaniya* (Feb. 1909) 32–42;

The brief revival of a socialist women's movement in the years 1912–1914 on Russian soil, though small compared with the majestic upsurge of the labor movement as a whole, relaid the foundations for political work among factory women that had been torn up by the reaction or left to rot by the indifference of the Party in the previous years. Organized around the celebration of the socialist International Women's Day, the revival gave the Russian movement a stronger universal dimension, and enabled later Soviet writers to claim some continuity between these events and the Bolshevik Women's Movement of 1917. Most important, the pre-war movement attracted, and was partially created by, the future leaders of the Communist women's movement: Zetkin and Kollontai in the International Women's Secretariat of the Second International; and a circle of women around Lenin, of whom Inessa Armand was to emerge as the most prominent.

In 1910, Clara Zetkin celebrated her triumph as the undisputed leader of the International Socialist Women's movement at the Second Conference of Socialist Women. Since the last conference in 1907, the movement had grown impressively and the "orthodox" German position on the woman question had gained supremacy. Zetkin capped her victory with a resolution condemning any kind of limited suffrage campaign "as a falsification and humiliation of the very principle of political equality for women." Zetkin then proposed the designation of March 8 as "International Women's Day" in the socialist movement, a female equivalent of May Day. Both the date and the idea were taken from a demonstration of American socialist women in New York on March 8, 1908 in opposition to the bourgeois suffrage movement there. The slogan of women's day was "universal suffrage" and its purpose was to attract more working women to the cause and to dramatize the political talents of women in the movement. Zetkin's proposal won the enthusiastic approval of the Conference. Beginning in 1911, and continuing annually up to the Great War, parades and demonstrations were organized in major industrial cities of Europe until their curtailment by the belligerent governments in 1915.[17]

No observance of Woman's Day in Russia before 1913 is recorded. The first link between the Copenhagen Conference and the women in Russia was provided by Kollontai, the only Russian at the Conference (as a delegate of the Petersburg textile union). She became a member of the International Secretariat and a contributor to *Gleichheit* and, though still a Menshevik, wrote an article in the Bolshevik organ, *Pravda*, explaining the purpose of the celebration in 1913. She also told Bebel about developments in Russia and he replied with a flattering letter describing Russian women as "the vanguard of

---

Kollontai, *K ist. dvizh.*, 19–20; A. Ivanova (a labor delegate) in *Zhenshchina v revolyutsii*, compiled by A. V. Artyukhina *et al.* (Moscow, 1959), hereafter as *Zhen. v rev.* (88–92). See also: Serditova, *Bolsheviki*, 62–69 and Itkina, *Kollontai*, 36.

[17] Kollontai, *Mezhdu. sots. soveshch.*, 24–29 (quotation, 29); *Kommunistka*, 8, 9 (Jan.-Feb., 1921) 1; K. I. Samoilova, *V obedinenii - zalog pobedy* (Moscow, 1921) 8–10; Bochkarëva, *Svetlyi put*, 33. The American origins of the holiday are mentioned by Krupskaya in her preface to Lenin, *Women*, 8.

the International Women's Socialist movement." But in a later *Gleichheit* article Kollontai declared that the decision to hold a celebration had been taken by the workers themselves. In the meantime, a so-called Third Women's Club had been organized by Bolshevik and Menshevik women in Moscow as part of the proletarian revival of 1912, with some 900 members of both sexes. Before being closed down by the police, it was able to stage a meeting in honor of International Women's Day. The much larger celebration in St. Petersburg, was masked as a legal "Scientific Morning Devoted to the Woman Question" at the Kalashnikova Bourse. We have the memoirs of a participant. A. N. Grigoreva-Alekseeva, a Petersburg textile worker and veteran of one of Ryabushinsky's mills, who treated the assembled crowd of women and policemen to a moving description of the life of a factory woman. There were no incidents, but the police, angered by the less than "scientific" tone of the meeting, made a few arrests. According to a Soviet account, similar efforts were mounted in Kiev, Samara, and Tiflis.[18]

The Bolshevik contributions to these activities seem to have been more or less spontaneous and locally inspired. There is little evidence of much interest among the leaders living abroad until 1913. There was, however, a series of articles in *Pravda* in May 1912 dealing at length with the exploitation of women's labor. According to an Old Bolshevik woman worker, it was the correspondence which this elicited from women workers that led Lenin to launch a journal for them;[19] another source suggests that it was the low political profile of women serving on the new insurance committees that inspired a special campaign among working women.[20] In any case, it was not until the Central Committee meeting of September 1913 at Poronino in Galicia that the Party opted for a "special" effort. Krupskaya spoke to the delegates on the need to organize women workers and the wives of workers; and Lenin gave instructions for the publication of a special journal, *Rabotnitsa*, devoted to this work. The editorial board—whose tripartite geographical character was to cause some awkwardness—was to consist of three groups of women: in Petersburg, Lenin's sister, Anna Elizarova, and her associates; in Cracow, Krupskaya and "Lilina" Zinoveva; and in Paris, Lyudmila Stal and Inessa Armand.[21]

Inessa Armand, known in Western historiography almost exclusively as a close friend of Lenin, was to become the first director of Zhenotdel, the Party apparatus for work among women in the Soviet period and was thus, with

[18] Kollontai's writings on these events are in *Stati*, 109–112 (and see 401, note 45). The Moscow club: Serditova, *Bolsheviki*, 76–78; Bochkarëva, *Svetlyi put*, 35–36; *Zhen. v rev.*, 112–16. The St. Petersburg meeting: A. N. Grigoreva-Alekseeva, "Zhenskoe utro," in *Zhenshiny goroda Lenina* (Leningrad, 1963) 65–70 and another version by the same writer in *Zhen. v rev.*, 93–98; Samoilova, *V obedinenii*, 11.

[19] E. G. Kovalenko, " 'Pravda' uchila nas borotsya," in *Zhen. goroda*, 58–64 (61).

[20] *BSE* (1st ed.), XXV, 233.

[21] The Porinino discussion are reported by G. I. Petrovsky in *Vospominaniya o Nadezhde Konstantinovne Krupskoi*, ed. A. M. Arsenev *et al.* (Moscow, 1966) 81–86. See also Levidova, *Krupskaya*, 101–102. For Stal, see *Zhen. russ. rev.*, 445–55, 569.

Kollontai, the major pioneer of women's emancipation in the new state. She was born in Paris in 1874 of French theatrical parents, but was raised in the home of a Russo-French industrialist's family (the Armands) near Moscow where her aunt had taken employment as a tutor. She received an exceptionally cosmopolitan education and when she was eighteen married one of the sons of the Armand family. She bore him five children, four of whom were to become communists.[22]

Inessa betrayed a strong "feminist" consciousness at a much earlier age than did Kollontai. As a child she was thrown into a fit of depression on hearing that a certain baby was refused baptism because it was illegitimate. And, on bearing her own first child, she was shocked to learn that church law prevented her from presenting her "unclean" body at the church for several weeks. Around the turn of the century, while still a liberal, Inessa Armand joined a Moscow feminist-charity group founded to assist prostitutes. She served as president for some time but at last became disenchanted with its meagre efforts and its futility. She was thus one of the few revolutionaries to graduate from the ranks of active feminism. According to one of her letters, she had been appalled at the age of fifteen by reading in Tolstoy's *War and Peace* that Natasha Rostova, on marrying, had become "a female of the species" (*samka*). Inessa Armand resolved to become a "human being" instead.[23]

By 1904, she had wearied of her role as a child-bearing *samka* and contracted a liaison with her brother-in-law. According to her Soviet biographer, her relations with him, though sexual, "did not resemble the adultery often found in bourgeois families"; that is, it was open and based on mutual love. She left her husband, though there was no divorce ("apparently because of the children") and they remained friends.[24] In the meantime early tenderness for servants and peasants, scenes of urban violence, revolutionary literature, and the iconoclastic milieu of the Armand family[25] combined to turn her into a socialist. In 1904, after her separation, she joined the Moscow organization of the Social Democrats and actively participated in the December Uprising of 1905. This was followed by the familiar pattern of arrest, exile, and emigration. Armand attended the feminist Women's Congress of 1908 but played no role in it. She did not meet Lenin until 1910 in Paris. While teaching at the

[22] Inessa apparently left no memoirs or autobiography other than a brief sketch written on four sheets of paper which now rest in the Central State Archive of the October Revolution. These have been used by Pavel Podlyashuk in his book, *Tovarishch Inessa: dokumentalnaya povest*, 2d. ed. (Moscow, 1965). It is superior to Jean Fréville: *Une grande figure de la Révolution russe: Inessa Armand* (Paris, 1957), a thin work, wrapped loosely around the story of Lenin and the Russian Revolution. For additional data, see Inessa Armand, *Stati, rechi, pisma* (Moscow, 1975) with a biographical sketch by her daughter; and Bertram Wolfe, "Lenin and Inessa Armand," *Slavic Review*, XXII, 1 (March, 1963) 96–114.

[23] Armand, *Stati*, 247.

[24] Podlyashuk, *Inessa*, 33.

[25] Buryshkin thus describes the Armands in *Moskva kupecheskaya*, 315. See her letters in Armand, *Stati*.

Longjumeau Party School, she and Krupskaya conceived the idea of political work among the Russian women living in Paris, an idea opposed by some of the Paris Bolsheviks but endorsed by Lenin. The Lenins then went to Galicia; she to Petersburg. When they met again in Cracow (1913), the plans for a women's journal were hatched. Inessa wrote several articles on women's work and suffrage for the journal (her first published work) and then set off on a tour of émigré colonies speaking on the woman question.

The final work of getting out *Rabotnitsa* (*Woman Worker*) in Russia was in the hands of the five Petersburg editors. Except for Kudelli, a veteran of the 1908 Congress, these women Bolsheviks were novices to the task of political work among women. Anna Elizarova, Lenin's older sister, had like her brothers been drawn to revolution by Populism in the 1880's; her career as a Bestuzhev student had been cut short in 1887 by her implication in the plot to kill the Tsar that had cost her brother Alexander his life. She was already fifty when assigned by Lenin to publish the new journal. Konkordiya Samoilova (1876–1921) was the daughter of a Siberian priest and a former Bestuzhevka, radicalized in 1898 by the Vetrova Affair. Elena Rozmirovich (1886–1953), who later married N. V. Krylenko, was currently serving as the secretary of the Bolshevik Duma fraction. Lyudmila Menzhinskaya (1876–1933) was a former teacher who had been attracted to Social Democracy by her childhood friend, Elena Stasova, and by her brother Vyacheslav, the future head of the Soviet political police. These women were all *intelligentki* and professional revolutionaries, serving as underground agents and journalists for *Pravda*, the Bolshevik organ. Their approach to the problem of organizing women, unlike Kollontai's and Inessa's, appears to have been simply a new Party assignment, much like any other, rather than as a deep personal cause arrived at through previous reflection. These circumstances, however, in no way dampened their enthusiasm for the job.[26]

The precedent of 1913 led the Committee to synchronize the debut of the journal with another observance of International Women's Day on February 23 (March 8 in the Western calendar) 1914. The police cunningly gave their permission to hold meetings, but then, on the eve of Women's Day, swooped down on the editorial board that was meeting openly in Kudelli's flat. All were arrested on an open warrant, except for Elizarova who, in an un-Bolshevik manner, had been late. On the way to the newly built women's prison on the Vyborg Side, one of her captors put to Samoilova a question which she recalled with ironic delight in later years: "Why, Madame, did you try to gather all our women together. Are you, like those foreign 'suffragettes' as they are called, desirous of throwing bombs at the government?" In spite of

---

[26] Ulyanova-Elizarova: E. Stasova, "Zhenshchiny semi Ulyanovykh," in *M. I. Ulyanova* (Moscow, 1965) 103–109; *Zhen. russ. rev.*, 473–88, 569. Samoilova: *Zhen. v rev.*, 104; V. Morozova, *Rasskazy o Zemlyachke; Klavidichka; Konkordiya* (Moscow, 1970), 317–541 (a fictionalized biography). Rozmirovich: *Zhen. russ. rev.*, 386–97, 567. Menzhinskaya: *ibid.*, 249–60, 564.

the liquidation of the editorial board and the arrest of some thirty women (eventually exiled), some of whom partially fulfilled the gendarme's fantasy by staging a seven-day hunger strike, Women's Day was celebrated in flash meetings around the city. And Elizarova, deep underground, finally managed to get *Woman Worker* published in spite of all obstacles. Among these, the most disheartening and the most serious for the future of the movement was the attitude of her male comrades who said to her: "Why a separate journal for you people when we don't have that kind of money?"[27]

Woman Worker appeared seven times between February 23 and June 26 when it ceased publication; some of the numbers were confiscated by the police. It contained articles on general topics (Bebel's *Woman*; the evils of feminism) and the more meaty reports of factory conditions, abuses of females and the like. These themes were taken up eagerly by other Party newspapers. *The Textile Worker, The Metal Worker*, and *The Tailor's Gazette* put out special issues for Women's Day. *The Northern Labor Gazette* and *The Path of Truth* printed poems and pathetic letters of lamentation from such anonymous contributors as "Metal Worker Shura," "Old Servant Woman," and "White Slaves." All this publicity came to an end with the onset of the war in the summer of 1914. In terms of the numbers of workers drawn into a Bolshevik women's movement by it, the results were insignificant. In this respect, as well as in regard to organization and communication, the Russian feminists were still far ahead of the socialists. But the Bolsheviks had taken up the idea and had worked out the beginnings of a technique. The editors of *Woman Worker* maintained contacts with groups of women workers in the capital from their place of exile in Novgorod. There would be no major observance of Women's Day in 1915 and 1916 but the holiday and the newspaper, under its old name, would be revived in the stormy days of 1917 as remembered methods of politicizing the women of St. Petersburg.[28]

In looking back at what came to be called the "proletarian women's movement" of the years 1905–1914, the picture is a mixed one at best. "Bolshevik feminism," as some Party members would like to have labeled it, appeared to have been surrounded by as much hostility and indifference as its more conventional rival—feminism *tout court*. Male workers continued to resent the competition of females, and would do so long after the Revolution. Male leaders of the various Marxist factions had little interest in organizing women. Some opposed it as a waste of time, energy, and funds; others as smacking too much of mere feminism—a movement that was held in contempt by every self-respecting socialist, man or woman. The Bolsheviks were no worse than

[27] The memoirs of Samoilova and Menzhinskaya are in *Kommunistka*, 8, 9 (Jan.-Feb., 1921) 12–15. See also *Zhen. russ. rev.*, 299 and *Zhen. v rev.*, 108–11.

[28] *Rabotnitsa* (SPB, 1914, 7 numbers). Only three of the seven were examined. The other newspapers are described, with excerpts, in *Iz epokhi 'Zvezdy' i 'Pravdy' (1911–1914 gg.)* (Moscow, 1921) 123–25. For the aftermath, see Samoilova, *V obedinneii*, 14–18. Some of the correspondence on *Rabotnitsa* has been published in Armand, *Stati*, 211–17.

other socialists in this regard. Indeed Lenin was more aware of and sympathetic to women than most of his colleagues in either the Menshevik or the
Bolshevik parties. But the awareness came late and had relatively little effect.
Most distressing of all, radical women who might have been useful in assisting political work among their less enlightened peers generally displayed a
curt disdain toward "women's" activity. Vera Zasulich, when asked for help
in Kollontai's short-lived women's club, replied that the enterprise was useless. It was against odds like these that women organizers among the Social
Democrats had to struggle in the years before the Revolution. Sadly enough,
they would have to repeat that struggle in the years after the Bolshevik victory.

3. THE FUTURE OF THE FAMILY

The picture of the Marxist doctrine on the woman question may be completed by looking briefly at its utterances on sexual and family relations, particularly as they would take shape in the framework of the socialist future. If
the politics of emancipation had excited angry rivalry between the feminists
and the socialists, the far more profound and ultimately decisive sexual question failed to do so. Neither gave it much public attention and thus found little
to fight about. There were differences between them on the subject, but they
failed to assume sharp and visible forms. Of far greater significance were the
psychological and ideological disagreements among the socialists themselves.
In view of the turbulent controversy that these contradictions aroused when
exposed to the light of post-revolutionary policy, it is important to examine
them here, at the time and place of their origin. In doing so, it is necessary to
be aware that Marxist sexual terminology is distressingly vague and inconsis-
tent, that the use of historical tenses and references to "the future" is often
muddled, and that some of the opinions cited in this section were published
long after they were uttered and were thus unavailable to the social architects
of the Revolution. These considerations help explain the bewildering use of
quotations from the Marxist masters by those on both sides of the polemical
barricades during the Soviet sexual revolution.

Socialists seldom ask the question: What of promiscuity for its own sake
without reference to marriage or love? The remarks of the German masters,
though scattered and sometimes published long after writing, leave no doubts
on this score.[1] Marx called love (not sex) a completion of and a complement
to the self; and his letters to his wife and his 1844 notes on human relationships between the sexes allow no latitude for the casual boudoir episode.
Engels, more specifically, contrasts mere sex (eros)—one-sided, light, fleeting—with "individual sex love" that is reciprocal, intense, and permanent.

[1] For a searching analysis of the sexual views of Marx and Engels as related to their lives, see
Meyer, "Marxism and the Women's Movement," in Atkinson et al., Women in Russia.

At the end of his celebrated analysis of the origins of monogamy, he predicts that love under socialism, "far from disappearing, will only begin to be completely realized." And men, he announced in tones that would have gladdened any feminist of the day, will become more monogamous, not women less so. Thus freedom simply means substituting sexual love ("by its very nature exclusive")—but not sex—for money.

Bebel, agreeing, added that, although sensual demands are normal and healthy, "excessive sexual passion is much more harmful than the lack of them." "Man," he explained, "is not a beast: for the higher satisfaction of his strongest demands, physical enjoyment is not enough; required here also is spiritual communion with that being with whom he establishes relations." Kautsky, in the language of simple programmatic explication, enshrined these views as official party dogma: "Socialists . . . maintain that ideal love, just the reverse of a community of wives and of all sexual oppression *and license*, will be the foundation of matrimonial connections in a Socialist Commonwealth, and that pure love can prevail only in such a system."[2]

When we step onto Russian soil, we find the atmosphere considerably more foggy. The moderate, no-nonsense outlook of the Germans was adopted, to be sure, along with the rest of Marxist theory. But this had to be grafted onto a tradition of sexual freedom inherited by the Russian left from the nihilists, who in turn had been inspired by the choryphaeuses of early French socialism. The result was an incipient dichotomy, still very blurred in these years, between the two traditions. The difficulty in sorting out the elements of a future schism among the Russians lies partly in the evasiveness of those who wrote on the subject, and partly on the very paucity of such writers. For the Mensheviks, there is only Kollontai; for the Bolsheviks, Lenin and Krupskaya. It is characteristic of the lack of attention given to the issue by the major leaders of the Social Democrats that the most detailed outline of the sexual culture of the future came from the pen of a now forgotten Marxist economist of the day, Andrei Isaev, in a book called *What Can Women Expect from Socialism?*.

Kollontai's views on sex and love were apparently given their first public utterance in a 1908 speech at the University of Dorpat on "The Family Question." Socialism, and only socialism, she said, would bring complete equality

---

[2] Marx: Bilshai, *O zhen. vop.* 110–11, 170–74. Engels, *The Origin of the Family, Private Property, and the State* (1884: 4th ed. 1891) (Moscow, 1952) 126–28, 125, 136, 135. Bebel, *Zhenshchina*, 142, 156, 150 (quotation). Kautsky, *The Class Struggle (Erfurt Program)* tr. W. Bohn (Chicago, 1910) 27 (italics added).

The most useful collection of Marxist "classic" writings on the woman question is that of Bilshai (Marx, Lenin, Engels). For those who do not read Russian, the following works may be of some use: *Woman and Communism: Selections from the Writings of Marx, Engels, Lenin, and Stalin* (London, 1950); *The Woman Question* (New York, 1951)—a similar selection (reprinted 1971); *La femme et le communisme: anthologie des grands textes du marxisme* (Paris, 1950); Clara Zetkin, *Lenin on the Woman Question* (New York, 1934); V. I. Lenin, *Woman and Society* (New York, 1938); *idem.*, *On the Emancipation of Women* (Moscow, n.d.). The best guide through Marx and Engels is still David Ryazanov's "Marks i Engels o brake i seme," *Letopisi marksizma*, III (1927) 13–35.

and independence for women, the state care of children, and full freedom in the area of love. The speech, we are told, was gleefully received by an audience of young people; but its ambiguity and brevity render it valueless. When writing *Social Bases*, Kollontai refined some of her explanations, though even here, she is still ambiguous. The main reason for this is that the author, determined to postulate a new "class" morality to replace all previous ones, felt compelled to launch an assault not only upon "bourgeois" marriage, a simple enough task, but also on the Russian tradition of "free love" that she identified with the bourgeois intelligentsia, particularly the proud, self-sufficient "emancipated" woman. Pages and pages of convoluted passages were devoted to proving that "free love," in and of itself, was not a sufficient "solution" to the sexual problems of the working class. To it she opposed a new "Proletarian morality." This had its roots in Engels and Bebel, both of whom proclaimed the working class to be the exclusive vessel of a pure sexual ethos, unsullied by property, litigation, or inheritance. Echoing this, Kollontai wrote that the life of the laboring man and woman offered "emphatically more suitable soil for working out the [sexual] psychology of the future than does that of the bourgeoisie."[3] But what is its sexual life, and its new morality?

As far back as 1869, in *Condition of the Working Class in Russia*, Bervi-Flerovsky described factory girls who did not hesitate to follow "the first call of love, the first heartbeats" without the sanction of matrimony. Workers far from their villages found it easy to strike up illicit liaisons, unmindful of church, of law, or of spouse back home. Kollontai found these unions based on affection quite natural; "the heart cannot wait" for conventional marriage. Indeed she claimed that working women found them preferable to wedlock, because of the relative freedom they afforded, and would marry only as a last resort, perhaps to help support a child. Pre-marital virginity played little part here, and a "girl with a past" could marry as freely as another. Kollontai was clearly exaggerating. But in plotting the future of these unions (which would be "purely moral") she was unable to foresee anything different in form from the traditional notion of "free love." "The ideal of free love, as envisaged by those women who struggled for emancipation undoubtedly corresponds to the norm of sexual relations which collective society will establish." Kollontai promised to explain later the differences between proletarian and bourgeois free love. But in the meantime, there was no doubt that her ideal of sexual life was *not* promiscuous pleasure for its own sake but a love relationship of two people, and that promiscuity, when practiced by the workers, had as its ultimate purpose the discovery of the ideal love partner.[4]

Although Lenin never wrote anything for the public about sexual intimacy, he expressed his views on the matter in two letters to Inessa Armand written in 1915 but not published until 1939. Inessa had been puzzling over the problem

[3] The report of Kollontai's speech is in *SZh* (Mar. 1908) 16. Kollontai, *Sots. osnovy*, 112–95. and quotation, 223; Engels, *Origin*, 118–19; Bebel, *Zhenshchina*, 173–74.

[4] Bervi quoted and commented on in Shishkin, *Revol. moral*, 49–50. Kollontai, *Sots. osnovy*, 219–23 (quotation, 219).

of sexual morality and had decided to write a pamphlet about it, partly as a guide for her young daughters. Writing to Lenin for advice, she used the term "free love" and claimed that (the quotation here is from Lenin's reply) " 'even a transient passion and love affair' is 'more poetic and purer' than 'the loveless kisses' (of philistine, very philistine) spouses." Lenin attacked such a view. On three occasions he identified "the demand [by women] for freedom of love" with bourgeois morality. In explaining, he allowed for freedom from material considerations, religious, social, and parental prejudices, and narrow bourgeois surroundings in love; but *not* (among other things) "from serious-ness in love." Lenin could not comprehend why Inessa contrasted transient passion with the loveless kisses of matrimony: " 'transient' (why transient?) 'passion' (why not love?)." He advised her to contrast it instead "to a prole-tarian civil marriage with love (adding, *if you absolutely must*, that a transient liaison [*svyaz-strast*] can be dirty and can be pure." From the letters Inessa was distinctly to the left of her idol in moral formulations. But she never wrote her pamphlet and, as far as it is known, never gave Lenin further trou-ble on the matter. Lenin's wife, Krupskaya, shared his views completely and wrote in 1911 that "a man sees in a woman, and *vice versa*, above all not a creature of the opposite sex, but a *person*."[5]

The form of relations between the sexes for the future predicted by most Marxists, then, was a "marriage," or love-union of some sort, rather than a series of love affairs. Though the terminology is exceedingly inexact, the dif-ference between these two life-styles is abundantly clear. But what form was the "marriage" to take? In the first place, as an equal member of socialist society, the woman of the future would have as much right to "choose" her mate as the man has. All socialists were in agreement on this. But the details of the marriage proposal and the wedding are revealed to us only in Isaev's social blueprint. The author, an extreme environmentalist, taught that the new socialist ethics would be marked by love of work, fair play, humanitarianism, tolerance, absence of greed, dignity, hatred of false patriotism, and cos-mopolitanism. Under these conditions, the woman, if possessed of a stronger personality, would feel free to say "I want to be your wife," and the socialist man, if disinclined, might refuse without insulting his suitor's dignity. Wed-dings were to be unencumbered by either legal formalities or nuptial solemnities—merely a simple declaration in the presence of a few friends. The wife could retain her own name if she so desired, and this predicted inno-vation found permanent acceptance in Soviet society.[6]

[5] The letters were first published in *Bolshevik*, No. 13 (1939) 58–62 and are reprinted in Bil-shai, *O zhen. vop.*, 179–83. For Lenin's alleged affair with Inessa Armand, see below Chapter XI. See also Podlyashuk, *Tovarishch Inessa*, 161–63; Krupskaya, *Izbrannye pedagogicheskie proizvedeniya* (Moscow, 1965) 123; and Armand, *Stati*, 208–9, 230, 238–39, 246–50.

[6] Bebel, *Zhenshchina*, 546–47 (on choosing a spouse). A. A. Isaev, *Chego ozhidat zhen-shchine ot sotsializma?* (Stuttgart, 1903) 8–10. For his general views on socialist morality, see: *O sotsializme nashikh dnei* (Stuttgart, 1902) esp. 268–309; and (as Isaieff) *Les Grandes hommes et le milieu social* (Paris, 1912).

But what of the marriage itself, the nature of its bond and its tenure? In 1842 Marx spoke piously of *"the moral beauty* that invested natural instinct with the ideal character of an instance of spiritual union—in a word the *spiritual essence* of marriage."* Engels, sketching out the history of monogamy, heaped scorn on it, the most caustic example of which was this typical piece of nineteenth-century quasi-biological irony: "And if strict monogamy is to be regarded as the acme of all virtue, then the palm must be given to the tapeworm, which possesses a complete male and female sexual apparatus in every one of its 50 to 200 proglottides or segments of the body, and passes the whole of its life cohabiting with itself in every one of these segments." And his nasty comments on its latest, bourgeois, stage are well-known. But in the end he admitted no other model acceptable to future lovers than the conjugal union stripped of its capitalist impedimenta. Bebel stated plainly that marriage ought to be entered into in all seriousness, with a mind to its obligations, and with an eye to permanence. And a German Marxist handbook of the 1890's—later translated into Russian—said that "socialism—and we stress this—does not seek to destroy or change the institution of marriage."[7]

But these suggestions, when placed beside the freedom and equality of the sexes to which all socialists adhered raise two more vexed and unavoidable questions: Is the marriage (or union) to be *strictly* monogamous, and is it to be indissoluble? The first of these has to do, of course, with adultery. Lenin, in his letter to Inessa Armand, stated flatly that adultery was not to be condoned (presumably even under socialism). Isaev, in a detailed description of how the future woman was to enjoy the companionship of a variety of male companions, was careful to point out that only one of them was to enjoy the charms of her flesh. Sex, in any case, would not play an excessively large role in the life of the socialist couple, he declared, since much of their energy would be deflected into public activity—an early adumbration of the theory of "revolutionary sublimation." Kollontai was bolder. She observed approvingly that among the proletariat husbands were not so shocked by the infidelity of their wives (and wives, presumably, less so). But her picture of the future was a blurry and undialectical vision of a "new" family life evolving out of present-day principles.[8]

On divorce, there is greater clarity. Marx, while opposed to whimsical treatment of marriage, conceded that it, like friendship, could be dissolved, and indeed that it was dead already if it was a haven of deceit. Engels, agreeing in principle, sounded rather reluctant to accept the practice in his correspondence with Karl and Louise Kautsky on the occasion of their divorce. In

---

[7] Marx, Bilshai, *O zhen. vop.*, 113. Engels, quotation, *Origin*, 54; comments on bourgeois marriage, 108, 118, 123. Bebel, *Zhenshchina*, 151–52. *Sprav. kniga*, I, 236.

[8] Lenin, Bilshai, *O zhen. vop.*, 180. Isaev, *Chego ozhidat*, 15–17. Kollontai, *Sots. osnovy*, 222, 216.

any case, he felt that men had greater responsibilities for preserving marriage bonds than did women. For Bebel, captivity in a loveless marriage was the greatest form of torture, thus making divorce a moral necessity. Isaev, brimming as ever with optimism, maintained that divorces would be few because the marriages would be sounder. But freedom of divorce there must always be, he warned, not only for the benefit of mismatched lovers but also for the protection of children from the baneful atmosphere of the loveless home. The dissolution, like the wedding itself, would be a simple announcement in the presence of friends. Kollontai found no need for a specific proclamation on freedom to dissolve a union. And Lenin, unconscious of any ambiguity, informed his readers in an unpublished comment of 1916 that "one cannot be a democrat and a socialist without demanding now the full freedom of divorce, for the reason that the absence of this freedom constitutes an extra yoke fastened on an already subjected sex, women—though it is not at all difficult to realize that *the freedom* to leave one's husband is in no sense *an invitation* to all wives to do so!"[9]

Most socialists seemed to endorse Bebel's belief that "marriage represents one side of sex life in bourgeois society and prostitution the other." Marxist pronouncements on that problem varied. The simplest version of the orthodox view is contained in Lenin's *Pravda* article of 1913: "as long as wage-slavery exists, prostitution must inevitably continue." Poverty and sexual inequality being the main villains, relief could come only after abolishing them—via the abolition of capitalism. But both Bebel and Engels also voiced their opposition to the police-medical inspection system the liquidation of which they made an immediate, minimal demand since, according to Bebel, it fostered belief in the legality and permanence of the vice and failed to stop disease. On this they were at one with most feminists.

Kollontai could hardly disagree, though in her remarks she observed that even among whores there was class differentiation and that the well-paid ones were able to avoid inspection through bribery.[10] Though far closer, both geographically and psychologically, to the problem of prostitution in 1905–1908 than the male leaders in emigration, Kollontai, like most other socialists, paid little attention to it. Her woman workers' club of 1908, though situated a short distance from the red light district, apparently concerned itself more with the women in the factories of the Nevsky District than those in the brothels on the Ligovka. Far distant were the days when the Bolshevik leaders would them-

[9] Marx, Bilshai, *O zhen. vop.*, 180. Engels, Letters to the Kautskys, October 11, 17, 1888 in *ibid.*, 175–76. Bebel, *Zhenshchina*, 165, 547. Isaev, *Chego ozhidat*, 10–14. Lenin: Bilshai, *O zhen. vop.*, 178–79 (written 1916; first published, 1924).

[10] Bebel, quotation, *Zhenshchina*, 226; Letter Engels-Bebel, December 22, 1892 in Bilshai, *O zhen. vop.*, 72–73. Lenin, *Emancipation*, 26–27; his oft quoted and anthologized *Rabochaya Pravda* article of the same year on the white slave traffic (in Bilshai, *O zhen. vop.*, 79–80) contains nothing of substance about the subject itself, though much about Lenin's attitude to private charity. Kollontai, *Sots. osnovy*, 160–70, 180–82; her remarks about the feminists in these passages are exceptionally unfair.

selves have to confront the realities of prostitution, abolition, regulation, disease, and prevention.

"How I eat, how I drink, how I sleep, and how I dress is my own personal business, just as my relations with a person of the opposite sex is also my own business." Thus wrote Bebel in 1879 about the privacy of sexual relations in the future. But compare Engels' words written five years later on the same subject. The new people, born and raised under socialism, "will establish their own practice and their own public opinion, conformable therewith, on the practice of each individual—and that's the end of it." With Bebel, there was no equivocation. But from the passage of Engels, one can surely build a case for establishing a "public opinion" about sexual matters in the coming age. This public opinion will, to be sure, be fashioned, as Engels says, out of the sexual practices of those who have never known the disgusting marketplace mentality of the bourgeoisie—but it will exist nonetheless as a norm, as a measure, in fact as a new Sexual Morality to be used as a means to judge "the practice of each individual." Otherwise the passage makes no sense. But the question that arises—quite apart from the substance of the new morality—is this: Why have an official morality or "public opinion," however pure and pragmatic its origins, unless it is to be used by society to frown upon those who transgress it?[11]

The social setting of the family and the role of woman as mother-housekeeper, though hardly separable from the sexual issues reviewed above, have peculiarities of their own. Most Marxist thinkers looked askance at sex for its own sake and child-bearing was to them one of the most important functions of sex and love. Speaking of "the duty of motherhood," Bebel conceded that there might sometimes be acceptable reasons for a woman to avoid it, but these did not include "convenience" or the preservation of one's figure. In the future, he said, regulation of the birth rate, resulting in smaller families than was now the case, would occur naturally (!) and "without the harmful effects of abstinence and without the unnatural use of birth-control devices." Lenin, for once, was less austere—or more realistic. Like all good Marxists, he violently opposed "social neo-Malthusianism," the notion that the production of human lives had to be deliberately and constantly restricted so that humanity could win the deadly race with a dwindling food supply. This he viewed simply as a deathwish of the decadent bourgeoisie and of "unfeeling and egotistical petty-bourgeois couples." But on the practical level he also demanded "the unconditional annulment of all laws against abortion or against the distribution of medical literature on contraceptive measures" to which all men and women had an elementary right.[12]

[11] Bebel, *Zhenshchina*, 574. Engels, *Origin*, 138.
[12] Bebel, *Zhenshchina*, 184, 579. Lenin, Bilshai, *O zhen. vop.*, 77–79 (a *Pravda* article of 1913 inspired by the debates on birth control at the Twelfth Pirogov Medical Congress in St. Petersburg in the same year).

Kollontai in these years gave little thought to abortion and contraception as boons for womankind. Like other socialists, she was concerned with the creation of new life and with making childbirth easier and pleasanter for all women. In *Social Bases* she took issue with Ellen Key's stress on maternity, with or without a husband, as the central focus of a woman's existence. On the other hand, Kollontai emphatically desired to make motherhood a possibility and a blessing for women of every class, married or not. Her main interest was in maternity benefits for working women. Before the War she produced a brochure entitled *The Working Woman as Mother* that contained the embryo of her massive study, *Society and Maternity* (1915). With her customary acidity, she described the easy lot of the expectant bourgeois mother, pampered and well nourished. To her she contrasted the haggard working woman, dry-breasted, sick, and over-worked, forced to return to the bench immediately after her confinement, with no hope of giving proper milk or care to the newborn child. Kollontai's demands were the blueprint of the future maternity welfare program in Soviet Russia: sixteen weeks fully-paid leave; free birth clinics; on-site nursing facilities and breaks.[13]

Except for those of Proudhon and his school, the socialist utopias of the nineteenth century—even the earliest of them, "Ruvarebohni" (1808)—tended to encapsulate the family in some kind of commune in order to release women for non-domestic pursuits. Engels, in *The Origin*, provided the Marxist version of this idea: "The individual family ceases to be the economic unit of society. Private housekeeping is transformed into a social industry. The care and education of the children becomes a public matter." Prior to the 1890's, most German socialists (Bebel was an exception) avoided the temptation to speculate about the details of future social life; this was a reaction against the excessive utopianism of their French forerunners. But in the 1890's, utopia building came into fashion once again, this time under the impulse of growing technology. Kautsky, in a preface to Atlanticus's *A Glimpse at the State of the Future* (1898), explained that the new utopians were trying to answer concrete questions of the workers about the coming dispensation. Bebel's *Woman*, for the first time enjoying wide legal circulation, rhapsodized over the missions of electricity to render cooking scientific, peel vegetables, wash dishes and finally abolish the kitchen, the slave-pen of women. Sharing Bebel's popularity among German workers was Edward Bellamy's *Looking Backward* (1888), in which the man of the year A.D. 2000, replying to a question about housework, replies: "There is none to do." Electricity has conquered all; women are freed for industry and are organized into their own "army" led by their own woman "general." The most complete picture was drawn by Lili Braun in *Female Labor and Housekeeping* (1901). In her view the unit of the future would be a modern building housing 50 to 60 families,

[13] Kollontai, *Sots. osnovy*, 197–204, 226–31; *idem., Rabotnitsa-mat* (1914) enlarged edition (Moscow, 1918).

265

with central facilities for laundering, dishwashing, and other domestic services. It would contain a communal kitchen and dining room where members could eat or "take out." It would also have a single playroom for all the children; and the whole operation would be run by a female director.[14]

The idea of collective living was hardly new to Russian radicals. Back in the 1840's, a Russian disciple of Fourier, Beklemeshev, extolled the logic of a big kitchen, a few large pots, and a handful of cooks replacing the absurdity of 200 kitchens, 200 pots, and 200 cooks. In the 1890's the German utopians were quickly translated and discussed; and Bellamy's book was read literally from Petersburg to Sakhalin even before the appearance of translations. Krupskaya's *Woman Worker* was the first Russian expression of the new tendency, though she passed rather lightly over the future. Isaev, on the other hand, described in detail the future forms of residential life. Most people would live in communes—modern apartment buildings—and eat collectively; some would retain separate dwellings and eat at a *stolovaya*, a public dining room; a few would live remote from the *stolovayas* and would have to cook at home. But in all cases, chores would be rendered easier by appliances, husbands would share any residual housekeeping duties, and woman would come to resemble man in everything except periodic pregnancies. Krupskaya believed that boys should be trained from childhood to help equally in housework. "The particularist, individual household economy" wrote Kollontai, "gives way to large-scale cooperative enterprises where, side by side with central heating and lighting for dozens of separate families, there will also be common kitchens and dining rooms." And Lenin, a great enthusiast for electric power, proclaimed that it would "relieve millions of 'domestic slaves' of the need to spend three-fourths of their lives in smelly kitchens."[15]

On the joys of collective living there was more agreement then than now among socialists. But one aspect of it, public (the words state, collective, or social are interchanged with it) childrearing, commanded a much more cautious approach than the collectivization of pots and pans. Most socialists endorsed the growing tendency of schools to become more numerous, more populous, and more versatile, but resisted the idea of any sort of state expropriation of children. They accepted a vision that included some form of public upbringing, though few felt constrained to provide details. Among them

---

[14] M. L., "Une Utopie rare: l'Utopie du Ruvarebohni," *Bulletin of the International Institute of Social History in Amsterdam*, I (Leiden, 1937) 22–36. Engels: *Origin*, 126 (and see also 244); his ideas on centralized housekeeping go back to before 1848 (Bilshai, *O zhen. vop.*, 88). Kautsky's preface to Atlanticus [Karl Ballod] *Ein Blick in den Zukunftstaat: Produktion und Konsum in Sozialstaat* (Stuttgart, 1898) vii–xiii. Bebel, *Zhenshchina*, 540–45. Edward Bellamy, *Looking Backward: 2000-1887* (New York, 1888) 118–19, 256. Lili Braun, *Frauenarbeit und Hauswirtschaft* (Berlin, 1891) esp. 21–26.

[15] Beklemeshev's comment from N. V. Riasanovsky, "Fourierism in Russia: an Estimate of the Petraševcy," *American Slavic and East European Review*, XII, 3 (1953) 289–302. Translations and discussions of Western Utopian writings: F. Engels, *Proiskhozhdenie semi, chastnoi sobstvennosti, i gosudarstva* (SPB, 1906); K. Kautsky, *Sotsialnaya reforma na drugoi den posle sotsialnoi revolyutsii* (Rostov-na-Donu, 1905); Petr Al. [G. A. Aleksinsky] *Nasha programma*

Bebel and Kollontai are notable because their positions, while not exactly contradictory, seem to be facing in different directions. Bebel, in lauding the value of the group outlook nourished in the children of a collective community, added three cautions: Parental tenderness cannot be replaced by group feeling; a child must remain at the mother's breast as long as necessary for his or her emotional well-being; only the parents should decide when *and if* their child is to be entrusted to public care.[16]

Kollontai's emphases are somewhat different. To fight egoism and to raise up true proletarian children, the family and the amateur mother will not suffice.

> In the hygienic, morally pure atmosphere of the nurseries and kindergartens, under professionally trained teachers, the child will be saved from the grim conditions in which proletarian children are now raised. These will be in the custody not of charity organizations (run by people of a different class) but in that of whatever collectives the future will organize. In these, the new generation will, from the earliest years, learn to value the beauties of solidarity and sociability [*obshchesvennost*], and become accustomed to looking at the world through the prism of the collective and not through his own selfish ego.

For the bourgeois "mommies" who raise their voices in fear at the specter of such socialization, Kollontai had nothing but scorn, particularly since wealthy women were more than willing to place their own children in the hands of nannies or in private day-nurseries in order to enjoy the freedom of leisure. But such mothers, nay all mothers, lacked the professional training necessary to care for children scientifically, she claimed. "To mend shoes, one has to pass through an apprenticeship," she wrote, quoting Zetkin; "but to guide such a delicate creation as the spirit of a child, one needs it would seem only a mother's instinct."[17] And so once again Kollontai appears, if still very dimly and tentatively, to be occupying the most leftward range of the theoretical spectrum in Marxism dealing with sexual and family matters. Only the Revolution would reveal that there were others, far to the left of her.

(programma maksimum i minimum RSDRP) (Moscow, 1906), who refers his readers (15, note) to Bebel, Kautsky, Atlanticus, and William Morris' *News From Nowhere* (serialized earlier in *Neue Zeit*) for details of life under socialism; E. Lozinsky, *O nastoyashchem i budushchem zhenskago dvizheniya* (N.p., n.d. 1903 or 1904), esp. 72–78 (on Lili Braun). For evidence of Bellamy's immediate popularity in Russia, see Chekhov's letter to A. S. Suvorin of December 17, 1890 in *Sobranie sochinenii*, 12 v. (Moscow, 1960–1964) XI, 473 and note 668–69. The first two translations (*Budushchii vek* and *Cherez sto let*) appeared in 1891.

Isaev, *Chego ozhidat*, 18–22. Krupskaya, *Iz pedagog.*, 448–51. Kollontai, *Sots. osnovy*, 217. Lenin, *Emancipation*, 24 (from a 1913 *Pravda* article).

[16] Bebel, *Zhenshchina*, 178, 519–21.

[17] Kollontai, *Sots. osnovy*, quotation, 217–18. The socialists had no monopoly on the belief in day nurseries and public care of children (see Lukhmanova, *Nedochety*, 53). For the more general remarks of Zetkin and Krupskaya, see the former's *Arbeiterinnen*, 23–39 and the latter's *Zhenshchina-rabotnitsa*, 19–20.

The musings offered above have been gleaned out of a relatively small body of writings. In general, socialists had little to say about sex; and this was in the true tradition of Russian radicalism which held that Chernyshevsky and Mikhailov, if not Engels and Bebel, had said it all. According to some of the old Mensheviks and Bolsheviks, sex was considered personal and was not subjected to the intense philosophical inspection accorded it by earlier generations. The Social Democrats taught that women were to be regarded as equals, to be called "comrade" rather than *baba* or auntie, and that was that. The Socialist Revolutionaries who wrote about it offered nothing original or important. B. German's *Biology and Socialism*, couched in Lavrovian terms, predicted that with the disappearance of physical dangers from nature, the parental instinct of protecting children would atrophy and with it personal child care. Public rearing would then be a blessed release of the mother from domestic concerns. N. S. Rusanov simply stated that sex, like religion, should be a personal matter, and he believed that women deputies in a future Duma would call for "neutrality" on the part of the state in marital affairs. This was perhaps the most inaccurate of the predictions made in pre-revolutionary years about the woman question.[18]

From the Anarchists very little on the woman question can be found; and nothing by the women themselves. Matrëna Prisyazhnyuk, the Ukrainian terrorist, said: "My ideal is the free development of the individual personality in the broadest sense of the word, and the overthrow of slavery in all its forms." More than this we do not have from Anarchist women. In 1908 the Kropotkinist, I. S. Vetrov, simply repeated the Marxist demand for the liberation of women from "the humiliating yoke" of household work, a theme repeated in Boris Frommett's *Life Under Socialism* and the Gordin brothers' *Union of the Five Oppressed* (both 1917). Under socialism, "marriage will no longer be hard labor and torment [for women]" wrote Frommett; and if it becomes so, it will be easy to escape from it. The Gordin brothers, with considerably more originality, listed woman as one of "the five oppressed" (with the worker, the young, the minority, and the personality) and identified her oppressor not as capital or wage-slavery but as "the bandits, rapists, bastards, cads, and literary seducers" who wished to dominate and conquer her (*vlastvovat*), in short as male sexual authoritarianism.[19]

Nowhere did socialist leaders or theoreticians preach community of wives or anything like it. Indeed, they were hardly more radical than the average member of the advanced Russian intelligentsia in matters of sex. But this did

[18] On the use of the word "comrade," see Shishkin, *Revol. moral*, 271. B. German, *Biologiya i sotsializm* (Geneva, 1904) 246–47. N. Kudrin [Rusanov], *O ravnopravnosti*, 24–27.

[19] The quotation from Prisyazhyuk's 1908 speech at her trial for assassination in Kiev from Paul Avrich, *The Russian Anarchists* (Princeton, 1967), 66. I. S. Vetrov [Knizhik] *Ocherk sotsialnoi ekonomii s tochki zreniya anarkhicheskago kommunizma* (Paris, 1908) 15–17. Boris Frommett, *Zhizn pri sotsializme* (Petrograd, 1917) 25–27. A. L. and V. L. Gordin, *Rechi anarkhista* (Moscow, 1919)—a collection of articles—71–73, 100–14 (quotation, 106), and 116–17.

not save them from religious and conservative accusations of promoting debauchery, present and future. Father Albitsky, in a 1907 critique of socialism, stated flatly that socialists taught "free love" (here meaning promiscuity) and implied strongly that most of them embraced the idea of sharing wives and children. In Marxist musings on the probability of smaller families in days to come, he found further proof that sexual relations in the future state would resemble those of cattle—"or, better to say, a pig-sty." Similarly, Kuzmin, in *Woman in the Teachings of the Social Democrats* (1907), called socialists "dark people" who were trying to undermine the state by destroying the family, by luring women away from their lofty "natural" functions, making prostitutes of all women, and introducing into society "the moral equality of the gutter." His evidence for all this, incidentally, was not Marxist writings, but a few decadent novels and tales of sexual freedom. Kuzmin had a deep-seated aversion to the entire socialist world outlook—particularly to its atheism and materialism. To a certain kind of pious moralizer, such an outlook must inevitably lead to the basest forms of behavior, regardless of what the socialist philosophers may say, or neglect to say, about such behavior. Kuzmin and Albitsky—there were others—were the intellectual descendants of Professor Tsitovich and the anti-nihilist mud-slingers of the 1860's and they were also the forerunners of the anti-Soviet propagandists of the early Soviet period who saw in the Bolsheviks an assembly of depraved monsters presiding over the orgies of a corrupted nation.[20]

4. WOMEN UNDERGROUND: A SKETCH

The "proletarian women's movement" was a special effort within the Social Democratic Party to fight against feminism and to build (class) consciousness. Its historical shift from negation to action can be seen in its tactics and symbols—antifeminist campaigns and the Women's Congress caucus in 1905–1908 to Women's Day and *Rabotnitsa* in the years 1912–1914. Its ranks were filled with women workers; its leaders almost exclusively *intelligenki*. Outside this tiny movement existed a community of radical women, largely unaware of the special women's work within Social Democracy—or aware only to the point of hostility. Though there was occasional overlap between

[20] Petr Albitsky (Father), *Khristianstvo i sotsializm* (Nizhny Novgorod, 1907), 63–73. Kuzmin, *Zhenshchina*, 3–7 (quotation, 5); his reactionary political views may be examined in his *Narod i vlast* (SPB, 1907).

The only reference I have ever seen to separating children from their parents and mixing them to prevent any future claims (done in the name of an "all-human" [*obshchechelovecheskaya*] goal is in a play of the well-known writer, N. Minsky [Vilinkin], *Alma* (SPB, 1900). But the bearer of the play's message is not, apparently, Alma, the collectivizer of children (she changes her mind later on and cannot find her own), but a pediatrician who voices his belief that "the only thing that is great and powerful is instinct and the instinct of motherhood is greater than any other" and that the so-called all-human impulses "tie people together mechanically as cities are tied together by telegraph wires, while instinct is not a wire but a living nerve" (104).

the two groups, they were fundamentally dissimilar. Not only was the purely radical community larger numerically than the Marxist women's movement, but it was broader, including Socialist Revolutionary and Anarchist as well as Social Democratic women. Furthermore, its traditions, recruitment techniques, and ethos were indigenous, stretching back to the 1860's—in contrast to the recently imported Marxist effort for women. Indeed it is this element of the women's movement in Russia—radical womanhood or "the common cause"—that distinguishes it so sharply from other European countries which might have had their proletarian women's movements, but nothing comparable to the ample cohort of Russian women who spent most of their adult lives in underground opposition.

The new generation of female radicals differed in several ways from its Populist predecessor. It was larger, though how much larger it is hard to say, partly because of the problems of defining the word "revolutionary." To a much greater extent than in earlier generations, many persons wore that epithet lightly or were readily endowed with it by the authorities. It is difficult to draw sharp lines in that blurry region where "true" revolutionaries intermingled with the broad left, or the democratic intelligentsia. But even a fairly narrow definition—women who engaged in illegal activities, worked for the overthrow of the government, and accepted violence—would supply us with a complement of Social Democratic, Socialist Revolutionary, and Anarchist women big enough to outnumber their Populist forbears. Since the revolutionary movement became nationalized, so to speak, in this period, its geographic spread and its ethnic composition was considerably broadened. The social level of women revolutionaries in 1905 was slightly lower than those of the 1870's and the new generation contained more women of the Western borderlands, more Jews, more daughters of "middle-class" families as well as a thin stratum of workers and proletarianized peasant women.[1] The following sketch deals with two clusters of radical women which in some ways are distinguishable from one another: the devotees of the *narodnik* tradition, flowing chiefly into the Socialist Revolutionary and Anarchist movements; and the professional agents of Social Democracy.

The Socialist Revolutionary Party was one of the most bizarre collection of radicals ever seen in Russia—a land of theatrical revolutionaries. It is particularly difficult to gauge how many women—or men for that matter—were genuinely active members. A large number of feminists were Socialist Revolutionary in their general outlook, but this meant little in terms of energy donated to the Party. Olga Volkenstein, for example, was a "female Socialist Revolutionary" (*eserka*), but it was the feminist groups that claimed her journalistic talents. A woman, Lyubov Rodionova-Klyachko, founded the leading

[1] This impression is confirmed by a recent statistical study by Amy Knight: "Women in the Russian Revolutionary Movement, 1881-1917," to appear in Glickman and Stites, *Women*.

Socialist Revolutionary group and its journal. But, as with the other parties, the men assumed the dominant positions. According to the tabulations and estimates (including an assessment of the gender of pseudonyms) made by Amy Knight, 18 or 9.2 percent of the 196 mandated delegates to the congresses and conferences of the years 1905–1908, were women; and 8 or 12 percent of the 66 consultative delegates were women. These percentages are higher for women than those of analogous Social Democratic congresses. But the female delegates had little enough to say. Chernov, Gershuni, the Gots brothers, and Azef the police spy were the undisputed leaders in the formative years.[2] The Party attracted many female students and professional women; and many an upper-class woman who, in a Western society, would have been a liberal at most. The Socialist Revolutionaries maintained no "fraction" in the feminist organizations, but they did have one in a small Petersburg charity group called Women's Mutual Aid. In the countryside, the typical *eserka* was either a salaried staff worker ("third element") in the *zemstvo* doing medical, technical, or clerical work, or a village teacher. The Socialist Revolutionary Union of Schoolteachers was its one auxiliary wholly dominated by women; in 1905, the Socialist Revolutionaries were so strong that they easily captured the National Union of Schoolteachers. During times of ferment socialist revolutionary women moved out of their bases in school and *zemstvo* office to spread inflammatory propaganda among the rural population.[3]

Terror made the Socialist Revolutionary woman, with a few Anarchists and Bolsheviks, the center of public attention in the first decade of the twentieth century. The magic of the deed was evoked by a series of murders of state officials, by Socialist Revolutionaries, carried out by teams of men and women. One of the latter, Mme. Averkieva, a veteran of the *narodnik* trials, and a mother of revolutionaries, refused "to talk" (via the prison "telephone") with a Social Democrat incarcerated in a nearby cell because *Iskra* had denounced terror. An early outrage involving women was the bombing of an Odessa café in late 1905 by an Anarchist group; one of the captured women was hanged. The Socialist Revolutionaries employed a bit more discrimination: In July 1906, a female member of a Socialist Revolutionary "flying combat detachment" threw a bomb into the headquarters of the Odessa Military District, and then shot herself at once. By the end of 1906, the Butyrka Prison was holding a half-dozen terrorist women (as young as eighteen) who had killed or tried to kill government officials. A typical Socialist Revolu-

[2] For the Socialist Revolutionaries before 1905: Zilli, *Rivoluzione*, 1, 285–300, 439–42. After 1905: Oliver Radkey, *Agrarian Foes of Bolshevism* (New York, 1958). The congresses: Knight, "Women in the Russian Revolutionary Movement."
[3] There is some description of local Socialist Revolutionary activity in A. N. Stepanov, "Kritika V. I. Lenina programmy i taktiki eserov v period novogo revolyutsionnogo podëma (1910–1914 gg.)," *Bolsheviki v borbe protiv melkoburzhuaznykh partii v Rossii (1910–1920 gg)* (Moscow, 1969) 28. Bernard Pares observed in 1904 that in the villages the schoolmistress "was almost certainly a Socialist and very likely a Marxist." (*My Russian Memoirs*, London, 1937, 65). If true, it ceased to be so after 1905 when that profession was completely dominated by the SR's.

tionary assassin was Zina Konoplyanikova, the village schoolteacher who killed the pacifier of the Moscow Insurrection of 1905, General Min. Tyrkova, who had met her in prison in 1903, recalled an utterly rebellious young woman who nevertheless spoke tenderly of her peasant mother from whom she hid her radical tendencies until she was hanged at the Schlüsselburg Fortress.[4]

The twenty-one year old Tolya Ragozinikova, ignoring the later pronouncements of Zasulich against terror, attempted to emulate her. Hearing that corporal punishment was being used on prisoners, she walked into the Okhrana headquarters in Petersburg with thirteen pounds of dynamite in her bodice and shot the prison administrator. The impetus was love. "I did what I could," she wrote to her family, "and this gives me peace and courage. . . . Only a higher duty forced me to this deed. No, not even duty, but love, a great love for mankind. For its sake I sacrificed all I had. How good it is to love people. How much strength one gains from such love." Lidiya Sture, a Bolshevik Bestuzhev student, helped a Fighting Detachment to prepare the attempted assassination of the Minister of Justice, Shcheglovitov (a fact that might partially explain his later attitude toward women's rights). Before she was hanged, she asked her father to send ten rubles a month to the scholarship fund for Bestuzhev students. She was the inspiration for Andreev's character, Musya, in *The Seven That Were Hanged*.[5]

Towering above these was Mariya Spiridonova, the eldest sister in a fairly well-off family of Tambov. Not yet twenty, she joined the Socialist Revolutionary Party, seeing in it the embodiment of "the social trinity"—peasant, worker, and intellectual. At the instance of her local committee, she set out to assassinate General Luzhenovsky who had subjected her province to punitive raids in 1905. On the railway station platform of Borisoglebsk, she shot him in the the face with her revolver—a silver-plated replica of which she was later given by her admiring comrades. Soldiers dragged her face down on the stone steps, extinguished cigarettes on her breasts, pulled out her hairs, whipped her, tore out her flesh, and asked her how many lovers she had had. Her beating caused her completely to forget the French language. When the details became known, there was a burst of public indignation in Russian society, and protests were arranged as far away as Trafalgar Square. The Union for Women's Equality praised her courage. Her victim was forgotten. She was spared the death penalty and proceeded triumphantly to Siberian exile amid the cheers of her admirers. Ten years later she would retrace the same route, again in triumph, leaving in her wake the ruins of dynamited prisons.[6]

Women politicals became so numerous that the government had to build a

[4] Zakharova-Tsederbaum, *Iz epokhi*, 70 (on Averkieva); Avrich, *Russian Anarchists*, 67; *Tovarishch*, August 3, 1906; 1; Figner-Brupacher, 7; *SZh*, (Nov. 1907) 10; I. Steinberg (Shteinberg), *Maria Spiridonova* (London, 1935), 45. Konoplyanikova: Trykova, *Na putyakh*, 142.

[5] Ragozinikova: Steinberg, *Spiridonova*, 89 and *idem, In the Workshop of the Revolution* (London, 1955) 214–16. Sture: *Kursy*, 63–64.

[6] Steinberg, *Spiridonova*, xi–44; V. Vladimirov, *Mariya Spiridonova* (Moscow, 1905).

new Women's Prison on the Vyborg Side. Some penal reforms were made. Women convicts were no longer allowed to be shackled, an innovation that prompted the chief of the tsarist prison administration to complain to the Duma. "Experience shows," he said, "that women, in terms of criminality, ability, and possession of the urge to escape, are hardly distinguishable from men." The Socialist Revolutionary Party, by 1908, had not become inactive; but many of its women fighters were gone—dead, or languishing in prison or in distant Siberian settlements. One of these was the "commune" organized by Spiridonova and her comrades at the Maltsev hard-labor settlement for women, some seventy female prisoners, mostly Socialist Revolutionaries and Anarchists. They organized their lives cooperatively, planned escapes, and read to each other—not Spencer, Darwin, Marx, or Lavrov, but the Bible, Indian philosophy, Pascal, Nietzsche, Dostoevsky, Solovëv, Merezhkovsky, and even Mach and Avenarius. Personal behavior in the commune was conducted according to a cult of moral integrity so exalted that some saw in it an excessively morbid spirit of self-analysis. Two veterans of these settlements were to have dramatic moments in 1918. Anastasiya Bitsenko, the Socialist Revolutionary assassin of General Sakharov, was unimpressed by the cult at Maltsev; she later went over to the Bolsheviks and startled the German officials at Brest-Litovsk by appearing in the peace delegation as the representative of toiling women. The other was Feiga Roidman, an Anarchist arrested for making bombs in a Kiev laboratory. Her penchant for political murder would bring her briefly to the center stage of world attention in August 1918 as Fanya Kaplan, the would-be assassin of Lenin, and then to oblivion.[7]

Women were present in the first Social Democratic circles (*kruzhki*) that began competing with the old populists in the 1890's. Here future Bolsheviks, Mensheviks, and "economists" worked together in a free and friendly fashion. Revolutionary romances blossomed; and when schisms erupted, wives usually followed husbands. Krupskaya and Lenin were a typical couple of this milieu. The Nevzorova sisters, a dentist, a teacher, and a chemist, blended radicalism with professional life and began their political careers by teaching simple workers all they knew about anthropology, history, and economics from the Marxist point of view. From the tiny circles of the Smolenskaya Sunday School, they branched into agitational work near the factories; then came arrest, exile, or emigration. Around them fluttered older and more cautious figures, such as Mme. Davydova and A. M. Kalmykova, who acted as early patronesses of legal Marxism.[8]

[7] Quotation on shackling cited in *Zhen. goroda*, 33. On the Maltsev Commune: Steinberg, *Spiridonova*, 95–99. Kaplan was incarcerated with these women at Akatu before the transfer to Maltsev: *ZhD*, (Dec. 15, 1913) 21–22.

[8] A good introduction to the circles is Allan Wildman, *The Making of a Workers' Revolution* (Chicago, 1967), *passim*. For some of the women, see: Krupskaya, "Pyat let raboty v vechernykh smolenskikh klassakh," 222–39; the works on Krupskaya cited in Chapter VIII, 1 n. 12; the brief

The founding of *Iskra* and of a national Social Democratic Party at the opening of the century created a type known as "the *Iskra* girl" (*Iskrovka*), the well-dressed young lady, skirts bulging with illegal newspapers, who ran the route from Poland or Finland across the frontier into Russia. The best known was Elena Stasova (1873–1966), the archetypical "professional" radical. Her uncle was the famous music critic; her aunt a founder of Russian feminism. The family apartment on Furshtadskaya (near the old American Embassy) was a center of culture, philanthropy, and parlor radicalism, nourished by Elena's mother, a typical *kulturnitsa* of the 1890's, and her father, a liberal lawyer. Somewhat boyish and of a practical bent, Elena tried medical studies for a time, then taught at the Smolenskaya Sunday School in Petersburg. In 1896, she began serving the Party as an archivist, became a member in 1898, and two years later took up work as a full-time *Iskra* agent, moving constantly from city to city and back and forth across the frontier. Her memoirs offer a wealth of detail about the underground ways of a conspirator, about secret codes, methods of concealment, and smuggling. More important, they reveal Stasova's special revolutionary personality. In it we find neither brilliant intellectuality, nor grand flights of passion, but caution, precision, iron reliability, devout attention to detail, acute powers of observation, and a worship of punctuality. She was the ideal agent, fully deserving of her honorary title in the Party, Comrade Absolute.[9]

Menshevik women tended to be somewhat more intellectual, a bit "softer" in revolutionary outlook and personality, and often Jewish. The best example is Eva Broido. Born of a prosperous Jewish family of Vilna Province, she studied pharmacy and read Pisarev who "caused an upheaval in all my ideas on life." Still innocent of politics, she felt "a preoccupation with the ideas of freedom, . . . a vague desire for an ideal country, peopled with perfect men and women, a passion for knowledge which would show the way to a better and more glorious future." On a visit to a Social Democratic bookstore in Berlin, she found Bebel's *Woman* that made the "greatest impression" upon her, indeed made her a socialist; she later translated it into Russian. In Petersburg Broido divided her time between a pharmaceutical business and illegal agitation in the factories. Personal contacts were predominant in making her choice between Bolshevism and Menshevism (she married Mark Broido); but she also observed that in Baku the Menshevik organizations were always democratically electd, with "no dictators." In her memoirs, Broido

---

sketch of the Nevzorova sisters in *Zhen. russ. rev.*, 271–77; and Knight, "Women in the Russ. Rev. Movement." Davydova, the mother-in-law of Tugan-Baranovsky, founded *Mir bozhi*; Kalmykova, a wealthy widow, propagandist, and patroness was already fifty in 1899.

[9] There is an extensive literature on and by Stasova. This account is drawn from her memoirs, *Stranitsy zhizni i borby*, 2d printing (Moscow, 1960) 3–44. An amplified version (*Vospominaniya*, Moscow, 1969) contains more detail but adds nothing new to the picture. Of the many biographies, A. A. Isbakh's is perhaps the least satisfying: *Tovarishch Absolyut* (Moscow, 1963), and that of S. M. Levidova and E. G. Salita, the most: *Elena Dmitrievna Stasova* (Leningrad, 1969).

emerges not only as an honest and sincere socialist but also as somewhat unstable, subject to frequent fainting and fits of depression that sometimes brought her to the verge of nervous collapse. A greater contrast between this personality and that of the iron-clad self-assurance of Stasova would be difficult to find in the whole of the Social Democratic movement.[10]

The events of 1905 turned a large number of educated women into temporary "revolutionaries." Actresses, teachers, schoolgirls, and even ballerinas like Pavlova and Karsavina, found an excuse to join the large-scale strike movement. The phenomenon was so universal that wags were led to announce that pregnant women had refused to give birth until a constitution was granted. Most active among the females were the students who struck in February and who formed medical first-aid units in October 1905 to minister to wounded comrades. Two non-Party Bestuzhev students assisted a Bolshevik urban guerilla group (*boevaya gruppa*) in preparing an armed insurrection at Kronstadt. Both of them were placed before a firing squad, though one was known to be pregnant. In Ivanovo-Voznesensk, the Bolshevik Olga Genkina was torn to pieces by Black Hundreds when caught with a suitcase full of weapons. For some female Bolsheviks 1905 was a proving ground. Varvara Yakovleva, a Moscow science student, was pulled out of a May Day parade by hefty armed men who jumped up and down on her breasts, causing an injury that led to tuberculosis. A dozen years later, Yakovleva attained considerable notoriety in the Petrograd Cheka. Rozaliya Zalkind (Zemlyachka), daughter of a wealthy Jewish Kiev merchant, served as an *Iskra* agent, held responsible posts in the Bolshevik Party, and was entrusted with difficult assignments. Among these was helping to direct the Moscow uprising of December 1905 and carrying out a purge of the Moscow organization after its failure. Her deployment of armored trolley-cars on the streets of Moscow was a rehearsal in miniature of the days when, as a leading political commissar in the Civil War, she would assist in disposing of armored trains and divisions of men.[11]

The "professional" Social Democratic woman revolutionary was economically independent and educationally fit to carry on continuous revolutionary activity as a way of life full-time, or at least most of the time. The professional had to be free to travel and take up a new Party assignment (*kommandirovka*) at rather short notice. These attributes distinguished them from proletarian radicals. To say that the woman professional was drawn largely from "the intelligentsia" is almost circular; however, the composition

[10] Broido, *Memoirs*, 1–142 (quotation, 9).

[11] Tamara Karsavina, *Theatre Street* (London, 1930) 190–96. The anecdote is told by Gurko and is quoted in S. Harcave, *First Blood* (New York, 1964) 198; *Kursy*, 54–64; *PZhK*, VIII (1906) 390–91; *Svetlyi put*, 16. Yakovleva: B. N. Jakowlewa, [V. N. Yakovleva], *Levenslauf einer Bolschewikin* (Moscow, 1934) 3–20; Zemlyachka: *Zhen. russ. rev.*, 146–57; Z. Bobrowskaja [Ts. Zelikson-Bobrovskaya], ed., *Bolschewiki in zaristischen Russland: aus Memoirer alter Bolschewiki* (Hamburg, 1932) 227; Keep, *Rise*, 265–66; Solomon Schwarz, *The Russian Revolution of 1905* (Chicago, 1967) 218.

of this class is more variegated in this period than in the heyday of Populism when gentry women still predominated both in numbers and in importance. The educational level of the new generation was still high, with the liberal professions still fairly well represented though somewhat diluted by sub-professionals (midwives, druggists). Jewish women held a clear and visible second place to Russians in numbers, and often very close to them in importance.[12]

Recruitment into radicalism begins with a temperament for action and the idealism of youth. There is no mystery to the widespread attraction which young women felt for revolution; it was the mood of their generation. The tradition of sexual equality simply made the doors easier to open. In this there was no difference between 1900 and 1870. The difference was in magnitude: Everything about the liberation movement was bigger, more desperate, and more promising than it had been a generation earlier. There was also more contact between the sexes in the universities, at work, in volunteer organizations. S. I. Gusev's conversion of his fiancée from burning but ill-defined Populism to burning and precise Marxism was re-enacted dozens of times.[13] The medical assistant, Lyudmila Gromozova, told a courtroom audience in 1904 how she had been inspired by the stories of Saltykov-Shchedrin and Uspensky, seen the horrors of Russian society as a village teacher, felt the bitter disillusionment of small deeds, and arrived at the capital a fully made revolutionary. Only then did she discover Marxism, which gave her the method of struggle.[14] Marxism drew to itself legions of dedicated young people, but people already possessed of the psychological tendency to revolt and who saw in Marxism something more real and respectable than the hazy romanticism of the Populists. Of these, the ones made of tougher fibre seemed to gravitate toward Bolshevism.

As in the past, women played a variety of revolutionary roles. Wealthy dilettantes made donations; the well-connected established the necessary liaisons with society. Those who had a deeper committment usually began political work as organizers and teachers, shifting in the mid-1890's from narrow "circle" activity to mass agitation (a shift reflected also in the evolution of teaching materials from big books like *The Gadfly* and *Spartacus* to one-page flysheets). Some women skipped this stage and went directly to communications, acting as couriers and smugglers and forming the links of the human chain which bound the labor centers together and to the emigration. When not on the move, they maintained conspiratorial flats where they hid weapons or literature. Those who displayed administrative talents were assigned by the émigré Party leaders to hold meetings, convey instructions, make appointments and transfers, purge undesirables, and plan operations. When armed violence was scheduled, as in 1905, women gave medical and

---

[12] See Chapter V, 3 above and Knight, "Women in the Russ. Rev. Movement."
[13] The conversion is described in *Leningradki*, 100.
[14] Lyudmila Gromozova, *Rech* (Geneva, 1904).

logistical support and when necessary fought on the barricades as well. Upon this pool of female administrative and military talent, the Bolsheviks were to draw heavily during the Civil War.

Most radical women married men of the same political faith. Intermarriages like that of Sukhanov and Flaxerman (a Menshevik and a Bolshevik) were exceptional, it would seem. Weddings were often concluded behind bars or in Siberia. Eva Broido relates with some irony how a *minyan* was assembled for her wedding in a penal colony. One revolutionary mother bore and raised her son in a prison cell; when they were released, the five-year old child was terrified of the open spaces. Children of underground couples had to be taught the virtues of secrecy and furtive ways and to help conceal incriminating materials when the gendarmes appeared. The little daughter of the Bolshevik agent, Drabkina, wondered why her mother sewed mercury caps and fuses into her brassiere and why she seemed to gain and lose weight as she traveled from flat to flat; and she was genuinely confused by the fact that her parents, who taught her always to be truthful, were forever lying about their comings and goings. Among female radicals, sexual irregularity was as rare as treason. Though there were women like Inna Smidovich, the "sailor's girl" of Odessa who posed as a whore in order to gain access to military barracks, there is no evidence to support the perennial legend of revolutionary women trading their bodies in return for military information or to convert the troops.[15]

In the end, these young women, who bore such strange underground code names as Bunny, Falcon, Gangster, and Beast, were important to the revolutionary movement, though somewhat less than they had been a generation earlier.[16] Again the men were in charge both of long-range policy and, in most cases, of everyday operations. Apart from the psychological advantages that their presence lent to the movement, the female cadres provided it with a significant reserve of talent, but at the second level of leadership. This pattern was to be repeated in the Civil War when the same female commissars stood beside, but slightly behind, male military commanders. And it would be continued further in Soviet society as a whole after the Civil War when the trained communist woman acted out the role of deputy, assistant, or vice-director in almost every walk of life.

[15] Broido, *Memoirs*, 26; E. Ya. Drabkina, "Tovarishch Natasha," *Leningradki*, 97–108; A. N. Emelyanov, "Raskaz o moei materi," *ibid.*, 70–80.

For elements of the legend of the-radical-as-prostitute, see 121 above and a variant of it, 171. Kuprin, in one of his versions of *Yama*, saw fit to give it popular expression by relating the tale of "Magda," a gentry music teacher turned socialist. She does a spell in a brothel in order to learn to pass as a prostitute, then moves among the sailors of the Black Sea ports spreading political propaganda. See Guerney's translation, 49–65; it does not appear in the Soviet edition based on the 1917 text (see full references to *Yama* in Chapter VI, 2).

[16] If we compare the statistics of Knight with those few which I compiled for the 1870's, we see at once that, whereas in the earlier period, the percentage of women rose as we approach the top of the hierarchies, in the later period it declines. In both periods, rank and file percentage for women hovered around 15 percent. In the Executive Committee of the People's Will, it rose to over 30 percent; in the leading bodies of Social Democracy and the Socialist Revolutionaries, it declined.

IX

Women Against Women

The feminist, Doroshevskaya: Everywhere women are subjected; everywhere they struggle for their rights. Women from America and England arrive here and are in complete solidarity with us and wish us well in our struggle. *Men cannot defend our interests*; they do not understand us.

The Bolshevik, Nikolaeva: You have not come here to defend our interests. You need our votes to defend your capitalist interests in the Constituent Assembly. You won't get them. We have learned how to struggle against you.

—*From a Debate at the Petrograd Conference of Women Workers, November 12, 1917.*

1. PATRIOTS AND PACIFISTS

The convulsions of 1914–1920 lend to the preceding years the appearance of tranquility itself. The Great War, the Revolution, and the Civil War unleashed massive stores of social energies and emotions and ended in a drastic re-assortment of the classes, estates, constituencies, and nations that made up the Russian Imperial community. In the first of these cataclysms, the Great War of 1914–1918, it is essential to remember that for large numbers of influential people in the warring states, it was initially a positive event—an opportunity, a liberating device, a catalyst for desired social or political re-arrangements. Having fixed our historical gaze so long upon the horizontal aspects of war—treaties, war aims, campaigns, and conquests—its vertical side is sometimes forgotten. In Russia as elsewhere, bureaucrats and party leaders, business and labor, revolutionaries and minorities, saw in the war—whatever their moral view of it—the main chance for advancing their sundry claims, whether of national liberation, national retrenchment, or private gain. "War as opportunity" is a major theme in the social history of all the belligerents.

The women of the Russian intelligentsia succumbed to the first euphoric waves of patriotism that swept over Russia. A few were unable to resist the kind of patriotic silliness that led the rulers to change the name of St. Petersburg to Petrograd: Even before the War, Countess Ditrikh of the Union of Russian Women flaunted the costume of the *boyarina*, proclaiming that "the Russian woman must, even in her dress, be true to her fatherland"; and the usually sensible Karsavina decided to drop from her repertoire the music

278

composed for her by Richard Strauss. A week after hostilities began, *Women's Cause* set the new tone by invoking the image of Roman matrons handing husbands and sons into the maws of war and declaring that Russian women would fight too but "with love and mercy." A new seriousness enveloped the journal and the fashionable pastels of early 1914 now gave way to a severe cover picture of Grand Duchess Sergei "called to war." Russian women had continued the tradition of military nursing even during the unpopular Japanese War; and a few had volunteered for the Balkan Wars. Now it became a veritable status symbol. Even the "spoilt beauties of the Smart Set," Muriel Buchanan tells us, abandoned the round of bridge, gossip and flirtation and went to work in hospitals. The women of the Imperial family set the trend, taking honorary charge of Red Cross units, hospitals, medical trains, sometimes lavishing special attention on "favorite" regiments.[1]

Some Romanov women went beyond this well-meant but highly personal brand of charity. Grand Duchess Mariya Pavlovna, sister of Rasputin's assassin, was recovering from a loveless marriage. At twenty-four, lonely, useless, and embarrassed by her divorce, she enrolled as a nurse and was sent to the front. The war was Mariya Pavlovna's introduction to Russian life. "Little by little," she recollected, "I spread my wings and tested my strength; the walls which for so long had fenced me off from reality were now finally pierced." At the other end of the political spectrum was Lenin's sister, Mariya Ulyanova (1876–1937), a former Bestuzhev student and veteran Bolshevik agent. Harassed by the police, she enrolled as an army nurse to deflect suspicion from herself. She served on a Sanitary Train, bringing showers, delousing equipment, and medicine to the troops. Between Mariya Romanova and Mariya Ulyanova, a host of women from almost every stratum of society served as volunteer nurses: students, doctors, journalists, women writers, and figures from the cultural world such as the wife and daughters of Chaliapin. Many died in service; some were mistreated when captured by the Germans. One nurse was so dedicated that she could not visit her dying mother. "You who gave birth to me, excuse me; I cannot leave the soldiers. They need all my strength." Such devotion was sorely tested by the inter-service rivalry, the sloth, and the corruption which permeated the medical military establishment.[2]

In 1915, the Zemstvo Union's Automotive Service opened drivers' courses

---

[1] The note on Ditrikh is from Elets, *Povalnoe bezumie*, 304; on Karsavina, *ZhD* (Sept. 15, 1914) 26. See the first wartime issues of *idem*. (Aug. 1, 1914) 22, and (Aug. 15, 1914). On nurses in 1904 and 1912; *ZhV* (Sept. 1904) 19–22; and *ZhD* (Oct. 15, 1912) 24. The popularity of volunteer nursing in society and at court is described in Meriel Buchanan, *The Dissolution of an Empire* (London, 1932) 117–25.

[2] Princess Marie, *Education of a Princess*, quotation, 229. *M. I. Ulyanova* (Moscow, 1965) 7–12; *ZhD* (Sept. 15, 1914) 25, and (Dec. 1, 1914) 3: N. Ardashëv, *Velikaya voina i zhenshchiny russkiya* (Moscow, 1915), quotation, 10. The ineptitude of the medical services is described in M. V. Rodzianko, *The Reign of Rasputin*, tr. C. Zvegintzoff (London, 1927) 113–17. Instances of discrimination in taking on volunteers in *Ocherk deyatelnosti petrogradskoi oblastnoi organizatsii Vserossiiskago Soyuza Gorodov za pervyi god voiny* (Petrograd, 1916) 91.

for women and made the interesting discovery that women were slightly inferior to men in performance, but much superior in theoretical knowledge, diligence, and zeal. All fifty-eight women students passed and the female military driver now became a fairly common sight. One was E. P. Samsonova, a former Bestuzhev student who in 1912 became Russia's first woman pilot. Her application to become an army aviator was refused and she settled for nursing and driving. Princess E. M. Shakhovskaya, another flier, was luckier and was assigned to active duty. Women soldiers were far more numerous. The first was Anna Krasilnikova, a twenty-year-old miner's daughter who tried to enlist, was refused, and then dressed up in a man's uniform. She managed to fight in nineteen battles and won the St. George Cross, Fourth Class. Other young women followed the same course. They were mostly uneducated and of low social standing. The government had no consistent policy on female combatants, and new names continued to appear in Russian journals.[3]

The most famous of these was Mariya Bochkarëva, the founder of the women's batallions in 1917. Daughter of a former serf of Novgorod Province, she began working at the age of eight. Seduced at fifteen, her subsequent love life would provide material for a string of cheap films. Beaten by a drunken lover, betrayed by another, sold into a brothel, even seduced by a Siberian governor, she found herself in 1914, aged twenty-five, at the end of her rope (indeed one of her husbands had tried to hang her). Bochkarëva's account of the early years was true, and she emerges as a naïve, religious, patriotic, superstitious, ambitious, and sometimes cruel woman. The news of the Great War brought her back to life. "The spirit of sacrifice took possession of me," she recalled. "My country called me. And an irresistible force from within pulled me. . . ." Though quite capable of posing as a man, Bochkarëva received permission to enlist as a woman soldier. Despising nurses and women of the auxiliary services, she threw herself into battle and soon became an authentic and much decorated heroine, specializing in crawling under enemy machine gun fire to rescue wounded comrades. A combination of disgust with defeatist agitation in the ranks and a desire to be feted by the politicians of Petrograd prompted her to leave the front in 1917—but only temporarily.[4]

On the home front, an even larger number of women were pulled into the war effort. The Union of Zemstvos employed 30,000 women in 1916; the Union of Cities and the Red Cross, some 10,000. Women dominated the Emergency Relief to Refugees Committee in Moscow. Essential utilities and transport, abandoned by male draftees, were now staffed by women. Of the

---

[3] The drivers' school: Tikhon Polner, *Russian Local Government During the War and the Union of Zemstvos* (New Haven, 1930) 255. The pilots: *Zhenshchina i voina*, 1 (Mar. 5, 1915) 5 and Ardashëv, *Velikaya voina*, 13. The soldiers: *Zhen. i voina* 1 (Mar. 5, 1915) 11, 14 and *ZhV*, (Jan. 1915) 21, (Mar. 1915) 73, (Apr. 1915) 94.

[4] Maria Botchkareva [Mariya Bochkarëva] and Isaac Don Levine, *Yashka: My Life as Peasant, Officer, and Exile* (New York, 1919) 1–99 (quotation, 66). The name "Yashka" was borrowed from one of her husbands.

1,250 Moscow telegraph employees, 700 were women. The trolley-car lines, opened about five years before the War, were considered "obviously not for women" until 1914. Now women served as conductors, cashiers, and traffic controllers. The woman streetcar conductor, a favorite stereotype in Western commentaries on women's equality under communism, was a common sight on the streets of the two capitals years before Soviet power was established. War wives replaced the carters, janitors, and gatekeepers called to the colors. Female personnel in Moscow offices increased as much as 80 percent. All this was not, of course, unique to Russia; feminists and others published reports on home-front and auxiliary women's work in the warring nations.[5]

From April 28 to 30, 1915, a Women's International Congress for Peace met at The Hague; but conspicuously absent were representatives of English, French, German, and Russian feminism. Organized women had long taught that women's suffrage would help end the scourge of war, though only one, Jeanette Rankin, had a chance to prove it when, as the first American woman elected to Congress, she voted against her country's entry into the War. Among feminists, peace had shared the program with purity and sobriety in the last years before 1914. At the Rome Congress of the International Council of Women, held a few months before the War, the Frenchwoman Marie Verone and the German Regina Deutsch ended their speeches with a pledge to peace and then crossed the platform to embrace amid thunderous applause. Before the year had ended all the major feminist groups of the belligerents had given a new pledge—to support their respective governments. Militant feminists outdid moderates in their patriotism in England where suffragettes pinned white feathers on London draft evaders.

In Russia, as early as 1899, the women's committee of the Russian League of Peace, a short lived effort of Shabanova and Filosofova, promised to show firmness in the "humanitarian enterprise" of peace. In 1904, the feminists, in the spirit of the movement, withheld support for the unpopular war with Japan. After the Bosnian Crisis of 1908 and the ensuing war scare, Tyrkova wrote a sweeping condemnation of militarism, with its frightful weapons, its waste of brains and talents, and its destruction of the lives produced by women. Only in 1912 is there an indication of what is to come. Vera Kirsanova, a frequent contributor to *Women's Cause*, explained in its pages that although women oppose war in principle they ought to support the Slavic belligerents of the current Balkan War because it was one of self-defense(!).[6]

[5] *ZhD* (Oct. 1, 1915) 1–2, and (Oct. 15, 1916) 8–10; *Zhen. i voina*, 1 (Mar. 5, 1915) 12–14; Ardashëv, *Velikaya voina*, 6–15. For similar efforts in other states, see F. T. Jesse, *The Sword of Deborah* (London, 1918) and Agnes von Harnack, *Der Krieg und die Frauen* (Berlin, 1915); K. Chukovsky, *Angliya nakanune pobedy* (Petrograd, 1916 or 1917); A. Bystrov, "Novaya Zhenshchina," *ZhD* (Feb. 1, 1916) 8–9.

[6] The Europeans: *ZhV* (July, Aug., 1915) 140–41 and Schreiber, *Journey*, 24–26. The Russians: *Zhenskoe delo* (June 1899) 69–90; Shabanova, *Ocherk*, 24; Tyrkova, "Voina," *SZh* (Mar. 1909) 1–2; Kirsanova, "Idoly i zhertvy," *ZhD* (Oct. 29, 1912) 2.

When the War opened, Anna Shabanova of the Mutual Philanthropic Society began at once to support the war effort. Before a year was out, she had made liaison with the various voluntary organizations and had set up a number of war-related enterprises caring for war victims, refugees, abandoned children, and (Russian) POW's. Shabanova also worked with the War Industries Committee in training women in military supply. There was hardly a home-front activity for which she did not offer the services of the Society. "Let us prove ourselves worthy of citizenship," Millicent Fawcett of England had said to women in World War I. Shabanova, in a speech to the Electoral Rights Section of the Society, made it abundantly clear that her efforts were at least partially inspired by the hope that they would be rewarded by the granting of women's suffrage. The patriotic activities of women, she said, noble and necessary as they were, had diverted women's thoughts and actions away from the women's cause. What is the sense, she wondered, in women giving so much when they receive so little voice in their own affairs. They could really expect no gratitude, no automatic granting of the vote unless they tied their wartime contributions to the specific promise of the enfranchisement of women.[7]

Shishkina-Yavein's League for Women's Equality, whose war efforts paralleled those of the Society, uttered similar sentiments in a summons to "the daughters of Russia" issued in August 1915.

> We women have to unite: and each of us, forgetting personal misfortune and suffering, must come out of the narrow confines of the family and devote all our energy, intellect, and knowledge to our country. This is our obligation to the fatherland, and this will give us the right to participate as the equals of men in the new life of a victorious Russia.

The League called for a "women's mobilization" along the lines of that attempted by Christabel Pankhurst in England; a campaign to draw all of Russia's women into some kind of war work. All this was accompanied by a constant refrain of addresses and complaints to the Duma, particularly the Progressive Bloc, blaming it for ignoring the wartime accomplishments of women. "Is it really possible," asked one of these, "that Russian woman, who has undergone so much for the country, can be forgotten?" Pokrovskaya's *Women's Messenger*, speaking for her Women's Progressive Party, voiced similar sentiments. The strongest expression of feminist-patriotism appeared in the first issue of a new journal, *Woman and the War*, edited by the Muscovite, A. I. Yakovleva. The leading articles called the War a moment of liberation and a vast opportunity for women. Yakovleva warned that men, out of fear of women's newly exhibited powers, would try to deny

---

[7] Published reports of the Society's activities appeared regularly in *ZhD*; a complete list with detailed financial accounting is in "Otchët za 1915 g," in TsGIAL, f. 1075, op. 2, No. 53. Shabanova's speech in "Otchët otdela izbiratelnykh prav za 1914 god," in TsGIAL, f. 1075, op. 2, No. 43, 7–9.

them their rights; and so women would have to hold on to the positions won during the fighting.[8]

Feminists were apparently united in a program of giving full support to their beleaguered country for the duration in the hope that they would soon reap a reward in the form of women's suffrage. In January 1915, Shabanova presented the City Duma with an imposing list of all the tasks that women had performed since the declaration of war and a request for female municipal suffrage. The City Fathers were impressed and agreed in principle, subject to the approval of the Ministry of the Interior. The League appealed to the Ministry itself. All the groups continued courting Duma members whom they invited to their meetings. But to all requests for their enfranchisement, whether municipal, district, or national, the government's reply was that few other countries had such an arrangement and that, in any case, the instability and imbalance of Russia's electorate was such that to introduce women voters now would lead to the exacerbation of political passions.[9]

Until the February Revolution, the feminists had to be content with gains in educational and employment opportunities. These were impressive enough. In the Minister of Education, Count Ignatev, the feminists at last found a sympathetic friend. Before his dismissal at the end of 1916, he broadened the teaching opportunities for women graduates and even, in response to pressure from the League, granted women free access to the universities, though only after qualified men had been placed. The demand for women engineers in rail and water transport became so great that, at the urging of the Ministry of Transport, the Ministry of Education gave graduates of the Women's Technical Institute rights of full-fledged engineers. Thousands of women poured into the voluntary organizations; Shishkina-Yavein herself volunteered for army hospital work. During the War, the Menshevik Vera Aleksandrova—the future wife of Solomon Schwarz—found herself with two jobs, one with the War Industries Committee and one with a newspaper; at night she attended university courses, and was even able to consider an immediate change of activity by going to the front as a nurse. There was no excuse for an educated woman to be idle, if she did not wish to be. As *Women's Cause* put it in a letter to a jilted wife, jobs were now so numerous that women no longer need contemplate the future with despair after an unlucky marriage. Though idle-

---

[8] Details of the League's wartime contributions may be found in every issue of *ZhD* from September 1914. For its political ambitions and lobbying see *ibid.* (Aug. 15, 1915) 1–2 (the summons with commentary) and: *ibid.* (Sept. 1, 1915) 1–2; (Nov. 15, 1915) 16–17; (May 1, 1916) 16; (Dec. 1, 1916) 14–15. The cited note to the Progressive Bloc is from the League's *Otchët R.L.R.Zh. za 1914 i 1915 gg.* (Petrograd, 1917) 32–34. *Zhen i voina* 1 (Mar. 1915), editorials, 3–4 and backcover. Pokrovskaya, in her opening comment on the war (following a warm tribute to the deceased pacifist, Bertha von Sutner, in the previous issue), declared that the cruel rigors of war "were clearing from women's path some of the obstacles which had previously blocked their aspirations to engage in every sort of work and was giving them access to professions once closed to them." *ZhV* (Sept. 1914) 173.

[9] For a few examples of lobbying and its fruits: *ZhD* (Mar. 15, 1916) 11–13; and (Oct. 15, 1916) 15; TsGIAL, f. 1075, op. 2, Nos. 45, 48, 52.

ness and conspicuous consumption among privileged women continued, it was clear that this war was giving the female intelligentsia of a non-radical persuasion an outlet for their talents never seen before in Russian social history. Would the trend have continued after the War had there been no Revolution?[10]

The European socialist movement, already deeply divided in social texture, temperament, and philosophy, was shattered by the War of 1914. Chauvinists, defensists, defeatists, internationalists, and "Zimmerwaldists" of several varieties appeared on the scene, hawking their ideological wares. Vera Zasulich voiced the view held by many older socialists who could not bear to see Russia defeated by the Prussian Junkers. A German victory, she said, could only weaken Western democracy and menace the future of the proletariat. Mensheviks like Aleksandrova and Dubnova recall how they had been infected by patriotic enthusiasm at the beginning of the conflict and then had turned in revulsion against war.[11] In Europe, the future Communists Zetkin, Balabanova, and Kollontai were sickened not only by the war, but even more so by the nationalist attitudes of their former socialist comrades. A scheduled summer Conference of International Socialist Women in Vienna had to be cancelled; and the International Women's Secretariat, shorn of the leadership of the bedridden Zetkin, was in disarray. Into this void stepped Lenin and the group of women who had founded *Rabotnitsa* earlier in the year. Anticipating the more famous conferences that were to follow (at Zimmerwald and Kienthal), he suggested to Armand and Krupskaya that they summon an International Women's Socialist Conference at Berne for the purpose of winning women over to his anti-war theses. This was the genesis of the first episode in the history of the so-called Zimmerwald Movement.

Inessa Armand and Krupskaya wished to invite only left socialists who unequivocally opposed the War; but they offered the job of organizing the conference to Zetkin, who insisted on a broader base in order to impress public opinion. She was assisted in the preparations by the Russian-Italian socialist, Angelica Balabanova. The conference opened in Berne on March 26, 1915, with about two dozen delegates from the four major belligerents and a few of the smaller neutrals; it was hardly representative of anything more than the inclinations of the organizers. The history of its proceedings is a bit murky, though its outcome is clear enough. Three main positions on the War emerged. The Russian delegation (four Bolsheviks, two Mensheviks), led by Armand, Krupskaya and orchestrated by Lenin from a nearby café, wanted a

[10] *ZhD* (Mar. 1, 1916) 17; *ibid.* (Sept. 15, 1916) 16; *Pervye zhen.-inzh.*, 22; Vera Aleksandrova, *Perezhitoe (1917–1921 gg.)* (New York, 1962) 5–11. The *ZhD* letter is in (Aug. 1, 1915) 14; complains about growing luxury among women in *ibid.* (May 15, 1916) 15 and (Oct. 15, 1916) 8–10.
[11] Zasulich, "O voine," in *Samozashchita: marksistskii sbornik* (Petrograd, 1916) I, 1–3; Aleksandrova, *Perezhitoe*, 5–17; Dubnova-Erlikh, *Obshchestvennyi oblik*, 4.

clearcut condemnation of the War and a summons to the workers to revolutionary combat against their rulers at home. The moderates, led by the English delegate, preferred a simple denunciation of the War devoid of any summons to political action. Zetkin, ailing and desirous of unanimity, pleaded with Lenin to compromise. A watery anti-war resolution was passed, evoking some scorn from Lenin and a demand that his version be read into the minutes. The women of the Russian delegation had the final word on the resolution: "We reject it on the grounds that it is incomplete and insufficient, but we do not rule out future cooperation. . . ."[12]

But the main purpose of the Conference, to publicize women's opposition to the War, had some success. Louise Saumoneau, a leader of the *Comité d'Action féminine socialiste pour la Paix et contre le Chauvinisme*, returned from the conference to begin pacifist propaganda and was arrested; she later became a Communist. Her Russian friend, Serafima Gopner, spread anti-War messages among émigré Russians in Paris who had enlisted in the French army. The Zimmerwald Movement, built up by leftist anti-War socialists after the Berne Conference, made a special effort to draw women into its orbit. A 1916 draft leaflet, "From French Women to German Women," spoke of the "fraternity of sorrow" that linked the two nations, and it made a frank emotional appeal to the women of Germany to join those of France in ending the war. Clara Zetkin's *Women of the Working People, Where are Your Husbands? Where are Your Sons?* contrasted the international conspiracy of capital with the international community of working men and women. In the spring of 1915, German women demonstrated in front of the Reichstag; the following year witnessed rioting and strikes in Austria and France. Italian pacifist women, even before their country entered the War, demonstrated against its intention to do so by lining railway tracks with their bodies.[13]

Among Russian women, the most vigorous anti-War propagandist was Kollontai. The declaration of war caught her in Berlin but she made her way at once to Sweden where she was arrested for socialist anti-War agitation. Upon

[12] This account is drawn from the following, rather sketchy, sources: Levidova, *Krupskaya*, 108–109 (with the Bolshevik reply to the resolution); Fréville, *Inessa*, 85–94; Podlyashuk, *Inessa*, 137–44; Angelica Balabanoff [Anzhelika Balabanova], *Impressions of Lenin*, tr. Isotta Cesari (Ann Arbor, 1964), xv of preface by Bertram Wolfe and 40–41; *idem.*, *Iz lichnykh vospominanii tsimmervaldtsa* (Moscow, 1925) 47–54; Ya. G. Tëmkin, *Tsimmervald-Kintal* (Moscow, 1967) 22–23. There are some discrepancies on the makeup of the Russian delegation. Lenin's resolution and his comments are printed in Bilshai, *O zhen. vop.*, 81–84. See also Armand, *Stati*, 220–29.
[13] Saumoneau's activity noted in Horst Lademacher, ed., *Die Zimmerwalder Bewegung: Protokolle und Korrespondenz*, 2 v. (The Hague, 1967) II, 99, n. 1; Gopner's in *Zhen. russ. rev.*, 92–97. The leaflets, "Des femme françaises aux femmes allemandes" (typescript) and "Frauen des Arbeitenden Volkes! Wo sind eure Männer? Wo sind eure Söhne?" are in the Archive Robert Grimm; Zimmerwald Bewegung, H-19 and I-30 [1915] in the International Institute of Social History in Amsterdam; the latter is also reprinted in Lademacher, *Zimmerwalder Beweg.*, II, 59–61. The women's antiwar demonstrations are described in Kollontai, *Polozhenie*, 136. See Armand's anti-war article in *Stati*, 31–33.

her release (and "eternal banishment" from Sweden), she made her way to Denmark; harried by police there also, she moved on to Norway. Though a member of the International Women's Secretariat and a bitter foe of the War, she was unable to attend the Berne meeting. There is much in Kollontai's biography that helps to explain her switch to Bolshevism. Above all, was her disgust with the Social Democrats of Europe, her isolation and broken friendships, and the stirring appeal of Lenin. By the middle of 1915 she was a convinced Left Zimmerwaldist and a Leninist; because of her contacts and linguistic abilities, she became Lenin's agent in Scandinavia, coaching Nordic delegations to the Zimmerwald conference and spreading the Leninist line throughout Norway and Sweden. At the invitation of a group of émigré socialists in America, she made a tour of that country in late 1915 and early 1916, sweeping through some eighty cities, where she passionately denounced the War in four languages. Her attacks against the defensists were so vitriolic that some thought her a German agent. She returned later the same year and made some observations of the American feminist movement that served to reinforce her hostility to bourgeois women's movements.[14]

Kollontai's comments on the War have more emotional than intellectual power. Two years earlier, at Basel, she had been converted to the belief in the international solidarity of the working class and its relentless hostility to war; in 1914 she was ready to concede that the ruling classes had known better than the socialists how deeply the workers had been conditioned to nationalism by the family, the schools, the church, and the press. In striking contrast to the euphoric phrases of the feminists, Kollontai revealed a profound feeling of disappointment and despair at the specter of a shattered international proletariat and the destruction of productive forces and human lives. "We need these lives," she said, "in order to build that army which will lead the fight against imperialism and capitalism." All the bitterness that she felt and her burning hatred of the belligerent governments were poured into her major anti-war pamphlet, *Who Needs War?* which ended with the words "our enemy is in the rear." It was standard Leninism; but its simple language and its simplistic themes of capitalist greed and proletarian blood made it eminently suitable for mass consumption. It enjoyed many translations. And its second Russian edition, published illegally in Petrograd in 1916, was widely circulated by the Bolsheviks in the capital.[15]

How much influence did such propaganda have among women inside Russia? Among the intelligentsia, apparently, very little. Even the segment potentially most susceptible to it, the female students of the capital, were overwhelmingly under the spell of patriotism, not Bolshevism. Even communist

[14] A concise account with a guide to the literature is G. D. Petrov, "A. M. Kollontai v gody Pervoi Mirovoi Voiny," *Istoriya SSSR*, No. 3 (May-June 1968) 83–97.

[15] Kollontai, *Stati*, 106–108, 128–32 (quotation, 132); *idem.*, *Komu nuzhna voina?* (Helsinki, 1917; 1st ed. Berne, 1916); Itkina, *Kollontai*, 67–68.

historians concede that the majority of Bestuzhev women supported the War, matching the feminists in patriotic rhetoric and far outdoing them in deeds. On International Women's Day, 1916, a group of Bolshevik students posted the following proclamation of the Petrograd committee of the Party:

> Comrades, Working women! This the day of our solidarity; the day when the working woman, breaking her ancient bonds of submission, slavery, and humiliation, proudly joins the ranks of the international proletariat for the struggle with the common enemy—capital. Working women! The government has sent our sons to their crucifixion for the sake of capital. So build your own organizations, band together in workshop and factory, office and shop, and let us roar in the face of insatiable capital: 'Enough blood! Down with the war. Bring the criminal autocracy to justice!'

Pro-war *bestuzhevki* tore it down; and when it was reposted, tore it down again. A year later, Bolshevik women students managed to gather 385 supporting votes at a flash meeting in opposition to the War; but the next day, the patriots answered with a 1,000 in support of it. But the few hundred Bolshevik stalwarts did provide the Party with talent needed to replace the professionals incarcerated early in the War. In 1917, these skills, political and medical, would be put to good use.[16]

The women workers themselves were another story. Their numbers swelled enormously during the War. Mass conscription lowered the number of males in inspected industries by 12.6 percent between 1914 and 1917; for the same period, the number of females rose by 38.8 percent. Women made up a third of the labor force at the start of the War and about half of it by 1917. In the summer of 1915, the War Industries Committee passed a resolution calling for "the removal, for the duration, of the restrictions laid down in the charter of industry in regard to female and adolescent labor to the extent that it does not impair their health." This opened the doors for swarms of women to enter industries where they had rarely been seen before. Percentages of increase in the metallurgical, mining, and lumber industries grew astronomically; scores of textile mills and even whole towns were now populated almost exclusively by women. In Petrograd, there were 50,000 women workers in 1916. But as a whole, the economic position of the working woman did not improve. Indeed in the early months, a fairly large group of women became unemployed as a result of the wartime collapse of certain areas of trade and industry (those engaged in the production and distribution of alcohol were among the first to go). Mothers with husbands at the front and unable to support their children

---

[16] On these events, see *Kursy*, 28–29, 69–72; *Pamyatniki agitatsionnoi literatury Rossiiskoi Sotsial-demokraticheskoi rabochei Partii*, vol. VI *(1914–1917)*, *Period voiny*, pt. 1, *Proilamatsii, 1914* (Moscow, 1923), vii–viii, 266–67, 287; Serditova, *Bolsheviki*, 123. The proclamation was issued in the name of the "organization of women workers" of the Petrograd Bolshevik Committee; the text is here cited from A. Shlyapnikov, *Nakanune 1917 goda* (Moscow, 1920) 158.

on the government allotment were soon drawn into industry. But wages remained largely constant—and lower than men's—while prices climbed.[17]

The government, the voluntary organizations, and the feminists, were alive to the plight of working women. At the urging of the League and the WIC, the government introduced women factory inspectors into those industries where large numbers of women were employed. Soldiers' wives had been granted allotments at the beginning of the war, and these were often supplemented in many places with free or cheap dining facilities, nurseries, and dormitories set up by the semi-public wartime committees. The government, responding to the enormous battlefield losses, also made modest efforts to increase maternity benefits and protection for women in industry. Of great practical significance also for the working wife was the establishment of prohibition at the outset of the War. Though the feminists had never managed to launch a temperance movement of any size, there is a bit of evidence that the women workers would have taken the issue into their own hands had the Tsar not signed the anti-alcohol decree in 1914.[18]

In the early days of the February Revolution of 1917, General Knox told the daughter of the British ambassador in Petrograd that "the trouble" had begun when a woman in a food line threw a stone through a baker's window. As a matter of fact, such incidents had been commonplace in Russia for the two preceding years. So-called food pogroms began occurring as early as the spring of 1915. In Petrograd on April 6, when the sale of meat was suspended for one day, women smashed and looted a large meat market; the scene was repeated in Moscow two days later over a shortage of bread. During the disturbances, the commandant of the city was badly cut by flying cobblestones. Later in the summer it happened again in the turbulent Khitrova Market. Similar events occured in the following year. The number of strikes in which women participated is too large to allow adequate treatment here. The June 1915 strike in Ivanovo-Voznesensk began as a "flour strike"; a month later it erupted again as a political demonstration to end the war and free jailed workers. Thirty people were killed. The simultaneous strike in Kostroma was met by armed repression and followed by a mass funeral and another strike in

[17] Figures on the growth of female labor: Rashin, *Formirovania*, 243, 246; Florinsky, *Russia*, II, 1354; *Izvestiya Moskovskago Voenno-Promyshlennago Komiteta*, No. 25-26 (July 1916) 30. The WIC resolution is from *ibid.*, No. 25–27 (July 1915) 8. The negative side of the female labor intake is well documented in the wartime study made by Z. Lilina (Zinoveva), based on official, industrial, and press reports: *Soldaty tyla: zhenskii trud do i posle voiny* (1916) (reprinted, Petrograd, 1918) 38–39, 41, 54–57.

[18] For various measures aimed at improving the welfare of working women and soldiers' wives, see *ZhV* (Jan. 1915) 1–5; *ZhD* (Nov. 15, 1915) 1; *ibid.* (Sept. 15, 1916) 10–12: TsGIAL, f. 1075, op. 2, n. 54; and Polner, *Russian Local Government*, 135, 139, 140. On July 5, 1914—a Saturday and a payday—about fifty women workers of Petrograd entered a tavern in the vicinity of the Novy Aivaz Factory, poured beer on the floor, smashed vodka bottles, and herded their husbands outside; the men obeyed without opposition. *ZhD* (Aug. 1, 1914) 22.

which working women addressed a circular to the soldiers asking them for protection instead of bullets.[19]

The Petrograd Women's Day disorders of February 23, 1917 combined all these elements: "food pogroms", an economic strike, a political strike, and the massing of women. But it was also the first day of the Russian Revolution.

2. FEMINISTS V. BOLSHEVIKS

In most accounts of the revolutionary year, women appear on the scene as historical agents only twice: on February 23 when women workers and soldiers' wives poured onto the streets of Petrograd for International Women's Day; and in the final act when the so-called Batallion of Women helped defend the Provisional Government in the Winter Palace in October. The historical distance between these two events is immense and there is no sense in trying to magnify the role played by the female half of the population during this crucial segment of Russia's modern Time of Troubles. With few exceptions, the political forces in the struggle for power were led by and overwhelmingly composed of men: government, parties, soviets, army, peasant associations, national organizations, cooperatives, industrial enterprises, and trade unions. But this should not obscure the fact that the two episodes involving women had an organic socio-political relationship to one another, and to the two-pronged women's liberation movement. That this relationship has not been made apparent in the literature on the Revolution is hardly surprising; in a titanic and even world-shaking upheaval, a great many social problems appear to be of marginal significance. Purely political accounts of the Revolution have naturally allowed working women to drop out of historical sight after February 23 and have also ignored the origin and political meaning of the women's military formations. These matters must now be brought into focus and set within the context of the clash between the Bolsheviks and the feminists. The clash was episodic and sporadic; and there was hardly more direct contact between the feminists and their socialist enemies than there had been in the pre-revolutionary years. Yet nothing shows more clearly than these eight revolutionary months the fundamental differences between them.

The first episode of the Revolution was the disorder that broke out in the capital on February 23, the date which had been periodically observed in Russia since 1913 as International Women's Day. Shortly after the event, Pitirim Sorokin made the following entry in his diary.

If future historians look for the group that began the Russian Revolution, let

[19] Meriel Buchanan, *Dissolution*, 163. The food riots are reported in Lilina, *Soldaty*, 69–70; Kollontai, *Polozhenie*, 136; Serditova, *Bolsheviki*, 106. For strikes, see *Svetlyi put*, 47–48 and P. Ya. Voronova, "Zarya novoi zhizni," in *Oktyabrëm rozhdennye* (Moscow, 1967) 71–78.

them not create any involved theory. The Russian Revolution was begun by hungry women and children demanding bread and herrings. They started by wrecking tram cars and looting a few small shops. Only later did they, together with workmen and politicians, become ambitious to wreck that mighty edifice the Russian autocracy.[1]

Some rather impressive volumes have been written in an effort to disprove the simplicities contained in this statement. Yet it is essentially true. There will never be any way to measure how much the working women and the masses in general desired to "wreck" the autocracy; but wreck it they did. By providing, almost by accident, a large-scale instance of unpunished civil disorder, they demonstrated the hopeless inability of the government to preserve law and order at the very center of its power.

The Bolshevik women's movement has no claim to revolutionary laurels on this occasion for the simple reason that it had ceased to exist. The *Rabotnitsa* group had been arrested in 1914 and Women's Day was observed in the two succeeding years only by proclamations and flash meetings. An employee of the Petrograd Pipe Factory, Melaniya Savchenko, recalls how her group of workers and a few women medical students distributed the 1915 Women's Day Proclamation to her co-workers; but before the next one in 1916 they were all in jail, where they remained until February 27, 1917. This was a common fate for wartime underground workers. By January 1917, the interminable food lines had shortened the tempers of lower-class Petrograd women (a psychological fact which is wholly unrelated to George Katkov's demonstration that there really was no shortage). On January 9, they were on the street for the ritualistic commemoration of Bloody Sunday. A month later, the Putilov strike added the necessary spark to the tinder. The largely female staff of the Vasilevsky Island trolley-car park, sensing general unrest a few days before February 23, sent a woman to the neighboring encampment of the 180th Infantry Regiment to ask the soldiers whether they would shoot at them or not. The answer was no, and on the twenty-third, the trolley-car workers joined the demonstration.[2]

If there was plan and reason to all this, it certainly did not issue from the Bolshevik organization. On the eve of Women's Day, Kayurov of the Party's

---

[1] Pitirim Sorokin, *Leaves from a Russian Diary* (Boston, 1950) 3.

[2] Savchenko's memoir and A. I. Rodionova's account of the trolley park episode are from *Zhen. goroda*, 71–76 and 87–92 respectively. Discontent among Petrograd women before February 23 is observed in *ZhV* (Jan. 1917), 1–2 and N. Sukhanov, *Zapiski o revolyutsii*, 7 v. (Petrograd, 1919) I, 14. According to an Okhrana report of January 1917, "mothers of families, exhausted from the endless queues at the shops, suffering at the sight of their sick and half-famished children, at this moment are much closer indeed to revolution than are Mssrs. Milyukov, Rodichev, and Co.; and of course they are more dangerous because they constitute a mass of inflammable matter for which only a spark is sufficient to cause it to burst into flames." This is quoted in Zoya Igumnova, *Zhenshchiny Moskvy v gody grazhdanskoi voiny* (Moscow, 1958) 11. George Katkov's comments on the non-existence of food shortages in Petrograd on 338–39 of his *Russia, 1917*.

Petrograd Committee advised a group of women workers from the Vyborg District who wished advice on how to celebrate the holiday "to refrain from isolated actions and to follow only the instructions of the Party Committee." When they decided to strike anyway, he was furious. Shlyapnikov reports that the organization could not even produce a Women's Day Proclamation because the press was not working. The *mezhraionka*, an independent Menshevik group, filled the gap with a flysheet addressed to women and opposed to the war. The women of the Vyborg textile concerns, with little guidance from Social Democrats of either persuasion, celebrated Women's Day around the theme "War, High Prices, and the Situation of the Woman Worker." At one of these, the cry "To the Nevsky!" was taken up and the celebrating strikers joined the throngs of queue-weary housewives to surge across the Neva bridges. Once in the center, the procession of women and children merged in the general demonstration. According to Trotsky, women then played a key role in the relations between worker and soldier who faced each other on the turbulent streets. "They go up to the cordons more boldly than men," he wrote, "take hold of the rifles, beseech, almost command: 'Put down your bayonets—join us'."[3]

The interesting question in all this is really not "whether" or "how much" the Petrograd females contributed to the overthrow of the autocracy, or even to what extent they were influenced by wartime Bolshevik propaganda, but rather, for historians of the women's movement: Who, after these events, recognized the revolutionary potential of working women and soldiers' wives? Who catered to their immediate needs? Who was able to command their allegiance in the deadly sequence of revolutionary events that was to follow?

At the time of the February Revolution, the feminist organizations appeared to be operating well, especially when compared to the defunct Bolshevik women's group. The Society, the League, and the Progressive Party were still functioning with euphoric vigor under their pre-war leaders, Drs. Shabanova, Shishkina-Yavein, and Pokrovskaya. Both *Women's Cause* and *Women's Messenger* continued to appear regularly. The War had generated new interest in feminism, and women's groups were mushrooming rapidly. Even before the February uprising, Shabanova, in an effort to unify these groups, took advantage of the incompetence in the Ministry of the Interior and announced the founding of an All-Russia Women's Society—later renamed the National Council of Women and affiliated to the International Council. Filosofova's dream had come true, at least on paper. In May the Council was "recognized" by the Provisional Government and gratefully named Paul Milyukov as its president! Though boasting some thirty branches, the Council held its first

[3] Kayurov cited in *ibid.*, 341; A. Shlyapnikov, *Semnadtsatyi god*, 2d ed. (Moscow, 1920–1927) I, 60, 240–41; L. D. Trotsky, *The History of the Russian Revolution* (1932) tr. Max Eastman, 3 v. (Ann Arbor, 1964) I, 109.

meeting only in December 1917—far too late for it to have further meaning. In May, Shishkina-Yavein, reorganized her League as the Republican Union of Democratic Women's Organizations with a program of labor and land reforms, a democratic republic, and war to victory—a program identical in spirit to that of the non-socialist radical democrats who would dominate the Provisional Government. In the feminist tradition, the new Union appealed to all democratic women, including those of the trade unions and the "less conscious" and sought "unity of persons of different parties and persuasions." Meetings and conferences now abounded; but the feminists were much more successful in winning the allegiance of prominent *intelligentki* like Figner, Breshkovskaya, Kuskova, and Lyubov Akselrod, than in making any headway among the female masses.[4]

The League lost no time in promoting the major feminist issue: the suffrage. Right after its formation and its somewhat vague declaration about a Constituent Assembly, the Provisional Government received a note from the League asking for a statement on women's right to vote in the Assembly. This was followed by a visit to Prince Lvov, the Premier, in pursuit of the same goal. Lvov was vague and refused to issue an additional statement. Losing patience, the League organized one of the earliest mass demonstrations in revolutionary Petrograd. It began on the morning of March 20 with speeches at the City Duma by Tyrkova, Shishkina-Yavein, and Vera Figner, whom the feminists had won to their cause. The alliance between the old terrorist Figner and the non-revolutionary feminists was more natural than one would think. Figner, unable to comprehend any of the revolutionary parties, was no doubt attracted by the democratic program of the women whose acquaintance she had made as early as 1906; the feminists were delighted to adorn their rostrum with an authentic and venerable relic of the Russian Revolution, particularly one whose radical impulses had mellowed with age. Some 40,000 women—students, older women of the intelligentsia, workers—proceeded from the City Duma to the Tauride Palace to confront the Provisional Government with their demands. The parade was led by a motor car holding Figner, Shishkina-Yavein, and some Bestuzhev students and was guarded by a female militia mounted on horseback. The marchers carried streamers with such messages as "The Woman's Place—Is in the Constituent Assembly," and "War to Victory."

This impressive demonstration of feminist street politics had a disappointing, if not wholly unsuccessful, outcome. At the Tauride the demonstrators,

[4] From 1917 onward, Russian sources on the feminists begin to thin out considerably. For the All-Russian Women's Society (Vserossiisskoe Zhenskoe Obshchestvo), see *ZhD* (Nov. 1, 1916) 16, *Ius Suffragi* (May 1, 1917) 120 and (Jan. 1, 1918) 61. The latter publication is the monthly journal of the International Women's Suffrage Alliance. On the League and its Republican Union (Respublikanskii Soyuz Demokraticheskikh Zhenskikh Organizatsii), see *Ves Petrograd na 1917 god* (Petrograd, 1917) I, 1118–19 and *Rabotnitsa*, 4 (May 30, 1917) 10–11 and 5 (June 14, 1917) 9–10. At a Moscow feminist congress in April, the absent Shabanova was chosen as honorary president and Shishkina-Yavein as actual president: *Ius Suffragi* (June 1, 1917) 135 and *ZhD* (Apr. 15, 1917) 14–15. See also Armand, *Stati*, 36–38, 168.

who filled the broad Shpalernaya and the horseshoe driveway, had to wait for several regimental parades. Then Shishkina-Yavein made a stirring speech to Chkheidze of the Soviet and Rodzianko of the Provisional Government, full of references to Figner and other heroines of the Revolution and ending with a categorical demand for a statement on women's suffrage. Chkheidze, as always cautious and politic, uttered the words "we will struggle together with you for your justly deserved rights" which evoked a shout from the crowd "against whom?" Rodzianko temporized as well; but both won applause from the assembled feminists and from Figner, who remained in the car to avoid the press of the crowd. Two dissonant notes were sounded. Some soldiers thought that the women ought to wait until the War was over before presenting their demands. A Bolshevik woman emerged from the crowd and attempted to divert the attention of those present from the useless demands of the feminists to the horrors of the War. The feminists were outraged and an obliging ruffian pulled the orator off the Tauride steps. It was perhaps the closest that the Bolsheviks and feminists had ever come to pulling out each others' hair. According to Kollontai, the solidarity of the demonstration was broken and several women bystanders showed their sympathy for the silenced Bolshevik speaker. In the meantime, the League organizers repaired to Rodzianko's office inside and were given further vague assurances.[5]

Antifeminism was by no means dead in Russia, even among those who embraced the cause of human freedom. Zinaida Gippius, who witnessed the women's demonstration from her "tower" near the Tauride Palace, made some acid comments about it in her diary. Women, she said, "show their 'humanity' very badly" by expecting to receive emancipation as a right instead of working for it and recognizing its responsibilities. And showing a lack of logic as great as her lack of awareness of how much Russian women had worked for their rights, Gippius testily advised them to focus upon "all-human" freedom and not on a feminist struggle that only alienates men. As the feminists had predicted, many had forgotten already the wartime sacrifices and accomplishments of women. A "populist" who, as he explained, "had never opposed women's suffrage in the past," telephoned the editor of *Women's Cause* in order to express his fear that granting women suffrage in the elections to the Constituent Assembly might lead to the restoration of the monarchy. Many members of the intelligentsia, including some in the Soviet, shared this view and suggested that the Assembly itself ought to decide the issue.[6]

But the parties in power had committed themselves for too long to the idea

[5] This account of the ceremonies and the march is drawn from *Rabochaya gazeta* (Menshevik) (Mar. 19, 1917) 3; *Rech* (Kadet) (Mar. 21, 1917) 5; *Ius Suffragi* (Nov. 1917) 26–27; and Kollontai, *Rabotnitsa za god revolyutsii* (Moscow, 1918) 8–10. The Bolshevik agitator described in the third person by Kollontai may have been herself as she hints in another source (see below). Another, more violent, clash between bourgeois and working women is described in R. Drumm, "Bolshevik and Feminist Attempts to Organize Women, 1917," (typescript), 17.

[6] Gippius, *Sinyaya kniga: peterburgskii dnevnik, 1914-1918* (Belgrade, 1929) 125–26; "Zhenshchiny i Uchreditelnoe Sobranie," in *ZhD* (May 1, 1917) 1–2.

of women's equality for them to back out now. All the socialist and "democratic" groups endorsed the idea in their programs. Brochures on the subject flooded the country as in the days of 1905. By the end of the summer, the central committees of all major parties contained women: Kollontai for the Bolsheviks; Broido and Plisetskaya for the Unified Mensheviks; Breshkovskaya (though only honorary) for the Socialist Revolutionaries, and Spiridonova for the Left Socialist Revolutionaries. Tyrkova, a long standing member of the Kadet Central Committee, was joined by Petrunkevich's stepdaughter, Countess Sofya Panina a well known figure in Russian philanthropy. Some of these women ran successfully for seats in the City Duma elections in the two capitals, their right to do so having been granted by the Provisional Government in the spring. The Special Conference on the Electoral Law for the Constituent Assembly reviewed the question of women's suffrage. According to Kadet accounts, it received no "serious opposition," and on July 20 the government ratified its decision to give the vote to all adults over twenty years of age. Russia thus became the first belligerent (and the first large country in the world) to establish genuine universal suffrage.[7]

Tyrkova, with some irony, tells how this news of the long awaited feminist victory was received by the woman on the street. After Prince Lvov made the announcement,[8] one of the feminists, in a flurry of enthusiasm, approached a crowd of women queued up at a bakery. "I congratulate you, citizennesses," she announced. "We Russian women are going to receive [our] rights." The women, tired of waiting in line, looked at the lady with indifference and lack of comprehension. Then a nearby soldier smirked and said: "Does that mean I can't hit my wife?" At this, the crowd livened up. "Oh no you don't, honey,"

[7] For comments on women by some of the smaller parties, see *Sbornik programmov russkikh politicheskikh partii* (Petrograd, "Skitalets," 1917) 14 (Radical Party); a publication bearing the same title, place, and date issued by 'Politicheskaya Biblioteka dlya Vsekh,' 27–28 (Republican Democratic Party); *Programmy politicheskikh partii*, ed. S. S. Zak, 2d ed. (Odessa, 1917) 49 and *Programma Trudovoi (narodno-sotsialisticheskoi) Partii* (Odessa, 1917) 1 (Trudoviks). These joined the major liberal and socialist parties (whose programmes remained unchanged on this issue) in giving support—with minor variations in wording—to political equality for women. Among the numerous brochures giving favorable attention to the matter, see: G. Lvovich, *Vseobshchee, pryamoe, ravnoe, i tainoe izbiratelnoe pravo* (Odessa, 1917); M. Gernet's *Ravenstvo* (Moscow, 1917), and Olgovich [Olga Volkenstein], *Osvobozhdenie zhenshchiny* (Petrograd, 1917).

On the final granting of the suffrage, see: Tyrkova-Williams, *From Liberty to Brest-Litovsk: The First Year of the Russian Revolution* (London, 1919) 197; P. Gronsky and N. Astrov, *The War and the Russian Government* (New Haven, 1929) 87–89; R. Browder and A. F. Kerensky, eds., *The Russian Provisional Government, 1917: Documents*, 3 v. (Stanford, 1961) I, 455, doc. 421. The final decree reads as follows: "The right to participate in elections to the Constituent Assembly shall be enjoyed by citizens of Russia of both sexes who have reached the age of twenty by the day of the elections."

[8] The terms of the government's decision were communicated to the feminist leaders by Prince Lvov before he resigned; it was promulgated under Kerensky's premiership. The composition of the feminist delegation to Lvov attests to the extent of unity of purpose attained by them by 1917: Shabanova, Shishkina-Yavein, Pokrovskaya, and Tyrkova.

they shouted. "None of that. You just try it. Nothing doing. Let ourselves be beaten any more? Not on your life. Nobody has the right now."[9]

The Provisional Government continued to sandwich in, between military and political crises of the highest order, pieces of legislation that further equalized the status of Russian women. In June women lawyers were given full rights to serve as attorneys before the bar and women the right to serve as jurors. In August women were granted equality of opportunity, pay, benefits, and titles in the civil service; this was a particular boon for schoolteachers, the largest group of female civil servants, who for the first time found themselves equal with men. The Ministry of Education, where Countess Panina served as Deputy Minister, drafted a project for transforming the Women's Higher Courses into genuine women's universities, equal in every way to those of men.[10] It seems fairly apparent that the Provisional Government, had it retained power longer, would have, under the constant surveillance of the feminists, established at least the mechanics of the emancipation as conceived by feminists everywhere. But the Provisional Government was destroyed by the Bolsheviks, who had their own program of female emancipation, and by the War, to which the Russian feminists turned their attention again after achieving their main political aims.

The Great War that had split the Russian intelligentsia asunder in 1914 continued to do so through the revolutionary months of 1917. Members of its "patriotic" wing, including many self-styled socialists, were horrified by fraternization, desertion, and the talk of a separate peace, though the vast majority of them voiced their concern exclusively by means of the spoken and printed word. Bolder spirits among them, however, hastened to enroll in the All Russian Volunteer Revolutionary Army that was being formed to defend the fatherland against Teutonic aggression. To stiffen its back, special units were organized by such groups as bearers of the St. George Cross, escaped POW's, and the wounded. A host of socialist political commissars were sent to the front to counter the defeatist propaganda of the Bolsheviks. Among them were the venerable old revolutionaries, Lev Deutsch and Vera Zasulich, whose League of Personal Example served as the propaganda section of the nascent revolutionary army. Some of the new special combat formations called themselves "Shock Battalions" or "Death Battalions" to underline their savage determination to perish in defense of the country if necessary. It was in this atmosphere that a Women's Battalion was formed in May 1917, one of the earliest of these volunteer units.

The idea came from Bochkarëva. During one of her frequent visits to the capital, Rodzianko asked her how to bolster the morale of the soldiers. She

[9] Tyrkova, *Osvobozhedenie zhenshchiny* (Petrograd, 1917) 15.
[10] *Russ. Prov. Gov.*, I, 225, 239; *ZhV* (July-August 1917) 96.

WOMEN'S MOVEMENT 1881-1917

suggested forming a "Women's Battalion of Death" under her command to serve as a model of valor and to shame the waverers. Kerensky and Brusilov approved and Bochkarëva was invited to announce her plan to a large patriotic rally at the Marynsky Theater on May 21. With considerable trepidation, this simple soldier woman mounted the rostrum and uttered the following words: "Men and women-citizens! . . . Our mother is perishing. Our mother is Russia. I want to help save her. I want women whose hearts are pure crystal, whose souls are pure, whose impulses are lofty. With such women setting an example of self-sacrifice, you men will realize your duty in this grave hour." Her voice choked with emotion and she could say no more. But her few words and gestures were more than sufficient in the exalted atmosphere of that assembly. Fifteen hundred women enlisted in the Women's Battalion that very night. Quarters were quickly arranged at a girls' institute, not far from the Marynsky Theater, and 500 more volunteers appeared the next day.[11]

This response was gratifying even though the quantity far exceeded the quality of the volunteers. The recruits were given medical examinations, short haircuts, and uniforms and divided into companies and platoons. Male instructors were provided by the Volhynia Regiment; female cadres from among the better educated of the volunteers. Yashka—answering to the title "Gospodin Nachalnik"—ruled her two 1,000-woman batallions with an iron hand. When a male officer had voiced his fear that the women's battalions might yield many little soldiers for the Russian army, Yashka stated clearly that the strictest moral discipline would prevail. She cashiered eighty girls in the first two days and used face-slapping and standing-at-attention to punish miscreants, particularly those with a tendency to flirt with the instructors. As far as she was concerned, sex was to be outlawed for the duration of the War. But Bochkarëva's autocratic methods triggered a mutiny. "Democratic" volunteers within and Bolshevik agitators from without spread dissent in the ranks, by demanding soldiers' committees or disbandment. Bochkarëva ejected the Bolsheviks and fought strenuously against the establishment of committees; but this agitation and her draconian discipline lost her all but 300 of the original 2,000 recruits.[12]

Who were these women? The paucity of our sources here precludes anything more than an impression. According to Bochkarëva, the original group included women of prominent families, university graduates, peasants like herself, and servants. Those who remained loyal to her and went into battle were, she claimed, mostly peasants, "but very devoted to mother Russia." A handful of well-born ladies acted as her assistants. But Bessie Beatty, a journalist who spent some time at camp with the group and who was more curious than Bochkarëva about these matters, met stenographers, dressmakers, fac-

[11] Bochkarëva, *Yashka*, 157–64 (quotation, 162).
[12] *Ibid.*, 165–83. Bochkarëva's fight against army committees led her into titanic personal struggles with Kerensky.

tory workers, students, nurses, and a doctor, as well as peasants. Aside from a Pole, a Cossack, a Japanese, and perhaps one Jew, they were all Russian. They ranged in age up to thirty-five with one or two exceptions, but were mostly rather young. Kollontai claimed at the time that these women, lacking as they did the proletarian element—this was largely if not wholly true—also lacked consciousness and had been drawn to battle through personal sorrow or failure in love. Observations by others seem to bear this out also, though there is no denying that the escapist motive—very strong in Bochkarëva for example—was also combined with a genuine, even fanatical love of country. Those screened out by the leader's perhaps excessive disciplinary zeal would appear to have been better educated representatives of the patriotic intelligentsia. They doubtless found their proper place in the other formations modelled on that of Bochkarëva, but not dominated by her.[13]

The feminists were enraptured by Bochkarëva's Battalion of Death. While Pokrovskaya lavished praise upon it in the pages of *Women's Messenger*, Shabanova tightened the knot that bound feminism and defensism together by acting as hostess to Emmeline Pankhurst who arrived in the capital in June. Mrs. Pankhurst, the fiery suffragette now turned patrioteer by the War, had been sent by Lloyd George on a semi-official mission to bolster the pro-victory spirit of Russian women and their fighting men. The moral union of Entente and Russian feminism was cemented socially in the dining room of the Astoria Hotel when Pankhurst and Bochkarëva dined together as the guests of Anna Shabanova. The Russian feminist leader escorted Mrs. Pankhurst to the barracks of the Women's Battalion and to various patriotic rallies designed to raise funds in support of it. At one of these, Pankhurst asked the following question: "Men of Russia, must the women fight? Are there men who will stay at home and let them fight alone?" When the colors of the Battalion were consecrated at St. Isaac's Cathedral, Shabanova and Pankhurst were on hand; the latter took their salute as they returned to their quarters. Two days later, Shishkina-Yavein's League of Women's Equality arranged a farewell ceremony at Kazan Cathedral whence the female troops made the march on foot to the Warsaw Station.[14]

[13] *Ibid.*, 177–201; B. Beatty, *The Red Heart of Russia* (New York, 1919) 96–100; Kollontai's article on the Women's Battalions in *Rabotnitsa*, 6 (June 25, 1917) 7–8; Buchanan, *Dissolution*, 216–17; Claude Anet, *La Révolution russe*, 4 v. (Paris, 1917–1919) II, 27–28. Anet, like most male foreign observers, was appalled at the idea of women in uniform. According to the engineer Bainovskaya, Bochkarëva once visited the Women's Technical Institute in order to recruit the students "for faith, Tsar, and fatherland" but with no success (*Pervye zhen.-inzh.*, 32).

[14] Bochakarëva, *Yashka*, 168; *ZhV* (July-Aug. 1917) 93–94; David Mitchell, *Women on the Warpath: The Story of the Women of the First World War* (London, 1966), which contains a brief undocumented account of Pankhurst's visit to Petrograd, 65–68 (quotation, 68); *Rech* (June 24, 1917) 5. The Battalion saw action in July, fought valorously, and incurred a large number of casualties. But the combination of German strength and Russian front-line democracy rendered their efforts at "personal example" useless. After the battle, Yashka, who was wounded, was sent back to Moscow to recuperate. Bochkarëva, *Yashka*, 184–218. Casualty estimates in Beatty, *Red Heart*, 109 and Louise Bryant, *Six Red Months in Russia* (London, 1918) 210.

Russians opposed to the War looked upon the use of women at the front with distaste. "In the organization of these battalions," said the Petrograd Committee of Peasant Deputies, "we see not only a completely inappropriate and inadmissible vaudeville show, but also another clear and deliberate effort of the bourgeoisie to employ every means to prolong this horrible war until they get what they want." While roundly condemning the regime for exploiting these women, the peasant delegates did not fail to salute the bravery and revolutionary enthusiasm of the women themselves. These comments were answered by a correspondent of *Women's Cause* who stated flatly that women had the right, as equals, to defend their country if they chose to do so. But the same reporter also conceded that the effort had failed to achieve its main goal: boosting combat morale by example. The Bolsheviks were harsher. "Have we become so small," ran a *Rabotnitsa* appeal to mothers of enrollers in the Women's Battalions, "that mercy means nothing to us, that love and sympathy for those dear to us no longer prevail and have given way to an obscene and sordid thirst for blood alone?"[15]

Neither criticism nor failure at the front dampened enthusiasm of feminists and volunteers for the women's military movement. Emulating the patriotic gesture of Lili Braun, the one-time colleague of Zetkin in the German socialist women's movement, Olga Nechaeva of the Russian Union of Democratic Women's Organizations laid before Kerensky a project for the conscription of women for non-combatant service. By its terms women from eighteen to forty-five years of age (excluding workers, peasants, and mothers of children under five) were to be drafted for certain state jobs to release the male incumbents for combat duty. In reporting on the plan, Tyrkova made no effort to conceal the link between this patriotic gesture and the aspirations of the feminists. She voiced the hope that it would utilize the energies of currently unemployed urban middle- and upper-class women. Nechaeva, the old feminist colleague of Filosofova and Shabanova, was named by Kerensky to head a commission to examine the possibilities of replacing men by women in the War Ministry. From the muteness of the sources, it can be assumed that the project died. In any case, no large-scale recruitment of women for behind-the-lines service took place before the October Revolution.[16]

Individual enlistment by females in combat units, on the other hand, increased rapidly throughout the summer. Women's battalions modeled on Bochkarëva's sprang up in Moscow, Perm, Odessa, and Ekaterinodar; smaller units, such as machine gun detachments and communications companies, appeared in several cities, including Kiev and Saratov. Small units were so numerous in the south that a Black Sea Women's Military Union was

[15] *Rabochaya gazeta*, 95 (July 1, 1917) 3; *ZhD* (July 15, 1917) 10 and (Aug. 1, 1917) 1–2. *Rabotnitsa* quoted in N. D. Karpetskaya, *Rabotnitsy i Velikii Oktyabr* (Leningrad, 1974) 90.

[16] Tyrkova, "Zhenskaya povinnost," in *Rech* (June 10, 1917) 3; Frank Golder, ed., *Documents of Russian History, 1914-1917* (New York, 1927) 422.

formed. The wartime phenomenon of individual enlistments by females in male units now gave way to sexually segregated outfits. Apparently, many women no longer trusted men to win the war. "In the last analysis," wrote Tyrkova, "woman is directing her energy towards military tasks because she has become bitterly disillusioned and sometimes even hostile to the harmful weakening of male energy." By August there was a Women's Military Union whose Petrograd Organizational Committee headed by an Army nurse, E. M. Malison, summoned Russia's first (and only) Women's Military Congress (August 1-5, 1917) in the capital. The delegates represented various women's battalions, local military unions, and nursing and medical units; the rostrum was suffused with the spirit of feminism and Socialist Revolutionary style patriotism. Nechaeva and other feminists reported on plans for female mobilization and the perennial Breshkovskaya recalled the glowing days of her revolutionary youth, linking those heroic exploits with the current struggle for a Russian victory. The Congress dispersed in an aura of optimistic patriotism, but there is no evidence of further organizational activity.[17]

Information on the fate of the local women battalions is scant. Beside Yashka's original Petrograd unit, only one (the Perm Battalion) is reported to have gone into action. The Moscow Battalion, probably the largest, reached full strength (1,000–1,500 effectives). According to Yashka, who was greeted by its members with great hostility, it was corrupted by a silk stocking and high-heels mentality. The only estimate of total enrollment in the battalions is Bessie Beatty's figure of 5,000 in the fall of 1917. Yashka Bochkarëva returned to the front with her unit in the hope of going into combat again. But the spirit of desertion was much stronger than that of defense. She was threatened and insulted and twenty of her women were lynched by Russian soldiers. Sickened by the disintegration of the army, she dispersed the remnant of her unit. Yashka went off to find Kornilov after the October uprising and later fought on the White side during the Civil War.[18]

The last episode was the defense of the Winter Palace against the Bolsheviks on October 25. The unit involved was not the Women's Battalion, but a company of privates detached from one of the later Women's Battalions formed in Petrograd after Bochkarëva's departure for the front. According to Beatty, its 1,100 soldiers were of a higher caliber than Yashka's and were well trained by an officer, Prince Kudashëv. The Battalion was slated to go to the front on October 24, but, according to Tyrkova's account—one of the few reliable ones—Kerensky ordered it to the Winter Palace to defend the Provi-

[17] The Congress is covered in *Rech* (August 1, 2, 3, and 6, 1917) 3, 4, 5, respectively. A brief hostile account is given by a Bolshevik nurse in *Leningradki*, 182–84. The Tyrkova quotation is from *Rech* (June 10, 1917) 3.

[18] The note on the Perm battalion is in *Ius Suffragi* (Nov. 1, 1917) 27. The Moscow Battalion is described by Bochkarëva in *Yashka*, 222 and Beatty, *Red Heart*, 112. After a short visit to the United States with Mrs. Pankhurst on a patriotic speaking tour, Bochkarëva returned to Russia. She is last mentioned at the mouth of the Ob in 1919 on her way out (Pares, *Memoirs*, 558).

sional Government. But the commander refused, Tyrkova tells us, and agreed only to send one company of 135 privates "to guard the motor cars which fetched benzine from the stores where the workmen were on strike." These women, continues Tyrkova, had no desire to defend the Government (or any government), but were drawn into the struggle against their will. General Knox, the British military adviser, claimed that the women were mostly of the intelligentsia, an assessment which accords with Lenin's later saucy description of them as "the ladies of the 'constitutional democracy'." But the journalist Albert Rhys Williams recalled that they were mainly of proletarian stock. No statistical data about them are on record. All accounts agree, however, that, whatever their initial reluctance might have been, they fought with the same valor displayed elsewhere by Russian women on the battlefield.[19]

Tales of mass rape, torture, and defenestration of these women after the capture of the Winter Palace circulated for a long time. Three women were supposed to have been stripped and tossed into the Neva from the windows of the Palace—a difficult feat in view of the width of the embankment. Sorokin began composing atrocity stories even before the events took place. But other hostile sources—Tyrkova, Sisson, Meriel Buchanan—mention no deaths or injuries. The facts, as established by the Bolshevik Dr. Mandelbaum and others are probably as follows: There were three cases of rape but no deaths or other injuries; there was one suicide; the women were all subjected to beating and verbal abuse by their captors but otherwise remained unharmed and were soon released to return to their camp outside the capital. After a few weeks, the Battalion was disbanded.[20]

There is little else to record about the activities of the feminists and other anti-Bolshevik women before the October Revolution. In the face of the Bolshevik threat to seize power and end the War, the remaining distinctions between the "bourgeois" feminists and the women of the moderate socialist parties tended to dissolve. In the Council of the Republic, for example, women were represented both in the democratic and in the privileged (or "bourgeois") curias of that body. But women speakers of the former found their warmest response on the right: Kuskova of the Cooperative Union, made a strong "defensist" speech; and the long-time Menshevik philosopher,

---

[19] Beatty, *Red Heart*, 113–14; Tyrkova, *From Liberty to Brest-Litovsk*, 250–56 (quotation, 255); Alfred Knox, *With the Russian Army, 1914-1917*, 2 v. (London, 1921) II, 711; Lenin's words, as reported by Clara Zetkin, were " 'kadetskie' damy" (Bilshai, *O zhen. vop.*, 186); A. Rhys Williams, *Through the Russian Revolution* (Moscow, 1967) 137–38.

[20] Sorokin's account of the defenders (whom he calls a "regiment of women soldiers") is typical of the distortions which gained circulation at this time: *Leaves*, 103. More balanced versions are: Tyrkova, *From Liberty to Brest-Litovsk*, 256–59; Knox, *With the Russian Army*, II, 711–14; Edgar Sisson, *One Hundred Red Days* (New Haven, 1931) 102; S. I. Strievskaya, "Smolnyi—Komnata 43," in *Leningradki*, 93–94. The official findings of the City Duma investigating commission are summarized in John Reed, *Ten Days That Shook the World* (1919) (New York, 1935) 337 and W. H. Chamberlin, *The Russian Revolution, 1917–1921*, 2 v. (1935) (New York, 1965) I, n. 14 on 333–34 (based on Reed).

Lyubov Akselrod, voiced the view of right Menshevism by declaring publicly that Marxists had always been closer to liberalism than to anarchism, especially in time of revolution.[21]

A last glimpse at the League for Women's Equality—its electoral list for the Constituent Assembly—shows that both socially and politically it was more "democratic" than it was "bourgeois." Of the ten candidates, two were doctors, three were teachers or professors, one was a journalist, and three were actively engaged in public or social work (cooperatives, trade unions, and so on). By political persuasion, the list was a mild mixture of feminists, liberals, and moderate socialists: Shishkina-Yavein, President of the League; Kuskova of the Cooperative Central; A. Ya. Efimenko, the historian; A. Kalmykova, an early patron of "legal Marxism"; E. N. Shchepkina, Lecturer at the Bestuzhev Courses and feminist official; L. M. Gorolits-Vlasova, Instructor at the Women's Medical Institute; Mariya Chekhova, teacher, former President of the Union for Women's Equality. The other three are described as a literary figure, a Kiev doctor, and a trade union activist.[22]

Before turning to the chronicle of Bolshevik women's activity in 1917, a word of caution is in order. The sources for it, in contrast to those for the feminist movement, are relatively plentiful. Memoirs abound and the newspapers and journals of the period are readily available. Party archives are apparently loaded with materials; a good many female graduate students in Party History Departments of Soviet universities and institutes have used them in preparing their theses. This, when set beside the paucity or unavailability of sources for the feminists and Menshevik women's groups, gives a distorted impression of the magnitude of difference between the Bolshevik women's effort and all others. In order to maintain some balance, preference has been given to contemporary sources and memoirs over the greatly repetitive and one-sided accounts found in many Soviet secondary works on the subject. But even after this is allowed for, it is clear that the Bolsheviks never had any real competition as organizers and propagandists among women of the urban lower classes in 1917.

At a March 13 Plenum of the Petrograd Committee of the Bolshevik Party, Slutskaya—a veteran of the 1908 Congress—proposed the creation of a Bureau of Women Workers and a revival of the defunct *Rabotnitsa*. The Committee assented and two days later she reported on the formation of the Bureau. Her assurance to the Committee that the Bureau would not act inde-

---

[21] The League with two delegates and the Republican Union with one counted as "bourgeois" organizations and were represented in the privileged curia; unnamed women's groups were represented in the democratic curia by one delegate (Milyukov, *Istoriya vtoroi revolyutsii*, 1 v. in 3 pts. (Sofia, 1921–1924) l/3, 122–26. Speeches of Kuskova and L. Akselrod reported in *Rech*, (October 13, 1917) 2–3; other favorable comments on them in Milyukov, *Istoriya*, l/3, 126 and Buryshkin, *Moskva*, 346.

[22] *Ius Suffragi* (March, 1918) 94.

pendent of the Party was a ritual that would have to be repeated again and again over the next dozen years. In April and May, the women's Bureau established agitational bureaus, commissions, and groups in the districts of Petrograd and a staff of teaching cadres at the center. Eventually women's commissions sprouted up at district Party levels (*raikom*), though the organizational terminology remained fluid and imprecise for months. Clubs and trade unions were also used to draw non-Party working women into party activities. On May 10, the second stage in the organization of a women's movement in the Party took place with the revival of *Rabotnitsa*. Heading it were the woman worker and graduate of the Longjumean Party School, A. Vasileva, assisted by the veterans of the 1914 *Rabotnitsa*: Samoilova, Nikolaeva, Stal, Elizarova. Kollontai, who had arrived in mid-March, became a major contributor and agitator. Between missions to Sweden and Finland, agitational sorties among the Baltic sailors, and other party assignments, the forty-five-year-old Kollontai dashed about the capital leaving behind her a trail of explosive rhetoric.[23]

Rabotnitsa appeared several times a month with a circulation of between 40,000 and 50,000. It advanced the Bolshevik program in terms women could understand, laying stress on the War, high prices, and labor conditions. When a band of military cadets raided its offices during the July Days, the editors concealed the type and the stock until after the turmoil was over and resumed printing. In the industrial and military districts of the city, energetic women Bolshevik officials supplemented the work of *Rabotnitsa* with their own campaigns: Krupskaya and Zhenya Egorova (*nom de guerre* of the Latvian Bolshevik, Ella Liepin) in the critical Vyborg District; Slutskaya on Vasilevsky Island; Lyudmila Stal on Kronstadt naval base; and Anna Itkina in the Narva District. Inessa Armand had travelled on to Moscow and there headed up a similar group around the journal *Life of the Woman Worker* (*Zhizn rabotnitsy*).[24]

The *Rabotnitsa* group adopted an activist style of work. After writing copy for the paper in the morning, the editors would travel to the factories and shops to talk personally to the working women. Agitation was legal for the first time in the history of the revolutionary movement; the Bolsheviks aspired to make it systematic and scientific. A women's school was established where seasoned revolutionaries turned women workers into agitators. Graduates of

[23] Karpetskaya, *Rabotnitsy*, 41–44. On Kollontai in 1917: I. Dazhina, "V vodovorote novoi Rossii: pisma A. M. Kollontai V. I. Leninu i N. K. Krupskoi v Shveitsariyu," *Novyi mir*, 4 (Apr., 1967) 235–42; Kollontai, "Avtobiog. ocherk," 295–99; Itkina, *Kollontai*, 81–83; E. I. Breslav, "A. M. Kollontai v 'Pravde' 1917 goda," *Zhurnalistika i zhizn* (Leningrad, 1967) 96–118.

[24] Kollontai, *Rabotnitsa za god*, 12–13; *idem.*, "Avtobiog. ocherk," 296–97; *Zhen. v rev.*, 119–20; *Okt. rozhd.*, 48–54 (Egorova), 44 (Slutskaya) 55–59 (Stal); Stasova, *Vospom.*, 260 (Itkina); Bobrovskaya, *Lenin and Krupskaya*, 29–30 (Krupskaya). Circulation figures for the two journals are from *Protokoly VI s"ezda R. S.-D. R. P. (Bolshevikov)* (Moscow, 1919) 129 (the figure for *Zhizn rabotnitsy* is 15,000).

its courses were then sent back to their factories to make speeches and new recruits, to teach others, to distribute *Rabotnitsa*, and to report back to the center. *Rabotnitsa* was thus the hub of an agitational network that, while modest in size and efficiency in the tumultuous months of the Revolution, could serve as a model for post-revolutionary mobilization. The whole enterprise was a stage along the road from the old underground circle of the 1890's to the Moscow-based network of training centers known as the Zhenotdel. The propaganda theme throughout the year was the solidarity of women workers with their menfolk in opposition to the War and to those, like the feminists, who supported it.[25]

The movement took the same form as it had in 1905–1907: assault upon the feminists and propaganda among the female masses. The former task came naturally to Kollontai, and on the very day after her arrival in Petrograd she was at the Tauride Palace for the feminist demonstration agitating in the halls and on the street against collaboration with the Government. At one point, she reports that some soldiers threatened to bayonet her. The next day she wrote a bitter commentary on the efforts of the "upper-class ladies" (*barynki*) of the League to extract a commitment to their suffrage right from Rodzianko. "The Constituent Assembly is not a club whose key is in Mr. Rodzianko's pocket," she explained in *Pravda*; "and neither he nor the entire Provisional Government can prevent this or that segment of the population from entering it." In Petrograd and Moscow, feminist meetings were attended by Bolsheviks and women workers who read anti-feminist resolutions and urged the assembled listeners to focus on war and on exploitation. When the feminists held an "All-Russian Women's Congress" in April in Moscow, a delegation led by Inessa repeated the tactics of 1908 and walked out after reading their prepared statements.[26]

In the pages of *Pravda* and *Rabotnitsa* the Bolshevik women leaders applied the political and economic positions of the Party to the woman question. Simply written brochures like Kollontai's *The Working Woman and the Constituent Assembly* reduced revolutionary complexities to everyday categories that any proletarian housewife could understand: hungry children, a husband at the front, and the political dichotomy between peace-bringing Bolsheviks and capitalist war profiteers. Though circulation of such materials was wide and relatively easily accomplished, conspiratorial methods still were used: Stanislava Vishnevskaya, an illiterate worker, insisted on masquerading as a gypsy fortune-teller and made her rounds of the women's mills with a pack of cards and a basket of agitational literature. Mass rallies were

[25] Karpetskaya, *Rabotnitsy*, 44–51.

[26] Kollontai, "Avtobiog. ocherk," 295–96; *Pravda*, 14 (March 21, 1917) 1–2 (quotation, 2). See another anti-feminist article in *ibid*. (April 7, 1917) 1. The Moscow events are related in A. T. Barulina, "Rabota petrogradskoi i moskovskoi part-organizatsii sredi zhenshchin-rabotnits (mart-oktyabr 1917 g.)," in *V borbe za pobedu Oktyabrya: sbornik statei* (Moscow, 1957) 184–208 and Podlyashuk, *Inessa*, 176–83.

arranged at the Cinizelli Circus and the Cirque Moderne that attracted large numbers of women.[27] If the role played by working women in the various uprisings comprising the October Revolution and their subsequent defense of it is judged, it may be concluded that large numbers of them had, like the author of *Why I Became a Communist*, come to see Lenin as "the most furious foe of capital" and, by association, of the War.[28]

Judging from the fragmentary sources available, which may well be misleading, the Menshevik effort to win the loyalty of working women was singularly unimpressive in Petrograd. Their press offensive dealt heavily in economics and tended to avoid hard issues and organizational questions; and their economic program for women was after all identical to that of the Bolsheviks. Lack of unity played its role also since some Menshevik women apparently agreed to work with the feminists and others did not. It was only during the reaction following the July Days that Menshevik and Socialist Revolutionary agitation among women workers outstripped that of the Bolsheviks. At the New Prometheus factory, anti-Bolshevik feelings were so high that Bolshevik agitators were met with flying objects. The Unified Menshevik group, which had a kind of women's sector led by Eva Broido, was the first to call for a conference of Petrograd women workers (in October). This conference adopted a resolution on establishing special commissions for agitation and organization of working women. But their organizational schemes were not matched by much activity.[29]

An illustration of the Bolshevik talent for establishing links with the urban masses by connecting their own political slogans with economic grievances is the campaign of the Bolshevik women leaders on behalf of two of the most backward, neglected, and even despised elements of the female population: laundresses and soldiers' wives. In Petrograd, thousands of washerwomen sweated and labored between thirteen and fourteen hours a day for their thirty kopecks in the steamy cellar laundries, which bore such enterprising names as "Record," "Progress," and "Niagra." The hopeless grind of their occupation has been captured in Arkhipov's popular painting, *The Laundresses*. In 1913, the Bolsheviks had made an effort to organize them, but when a delegation

[27] See *Pravda* 14 (March 26, 1917) 1–2, *ibid.*, 14 (June 8, 1917) 2–3; and *ibid.* (June 30, 1917) 3–4. Kollontai's brochure is *Rabotnitsa i Uchreditelnoe Sobranie* (Peterburg [sic], 1917). For various descriptions of agitation among working women, see *Zhen. v rev.*, 142; Itkina, *Kollontai*, 75–76; *Rabotnitsa*, 3 (May 20, 1917) 3–4; Krupskaya, *Zhenshchina* (1937), 21–22; Dridzo, *Krupskaya*, 88–100.

[28] This simple assessment of Lenin's meaning in the Revolution is from A. Beryushin, *Pochemu ya stala kommunistkoi* (Moscow, 1919), a vivid testimonial of a young Bolshevik convert who was seventeen at the time of the Revolution.

[29] Samples of Menshevik literature and activity vis-à-vis the women's movement in 1917: *Chego khotyat sotsialdemokraty* (Odessa, 1917) 10; *Rabochaya gazeta*, March 7 and March 21, both 1917 *passim*; *Zhen. v rev.*, 131–32, 136; *Novaya zhizn* (Oct. 14, 1917) 3; "Moscauer Organization; Petersburger Organization; Menscheviki-Oboronzy; Mensch. Internat." Folder 1–3 and "Parteitage u. Konferenzen der Menschewiki, 1917–18," Folder 1–3 in the International Institute of Social History, Amsterdam.

requested permission from the police to found a library, the refusal was accompanied by the ironic question "What kind of literature are they going to read over their washtubs?" After the February Revolution, the laundresses organized and sent their demands to the Provisional Government: better working conditions and the establishment of public laundries on a city-wide basis. When these demands were refused as untimely, the women went out on strike. Through Kollontai Lenin was won over to the cause and the Bolsheviks gave it full support. In return, the strikers added the Bolshevik positions on the War, the Soviets, and the "compromisers" to their own economic demands. In the end, the owners were forced to give way, and the main demands of the strikers were met.[30]

Before the War, the "soldier's wife" (*soldatka*) had ranked only a few social millimeters above the prostitute with whom she was often bracketed. When the War converted millions of peasant and working-class women into *soldatki*, the social stigma was forgotten and soldiers' wives were issued a monthly allotment of some seven to nine rubles. By the spring of 1917, this was virtually wiped out by the inflation and a group of Petrograd wives applied to the authorities for assistance. Meeting with no encouragement, they arranged a march to the Tauride, but in contrast to the feminist's march of a month before, this demonstration addressed itself to the Soviet and not the Provisional Government. There was a brief flurry of concern in the Soviet Executive Committee over the issue. The Menshevik Dan, speaking for the majority, called the *soldatki*'s request for an increase in the allotment to twenty rubles empty and naïve: Kollontai hotly opposed him on this and advised the angry soldiers' wives to take over the machinery of distribution themselves. Later an informal allotment committee, composed of Kollontai, some thirty-five *soldatki*, and a few members of the Executive Committee, was organized. Similar arrangements, such as the Union of Soldiers' Wives, in Kharkov, were made in other cities. These groups formed natural recruitment pools and agitational bases for the Bolshevik women in their verbal assaults upon the government and its feminist supporters.[31]

The Bolsheviks, like most other socialists, were hostile to the Women's Battalions—which they called "Shame Battalions"—and fought against their formation; but their hostility was directed against the cause for which the battalions fought, not against the principle of women in combat. The Bolsheviks, like all revolutionary groups of the militant left since the 1870's, had willingly enlisted the services of their female comrades in carrying out armed actions. Women Bolsheviks, as well as Anarchists and Socialist Revolutionaries, had

[30] V. R. Novik-Kondrateva, "Slovo o prachkakh," in *Leningradki*, 61–69; Kollontai, *Za god revol.*, 11; *idem.*, "Avtobiog. ocherk," 296; Breslav, "Kollontai v 'Pravde,'" 106–107.

[31] In Petrograd: *Rabochaya gazeta* (March 19, 1917) 3; Kollontai *Polozhenie*, 135; *idem.*, *Za god revol.*, 10–11; Breslav, "Kollontai v 'Pravde,'" 109; M. P. Dvoretskaya, "Soyuz soldatok," *Zhen. goroda*, 77–86; Dridzo, *Krupskaya*, 92. Elsewhere: *Zhen. v rev.*, 146–50, 172–77.

long proved their worth as fighters, assassins, planners of insurgent operations, and support elements in street fighting. In September, against Kornilov,
and in the October Uprising of 1917, they repeated their exploits of 1905–
1907 on a larger scale. Soon after the February Revolution, with the formation of workers' militia groups (later called the Red Guard), medical units,
made up of factory women and trained by Bolshevik medical students, were
attached to them. During the October days, the hastily trained nurses and
"medical orderlies" (*sanitarki*) of Petrograd took up positions around the beleaguered Winter Palace in order to treat the wounded Red Guards who were
storming it. After the seizure of power, these groups were amalgamated into a
Proletarian Red Cross and later incorporated into the Red Army. A few
women were among the troops who invested the Palace. There was little
bloodshed on either side, but it is worth noting that there were more armed
Bolshevik women involved in the October 25 events than there were members
of the Women's Battalion.[32]

In the Moscow Uprising of 1917 where there was real fighting, women
played a more direct role in the operations. At the administrative level, a
number of women intellectuals and workers held important positions in the
Soviet, the Party Organization, the Military Revolutionary Committee, and
the so-called combat party center; these included the tough underground veterans, Zemlyachka and Yakovleva, and the future Zhenotdel leaders,
Smidovich and Varentsova. When the hostilities began, women of the
trolley-car parks prepared medical, reconnaissance, and "armored" trolley-
cars and took advantage of their functions as trolley-car drivers to scout
enemy positions in the vicinity of the Kremlin. Most of the women insurrec-
tionaries staffed the supply, feeding, communication, and medical points. An
early female martyr of the Revolution, the Bolshevik student Lyusik
Lisinova, was hit by an enemy bullet while working in this way. Similar
scenes were acted out in other industrial centers where uprisings occurred,
particularly in the towns of the Moscow Province textile belt.[33] All this was
not merely the climax of Bolshevik women's activity in 1917—as well as of
the tradition of female militance in the revolutionary movement inaugurated
by Zasulich and Perovskaya—but also a prelude to the much greater epic of
militarism, ferocity, and valor displayed by Russian women on the battlefields
of the Civil War.

3. THE VANQUISHED

"Everywhere women are subjected; everywhere they struggle for their

---

[32] "Proletarskii Krasnyi Krest," *Zhen. goroda*, 106–12; M. F. Spetsova-Vasileva, "Vragi
boyalis nas," *Leningradki*, 170–76; Kollontai, *Za god revol.*, 14; Karpetskaya, *Rabotnitsy*, 114.
[33] *Okt. rozhd.*, 61, 63, 67; *Zhen. v rev.*, 143–44, 158–63; L. Petropavlovskaya, *Lyusik
Lisinova* (Moscow, 1968); Igumnova, *Zhen. Moskvy*, 18–19.

rights. Women from America and England arrive here and are in complete solidarity with us and wish us well in our struggle. *Men cannot defend our interests*; they do not understand us." In this, one of the last official statements by a Russian feminist, is a capsule summary of the views that set her group off from the women of the Bolshevik persuasion. The occasion was the First Conference of Working Women of the Petrograd Region, held in the capital on November 12, 1917—just a few weeks after the change of power. The purpose of the meeting, organized by the *Rabotnitsa* group, was to persuade those assembled to vote for the Bolshevik list and not for that of the League for Women's Equality in the elections to the Constituent Assembly. The League speaker, a Dr. Doroshevskaya, prefaced the remarks quoted above with the affirmation that she was not a parasite but a professional and a self-supporting mother who had been abandoned by her husband. The intimate connection between personal misfortune and social-political outlook—more prevalent in history than is sometimes allowed—was easily visible here. But the pathos of Dr. Doroshevskaya's position in life could hardly have been sufficient to win acceptance of her program for the emancipation of women by the chamber maids and factory women who reluctantly listened to her. Kollontai, having a moment of triumph, had to persuade the conference to hear the feminist out in order to know "our enemy." The speech marked, practically speaking, the end of Russian feminism.[1]

Little is known of the subsequent fates of the feminist leaders. Olga Volkenstein stayed in Soviet Russia to die in the blockade of Leningrad in 1941 or 1942. Anna Shabanova, the oldest and most conservative of them, also remained. She apparently returned to pediatrics and her last work on the subject was published in Russia in 1926. In the emigration, only marginal figures—that is, feminists whose main activities lay elsewhere—maintained prominence. Kuskova emigrated in 1922 and died in 1958. Milyukova was chairman for a time of the London Russian Red Cross Relief Committee; she died in Paris in 1935. Tyrkova, who left Russia in March 1918, wrote for the Russian Liberation Committee in London and wrote a vitriolic study of Bolshevism entitled *From Liberty to Brest-Litovsk*. She later served as a correspondent and editor of the *Times* and died in 1962. Pokrovskaya's fate is not on record. Shishkina-Yavein emigrated to Bulgaria during the Civil War. When the typhus epidemic struck, she traveled with her husband and two children to Estonia where her family (or her husband's) had an estate. Finding it destroyed, she went to work in a quarantine compound, but, as a Russian refugee, she was not permitted to practice medicine in the new Estonian state. By 1921, her husband having died, she was left in exceedingly dire circumstances. In 1920, she wrote the last official greetings from her League to the Geneva Congress of the International Women's Suffrage Association. No

---

[1] The episode is described in *Rabotnitsa*, 12 (1917) 10–15 and 13 (1917) 10–12 (Doroshevskaya's words, 11 of the latter).

Russian attended the Congress. After this, there is no longer any record of Shishkina-Yavein, the League, or any of the other feminist groups.[2]

The paucity of sources does not permit speculation on how many former feminists went into emigration as compared to the number of those who, like Shabanova, stayed on and worked under the Soviet regime. Most of the adult females who emigrated appear to have been wives. Hundreds of them tasted deprivation, particularly in the early years. The streets of Istanbul witnessed the piteous spectacle of refined and educated Russian women—some of whom had perhaps fought prostitution in pre-revolutionary Russia—selling their bodies in order to feed a child or a disabled husband. Later on, many Russian émigré women were able to enrich the culture of their adopted lands in more suitable occupations. From what we in the West have observed of the women of this epoch, it is perfectly clear that most of them were able to retain the honest pride, the dignity, and the high-spirited independence that had been the hallmark of Russia's educated women for generations. Frithjof Nansen and his associates who defined the legal status of the Russian émigrés deserve credit for allowing Russian women to retain the liberal property rights that they had enjoyed under traditional Russian law, even while living in countries like France whose legal code was so different.[3]

Socialist Revolutionaries and the older populist figures present a more varied story. Zasulich, who spent most of her remaining years in emigration, inherited from the 1870's the impeccable probity of the *narodnik* tradition but a thorough disillusionment with populism in general and with terror in particular. Under Plekhanov's influence she gradually turned to Marxism and remained his undaunted ally right up to the Revolution. Zasulich's firm adherence to the nihilist ethical code of her girlhood, her personal modesty, and her scrupulous fairness in judging other comrades earned her in some quarters the sobriquet of "the Socrates of Russian Social Democracy." From this same code arose her utter hostility to decadence or any form of sexual irregularity and her idealism and contempt for bourgeois material comfort. Her ironic triumph as a propagandist came in 1901 when she, the fabled terrorist of bygone days, wrote an article for *Iskra* definitively condemning individual terror as a political weapon. Zasulich, ever following Plekhanov, remained as far from Bolshevism as it was possible for a socialist to be; she died in Petro-

[2] The data on Volkenstein and Shabanova were supplied to me by the reference librarian of the Social-Economic Reading Room of the Saltykov-Shchedrin State Public Library in Leningrad. For Milyukova, see *The New Russia* (Nov. 11, 1920) iii (a London émigré weekly) and the obituary cited above in Chapter VII, 2, n. 15. On Tyrkova, Arkady Borman (her son), *A. V. Tyrkova-Vilyams* (Louvain, 1964) chs. 11–20. On Shishkina-Yavein and the last echoes of Russian feminism: *Ius Suffragi* (June 1921) 134; Ida Husted Harper, *The History of Woman Suffrage*, 6 v. (New York, 1922) VI, 862, 789; and *Report of the Eighth Congress of the International Woman Suffrage Association . . . Stockholm* (Manchester, 1920); *ibid.* for the ninth congress at Rome (Dresden 1923) and the Tenth at Paris (London, 1926).

[3] *Russian Life*, 1 (Sept.-Oct., 1921) 105 and 3 (Jan. 1922) 178 (a London émigré monthly); W. Chapin Huntington, *The Homesick Million: Russia-out-of-Russia* (Boston, 1933) 25–26, 83, 272; the sensitive Soviet film, *Beg* (1971).

grad on May 8, 1919, and was buried near her teacher in Volkovskoe Cemetery. In commenting on the death of a woman who had devoted the last forty years of her life to the working class, a *Pravda* obituary had these words to say about her: "In later years, V. I. Zasulich broke with the revolutionary proletariat. But the proletariat values her great services in the past. They will never forget her name." Thus the terrorist came to take precedence over the Marxist scholar.[4]

Vera Figner had entered the Schlüsselburg Fortress when she was 32; she emerged twenty years later, in 1904, an old woman seeking to begin "her third life." The sustained incarceration had shattered her nervous system. She wandered sadly from one place of exile to another under police surveillance. An ironic blow struck her in 1905 when her ancestral home near Kazan was burned to the ground by insurgent peasants. During a brief visit to Moscow, Figner was feted by the intelligentsia, flocks of Bestuzhev women, and the Union for Women's Equality. But like Zasulich, she remained lonely and disoriented for a time. She left Russia and finally joined the Socialist Revolutionaries in 1908. But, as a seasoned conspirator, she was disenchanted by its amateurishness in the Azef affair and resigned. In 1917, Figner tried to come to grips with the problem of the old revolutionary set loose in the hurricane of a revolution not of her making. "The overturn of October 25, from which our great social revolution began, was a great shock for me. I was not prepared for it. To read at the age of nineteen or twenty the story of the struggle of the revolutionary parties in the French Revolution is one thing; to live through revolutionary events personally is quite another." Though courted by the regime, Figner refused to become a Communist. But she stayed in Russia, busied herself with literary work in the Society of Political Exiles, and even tried to attract other old *narodniks* back to Russia. When the Germans were approaching Moscow in 1941, the authorities sought to evacuate the feeble old heroine. "Concern yourself with the living," she told them. She died the following year at the age of ninety and was buried with honor in the Novodevichi Cemetery.[5]

Breshkovskaya was the only one of the three veteran populists to adhere

[4] Some idea of the reputation which Zasulich enjoyed among Russian Marxists of all shades may be gotten from the following: K. I. Zakharova-Tsederbaum and S. O. Tsederbaum (Martov's sister-in-law and brother), *Iz epokhi 'Iskry' (1900–1905 gg.)*, ed. V. I. Nevsky (Moscow, 1926) 10–11; Broido, *Memoirs*, 65; Krupskaya, *Memoirs*, 53; Lyubov Akselrod [Ortodoks], *Etyudy i vospominaniya* (Leningrad, 1925) 37–46; and the brief memoirs in *Gruppa 'Osvobozhdenie Truda': iz arkhivov G. V. Plekhanova, V. I. Zasulich, L. N. Deich*, 6 v. (Moscow, 1923–1928) II, 160–67 and III, 68–81. Obituary: Kovnator, intro. to Zasulich, *Stati (Pravda*, [May 10, 1919] 18).

[5] The basic source, *Posle Shlisselburga* (Leningrad, 1925), details only the first few years after Figner's liberation; the German version was used: *Nach Schlüsselburg* (Berlin, 1928). This must be supplemented by M. N. Figner, "Posle Shlisselburga," in Figner, *V borbe* (Lenigrad, 1960) 185–227 (quotation, 212). See also Lidiya Dan, *Iz vstrechi s Veroi Nikolaevnoi Figner* (New York, 1961) and Figner, *Les prisons russes* (Lausanne, 1911). I am indebted to Margarita Nikolaevna Figner (V. F. Figner's niece) for additional details on Figner's last years which she related to me in January 1968, in Leningrad.

wholly to former traditions. After twenty years in the camps of Siberia, she returned to Russia as iron-willed as ever and bursting with the revolutionary energies she had stored up during captivity. Joining radicals half her age, she helped to form one of the local circles which became a nucleus of the Party of Socialist Revolutionaries. Then she was off to America to make speeches and to raise money for the liberation of her country, moving freely and indiscriminately among workers, liberals, and "bourgeois" feminists. On her return to Russia, she inspired the "maximalist" wing of the Socialist Revolutionary Party with the idea of agrarian terror while at the same time opposing individual terror or political assassination. This drew from the terrorist leader, Evno Azef, the comment that "the old woman has gone out of her mind." Breshkovskaya, fondly recalling her Bakuninist days of youth, longed to do something daring and she took as her slogan "To arms! To the people!" But the Party leader, Chernov, was right when he wrote that all this really reflected Breshkovskaya's lack of faith in all organization. Unfit for administrative responsibility, she was also "alien to theory, to strategy, to tactics," said Chernov. "She was rather a witness, an apostle, converting people by her words and, even more, by her living example." But even this function was lost when, in 1908, this woman of "extraordinary revolutionary passion"—the phrase is Valdo Zilli's—was again arrested and removed from the political arena.

The puzzle of Breshkovskaya has yet to be unraveled. It arises from the contradictions between the ultra-radical flamboyance of her youth and the conservative nationalism of her later years. Her passionate love of the peasantry was sharply at odds with her strident support of a war which was slaughtering them like sheep. Her early anarchism and anti-liberalism gave way in 1917 to state worship and idolatry of the Entente and its brand of liberal democracy—though this was accompanied by a moralistic populist hatred of Petrograd and its rotten Westernism. Behind the personal image of the sweet old *babushka* ("the patented grandmother of the revolution" in the sardonic phrase of one Bolshevik observer) that has been dished up in popular Western treatments of her, there is a vitriolic woman who spat her venom freely at Chernov and other hated internationalists in her own Party, and who was perfectly willing to act as the purveyor of Allied funds donated to support pro-war politics in Russia. Such transformation, indeed confusion, of values was hardly peculiar to Breshkovskaya in 1917; but, perhaps she is the most disturbing example of that ideological disorder which was so characteristic of Russia's last populist party.[6]

[6] Zilli, *Rivoluzione*, I, 286–87; *A Message to the American People* (New York, n.d. 1919 or 1920) 5; *For Russia's Freedom* (Chicago, 1905); V. M. Chernov, *Pered burei: vospominaniya* (New York, 1953) 204–205, 215, 316. Azef's comment is reported in *ZhD*, 2 (Jan. 15, 1914) 20. Breshkovskaya left Russia in December 1918 and died sixteen years later in Czechoslovakia at the age of ninety. V. G. Arkhangelsky (a Right Socialist Revolutionary) has written a straightforward and sympathetic account of the last years: *Katerina Breshkovskaya* (Prague, 1938) 99–213. But see also the comments of Edgar Sisson, *One Hundred Red Days* (New Haven,

Mariya Spiridonova's integrity and consistency has been somewhat obscured by a political style and personality which was, even by Russian standards, theatrical. Emotionally overheated by long years in the exalted atmosphere of Siberian women's prisons, Spiridonova, on being released by the Revolution of February 1917, ordered the Chita prison to be blown up, and later begged her friend Steinberg of the Left Socialist Revolutionaries, Justice Minister under the Bolsheviks, to repeat the operation on the Peter and Paul Fortress in Petrograd. Looking for all the world like "a little old-maid schoolteacher of a past generation" (George Sisson), she would open meetings by striking the rostrum with a small silver revolver presented to her by friends as a memento of her 1905 exploit, and then proceed to address her comrades in deeply passionate, sometimes hysterical cadences. Her views—simple, idealistic, sometimes utopian—were moored to a personality whose salient features were the distilled essence of Russian radicalism: sincerity, probity, love of "the people," and firmness of will. Like Breshkovskaya, Spiridonova stressed the role of personality in history; unlike her, she managed to keep her personality together and her ideals in focus all through the maelstrom which engulfed them both.[7]

As the *de facto* leader of the Party she helped found late in 1917, the Left Socialist Revolutionaries, Spiridonova willingly conceded the identity in immediate goals between her Party and the Bolsheviks. But in doing so—at the Left Socialist Revolutionaries' first congress—she voiced her reservations. "We have entered a new phase of history . . ." she said; "that of bitter class struggle. But because of that it is our duty to cleanse the air, to refill our souls with idealism from that treasure left us by the martyred fighters of the past. The final goal is the *human personality*. We fight not only that all men might eat; our goal stands much higher: we fight so that in this economic struggle man may triumph and may rise as a moral human being. . . ." In justifying the alliance with the Bolsheviks whom most Socialist Revolutionaries considered ruthless and materialistic, she said:

> Today the Bolsheviks have the support of the masses of the people, but that is temporary—temporary because everything there [among the Bolsheviks] is hatred and bitterness. Such emotions, aroused by selfish interests, may be useful when the fight is on the barricades. But in the second phase of the struggle, when organic building begins, when a new life must be erected on

1931) 44–50 and Radkey, *Agrarian Foes*, 189 with note, 193, and 378–79, 396, and 399. Of her own writings of 1917, the following are typical and revealing: *O voine* (Simferopol, 1917) and *Obyazannosti svobodnykh grazhdan* (Simferopol, 1917). In the latter (11), she proposes compulsory state teaching liability for all women university and high-school graduates.

[7] Sisson's words quoted from *One Hundred Red Days*, 43. For varying assessments and descriptions of her behavior, see: Radkey, *Agrarian Foes*, 348, 472; Sorokin, *Leaves*, 51; Steinberg, *Spiridonova*, 158–221 and *passim*; and *idem.*, *In the Workshop of the Revolution* (London, 1955) 66, 196–214. Spiridonova's comment on personality in history is her speech at the first Congress of the Left Socialist Revolutionaries: *Protokoly pervago s"ezdi Partii Levykh Sotsialistov-Revolyutsionerov (Internatsionalistov)*, Petrograd, 1918, 35.

the foundations of love and altruism, the Bolsheviks will go bankrupt. But we, who wish to retain the message of our pioneers [the populists], must always think of the second phase of the struggle.[8]

The break with the Bolsheviks came over the issue of Cheka terror and the German occupation of the Ukraine (which followed the Treaty of Brest). Individual terror was the traditional weapon of the Socialist Revolutionaries—its three female candidates to the Constituent Assembly were convicted assassins; and the murder of German officials in the occupied area—where, in Spiridonova's words, "there is not a peasant whose back is not scarred"— were either ordered or endorsed by her.[9] It was a re-enactment of 1905. Criticized by the Bolsheviks, she wrote a well-known letter on terror and its moral imperatives:

> You call this terror. But in the history of the Russian Revolution, this word has never meant to signify revenge or intimidation (that was its least important purpose). It did not mean only the liquidation of one of the people's hangmen. No. The most important element in the terror was protest against the oppression of despotism, an attempt to arouse indignation in the souls of humiliated men and women, to fire the conscience of those who stood silent in the face of this humiliation. That is how the terrorist advanced on the enemy. And almost always did the terrorist combine his deed with the voluntary sacrifice of his own life and freedom. I believe that only thus was it possible to justify the terrorist act of the revolutionary.[10]

Spiridonova's rejection of Bolshevism and justification of terror were embodied in Fanya Kaplan's attempt of August 30, 1918, upon the life of Lenin. Very little is known about Kaplan, often incorrectly called Dora Kaplan in foreign accounts. She was born Feiga Efimovna Roidman in 1890, the daughter of a Jewish teacher from Volhynia. Though associated with both the Anarchists and the Socialist Revolutionaries, she was never a member of either party. Her politics, like that of many a young exalted terrorist, seems to have consisted in combating perceived despotism with dynamite and the revolver. She shot at Lenin, according to her own testimony, because he had made peace with the Germans and betrayed the Revolution. There are indications that she was unstable, and the act appears to have been a lone venture. Both the would-be assassin and the Socialist Revolutionaries denied any mutual connection, though the Bolsheviks have always insisted on a conspiracy. If, as official sources have it, she was shot soon afterward, she was the first revo-

[8] Both passages from Steinberg, *Workshop*, 122–23.

[9] The three women were: Spiridonova, Izmailovich, Bitsenko. Kollontai and Nikolaeva were on the Bolshevik list; Panina on the Kadets'. Spiridonova's reaction to German occupation and the quoted words in James Bunyan, ed., *Intervention, Civil War, and Communism in Russia* (Baltimore, 1936) 201–202, 208–209, 219.

[10] Steinberg, *Workshop*, 132.

lutionary woman to perish in this way under the new regime, a sobering thought that evoked from Krupskaya the comment: "A revolutionist executed in a revolutionary country! Never!" Spiridonova, and Lenin too by the way, opposed the execution, and the former suggested that an act of mercy toward an old revolutionary fighter would have been appropriate "at a time of general madness and frenzy." There was no act of mercy, as such, but it might be that Kaplan was not shot but remained alive in captivity long after the event.[11]

A similar fate awaited most of the other activist Left Socialist Revolutionary women. By 1920, Spiridonova was permanently in jail, after several shorter spells during the Civil War. The American anarchist Emma Goldman asked Zetkin to intercede for her, but Trotsky thought her too dangerous to be released. She died in captivity sometime between 1937 and 1941. Her friend, Irina Kakhovskaya, the assassin of General Eichorn, fought against the Whites in the Civil War and even planned an assassination attempt on Denikin; like many Socialist Revolutionaries and Anarchists, she looked upon the Whites as a greater evil than the Bolsheviks; and like them also she found herself in a Cheka prison at the end of the war. Long before Stalin assumed power the prisons and camps of the Revolution were filled with revolutionary women who maintained their moral outlook, as well as their clandestine organizations, well into the Stalinist Terror and were as truly the inheritors of the women's radical tradition as were the Bolshevik women (some of whom would share cells with Socialist Revolutionary women during the 1930's).[12]

[11] The official Bolshevik account is I. Volkovicher, "K istorii pokusheniya na Lenina," *Proletarskaya Revolyutsiya*, 6–7 (18–19) 1923, 275–85. "Fanya Kaplan" seems to have been her revolutionary *nom de guerre* after 1905, though a number of journalists report her at the time as "Dora," a name she may have been given at the time of her arrest. Krupskaya's exclamation is recorded by Balabanova in *Impressions of Lenin*, 13; Spiridonova's words are reproduced in Steinberg, *Workshop*, 151. Pavel Malkov, former commandant of the Kremlin compound, claims to have executed her personally in the courtyard of the Kremlin beside a truck whose running engine muffled the noise of the shot. When he asked Sverdlov where to bury her, the latter is said to have replied: "We will not bury her. We will destroy her remains without a trace." *Zapiski Kommandanta Moskovskogo Kremlya* (Moscow, 1959) 159–61.

No written evidence of the non-execution of Kaplan has been seen, but a number of credible Soviet Russians—officials and ordinary citizens—have stated that she was never shot. An acquaintance claims to have seen her working as a librarian in a labor camp right after World War II.

[12] Emma Goldman, *Living my Life*, 2 v. (London, 1932) II, 915. Steinberg, a good friend, last heard from Spiridonova in 1931. K. Gusev, in *Krakh levykh eserov* (Moscow, 1963), places her death in 1941 (248). Robert Conquest, on the basis of a Polish prison memoir, suggests that she may have been liquidated in 1937 for refusing to cooperate in the Bukharin frameup which tried to link him to the Socialist Revolutionaries and to plans to kill Lenin (*The Great Terror* [Harmondsworth, 1971] 399).

For Kakhovskaya, see Steinberg, *Workshop*, 177–79. Reports of incarceration and mistreatment of SR women in the 1920's: Olga Kolbassine-Tchernoff [Kolbasina-Chernova], *Les prisons soviétiques* (Paris, 1922) 26–28; *Partei der Linken Soziale-Revolutionäre* (Berlin, 1922) 3. The fullest memoir of the period is Ekaterina Olitskaya, *Moi vospominaniya*, 2 v. (Paris, 1971). Portraits of SR women in Stalin's prisons may be found in Evgeniya Ginsburg, *Into the Whirlwind*, tr. P. Stevenson and M. Harari (Harmondsworth, 1968) 87, 93, 227, *passim*.

PART FOUR

Women's Liberation

X

Bolshevik Liberation

"Don't make an issue of my womanhood."
—*Ninotchka* (1939) C. BRACKETT, B. WILDER,
and W. REISCH.

1. THE LIMITS OF EQUALITY

"The future historian," said Kollontai after the Civil War, "will undoubtedly note that one of the characteristics of our revolution was that women workers and peasants played not—as in the French Revolution—a passive role, but an active important role." The following paragraphs may serve as a gloss on this remark. Though there was a good deal of spontaneous activity among the women of the Red side, Bolshevik women organizers—Kollontai foremost among them—did not leave much to chance. In a propaganda pamphlet of 1920 addressed to women, Kollontai directly invited working and peasant women to support the Red Front in every possible way including combat. Conscious of her own former anti-war propaganda, she was careful to point out the difference between the exploitative character of the Great War and the liberating and defensive nature of the present one, tying together the thesis of women's capacity to fight with the need to defend the equality that they had won in the Revolution. The Soviet publicist, V. Bystryansky, began his argument in *Revolution and Woman* (1920) with a reference to Fourier's statement about measuring a society's level of progress by examining the level of women's emancipation in that society, and made flattering comments about the military potential of women. Variations of these themes were the stock in trade of propagandists such as Krupskaya, Balabanova, and other Bolshevik women who held important propaganda posts during the Civil War.[1]

What is striking about Russian women's participation in this War is the variety and novelty of the functions that they performed. As in the past, women carried out every conceivable support task on the home front, ranging from feeding and sanitary operations to building fortifications and digging trenches in beleaguered cities. As in World War I, women served in medical and combat capacities, but on a broader scale and in a much more organized context. Propaganda, psychological warfare, espionage, and police work—

---

[1] Kollontai, *Polozhenie*, 200; her pamphlet, *Rabotnitsy, krestyanki i krasnyi front* (Moscow, 1920); Bystryansky's, *Revolyutsiya i zhenshchina* (Petrograd, 1920).

known previously to only a few exceptional women—now recruited large numbers of them. Women's participation was erratic and tentative during the first year of the War. In October 1919, the Zhenotdel gave greater definition to the functions of women and set up the machinery for large-scale and orderly recruitment. By the end of the war in 1920, conscription of young women for non-combatant service had begun, and high-ranking posts in Military Revolutionary Committees and Political Departments of the Red Army were occupied by women.

In the early days of the Red Army, there were apparently some female medical personnel left over, voluntarily or otherwise, from the tsarist and Kerensky days. According to the historian Igumnova, these women were hostile to the Red soldiers and often deserted their wounded. In 1919, special short courses were set up for workers in first-aid and sanitation, which turned out some 6,000 graduates, mostly from Moscow, ranging in age from seventeen to forty, and non-Party. The women received rifle training and political indoctrination; some of them were appointed political commissars of hospitals. These raw volunteers merged with medical students and Red Guard nurses from the October days to form an effective medical arm. Captured nurses were often treated with special brutality by Whites. Near Petrograd in 1919, three nurses were hanged in bandages from the beams of their field hospital with their Komsomal pins stuck through their tongues. Those who survived frequently went on to do cultural, medical, or Zhenotdel work in the 1920's. This tradition (which had helped launch the woman question during the Crimean War) was one of the first to be unostentatiously taken over by the Bolsheviks and adapted to revolutionary purposes.[2]

Women in combat was another. Although we find instances of women who, like Bochkarëva, joined the army disguised as men, most of the fighting female soldiers were accepted as such. They fought on every front and with every weapon, serving as riflewomen, armored train commanders, gunners. The female machine gunner of the Red Army became a stock character in early Soviet literature. Though the total number of fighting women (as opposed to auxiliaries) was certainly larger than it was in Kerensky's army, the idea of large all-women units like the Women's Battalions does not appear to have caught on. More typical were the company-sized detachments of 300 or so which sprang up bearing names like Communist Women's Combat Detachment or Communist Women's Special Purpose Detachment; they performed police work in the towns, and combat duty in time of enemy siege. But there were also front-line units whose performance compared favorably with that of the Women's Battalions. During the Polish campaign when a reg-

[2] On Red Sisters: Kollontai, *Rabotnitsa i krestyanka v Sovetskoi Rossii* (Petrograd, 1921) 10–11, where the figure of 6,000 is given; Igumnova, *Zhenshchiny*, 46–64; claims that 50,000 nurses were trained in 1919–1920; N. A. Koshcheev, *N. K. Krupskaya v prikame* (Izhevsk, 1966) 55; *Leningradki*, 173–75; *Kommunistka*, 8–9 (1921) 40–41; *Zhen. goroda*, 156.

iment began to falter, the situation was saved by the aggressive onslaught of a company of women, all but one of whose members perished in the assault.[3]

Women took naturally to irregular warfare, an activity unknown to them since the days of 1812 when the Baba-Bogatyr Vasilisa (the peasant wife of a village elder) and her associates pitch-forked, scythed, and burned alive the stragglers from Napoleon's army. According to the memoirs and accounts of the Civil War, the rough, comradely ways of partisan life were congenial to women. They paid dearly for it when caught: The captured women of a Yakutsk group were frozen alive into icy status. Scouts and spies were hard to recruit and easily lost and this led underground Red networks in the White areas to make thorough use of female agents to gather intelligence and spread subversion. In Chita, Bolshevik women "socialized" with Cossacks and Japanese officers. In Odessa and Baku, educated women spun out anti-interventionist arguments to French and British soldiers in their own language. This work was considered so crucial that Lenin ordered the establishment of a special school for training disorganization and espionage personnel to work behind Denikin's lines. The school, hidden in a secret wing of a Moscow house, was headed by the Georgian revolutionary, Kamo, who trained young women from the Caucasus in the arts of simulation, sabotage, and holding up under interrogation. Its graduates became members of the First Partisan Special Purpose Detachment and were sent off on a variety of intelligence missions.[4]

The most colorful of the partisan-spies was Larisa Reisner, the prototype for the heroine of Vishnevsky's play, *Optimistic Tragedy*. Born in Lublin, she was the daughter of a law professor, was educated in Europe and Russia, and was active in social democratic journalistic circles. By all accounts, a strikingly beautiful woman, she was twenty-two at the time of the Revolution. Her first job in the new state was to help draft the decree separating Church and State; later she worked on the Constitution of 1918 and on alphabet reform with Blok and Mayakovsky. Restless, and intoxicated by power, she strapped on a mauser and took up a post as head of the intelligence section of the Volga Fleet and specialized in organizing and performing espionage work behind enemy lines. She was married to the commander of the fleet, the Bolshevik sailor, Raskolnikov. After the Civil War, she was unable to adjust to the New Economic Policy, which she loathed—a loathing shared by many who had had partisan experience. Reisner spent her remaining years traveling with Karl Radek whose mistress she became. She died in 1926; both the men in her life were destroyed (in one way or another) during the purges.[5]

---

[3] Halle, *Woman*, 99; *Zhen. v rev.*, 261–63; *Docheri revolyutsii: sbornik* (Moscow, 1923); *Zhen. goroda*, 127–30, 153, 155; *Kommunistka*, 8–9 (1921) 41.

[4] On Vasilisa: *ZhD* (Aug. 15, 1912) 5. Episodes of irregular warfare: Krupskaya, *Zhenshchina* (Moscow, 1937) 9; *Oktyabrëm*, 89–95, 118, 122–27, 155–60; *Pravda stavshaya*, 113–24, 132–42, 186–90, 199; *Zhen. v revol.*, 226–33.

[5] *Leningradki*, 162–69; *Pravda stavshaya*, 78–88; *Vospom. o Krupskoi*, 473; Nadezhda

As impressive as the purely military effort of Russian women was during this War, it was the political work of women in the Red Army that probably had the greatest impact on its outcome. The Whites suffered grievously from the absence of skilled and coordinated propaganda machinery; the Bolsheviks, whose daily bread had been propaganda and agitation in the long years of preparation, perceived its military importance at once. Women, who had long since proved their effectiveness in agitation, were immediately recruited. Kollontai, after her brief fling as a cabinet minister, threw herself into the work with great energy. Under a variety of auspices, and bearing different titles, she roamed the front with her sailor-husband, Dybenko, on an especially equipped Agitational Train (*Agitpoezd*), dispensing political instructions and Bolshevik propaganda. Her 1919 pamphlet, *Be A Stoic*, addressed to potential deserters, is as much a classic of patriotic pro-war literature as her 1916 pamphlet, *Who Needs War?*, was a classic of anti-war writing. A comparison of the two clearly shows that Kollontai, like the feminists before her, believed that some wars were better than others. Balabanova and Krupskaya, her colleagues during World War I, carried out similar missions in support of the Red Army, the latter traveling through the vast Kama basin on an Agit-Boat.[6]

Political work in the Red Army itself was carried on through the "political sections" (*politotdely*) in each unit. These were coordinated at the center by the Agitational Department of the Bureau of Military Commissars in Moscow, headed by Varya Kasparova, chief organizer of the *politotdels*. Women trained there and at the Central Executive Committee's School for Agitators and Instructors (also headed by a woman) were sent out to head up or staff the Front, Army, or lower level unit *politotdels*. A typical *politotdel* was a mobile group of 20 or so, with a "leader" (*nachalnik* or *zaveduyushchii*) and a wagon-load of political literature geared to the interests of the soldiers. Propaganda teams or individual instructors would visit the front-line units to give lectures, pep-talks, or visual presentations about what precisely the Red Army men and women were fighting for. *Politotdel* people were also used to politicize or neutralize the local population. The women who achieved a high rank in the *politotdel* hierarchy were generally veterans of the revolutionary movement and skilled labor agitators. In this, as in so many other matters, the Civil War was conceived of as simply the continuation, on an intensified scale, of the revolutionary movement. Social-political continuity was further maintained when many of the commissars of the Civil War went on to take up positions in the Zhenotdel in the 1920's. Thus the Civil War, still curiously neglected as a crucial stage of the revolutionary process, was both a proving

Madelstam, *Hope Against Hope: A Memoir*, tr. Max Hayward (Harmondsworth, England, 1975) 128–32.

[6] Kollontai: her pamphlet, *Bud stoikom bortsom!* (Moscow, 1919) and Itkina, *Kollontai*, 94–97. Balabanova: *Impressions*, 77. Krupskaya: Dridzo, *Krupskaya*, 102–104.

ground for a generation of underground fighters and a training ground for future social mobilizers.[7]

The most prominent of the full-time women "commissars" (the term was loosely used; here it refers to the head of a *politotdel*) was Zemlyachka, the former *Iskrovka* and veteran of the 1905 Moscow uprising. Now in her forties, the only vestige of her bourgeois origins (see above, p. 275) was the pince-nez that she wore in grotesque contrast to her short hair, boots, pants, and leather coat. Merciless to her enemies, Zemlyachka would unblinkingly order the shooting of one of her female comrades caught at treason or would preside, with Bela Kun and others, over the execution of thousands of White officers and members of the "bourgeoisie" after the conquest of the Crimea. As commissar of the VIIIth and later the XIIIth Armies, she was also merciless to inefficiency, dirt, corruption, "partisan" tendencies, or any attempt to treat her as anything but an equal. "What do you take me for? An *institutka*? A bread-and-butter miss?" she once asked of a commander who had displayed ironic anti-feminism toward her. Zemlyachka and others like her had to work hard to overcome the double hostility of some officers whose hatred of "commissars" (dating from the time of Kerensky) was now compounded by a hatred for female busybodies.[8]

A number of women worked in the Cheka during the Civil War, though data on them is very scanty and unreliable. Contemporary anti-communist verbal cartoons of them are numerous, but mostly, it would seem, fanciful. Waliszewski, for example, reports that a certain Grebennikova, "cigarette in mouth, enormous revolver at the belt," forced Red Guards to violate women and children before executing them. The anti-Bolshevik (and anti-Semitic) English journalist, Hodgson, reports the story of "a young Jewish girl who was known as Rosa" who shot her victims joint by joint or boiled the skin off their arms (the well-known "glove trick"). Of the genuine articles, only the Chekist Kseniya Ge, hanged in 1919, has come down to us enshrined in Soviet hagiography. Varvara Yakovleva, veteran with Zemlyachka of 1905, headed the Petrograd branch of the Cheka late in 1918. Although hard evidence of her brutality is lacking, there is no reason to disbelieve the fact that Yakovleva (a future purge victim also) was directly responsible for a large number of Cheka executions in Petrograd. The Bolsheviks did not deny the value of terror, whether administered by men or by women.[9]

How many and what kind of women fought in the Civil War? The numbers are, if accurate, impressive, however paltry they may appear beside the number of male participants. A. P. Bogat's figure for 1920, certainly low, is

[7] *Pravda stavshaya*, 34–47, 71, 114–15; *Zhen. v revol.*, 43–51; Kollontai, *Rab. i krest. v. Sov. Rossii*, 10.

[8] *Pravda stavshaya*, 7–27; Chamberlin, *Russ. Revol.*, II, 74 on terror in the Crimea.

[9] K. Waliszewski, *La femme russe* (Paris, 1926) 205; J. L. Hodgson, *With Denikin's Army* (London, 1932), 73; E. Didrikul, "Kseniya Ge," in *Kommunistka*, 8–9 (1921) 38–40. On Yakovleva, see *BSE*, 1st ed., LXV, 464. Women in "special purpose" units were sometimes used to execute bandits: *Pravda stavshaya*, 150.

73,858, of whom 1,854 became casualties (Kollontai's estimate), and of whom 55 were awarded the Order of the Red Banner. The scant evidence about recruitment, social composition, and function-as-related-to-background points again to the conclusion that socially the Civil War was the Revolution played over again in military costume. Women holding high rank and responsibility were mostly of the same background of those who had done so in the revolutionary labor movement: students, intelligentsia, and politically trained workers, with an ample sprinkling of Jews among the first two groups. Women in the ranks tended to be workers, servants, wives of soldiers on active duty or war widows. In relation to the men, women tended to: fill middle ranks rather than high and low ones; perform support and political rather than combat functions; and, as officers, hold staff rather than line positions. And this had also been generally true in the revolutionary movement from the very beginning. Ease of promotion and frequency of transfer over vast distances introduced to Russian women of that epoch a mobility, social and geographic, unknown to their sex anywhere else in the world.[10]

The image of the revolutionary woman as the tough-willed equal of men persisted and deepened in the crucible of this bloody war. "Happiness in those years," recalled a former nurse of the Ural front, "was understood not as a pretty dress, a successful marriage, or a cozy flat with a grammophone; happiness was working at the front among the wounded, the dying, the stricken." Sexual life was not altogether ignored, as we shall have occasion to note elsewhere, but the defeminizing element among revolutionary women, dating from the nihilist days, displayed itself in dress style and in the emulation of "military" virtues. When a young woman combatant, equipped with over-sized *papakha*, leather coat, and Browning, was detected by her comrades as a "little girl" (*devchina*), she proudly replied, "I am not a little girl now; I am a soldier of the Revolution." Allegations of feminity were resented, and male resistance to the idea of women in combat vigorously and successfully opposed. But the no-nonsense personality of the Bolshevik "woman commissar," as caricatured by amused but uncomprehending Western journalists and film-makers in the early Soviet years, was forged not so much by the Civil War as by a half-century of conditioning in the revolutionary movement.[11]

[10] A. P. Bogat's figures in *Oktyabrëm*, 112; Kollontai's in *Rab. i krest. v Sov. Rossii*, 11.

[11] *Pravda stavshaya*, 204 (quotations), 205, 222; *Oktyabrëm.*, 134 (quotation). Outlandish amazon costumes like the one described in Lavrenëv's *The Wind* (1924)—"pink hussar breeches with silver stripes, patent leather boots with spurs; she had a silver mounted saber hanging at one side, a sheathed automatic pistol at the other, and her black, shaggy Cossack cap sported a red bow"—do not seem to have been the rule among real women of the Civil War (this quotation is taken from Xenia Gasiorowska, *Woman in Soviet Fiction, 1917–1964* [Madison, 1968] 144). Even before the Bolshevik Revolution, the Kadet, Countess Panina, affected "a workman's blouse and leather skirt" as Assistant Minister of Welfare in the Provisional Government: Bette Stavrakis, "Women and the Communist Party in the Soviet Union, 1918–1935" (Ph.D., Western Reserve University, 1961) 25. The iconography of the period shows that most women wore simple soldier's tunics or leather jackets, with pants, boots, and greatcoats.

The role of women in the political life of the country in the generation following the Revolution may be seen in two fairly distinct stages. In the first, roughly 1917–1923, a small but visible group of women held responsible positions during and immediately after the Civil War. After 1923–1925, when there were no more prominent individual Bolshevik women even close to the seats of power, a second stage began. Women were then and for the future absent both from positions of power and prestige and largely from public prominence; but at the same time, the lowest strata of women had begun to stir and to participate in a limited but real way in the political process, such as it was. And a modest number of women were permanently lodged in the middle range of political and administrative authority. The "major" women Bolsheviks as a group were clearly less eminent than the men on any reasonable list of leading Bolsheviks. There are, however, a few who, in terms of political work, public image, or both, may be set off from other Bolshevik women: Stasova, Armand, Balabanova, Kollontai, and Krupskaya, all born between 1869 and 1878, and all possessing revolutionary credentials dating from the turn of the century or earlier (though only Krupskaya and Stasova could claim to be Old Bolsheviks).

Elena Stasova was at the very center of events in 1917, serving as the functioning Secretary of the Party during and immediately after the Revolution. Her reputation as storehouse of the Party's traditions had made her the logical candidate for the job. When the government moved to Moscow, however, Stasova remained behind; Lenin had found a more effective administrator in Yakov Sverdlov who had a talent for making policy as well. When Sverdlov died in 1919, Stasova resumed her work in the Secretariat under the tripartite management of Krestinsky, Preobrazhensky, and Serebryakov. But in 1920, when the staff was reorganized, Stasova resigned and requested a chancery position in one of the higher Party organizations. Krestinsky suggested instead that she go to work in Zhenotdel—a suggestion that Stasova immediately declined. Having worked at the center of political life, she perhaps resented being shunted off to what might have seemed mere auxiliary work. Stasova eventually found a congenial assignment as leader of the International Red Aid (MOPR)—a Comintern version of the old political Red Cross. From 1920 onward, she had no impact on the Soviet political scene. Here is a clear case of a woman who, in spite of certain administrative talents, was by her own admission always hazy on matters of theory and thus ultimately unsuited for top leadership in a Party which was still composed largely of intellectuals.[12]

Inessa Armand died of cholera in 1920. She had been second only to Kollontai in energy and range of political work. In addition to founding and directing Zhenotdel, Inessa held important posts in the highest Party, Soviet,

---

[12] Stasova, *Stranitsy*, 87–127; Levidova and Saliga, *Stasova*, 223–332.

and economic agencies of Moscow Province; and she helped shape the international communist movement by organizing foreigners of Bolshevik sympathies into the Club of the Third International. Her political prominence was clearly enhanced by her exceptionally close relationship with Lenin (and Krupskaya). The notion, however, that Inessa had been Lenin's mistress—though gaining acceptance among a number of Western students—has no relevance to the question of her political importance, and the evidence is flimsy and unconvincing.[13]

Angelica Balabanova (Balabanoff), whom we have met briefly in connection with World War I, was an almost archetypical radical Russian woman. Brought up amid the luxury of a large Ukrainian manor house, she had felt the stirrings of revolutionary consciousness early, perceiving, as she says, the "difference between those who could *give* and those who had to *receive*." "My ardent desire," she recalled, "was to escape my conventional and egoistic milieu in order to devote myself fully to a cause from which I could live and die. This was not self-abnegation, but a wish to live a life which would make me *useful* to the suffering masses." The route of her "escape" took her to Brussels and then to Italy where she became a key figure in the socialist movement, acting for a time as Mussolini's secretary. After 1917, she came back to Russia and served in a number of posts including Foreign Minister of the Ukraine and Secretary of the Comintern. But her ardent service to the Bolshevik regime did not prevent her from repudiating it when it failed to meet her expectations. "The deformation of the October Revolution," she wrote, "progressed at the same rate at which the individual replaced the masses. This substitution, which was made at the outset in good faith, was bound to degenerate in time." In 1921, she resigned her positions and left Soviet Russia forever.[14]

Kollontai was by far the most active and versatile of the Bolshevik women of this era. A member of the tiny Central Committee at the time of the overthrow, she was soon appointed Commissar of Public Welfare. During her brief tenure as Commissar, Kollontai betrayed some administrative vacillation. At first she was reluctant to use force in dealing with left-over recalcitrant civil servants of the tsarist days. Lenin chided her by asking if she thought a revolution could be made with white gloves. But when she took some rather strong public measures against the Orthodox Church, he warned her to exercise tact when dealing with religious sensibilities. But it was her marriage to the younger revolutionary sailor, Pavel Dybenko—the romantic aspects of which will be explored later—that undercut the confidence that the Party leaders had briefly shown in her. Her association with him and his reckless and erratic behavior brought no credit upon her political reputation. "I

[13] The alleged Lenin-Inessa affair is discussed, with references to the literature, in my review article: "Kollontai, Inessa, Krupskaya."

[14] Quotations: Balabanova, "Note autobiografiche," in *I buoni artieri*, 3 pts., ed. A. Schiavi (Rome, 1957), pt. I, 9, 13; and *idem*. (Balabanoff), *Impressions*, 120.

will not vouch for the reliability or the endurance" said Lenin a few years later "of women whose love affair is intertwined with politics." Not that her revolutionary career was over by any means. She served as Commissar for Propaganda in the Ukraine, toured the front with Dybenko on an agit-train, and headed Zhenotdel.[15]

Kollontai's exit from Soviet politics came in 1922, in connection with her role in the dissenting Workers' Opposition Group whose leader, Shlyapnikov, was her former lover. Kollontai herself drafted the program and distributed it to Party members in 1921. It was as much a product of her longstanding faith in the creative powers of the proletariat, first enunciated in *Social Bases*, as it was a tract for the times. Against the increasing centralism, authoritarianism, and bureaucratism which had overtaken the Party during the Civil War, she proposed "the collective, creative effort of the workers themselves." Her most suggestive theme was that collective, interpersonal relations among the producers generated great productivity, and that this productivity was diminished by the alienating presence of authoritarian officials—"the bosses and the bureaucrats." Kollontai's form of syndicalism, shared by many in the Russian labor movement, was seen by Lenin and others as a menace to unity and discipline in the Party. Lenin displayed his fury at the fateful Tenth Party Congress; when Kollontai persisted in her efforts to disseminate her ideas, she was removed from her posts and sent off to Norway on a minor diplomatic mission. She was eventually promoted to Soviet ambassador to Sweden; but her career as a Bolshevik political figure was over.[16]

As Lenin's wife, Krupskaya had been a key organizational figure of the early Bolshevik movement in emigration because of her network of correspondence with agents in Russia. But after Lenin and Krupskaya arrived in revolutionary Russia, Stasova, not she, was appointed to head up the Secretariat of the Party in the Kseshinskya Palace. Krupskaya's main work and her abiding concern both before and after Lenin's death was propaganda and education. By her own admission, high politics held little interest for her, and she was almost reprimanded by the Central Committee for failing to attend Party meetings regularly. On the other hand, she was certainly a good deal more than "first lady of the great Russian state" (Zetkin's pious phrase). Her pedagogical and journalistic activities contributed much to the training and liberation of women. After her well-known clash with Stalin during Lenin's illness, she did emerge as a potential rallying point for oppositional elements;

[15] Itkina, *Kollontai*, 85–91; Kollontai, *Vospominaniya ob Iliche* (Moscow, 1959) 3–6; "Pervie posobie iz Sotsobesa," *Moskva*, 9 (1957) 156–58.
[16] Kollontai, *Rabochaya oppozitsiya* (Moscow, 1921). For its importance in the history of the Party, see R. V. Daniels, *Conscience of the Revolution* (Cambridge, Mass., 1960) 128–63 and Avrich, *Russian Anarchists*, ch. 8. For the Party's reaction to Kollontai, see: Itkina, *Kollontai*, 106–107; Balabanoff, *Impressions*, 98; *Desyatyi S" ezd RKP (b). Mart 1921 g.* (Moscow, 1933) 115–27; and *KPSS v rezol. i dok.*, I, 650–53. See the very interesting treatment in Barbara Clements, "Kollontai's Contribution to the Workers' Opposition," *Russian History*, II, 2 (1975) 191–206.

but by 1925, this was all over, and she had come to realize that she was far from being a political match for the wily Stalin.[17]

As early as 1924, the British journalist Lancelot Lawton observed that there were no great women leaders in the Soviet Union.[18] The tradition of women as secondary figures in the revolutionary movement was stronger than the impulse to introduce complete equality of the sexes.[19] The Soviets never succeeded in matching educational and economic equality of the sexes with political equality on any level. Women's role in the Communist Party offers a revealing example of this. Before the October Revolution, only three women had ever been members of the highest bodies of the Party. Stasova became a candidate member of the Central Committee (1912). In August 1917, she was re-elected along with Yakovleva; at the same time Kollontai became the first full member of her sex, but was dropped early the following year. From 1918 until Lenin's death in 1924, no women appeared in the leading bodies—Central Committee, Orgburo, Politburo, Secretariat—except Stasova who sat on the Central Committee in 1918 and 1919. From 1924 to 1939 there were only four women members of the Central Committee: the Zhenotdel leaders Nikolaeva (three times) and Artyukhina (twice); Krupskaya (three times); and the former textile worker, Anna Kalygina (once). Typical ratios of women to men on the Central Committee were one to fifty, one to sixty-three, one to seventy, and two to seventy-one. In addition to this, Artyukhina served a few times on the Orgburo and as a candidate secretary. Before 1956, no woman ever sat on the Politburo or the Presidium, the chief policy body of the Party.[20]

At lower levels of the Party, the situation was not significantly different. By the 1930's, women held about one-sixth of the administrative posts; few rose higher. Prior to 1939, the number of women delegates at Party Congresses never reached 10 percent of the total. Through the 1930's there was even a slight decline in the number of women in responsible Party posts. The rank-and-file also remained predominantly male. After seven years of Soviet power in 1924, only 8.2 percent of the Party membership was female. By 1932 this proportion had doubled; but thereafter its rise was imperceptible. Even after the great blood-letting and the decimation of the male population in the years 1936–1945, the percentage was only seventeen, one percentage point more than in 1932. A notable feature of the women's segment of the Party in the early years was that it was more urban (c. 85 percent) than the male (c. 75 percent), though this difference diminished in later years. Ethnically, the female segment resembled the male: heavily dominated by Russians and by women from the western borderlands (Poles, Balts, Jews). In the non-Russian

[17] McNeal, *Bride of the Revolution*; Sheila Fitzpatrick, *The Commissariat of Enlightenment* (Cambridge, 1970); the later chapters of the Soviet biographies cited in Chapter VIII, 1, note 12; Balabanoff, *Impressions*, 4, 65; and Zetkin, *Vospominaniya o Lenine* (Moscow, 1966) 8.
[18] L. Lawton, *The Russian Revolution (1917–1926)* (London, 1927) 236.
[19] On this, see McNeal's "Women in the Russian Revolutionary Movement."
[20] These data are drawn from Daniels, *Conscience*, 422–33 and *passim*.

regions (particularly the Soviet East), over 60 percent of the women Communists were outsiders.[21]

Women were more, but not much more, prominent in the government than in the Party. Nobody ever challenged the notion that women would be granted complete civil, legal, and electoral equality in the new state. These were first decreed in January 1918 and incorporated a few months later in the Constitution. But there was little practical equality in the administration of the state machinery. No woman ever held the post of President (that is, Chairman of the State Presidium, a ceremonial post) or Premier (Chairman of the Council of Ministers or Peoples' Commissars), though one woman, Zemlyachka, did serve as a Deputy Chairman. Kollontai was the first woman People's Commissar, but lost her title within a few months; and no woman held a similar office until 1956. A number of women served as Commissars in the Union Republics. But in general, cabinet positions remained the preserve of men. Marital nepotism had some place in Soviet life, but the wives of well-known Soviet leaders like Lenin, Trotsky, Zinoviev, and Kamenev, busied themselves more with education, welfare, and cultural work than with politics. Foreign observers in the 1920's noticed that women were more prominent in the political police than in other state organs, though here they were more often mere agents. The army, once the Civil War was over, rid its ranks of female commanders, soldiers, and commissars. As Kollontai observed in 1922, the Soviet state was run by men, and women were to be found only in subordinate positions. And so it has remained, for the most part, until this day.[22]

The regime's efforts to include women in political work often took the form of tokenism as when Anastasiya Bitsenko, the indomitable old SR terrorist, was sent along with the delegation to Brest-Litovsk. The people's "troika"—a worker, a sailor, and a woman—made its appearance around Soviet Russia as a living symbol of newly liberated social groups. But the real pattern was reflected in such situations as the Vladivostok Soviet, led by a man and assisted by three women students;[23] or in Trotsky's dictating a sketch of the *Russian Revolution* to female stenographers; or in the innumerable episodes from early Soviet literature where women acted as the helpmates of the embattled male Bolshevik commissars and officers. No one could really expect Russian women, more backward than men in culture and political experience, to take over the reins of Soviet politics. But it is equally clear, in hindsight, that many outstanding female talents were not fully utilized by a regime "too busy" to insure female equality at every step of the way.

[21] The figures are from: Walter Batsell, *Soviet Rule in Russia* (New York, 1929) 662; André Pierre, *Les Femmes en Union soviétique* (Paris, 1960) 126–27; Merle Fainsod, *How Russia is Ruled* (Cambridge, Mass., 1953) 217–31; Stavrakis, "Women," 206, 210, 219, 238; *Svetlyi put*, 89–91.
[22] *L'égalité de la femme*, 17, 29; *Oktyabrëm*, 152; Monkhouse, *Moscow*, 274; Kollontai, *Polozhenie*, 200, 205.
[23] Rhys Williams, *Through the Russian Revolution*, 200.

The growth of the proportion of women in local and regional Soviets—to say nothing of those at higher levels—was painfully slow. By 1926 only 18 percent of the deputies to city Soviets and 9 percent of those of rural Soviets were women. It would take a long steady rise before these figures would reach a combined percentage of 40 percent in the 1950's. The obstacles were imposing. Jessica Smith relates how local women would usually choose a popular *baba*, regardless of her aptitude for politics; and the men in the Soviet would offer no encouragement, saying that women were good for only one thing. Large numbers of women stayed out of the local political process for a long time and were passive when they were elected. Yet the regime persisted in its campaign to draw women into politics. Resolutions of Soviet Congresses and the Council of Peoples' Commissars and the speeches of Lenin reiterated the theme year after year. During the 1930's Chernyshevsky's principle, newly applied to state affairs, of "bending the reed back the other way" was invoked; and a policy of rapid and deliberate promotion of women in the bureaucracy was adopted. The "promoted woman" (*vydvizhenka*)—the modern-minded, business-like female administrator sprung from some obscure corner of the working classes—took its place in the new Soviet lexicon of female types.[24]

But inequality remained not only in the state apparatus but also in other social pyramids. In trade unions, where women's membership in 1913 had run from 5 percent to 17 percent in various unions, it had risen only to 22.2 percent by 1922. And it took another forty years before this reached the more natural figure of 50 percent. In trade union leading bodies the percentages were and remain much smaller. The same situation prevailed in industry, education, and a whole range of other public institutions. The pattern established in the first fifteen years of Soviet power—a man at the top, women in subordinate roles—has persisted down to the present though always accompanied by a steady increase in the representativeness of women.[25]

When in the nineteenth century radical women had decided to tie their fate to the "common cause"—a cause initiated, defined, and dominated by radical men, they had been willing to contribute their skills and energies without demanding full and immediate equality of role and decision making within the movement. Doubtless they expected that the Revolution would deliver complete political equality with men, though few ever speculated much about the problem. Total justice was total justice. Having declined to press the point (as the feminists had tried to do in World War I via their patriotism), those who wished to achieve full equality in power were hard put to realize their program in the post-revolutionary environment. Other Bolshevik women turned their efforts to removing the social and educational obstacles that hindered Russian women from realistically asserting their pretensions to equality.

[24] Pierre, *Les Femmes*, 131–32; Stavrakis, "Women" 228–32; Jessica Smith, *Woman*, 35; *Svetlyi put*, 196ff.; V. N. Tolkunova, *Pravo zhenshchin na trud i ego garantii* (Moscow, 1967) 45; Halle, *Woman*, 285–88 (on the *vydvizhenka*).
[25] *ZhD* (Mar. 15, 1913) 21: Stavrakis, "Women" 234–37; Dodge, *Women, passim.*

2. ZHENOTDEL

Whenever a revolution has been preceded by a long established underground movement, the structure of that movement—just as much as its leadership and its ideology—super-imposes itself on the political life of the new society. This is why Bolshevik Russia became a land of committees, commissions, congresses, and cells. Before 1917, the Bolshevik Party had been a congeries of local committees directed from the center by a small group that communicated with its branches by means of a newspaper (for general ideas) and peripatetic agents (for specific instructions); feedback to the center came through correspondence and rare congresses and conferences. After 1917, the Bolsheviks used these devices (now amplified by railroad, telegraphy, and wireless) of political organization and communication for social mobilization of the country in the same way that they had used them to destroy its former regimes. The "novel" methods of social communication all had their counterparts in the history of the revolutionary underground. The techniques of Zhenotdel—the post-revolutionary organ responsible for women's liberation in Soviet Russia—were no exception. They were summarized long before Zhenotdel came into existence in a list of instructions given by Klavdiya Nikolaeva to women workers in May 1917: Organize Social Democratic groups in your factory; appoint a liaison to *Rabotnitsa*; arrange meetings.[1] It was all there—organization, filtering down of leaders, responsibility to the center (an editorial board), communication back to the rank and file through liaison and newspaper, and processing the instructions at local meetings. And it had been there, in embryo, for a generation.

But would the machinery be used? And to what end? That the "proletarian women's movement" would continue after the Revolution was a tacit assumption of its leaders and was inherent in the revolutionary movement itself. Kollontai, in 1921, spoke in retrospect of the hostility to the regime nourished by the vast majority of women and of their fears that it would uproot the family, decree the "heartless" separation of children from parents, and destroy the church. In 1918, she was already aware of the danger of disillusionment among the masses of women and of the need for long-range and patient work among them. Lenin, though he had little time to voice his opinion on the matter in the first years of Soviet power, was in full agreement with Kollontai, Inessa, and the others on the need for active liberation of Russian women—in life as well as in law. Thus the formal, legislative program of emancipation (the only one usually noted by historians) had to be given meaning in a social revolution from below. This is the true historical context of the Zhenotdel.[2]

A year of false starts and confused work, understandable under the circumstances, followed the October overturn. The first tentative step was a twelve-day Conference of Women Workers of the Petrograd Region held in mid-November 1917. Nikolaeva, veteran anti-feminist agitator of 1905–1908,

---

[1] *Rabotnitsa* (May 20, 1917) 3–4. See Chapter IX/2 above.
[2] Kollontai: *Rab. i krest.* (1921) 4–5; *Rabotnitsa za god* (1918), 18–19.

presided; Kollontai and other *intelligentki* assisted. Some of its substantive resolutions, such as the one on maternity protection, were used as working drafts for Soviet decrees on women that soon followed. But organizational formulas concerning the creation of women's groups in Party committees produced nothing. A national congress, planned for Women's Day 1918, did not take place. Other local meetings in the spring of 1918 had few results. According to Kollontai, the idea of an "All-Russian" Congress of Women was again suggested to her by an old woman textile worker in Ivanovo during an agitational visit. Lenin agreed but with the usual proviso that this would not blossom into a separate feminist movement outside the Party. A commission including Inessa Armand, Kollontai, Sverdlov, and Nikolaeva planned the Congress, sent agitators into the provinces, and—in the haphazard manner of the day—arranged for local election of delegates. The program presented to the Congress was an imposing one: to win the support of women for Soviet power; to combat domestic slavery and the double standard of morality; to establish centralized and collective living accommodations in order to release wives from household drudgery; to protect woman's labor and maternity; to end prostitution; to refashion women and thus "give communist society a new member."[3]

Though the organizers had prepared for only three hundred delegates, over a thousand appeared, a motley array of red-kerchiefed women—mostly workers—wearing sheepskins, colorful local costumes, or army greatcoats. They squeezed into the Kremlin Hall of Unions, draping themselves on the red plush upholstery and creating a great deal of noisy disorder in the early moments of the Congress. Sverdlov welcomed the delegates; Nikolaeva presided. Kollontai delivered a speech that became her most widely quoted (and misunderstood) work: *The Family and the Communist State*. Inessa's attack upon pots and pans and upon individual housekeeping, and her warm endorsement of communal services and nurseries evoked the cry, "We won't give up our children," from some women. Lenin's appearance created a sensation. Smiling, he held up his watch when the storm of applause showed no signs of abating. His speech was a little more than a brief and general endorsement of emancipation and an appeal to women to support the regime. Yet no head of state had ever said anything like it in the history of the woman question. Most delegates displayed little ideological awareness and focused mostly on specific grievances; but they sang the "Internationale" with gusto and shouted roaring approval when someone proposed outlawing the word *baba*. (*Baba*, depending on the context, can mean "grandmother," "peasant woman," or simply "old woman." A slang term used demeaningly and / or humorously by males for adult females in general.) It was the first taste of

[3] For the rather skimpy history of this first year, from various vantage points, see: Kollontai, *Rabotnitsa za god*, 22–28 (with program summary); *idem., Tri goda diktatury proletariata* (Moscow, 1921) 15–16; *idem., Rab. i krest.*, 3–4; *Svetlyi put*, 67–68; Igumnova, *Zhenshchiny*, 21–22; Itkina, *Kollontai*, 84–96; Levidova, *Krupskaya*, 147; Podlyashuk, *Inessa*, 217–19; and A. E. Arbuzova. "Vmeste s partiei," *Zhen. goroda*, 113–21.

politics for most of them; and the first journey outside the world of the village for many. For the organizers, it was a heady exercise in agitation as well as a clear demonstration that their work had only begun. It had been ten years since the last general women's congress in Russia. The lorgnetted and furred ladies of 1908 had been replaced by the stern workers and commissars of 1918 (Kollontai, in deference to the occasion, wore a modest black). But the major contrast lay in the fact that the 1908 Congress had marked the pinnacle of the feminist movement—a movement that was brave and sincere, but weak and vastly out-weighed by a government basically hostile even to its limited goals. The 1918 Congress was a beginning, an open manifestation of the fact that some Bolshevik leaders actively supported the cause of liberation, as they understood it. Before the Congress adjourned, it resolved to set up permanent machinery to carry out its goals.[4]

This machinery at first took the form of "commissions for agitation and propaganda among working women." The term "commission" indicated an *ad hoc* body attached to regular Party organs; the word *rabotnitsa* became the stylized designation of all employed females of whatever station. The Central Commission, headed by Inessa, Kollontai, and Moirova, created local branches at the lower Party levels. Emelyanova's research in provincial Party archives indicates that the establishment of women's commissions, a slow and tedious process, was often hindered by local resistance to the whole idea. But it was approved by the Eighth Party Congress in 1919. Later that year, the Commission was given a higher status by reorganizing it into the "Women's Section or Department" (*zhenskii otdel*; or *zhenotdel*) of the Central Committee Secretariat. Inessa Armand was named its first director (*zaveduyushchaya*) and held the post until her death in 1920. Using techniques developed during the revolution, Armand and her staff in Moscow made appointments and established a network of local zhenotdels. Party members and unpaid volunteers, known as "womorganizers" (*zhenorganizatory*), staffed the local bodies. The entire hierarchy of women's sections was known collectively as the Zhenotdel.[5]

During the Civil War, Inessa used the Zhenotdel to mobilize women in

---

[4] Details of the Congress are from: E. D. Emelyanova, *Revolyutsiya, partiya, zhenshchina: opyt raboty sredi trudyashchikhsya zhenshchin (oktyabr 1917-1925 gg.)* (Smolensk, 1971) 74–87. *Svetlyi put*, 79–81; Halle, *Woman*, 94–95; Stavrakis, "Women and the Communist Party," 97; Kollontai's brief memoir in *O Vladimire Iliche Lenine: vospominaniya, 1900–1922 gody* (Moscow, 1963) 221–23; Podlyashuk, *Inessa*, 220–23 (quotation); *Zhen. v rev.*, 187–200.

[5] On the history of Zhenotdel, there is, in English, the Stavrakis dissertation; but it suffers from repetition and insufficient analysis. More concise and valuable is Carol Eubank, "The Bolshevik Party and Work Among Women, 1917–1925;" a paper read at the Stanford Conference on Women in Russia, June 1975, to appear in the journal, *Russian History*. A brief chronological outline is "Zhenotdely," in *BSE*, 2d ed., XVI, 62. Biographies and contemporary writings of Communist women leaders (especially Kollontai and Inessa), recollections of or about lower level figures written much later, the press, published Zhenotdel internal documents, archival sources, and the few secondary works have been used.

On the origin of Zhenotdel: Kollontai, *Tri goda*, 16; *KPSS v resolyutsiakh i resheniyakh*, chast I, *1898–1924* (Moscow, 1954) 453; *Zhen. russ. rev.*, 40–42; *Zhen. v rev.*, 150–51; *Svetlyi put*, 81–82; "Zhenotdely," 62; Podlyashuk, *Inessa*, 225–27; *Bez nikh my ne pobedili by* (Moscow, 1975); Armand, *Stati*, 33–176.

support of the Red Army and the new regime. Propaganda teams, like the ones headed by Krupskaya and Kollontai, threaded their way on agit-trains and boats through the Red areas, stopping at remote villages to regale the population with poster art, song-and-dance groups, and speeches. The popular "Natasha" (K. I. Samoilova), known affectionately among Russian women as "our own mother," sailed up and down the Volga with a plea for support and a promise of liberation which she proclaimed from the decks of the *Red Star*. She died of cholera during one of her cruises. At the local level, "volunteer Saturdays" (*subbotniki*) and "days of wounded Red Army Men" were launched to recruit previously inactive women in jobs like sewing underwear, bathing soldiers, and bandaging wounds. Recruiting work grew very slowly; and the Party sometimes tended to use Zhenotdel workers exclusively in such endeavors as food distribution, child and orphan care, and the struggle against illiteracy and superstition—areas of activity that, in the context, were really the Soviet equivalents of *Küche, Kinder*, and *Kirche*. Inessa Armand drove herself to exhaustion working fourteen to sixteen hours a day. By a stroke of fate, she was ordered by the Party to the Caucasus for a rest. There, in the fall of 1920, she took cholera and died.[6]

Kollontai was chosen to succeed her. If she had been bypassed in 1918, it was probably only because of the Party's, especially Lenin's, greater confidence in Armand's reliability and obedience. Kollontai and Inessa had helped forge the women's movement, separately before the Revolution and together after it; and they shared the same philosophy of women's liberation.[7] Kollontai held no brief for a "feminist" movement separate from or outside the Party; she even hoped to dissolve some of the purely "female" features of Zhenotdel work (such as the "women's pages" in Party newspapers). But she was equally firm in resisting any suggestions of liquidating the Zhenotdel itself. Passivity and lack of consciousness were the hallmarks of Russian women. She told Emma Goldman (who refused her invitation to work in Zhenotdel) that women "were ignorant of the simplest principles of life, physical and otherwise, ignorant of their own functions as mothers and citizens." It was imperative, then, to raise the consciousness of these women and to deal with specifically woman-related problems, such as maternity care, in their own special way. This, she said, was not feminism.[8]

Kollontai was right. It was not feminism, at least as the word was then understood. The feminist movement in Western Europe and America, from 1848 to 1920, had ultimately settled on the vote as the capstone of emancipation.

[6] For the Zhenotdel in the Civil War, see: Kollontai, *Rab. i krest*, 6–7, 31–32; *idem., Polozhenie*, 183ff.; *Tri goda*, 19–22, *KPSS v resol. i resh*., 1, 503; *Svetlyi put*, 68–78; Igumnova, *Zhenshchina*, 31–49. For Inessa's last years: Fréville, *Inessa*, 121–79; Podlyashuk, 187–230; Balabanova, *Impressions*, 14. For Samoilova: Morozova, *Rasskazy*, 514–24.

[7] The apparent identity of their basic outlook is all the more impressive in view of the fact that they did not get along very well together and disagreed openly on a number of matters. This discord is described, all too sparingly, by Polina Vinogradskaya in her *Pamyatnye vstrechi* (Moscow, 1972) 196–98.

[8] Kollontai, *Rab. i krest*., 3, 23–27. Her words to Goldman in the latter's *Living My Life*, II, 756–57.

After acquiring it, no feminist movement in the West, until recent years, made many further steps toward realizing economic or sexual liberation; even less did it engage in any mass movement for the liberation of women of the working class or minorities. Bolshevik "feminism" reversed the social timetable of Western feminism. For the latter, political emancipation was the goal; for the former, it was only the beginning.

During her manifold assignments of the Civil War period, Kollontai had always (except during a serious illness) kept in touch with Zhenotdel activities. After her appointment, she led Zhenotdel with the abundant optimism, energy, and talent which she had displayed in other realms of revolutionary work. Her two year tenure as its leader (1920–1922) also happened to be a period of deep emotional and political tribulation for her. Kollontai's most important practical accomplishment was to turn Zhenotdel's energy away from wartime auxiliary work (the War ended in 1920) toward the subtler tasks of psychological and social demobilization. More spectacular and in the long run just as important was initiating the liberation of the so-called women of the East—the Muslim, Christian, Jewish, and Buddhist women of the non-western borderlands of Caucasia, the Volga, and Central Asia who were subjected to codes of sexual behavior unknown in the rest of Russia. The most severe of these was the Muslim *şeriat* that in practice gave women no status and no purpose other than as pleasure-giver, servant, housekeeper, and childbearer. Their isolation and untouchability was symbolized by "the veil" in all its varieties, the most severe of which was the *paranja*, a heavy horsehair garment that hung from the nose to the floor. Aside from serious organizational work among these women, Kollontai also brought some of them to Moscow for congresses where the exotic guests would tear off their face coverings before a startled audience. Criticized by some for excessive theatricality, Kollontai told Louise Bryant that "all pioneering work is theatrical."[9] It was not the last time that an article of women's clothing would be seen as an enslaving, sexist fetish; and the doffing of the veil became the favorite gesture of baptism into free womanhood in the Soviet East.

Kollontai's key role in the Workers' Opposition Movement (see above) brought about the end of her political duties in Russia and her fall from grace. She was sent abroad and, from a minor diplomatic post in Norway, she managed—on sheer merit and loyalty—to work her way up to an appointment as the first woman ambassador (to Sweden) in modern history. She also resumed her writing on liberation, writings that were to play a fateful role in the moral revolution of the 1920's. But her removal from Zhenotdel was a blow to the women's movement in Russia and to the still shaky Zhenotdel. Party authorities may have wished to replace her with someone of near comparable stature. Balabanova states that she was asked to take over Kollontai's posts, but that she had refused on the grounds of possessing neither the interest nor

---

[9] Louise Bryant, *Mirrors of Moscow* (New York, 1923) 121–22. The *paranja* and other traditional garments worn by Muslim women of the Russian Empire are on display at the Leningrad Ethnographic Museum.

the talents that Kollontai had shown. Stasova had expressed similar sentiments earlier when advised to go into "women's" political work.[10] The fact
that Krupskaya, the only other major female, did not offer herself meant that
the post had to fall to lesser figures. It was an early sign of the incipient decline of the Zhenotdel as a political force. The successors of Armand and Kollontai, though competent revolutionaries, were distinctly less prominent.

The first of these was Sofya Nikolaevna Smidovich, a Tula woman of the
same age as her predecessor, and like her also a Social Democrat since 1898.
But Smidovich had had only a high school education and her interests were
narrower than those of Armand or Kollontai. She and her husband were a
fairly well-known Bolshevik couple in the years 1905–1917. After 1917,
Smidovich worked with Inessa Armand on the Moscow committees and on
the Zhenotdel, agitating among the often hostile women factory workers.
From 1919 to 1922, she headed the Moscow Regional Zhenotdel. A prim
figure with auburn hair pulled into a bun, long dress, and dark blouse,
Smidovich despaired of the cynicism that people displayed toward the abandoned and delinquent "homeless children" (*bezprizornye*). She once overheard a Moscow citizen urge bystanders to douse with kerosene and ignite a
pair of snarling young hoodlums. Smidovich, a wife and mother of three and
aged fifty, appeared to be much more concerned with the care of single
mothers and abandoned children than she was with the theoretical sexual
rights publicized by the new regime. After her sojourn as head of Zhenotdel
(1922–1924), she became an outspoken opponent of the loose sexual tendencies of the time.[11]

Klavdiya Nikolaeva, long a central figure in the Bolshevik women's
movement, succeeded her. The first worker to head Zhenotdel (from 1924 to
1927), she was a veteran of the feminist Congress of 1908, an editor of the
1914 *Rabotnitsa* and of its 1917 reincarnation. Like her mentor and friend,
Kollontai, Nikolaeva was in opposition for a while (after the Fourteenth Congress of 1925) but soon returned to the fold and, again like Kollontai, survived the purges and held high Party posts until her death. Her successor in
Zhentodel in 1927 was Aleksandra Vasilevna Artyukhina who was of the
same generation (b. 1889) and class background (a Petersburg textile worker).
Artyukhina, much decorated and honored in her later years for economic and
trade union work, was the last head of Zhenotdel when, in 1930, it was rather
suddenly dissolved.[12]

How did Zhenotdel work? Its central headquarters—called *Tsentro-Baba*
by certain witty comrades—were located in a flat in Moscow at Vozdvizhenka

[10] Balabanova, *Minnen och upplevelsen*, tr. Leif Bjorke (Stockholm, 1927), 207; Stasova,
Stranitsy, 110.

[11] A. Arenshtein, *Rannim moskovskim utrom* (Moscow, 1967) and *Zhen. russ. rev.* 425–33,
568.

[12] Nikolaeva: *Leningradki*, 139–49; *Zhen. russ. rev.*, 290–303, 566. Artyukhina: *Oktyabrëm*,
12–33; *Zhen. Goroda*, 394.

No. 5 near the Kremlin. The staff included, at least according to the table of organization, twenty-two paid workers: the director, a deputy director, assistants, and secretaries. The director, who was answerable to the Party Secretariat, supervised not only all the internal affairs of the Zhenotdel proper, but extended her influence into every corner of life where women, qua women, were involved. For example, she maintained close and continuous contact with such related bodies as the Maternity and Infancy Section of the Ministry of Health, the Commission for the Struggle Against Prostitution, the Komsomol, the Party central, and a large assortment of bureaucracies dealing with food, insurance, education, welfare, Soviet, trade union, and even literary matters. Bolshevik women leaders with their own particular responsibilities and interests—V. P. Lebedeva (maternity), Krupskaya (education), and Mariya Ulyanova (journalism)—inter-locked their activities with those of the Zhenotdel. Thus the full machinery of the Bolshevik women's movement extended out beyond the organizational frontiers of the national network of Zhenotdels.[13]

Lower echelon leaders of Zhenotdel came from revolutionary backgrounds similar to those of the directors. Lyudmila Menzhinskaya, deputy director under Kollontai and Smidovich, was a party journalist and co-worker on the original *Rabotnitsa*. Her successor, V. A. Moirova, was the daughter of an Odessa laundress. She attended the Moscow Higher Women's Courses and joined the Party in 1917; another protégé of Kollontai, she was appointed head of the Ukrainian Zhenotdel and later moved up to deputy at the center. A typically vigorous Zhenotdel leader at the provincial level was Olga Varentsova, a veteran revolutionary of the Ivanovo region who had helped to make that heavily female area a Bolshevik stronghold long before the Revolution. With her straight hair, gray knitted blouse, and worn-out shoes, Varentsova was the very model of the "Zhenotdel functionary" (*zhenotdelovka*). Another provincial head was Anna Pankratova of Odessa (1897–1957), later a well-known historian. *Zhenotdelovki* at the grass-roots level were usually communist working-class women or professional revolutionaries and veterans of the Civil War. As a group, cadres appear to have been unusually young.[14]

From the Moscow center radiated the impulses of propaganda, agitation, and mobilization that were transmitted by local branches out among the female masses. In pre-revolutionary times, propaganda had denoted the conveyance of a large number of ideas to the few; agitation, the presentation of one main idea to the many. In Zhenotdel, the printed word was the vehicle of propaganda because it imparted theory, news, and instructions to a relatively small number of literate women. Marxist classics on the woman question, distilled into little brochures, were widely circulated. *Rabotnitsa* remained the

[13] Itkina, *Kollontai*, 103–104; *Doklad otdela po rabote sredi zhenshchin TsKRKP* (Moscow, 1922).
[14] *Zhen. russ. rev.*, 564–67; *Leningradki*, 59, 409; *Oktyabrëm*, 141–42; *Pravda stavshaya*, 157–58; Bolshevikov, *Varontsova* (Moscow, 1964) 48–61.

WOMEN'S LIBERATION

central organ; Krupskaya's *Kommunistka*, its theoretical journal. Interior bulletins and local women's magazines like *Peasant Woman, Delegate, Red Siberian Woman*, raised the total circulation of the eighteen women's publications to 670,000 in 1930. When the leaders found out that women still read fashion magazines, they added fashion pages to their own publications. Regular Party organs added "pages for women" modeled on Ulyanova's "women's page" in *Pravda*. Female "factory and village correspondents" (*rabkors* and *selkors*) were encouraged by Ulyanova and Krupskaya to add their voices, and complaints, to the general discussion.[15]

But printed propaganda did not suffice in a land of largely illiterate females. "Going out among the people" face-to-face was the answer. Techniques varied according to geography and circumstance. Wherever the railway track went, the agit-train followed; in the vast Kama and Volga basins, the agit-boat served better. In Central Asia "the peripatetic tent" was the mobile headquarters of Zhenotdel activists seeking out isolated communities of oppressed women. In a Petrograd speech of 1920, Zinoviev, Party chief of the region, suggested that, since most women workers could not read, and did not come to meetings on their own, the Party would have to go to them by sending propaganda units to the bath-houses where women always congregated to gossip. In the towns, leather-coated and booted Komsomol women would gather at local Zhenotdel headquarters, usually no more than a room, to receive instructions and then go off to the factories and neighborhoods to organize women, hold meetings, or set up reading rooms. The process was paralleled, with much greater difficulty, in the villages. At the end of the agitational trail stood the peasant or working woman, the object of this large-scale exercise in social communication. The tobacco worker, former Socialist Revolutionary, Civil War veteran, and head of a local Zhenotdel, Vera Alekseevna—a worthy successor to Chernyshevsky's Vera Pavlovna—invited women to a sewing circle where she lectured to them on politics, cooperation, and hygiene.[16]

But even talking to women face-to-face was not enough—as Chernyshevs-

[15] For various descriptions of Zhenotdel communications techniques, see: Kollontai, *Rab. i krest.*, 15–16; W. Chamberlin, *Soviet Russia* (Chautauqua, N.Y., 1931) 374; Jessica Smith, *Women in Soviet Russia* (New York, 1928) 59; D. A. Ershov, *Mariya Ilinichna Ulyanova* (Saratov, 1965) 83–84; *M. I. Ulyanova, sekretar 'Pravdy'* (Moscow, 1965) 68–69, 235. Recommended readings for Zhenotdel workers included shorter works by Bebel, Zetkin, Kollontai, and Lilina Zinoveva (*Kommunistka*, 8–9, Jan.-Feb. 1921, 59). Precise and illuminating data on Zhenotdel techniques and materials may be found by examining the following representative handbooks: *Sbornik instruktsii otdela TsKRKP po rabote sredi zhenshchin* (Moscow, 1920); *Sputnik organizatora krestyanok*, 2d ed. (Moscow, 1927); *Programmy dlya kursov perepodgotovki rabotnikov sredi zhenshchin, 1928 g.* (Moscow, 1928); and *K perevyboram delegatskikh sobranii, 1929-30 goda* (Moscow, 1929).

[16] Chamberlin, *Soviet Russia*, 374; G. Zinovev, *Novye zadachi nashei partii ot voiny k khozyaistvy* (Moscow, 1920) 19–20; Arenshtein, *Rannim*, 176–77; Smith, *Woman*, 57. A scale model of an agit-train of the Civil War period may be seen at the State Museum of the History of Leningrad.

ky's heroine had also realized.[17] The key to winning the Russian woman was to draw her directly into the work of liberation; to make her a subject rather than an object. The first technique tried was "women's sections" made up of volunteers for active Party work. It failed because it attracted only those women already interested in public activity and had no effect on the masses. Later Inessa Armand and her colleagues adopted the technique of "delegate meetings" designed as a continuous school in politics and liberation. Organizers would hold elections among the women of, say, a factory; workers would choose one of their number as delegate to the Zhenotdel for a period of three to six months. The election itself was a step toward consciousness. "When the gray, backward, non-Party woman elects her representative, she feels she has accomplished an act of politics," wrote Kollontai.[18] The delegate, with a red headscarf as her badge of office, would then serve as observer-apprentice in various branches of public activity: factory, Soviet, trade union, public service bodies (especially schools, hospitals, and catering centers). After her sojourn in the world of practical politics, she would then report back to the Zhenotdel and to her own constituency about what she had seen. She had thus, in one season, acted as an elected politician, an administrator, a propagandist, and a critic. Her electors, caught in the game of politics, now took their turns as the next delegates.

Organizing delegate points was hard work, especially in the countryside. A Ryazan Province woman tried to make a public announcement at the village meeting with no results; she had to go door to door reading excerpts from leaflets to arouse the curiosity of the village women. Shyness was a common retarding factor. "I can't manage it," claimed Mariya Suvorova, a shoe-factory employee elected as delegate; "I'm badly educated." Her comrades persuaded her and she spent the next months visiting the court, the cooperative, the health section (of the Soviet), and the schools, discovering and reporting on a number of deficiencies. Such delegate reports were supposed to control and improve the quality of administration as well as to train women in public responsibilities.[19]

Understandably, friction sometimes arose between over-worked and harassed administrators (mostly men) and the unseasoned delegates. And often the delegate was shunted off to trivial routines to get her out of the way of day-to-day business. But as a rule, she saw much and reported honestly. And there can be little doubt that the delegate meeting system played an important role in raising the consciousness of many a "backward" woman, by exposing her directly to the realities of administrative life—hitherto an arcane world

[17] Chernyshevsky, *Chto delat?*, 196. See Armand, *Stati*, 114–23.

[18] Kollontai, *Rab. i krest.*, 29–30.

[19] The Ryazan organizer: Levidova, *Krupskaya*, 256; Suvorova: *Svetlyi put*, 86–88. For more on delegate operations, see [Inessa Armand], *Otchët o pervoi mezhdunarodnoi konferentsii kommunistok* (1920), Moscow, 1921, 83–85; *Zhen. v rev.*, 279–82 and 330–34; *Zhen. goroda*, 166–76.

beyond her ken. She became, in the words of a Zhenotdel leader, "a menace to bureaucrats, drunkards, kulaks, sub-kulaks, and all who opposed Soviet laws." Zhendelegatka took its place beside *komsomolka* in the lexicon of Soviet female types of the 1920's. Sometimes the delegate would become so immersed in public work that she would neglect home and family concerns, and episodes of domestic discord between delegate (or Zhenotdel activist) and bewildered husband festooned the pages of early Soviet novels and stories.[20]

The completion of a delegate's education and the closing of the circle of social mobilization was the periodic conference or congress where women of different regions could—as the old feminists had done—see new faces and share experiences. "A woman who has gone to Moscow from some remote village," Kollontai told Louise Bryant, "is more or less something of a personage when she returns and you can be sure that the journey is an event in the whole village." The number and variety of such conferences were enormous. In the Civil War, non-Party conferences were used by Bolshevik women to win uncommitted women away from rivals like the Socialist Revolutionaries and Mensheviks. Yuliya Grinfeld, an Odessa Menshevik, recalled such a conference held there in 1920 where claques of Bolshevik women were planted around the hall to shout down the Menshevik speakers. When Grinfeld took the floor, the Bolshevik chairman, persisted in pulling at her skirt and finally tore it. Thus women's congresses in Soviet Russia never became forums of free debate in the Western sense at all, but rather demonstrations of solidarity and celebrations of communist consciousness. The last important one of the period was the 1927 Congress of Women Deputies to the Soviets, a massive witness to the work that had been done in the past ten years. Though it did not fail to point out lingering shortcomings and male prejudice, it possessed, in the words of William Henry Chamberlin, an eyewitness, "a sense of power and achievement" and "a note of almost touching faith in the new Soviet gospel."[21]

A fair example of Zhenotdel operations at a lower level were those of the Ukraine, headed from 1926 to 1930 by Olga Pilatskaya, an old Bolshevik since 1904 and one of the organizers of the 1917 seizure of power in Moscow. She had become hostile toward "bourgeois" feminism during a pre-revolutionary visit to England. She was sharp and direct, avoided clichés, and encouraged the shy to assume responsibilities. To her staff she was loyal in defending them against slander; to her superiors, the male Party heads in Kharkov and Moscow, she was totally submissive in lashing out at opposition elements. Her two assistants maintained a card file of cadres that was used for assignments, transfers, and promotions (and, doubtless, purges of opposi-

---

[20] Chamberlin, *Soviet Russia*, 373; N. Astakhova and E. Tselliarius, *Tovarishch Olga* (Moscow, 1969) 130 (quotation). The delegatka is celebrated in Mayakovsky's well-known poem "Vladimir Ilych Lenin." For fictional treatment of family discord, see the following chapter.

[21] Bryant, *Mirrors*, 121; Yu. Grinfeld, *Iz vospominanii o borbe za svobodu i narodovlastie v Odesse, 1918-1920 gg.* (New York, 1962) 42–44; Chamberlin, *Soviet Russia*, 378.

tionists when the occasion arose), and also prepared curricula for the Zhenotdel educational program. The two-room headquarters served as a rallying center for rustic visitors lost in the bustle of Kharkov. From it issued the papers, *Selyanka* (*The Peasant Woman*) and *Komunarka*, and teams of organizers who made their way to the local centers and villages.[22]

Provincial Zhenotdels were assigned only eight full-time people in the organizational setup. Since five of them sat in the center, this meant only one instructor or *zhenorg* for every three districts of a province. Furthermore, Stavrakis' study indicates that Zhenotdel, like most analogous Party organizations, suffered from personnel deficiency, shortage of funds, jurisdictional overlap, and superficiality at the grass roots level. The areas of greatest resistance to its efforts were the villages and the non-Slavic borderlands. The Ukrainian organizer, Kiselëva, walked miles from *raikom* headquarters to the little village of Sripal to gather the women into a reading cabin in order to organize them. The menfolk surrounded the cabin and shouted, "We'll beat you up if you touch our wives." In Chigirin district, three Zhenotdel workers were killed in one year by "bandits." At the beginning of collectivization, women organizers in the Ukraine had to dispel the rumors which said that in the new kolkhozes the young women would be "shared" by the men and the old ones boiled down for soap. Everywhere, men (invariably called "kulaks" in the literature) fought efforts of the Zhenotdel to organize and politicize their wives.[23]

Of vastly greater difficulty was Zhenotdel work among "eastern" women. Kollontai's congresses were only the beginning. These women could barely hint, and only after patient prying, at the kind of life they had had under the traditional order. "We were silent slaves," said one. "We had to hide in our rooms and cringe before our husbands, who were our lords." Another recalled: "Our fathers sold us at the age of ten, even younger. Our husband would beat us with a stick and whip us when he felt like it. If he wanted to freeze us, we froze. Our daughters, a joy to us and a help around the house, he sold just as we had been sold." These words were spoken to Clara Zetkin who inspected the Zhenotdel operations in the Caucasus during her recuperation there in the early 1920's. Lacking in native Bolshevik cadres, Zhenotdel sent out Russian revolutionaries and educators to take up the work. Typical of these was Nadezhda Kolesnikova, veteran propagandist and wife of one of the fabled Twenty-Six Commissars. Another was Olga Chulkova, a librarian-teacher and Bestuzhev graduate, who worked from her Zhenotdel base in Sukhumi to organize the women of Abkhaziya. Teams were sent out into the

[22] Astakhova, *Tov. Olga*, 115–17.

[23] *Byulleten No. 15 otdela TsKRKP po rabote sredi zhenshchin* (Moscow, 1922) 12–13; Stavrakis, "Women," *passim*; Astakhova, *Tov. Olga*, 122, 140 (for the quoted anecdotes); *Zhen. v rev.*, 263 (Chigirin incident). For more on local Zhenotdel operations: *Byulleten 5/6* (Moscow, 1922); *Zhen. v rev.*, 272–76, 283–87, and 296–301; the Zhenotdel documents in the Smolensk Archive, dating from 1922 to 1934, indexed on page 17 of the archive guide; Armand, *Stati*, 94–98, 123–39.

mountain villages and women who had never left their native settlements before were brought down to Sukhumi. Some were shuttled off to Moscow to study; the rest went back to the mountains to organize day nurseries.[24]

As Bette Stavrakis has observed, the lack of native Bolsheviks, the difficulties of language, the size of the territory, the prevalence of illiteracy, the varieties of religion, the tenuous communist control of some areas, and, most important, the ferocious hostility of the males, led the Zhenotdel leaders to adopt methods in accordance with the local situation. These included secret visits, rendezvous in bath-houses, and small groups or *artels* in the initial stages, and the "women's clubs"—social covers for political consciousness raising. In Batumi, the woman's club used male speakers at first until the first shrouded woman stood up and tore off her veil; in Baku it had thousands of members and became the school, church, and social center for women, replacing the gossipy bazaar. Zhenotdel workers appeared in places where a city person had never been seen before; in Central Asia they wandered over the steppe in makeshift transport, stopping at camp, *aul*, and oasis to lecture with the magic lantern (as the Sunday School teachers of Petersburg had done in the 1890's) or to show a motion picture featuring a Muslim heroine who refused to marry the old man who had bought her.[25]

Men reacted to all this with savage violence. Women coming out of the club at Baku were assaulted by men with wild dogs and boiling water. A twenty-year-old Muslim girl who flaunted her liberation by appearing in a swimsuit was sliced to pieces by her father and brothers because they could not endure the social indignity. An eighteen-year-old Uzbek woman activist was mutilated and thrown into a well. Central Asia witnessed three hundred such murders during one quarter of 1929 alone. The Presidium of the Soviet Central Executive Committee, after consulting with the Zhenotdel, decided to classify such crimes as "counter-revolutionary offences." Yet, in spite of the danger, hundreds of native women volunteered as translators and assistants and eventually worked their way into administrative Zhenotdel positions. And each May Day or International Women's Day, thousands of women would assemble in the market places of "eastern" Soviet lands and defiantly tear off their chadras, paranjas, and veils. If it had accomplished nothing else, Zhenotdel would deserve a place in social history for having brought this about.[26]

[24] The quotations are from Ilberg, *Tsetkin*, 184–85. Kolesnikova: *Zhen. russ. rev.*, 181–96; and R. G. Suny, *The Baku Commune, 1917–1918* (Princeton, 1972) 210, 231, 252–56. Chulkova: *Bestuzhevki*, 14–18.

[25] Stavrakis, "Women," 172–87; Ilberg, *Tsetkin*, 182–86; *Pravda stavshaya*, 125–31; Chamberlin, *Soviet Russia*, 378–80.

[26] R. Schlesinger, *The Family in the USSR* (London, 1949) 196–98; W. Reich, *The Sexual Revolution*, 4th ed. (New York, 1969) 213–14; E. J. Dillon, *Russia Today and Yesterday* (London, 1929) 220–23. For additional information, see: F. Halle, *Women of the Soviet East* (New York, 1933); a recent valuable collection of documents—*Velikii Oktyabr i raskreposhchenie zhenshchin Srednei Azii i Kazakhstana (1917–1936 gg.): sbornik dokumentov i materialov*, ed. Z. A. Astapovich *et al.* (Moscow, 1971); and the extremely interesting and provocative interpre-

The variety of enterprises engaged in by the Zhenotdel was enormous: child and orphan care, school service and inspection, food distribution, housing supervision, preventive medicine and public health, anti-prostitution campaigns, war work, education, legislation, placement, family service, and mass propaganda for every campaign that the Party decided to undertake. Some of this resembled the kind of activity which traditional feminists had busied themselves with. But, as an arm of the Party, Zhenotdel had better resources to help it unlock the energies of the most backward and remote communities of Russia's women. In doing this, Zhenotdel served not only the cause of women's liberation but also the regime as a whole by helping to create new reserves of skilled and politically conscious labor. Why then was the Zhenotdel apparatus dissolved in 1930?

One could easily assemble an impressive chain of quotations from Lenin showing that he gave his unqualified support to the Zhenotdel, whose meetings he addressed on a number of occasions. His strongest statement on the subject, made to Zetkin in 1920, will suffice:

We derive our organizational ideas from our ideological conceptions. We want no separate organizations of communist women! She who is a Communist belongs as a member to the Party, just as he who is a Communist. They have the same rights and duties. There can be no difference of opinion on that score. However, we must not shut our eyes to the facts. The Party must have organs—working groups, commissions, committees, sections or whatever else they may be called—with the specific purpose of rousing the broad masses of women, bringing them into contact with the Party and keeping them under its influence. This naturally requires that we carry on systematic work among the women. We must teach the awakened women, win them over for the proletarian class struggle under the leadership of the Communist Party, and equip them for it. . . . It would be silly to ignore them, absolutely silly. We must have our own groups to work among them, special methods of agitation, and special forms of organization. This is not bourgeois "feminism"; it is a practical revolutionary expediency.[27]

Lenin's views, clearly revealing an instrumentalist outlook toward women, were a direct outgrowth of the Russian revolutionary tradition, and were shared by the Zhenotdel founders and leaders.

But the "anti-feminist" current, which had appeared among Social Democrats as far back as 1905, persisted among certain Soviet leaders after the Revolution as well. Zinoviev and Rykov, for instance, opposed the summoning of the 1918 Women's Congress. The trade union opposition was more serious: under the banner of anti-feminism, the leaders called for the abolition of Zhenotdel. This was partly anger over jurisdictional overlap—a common

tation of Zhenotdel and Party policy vis-à-vis Eastern women by Gregory Massell: *The Surrogate Proletariat* (Princeton, 1974).

[27] V. l. Lenin, *On the Emancipation of Women* (Moscow, n.d.) 106.

cause of inter-organizational friction in those years; but at a more menacing level, it reflected rank-and-file workers' hostility to female competition in the labor market. Antagonism in the Party to Zhenotdel and its work sometimes took contrasting forms. Some male Bolsheviks opposed, for example, the celebration of International Women's Day, calling it a trivial waste of effort and forgetting, as a Bolshevik woman pointed out, that this was to be a holiday of general consciousness raising for men and for women. Others, according to the observations of David Ryazanov in the mid-1920's, "preferred complete division of labor between men and women" with Zhenotdel dealing with the woman question and the "Muzhotdel" (meaning the rest of the Party) dealing with "male" problems (meaning the important ones). Resistance to special work among women by communists at the local level has been amply documented by Carol Eubank and others.[28]

The Party generally upheld—if sometimes in rather tortured phrases—the special machinery it had created for political work among women. But, beginning with the Eleventh Congress (1922), its affirmations of the need for Zhenotdel were accompanied by complaints about its shortcomings. The Twelfth Congress in 1923 adopted a resolution which lamented the fact that certain conditions encouraged the growth of "feminist tendencies." "These tendencies," it warned, "permit the formation of special societies which, under the banner of improving the women's way of life, actually could lead to the female contingent of labor breaking away from the common class struggle." But the way to fight this, it concluded in rather irresolute tones, was to keep Zhenotdel and to forge stronger links between the women and trade unions, co-ops, and Soviets. A circular letter of 1927 from the Central Committee to local Party organizations noted their failure to make sufficient use of the Delegate Meeting to mobilize women around pressing tasks of the Party. What these watery resolutions, double-edged statements, and perennial complaints reflected was an obvious tension among the leadership over the question of retaining a useful piece of political machinery or dismantling it. How the leadership divided over the issue has never become public record.[29]

An interesting, though not particularly illuminating, prelude to the 1930 liquidation of Zhenotdel, was the abolition, in 1926, of the International Women's Secretariat. This was an outgrowth of a series of congresses of international communist women, sponsored by Zhenotdel and affiliated with the Comintern Congresses which usually preceded them. Inessa Armand dominated the first, held in 1920 in Moscow, and caused some distress among the

[28] The opposition of Rykov and Zinovev to the congress is recorded in a memoir written much later by Kollontai and printed in *O Vladimire Iliche*, 221–23. A year earlier, Zinovev and Kamenev and Rykov had been censured by the Petrograd conference of women for their failure to endorse Lenin's political decisions (*Svetlyi put*, 68). Some of the hostility to Zhenotdel on the part of Party leaders must surely have arisen from such personal grounds. Itkina, *Kollontai*, 102; *Kommunistka*, 8–9 (Jan.-Feb., 1921) 1–3; Samoilova, *V obedinenii*, 5; D. Ryazanov, "Marks i Engels o brake i seme," *Letopis marksizma*, III (1927) 26; Eubank, "Bolshevik Party," 3, 4, 10.

[29] The quoted resolution is in *KPSS v resol. i reshen*. I, 754–55; see also the resolution of the previous congress in *ibid.*, 648. The circular letter is described in *Svetlyi put*, 86. See also Stavrakis, "Women," *passim*.

German delegates by flatly condemning the Second International (and thus by implication, its dominant force, the German Social Democratic Party). The German comrades managed to get an amendment accepted exempting Clara Zetkin and her work among women from this sweeping indictment. When Inessa died, Zetkin, an ardent supporter of Soviet power and a regular visitor to Russia, became head of the permanent Secretariat established by the congress and approved by the Comintern of which it was an organ. Kollontai, as head of the Russian Zhenotdel, became her deputy. E. H. Carr talks about a "struggle" between them in 1920–1921, but without advancing either evidence or specific issues. The only substantive issue that divided them was their attitude toward cooperating tactically with bourgeois feminist groups. Zetkin, the original embodiment of animosity toward feminism, favored cooperation and united front; Kollontai fully opposed it, thus teaching the teacher. If there was a struggle, Kollontai lost, but again because of her role in an opposition movement in Russia. Zetkin's victory, if that is what it was, was hollow in any case. Within two years, the International Women's Secretariat was in Zhenotdel hands again (those of its head, Nikolaeva) and in 1926 it was downgraded to a Women's Department of the Executive Committee of the Communist International.[30]

By the end of the 1920's, the Zhenotdel had lost much of its original verve and power. As early as 1922, Smidovich proclaimed that it would be "better to liquidate" it than to grant it half a life. Indeed, there was a widespread movement among local party organs in the early 1920's to liquidate the Zhenotdels and to subsume their work under propaganda and agitation sections. The furious pace of industrialization and collectivization beginning in 1928 posed tasks of mass mobilization which were, in the minds of some, much too imposing to be handled by Zhenotdel. One Party figure, according to Kaganovich, felt that "Zhenotdel was no longer a center of progress, but rather a brake to it." In late 1929, the Secretariat of the Central Committee, which had (since 1924) included sections for Organization-Assignment, Agitprop, the Press, the Village, Accounting, Statistics, Information, Administration, and Women, was reorganized. Agitprop was split into two new sections for Agitation-and-Mass-Campaigns and Culture-Propaganda; the Women's and Village sections were abolished and their work subsumed under Agitation-and-Mass-Campaigns. Kaganovich, in reporting on this decision, mentioned that some comrades had applauded the abolition of Zhenotdel as long overdue while others had lamented the decision. Both were wrong, he said; Zhenotdel had been necessary and had done enormously important work in its time; but now there was a solid cohort of liberated women and a special organ was no longer needed because the Party as a whole would assume this work. Artyukhina, the last head of Zhenotdel, endorsed this explanation and insisted that the Zhenotdel had not been liquidated because it was in any way considered harmful. But for many Zhenotdel workers, it was a sign of the end

[30] For information on this episode, see: [Armand], *Otchët*; Kollontai, *Rab. i krest.*, 25; Carr, *Socialism in One Country*, 3 v. in 4 (London, 1958–1964) III, 976–86.

of political work among Russian women and thus the end of much that was of value for them. For the historian, it plainly marks the end of the Proletarian Women's Movement that had its dim beginnings among the textile workers and intellectuals of Petersburg in 1906.[31]

Strictly speaking, special political work among women did not die out with the abolition of Zhenotdel. It was carried on by Zhensektors, attenuated successors to the local Zhenotdel organs; and by the Delegate Meetings which were retained for the rural areas until 1934. Women's departments were retained until the 1950's in certain regions inhabited by non-Russian nationalities. Political work among Russian women continued, and continues, in other forms. Cultural, political, and professional organizations composed largely of women abounded, as did mass campaigns and special women's publications. International Women's Day (March 8) remained one of the three major Soviet political holidays. But more and more these activities were tied to the general tasks of the nation and the Party rather than to any specifically female interest. As early as March 1930, for example, the International Women's Day slogan was "100% Collectivization!"[32] This did not mean that all the legal, economic, and educational rights bestowed upon women by the Revolution and put into life by Zhenotdel were taken away again after 1930. It does demonstrate, however, that the new rulers of Soviet Russia put no faith, to say the least, in *any* sort of autonomous political activity for women, even within the Party; and that they wanted no potential base of opposition to the frenzied policies upon which they were about to embark. The abolition of Zhenotdel was clearly a political act that had little bearing on the level of emancipation which Russian women had achieved by 1930. The fact that certain educational, professional, and economic benefits for women date from the period after 1930 does not alter the other fact that henceforth much of what Soviet women gained would be granted to them from on high by a Party largely made up of and led almost exclusively by men.

A final word about Zhenotdel. There can be little doubt that it made an enormous impact on Soviet society, particularly in the cities. Its frequent mention in Soviet literature attests to its prominent place in everyday consciousness. Fictional treatment of Zhenotdel varied. Sometimes it was used merely as a backdrop; often it was a cause of domestic friction or an object of ridicule—and just as often as a problem-solver and proper haven for the newly conscious Soviet woman, but always a symbol of newness on the social landscape.[33] The images were never far from the reality; Zhenotdel was an engine

[31] For data on the liquidation tendency in 1921, see Molotov's critical comment on it in Smolensk Archive, WKP, 420 (1932 [1922]), no. 21; Eubank, "Bolshevik Party," 14, and Emelyanova, *Revolyutsiya*, 108–10. Stavrakis, "Women," 85, 107, 109, 110, 115, 121; *Kommunistka*, 2, 3 (1930) 3–7 (Kaganovich's report and Artyukhina's comment); "Zhenotdely," in *V edinom stroyu* (Moscow, 1960) 174–75.

[32] Levidova, *Krupskaya*, 262. See also Smolensk Archives, WKP, 429 (1932), 430 (1933), 432 (1933).

[33] A very useful guide to the fictional treatment of women in these years is Gasiorowska, *Women in Soviet Fiction*.

of mobilization in an environment of extreme social backwardness. Organizational and communication skills enabled it to go beyond the specific social task—the "small deed" of the nineteenth-century intelligentsia—toward the larger goal of mass socialization. As an arm of the Party, it lacked the independence and perhaps some of the imaginative initiative of prewar feminism; but, in spite of weaknesses noted above, the Zhenotdel surpassed the feminists in power and prestige. Zhenotdel represented a combination of class and sexual struggle and thus was a working out not only of Marxist notions about the female half of the labor movement, not only of the revolutionary Populist tradition of the "common cause," but also, in some ways, of the much more feminist belief, given expression by Lenin in 1919 that "the emancipation of working women is a matter for the working women themselves."[34] The successes registered by Zhenotdel in raising the consciousness of poor and backward women were proof enough that there was something more to female emancipation than winning the suffrage. But its abolition in 1930 was also proof that without political equality, the "common cause" for which women had fought for three generations would always be defined by men.

The main outlines of post-revolutionary liberation had been drawn in the first dozen years of the new regime. Without missing a historical beat, Bolshevik women, having assisted in the establishment of Soviet power, had gone on to defend it in the Civil War. During it, and for a few years afterward, some of these women had participated in the high councils of the Party and exercised some influence in the new regime, while others had devoted their energies to the task of liberating and mobilizing their less conscious sisters among the workers and peasants. By 1930 the woman-run machinery for liberation—the Zhenotdel—had been dismantled and the woman question was officially considered "resolved." Long before 1930, women, while continuing to occupy intermediate positions in the Party and the government, had disappeared from the genuine seats of power altogether. Major changes in women's status were henceforth to be made almost exclusively by men in accordance with what they perceived to be "larger" considerations—industrialization, defense, and reconstruction. The changes that will be summarized in the final chapter of this book were substantial and enduring, if not always salutary in their mode of application. But they were not the result of a conscious and self-directing women's movement any more. They were policies, flowing out of the broader modulations of Soviet economic, military, and political history, which were made by men for women. But accompanying the rising and declining fortunes of an autonomous women's movement in the first generation of Soviet power was a revolution in sexual theory and behavior that would have a profound effect upon the outcome of the woman question in Russia.

[34] Lenin, *Emancipation*, 68.

345

XI

The Sexual Revolution

> We think that the approaching century will be an era of deep colli-
> sion between the religious sacramental essence of marriage and
> our civilization which is typically and characteristically atheist and
> sexless.
>
> —V. V. ROZANOV

1. KOLLONTAI AND THE NEW MORALITY

Since the sexual excesses of the 1920's were often traced to the theories and
the personal example of Kollontai, it is essential to look at them in some detail. With a few recent exceptions, Western writers are of no help, and are
often perpetuators of misleading clichés. One of the earliest (1917) charac-
terizations of Kollontai by a Western scholar (at the time, 1917, a Russian
observer) was that of Pitirim Sorokin. "It is plain," he wrote in his diary,
"that her revolutionary enthusiasm is nothing but a gratification of her sexual
satyriasis. In spite of her numerous 'husbands,' Kollontai, first the wife of a
general, later the mistress of a dozen men, is not yet satiated. She seeks new
forms of sexual sadism." Modern writers, though softening the language,
have done little to modify this inaccurate picture of Kollontai. André Pierre,
for instance, claims Kollontai preached that "relations between the sexes must
be purely biological." Theodore Von Laue sums up her beliefs in one word,
"libertinism," and adds that "the maternal instinct was merely a bourgeois
relic to her." Georg von Rauch tersely calls her the "great prophetess of free
love"; and Robert Daniels introduces her as the "mistress of Shlyapnikov
(among others, as she practiced the free love which she preached)." E. H.
Carr, the doyen of British historians of Russia, barely veils his hostility to
Kollontai when he writes that she "preached the uninhibited satisfaction of the
sexual impulse, supported by the assumption that it was the business of the
state to take care of the consequences." These are a few examples. In all of
them one feels either a salacious delight in finding an element of sexuality in
the Revolution or a righteously judgmental attitude toward a woman who
"practices what she preaches."[1]

---

[1] Sorokin, *Leaves*, 59; Pierre, *Les femmes*, 23; Theodore Von Laue, *Why Lenin? Why Stalin?*
(New York, 1964) 217, 158; G. von Rauch, *History of Soviet Russia* (New York, 1957) 140;
Robert Daniels, *Conscience of the Revolution* (New York, 1969) 127; E. H. Carr, *Socialism in
One Country*, I, 31.

What *did* Kollontai practice? Her writings on sex cannot be fully under-stood outside the context of her personal life both before and after the Revolu-tion. Many writers have alluded—with a brand of irony reserved for women—to her numerous lovers. But even the most gossipy accounts, taken together with her own memoirs, yield no more than four men in her adult life: two husbands and two lovers. The husbands were Kollontai and Dybenko; the lovers, Shlyapnikov and an unidentified figure of the emigration years. About the last mentioned, there is some information from Kollontai herself who does not name him. He appears to have been the Menshevik economist, P. P. Mas-lov (though this is not proven) and he figures as the hero, Senya or S.S., in Kollontai's semi-autobiographical story, *Great Love* (1923). More important than his identity, however, is the author's reaction to her sad affair with him, which took place around the years 1910-1911. The heroine, Natasha-Kollontai, gave herself body and soul to her lover, but wished also to be re-spected as an intellectual, a comrade, and a Party worker; Senya, a weak and selfish married man, treated her mainly as a woman and a sexual object. She broke off the affair and went back to political work. It was during the rebound from this affair that Kollontai wrote her most important pre-war articles on sex.[2]

About Kollontai's affair with Shlyapnikov, there is no mystery: they lived together in Norway during World War I, and were close again in 1920–1922 when they collaborated in the Workers' Opposition Movement.[3] In the stormy years of Revolution and Civil War that divided these two periods, Kollontai's famous romance with the sailor, Pavel Dybenko, blossomed. Though seventeen years older than he, she was attracted by his primitive strength and revolutionary energy—and he presumably by her feminine charm and politi-cal literacy. They eschewed formal marriage at first; then, either under the pressure of gossip, or out of fear of being captured and separated by counter-revolutionaries, they married. The Party leaders were not entranced with Kol-lontai's romance in time of revolution, and their dissatisfaction was increased when Kollontai tried to interfere with the decision of a Party tribunal that tried Dybenko for various breaches of discipline and lapses of judgment while Commissar for Naval Affairs. Both vociferously opposed the Brest-Litovsk peace settlement and both resigned their government positions. Later they were posted together to the Ukraine for military propaganda work, Kollontai acting as Dybenko's ideological mentor as well as his political commissar and wife. They scoured the Ukraine on an agit-train and were eventually parted by the hazards of war. After the War, she began hearing rumors about Dybenko carousing with younger women. This hurt her terribly, coming as it did in the middle of the most serious political crisis of her life—the Workers' Opposi-

---

[2] For this affair, *Great Love*, and the misinterpretations built on it about Lenin and Inessa, see Stites, "Kollontai, Inessa, Krupskaya."

[3] This information, based upon personal interviews, was kindly supplied to the author by Dr. Kaare Hauge of Oslo.

tion debacle, a near rift with Lenin, and her own subsequent break with the Opposition. By 1923, her second marriage was finished. Kollontai was fifty. Her love life was behind her; and her major ideas on the subject had been uttered.[4]

An adolescent love affair, an early and unsuccessful marriage, a serious affair in her late thirties, another one in her early forties, and a final second marriage at age forty-six—this is the public record of Alexandra Kollontai's amourous career. Perverted? Promiscuous? Abnormal? Compared to other European women—and not only continental ones—of her class, education, and intellectual scope, Kollontai's behavior could hardly be called outrageous, though it was perhaps more open than that of most. She was, by all accounts, a vivacious, attractive, and sensitive woman—one who even as a little girl had needed love but who could not be chained by it if it became oppressive. In the end, it would seem that what appalled her critics was not that she practiced what she preached, but rather that she preached what she practiced.

The correct dating of Kollontai's works is crucial in understanding why she said certain things and what she meant by them at the time of writing. Chronologically her pre-war writings seem to belong to the previous discussion of Kollontai's views of the future of sex relations. But since Kollontai saw fit to republish them together after the Revolution under the misleadingly unifying title of *New Morality*, and since the work was widely circulated and frequently cited, it is sensible to treat its three component articles as a major part of Kollontai's sexual doctrine as of the moment of re-publication— keeping in mind that the earliest of them was written seven years before. *New Morality* invites discussion in the later context, also, because one of Kollontai's best known writings on sex of the Soviet period, "Make Way for the Winged Eros," draws much of its psychological imagery from the earlier works. The novel elements in these articles are a psychology of erotic technique, and a strong appeal for women's independence from enslaving love affairs.

The first was elaborated in a 1910 review of Grete Meisel-Hess' *Die sexuelle Krise* (1910). Meisel-Hess was a Berlin-based native of Vienna who, in the years before and during World War I, wrote tracts assaulting bourgeois hypocrisy in marriage and the double standard of morality. Her works were serious and, for the time, original; she was one of the first in a long line of thinkers who tried to combine the insights of Viennese psychoanalysis with the teachings of socialism. Kollontai, while vaguely referring to needed corrections and modifications of Meisel-Hess, generally endorsed her main ideas

---

[4] This brief account, far from definitive, has been pieced together from data in Kollontai "Avtobiog. ocherk," 299–302; Palencia, *Kollontai*, 160–65, 176–77; Mindlin, *Ne dom*, 288–317 (the fullest account), and 359–75; Itkina, *Kollontai*, 98–100. Additional, and sometimes conflicting, bits of information can be found in: Bryant, *Mirrors*, 115; Rhys Williams, *Through the Russian Revolution*, 29; Claude Anet, *La Révolution russe*, 4 v. (Paris, 1917–1919) IV, 51–52; and a clipping from *Golos russkoi kolonii* (Helsinki, n.d., but early 1918) in the National Archives of Finland, 836/1.

and called the book "the thread of Ariadne" through the complex maze of contemporary sexual problems. Indissoluble marriage, according to Meisel-Hess, failed to allow for accidents of mating and incompatibility; and by trapping people together in constant proximity, eroded the original tenderness between the partners. Prostitution was even more dehumanizing. Kollontai, commenting on this, first used the figure of "winged Eros": "Prostitution," she wrote, "suffocates love in human hearts; from it Eros flies in fear of soiling her golden wings on the unclean couch." Kollontai also observed that in the act of prostitution, the man invariably deprived his partner of orgasm because of his selfish objectification of the woman. The third sexal alternative, the "free union," was also seen by Meisel-Hess (and Kollontai) as an inadequate outlet for love and Eros in the modern world—chiefly because it was too all-consuming.

Required was a re-fashioning of the human psyche in Meisel-Hess' emphasis, and an economic and social transformation, in Kollontai's. In the meantime, women who rejected the erotically deadening life of the prostitute or the wife and who also refused to go through life in a state of sexual hunger could know the delight of sex and realize their "love potential" by means of what Meisel-Hess called "love-play." As Kollontai explained, this was not the suffering and tragic "great love" (*bolshaya lyubov*—words she used as the title of one of her last works of fiction); not the all-consuming lover-mistress relationship usually meant by the term "free union"—a relationship that drained the energy of both lovers and demolished the ego of the woman. Nor was it simply crude, physical sex: the fictional hero, Sanin, observed Kollontai, would have been a poor partner in the act of "love-play." It was rather an "erotic friendship" schooled in the arts of love that "requires attentiveness, sensitivity, sharp awareness and a profound penetration of the partner's soul rather than the eternal smiles and roses." "Love-play" allowed for intense and tender passion without incarcerating or annihilating the soul of the love partner.

In the future, said Kollontai, "there is no doubt that love will become the cult of mankind." Not suffering love, but bright, joyous and life-enriching love. The forms of love—Meisel-Hess speaking, Kollontai endorsing—would be varied and limited only by two considerations: no violation of the human race (by consanguine intermarriage); no arrangements based on money. The monogamous union based on the "great love" would be the ideal, but as the human psyche became more complex, variations of this would become inevitable, including "successive monogamy" and a whole spectrum of forms of sexual unions and relationships. All of these would presuppose the "sanctity of motherhood" and the care of mother and child, morally and materially, by society.[5]

[5] "Lyubov i novaya moral," in *Novaya moral* (Moscow [1918] 1919, 36–47 [quotation, 47, 40, 44, 45]). Originally published in *Novaya zhizn* in 1911 as "Na staruyu temu"; tr., with some errors, by Alix Holt in *Sexual Relations and the Class Struggle; Love and the New Morality*

The second and closely related major theme in Kollontai's writings on sex in these years was that of "the new woman," contained in a review essay of that title in 1913. Surveying some two dozen tales and novels of the early twentieth century, Kollontai saw emerging from them a new fictional type: the "bachelor woman" (*kholostaya zhenshchina*). One could see their real-life prototypes in their millions, she wrote: dressed in gray, by day occupying the offices and factories of the great cities, by night their tiny rooms; living alone—but working and free. These were the modern "single girls," self-reliant and self-confident, living side by side with the women of the old type—the weak, the dependent, the deceived, the abandoned, the betrayed. George Sand's heroines dwelling in the midst of the Emma Bovarys. Kollontai praised Tatyana Shchepkina-Kupernik's *One of Those* because its heroine. like Kollontai, left her husband when his presence interfered with her work. It was the victory of personality over love, a victory for which Kollontai struggled during much of her adult life. The New Woman had to triumph over emotion, to display resilience, control, strength, toughness of mind. Above all, her personality had to survive.

If a woman did have a romantic relationship, said Kollontai, it had to be equal and had to leave the woman's ego intact. Refusing to accept Mme. de Staël's verdict that "for a man love is only an episode while for a woman it is the whole story," Kollontai pushed love *and sex* to the side. "Love affairs, passion, romance are only the episodes of life. Its real content is that 'holy cause' which the new woman serves: the social idea, science, calling, creativity. . . . And this cause, this goal, is often more important, more worthy, and holier for the new woman than all the joys of the heart, all the pleasures of passion." To ensure equality, independence, and her holy mission, a woman had to evince "self discipline instead of emotionalism, recognition of the value of freedom and independence instead of submission and a faceless personality, assertion of individuality instead of the naive attempt to absorb and reflect the alien nature of the 'beloved,' insistence on her right to earthly happiness instead of the hypocritical donning of the mask of virtue, and finally, a willingness to put the expression of love in a subordinate place in her life. Before us stands not a mate—the shadow of a man; before us stands a personality—a Woman Human Being."[6]

Five years elapsed before Kollontai returned to the subject in her well-

---

(Montpelier, England, 1972) 15–26. There is an English edition of Meisel-Hess' book: *The Sexual Crisis*, 2d ed., tr. E. and C. Paul (New York, 1917). See also her *Sexuelle Recht* (Berlin, 1912) and *Krieg und Ehe* (Berlin, 1915).

[6] "Novaya zhenshchina," in *Novaya moral*, 3–35 (quotation, 24, 29). It first appeared, with the same title, in *Sovremennyi mir*, 9 (1913) 171–86 and has been translated, via German, by S. Attanasio in A. Kollontai, *Autobiography of a Sexually Emancipated Communist Woman*, ed. I. Fetscher (New York, 1971) 51–103. The third essay comprising *Novaya moral* (48–61) is of little consequence; it first appeared in *Novaya zhizn*, 9 (1911) as "Polovaya moral i sotsialnaya borba," and appears in English translation in the Holt pamphlet cited above (1–13). See Stites, "Kollontai, Inessa, Krupskaya," for critical comment.

known speech of 1918, *The Family and the Communist State*—her first writing on the problem since 1908 to have wide circulation in Russia, and the first ever of a popular nature. Apart from remarks on socialist care of children, its main focus was on the form of socialist marriage rather than on sex in the broader context. The "old type of family" or "former family"—not the family *tout court*—was described as a microscopic state where husband ruled wife and children; and as the social incubator of future citizens. It was to be abolished: public upbringing of children would replace its traditional function; equality of sexes would dethrone its traditional ruler. The remaining relationship, still defined as "marriage" by Kollontai, would be a "comradely and warm union of two free and independent, laboring, equal members of communist society."

> In place of the indissoluble marriage based on the servitude of woman, we shall see rise the free union, fortified by the love and the mutual respect of the two members of the Workers' State, equal in their rights and in their obligations. In place of the individual and egotistical family, there will arise a great universal family of workers, in which all the workers, men and women, will be above all, workers, comrades.

Kollontai's vision of marriage under socialism—in reality the free union that was unworkable under capitalism—was taking shape; but a precise sexual definition, its tenure, the rights and rules of its members were still left undetermined.[7]

Kollontai wrote nothing during the next two years about the sexual problem. To Polina Vinogradskaya, however, she said that under communism marriage would not take the form of an extended union; to Marguerite Harrison of the *Baltimore Sun*, she expressed hostility to "the family"—presumably the present one—and said that sex existed merely for reproduction and should suffer no restraints. In print, Kollontai was more diffident and refined. In a 1921 book about prostitution, she once again described communist marriage. "At the base of the marriage relation," she wrote, "will lie a healthy instinct for reproduction, embellished with the charming colors of young love, with the ardent tones of passion, with the tender blossom of the harmony of souls and the sympathy of spirits, or with the hotly burning, but quickly extinguished, fire of physical attraction." In a lecture course of the same year, Kollontai further defined the image of the new marriage: premarital sex was condoned; notions of illegitimacy, alimony, and regulation of sex were not. An offhand comment in her book, *Prostitution*, left no doubt that arrangements other than marital were compatible with the life of a good communist. "The collectivity," she says, "is not concerned with its length or the character of its attraction—as long as it is not based upon purely material bar-

---

[7] The first quotation is from the original Russian edition: *Semya i kommunisticheskoe gosudarstvo* (Moscow, 1918) 21; the other is from Schlesinger's *Family*, 68, 69. There is a complete, but very bad, English version: *Communism and the Family* (London, n.d.).

gains between the partners. But it can be passion or even fleeting physical attraction."[8]

Kollontai's last major statement on sexual morality, "Make Way for Winged Eros" (1923), a vividly painted contrast between vulgar love (wingless Eros) and sublime proletarian love (winged Eros), provides the key to her views. It is at once a synthesis of her earlier notions and an end to her search down through the years for an authentic communist morality. Ironically, though one of the main targets of attacks upon her, this article clearly acquits Kollontai of the charge of being the ideologue of the sexual abuses and the cynicism that bespattered the moral life of Soviet youth in the 1920's. Through it runs an unsparing critique of that base, vulgar sexuality that had captivated Sanin's generation and that again was exalted to a philosophy of life by the new Soviet youth. The crude, soulless sex act, the casual, unfeeling lovemaking—wingless Eros—was by origin an excrescence of bourgeois society, Kollontai wrote. But in Russia, amid the harshness of revolutionary violence, the turbulent din of battle, and the hectic timetable of the Civil War, it appeared again, appealing to those beleaguered heroes and heroines who had no time for the sweet delights of tender love. Kollontai spared no words in cataloguing the various manifestations of the wingless Eros; it was the "naked instinct of reproduction," unhealthy satisfaction of the sex drive for its own sake, coarse lust, quick pleasure, "mere possession" of someone's body, whoring. And she condemned it unequivocally as wasteful of energy, debasing to the spirit, and inimical to the principle of sexual equality.

Winged Eros was the antipode of all this. Its conceptual fogginess does not permit precise analysis, but amid its diaphanous terminology two shapes assumed some substance. The first was the tender eroticism of "love-play." The second, which almost obscured it, was *lyubov-tovarishchestvo*—"love-comradeship" or "the love collective," the ultimate goal of communist workers. "Love in its present form," wrote Kollontai, "is a very complex condition of the soul, long since detached from its original impulse—the biological instinct of reproduction—and often in sharp opposition to it. Love is a conglomerate, a complex combination of friendship, passion, maternal tenderness, affection, sympathy of spirit, concern, attraction, habit and many, many other nuances of feelings and experiences." People were conflicted, she continued, by their simultaneous feelings for work, for lover, for child, and for the collective; and the most tempestuous of these conflicts was the simultaneous fondness for two people of the opposite sex. This was not the cheap adultery or the multiple affairs of bourgeois life; it was a genuine and inevitable feature of life in an age of increasing human association and psychological complexity. Must the worker fear and suppress such natural feelings? asked

[8] P. Vinogradskaya, *Pamyatnye vstrechi* (Moscow, 1972) 53; M. Harrison, *Marooned in Moscow* (New York, 1921) 79; Kollontai, *Polozhenie*, 188, 191–92. Quotations are from *Prostitutsiya i mery borby s nei* (Moscow, 1921) 22, 18.

Kollontai. No. In the collective, "the more such threads connecting soul to soul, heart to heart, and mind to mind—the more strongly will the spirit of solidarity be inculcated and the easier it will be to attain the ideals of the working class—comradeship and unity." Exclusiveness and ownership could not be the bases of love among the workers, she adds. They would see the beauties of "the many-sidedness and many strings of the winged Eros" within the larger loving embrace of the "love-collective," the final form of human love; and they would do so whether their love took the shape of long alliances or brief liaisons.

> In this new society where spirit and emotion is shared—begins the rhapsodic peroration—in the atmosphere of joyous unity and comradely collective living for all productive members, Eros will occupy a worthy place and be the source of emotional experience and of ever increasing happiness. What will this transformed Eros be like? The most daring fantasy cannot depict it. But one thing is clear: the more tightly welded are the new human bonds of solidarity, the loftier will be their spiritual and soulful bonds in all areas of life, creativity, and living—and the lower will be the place occupied by love, as that word is presently understood. Contemporary love always sins in absorbing the thought and feeling of "the loving hearts," thus isolating them and setting them apart from the collective. Such alienation from the collective—the interests, aims, and aspirations of all of whose members are woven in a dense web—will become not only needless but impossible. In this new world, the accepted, normal, and desirable forms of sexual relationships will, apparently, be based upon healthy, uninhibited, natural attractions of sex (free of perversion and excess) and thus upon a "transformed Eros."[9]

This final vision of Kollontai pulled together the strands of her earlier ideas. The proletariat would evolve its own morality and would brook no interference or regulation, and indeed would require none. Independence of women would encourage both sexes to keep sex in its proper, and subordinate, place in life. The brutish physiological approach to sex would give way to the winged Eros, an enriching and enrapturing experience of emotional and physical eroticism. The sexual code of communism would allow for manifold varieties of marital and non-marital love and sex combinations, and all "loving hearts" would be supported and nourished spiritually in the "love collective." Kollontai's essay was a striking juxtaposition of ideas that had been voiced earlier by Bebel and Meisel-Hess, and by Enfantin, Fourier, and Chernyshevsky. Enfantin's "priest-couple" and Chernyshevsky's *tsaritsa* were

---

[9] "Dorogu krylatomu erosu," *Molodaya gvardiya* (May, 1923) 111–24 (quotations, 120, 121, 123). It is the third in a series of "Pisma k trudyashcheisya molodëzhi" ("Letters to Toiling Youth"), of which the first two deal with general moral principles: Apr.-May, 1922, 136–44 and Oct.-Dec., 1922, 128–36.

demoted from their authority to bless, regulate and orchestrate love just as emphatically as were God, the Church, and the State. This was to be the sole concern of the workers within their love-collective. But this was all clearly an image of the future, a future wherein all the other requirements for full freedom and honesty in love and the complete emancipation of women and men have been met. It could not be taken, except by artful hypocrites or blunt-minded puritans, as an invitation to the kind of misanthropic carnal adventurism that re-emerged in Russian society after the Revolution. For in it there was no trace of a doctrine that taught either the compulsive promiscuity of the biological interpretation of love, or a cynical "revolutionary" apologia for such an interpretation.

Kollontai's last and terse word on sex was an updated version of the preface she wrote in 1913 to Bebel's *Woman and Socialism* whose most ardent passages are devoted to his campaign against the double standard and on behalf of privacy and freedom in sexual relations. In her 1923 revision, Kollontai cited and underlined these words from his book: "the satisfaction of sexual desires is just as private and as personal as the satisfaction of any other natural demand of the human organism."[10]

Kollontai's comments on maternity and the family, though more specific and aired in rather different contexts than most of her remarks about sex *per se*, further explain her general moral stance. Despite reservations about sexual love consuming too much energy, Kollontai seems to have shared the view of some Russian religious thinkers, notably Solověv and Rozanov, that sex love was higher, theologically speaking, than maternal love. "Although I personally raised my child with great care," she tells us in her memoirs, "motherhood was never the kernel of my existence."[11] In this respect she differed greatly from many of the sexual reformers of the "Right to Motherhood" movement of pre-war Europe who saw mother-love as a surrogate for sex. Kollontai has been accused both of ignoring or rejecting the maternal instinct of women altogether and of sponsoring laws requiring "that little girls of twelve were to become mothers."[12] Both belong in the realm of fantasy.

Kollontai ardently believed in the natural and sacred function of motherhood and said so many times. Her largest book and much of her political effort after October was devoted to ensuring adequate medical care for working mothers. She also believed that society had an obligation to assist mothers by helping to raise their children. But her belief bore a qualification rarely mentioned in comments about it or about her: The state would *not* take children

---

[10] "Velikii borets za pravo i svobodu zhenshchiny," in A. Bebel, *Zhenshchina i sotsializm* (Moscow, 1923) 7–17 (quotation, 15–16). The passage is not included in a recent edited version of this preface (taken from a 1918 Prague edition of Bebel) printed in Kollontai, *Stati*, 113–24.

[11] *Autobiography* (Fetscher), 11. Solověv on the two forms of human love: Khvostov, *Zhenshchina*, 286–87.

[12] This charge is mentioned by Kollontai in *Autobiography* (Fetscher) 38.

away from their parents, and all public child-rearing arrangements would be voluntary on the part of the parents. Her primary concern was that every woman would have the right and the genuine opportunity to have children and to be sure that they would be cared for. "Every mother must be convinced that once she fulfills her natural function and gives a new member to communist society, i.e. a new worker, the collective will love and attend to her and her child." Marriage and sex were personal affairs; but motherhood, she said in words almost identical to Lenin's, was a social concern.[13]

Kollontai supported the abortion law of 1920 as a matter of principle but, like most Bolsheviks, saw it as a necessary and temporary evil. She considered childbirth the natural right and duty of the woman, entailing certain obligations. The first was to care for herself during pregnancy, "remembering that in these months she no longer belongs to herself; she is serving the collective and 'is producing' from her own flesh and blood a new unit of labor, a new member of the labor republic." After childbirth, the communist mother was obliged to nurse and surround the child with tender maternal love; only then did the mother have the right to say that her social obligation to *that* child was fulfilled. Thereafter, the natural and persistent instinct to care for children and to love them was to be generalized and directed toward all the children of the collective. After returning from human reproduction to economic production, the mother was to serve as part-time assistant in schools, nurseries, and children's homes in addition to maintaining, if she so wished, a special relationship to her "own" child. Avoidance of maternity (as through abortion) or of any of these duties was seen by Kollontai as a selfish and immature lack of responsibility.[14]

In Kollontai's last formulations on collective living, she singled out the kitchen, far more than the nursery, as the prison house of women. "Let men learn to value and love a woman not because she is good at kneading dough," she told her auditors in an oft-quoted remark; "but because she is attractive and has personal qualities, because of her 'self' . . . 'The separation of the kitchen from marriage' is a great reform, no less important than the separation of Church from State, at least in regard to the historical destiny of woman." Here Kollontai echoed Lenin, whose hatred for individual kitchens was almost obsessive. Collectivizing the kitchen was only the first step in lightening the load of the working woman and mother. The commune—sometimes referred to as "hostel" or "communal apartment house" (*obshchezhitie*, *dom-*

<hr/>

[13] *Communism and the Family*; quotation from Kollontai, *Za god revol.*, 28. It was this belief which impelled Kollontai in 1926 to launch her last public campaign on behalf of women. During the marriage code debates of that year, she advanced the idea of a tax-financed public maternity insurance fund which would release *all* pregnant women from dependence upon alimony and would put state support in its place. Her suggestion is treated at length and in context in Beatrice Farsworth, "Bolshevik Alternatives and the Soviet Family: the 1926 Marriage Law Debate," in Atkinson *et al.*, *Women in Russia*.

[14] Kollontai, *Polozhenie*, 173–79 (quotation, 173).

kommuna)—was the next; only in such living arrangements could housekeeping be delegated to specialists—in other words to professional cleaning women. Kollontai saw full-time housekeeping as a labor specialty like any other and not in itself demeaning. What was demeaning was the wasteful and repetitive labor that placed a double burden on the working woman. Kollontai presumably envisioned the labor collective and the living collective to be coterminous: "a family of a collective of toilers, wherein it is not the blood relationship, but rather the common labor and the unity of interests, aspirations, and goals which will bind the members tightly together and which will make true spiritual brothers of them."[15]

Kollontai's six works of fiction (all published in 1923) are really only simple commentaries on the ideas outlined above. The story "Twenty-two Pages" was an illustration of how love affairs could interfere with the independent work of a woman and thus her self-esteem. Its heroine, a young Soviet student locked in a romance that has kept her from writing more than twenty-two pages, broke with her lover and returned to her desk. "Conversation Overheard" described the problem of a woman caught in a conflict between her stable relationship with an old comrade and a fleeting, but in the long run unsatisfying, attraction for a more dashing figure. In the end, she chose the new romance, realizing how shallow it would be. *Great Love* was the autobiographical novella which recalled Kollontai's love affair with Maslov before the Revolution. "Sisters," published in another collection, was a slight tale about two victims, one a wife the other a prostitute, of a former revolutionary corrupted by the poisonous influence of the semi-capitalist New Economic Policy (NEP).[16]

In the story, "Vasilisa Malygina"—a last major attempt to grapple with the new morality in everyday Soviet life—Kollontai swung back to the persistent theme of independence. The heroine was a worker, a new communist woman with high ideals and a genuine love for a fellow revolutionary whom she "married." But the man, like all Kollontai's heroes, was weak and corruptible. After the fervor of the Civil War, he settled into comfortable work in the morally corrosive atmosphere of NEP and began to betray her, as well as his own earlier ideals. Vasilisa's rival in love was described contemptuously as a Nepka (literally, "woman of the NEP")—well-dressed, made-up, and properly seductive—in contrast to Vasilisa whose breasts have been hardened by years of work and struggle. Vasilisa left her man and found fulfillment in

[15] *Ibid.*, 167–68, 185–89. See also her 1918 article, " 'Krest materinstva' i sovetskaya respublika," in *Stati*, 237–42.

[16] The first three of these stories make up *Zhenshchina na perelome (psikhologicheskie etyudy)* (Moscow, 1923) 3–13, 14–18, and 19–96, "Bolshaya lyubov" being republished later as a book, in slightly revised form (Moscow, 1927). The English translation by Lily Lore is *A Great Love* (New York, 1929); see reference in note 2 above. "Sisters" appears (52–66) in the collection cited in the following note.

the establishment of a commune. Pregnant, she decided to have her baby and raise it herself with the aid of her communal comrades—in contrast to the Nepka who, pregnant by the same man, chose to have an abortion. Vasilisa fought hard to make the commune a success in the face of petty egoism and, in her efforts to teach other women how to attain their freedom, took her place in Russian fiction as the modern Vera Pavlovna.[17]

The best known and most misinterpreted of Kollontai's stories was "Love of Three Generations" that was both a further instance of Kollontai's repudiation of the "wingless Eros" of the Civil War period and a statement of her own tolerant confusion vis-à-vis the more radical sexual ethos of the new generation. The three generations of the story were vivid illustrations of the changing revolutionary attitude toward sex from the 1860's to the 1920's. The heroine's mother, a late *narodnitsa*, shared the nihilist no-nonsense ethic of the 1860's and lived in *de facto* monogamy with a married man until he betrayed her. The heroine Olga—representing the middle generation and clearly a partial self-portrait of the author—contracted a revolutionary marriage but then carried on an affair with a married man (who bore strong psychological and circumstantial resemblance to the anti-hero of *Great Love*) behind the back of his wife, an arrangement which her old mother could not condone. After the Revolution, Olga's daughter Zhenya shocked them both by the novelty of her sexual ideas and the boldness of her behavior (the former distinctly growing out of the latter). She had quick affairs during the Civil War—no time, she said, for anything more than that. On leave, she managed to sleep with her mother's lover (a worker whose relationship to Olga resembled that of Dybenko to Kollontai) while simultaneously having relations with another comrade her own age. She had an unwanted pregnancy and decided on an abortion, vowing next time to "use something." Olga was hurt and appalled by all this but, recalling that she had once scandalized her own mother, an "advanced woman" of a bygone age, she tried to show tolerance and understanding toward the morality of Zhenya and her generation—a morality that, if not new, was certainly far "in advance" of her own in its light-minded attitude to sex. A careful reading of this story in the context of Kollontai's other writings should be sufficient to dispel the double myth surrounding it which says that it contains the origin of the "glass of water" theory of sex and that Zhenya was simply echoing the views of the author.[18]

The purpose of the preceding exposition of Kollontai's vision of the New Morality has not been to exhaust it by thorough analysis or to evaluate it in the light of the sexual theories of her time and of the present, though this certainly

---

[17] "Vasilisa Malygina," *Lyubov pchël trudovykh* (Moscow, 1923), 67–303. Translations: as *Free Love* by C. Hogarth (London, 1932) and as *Red Love* (New York, 1927).

[18] "Lyubov trëkh pokolenii," in *ibid.*, 3–51. In real life, a similar instance of distress at the sexual behavior of their niece and daughter by Vera and Lidiya Figner during the Civil War is recorded by L. Dan in *Iz vstrechi*, 5–6.

deserves to be done.[19] Rather, it has been an attempt to correct some of the myths and misinterpretations of her life and thought that began to appear immediately after the Revolution, in particular, the belief, long held both in the Soviet Union and in the West, that Kollontai was responsible for the abuses of the sexual revolution in Russia and that her teachings led directly and logically to the moral anarchy and the abysmal lack of human decency that accompanied it. It is true that her work, even when treated carefully, fairly, and fully, is replete with ambiguities and latent contradictions. Anyone—and this includes almost the whole of the pre-revolutionary intelligentsia—who advocates honesty, sensitivity, and seriousness in regard to sexual behavior and also insists upon complete freedom from social judgment or control is bound to meet with conflicts when facing the realities of sexual life, particularly when it is played out in the atmosphere of a revolutionary reconstruction of society. This became abundantly clear when the Revolution was forced to confront the prosaic and often sordid details of everyday sexual and marital life. But it is also true that Kollontai was alone in attempting to graft a healthy and enriching notion of Eros on the exemplary but narrow socialist ethos derived from Russian traditions and from Marxism; and alone also in endeavoring to discover and predict, however tentatively and hazily, new ways of realizing and combining sexual honesty, erotic joy, and personal autonomy. As is often the case with prophets, her main ideas remained unread, distorted, or misunderstood.[20]

2. LIFE WITHOUT CONTROL

What effect did the Revolution have upon sexual life? Revolutions require lavish outlays of energy and time and a near total mobilization of the personality. During the Civil War sex was either pushed to the side or pursued casually and coarsely. Kollontai and Lenin had cause to complain about the coarseness at the end of hostilities. But it is the notion that the "front abolished sexuality" that has become the accepted image popularized in fiction. There was some truth in the image: 53 percent of the male respondents to a questionnaire recorded their belief that "the Revolution" had weakened their sexual impulses. A female veteran of the conflict writing many years later recalled her

[19] Two recent attempts are: K. Bailes, "Alexandra Kollontai et la Nouvelle Morale," *Cahiers du Monde russe et soviétique*, VI, 4 (Oct.-Dec., 1965) 472–96; and B. Clements, "Emancipation through Communism: the Ideology of A. M. Kollontai," *Slavic Review* (June 1973) 323–38.

[20] Kollontai's retrospective assessment of her own attempts to combine love and revolution is essentially negative. "Love," she wrote in 1926, "with its many disappointments, with its tragedies and eternal demands for perfect happiness still played a very great role in my life. An all-too-great role! It was an expenditure of precious time and energy, fruitless and, in the final analysis, utterly worthless." Fetscher, *Autobiography*, 7. See also *ibid.*, 8, 22, 26 and Palencia, *Kollontai*, 137 for similar remarks. The judgment is relevant, honest, and understandable—particularly at Kollontai's stage of life and career. But it would be unwise to make it the basis for a critique of the substance of her teachings.

own experience. "Once," she wrote, "I chanced to read a story wherein the author was rather ironical about a commissar who rejected love because it interfered with his total dedication to the cause of the Revolution. Perhaps in those days we did overdo this kind of thing a bit. But now it is eminently clear to me: we were victorious even under incredibly difficult circumstances because we knew how to overcome personal concerns and attachments."[1]

The establishment of NEP brought a transformation in the socio-psychological tone of life. The days of drama were over. Lenin was telling the Party to take up a "prosaic task" and "petty affairs." Many were unable to make the required transition from the bracing air of the battlefield to the stuffy atmosphere of a Soviet office. A depressing pall, described by the sociologist Volfson as "a demobilization of will and nerve," descended upon young people. Heavy with disillusionment and cynicism, it was strongly reminiscent of that cloud of cultural despair which had enwrapped Russian youth after the Revolution of 1905. Even the forgotten *Sanin* reappeared in Moscow bookstalls; and a rash of suicides in the mid-twenties added another poignant detail to a tableau whose acrid colors recalled the prewar days of decadence.[2] To the gruff and hasty sexuality of the Civil War was now added a large dose of callousness.

Unlike the Saninists of a bygone day, the Soviet sex heroes defended their raw desires by reference to socialist ideology. Obeying a deep iconoclastic strain in the Russian radical tradition, the new generation displayed fierce hostility to old values, particularly those related to the beautiful, the aesthetic, and the romantic. Neckties, combs, and neat clothing were relegated to the trash heap and the neo-nihilistic aversion for the refined and the exalted was extended to matters of love and sex. "The young people seem to think that the most primitive view on questions of sex is communist," complained Sofya Smidovich in 1925. "And that everything which goes beyond the primitive conception which might be suitable for a Hottentot or still more primitive representative of man at his earliest phases implies something characteristic of the petty bourgeoisie, a bourgeois attitude towards the sexual problem." "We don't recognize love," runs a famous passage in Gumilevsky's *Dog's Alley* (1927); "it's all bourgeois goods, petty bourgeois business." In a questionnaire of the 1920's, 48 percent of the respondents declared that love did not

[1] The first quoted phrase is from L. Fridland, *S raznykh storon: prostitutsiya v SSSR* (Berlin, 1933) 148. The quoted passage, from A. Prokhorova, "Doroga dlinoyu v zhizn," *Pravda stavshaya*, 89–90. Questionnaire data from I. Gelman, *Polovaya zhizn sovremennoi molodëzhi* (Moscow, 1923) 79. For fictional illustrations see Vishnevsky's perennially popular play, *Optimistic Tragedy* and discussion of other works in A. M. Van der Eng-Liedmeier, *Soviet Literary Characters* (The Hague, 1959) 30–32.

[2] Lenin's words and the mood they engendered from Carr, *Socialism*, I, 21 and ff. S. Ya. Volfson's phrase is from his *Sotsiologiya braka i semi* (Minsk, 1929) 418, a work rich in illustrations of the atmosphere of depression. On *Sanin* and the suicide vogue: Lawton, *Russian Revolution*, 237; Carr, *Socialism*, I, 25, and II, 218, n. 2; Victor Serge, "Vignettes of NEP," in *Verdict of Three Decades*, ed. J. Steinberg (New York, 1950), 138–43.

exist. In another of 1929, typical comments were: "love is the instinct of sex needs," "there is no love—only sexual needs," and "only physiology—nothing more."[3]

In Vera Ketlinskaya's "Natka Michurina," we find the following speech. "Listen Natasha, darling, you think just like a woman; and you just can't understand that it's old fashioned and silly to think that way. Why do we have to be tied to each other? You like Silantiev—O.K., that's your business. Last night I gave pleasure to Ivanova and to myself—what's wrong with that?" The Komsomol poet, Kuznetsov, put it another way:

> When the fires of my passion
> Are briefly banked in your embrace,
> We are comrades as before
> As if naught had taken place.

"I want to be free," explained a student in 1929. "I want to work and to study. I've got a girl—and we're intimate. But I don't want to marry. Then you get tied down too early. For me, sex life is a secondary matter." Said a Komsomol worker: "Me marry? For what! I want to live free and be active in public affairs. I need society. It's important for me. I can't get along without sexual life, without love; but it musn't tie me down." The best solution to the problem, in the view of a twenty-two-year-old male student, was to set up "special houses for sexual intercourse," not brothels, but stations analogous to maternity clinics where people could register, be examined, and have their pleasure.[4]

Behavior did not always match attitude, but there was a sharp lowering of the age of sexual activity, and students, Komsomols, and young workers were frequently censured as a group for sexual miscreance. With mixed dormitories, a foreign journalist observed, coeducation often meant cohabitation. The result was "liberty, equality, and maternity"—equality for the sexes, liberty for the man, and maternity for the woman. Hostels became the scenes of squalor, promiscuity, and drink—"I'd work sixteen hours at the factory," a young woman complained, telling of dormitory life, "so as not to go home. In the entryway, guys would chatter and grab girls. Many have already fallen. I'd be glad of a chance to move out of the dorm. But the dorm-commandant, refusing to correct matters, says maliciously 'We'll hang a red light in front of

[3] Smidovich quoted in Halle, *Woman*, 115; L. Gumilevsky, *Sobachii pereulok* (Leningrad, 1927) 14; questionnaire figure from Volfson, *Sotsiologiya*, 420. The 1929 responses are reported in *Zhizn bez kontrolya (polovaya zhizn i semya rabochei molodëzhi)*, ed. Vera Ketlinskaya *et al.* (Moscow, 1929), an unusually rich source of data drawn from a 1929 Komsomol conference on morality held in the Vyborg District of Leningrad, and from which I have taken the title of this section. Hereafter cited as *Zhizn*.

[4] Ketlinskaya (the same who edited the above cited work) cited in Fridland, *S raznykh storon* 142; Nikolai Kuznetsov, "Komsomolskaya lyubov," in *Na puti k novomu* (Moscow, 1925) 208. Student and worker comments from *Zhizn*, 44, 57. The proposal for a sex station is reported in Ella Winter, *Red Virtue* (New York, 1933) 127.

the entrance for you'.'" Callousness toward women became a style of life. One man seduced a sixteen-year-old girl with promises of marriage and afterward said to her: "You little whore, giving yourself up without any resistance." Another ensnared a twelve-year-old with wine and promises of wedlock only to desert her. Young girls polled at a symposium on morality in 1929 expressed the opinion that most men were depraved, "chase skirts," and were "after only one thing" from a girl. A young communist leader was cited at a congress for pimping Komsomolkas, and Party members themselves were involved in sexual scandals. Even the old story about "Leagues of Free Love" made its appearance in the Soviet press.[5]

Women also came in for their share of censure, but the vague and general nature of the complaints leveled at them make it difficult to know precisely who, how many, and in what ways they shared the new sexual ethos. Out of the welter of criticism, two types emerged. The first, interpreted as a poisonous vestige of the past, was usually called "Soviet Baryshnya" a type defined as early as 1920 by Angelica Balabanova as "a 'young lady' (*devitsa*) from a former petty-bourgeois or bourgeois family," accustomed to idleness and to being kept by men of wealth and position. The "lady typist" (*pisbaryshnya*) was a variant of this—the ubiquitous "office girl friend" who battened off the income and privileges of her boss. Kollontai used the terms Nepka and "career prostitute" to describe similar types. Epitomized by Kollontai's Nina in her "Vasilisa Malygina," these ghosts of a bygone moral epoch sold themselves for French perfume, high boots, silk stockings, and other items of NEP conspicuous consumption. They were fox-trot heroines, Soviet flappers, and latter-day versions of the flirting tango dancers and goodtime girls of pre-war days. Between them and ordinary prostitutes, the line was exceedingly thin; to communist critics non-existent.[6]

Of quite a different order were Bolshevik and working women who rivaled men in their emphatic repudiation of old-fashioned notions of love. The female characters in Pantaleimon Romanov's novels were often cited as the archetypes. "I am far from any kind of sentiment," proclaims one of them;

[5] Early sex: *Zhizn*, 15–17, 24–25, 34, 37; Gelman, *Polovaya zhizn*, 49, 56, 59, and *passim*. Dormitory life: Lawton, *Russian Revolution*, 326; Serge, "Vignettes," 149–51; and *Zhizn*, 21 (quotation). Komsomol and Party incidents in R. Fisher, *Pattern for Soviet Youth* (New York, 1959) 156 and M. Fainsod, *Smolensk Under Soviet Rule* (Cambridge, Mass., 1958) 206–207; the report on free love leagues is mentioned in P. Vinogradskaya, "Voprosy morali, pola, byta, i tov. Kollontai," *Krasnaya nov*, 6, 16 (Oct.-Nov. 1923) 187. Sheila Fitzpatrick has shown, by analyzing student questionnaires, that sexual behavior among university students in Moscow and Odessa lagged behind the image which it had in fiction and journalism: "Sex and Revolution: Sexual Mores of Soviet Students in the 1920's," a paper read at the American Association for the Advancement of Slavic Studies conference, Atlanta, October, 1975.

[6] Balabanova's definition is in her *Ot rabstva k svobode* (Moscow, 1920) 19 (a brief and standard pamphlet on Bolshevik liberation of women); G. Grigorov and S. Shkotov mention the term "sovietized lady" (*osovetivsheisya baryshnya*) in *Staryi i novyi byt* (Moscow, 1927) 173. To this day, the word *sekretutka*, combining "secretary" and "prostitute," is sometimes used ironically to refer to sexy office types.

"far from regretting the loss of my innocence, and certainly free of any pangs of conscience over my 'fall'." In her circle, she tells us, there was "no knowledge of love—only sexual relations. Love is scornfully relegated to the realm of 'psychology', whereas among us only physiology has the right to exist. Girls sleep with boys for a week, a month, or sometimes, just by chance, for a night. And in all these affairs, those who seek to find in love something more than physiology are laughed at as deformed and mentally retarded." Another character, from the notorious *Comrade Kislyakov* (1930), tells of women who "look upon everything with cynical simplicity. Sleeping with men means nothing to them. And they see an affair as light satisfaction." In real life, there was evidence of "loose" sexual behavior among women of this period, behavior sometimes accompanied by proud justification for it. Certain Komsomolkas looked upon the family as a millstone, and preferred to retain their mobility and independence with or without a child. A working girl informed the world that she needed sexual variety, which she characterized as "play in love" (*igra v lyubov*)—a phrase as distant from Kollontai's *lyubov-igra* psychologically as it is close to it linguistically.[7]

But the purely physiological view of sex that often buttressed the male preference for short, non-committal relations was not widely shared by urban female youth, to say nothing of the older generation and of village women. A youth questionnaire of 1922 revealed that a third of those women who avoided marriage did so because of an absence of love (as compared to 12.3 percent of the male respondents); and that 81 percent preferred either marriage or a long-term arrangement to brief liaisons (compared to 72 percent of men). An anguished Komsomolka wrote to Krupskaya in 1925 asking her for an affirmation of her crumbling belief that love did indeed exist as something more than just casual sex. Even the heroine of *Without Cherry Blossom*, thought to be the very voice of the physiological love ethic, admits later in the story that for her, something more than physical attraction was required in a man—"mind, talent, spirit, tenderness." By the end of the 1920's, it was clear that brief liaisons did not really correspond to the psychological make-up of most women, and that marriage in one form or another was to remain a persistent element in Soviet sexual culture.[8]

What changes did matrimony undergo as a result of the Revolution? The historical precedent of European revolutions suggested that, at the least, mar-

---

[7] P. Romanov, *Bez cherëmukhi: sbornik rasskazov* (Moscow, 1927) 5, 9–10; *idem, Tovarishch Kislyakov* (Berlin, 1931) 109 (and see also 158). For "loose" behavior and advanced opinions, see: Grigorov and Shkotov, *Staryi i novyi byt*, 164 (quotation, 165–66); I. Bobryshev, *Melkoburzhuaznye vliyaniya sredi molodëzhi* (Moscow, 1928), 101–103 and *passim*; and *Zhizn*, 14, 61, 75–76.

[8] The query to Krupskaya and other evidence and opinion supporting the conclusion of this paragraph: Levidova, *Krupskaya*, 276; Gelman, *Polovaya zhizn*, 67, 84, 95, 124; Fridlander, *S raznykh storon*, 142–44. The Romanov quotation is from *Bez cherëmukhi*, 20.

riage would be secularized, divorce would be made easier, and the juridical category of illegitimacy would be abolished or upgraded. Russian society was clearly sympathetic to this. When the Bolsheviks took up the problem, Kollontai participated in framing the new laws. The main author of the decrees, however, was A. G. Goikhbarg, a former Menshevik law professor who served as a jurist in the Left Socialist Revolutionary Commissariat of Justice in 1917. In a pre-war lecture on family law, Goikhbarg had lamented the inferior position of women as reflected in the tsarist code and had proclaimed the need to restore to the wife her own personality. Thus the new Soviet laws, incorporating views of the Bolshevik Kollontai and the Menshevik Goikhbarg, and promulgated under the auspices of the Left Socialist Revolutionary Commissar, Steinberg, seems to have been an accurate reflection of the sentiments of the Russian left on matrimonial matters.[9]

The decree of December 20, 1917, later amplified in the Family Code of 1918, broke new ground in a number of ways. By exclusively recognizing unions recorded in the Civil Registry Office (whose Russian initials are ZAGS), it tore from the Church its historic monopolistic right to sanctify matrimony. Henceforth, church ceremonies were optional but devoid of legal force (except for those held prior to the law). By invalidating the old code with its language of dominance and submission, by allowing spouses to choose either name or a combination of the two as their marital surnames, and (via a commentary) by forbidding either spouse to interfere in the other's business, friends, correspondence, and even residence, it enshrined in law an idea of sex equality in marriage first advanced six decades earlier. Other features of the law were not so revolutionary: the age of consent, the prohibition of bigamy and consanguine marriages, the requirement of free consent, and the provisions for separate property of the spouses were all adapted—with minor changes—from the old tsarist code. Even the right of a wife to mobility, occupation, and separate quarters dated from late tsarist Duma legislation. As a whole, the new code was a reasonable, progressive synthesis of old laws and old ideals and was, as Goikhbarg announced triumphantly, "almost completely free of male egoism," establishing marital relations wherein "the spouses do not lose or lessen their own identity as free and equal and independent personalities."[10]

The wedding ceremony at the ZAGS office—lasting about twenty minutes—emphasized simplicity, privacy, and a low level of civic importance. The speed of the ceremony also reflected its revolutionary origins; even

[9] Kollontai's role: Itkina, *Kollontai*, 92. Goikhbarg: his *Novoe semeinoe pravo* (Moscow, 1918) 40–41 and his *Brachnoe, semeinoe i opekunskoe pravo Sovetskoi Respubliki* (Moscow, 1920) 7–16; *BSE*, XVII (1930); V. Bonch-Bruevich, *Na boevykh postakh* (Moscow, 1930) 165–66; Lawton, *Russian Revolution*, 223.

[10] The decree is in *Sobranie uzakonenii i rasporyazhenii Rabochego i Krestyanskogo Pravitelstva*, 2d ed. (Moscow, 1919), No. 11, art. 60, 161–63. Commentary in Goikhbarg, *Novoe* (quotation, 51) and *Brachnoe* (quotation, 151).

Sorokin had wed between political meetings during the hectic days of the Provisional Government. In the 1920's, the Komsomol and Zhenotdel made a lukewarm effort to promote the so-called Red Wedding—a more elaborate and festive procedure held in a factory or civic building complete with red bunting, crowds of co-workers, and vows dealing more with social goals than with binding mutual fealty. The novelist Brykin reproduces such a vow in *Dog's Wedding* (1925). "Do you promise," asks the officiator, "to follow the path of Communism as bravely as you are now opposing the church and the old people's customs? Are you going to make your children serve as Young Pioneers, educate them, introduce scientific farming methods, and fight for the world revolution? then in the name of our leader, Comrade Vladimir Ilych Lenin, I declare the Red Marriage completed." But, except among Komsomols, the Red Wedding failed to catch on and the ZAGS procedure remained the norm for decades. Couples were still free to supplement this with a church service if they chose to, but this practice also declined through the years.[11]

Data about "good" communist marriages are rather hard to find. But there are sufficient indications that for many women, the old dream of Vera Pavlovna and of Kollontai about a "room of one's own" became a reality with the Revolution. As with revolutionary couples before 1917, this was not always by choice but by the force of circumstances (educational plans, jobs, housing shortages), with couples living across town from each other or—for more than a few—with one in Moscow and the other in Tashkent or Khabarovsk. Some women preferred this arrangement. A worker interviewed by Ella Winter wanted her own room, name, job, and freedom; when her husband objected, she left him. Another explained her motivation. "I won't have Jura live with me in my room," she said. "I've only one room, and I don't want to wash and cook and darn for him. Of course, I don't mind if he comes in the evening and washes up his plate and cup; but I don't want him to be there always. I want it to be a fresh conquest each time." Couples who did live together sometimes shared the housework. "When I go home," said an exceptional communist husband, "I'm not afraid of women's work. I do the dishes and clean the floor." One idealistic pair even arranged their marital life on the basis of Scientific Organization of Labor—the American born time-motion efficiency system then popular in Soviet industrial circles.[12]

There is more information about strained marriages. Of the traditional "causes," male drinking and infidelity led the lot. A 1929 opinion sample showed that 53 percent of unhappy marriages were traceable to vodka. According to a foreign observer, housewives of Leningrad's Red Putilov district asked the Party to deduct for them a portion of their husbands' wages so that

[11] Sorokin, *Leaves*, 52. On Red Weddings, see: Pierre, *Les Femmes*, 58; *Zhen. v rev.*, 276; Smith, *Woman*, 93. The Brykin passage is from Gasiorowska, *Women*, 24.
[12] Kollontai, *Polozhenie*, 190; Winter, *Red Virtue*, 130, 136 (quotation), 148; *Zhizn*, 77 (quotation), 80.

they would not drink it all up; and a Komsomol woman admitted that she had to buy her husband a bottle every payday in order to keep him home. Extra-marital sex, particularly among men, seems to have increased since the Revolution. Statistics were offered showing that husbands who had begun their sex lives early were likely to continue their promiscuous mode of life after marriage. This was hardly a revelation: Tolstoy had lamented the perfectly obvious phenomenon a generation before in *Kreutzer Sonata*. What made it serious was the fact that the age of initial sex contact had dropped sharply since the Revolution.[13]

Of greater interest were those connubial problems directly traceable to the emancipation of women. The sociologist Volfson spoke of marital "scissors" crises wherein the husband was more politically developed than his wife—though this was really an old problem in a new setting. More serious was the reverse situation or even that in which the wife merely sought civic equality with her husband. Kollontai tells of a man who complained because his wife, a "new woman," neglected home and children for the sake of public activity; and of another so enraged by his spouse's Zhenotdel work that he burned her official files. A host of complaints were registered by husbands at the Vyborg District conference on morality. "Why did I get married?" asked one, because he returned home only to find his dinner not ready. Others, when asked what kind of marriage they wanted, replied: "where the wife prepares everything"; or that "the wife must be less developed than the husband." For too many men, lamented the organizers of the poll, "a clean pair of socks is higher than the spiritual growth of one's wife." When wives resisted this attitude, they were often beaten or forced to give up their social work.[14]

But there were also cases of successful resistance. Before the Revolution, the Bolsheviks had made efforts to defend working women from abuse and wife-beating. This work was continued with greater élan and consistency by Zhenotdel, which acted as legal aid in court cases involving domestic disputes. "A guy can't even beat his woman, nor make her work—not even argue with her," sighed a character from Kochin's *The Gals* (1929) "They've made up special laws for women in Moscow." For some wives, these "special laws"—in reality only the operating code of Zhenotdel—were seen as their greatest gain from the Revolution. "We're not afraid anymore," said one of them. "That's the main thing. We're not afraid of our husbands. We don't have to ask permission for everything we do."[15]

[13] *Ibid.*, 17, 43, 73–74; Serge, "Vignettes," 144; Fridland, *S raznykh storon*, 169. For the role of alcohol in a "backward" workers' family, see E. O. Kabo, *Ocherki rabochego byta*, I (Moscow, 1928) 29–34.
[14] Volfson, *Sotsiologiya*, 393–94; Kollontai, *Rab. i krest.*, 34; *idem*, *Polozhenie*, *passim*; *Zhizn*, 65–66 (quotations), 67, 68, 72, 90, 96.
[15] Pre-revolutionary Party defence of wives mentioned in Shishkin, *Moral*, 271–73. Zhenotdel activities: Schlesinger, citing the 1925 marriage reform debates, in *Family*, 97; Kochin's *Devki* quoted in Gasiorowska, *Woman*, 79. The concluding statement in the paragraph was made by a *delegatka* to Jessica Smith (*Woman*, 39).

In the villages the revolt in matrimony blended with old traditions of *baba* intransigence. The first rebellious peasant woman in Soviet fiction is Neverov's "Mariya Bolshevichka" (1912), a formerly submissive wife who learns to read, becomes active in Zhenotdel politics, and revolts against her husband. Village studies of the 1920's tell of generational struggles, fragmentation of families, and insurrections of wives and daughters. "Now that we have Soviet Power/My husband I don't fear," ran the lyric of a popular village song. Jessica Smith heard of instances of peasant women beating their husbands and of the latter running to Zhenotdel to complain of mistreatment. The most famous gesture of organized wifely resistance to brutish husbands was a sexual strike in Bryansk Province in the mid-1920's. In a lively blend of Lysistrata and Mirabeau, the harried women presented the following ultimatum to their husbands. "We agree to work at home and be our husbands' helpers, but demand in return that we shall not be given over to our husbands' wills, that they shall not be so free with their hands, and call us such names as 'old hag,' 'bitch,' 'slut,' and other unmentionable ones. And this too we add—we shall not disperse, and not return to our husbands until they have all signed their names to this paper."[16]

Unfortunately, in far more cases and in far more serious ways, women were losers in the marital system. It was not the quality of marriage, but the effects of its dissolution or malfunctioning and the resulting victimization of women and children that caused public concern. What generated the greatest dismay were the so-called *besprizorniki*, the orphaned, abandoned, homeless, or generally neglected children. The phenomenon was not a novel outgrowth of the Revolution. Its main features, its locales, its very name were well known to pre-revolutionary Russia. But the ranks of the pre-war *besprizorniki*, were swollen enormously by the ravages of war, social strife, and famine until they reached the figure of 7,000,000 in 1921. By the mid-1920's it was an issue of the first magnitude: gangs of homeless children, vicious and undomesticated, roamed the countryside armed with weapons of the recent wars in search of loot; others infested squalid city slums like Moscow's Khitrovo Market.[17]

Homeless children were the direct victims of the violent upheavals that had shaken the Russian population since 1914. But their numbers were constantly augmented by children abandoned by mothers (or both parents) unable or unwilling to care for them. Neither contraception nor the abortion law had any

[16] Gasiorowska, *Woman*, 35, for a discussion of Neverov's story. Details of village life and female revolt: Volfson, *Sotsiologiya*, 398–401 and Smith, *Woman*, 34, 45–46 (the ultimatum). For other instances, see Astakhova, *Tovarishch Olga*, 127–28, 130.

[17] See *Trudy Pervago Vserossiisskago S" ezda po Borbe s Torgom Zhenshchinami*, II, 612, and *ZhD* (Dec. 15, 1913) 20 and *ibid*. (Dec. 1, 1914) 10–12 on prerevolutionary *besprizorniki*. Specialized and popular Soviet treatments include G. Belykh and L. Panteleev, *Respublika ShKID*, 6th ed. (Moscow,1932); the film *Doroga zhizni*, and the various pedagogical works of A. S. Makarenko. Figures are from Madison, *Social Welfare in the Soviet Union* (Stanford, 1968) 39.

marked effect on the increase of potential *besprizorniki*. Fathers frequently threw their wives out when a child was born and denied both of them support. Mothers who were unable to raise a child often abandoned it or gave it to an orphanage. Many were overcrowded. Since adoption was ruled out by the 1918 Family Code, there was literally no place for thousands of children to go except the streets. In the minds of the jurists and social workers who had to process cases of desertion, non-support, and abandonment, the relationship between marital instability and the growth of the *besprizorniki* was intimate and direct.[18]

To legal reformers, the crux of the matter was the undefined and vulnerable status of the wife in a so-called *de facto* or "unregistered marriage" *(fakticheskii brak)*. Such unions had a respectable pedigree among the revolutionary intelligentsia who often preferred them to church marriages or who required them for conspiratorial purposes. The Code of 1918 made no mention of them; but they were accepted among urban people as having the same moral, if not economic and juridical, validity as those recorded in ZAGS. In spite of the ease of registering a marriage, many people (especially men) preferred no registration at all. Abuse was easy. Although the father of a child was responsible for its support, paternity was harder to prove in an unregistered union and the amount of support was small. Registered wives were also victimized in the early 1920's—partly due to the separate property law—but the impetus of the 1926 marriage reforms was clearly the insufficient legal recognition and protection of the unregistered wife.

The reform party was led by the Commissar of Justice himself, Dmitry Kursky, whose aim was to revise the Family Code of 1918 by extending legal recognition to *de facto* marriages and making them equivalent to registered ones in terms of material consequences. *De facto* spouses were to have the same right of support and property division as legal spouses in the event of separation, so that an employed man could not walk out on a dependent wife and leave her with nothing. In order to encourage registered marriages— which the jurists preferred—divorce was made easier. The draft was presented to the Central Executive Committee of the Soviets in October 1925 and it triggered off a lively debate. Some deputies and President Kalinin thought the issue ought to be debated nationally. This was done; and after a year of widespread public discussion in meetings and in the press, the Committee reassembled to reconsider the draft, modified meanwhile by the Council of People's Commissars. The opinions voiced during these debates are illuminating.[19]

---

[18] General information from: Boris Sokolov, *Spasite detei! (o detyakh Sovetskoi Rossii)* (Prague, 1921), *passim* and especially 67–69, a temperate anti-Soviet account written from the point of view of a Socialist Revolutionary; Carr, *Socialism*, 1, 35 (on adoption); *Zhen. v rev.*, 219–25; B. S. Ginzburg, *Sud nad materyu podkinuvshei svoego rebënka* (Moscow, 1924).

[19] Background of the Code and selections from the debates in Schlesinger, *Family*, 81–153, Halle, *Woman*, 116–17, and P. Stuchka, preface to *Brak i semya* (Moscow, 1926).

Kursky repeatedly and unequivocally described the new draft as a device for the "protection of the weaker party," women and children, and claimed that the 1918 laws had in practice worked "against the interests of women." The unregistered marriage was a fact of Russian life, he reminded his listeners (at that time there were about a quarter of a million unregistered spouses); and to deny legal and economic rights to women who were wives in all but name would be a gross injustice. His colleague, Brandenburgsky, answering objections that recognizing *de facto* marriages encouraged moral instability, announced in very unjuridical tones that "the establishment of continuous and stable marriages cannot be made a function of the law." Opinion in the towns, Kursky reported, was overwhelmingly behind the new code, though it is clear from other indications that urban males were far less enthusiastic about it than were urban females.[20]

Opposition by peasant deputies of both sexes was generally directed at immorality in the towns, the growth of desertion, and the high divorce rate; and specifically at the peasant household's financial liability in cases of broken marriages. In the 1922 Land Code, as the price of retaining the traditional economic and juridical solidarity of the peasant family (*dvor*), it had been made responsible for meeting support or alimony payments for any of its legally married members if the individual concerned defaulted. The 1926 Code would apply this liability to unregistered spouses as well. What would happen to farm and household property if any old *baba* came along claiming to be a *de facto* wife? Peasant women deputies conjured up colorful images of cutting up the cow into three parts or otherwise disastrously partitioning family wealth in order to meet such claims. The conservative feelings of the peasant deputies were representative. The Ukraine, a peasant colossus, did not even adopt the Code and retained the distinction between legal and unregistered marriages.[21]

A third point of view was that the 1926 Code did not go far enough in protecting legally unmarried women. According to the draft, a *de facto* marriage had to be established by the authorities on the basis of very specific evidence: cohabitation, a common household, and testimony thereto by witnesses and documents—in short, an open marital face to the outside world. Some thought these criteria should be broadened. Yury Larin reminded everyone that many couples who lived apart on principle or by necessity could not thereby fit the definition of *de facto* married people. A Viatka woman protested the fact that "casual" marriages were not included in the new law and insisted that such unions, when dissolved, were the source of the *besprizorniki* problem. Kol-

[20] Schlesinger, *Family*, 84–87, 114, 119, 126 (Kursky), 104 (Brandenburgsky).

[21] *Idem, Family*, 105–106 (examples of peasant opposition), 121–26 (Kursky's report); Shinn, "Peasant Household," 610–12; G. K. Matveev, *Istoriya semeino-brachnogo zakonodatelstva Ukrainskoi SSR* (Kiev, 1960) 20–40. It was also opposed by some older Communists on the grounds that it would encourage irresponsibility.

lontai, in a series of articles, insisted that all sexual liaisons be given equal legal status and that society be liable for the children which issued from them. A representative of Zhenotdel, apparently voicing a general concern within that body, expressed dissatisfaction with the restrictive definition of *de facto* marriage. This is perhaps the closest thing we have to the pulse of urban working and white collar women—the principal victims of husbandly irresponsibility and desertion. Aside from this complaint however, Zhenotdel officially supported the new laws.[22]

The change in divorce procedure aroused as much interest as the issue of *de facto* marriage. Goikhbarg's 1917 Decree had been designed to abolish the old system whereby, in his words, "people alien to each other were chained together like prisoners to a wheelbarrow." The new procedure was mercifully simple: if by mutual consent, dissolution on the spot; if by a single claimant, by a brief court hearing. No grounds, no contest, no evidence or witnesses, and no bitter, painful recrimination, at least in public. Where children were involved, custody and support were decided individually by the courts. By abolishing the concept of guilt, the humiliating delays, and the publicity, and by allowing release at the behest of either spouse or both, Soviet Russia became the only country in the world with full freedom of divorce; only the Mexican state of Yucatan in the years 1923–1926 could equal it in liberality. The measure won the general approval of the Russian urban intelligentsia, Bolshevik and otherwise, who despised the hypocrisy of tsarist and western bourgeois marriage laws.[23]

When the 1926 Code was being drafted, it was decided to simplify divorce even further. Since *de facto* marriage was now to be endowed with a quasi-legal status, with a beginning (coming to live together), a sexual content (cohabitation), an economic content (joint household), and an economic aftermath (support and division of property), it ought to have a legal termination as well. Thus "registered divorce" was made available to the *de facto* couple. Since the drafters also wished to make registered marriages as attractive to prospective couples as the looser arrangement, henceforth married people (of either persuasion) could part officially at the ZAGS office. If only one spouse wanted the dissolution and the other did not appear at the office, the latter was notified by a printed form—thus the so-called "postcard divorce." When this aspect of the code was questioned, Brandenburgsky had this to say: "If you object to a frequent change of spouse, with what weapons do you propose to fight it? For if today we set down a law with whatever norms you like, whatever rule of divorce you choose, it will not be a new one, it would be very old." The well-known jurist Stuchka endorsed complete freedom of divorce

[22] Schlesinger, *Family*, 131–33, 135–36, 139–40, 143–44; Smith, *Woman*, 105–10, 119. For Kollontai, see 13, Chapter XI/1, n. 13.

[23] Goikhbarg, *Novoe*, 4; *Sob. uzakon.*, No. 10, art. 152, 150–52; J. K. Folsom, *The Family* (New York, 1934) 365 (on Yucatan divorce); Lawton, *Russian Revolution*, 225.

by referring to the just published statement of Lenin on divorce (first made in 1916) without, however, showing any awareness of how ambiguous that statement was.[24]

The new laws were promulgated in January 1927. In comparison with both Roman and Anglo-Saxon legal traditions, the code was truly radical. Western family law was generally designed to penalize extra-marital unions by means of property, inheritance, legitimacy, and even fornication laws. The Soviets, on the contrary recognized them as an established and by no means repugnant fact, and they extended protection to the potential victim of its legal fragility: the wife. The framers were optimistic that alimony would be easy to collect. At the behest of a woman deputy, they added a provision for a division of family property acquired during the marriage. Adoption of parentless children was now made legal. However, as several deputies pointed out, the new code was replete with unclear and ambiguous provisions, thus throwing the work of family adjudication onto untrained ZAGS officials and the courts. By introducing more freedom in personal relations, it also promoted more abuse. When a deputy voiced a hope that the courts would protect women from dandies and good-for-nothings who would exploit its loopholes, angry prophetic female voices shouted from the benches "they'll exploit it whatever happens."[25]

The major problem both before and after the issuance of the Code of 1926 was the multitude of divorces, desertions, betrayals of women—wives or otherwise—and the resulting economic and emotional suffering. The 1917 divorce reform had been followed by a rash of divorces, releasing no doubt hosts of prisoners long incarcerated in impossible marriages. By 1922, the first year of political and economic stabilization, the number of divorces was 122,479, distributed (very roughly) as follows: about 70,000 in the capitals; 30,000 in the other towns; and 20,000 in the villages. But in the years 1924 to 1927, the number of divorces trebled. The effect of the new legislation was graphically illustrated in the figures from Leningrad where the number of divorces jumped from 5,536 in 1926 to 16,006 in 1927. The working class was clearly in the vanguard. In two well-established proletarian quarters of that city (Moskovsky and Narva) there were fifty marriages of one or two days duration and another fifty of one or two weeks in December 1927 alone; in the following year the ratio of divorces to marriages was 4:5! A critic observed that a spouse could now go to work married in the morning and return home divorced. An American correspondent reported a case of a man arrested for marrying and divorcing five times in as many months. Figures from other quarters gave an equally disturbing picture.[26]

[24] Brandenburgsky: Schlesinger, *Family*, 103–104; Stuchka, *Brak*, 20. For Lenin's statement, see Ch VIII/3.

[25] Parts I and II of the code is printed in Schlesinger, *Family*, 154–68; see also 88–89, 96 (quotations), 116, 129 of the debates and Smith, *Woman*, 119.

[26] V. Bystryansky, *Kommunizm, brak, i semya* (Petrograd, 1921) 64–65; Carr, *Socialism*, I,

Even in the early 1920's armies of deserted and destitute women filled the streets of Soviet towns. By the end of the decade the situation was crying for correction. Legalization of *de facto* marriages had failed to make them more stable or the men in them more responsible; conversely it had facilitated irresponsibility among legally married men. A sample of 500 questionnaires about broken homes discussed at the Vyborg District conference showed that 70 percent of such separations were unilaterally initiated by men and only 7 percent by mutual agreement. Of the known causes (some 66 percent), 22 percent were traditional (alcohol and other women), 17 percent friction with in-laws, and 27 percent pregnancy. "If a child comes," young husbands complained, "that's the end of freedom." It was not, alas, the end of freedom to desert. The expected flow of support and alimony did not materialize. Support was hard to come by in practice; husbands were too poor, too sick, too mobile, or too irresponsible. And those men who took excessive advantage of the new dispensation often found themselves forced to share their meager incomes with a number of former spouses. As the sponsors of the Conference forlornly surveyed the moral ruin, they came to the conclusion that it was the result of too much free love—in practice as well as in theory.[27]

The reappearance of prostitution was a painful surprise to Soviet intellectuals—particularly since it was widely believed to have disappeared forever during the Revolution and Civil War. The Provisional Government, though abolishing the much-hated system of inspection and its yellow ticket, had not succeeded in abolishing the practice itself—a fact long predicted by defenders of the system. At about that time, the indignant Sorokin was accosted on the streets of Petrograd by a painted woman who hailed him with the words "Comrade! Let the Proletarians of all countries unite. Come home with me." On the eve of October, John Reed states, "prostitutes in jewels and expensive furs walked up and down, crowded the cafés." Praskovya Kudelli saw "women and girls, hardly more than children, carrying on with painted faces, half-drunk eyes, and cigarettes dangling from their hands." But during the Civil War prostitutes seemed to vanish from the streets of Soviet towns, while bordellos flourished openly in White centers such as Omsk, Rostov, and Vladivostok. The vice did not disappear altogether, as we know from Kollontai and other sources; but it definitely and visibly declined. "When the Bolshevik Revolution took place," wrote a prostitute in the pages of *Pravda*, "our earnings fell off; whether this was due to free marriages or the closing of 'corners' I cannot say." The decline was the result of a number of circum-

---

37; Kollontai, *Polozhenie*, 198; Lawton, *Russian Revolution*, 234; Volfson, *Sotsiologiya*, 410; Fridland, *S raznykh storon*, 131–32; *Zhizn*, 78, 99. The American correspondent was John Gunther: "Russian Children All Have Fathers," *North American Review*, CCXXIX (Jan. 1930) 45–48.

[27] *Zhizn*, 14, 53, 57, 97–98, 101 (quotation), 102; Halle, *Woman*, 278; Lawton, *Russian Revolution*, 237.

stances, later noted by Soviet doctors: a shortage of money, the impressment of some prostitutes into labor service, the flight or concealment of propertied people, and the nationalization or closure of hotels, cafés and other trysting places. Robbed of its requisite ingredients—a medium of exchange, buyers, sellers, and available beds—prostitution went into eclipse.[28]

With the establishment of NEP, the preconditions for prostitution were also reestablished and the trade began to thrive as of old. By 1921, according to Soviet statistics, there were 17,000 prostitutes in Petrograd and 10,000 in Moscow. In the next year the Petrograd figure had climbed to 32,000, grimly signaling the fact that the problem had again reached pre-revolutionary proportions. Bordellos were outlawed, but informal rendezvous managed to spring up. Volfson counted 446 in 8 Belorussian towns and 80 in Omsk. Where these were not handy, transactions were conducted in girls' rooms, courtyards, gardens, and forests; and the unattached "loners" despised before the Revolution by bordello women, now became the dominant type and reappeared in their old haunts: Trubnaya Square and Tverskoy Boulevard in Moscow; the Ligovka and Nevsky in Leningrad. The latter contained casinos, clubs, and hotel bars, frequented by foreigners and "Nepmen" (NEP businessmen), and celebrated in fiction. Drugs, gambling, and cheap vice were their stock in trade. Victor Serge vividly described the bar at the Hotel Europa with its soiled linen, dusty palms, and inscrutable waiters. "Thirty girls," painted and bejeweled, lounge about the Europa bar," he wrote. "Daughters of Ryazan and of the Volga, daughters of famine and revolution, who have only their youth to sell and are too thirsty for life to be among those on the suicide list." The proud capital, in this as in a hundred other ways, had become a twisted parody of its former self.[29]

Who were the Soviet prostitutes? According to Volfson's estimate for Moscow, 43 percent were of peasant origin, 14 percent working class, and 42 percent "former people"—the last group composed of 21 percent bourgeoisie, 14 percent merchant, and 7 percent gentry—a striking indication of how deeply the social overturn had affected Russia's old propertied orders. The remainder tended to be unemployed, currently unmarried, uneducated, nonparty peasants and workers, aged eighteen to twenty-five, with the peasant-worker ratio about 3:1. As of old, railway stations and night lodges served as

[28] Palencia, *Kollontai*, 27. Sorokin, *Leaves*, 33; Reed, *Ten Days*, 41; Kudelli in *Rabotnitsa*, 11 (Oct. 18, 1917) 10–12; Bystryansky, *Kommunizm*, 60 (the prostitute's letter); Fridland, *S raznykh storon*, 146–48; Lawton, *Russian Revolution*, 235; Bronner, *La lutte*, 25.

[29] Figures and locales: *Petrogradskaya Pravda*, 152 (July 11, 1921) and *Pravda*, 190 (Aug. 28, 1921) both cited in Bystryansky, *Kommunizm*, 60; Fridland, *S raznykh storon*, 149, 160, 179; Volfson, 433–40. The Leningrad scene: Charles Sarolea, *Impressions of Soviet Russia*, 3d ed. (London, 1924) 26; N. Gromov, *Pered razsvetom: putevnye ocherki sovremennoi Sovetskoi Rossii* (Berlin, 1927) 11, 23, 25–26, 33; Serge, "Vignettes," 142 (quotation) 144. The locale at the Europa Hotel described here is now occupied by the Sadko Bar and its two restaurants. A tragicomic tour through Leningrad's night spots may be found in V. Kataev's picaresque novel, *The Embezzlers*.

familiar points along the trail of recruiting fresh immigrants from the countryside.[30] Child prostitutes, byproducts of the orphan problem, reappeared in larger proportion that before when they had made up only 2 percent of the total. According to a study of homeless children, some 60 percent to 80 percent of all delinquent girls were prostitutes in 1920; and 88 percent of those who appeared before commissions on minors. By the early 1920's, thousands of children were pouring monthly into the crime-ridden warren of Khitrovo Market where the male children were apprenticed in petty theft and hooliganism and the females learned "the science of the streets."[31] The clients were of two general sorts. The first group were the beneficiaries of NEP—"knights of private capital," officials, and specialists who patronized the "silk stocking" girl and the "Soviet lady" (sovdama), thus refashioning a pre-revolutionary socio-sexual alliance. The second category was no more novel: students and workers who made use of cheaper prostitutes due to a lack of time, money, or energy. An active Komsomol, when queried about his visits to prostitutes, replied: "What do you mean? It's a social evil caused by economic fluctuations. When she invites me, why shouldn't I go? She earns money and I satisfy a need. I'm too busy to bother myself with courting or with love."[32]

There may have been fewer prostitutes per capita in Soviet Russia, as some observers believed, than in any other country of Europe,[33] but the Bolsheviks were frustrated throughout the 1920's in their efforts to reduce their numbers. One reason for this was the differences of attitude toward the prostitute herself: Was she a parasite or a victim? The various police establishments tended to take the former view. They repressed them during the Civil War and later proposed the establishment of a "morals police"—though whether this was meant to be a simple vice squad or the resuscitation of the police-medical inspection system is not clear. At least one doctor (Zalkind) thought prostitutes were of a certain "clitoris type" and thus incurable. But public policy rejected these conservative approaches and took its cue from Lenin who said "return the prostitute to productive work, find her a place in the social economy." Doing this was harder than saying it—as three generations of feminists, social workers, and medical officers had sadly learned.[34]

Because prostitution was linked to venereal disease, the Soviets finally

[30] Data on social composition from: Volfson, *Sotsiologiya*, 438; Halle, *Woman*, 234–35; Gromov, *Pered*, 25–26. Recruitment: Fridland, *S raznykh storon*, 77–90, 110, 139ff; *Zhizn*, 19–20.

[31] Sokolov, *Spasite detei*, 18–56 (*passim*); Fridland, *S raznykh storon*, 126.

[32] Description of clients in Volfson, *Sotsiologiya*, 433 (quoted phrase) and Fridland, *S raznykh storon*, 63–65. The Komsomol's remark in *Zhizn*, 20. Consorting with prostitutes was a ground for dismissal from the Party (Carr, *Socialism*, II, 216).

[33] Lawton said this (*Russian Revolution*, 238); Dillon (*Russia*, 30) noted their low visibility in 1928.

[34] Police policies and attitudes in Bryant, *Mirrors*, 124–26 and Volfson, *Sotsiologiya*, 435. Lenin's words date from 1920 (*Emancipation*, 96).

came to handle it primarily as a medical problem—which is exactly the way all governments had originally become interested in prostitution. The Health Commissariat set up a Central Council for Combating Prostitution. The preventive side of its work consisted chiefly in seeking better employment and educational opportunities for women, launching propaganda campaigns against vice, and—a direct borrowing from old-style philanthropy—meeting incoming peasant women at urban railway stations. The prostitute was to be immune from harassment or mistreatment and was officially viewed as a victim of circumstances. So were the patrons; though this was left unsaid. But pimps and proprietors of informal brothels and houses of assignation were to be given stiff prison sentences. In 1924–1925, over two thousand nests of vice were raided and closed. The main achievement of the Council was a network of prophylacteries combining features of V. D. clinics, workshops, and shelters. In them infected prostitutes were given maintenance, medical treatment, training, and eventually job placement.[35]

These measures, clearly different in spirit from the callous system of tsarist state regulation, doubtless enjoyed some success. But the scope was much too small to care for the problem in a meaningful way. Prophylacteries were woefully few in number; local councils were sluggish; and budgets were so tiny that Dr. Fridland likened the entire effort to "scooping out the sea," a favorite metaphor of pre-revolutionary socialists for philanthropy. Furthermore, the hostels and prophylacteries often evoked scorn and hostility from the inmates. "Let me go so that I can be free to live as I like and walk the streets," said one of them; "Who needs your sewing machines?"[36] A painful historical slap in the face of the revered Chernyshevsky by the realities of Soviet society. The Bolsheviks, heirs of an intelligentsia that for three generations had ridiculed charitable approaches to prostitution and had devised fictional utopias and *artels* as the right solution, now found that even their own state-sponsored synthesis of these two traditions would not suffice to liquidate a searing social cancer, without removing the deeper causes: female unemployment, abandonment of children, desertion of wives, poverty, housing shortage, overcrowded cities, and the presence in the midst of social squalor of men with money and women without it.

"A curious fact: in every great revolutionary movement the problem of 'free love' comes to the fore. For some it is a matter of revolutionary progress, liberation from old bonds of tradition; for others, an eagerly accepted teaching, conveniently covering every sort of free and easy relation between man and woman."[37] These words of Engels and his implied attitude toward his second category summarize a recurrent tendency of European social revolu-

---

[35] Halle, *Woman*, 223–67.

[36] Fridland, *S raznykh storon*, 56–61 (quotation 60–61), 92, 105; Volfson, *Sotsiologiya*, 438.

[37] The passage from Engels is in *O zhen vop.*, 129.

tions to unleash three kinds of forces: a genuine and healthy emancipation of certain previously locked up human energies; an excessive compulsion to transcend this level of emancipation and to reach toward utopian or anarchic extremes, and a countervailing force, frequently called "Thermidor," which draws its sustenance from pre-revolutionary social textures, which springs up initially to combat the excesses, but which transforms its defensive nature into an offensive against the emancipation itself. In the Russian Revolution, Kollontai, Zhenotdel, the bulk of urban women, and a large number of male Bolsheviks understood "free love" as a matter of Engels' "revolutionary progress." But by a large number of men—students, workers, young Bolsheviks—the "eagerly accepted teaching" was used to justify and defend base and selfish forms of sexual satisfaction.

There is no denying the impact that doctrine had upon sexual behavior in these early years of experimentation. "The Communist theory has outstripped our actual everyday life by ten years and in some respects by a century," wrote Trotsky as early as 1923. The theories, incapable of being correctly applied in the midst of poverty and disruption, were distorted and misapplied. "No one in his senses would pretend that the Bolshevik leaders encourage immorality," observed Lancelot Lawton the following year; "but so daring are the teachings of many of their disciples that when they are misunderstood very sad results ensue."[38]

The historian E. H. Carr, on the other hand, denies the importance of theory. Carr believes that the moral disorder and disruption were largely the fruits of war and revolution, and that they were "retrospectively justified in terms of socialist doctrine."[39] This particular judgment of Carr does not stand up well to historical scrutiny, especially since the works of Kollontai that he cites as "socialist doctrine" are later editions. The sexual revolution in all the forms it took was well prepared, theoretically and psychologically, by generations of Russian thought and literature, and not "retrospectively justified." Having said this, however, it would be foolish to deny the essential correctness of Carr's verdict on the deeper causes of the sexual upheaval—for it was precisely the atmosphere of heroic desperation in the violent years that gave impetus to the adventurous style of love and sex; and precisely the sudden termination of a violence seen as creative and grand that ushered in an epoch wherein Engels' "liberation from old bonds of tradition" were perverted into the vilest forms of sexual activity and thought.

But what of the Thermidorian impulse to lump teachings and excesses together and to combat them both? Maurice Hindus, an astute foreign commentator on Soviet everyday life, speculated on this problem at a particularly crucial moment in Russian history—1929. If, he mused, the sexual revolution

---

[38] Trotsky, *Problems of Life*, tr. Z. Vengerov (London, 1924) 25; Lawton, *Russian Revolution*, 230.

[39] Carr, *Socialism*, I, 31.

would lead to less promiscuity—that is, if "under the Russian condition of liberty, libertinism will diminish"—the result would be a new and higher form of monogamy and morality. If, however, it tended toward greater polygamy in both sexes, "then no doubt the Russians will curb personal liberty in matters of sex" and would introduce greater "discipline," "social censure," and ever increasing "external compulsion."[40] This is precisely what happened; but the elements of a Thermidorian reaction were clearly on display long before Hindus predicted its emergence.

3. THE SEXUAL THERMIDOR

Accounts of Soviet history mentioning the sexual revolution at all usually convey the impression that its "Thermidor" or reaction set in rather suddenly (in the mid-1930's), that it was a purely Stalinist reversal, that it was imposed against the will of the people, and that therefore it was a strictly negative phenomenon. All of these assumptions need to be qualified. The Thermidorian mood was born with the Revolution and was given voice as early as 1920 by the leader of the Revolution himself. Lenin's view, rooted deeply in the traditions of the revolutionary intelligentsia, found sympathetic vibrations among a large number of influential followers all through the 1920's and into the 1930's. Stalin, though he added his usual dose of harshness and firmness to the solution that he inaugurated, was also acting with the staunch approval of a wide circle of the Bolshevik intelligentsia of both sexes. Furthermore, although his measures may have cast a pall over the sexual energies and experimental tendencies of many people, they also helped stem the tide of sexual abuse and exploitation that had been raging in Russian society from the early days of Soviet power.

Lenin first spoke out against the excesses of the sexual revolution in an oft-quoted interview with Clara Zetkin in 1920.[1] Though not published until five years later—at which time it was warmly welcomed by sexual conservatives—his remarks were made just at the end of the Civil War and three years before Kollontai's Zhenya made her notorious apologia for sexual freedom in "Love of Three Generations," a work that Lenin apparently never read and certainly never commented on. Lenin leveled his criticism specifically at the loose sexual behavior of the Civil War years—the same "wingless Eros" that had distressed Kollontai. Though vague and ambiguous in places, Lenin's thoughts, the first on sex since his wartime letters to Inessa Armand, display a generally negative attitude toward "abnormal" and "excessive sex life," and a frankly hostile view of "preoccupation" with the sex question,

[40] M. Hindus, *Humanity Uprooted* (New York, 1929) 100.
[1] A convenient English edition is Zetkin, *Lenin on the Woman Question* (New York, 1934). The interview has been reprinted and translated for many anthologies (see the titles cited in Chapter VIII/3 n. 2). In view of its brevity, each quotation has not been cited.

even for purposes of discussion. "I mistrust those who are always contemplating the sexual question, like the Indian saint his navel," he told Zetkin, confessing also that "rooting about in all that bears on sex" was repugnant to him. He characterized the current attitude of youth toward sex as a "disease of modernity." "Promiscuity in sex matters is bourgeois," he announced. "It is a sign of degeneration." And, foreshadowing a dominant theme of the coming debate, warned that it "wasted health and strength" of the young.

The main thrust of Lenin's assault, however, was against the theoretical justification of such behavior by the so-called glass-of-water theory of sexual relations. "You must be aware of the famous theory," he said to Zetkin, "that in communist society the satisfaction of sexual desires, of love, will be as simple and unimportant as drinking a glass of water. This glass of water theory has made our young people mad, quite mad. It has proved fatal to many young boys and girls. Its adherents maintain that it is Marxist." Since Lenin did not indicate a source for this "famous theory," and since it has been frequently and erroneously traced to Kollontai, some clarification is in order. Though no specific enunciation of it anywhere except in the Lenin interview has been found, its central idea is a familiar feature in Russian musings on the meaning of sex and love, as exemplified both in the physiological notions of Gieroglifov during the high tide of nihilism and in the various analogies of sexual pleasure to tasting, devouring, having dinner, savoring cherries, drinking, breathing and the like in the decadent fiction of 1905–1914 (see Ch. VI/2). Nor was the specific image of slaking thirst a novel thing in utopian speculations about sexual rights. "I have no right to the ownership of the fountain that lies in my path," wrote the Marquis de Sade as early as 1795; "but I certainly have the right to make use of it; I have the right to enjoy the limpid water offered up to my thirst; in the same way I have no actual claim to the possession of such and such a woman, but I have an incontestable one to the enjoyment of her."[2] And Bebel wrote in the immensely popular *Woman and Socialism* that "of all the natural demands of man, sex—after eating and drinking—is the strongest."[3] It seems probable that the glass-of-water theory was no theory at all, and certainly not a new one; but rather a vulgarized slogan drawn from Bebel or from indigenous traditions and perhaps voiced at one time or another in the unfortunate form to which Lenin so indignantly objected.

"I think this glass of water theory is completely un-Marxist," complained Lenin. "Of course, thirst must be satisfied. But will the normal man in normal circumstances lie down in the gutter and drink out of a puddle, or out of a glass with a rim greasy from many lips? But the social aspect is most important of all. Drinking water is of course an individual affair. But in love two lives are concerned, and a third, a new life arises. It is that which gives it its

[2] Marquis de Sade, *Bedroom Discourses* (1795) cited in Manuel, *French Utopias*, 228, n. 4.
[3] Bebel, *Zhenshchina*, 142. Echoed by Kollontai in *Kommunistka* 12-13 (May-June 1921) 31.

social interest, which gives rise to a duty towards the community."[4] Lenin did not trace the pedigree of the idea, but he did make ironic references to the days of the "emancipation of the heart" and "emancipation of the flesh"— that is to George Sand and Enfantin—and added that the teaching then was "more talented than it is today." This and the previously quoted comment about distrusting "women whose love affair is intertwined with politics" are the only hints that he may have been aiming his shafts of disapproval at Kollontai (whom he never mentions). In any case, he left no doubt that, wherever the idea of communist promiscuity came from, and whoever was preaching it, "there is no place for it in the party, the class conscious fighting proletariat."

Lenin conceded that the revolutionary upheaval had caused young men, and women to rebel "with all the impetuosity of their years." He agreed further that to foster "monkish asceticism and the sanctity of dirty bourgeois morality" would be incorrect. How then avert the danger of sexual wildness among the young? How conserve the vast energies which were being squandered in unchecked sexual gratification? The answer of course was to divert those energies elsewhere—for self-perfection and for the Revolution. "Young people, particularly," he said, "need the joy and force of life. Healthy sport, swimming, racing, walking, bodily exercises of every kind, and many-sided intellectual interests." Here is the direct inspiration of the other famous theory: revolutionary sublimation. But Lenin planted no specific guideposts for the sexual behavior of men and women. Elsewhere in his conversation with Zetkin, he had pleaded for "clarity, clarity, and again clarity" on the sexual issue. But a singular lack of clarity characterized his terse and negative summary of sexual virtue: "Neither monk, nor Don Juan, nor the intermediate attitude of the German philistines."

Lenin also attacked "the decay, putrescence, and filth of bourgeois marriage with its difficult dissolution, its licence for the husband and bondage for the wife, and its disgustingly false sex morality and relations." But he said very little about the tenure of marriage or the frequency of divorce, confining himself chiefly to abusive comments on husbands who did not share household duties with the wife. "Very few husbands," he observed, "not even the proletarians, think of how much they could lighten the burden and worries of their wives or relieve them entirely, if they lent a hand in this 'woman's work'." As a result, "the domestic life of the woman is a daily sacrifice of self to a thousand insignificant trifles." Lenin's acid comments on individual housework, though repetitive and uttered mostly within a two-year period, are legion. "Petty housework," he said in 1919, "crushes, strangles, stultifies and degrades [the wife], chains her to the kitchen and the nursery, and she wastes her labour on barbarously unproductive, petty, nerve-racking, stultifying and crushing drudgery."[5] Lenin's solution to this, according to David

---

[4] See the almost identical remark by a socialist woman doctor, A. Omelchenko in *Svobodnaya lyubov i semya* (SPB, 1908) 25.

[5] Lenin, *Emancipation*, 61. For other examples, see 25, 67, 79, 81, 110.

Ryazanov, was drawn from Kautsky's 1903 work on the agrarian question. It was, briefly, "to shift the functions of house-keeping and education from the individual household to society," by means of collective kitchens, dining rooms, laundries, repair shops, crèches, kindergartens, and other pre-school facilities. But, as Ryazanov also observed, the disappearance of domestic repetitiveness did not mean to Lenin the disappearance of individual households and families.[6]

In the context of the Soviet sexual arena, Lenin appears to be a conservative. But he was no prude in the Western sense of that word. His troubled view of sexual dissoluteness not only was shared by a wide circle of Bolsheviks but also was deeply rooted in European socialist culture. From the moment of the first great sexual debate in the history of socialism between Enfantin and Bazard in 1831, that movement had advanced two views toward the impossibly difficult question of man-woman relations: that of Enfantin ranging toward more freedom and mobility in these relations; and that of Bazard who, like Lenin, preferred monogamy, constancy, voluntary and equal union, long marriages, and rarity rather than frequency of divorce. It is worth recalling that the two foremost representatives of the early Russian intelligentsia, Herzen and Belinsky, entered the debate with denunciations of Enfantin and George Sand respectively, though later modifying their views. Mikhailov, the pioneer of the woman question, advocated freedom of love while simultaneously proclaiming monogamy as the ideal relationship. Chernyshevsky did so as well in dramatic, if less precise terms. Among the German Marxists, standards of sexual morality were even more conventional. One must agree that Lenin in thought and (unless one accepts the theory that Lenin and Inessa were lovers) in life belonged to this latter tradition which—whatever label one might attach to it—relied far more upon personal restraint and conscience than upon categorical affirmations of personal liberty.

Lenin's views, published in 1925, afforded a basis for writers and officials critical not only of "life without control" but of Kollontai's "new morality" as well. But the voice of the sexual Thermidor began to make itself heard much earlier if only in a sporadic and general way. In tones redolent of the anti-Saninist sentiments of the past, Bystryansky in 1921 characterized the sexual effervescence as "the poisonous miasma of capitalism" that "continues to infect the social atmosphere." "Free love," lamented a Zhenotdel journalist, "is being interpreted by the best people as free vice." Bukharin, though an articulate and acerbic foe of the traditional family, secured a Komsomol resolution in 1922 condemning sexual immorality, and later launched an assault upon the "vulgar materialism" of the purely physical sex theories.[7] By 1923, the reaction had found a focus in Kollontai whose "Eros" articles

[6] Ryazanov, "Marks i Engels," 32.
[7] Bystryansky, *Kommunizm*, 59, 62. For Bukharin: Carr, *Socialism*, I, 30, 32 and Volfson, *Sotsiologiya*, 422.

and stories, her well-known romances, and her recent political demise made her the favorite target of the sexual right. Kollontai herself admitted that her "views were bitterly fought by many Party comrades of both sexes," even while she was abroad. The publication of her works met some resistance and, according to her long-time friend Maurice Body, a series of articles, appearing under the initials A.M.K. (but not written by her) advanced the most extreme notions of sexual behavior. She was reprimanded by the Party and only after an interview with Stalin did the false articles cease. But the attacks against her ideas had only begun.[8]

The most serious of them was written in the fall of 1923 by Polina Vinogradskaya, a former colleague of Kollontai in Zhenotdel. In her recently published memoirs, Vinogradskaya claims that both she and Krupskaya were appalled by the ideas Kollontai expressed at the meetings of the editorial board of *Kommunistka*, which included these three women and Inessa Armand. After the appearance of the "Eros" articles, Vinogradskaya decided to reply in print and, she says, her work was read and approved in advance by Krupskaya. In it, she called Kollontai "a twentieth-century George Sand" and "the Verbitskaya [a pre-revolutionary 'erotic' novelist] of our communist journalism," and called her ideas a concoction of feminism and communism. Vinogradskaya's article never rose above this level of criticism. The main fault of Kollontai, she wrote, was her over-concern with Eros and "the cult of love" and her lack of concern with "genuine problems": divorce, desertion, and abortion. Vinogradskaya simply overlooked the fact that Kollontai had in fact addressed herself to all of these problems in great detail. The critic advanced no specific alternatives of her own as guidance in the ways of love and sex, preferring instead to dwell upon the sexual anarchy that, she said, raged behind the façade of "ideal motifs of the communist program"—implying that Kollontai had composed or endorsed these "motifs." Vinogradskaya's remarks on Kollontai initiated the myth that most students of these years have taken as simple fact—that Kollontai's ideas contained the nucleus of the "biological" sexual theories of the time and thus caused the excesses which flowed from them.[9]

Recognizing the futility of mere criticism of Kollontai, of her "Zhenya," and of the glass-of-water (often co-mingled indiscriminately), writers began to construct an alternate philosophy of sexual life. "After long consideration," wrote a communist youth in 1922, "I have concluded that energy used in the satisfaction of the sexual appetite can be directed elsewhere and expended on more useful concerns." This idea was elaborated into a full theory of "revolutionary" sublimation by a circle of doctors led by Aron Borisovich

[8] Kollontai, *Autobiography*, 43; Marcel Body, "Alexandra Kollontai," *Preuves*, II, 14 (April 1952) 14. Though there is no reason to doubt Body on this score, *Pravda* for the time in question was checked and the "A.M.K." entries could not be found.

[9] Vinogradskaya, *Pamyatnye vstrechi*, 53 and her "Voprosy morali" cited fully in Chapter XI, 2, p. 361, n. 5 (quotations, 213, 186, 214).

Zalkind, the Bolshevik Freudian founder of the Society of Marxist Psychoneurologists. Zalkind accused contemporary sexual culture of stealing energy from work and love from the collective, and he accused Kollontai and others of placing false emphasis upon sex. "The collective, the purely revolutionary, is obscured when 'love' is too much in the ascendant." This directly contradicted Kollontai's belief that love, though varying in kind, existed in unlimited stores and indeed was brought to fulfillment within the context of the working commune. To Zalkind, love and sex, being functions of "the economy of class energy," resembled fixed capital which had to be invested in "class"-oriented pursuits and not squandered outside them. From this piquant position, Zalkind moved easily into traditional ideas of sex-conservation: sex should be prevented from premature development; once present, it should be used for its "main role"—the reproduction of children. Energy thus saved was to be harnessed to the revolution.[10]

The ideas of Zalkind, who perhaps aspired to become the Moses of the Soviet sexual wilderness, came to be known as "Zalkind's Twelve Commandments." His code forbade sexual experience before marriage at age twenty or twenty-five. Citing Tolstoy's *Kreutzer Sonata*, the commandments prohibited sex outside love and marriage. "Purely physical sexual desire is impermissible from the revolutionary-proletarian viewpoint." And sexual attraction to a class enemy was described as a depravity equal to the attraction between a crocodile and an orangutang. Even in marriage, the sex act should not be enjoyed too frequently and never with "perversions." Monogamy, said Zalkind, was the only state natural to a woman: Kollontai's Zhenya was a nymphomaniac. Parents should always be ready to support their children because the state could not. The last commandment was an ominous rejection of Bebel and the school of privacy: The class had the right to intervene in the sex life of its members.[11]

Even that progressive obeisance to liberalism, the insistence on complete equality in the marriage, is absent from Zalkind's ponderous clauses. The only sop to modernity is the banishment of jealousy from the bosom of the family; but the family portrayed and idealized by Zalkind consists of two semi-virgins who fight lust as ardently as they struggle against dirtiness, tardiness, and inefficiency in everyday life. Even as Zalkind wrote, similar ideas were in the air. "The sex instinct is restrained," said the principal of a Moscow school about the love life of his pupils; "and, in conformity with the well-known Freudian law, it is 'sublimated' by the social and political instinct." And in the wake of the twelve commandments, some Komsomol puri-

[10] The youth's remark is quoted by Gelman in *Polovaya zhizn*, 78. On Zalkind see *BSE*, XXVI (1930), 115–16. For the philosophical and psychological bases of his sex theory, see his: *Ocherki kultury revolyutsionnogo vremeni* (Moscow, 1924) 51–56; and his "Polovoi vopros s kommunisticheskoi tochki zreniya," in S. M. Kalmanson, ed., *Polovoi vopros* (Moscow, 1924) 5–16 (quotation, 13), a collection of conservative views.
[11] Zalkind, *Revolyutsiya i molodëzh* (Moscow, 1925) 77–90 for the "twelve commandments."

tans of Perm sent out teams at night to catch couples petting, throw bags over them, and bring them before the authorities.[12]

The deepest reservoir of hostility to sexual irregularity was the Russian villages where, for rural women, the everyday economic facts of life loomed greater than speculations on independence, modernity, and equality. "Marriage," said the lawyer Krasikov, voicing the peasant outlook in the 1926 debates, "in so far as it creates a family and a working union, demands that its bases be strengthened, that it be publicized, so that everyone should know that two given people are a married couple." Philandering had no place in village life, explained a woman deputy; women should unite in refusing the attentions of country Romeos. Divorce was worse, she said, allowable perhaps after a year of incompatibility—but after twenty years and five children? Another peasant woman summed it up this way. "Yes, it's all very well to talk about divorce but how could I feed my children? Two's better than one when it comes to that. Alimenta? Yes, I know about that—but what good would that do me when I know my husband has nothing in his pocket to pay me. And if my husband goes away, or if I get land somewhere else, how can I work the land alone? Together we can manage somehow." A similar expression of dependence and partnership was given voice in A. Yakovlev's *The Lot of a Peasant Woman* (1926): "A peasant family is like a cart: once you're harnessed, you've got to pull it for all you are worth, and no kicking either! It's not like in factory life here; we've got the land to consider."[13]

By the time of the new marriage code, high Party figures were alert to the issue and its main outlines, though not always sensitive to its nuances. The old Bolshevik, Lyadov, for example, rector of the Communist Academy, announced to students that Kollontai's Eros theory of love was simply an apologia for egoistic desire, though he admitted ironically that he did not know whether she had exalted "winged" or "wingless" Eros. Ryazanov, the eminent Marxist scholar, was fairer to Kollontai, but his comments left no doubt where he stood on the questions raised by her. "We should teach our young Komsomols that marriage is not a personal act," he pleaded in a speech opposing the new code, "but an act of deep social significance, demanding interference and regulation by Society."[14] Ironically, it was Commissar of Education Lunacharsky—a connoisseur of ballerinas—who launched the strongest statement about monogamy in these years. Speaking of the need to restore the demographic levels of 1913, he insisted that the state could not care for the new children because it could not even handle the hundreds of thousands of current homeless children. Nor could mothers without the constant help of husbands. "In our society," he wrote, "the only correct form of

[12] Sarolea, *Impressions*, 98; Smith, *Woman*, 131.

[13] Quotations: Schlesinger, *Family*, 95, 109; Smith, *Woman*, 31–32; Gasiorowska, *Women*, 28. See also Volfson, *Sotsiologiya*, 403–408 and Tchernavina, *We Soviet Women*, 167.

[14] M. N. Lyadov, *Voprosy byta* (Moscow, 1925) 16–18, 34–36; Ryazanov, "Marks i Engels"; his and Brandenburgsky's words quoted in Smith, *Woman*, 92, 116–17.

the family is the long-lasting paired family." Such a union, he continued, "in the name of a life in common, bearing and bringing up children, is the only form we need. And he who wishes to fulfill completely his obligation— political, labor, and human—must establish just such a family." Divorce should be an exceptional occurrence to be resorted to once or twice at most. He who abused it, he warned, was nothing more than a "counter-revolutionary of everyday life."[15]

The Komsomol leadership, no doubt because its rank-and-file was so often singled out in the criticism of loose behavior, took special pains to dissociate itself from it. Two Komsomol writers joined the campaign against "abnormality" in sex life, the "winged Eros," irresponsibility, cynicism, and promiscuity with an argument foreshadowing things to come. "Soviet society," they wrote, "needs technicians and engineers to build socialist industry; it needs good and well-trained cooperative workers, teachers to eradicate illiteracy and ignorance, social workers; it needs change to push the revolution along towards socialism. Can we build all this if youth—the trained reserve of socialism—allows much of its attention to be distracted by the problems of love, marriage, and the like?"[16] The Vyborg District conference of 1929 flung about anguished pre-revolutionary clichés about "accursed questions" and "Oblomovism," and concluded that life, now "out of control," would have to be placed back within the bounds of social regulation. "The 'free love' which many young men and women are inclined to praise often transforms itself into free depravity," the sponsors concluded. "The person who is physically and spiritually healthy, who is building a new life and desires a full-blooded and interesting one—both social and personal—has no time for sordid little affairs."[17]

By 1929 fanfares of indignant protest were blaring through the halls of the Communist Academy, the commissariats, and the universities. When Wilhelm Reich visited Russia that year, he discovered what he called " 'bourgeois' moralistic attitudes" among health and social officials. The most articulate voice of conservatism was the former director of Zhenotdel, Smidovich. "Every little *Komssomolka*, . . ." she complained, "every *rabfakovka* [female student in Labor Faculty courses] or other woman student upon whom falls the choice of this fellow or that, of the male—whence such African passions have developed among us in the north, I cannot judge—must comply with his wishes, otherwise she is 'petty bourgeois!' " Her article, Reich tells us, was displayed on German bulletin boards by the Communist Party of Germany as an example of official Party morality. On another occasion, Smidovich offered a glowing tribute to revolutionary love which she contrasted to the current vogue of "revolutionary" sex. "Of course," she said, "we older Communists believe that it is best to love one person and stick

[15] A. Lunacharsky, *O byte* (Moscow, 1927) 21–22, 37.
[16] Grigorov and Shkotov, *Staryi i novyi byt*, 157.
[17] *Zhizn*, esp. 5–59 (quotation, 58).

to him. It is harder for us than for other people to change around, because the ties we have are stronger. . . . It is no light thing to break up a union that is based on a life-time of struggle together for a common aim. What we seek first is a comrade—one whose thoughts and feelings we can share. If that feeling of mutual love goes, the marriage relation of course must stop."[18]

On the eve of industrialization, the public mood vis-à-vis the sexual revolution was one of troubled concern, but not of unanimous agreement as to the means of correcting the obvious abuses. Women, by way of opinion polls, were increasingly demonstrating their clear preference for love over simple physiology, for long relations over short ones, for one man over a series of lovers, and for marriage over all else; while men by their behavior continued to demonstrate their preference for the opposites. Official opinion sided with the women, but laid down no precise guidelines for improving the situation. There were outraged voices like that of Dr. Fridland who insisted that men who exploited women be put behind bars; but there were others, like Bukharin, who believed that Party interference in family matters was "petty bourgeois." Commentators saw moral anarchy on every side, but their suggestions for improvement were conventional pieties: sex education, physical culture, youth clubs, and a wholesome moral atmosphere at home. Soviet society, though noticeably perturbed, was apparently not yet prepared to give up the sexual and marital freedom it had won in the Revolution. The uneasy balance was neatly illustrated in a *Pravda* article of June 23, 1928 that called for a struggle on two fronts: against the unrestricted polygamy and free love of the "Mohammedans" and against the puritanical monogamy of the "Catholics."[19]

In view of influential public opinion on sexual intemperance and all that went with it, it is not surprising that the authorities eventually did something about it. The surprise is rather in the moderate and oblique legal form which the reaction initially took: a law abolishing free abortion and a mild tightening of divorce procedure. This has led some observers to the somewhat cynical conclusion that the regime was interested solely in high birth-rates and not in "morality" as such. But demographic considerations alone do not account for the vitriolic press campaign against irresponsible sexuality that preceded and accompanied the laws or for the theoretical re-definition of the family which endowed them with ideological legitimacy. During the early 1930's, opinion on sex, marriage, and the family crystallized among the leadership of the

[18] Wilhelm Reich's observations in *The Sexual Revolution* (1935), 4th ed. (New York, 1969) 186, 187, 189 and Ilse Ollendorff Reich, *Wilhelm Reich: A Personal Biography* (New York, 1970) 41–42. Smidovich's two quotations: Halle, *Woman*, 115 and Smith, *Woman*, 102–103. For more on Smidovich, see Farnsworth, "Bolshevik Alternatives." For other data on official views, see Z. Tikhonova, *Narodnyi Kommissar Zdorovya (o N. A. Semashke)* (Moscow, 1960).
[19] One of the polls referred to and Fridland's suggestions in his *S raznykh storon*, 134–75. Bukharin and *Pravda* both quoted in Volfson, *Sotsiologiya*, 382. See also *Zhizn*, 61, 105–10.

Party, though exactly how, and under what direct circumstances we cannot know on the basis of available evidence.

The attitude of Stalin—undisputed leader of state and Party—toward women, sex, and the family is of little help. He shared the Georgian male's good-natured contempt for the female sex, and he held a crudely cynical view of women who, like Kollontai, mixed love with revolution. He was coarse, and, in a personal way, deeply anti-feminist. On the other hand, Stalin was a Bolshevik and he shared his party's views of woman as a worker and as a potential equal of man in the productive life of an industrializing country. And he displayed little restraint in treating women as equals in the cruel repressions that he unleashed in the mid-1930's. Stalin was a supremely practical man, and to him women, like other Soviet citizens, were human materials to be fashioned according to his aims: the construction of the industrial base of socialism and an authoritarian political system with himself at its pinnacle. In one of his rare remarks about women and socialism, made in 1923, he said that women could help push industry forward or could impede it; help develop agriculture or impede its growth. She could, if conscious, contribute to the workings of Soviet political life, or, if not, impede its functioning; and could, as a mother, rear good Soviet citizens—or cripple their spirits. This double view of woman—as an active economic and political agent of society and as a mother and nurturer of new communists—remained unchanged and was the basis for Stalin's support of a policy bent upon curbing the sexual energies of a revolutionary generation.[20]

The family in tsarist times had been the basic nucleus of society, a state in miniature with its autocrat, its subjects, and its fundamental law. Divorce, wifely disobedience, and adultery were severely frowned upon—not least because they might have set up models for desertion, mutiny, or treason in the larger society. When the Soviet family exhibited signs of disappearing, those in authority no doubt perceived the crucial role that the family plays in any society as a microcosm of social order. No one has ever hated or fought anarchy as have the Bolsheviks; and anarchy in everyday life was totally incompatible with the discipline and organization needed in an industrial society. Repeated divorces, hordes of uncared for children and betrayed wives, and the lack of a family system frayed at the very fibre of social cohesion and fostered instability and lack of discipline. A firm family foundation, on the other hand, could produce a steady stream of new citizens, thus sustaining if not increasing the birth rate, and provided the shelter in which these children could be reared with minimum state investment. It thus promised an end to the *besprizorniki* problem. It also implied self-discipline and the attachment to a single job, responsibility, and good "bourgeois" life habits; and, perhaps most crucial, it provided a setting wherein men's and women's energy could be directed to production—and away from endless philandering, evading de-

[20] *Women and Communism*, 63–65.

385

serted spouses, or pursuing deserting ones with all the distractions attendant upon these activities. These considerations, together with an undeniably genuine concern over the victimization of women that the 1926 Code had not succeeded in diminishing, form the background of the marriage reform of the mid-1930's.

Abortion and divorce were the two elements of this reform. The decree "On the Protection of Women's Health" issued in November 1920 by the Commissars of Health and of Justice gave notice that its main purpose was to combat illegal abortions by providing safe and legal ones. It was seen as a temporary measure to be obviated in the near future by a massive protection for motherhood. Birth control would have been a more suitable response to the terrible conditions of childbirth in these years. But older Communists were generally negative about it and sales of contraceptives remained very low. Abortion could be had for the asking, and there were cases of women who had twenty or more. In Moscow, alone, there were 175,000 in 1930, dropping only to 155,000 by 1935, the last year of free abortions. The figure for all rural Russia was only 324,194. Most women gave "material conditions" as their reason; the rest offered shame, freedom, "aesthetics," and the need to devote time and energy to their children. Men often pressured women to abort. Due to the laxity in sexual relations, a man was sometimes unsure just whose baby was expected—a situation sadly and comically delineated in a masterful Soviet film, *No. 3, Meshchanskaya Street* (1927), which dealt with a not atypical *ménage à trois*.[21]

Until the mid-1930's public opinion was ambivalent on abortion. At the Ukrainian Conference of Gynecologists in 1927, all the speakers were hostile to abortion on medical grounds, but some insisted that legal restraint would only push it underground and would work economic hardship upon women. "No one of us men," said a doctor, "would accept a decision by some commission as to the social interest in his being married or not. Do not prevent women from deciding for themselves a fundamental issue of their lives." The conference opposed a "lighthearted approach" to abortion, but stopped short of recommending anti-abortion laws.[22] This Janus-like posture remained the prevailing one until April 27, 1936, when Stalin published the following words in the periodical *Labor*. "We need men. Abortion which destroys life is not acceptable in our country. The Soviet woman has the same rights as the man, but that does not free her from a great and honorable duty which nature has given her: she is a mother, she gives life. And this is certainly not a private affair but one of great social importance." On May 26, the Central

[21] Sokolov, *Spasite detei!*, 26; the decree: *Sob. uzakon.*, 90/471/475; Smith, *Woman*, 186–87; Winter, *Red Virtue*, 146–47; Reich, *Sexual Revolution*, 187; Halle, *Woman*, 139–43; Pierre, *Les femmes*, 27; Gelman *Polovaya zhizn*, 106; Schlesinger, *Family*, 175–76, 184; *Zhizn*, 47–50. On the Sovkino film of V. Shklovsky and A. Room, *Tretya Meshchanskaya*, see *Sovetskie khudozhestvennie filmy*, 4 v. (Moscow, 1961–1968), I, 230.

[22] Schlesinger, *Family*, 172–87; Smith, *Woman*, 183.

Executive Committee published the draft of a new family law drawn up in response to requests by many women designed to protect the health of working women by abolishing abortion on demand, by allowing it only for the most serious medical indications, and by surrounding the mother with a supportive network of material and social guarantees. Objections were still permitted and published, but they had no effect upon the law.[23]

The timing of the decree, in years of growing tension with Japan and Germany, and the transparently demographic terms of Stalin's statement have led some observers to see the anti-abortion law solely as a desire for a bigger population. But the official comments favoring the law reveal a much broader concern with ending the era of sexual adventurism and the re-establishment of the family. "There is no doubt" announced a *Pravda* editorial, "that it will serve as a further strengthening of the Soviet family," that it would discourage "free love" and "disorderly sex life." Furthermore, it concluded, "a woman without children merits our pity for she does not know the full joy of life. Our Soviet women, full blooded citizens of the freest country in the world, have been given the bliss of motherhood. We must safeguard our family and raise and rear healthy Soviet heroes!" Similar items in other papers, letters from readers, and a series of commentaries by Krupskaya dwelt on the same theme and underscored the fact that removal of the right to abortion was simply the first step in putting an end to unbridled passion, casual pregnancies, automatic abortions, and the general disrespect for women, love, motherhood, and the family.[24]

A tightening of the divorce regulations was the other major feature of the 1936 law. "It is high time," announced *Izvestiya* in 1935 "to declare frivolity in family affairs a crime, and unfaithfulness an offense against the morality of the Socialist regime." Leningrad's *Red Gazette* denounced the irresponsible use of divorce and the abandonment of families without support and warned that "a father who leaves wife and children and feels as free as a bird is a criminal."[25] In view of this menacing press campaign, the 1936 reform was rather moderate. Its purpose may be summarized as follows: to induce women to have the "natural" number of children; to alleviate their consequent material and moral vulnerability by (1) giving them greater assurance of the presence and assistance of a husband via the divorce clauses, and (2) establishing an extensive system of maternity welfare, child care, and financial support by the state; and finally, through these measures, to lay the foundations for a re-strengthening of the family. The first of these was effected by the article on abortions. The wife-mother was then buttressed from inside the marriage by a

[23] Reich, *Sexual Revolution*, 176; Serge, *Russia*, 24; *La femme et le communisme*, 57 (Stalin); Pierre, *Les femmes*, 28–31; Schlesinger, *Family*, 255–57, 265.

[24] Press notices in *ibid.*, 251, 254–55 (quotations), 258, 260–61, 265. For a sampling of Krupskaya's opinions: *Zhenshchina*, 22–23.

[25] The *Krasnaya Gazeta* item from Pierre, *Les femmes*, 25–26; *Izvestiya* quoted from Tchernavina, *We Soviet Women*, 196.

clause aimed at "combating light-minded attitudes towards the family and family obligations." The presence of both spouses at divorce proceedings and the recording of divorces in internal passports were required, and the law laid down a graduated scale of fees ranging from 50 rubles for the first to 300 rubles for the third divorce, and stricter provisions for alimony payments. The outer buttress consisted of monetary payments, family bonuses, and the expansion of the child care and pre-school networks. If the mother, as such, was henceforth to be enrolled in the ranks of the producers, she was also to be closely protected and paid for her services.[26]

In the new official image of the family, stability and productivity were stressed rather than freedom, equality, and independence. Krupskaya wrote in 1936 that marriage was based not only upon the satisfaction of normal sex instincts but also upon ideological affinity and a common goal: production. The sociologist Volfson, in 1929, had advanced the concept of a "sexual scissors" wherein the slow tempo of economic growth was outstripped by the rapid disintegration of the family. In the interval the state required the services of the family to take care of the children, but "in socialist society," he had predicted, "this 'natural category' [the family] will be consigned to the same place as that which Engels predicted for the State: it will be sent to the Museum of Antiquities." By 1937, Volfson found it necessary not only to correct the technical error in the above quotation (Engels' prediction for the state referred to the stage of communism, not socialism) but also to repudiate his scissors theory. Now, with the aid of insulting remarks on the "coarse, animal, anti-Marxist views" of Kollontai and others, Volfson exalted monogamy and reminded his readers that, while divorce and abortion must be the right of every citizen, they really ought never to be invoked. Another theorist accused Kollontai of having advocated separation of parents from children and the total shifting of child care from the mother to the state, and of denigrating maternal love. All of these charges were false, but the notion of the indissoluble link between motherhood, permanent marriage, and a strong individual family had become the established norm. Abortions dropped sharply after the decree without disappearing completely; mothers and huge families were glorified in the press; and the new family ideology was celebrated in novels that featured female characters yearning for motherhood. The indestructible Soviet family, nuclear but populous, cozy and proud, emerged to replace earlier revolutionary images.[27]

The 1936 Law did not alter the status of *de facto* marriages or put a first divorce beyond the reach of the masses. Complaints of this situation were being made when World War II intervened. After three years of devastating combat, loss of life, and tremendous geographic mobility, the authorities de-

---

[26] Schlesinger, *Family*, 271–79 (the law).

[27] Krupskaya, *Zhenshchina*, 21; Volfson, *Sotsiologiya*, 442–50; *idem.*, *Semya i brak v ikh istoricheskom razvitii* (Moscow, 1937) 214, 219–23 and *passim*; Schlesinger, *Family*, 280–347; Gasiorowska, *Women*, 191.

cided that it was time to tighten up the shackles of matrimony even more and to extend further incentive and protection to women with large families. The war dead had to be replaced within the context of the new Soviet family. Nikita Khrushchëv, a key figure in wartime administration, initiated the move, and this time there were no preliminary debates before the publication of the edicts in the summer of 1944. By their terms, mothers were to be awarded with a series of cash payments scaled to the number of children, decorated for especially prodigious feats of reproduction, and surrounded by a still denser network of crèches and other pre-school institutions and birth clinics. Conversely, the unmarried and childless were to be taxed. The new monogamy was given the supreme compliment of exclusive status by abolishing all the legal and economic rights that the *de facto* marriage had enjoyed since 1926, and by erecting obstacles to divorce unheard of in Soviet society since before the Revolution.[28]

This final capstone of the sexual Thermidor requires two comments. The divorce articles were certainly restrictive by Soviet standards. Both parties now had to appear in court—no longer at ZAGS—and to present their reasons; witnesses could be summoned and evidence presented; proceedings were advertised in the papers. The two-stage trial could drag out, especially if appealed or contested, and the fees beginning with 100 rubles for court costs and running, if successful, from 500 to 2,000 rubles were prohibitive to all but the most affluent or persistent. The jurist Sverdlov told an American legal scholar that this was a deliberate effort to discourage divorce. In this it was certainly successful: Many couples now simply separated and began other families outside the law rather than go through the agony and expense of divorce. On the other hand, the law was neither a reversion to tsarist times nor less liberal than those of most other countries. Sverdlov explained in 1946 that the measures were designed to fight light-minded behavior, but that divorces were always granted to childless couples by mutual consent, and frequently in contested cases as well. Denials occurred only where there were minor children and then not always. And there was no waiting period after a decision.[29]

The other major innovation, the non-recognition of *de facto* marriage, was also reactionary. By abolishing the legality of such unions, it made them adulterous and their progeny illegitimate. Though that term was never legally applied to such children, paternity search and alimony claims were disallowed outside registered marriages, and the child born out of wedlock after July 8,

[28] Schlesinger, *Family*, 348–62, 367–77 (the law). For intelligent commentary, see Peter Juviler, "Family Reforms on the Road to Communism," *Soviet Policy-Making*, ed. Juviler and H. W. Morton (London, 1967) 29–60.

[29] John Hazard, *Communists and Their Law* (Chicago, 1969) 274. Sverdlov's article in Schlesinger, *Family*, 377–90. Soviet marriage, even at its most restrictive stage, thus conformed to Judge Lindsey's once famous and notorious formula of "companiate marriage" for which he was labeled, among other things, a libertine and a Bolshevik: "legal marriage, with legalized birth control, and with the right to divorce by mutual consent for childless couples, usually without payment of alimony," Ben B. Lindsey, *The Companionate Marriage* (New York, 1927).

1944, could not claim the surname, the patronymic, the support, or the inheritance of his or her biological father. This was an undeniable return to "bourgeois" juridical traditions. But two articles compensated the unmarried mother financially in a manner not often encountered elsewhere. She was not only to receive the payments accorded to "legal" mothers for multiple births but also additional allowances for all her children in her capacity as an unwed mother. So stood the juridical status of the Soviet family until after the death of Stalin; the Thermidor had reached its limit.

The Soviet sexual Thermidor, like other historical phenomena bearing that poetic name, was reactionary. In this case it was a response to excessive interpretations of the libertarian slogans inscribed on the banners of the October Revolution and a search for half-forgotten moorings on which to fasten the floating and bobbing social energies cut loose by the tempests of that revolution. Like everything else about the Stalinist period, it was elitist and authoritarian, arising more from the perceived needs of the economy and the state than from the articulated wishes of the community to which it was applied. But it was not a mere whim of Stalin; nor was it a monolithic assault upon the pleasures of the flesh by a band of revolutionary ascetics acting out the prophetic gestures of a Rakhmetov. It was rather an ambiguous, pained, and often angry response by a large and representative segment of the ruling intelligentsia, who, as the self-proclaimed heirs of the nineteenth-century intelligentsia, were as appalled at the pseudo-principled carnality that raged around them as a Perovskaya, a Plekhanov, or a Kropotkin would have been in their day. That is why, after eighteen years of unfettered "revolutionary" sex, the Russian people—and notably its menfolk—were subjected to another eighteen years of "revolutionary" moral regulation.

The crucial question is: How did women fare in the Age of Thermidor? On the one hand masculine sexual chauvinism, with its trooping from one love-nest to another, its callous use of the female body, its cavalier rejection of finer sentiments, and its carefree lack of concern for the fruits and the sources of its pleasure, was at last—if not wholly banished from the realm of socialism—publicly and officially discredited, legally restricted, and financially penalized. But by any reasonable standards of judgment, including post-Stalinist Soviet ones, the effect of the reaction was to take away from Soviet women more than it gave them. In a number of mutually reinforcing ways, it tended to draw a line between the sexes and their respective roles which was wider and more visible than anything previously known in revolutionary imagery.

An early sign of this was the celebrated Conference of Wives of Engineers in Heavy Industry, held in Moscow in 1936, which glorified the "flower garden" brand of small deeds performed by the unemployed wives of the privileged members of Soviet society. Desperately hard-working factory women were now informed that "kept wives"—as long as they hung curtains in their husbands' enterprises—were as worthy of the people's recognition as they were. Another effort to deepen the gulf between the sexes was the war-time ordinance separating children in the schools according to sexes, with military training added for the boys, and home economics for the girls. The measure, though lasting only ten years, was a clear repudiation of the principle of equal co-education hallowed by the theories and practices of socialism and sex equality. Finally, the whole mystique of motherhood, bathed in a sugary solution of "momism" that would have sent a battalion of Philip Wylies into convulsions, transformed in the popular imagination the former image of the Russian Woman from one of power, work, and proud independence, into what one critic called "the Stakhanovite of the human reproductive machinery"—a secure, protected, but massively dependent child-bearing machine. Soviet iconographers of the time certainly never meant this image to be demeaning; but then neither did those of the nineteenth century who reverently slipped a pedestal beneath the image of woman that they had fashioned.[30]

When you are struck by a historical pendulum, as Soviet women were twice, it does not matter much whether it is swinging out to the left or back toward the right: it still hurts. The best feature of the Thermidor, it must be said, was that it did not last very long. When Stalin died in 1953, the slow ferment and the mild-mannered agitation commenced. Late Stalinist experience had shown once again that divorce and abortion laws could never really be successful in the face of large numbers of dissident people who evaded them. Reforms began. They restored some of the freedoms of the 1920's and rejected others. The settlement which remained was, in the last analysis, a compromise between communist ideology, Russian traditions, and the imperatives and complexities of modern urban industrial life.

[30] Schlesinger, *Family*, 235–50, 363–66. Quotation: Gordon, *Workers*, 335. The best sociological study of *The Family in Soviet Russia* is by Kent Geiger (Cambridge, Mass. 1968).

XII

The Revolution and Women

Love, work, and knowledge are the well-springs of our life. They
should also govern it.
—WILHELM REICH

1. THE REVOLUTIONARY SETTLEMENT

Revolutions, after detonating the fiercest explosions, have a way of settling
down and yielding up moderate regimes led by men (seldom by women) who
are moderate, fearful of extremism and violence, and exhausted by reigns of
terror, permanent purges, or cultural revolutions. The Russian Revolution,
though describing an arc of political terror and repression unparalleled in
human annals, was no exception. Few students would deny that the death of
the dictator in 1953 was a major turning point in Soviet history. Long before
the present moment, the signs were clearly visible that Soviet society was settling into a more or less stable pattern, and that the gains of the Revolution
had been tested and sifted—some being discarded as hopelessly romantic. As
far as women's equality is concerned, the depths of illiberalism had been
reached during World War II. But the central core of liberation had never been
seriously challenged; and after 1953, much of what had been lost was restored. Now, long after the great female commissars have left the stage, after
the heroines of two wars have died or returned to peaceful pursuits, after
the grim tyrant has fallen, and after the shrill vibrations of the sexual revolution
have subsided to a hum, the question may be asked: What did Russian Woman
get from the Revolution?

Early Soviet prophets and propagandists of women's liberation perceived it
as a process that would remove the social, psychological, and political obstacles to freedom and equality for women—obstacles that had loomed high before the Revolution in Russia and that continued to stand firm elsewhere in the
world. This meant, in the most concise terms, *total* equality with men in regard to opportunity for work and full development as a human being, except-
ing only those differences associated with biological roles of the sexes. Bolshevik leaders, men and women, rarely spoke of discrete aspects of the
woman question—work, education, power, and sex—since these were seen
as inseparable elements in the dialectic of exploitation and liberation. In the

early communist image, the liberated woman was inconceivable unless surrounded by an unbroken ring of social circumstance: cooperative housekeeping and public care of children to release her for work at any job for which she was qualified; the performance of any residual family chores by both spouses on an equal basis; educational machinery that would allow her to reach the summit of her natural abilities and to put them to the fullest use; the application of her previously locked-up energies to the task of building socialism. The spirit of this program may be tersely summarized in the formulas of three of its prophets: "Happiness is impossible without work" (Bebel); "from each according to his capacity, to each according to his work" (Marx); "it is now necessary to bend the reed the other way" (Chernyshevsky). The measure of its realization, however, would be determined as much by the requirements of a modernizing regime as by the formulas of liberation.

It ought to be noted at once that many Soviet women got nothing whatsoever from the Russian Revolution—and, in all too many cases, nothing but grief, pain, and a terrible death. Quite apart from the wretched survivors of the Old Regime who suffered discrimination, ostracism, and persecution from socialist society,[1] myriads of "good working women" were arrested, interrogated, tormented physically and mentally, torn from their young ones, cast into prison, sent out to camps, subjected to hideous conditions, starved, beaten, raped, and even executed by Communist authorities during the Great Terror. In their ranks we find not only Socialist Revolutionaries, Mensheviks, aristocrats, and Anarchists, but Communists—Party stalwarts, Zhenotdel leaders, and Civil War veterans; not only Russians but Tatars, Jews, Poles, Georgians, and Uzbeks; not only wives of oppositionists but workers, peasants, doctors, historians, geographers, agronomists, parachutists, and ballerinas. Every women's prison or camp-sector was a macabre tableau of the variety and the extent of women's participation in the economic, political, and cultural life of the nation; and a dreadful reminder that the Revolution could devour its offspring as readily as it could unshackle them.[2]

The structure of female liberation, having survived this and other nightmares of Soviet history, has become a permanent feature of the system, and no further whim or administrative fashion is likely to alter its basic form that is as much a part of Soviet life as is the absence of capitalism. At its base is the economic and educational equality of the sexes in law, embellished ideologically by a widely if not universally held conviction that woman is as capable as man in almost every field of endeavor now open to mankind. This notion is encased in the official myth that Soviet people of both sexes are better equipped than any other group in the world to cope with the new chal-

[1] See Tchernavina, *We Soviet Women, passim*, for examples of this.

[2] Evgeniya Ginzburg, *Into the Whirlwind*, tr. P. Stevenson and M. Harari (Harmondsworth, England, 1968); Olitskaya, *Vospominaniya*; *Zhen. goroda*, 165; Svetlana Allilueva, *Tolko odin god* (New York, 1970) 148–49; Robert Conquest, *The Great Terror, passim*.

lenges that science and technology may present to humanity in the near future. This sweeping confidence, particularly observable among educated women, is another legacy of the iron-willed optimism of the nineteenth-century radical intelligentsia. If the active phase of women's liberation accomplished nothing else, it must be credited with having transformed into a national myth the notions that women are capable of great economic wonders, that they must be allowed full play to their faculties, and that men have no right to hinder this process but rather every obligation to further it.

In regard to Soviet women's role in the economy, a major theme has been the changing relationship between levels of employment and the coverage of protective legislation. The ideal has always been full and equal employment for women and full comprehensive program of benefits and rules concerning the worker qua woman. In the 1920's and 1930's, these two goals were at odds. During NEP, the high rate of female unemployment was due both to the economic system itself that was quasi-capitalist and to male opposition to female competition for available jobs. This situation, aggravated by the Divorce Law of 1926, led many an unemployed and abandoned woman to desert her child, become a prostitute, or both. Neither laws to exempt women from layoffs nor Zhenotdel efforts to enforce them—admirable and novel though these were—had much effect. *De facto* inequality of wages for the same work—though illegal since the Revolution—also persisted until the 1930's. The regime devised special schools for women to upgrade their labor skills and periodically denounced obsolete male attitudes, but to no avail. The affirmative action of the Zhenotdel and other agencies was powerless to overcome the resistance of the productive system of the time.[3]

Women who did manage to work under NEP (less than a third of the labor force in 1928) benefited from the welfare and protective measures that the Revolution bestowed upon them. The earliest code (1918) mandated an eight-hour day and female factory inspectors, and outlawed night work and overtime as well as jobs injurious to women's health. Enforcement remained sporadic, however, even after the military emergency of 1918–1920 could no longer be used as justification. Officials in the Labor Commissariat and the trade unions opposed "excessive" protection as expensive; and so did some

---

[3] Lenin, *Emancipation*, 79; Kollontai, *Polozhenie*, 112, 145; *idem., Rab. i krest.*, 16–18. Carr, *Socialism in One Country*, I, 363, 367; Dodge, *Women*, 44, 55, 60–63; Schlesinger, *Family*, 133; Ershov, *Ulyanova*, 125; Astakhova, *Tov. Olga*, 118, 126; Manya Gordon, *Workers Before and After Lenin* (New York, 1941) 168; Smith, *Women*, 15–16; Margaret Dewar, *Labour Policy in the USSR, 1917–1928* (London, 1956), 139, 165, 219, 232; Tolkunova, *Pravo*, 10, 47–49, 94; *Svetlyi put*, 135–37.

I have not tried to repeat the detailed history of the advances made in the legal, educational, economic, and social status of women in Soviet times, partly because much of it was accomplished by the regime after the demise of the women's movement, and partly because this has been done in a number of important works published in English: Dodge, *Women*; Gail Lapidus, *Women in Soviet Society* (Berkeley, 1977); *Women in Russia* (to appear shortly; Stanford); Madison, *Social Welfare*; and the more popular treatment, W. Mandel, *Soviet Women* (New York, 1975).

women workers themselves who, in the face of unemployment, preferred an unprotected job to none at all. The crowning legislative achievement for women workers was the maternity insurance program designed by Kollontai before the Revolution and put into law at her urging shortly after the Women's Congress of 1918. The mother-care law provided for a fully paid maternity leave of eight weeks, nursing breaks and factory rest facilities, free pre- and post-natal care, and cash allowances. It was administered through a Commission for the Protection of Mothers and Infants (*Matmlad*)—attached to the Health Commissariat—and headed by a Bolshevik doctor and ex-revolutionary, Vera Lebedeva. *Matmlad*, with its network of maternity clinics, consultation offices, milk points, nurseries, and mother-and-infant homes, was perhaps the single most popular innovation of the Soviet regime among Russian women.[4]

With the onset of intensive forced industrialization in the 1930's, female employment rose and labor protection diminished. Beginning with the first Five Year Plan, the Party launched a massive campaign to draw women "from the household to the workbench"—thus repudiating the old Russian saying: "Woman's path, from threshold to stove." Propaganda, the price mechanism, and the opening of new jobs with free skill training—often on an affirmative action quota basis—were the prime mechanisms. The Commissariat of Labor, the *Sovnarkom*, and the Council for Labor and Defense all issued decrees on minimum percentages of women to be admitted to jobs, apprenticeships, and technical courses. By the end of the second Five Year Plan, the number of women had tripled since 1927. The invigorating martial atmosphere of the Civil War was reinvoked and Shock Battalions of women workers—sometimes outnumbering and outproducing men—made their appearance on the economic front. But the fury of industrialization and the driving authoritarianism of the Party in the 1930's also led to the reduction of women's labor protection rights. Between 1936 and the end of World War II, the coverage and leave time for pregnant workers was reduced, and various other measures and limitations to women's labor were curtailed. Although the protection norms were gradually restored after the War, it should not be forgotten that Russian women—apart from other sufferings they endured—were dreadfully overworked and underprotected in these years.[5]

Before World War II, women had already made up 45 percent of the working force; now that figure has gone over the 50 percent mark. Various data

---

[4] *Sobranie uzakonenii i raspryazhenii Rabochego i Krestyanskogo Pravitelstva, 1917–1918*, 2d ed. (Moscow, 1919) p. I, art. 10, pars. 7–10; Dewar, *Labour Policy*, 115, 160, 164–65, 177, 184, 189, 199–200; Dodge, *Women*, 57–59; Carr, *Socialism in One Country*, I, 369. For the origins and work of *Matmlad*, see: *L'égalité de la femme en URSS* (Moscow, 1957) 211; Kollontai, *Rab. i krest.*, 14; Tolkunova, *Pravo*, 148–49; Halle, *Woman*, 149–67; Smith, *Women*, 174–77.

[5] Dodge, *Women*, 64–67, 175–76; *Svetly put*, 139–45; Tolkunova, *Pravo*, 87–90; *La femme et le communisme*, 59; Halle, *Woman*, 324–27.

compiled since 1959 indicate that women, making up 53.8 percent of the population, also occupy comparable percentages in the economy: 51 percent of industrial and white collar and 53 percent of the collective farm jobs. Over 80 percent of able-bodied women are employed. Ten years ago, this was double the United States percentage. In health, education, and social work, women predominate by large percentages. On the other hand, the vast bulk of women are engaged in "material production," including agricultural and low-grade physical labor; and a sizeable number of white collar employees perform retailing and catering services that can hardly be called uplifting. It is also true that a good deal of the paid work done by women—probably more so than men's—is relatively unproductive by Western standards. Nevertheless, if we are to accept the assumption that the right and the opportunity to work and earn one's own money is at the heart of women's liberation, it is clear that Norton Dodge is right in concluding that few societies have done as much in this direction as has Soviet society.[6]

The wide range and rich variety of occupations open to and held by Soviet women is impressive. They not only play the violin, edit newspapers, perform surgery, and teach school; but also tear up streets with an air hammer, drive gasoline trucks, announce news on the radio, and fly around the earth in a spaceship. If Valentina Tereshkova-Nikolaeva, famous for the last-mentioned exploit, is a symbol of educated Soviet womanhood, it is not because of her personal valor—hardly a novelty to Russian women—but because of her technical education and her scientific curiosity, nurtured among Soviet girls from their earliest years. The immense variety of professional roles for women, and the large numbers of trained women technicians is the societal context that makes Tereshkova's career a natural phenomenon and not a freak.

In the Soviet Union, work for women is not legally mandatory. Jobs are contracted with each enterprise, and employment according to qualifications is guaranteed by the state. The wages and purchasing power of Soviet women are in no way comparable to those of the West; but they are comparable to those of Soviet men. The law and the constitution provide for the principle of "equal wages for equal work" and the principle is now strictly enforced. There are few other countries, even advanced ones, where such a principle prevails—either in law or in fact. The Soviet woman enjoys certain privileges connected with her right to work, the most important of which are maternity benefits. The latest (August 1973) version of Kollontai's law mandates for all working women a paid sixteen-week maternity leave, the right to perform light duties for a time after returning to work, free pre-natal, surgical, and other medical services, and either free nursery services or the alternate right to

[6] Dodge, *Women*, 44–45, 183, 198, 238–43; *Zhenshchiny i deti SSSR: statisticheskii sbornik* (Moscow, 1969) 82–83; *Soviet Life* (March, 1974) 7; V.I. Starodub, *Zhenshchina i obshchestvennyi trud* (Leningrad, 1975), *passim*.

stay home with the child for a longer period without pay but without loss of job or seniority. Unmarried mothers, divorced women, and widows receive more.[7] These measures, though heavily paid for through the price and wage system, afford the Soviet working woman with children a certain measure of security and self-respect.

Equal educational opportunities for women had been the main theme of the earliest musings over the "woman question" back in the 1860's; its high degree of realization has been one of the proudest achievements of the Soviet order. At the time of the Revolution, 14 of the 17 million illiterates in the country were women. Illiteracy was essentially a woman's problem, and to it were applied the energies and talents of women themselves. The All Russian Extraordinary Commission for the Liquidation of Illiteracy (Likbez), established in the Commissariat of Education in 1920, was run by a seasoned revolutionary woman, Anna Kurskaya. In 1923, voluntary "Down with Illiteracy" societies sprang up to assist the work of Likbez. Women wrote the texts and provided most of the teaching skills in both organizations; and the Zhenotdel detailed some of its personnel for anti-illiteracy work. The campaign, the largest of its kind ever mounted by a government up to that time, met with striking results: by 1926, 42.7 percent of Russian women could read; and by 1939, 83.4 percent. Illiteracy is all but abolished; and the old nineteenth-century principles of secular education have been achieved: it is universal, free, compulsory, and co-educational. The social investment has been massive—though even after fifty years half the female population had less than seven years of schooling, and pockets of undereducated and uneducated women are to be found throughout the eastern republics.[8]

Early decrees required co-education in all schools, equal admission for both sexes, with violations subject to criminal prosecution, and uniform curricula for boys and girls. Pupils were not divided by sex into future houseworkers and future career men. All were exposed to a variety of subjects including the natural sciences and technology. Girls whose latent talents for such specializations were awakened by this exposure were encouraged in believing that careers in them were as natural for girls as for boys. Equality of sexes in real life, as Krupskaya pointed out in 1921, had to be anchored in educational equality from the very earliest years. Thus the belief in the omnicompetence of women, long nourished by the female intelligentsia of the nineteenth century, was institutionalized in the Soviet educational system. The abolition of co-education by Stalin in 1943 did not succeed in permanently altering the principle of equality in education; even during the decade of its existence, curricula for boys and girls remained the same for academic subjects. From the

[7] Tolkunova, *Pravo*, 19, 24–25, 107–108; *Soviet Life* (March, 1974) 48–49.
[8] *Svetlyi put*, 169–72; Tolkunova, *Pravo*, 84–85; *Zhen. goroda*, 186–92; Dodge, *Women*, 140–59.

lowest grades, girls are exposed to a wide range of subjects, including science and technology.[9]

A particularly important aspect of educational equality was the effort to place women in so-called Specialized Secondary Schools, the intermediate training centers for scientists and technicians. By 1927, largely through the efforts of Zhenotdel, women already occupied 40 percent of the places in them. With the onset of industrialization, the government announced that a minimum of 30 percent of the enrollees in *all* such schools was to begin in 1929. By World War II, girls made up half the student body of specialized schools. Minimum quotas and affirmative action methods were also used to enlarge female enrollments in the universities and institutes and with similarly striking results. Estimates made in the mid-1960's of female enrollments in various disciplines of higher educational institutions show that 53 percent of the medical students, 75 percent to 80 percent of the biology students, 25 percent of the students in agronomy, about two-thirds of the chemistry students, almost half of the students in mathematics, and from 25 percent to 40 percent of those in the physical and geological sciences were women. These figures are strikingly high when compared with other countries. The result is an extraordinary large number of female scientists and technicians. According to Dodge, 63 percent of all specialists with specialized secondary education, 92 percent of the semi-professional medical personnel, and 75 percent of the planners, statisticians, and accountants were women. In fact more than half of the mental workers in Soviet Russia are women. And this is in a country where, two decades before the Revolution, a bewildered peasant could ask a woman pharmacist "Can it really be so, young lady, that a woman's mind can fathom such matters?"[10]

Soviet graduates entered a wide range of professional and semi-professional occupations after the Revolution. In medicine and technology, the difference between the Soviet way of utilizing the talents of women and that of the West is strikingly illustrated. The traditions of Russian women in the nineteenth century and the massive health problems that faced Russia on the morrow of the Revolution led naturally to the full use of women in the Soviet medical profession. As early as 1926, half the medical students were women; and by 1935, half the doctors. The percentage has risen steadily since then, and now medicine—doctoring as well as nursing—is considered to be

[9] The decree on education: *KPSS v rezol i resh.*, I, 419; on coeducation, Bunyan, *Intervention*, 528; also Dodge, *Women*, 100–22, 241–42; Krupskaya in *Kommunistka*, 8–9 (Jan.-Feb., 1921) 22–26. There is considerable evidence, however, that by means of illustrations and story situations, boys are presented as active figures and girls as nurturing and supporting ones in Soviet children's literature: Molly Rosenhan, "Images of Male and Female in Children's Readers," in Atkinson *et al.*, *Women in Russia*.

[10] Dodge, *Women*, 123–39, 184–99, 244; Halle, *Woman*, 319; Lesnevskaya, *Po neprotorënnei doroge* (see Chapter VI/1, n. 40 for the context and full citation). See also Astakhova, *Tov. Olga*, 119–31; *Zhen. goroda*, 204–206; *Svetlyi put*, 174–79. For recent material on female career aspirations, see: *100 intervyu s sovetskimi zhenshchinami* (Moscow, 1975).

largely a woman's profession. Many of the new Soviet women doctors were former revolutionaries or Civil War veterans who left the underground life or the hospital train to direct their energies into socially productive peacetime medical work. Engineers, technicians, and scientists had more obstacles to face than women doctors; but the initial hostility to them did not endure. In the Civil War they designed and built bridges and railroads; in the 1920's they helped electrify such vast wastelands as the Fergana Valley in Turkestan; and by the 1930's they had become a permanent feature of the industrial scene.[11]

Recent scholarship has also shown, however, that the rosy picture given in Soviet official statements—that of perfect equality of opportunity in school and workplace—does not meet the test of the evidence. The "double shift" and "the politics of sex" continue to inhibit women from greater productivity and promotion in their chosen professions. But there are even formal violations, though not publicized, of the prevailing doctrine of equality, as in the system of preferred acceptance of men in some higher educational institutions, deliberately contrived and—one student believes—motivated by the self-fulfilling belief that women are less productive after they graduate. However motivated, this is emphatically a betrayal of the egalitarian notions on women's education held by the Russian intelligentsia from the 1860's onward. There is also, though to a somewhat lesser extent than in the West, an informal but pervasive system of occupational segregation under which women are directed into relatively low-paying and low-status occupations, some of which (catering, medicine, teaching) have been effectively "feminized." This is one of the reasons for the still considerable income gap between men and women that prevails alongside the legal enforcement of equal pay for equal work.[12]

The Soviet solution of the woman question looks more impressive when measured against other times and other places. In spite of the successes of nineteenth-century Russian feminists, the number of women receiving higher and specialized training and then using their sorely needed skills remained minute before 1917. Presently, in the affluent democracies of the West—after a century of feminist activity—there is gross inequality, male monopoly of vast areas of life that in the Soviet Union would be open to women, and an enormous waste of talent, energy, and education. Some say that American

[11] The Soviet literature on professional women is large. For a sampling, see: *Bestuzhevki* (full citation in Chapter VI, 1, n. 41); *Zhen. russ. rev.*, 158–68, 562; *Skvoz gody i bury* (Moscow, 1969) *passim*; *Oktyabrëm*, 329–60; *Leningradki*, 269–91; *Zhen. goroda Lenina*, 275–71; Dodge, *Women*; Krupskaya, *Zhenshchina*, 10; *Pervie zhen.-inzhenery*, 24, 25, 27, 87, 93, 134, 178, and *passim*.
[12] Dodge, *Women*, 112–17. See also Richard Dobson, "Educational Policies and Occupational Achievements: the Performance of Girls and Women in the Soviet Educational System," in Atkinson *et al.*, *Women in Russia*. For a concise and valuable recent treatment of occupational segregation, see Gail Lapidus, "Occupational Segregation and Public Policy: a Comparative Analysis of American and Soviet Patterns," *Signs: Journal of Women in Culture and Society*, 1, 3, pt. 2 (Spring, 1976) 119–36.

and European women are grateful for their leisure and high standard of living, and would never want to experience the pressures and expectations to work with which Soviet women live. This may have been true a few years ago; but for a growing number of women in the West, it no longer is. The ferment in the United States is too well known to warrant comment here. In the Common Market nations of Western Europe, according to a European Economic Community study, three quarters of the women are not "employed" at all, though many of these actually work long hours in an unsalaried capacity on farms and in family businesses. For wage-earners, Article 119 of the Rome Treaty on equal pay for equal work has remained a dead letter. Evelyne Sullerot, author of the report, believes that many European women wish "to escape the boredom of the hearth and achieve the relative economic and psychological independence of a job."[13] In the Soviet Union the woman's choice of working or not working means, in practice, freedom to work for most women; in the West that choice, in large part, means mostly freedom not to work. Two questions are left. Can a woman be psychologically independent if she is not economically? Can she really be economically independent if what she spends has been earned by someone else?

"Peoples whose women have to work much harder than we would consider proper," wrote Engels, "often have far more real respect for women than our Europeans have for theirs."[14] Though it would be foolish to claim universal validity for these words of Engels, it does have a certain relevance to Russian society. In cultures where men hold almost all of the important occupations and have a monopoly on earning power, women are forced—often without knowing it—to define themselves in terms of someone else, a doer, a producer, a breadwinner—in other words, a man. Women, on the other hand, who do perform high-status work in such a society are encouraged by the surrounding value system to look upon themselves as freaks. It is only in societies where women's work and women's success is an accepted norm that the individual woman possesses the easy sense of dignity and worth that for ages has been associated with males. American and English wives, and a good many Europeans too, have a habit of introducing themselves as Mrs. So-and-So or as the wife of Dr. So-and-So. The unstated implication is: You might know my spouse, he is somebody; I am merely his wife. Russian married women rarely introduce themselves in terms of their husbands or anyone else; indeed, it is unusual for a husband to merit mention at all in an ordinary conversation. A Soviet woman has her own friends—male and female—her own work or cultural associations which the husband is not necessarily expected to share—not because he is "above" them but because he doubtless has his own. At the bottom of it all is the fact that the wife, in most cases, has her own job, her own identity, her own sense of herself.

[13] Reported in *The Times* (London), May 8, 1972.　　[14] Engels, *Origin*, 82.

The attitude is generally shared by men; otherwise it would have little chance of survival. There are, to be sure, Soviet men whose coarse, contemptuous, and "chauvinistic" attitudes to women are ever on display; and many others who mask such attitudes beneath the façade of courteous respect. But in comparison to such men in other societies, they are surprisingly few in number. A recent Civil War film, *White Sun of the Desert* (1972), featured a Bolshevik hero who, when placed in charge of a harem of ten wives lately delivered from a local chief, places them at once in a "First Dormitory for Liberated Women of the East" in front of which is placed a placard saying, "A Woman Is Also A Human Being."[15] One can easily imagine what Western film-makers, with an eye to their audiences, would make of such a plot idea. The film piously repeats an official image, to be sure; but it also reflects a widespread attitude among Soviet men, inherited from the intelligentsia and disseminated by the media. Respect for the personality of a woman may be partly related to the vestigial memory of women's role in the revolutionary movement and in the two great wars. But this respect could not be sustained (as evidenced by the Western experience of women's wartime service and its aftermath) unless women themselves possessed a substantial role in the productive and administrative life of the nation. The gallantry that an American or an English general shows to a lady is revealingly different from the respectful humility that a Red Army general exhibits in the face of a tongue-lashing by a female white collar employee.

This psychological nexus between the male and the female personality is at the root of what some observers and critics call Soviet puritanism. In fact the Soviet attitude about sex is neither puritan (a deeply negative feeling toward sex), nor Victorian (being, or pretending to be, ignorant about it). Current Soviet ideas on love and sex are full-blooded enough, though certainly more so in practice than in public utterances. They are however openly hostile to pornography and prurience and their principal enunciators are the spiritual heirs of those stunned members of the intelligentsia who fought frantically against the tide of Saninism so many decades ago. The anti-pornographic tradition of the intelligentsia goes back even further:[16] "Pornographic works [wrote Radishchev in 1790], full of suggestive descriptions, breathing forth vice, whose every page and line gapes with provocative nudity, are injurious to youth and to the emotionally immature. By fanning an already inflamed inquisitiveness, by arousing dormant sensations and wakening a peacefully slumbering heart, they lead to premature sexual ripening, deceiving the youthful senses as to their powers of endurance and leading them to early decrepitude." Artificial stimulation of the senses by means of female nudity, to a Soviet mind, is both degrading to the watcher and to the watched; and also conducive of generating passions which cannot be easily or licitly satisfied.

---

[15] *Beloe solntse pustiny* (Lenfilm, 1972).

[16] Alexander Radishchev, *Journey from St. Petersburg to Moscow*, tr. L. Wiener, ed. R. Thaler (Cambridge, Mass., 1966) 170.

The official line on sex teaches that abstinence is not harmful to the organism, that sex is best only when a person is physically and psychologically mature, and that promiscuity and pre-marital sex are bad—for girls and boys. There are even those who would amplify this by evoking the Domostroi when "the most sacred thing in a woman's life was trampled on."[17] But virginity before marriage is not nearly as important psychologically to a Soviet couple as it is—or was up until a few years ago—in the countries of the true Puritan and Victorian traditions. Pre-marital sex is discouraged, but in a rote sort of way. For example, Yury Gagarin, echoing Lenin, tells teenagers to prepare themselves for communism through study, sport, and helping around the house.[18]

Life does not fit squarely with the official ethos in the Soviet Union any more than it does in other societies. Sex before marriage is common among young Soviet women. It is not treated with quite the same circumspection, secrecy, guilt, and shame that used to surround it among American girls until a few years ago. Many unmarried couples live together in Russia, after a fashion; the difficulties arise more from logistical problems than from public opinion. The Thermidorean backlash against wild and irresponsible sex never cut that deeply into the thick flesh of Russian behavioral freedom. The film director, Larisa Shepitko, probably summed up the attitude of the young on this score in 1969 when she said that "any interference by society in an adult's personal life will be extremely dangerous until society itself becomes ideal. But in the ideal society interference in personal life will be obviously unnecessary." And yet there are few citizens in Russia today who would not be shocked by such Western radical sexual proposals as that voiced by the Dutch Provo feminist philosopher, Irene van de Weetering, who believes that all girls should experience love-making from puberty onward and should never marry without having enjoyed such experience. To young Komsomol girls, this and tales of nude encounter sessions, group sex, collective families, and wife-swapping were not only wholly repugnant but quite unbelievable.[19]

Marriage and the family are still the norm in Soviet life, still a goal—though not *the* goal—of most women. And this seems to be the case everywhere in spite of the waves of sexual rebellion that have crashed against them in this century. Social scientists, East and West, still seem to be in agreement that the family is the most constant of human relations. One of them predicts that in 1984, however many changes in our way of life will have evolved, "all sorts of small instruments will be shrilling away with their new

[17] *Current Digest of the Soviet Press* (Dec., 4, 1968) 11 (to be cited as *CDSP*).

[18] Gagarin's advice cited in *Chistyi istochnik: tvoi moralnyi kodeks* (Moscow, 1962) 28. This work and the two which follow will give the reader a reasonably complete picture of official Soviet views on sex morality and of the broader system of ethics of which it is a part: S. D. Laptënek, *Moral i semya* (Minsk, 1967) and V. G. Nesterev, *Trud i moral v sovetskom obshchestve* (Moscow, 1969). A concise and accurate summary of these views in English may be seen in Madison, *Social Welfare*, 68–69.

[19] Shepitko: *CDSP* (Dec. 4, 1968) 15. Van de Weetering: *Delta: A Review of Arts, Life, and Thought in the Netherlands* (Amsterdam, 1967).

tunes, but from the family ground bass we shall hear the same figure as to-day."[20] In retrospect, the Soviet sex and family revolution of the 1920's was not simply a violent excrescence of the Revolution or a "typically" Russian excursion into social fantasy. It appears to have been a part of a larger phenomenon of socio-sexual adjustment to industrialization which reached one of its peaks of activity and drama in the 1920's—in Germany, England, the United States, and elsewhere. Future comparative studies will no doubt disclose more similarity between these and the Soviet experience than is now thought to be the case. In all of them, the family and marriage were under assault, though this assault had a less ideological tone in the Anglo-Saxon countries than it did on the continent. In all cases, including the most danger-ous, the Soviet one, the victim of the assault survived, if in somewhat differ-ent size and shape.

The new marriage laws of 1968 have—fifty years after the first code—struck a balance between the radical thrust of 1916–1926 and the counter-thrust of 1936–1944. Divorce and abortion have been re-established on a free basis; but the *de facto* marriage has been kept outside the pale of the law. Marriage must now be preceded by a month's waiting period or "betrothal" designed to discourage whirlwind marriages. The measure has been seen by some young people as somewhat insulting and it is possible, under special conditions, to evade it. If the wedding takes place at ZAGS, a mere shuffling of documents and a nominal fee is required. The regime, however, encour-ages the more elaborate ceremony in a Palace of Weddings which usually in-volves a waiting list, more formal attire, and a ceremony which might include a best-man and bridesmaid, flowers, a "wedding taxi," the Mendelssohn pro-cessional, and a family banquet afterwards. In the marriage, the historic Soviet personal and property rights of women have been preserved intact. Separate households are not encouraged but are not prohibited, and more than a few couples, in line with an old tradition, find it more romantic and satisfy-ing to live apart and meet during holidays and vacations. Soviet married life varies as much as it does elsewhere and it would be silly to try to speak of a marriage style that was peculiarly Soviet or indeed of a typical Soviet wifely outlook on marriage. But the following brief remark sums up a good deal of what I have heard on the subject. A young woman explained to readers that she and her husband had the same schooling and earned the same wages, though she read a good deal and he spent his time on soccer and hockey. "Why," she then asked, "should he deserve more respect than I?"[21]

Neither Soviet nor any other society has solved the age-old marital prob-

[20] Michael Young, "Changing Patterns of Family Life," in *The World in 1984*, ed. Nigel Cal-der, 2 v. (Harmondsworth, 1965), I, 42–45.

[21] For detailed commentary on the law, see: N. A. Ivanova *et al.*, *Novoe zakonodatelstvo o brake i seme* (Moscow, 1970). Comments on the "betrothal" period in *CDSP* (Dec. 4, 1968) 12–14. An interesting sampling of Soviet couples' views of their own marriages may be found in Sture Stiernlöf, *Kvinner i Sovjet: Yrkesliv och Könsroller i första Socialiststaten* (Stockholm, 1970) 113–14 (quotation, 114). The description of the wedding ceremony is based on a personal experience in 1969.

lems of incompatibility, boredom, drift, dessication, and other seemingly immutable sources of matrimonial woe that continue to beset married couples everywhere. Neither work for women nor the high degree of equality in life have succeeded in liquidating these problems. In the light of this, the Soviets have settled on what seems to be a permanent and liberal arrangement for escaping from unfortunate unions by means of a reasonable, humane, and non-humiliating divorce. It is, practically speaking, a reversion to the Law of 1917. In retrospect, a recent Soviet writer concedes, the 1944 Law had led to non-registered unions and artificial buttressing of factually disintegrated families. The ferment for change began right after the death of Stalin with proponents of reform citing Lenin's ideal of free marriage and free divorce and conservatives countering with irrelevance, silence, and prolonged bureaucratic manoeuvers. In 1965, a decree simplified the divorce process considerably by reducing the two-stage hearing to one and cutting out some of the expense-laden items (such as publicity). Subsequent court experience and public opinion both pointed to further loosening, and new divorce clauses were included in the 1968 set of family laws. Divorce by mutual consent for childless couples can now be gotten, three months or more after the wedding, quickly and painlessly at a ZAGS office. Others must pass through a *pro forma* reconciliation attempt; but there are no grounds and each case is decided on a combination of economic, pediatric, and psychological merits in the local court. Divorce petitions are seldom denied and the decision may be appealed.[22]

Since 1965, when the Soviet divorce rate (1.6 per 1,000 inhabitants) was lower than the U.S. rate (2.4)—though double those of England and France—the rate has moved briskly up to 2.7 in 1967, slightly ahead of the United States'. The rates are highest in the Western border republics, lowest in the East; and much higher in the cities than in the country. Moscow's rate jumped from 3.6 to 6.0 in three years (1964–1967). Leningrad is only a fraction behind. According to a recent source, women initiate most divorce cases, and couples are particularly divorce-prone when the educational level of the wife exceeds that of her husband. Press complaints tend to confirm this. But in terms of causes of marital breakup, there are no surprises—they result from differences in personality and life-goals, tensions of work and study, the temptations of big city life, cramped housing conditions, the presence of in-laws, and multiple combinations of these—frequently irrigated with ample doses of spirits.[23]

The right of abortion on demand was restored to Soviet women even before the right of divorce. The twenty-year period in which it was outlawed revealed to the Soviet authorities that it led to illegal abortions and consequent

[22] Juviler, "Family Reforms," 33–53; *CDSP* (Nov. 13, 1969) 25–26; Ivanova, *Novoe*, 42–44.
[23] Juviler, "Family Reforms," 44; Madison, *Social Welfare*, 71–72; Stiernlöf, *Kvinner*, 110–111; Ivanova, *Novoe*, 10; *Soviet Life* (March, 1974) 13.

harm to women's health and safety—and after 1953 they were free to say as much without fear of being harshly contradicted. The Law of 1955 restored the right to be aborted for a number of medical reasons or, upon the woman's insistence, for social indications. Though Bernice Madison noted bureaucratic obstacles in the early 1960's, these have largely disappeared and the statement "women can decide to have or not to have a child and how many children to have" is now a description of reality. Soviet women endorse this arrangement—whatever their personal views about marriage and children— and find it incomprehensible that "rich" countries with superb medical establishments do not offer the same choice to their women. Abortions are common in Russia, and not only for over-burdened mothers of large families. Even though unwed mothers are rarely looked down upon there, most young women on the verge of entering this category would rather avoid doing so by means of abortion.[24]

A final word about women and sex. The Soviets have not succeeded in abolishing prostitution, in spite of all their efforts—positive and repressive— to do so. In the 1930's its incidence was reduced drastically and suddenly by a combination of rehabilitation and retraining, job placement, and detention of so-called incurables. But prostitutes have re-appeared in the last few decades, catering to the wealthy and powerful of the capital or to tourists. Though squads of prostitutes may no longer be seen parading along their old pre-revolutionary haunts—the Nevsky, the Ligovka, and elsewhere—they may be met in foreign bars or in cabs that cruise along Gorky Street in Moscow or around hotel entrances. There is nothing at all to compare to a Reeperbahn, a Pigalle, a Kurfurstendam, or an Amsterdam Canal Street in all of the Soviet Union. There are no brothels, though there are certainly places to sleep with girls who are willing to sell sex for foreign currency, gifts, and clothes. And there are pimps. But the overwhelming majority of Soviet women do not sell themselves—as whores, as kept wives, as sex symbols, as commercial live-stock, as dates to the highest bidders, as escorts, models, B-girls, or geishas—and do not allow themselves be packaged and merchandised by others. Though possessing little enough by Western standards, they have work, their own wages, and the respect of men and of society.

A major element in the indictment of manocracy by American feminists in recent years has been the over-feminizing of women by keeping them at home—surrounded by electrical fetishes and conveniences which wither mind and soul, and manipulated by commercial commands to consume, both at the expense of the unfolding of women's capabilities. Unlike her American counterpart, the Soviet wife does not enjoy the elegant leisure, the household

[24] David Heer, "Abortion, Contraception, and Population Policy in the Soviet Union," *Soviet Studies*, XVII, 1 (July, 1965) 76–83; Madison, "Russia's Illegitimate Children," 91–93. For a survey of abortion elsewhere, see David Smith, ed., *Abortion and the Law* (Cleveland, 1967); and for Soviet comment on birth control, which is being increasingly accepted and encouraged, see *CDSP* (Dec. 25, 1968) 11–12.

appliances, the luxuries, and a standard of material existence that is probably the highest in the world. But unlike the American housewife also, the Soviet wife has received official recognition of her worth as a human being, the right to work, to proceed up the ladder of professional opportunity to a certain point below the top, and a feeling of equality and independence vis-à-vis her husband or lover that is deeply rooted in the economic opportunities open to her. Exceptions of course exist in both societies. The idle Soviet women can still be seen occasionally gossiping in the courtyard and chewing sunflower seeds, even though they are perfectly capable of earning their own money. And American women more and more, especially among the young, are unwilling to marry the suburban home, the two-car garage, and the insurance policy. Many are determined today to learn, to work, to live, and to love according to their own design, without benefit of clergy or of the Advertising Council. Women at such a level of consciousness may have more in common with Soviet women, past and present, than they realize.

2. ACCOUNTS UNSETTLED

Some of the positive features of women's status in Soviet society have been discussed. Now it is necessary to look at the unfulfilled promises and the discrepancies between the Soviet doctrine of sexual equality and actual practice. Most of them fall into one or more of the following categories: village life where female inferiority persists; the so-called double shift that afflicts urban woman by saddling her with both job and housework; and the politics of sex that cuts across all social and economic groups.

Nowhere was the sluggish pace of liberation more apparent than among the peasantry. As late as six months after the Revolution, peasant women felt discrimination even in their execution: a peasant wife and her lover had been convicted of husband-murder; the lover was simply shot, while she was bound to his corpse and buried alive with it. And after a decade of revolution and years of hard work by Zhenotdel and other organizations, Krupskaya could still lament that Russian peasant women, though possessed of many admirable features, were "very backward in their development." Illiteracy, scarcity of opportunity for schooling, and the absence of alternative roles in village life ruled out vertical mobility; and horizontal mobility was blocked by rural attitudes toward divorce and desertion. Peasant men in Russia were not noted for pushing their women toward emancipation. Politics did not fit into the mosaic of the male peasant's image of the *baba*. Hostility to feminism was often exhibited over relatively minor things, like the participation of wives in International Women's Day. "They'll manage without you," decided the husband of one woman. "You're too dirty and stupid. It's just about enough for you to look after the cow." The literature is full of such episodes. The endless official resolutions and decrees availed but little, and by 1930, the vast majority of peasant women was still outside the pale of Party influence.[1]

Collectivization was preceded by the interesting phenomenon of "women's communes" whose impulse was the large number of unattached women left over from the conflicts of 1914–1920. In 1919, for instance, we hear of the Red Dawn Commune in the Kharkov area, where widows, single girls, and otherwise "lone" peasant women live together and collectively managed child care, feeding, and laundering; others of the same genre were the Free Labor Artel and the Rosa Luxemburg Collective for widows. By the end of the 1920's, the best known was the Artyukhina Women's Commune, organized in 1929 by a working woman out on the Salsk Steppe and composed of agricultural day laborers. One of the last such enterprises appeared in 1931–1932 with 424 women and 254 men, single and married, with a common kitchen, bakery, and laundry. But the vast majority of peasant women remained hostile to the commune as a form of social and productive life. They feared it as an alien civilization where atheism, plural marriage, nonmarriage, collective intercourse in an enormous bed with a hundred-meter blanket, confiscation of children, and a generally satanic carnal atmosphere prevailed. The institution upon which generations of socialists, from Chernyshevsky to Kollontai, had placed their hopes for the full emancipation of women failed to take root in the Russian countryside.[2]

Female cadres were not lacking for the collectivization drive: a half-million Zhenotdel-trained delegates; women leaders of rural Soviets; some 5,000 urban women who served as deputy chiefs of the Machine Tractor Stations' political departments; the *Zhensektor* of the *Agitmassotdel*'s women's shock brigades, including the Women of the Five-Hundred, agronomical wizards who could conjure up five-hundred centners of beets out of a mere hectare of soil; and finally women tractor-drivers whose archetype, Pasha Angelina, symbolized the marriage of backward humanity and moving metal in the headlong, though carefully mobilized, rush toward economic modernity.[3] How did the peasant women themselves take to collectivization? Aside from those millions who, with their husbands and families, were liquidated in the forced collectivization or starved by its accompanying famine, Russian women as a whole seem to have accepted the new dispensation without much hostility. Rural women were given legal equality in the household and sepa-

[1] The execution is reported in J. Bunyan and H. H. Fisher, eds., *The Bolshevik Revolution, 1917–1918: Documents and Materials* (Stanford, 1934) 290–91. *Vospom. o N. K. Krupskoi*, 85; Halle, *Woman*, 271–73 (quotation, 272); *Zhen. v Rev.*, 277; *Svetlyi put*, 198–99; Tolkunova, *Pravo*, 53; Stavrakis, "Women," 145, n. 32.

[2] *Oktyabrëm*, 262–69; Halle, *Woman*, 378–85; R. Wesson, *Soviet Communes* (New Brunswick, 1963), 214–17 and *passim*.

[3] *Svetlyi put*, 157–61; *Zhen. v Rev.*, 270–71; *Oktyabrëm*, 189–96; Tolkunova, *Pravo*, 90. For a sketch of Pasha Angelina, the first Soviet woman tractor driver, see *Skvoz gody i buri* 80–95.

rate earnings. This and the limited maternity benefits gave the peasant woman a measure of economic independence without recourse to the hated commune that would have robbed her of her home, her garden plot, and (she feared) her virtue. But the peasant woman was increasingly neglected and over-worked, and the role which the liberators had dreamed of for her in public life rather quickly faded without ever quite disappearing.[4]

Few major advances in peasant women's status have been registered since collectivization awarded them separate earnings, full legal and civic equality, a network of social security, and some models of educated and semi-professional technicians. In the mid-1960's, 83 percent of village women performed unskilled labor in the fields and barnyards as well as almost all of the housework. Few are engaged in specialized or mechanized occupations. Since World War II, the now legendary *traktoristka*, Pasha Angelina, has ceased to symbolize the realities of female performance in the countryside. There is less specialization than in the towns, and male attitudes continue to ensure that men get the complex and responsible posts. This is especially true in farm administration. "It turns out," observed *Izvestiya* in 1961, "that it is the men who do the administering and the women who do the work."[5]

This unbalanced economic arrangement is reinforced by (and itself reinforces) inequality in the home. Young women, even before marriage, are much less free in their socio-sexual behavior than urban ones, and village prudes are still ready to tar the gate of a house that shelters an "immoral" girl. Hard-dying folk traditions tend to reinforce older attitudes about courtship and marriage: The young people's club, for example, struggles to replace "the street," a charming but faintly sexist mode of wife-shopping; and bridal pairs still follow the correct proceedings in a dismal village ZAGS office with a walk around the church. In the home, the husband continues to be the *khozyain*, even by official definition—though now rather as a "spokesman" and responsible agent for the family than as the once omnipotent *bolshak*. A well-known Soviet ethnographic study, *The Village of Viryatino*, frankly describes the wife as a "housekeeper, child rearer, and the organizer of daily life." It seems likely that, given the cyclical and stable nature of agrarian life, the low investment of capital in the agricultural sector, and, the continuing need for masses of farm labor, this situation will not change significantly in the near future.[6]

The problem for urban women, the principal beneficiaries of the communist

[4] John Maynard, *The Russian Peasant and Other Studies* (1942; New York, 1962) 388–89, 413, 415; Dodge, *Women*, 65–66. For a more negative view of women's life on the kolkhoz, see Fëdor Belov, *The History of a Soviet Collective Farm* (New York, 1955). The best study of collectivization is Moshe Lewin, *Russian Peasants and Soviet Power* (New York, 1975).

[5] Dodge, *Women*, 168–70 (quotation, 170 from *Izvestiya*); Tolkunova, *Pravo*, 22–23, 181. Lapidus' more recent figures in "Occupational Segretation" do not change this picture.

[6] *The Village of Viryatino*, by P. I. Kushner, *et al.*, tr. Sula Benet (New York, 1970), cf. ch. IV with ch. X (quotation, 253); See also the article of S. Dunn on the family in *The Soviet Rural Community*, ed. J. Millar (Urbana, Ill., 1971) 325ff. and *Rabotnitsa* (May 1973) 8–11, 29.

program of emancipation, is of a different sort. Though enjoying more mobility, education, and variety of occupation than their village sisters, they have ironically far less time to pursue their jobs and career opportunities to the point where equality in Soviet life would become a fact. For the enormous category known as "family women," those with a husband, children, or relatives to look after, the major obstacle to equality is the "double shift," which forces the average Soviet housewife to work a full day in office or mill and then at once to begin her second shift with shopping, housework, and child care—bringing her total number of work hours up to twice that of the average person unencumbered with such duties. As Bette Stavrakis wrote some years ago, "the Soviets have not really refuted the theory that woman's place is in the home, but have expanded it into a new theory which holds that women's place is in the factory as well as in the home."[7]

The double shift, as it operates today, has no theoretical justification in socialist theory, which always taught that housework and child care would be shared with the wife partly by communal services and partly by the husband. The ideas of Bebel, Engels, Kollontai, and Lenin on this matter were repeated in Soviet declarations right up to the mid-1930's. The first post-revolutionary Party program hoped to abolish "the yoke of household economy by means of the House-Commune." *The ABC of Communism* (1920) wondered how the woman toiler would "realize her rights when she has to look after the house, shop, stand in line, wash, tend to the child, and bear the heavy cross of housekeeping." During the first Five Year Plan, laments and appeals rose to a crescendo. "Down with the kitchen!" exclaimed Ilin, the pedagogue of industrialization. "We shall destroy this little penitentiary! We shall free millions of women from house-keeping. They want to work like the rest of us. In a factory-kitchen, one person can prepare from fifty to one hundred dinners a day. We shall force machines to peel potatoes, wash the dishes, cut the bread, stir the soup, make ice cream." And slogans like "The Saucepan is the Enemy of the Party Cell" or "Away with Pots and Pans" became watchwords of economic and political agitation.[8]

This was not mere sloganizing. During the Civil War and again during industrialization, vast campaigns were mounted and energies expended in opening factory and neighborhood dining rooms. But strictly communal cooking and feeding in residential units never became a reality. In 1936 a *Pravda* editorial denounced a blueprint for an apartment house without individual kitchens as a "left deviation" and an attempt to "artificially introduce communal living." The "house commune" (*dom-kommuna*) or communal apartment house, never materialized in the cities; and during collectivization its rural counterpart, the "commune" (*kommuna*) was abandoned in favor of the

---

[7] Tolkunova, *Pravo*, 168; Stavrakis, "Women," 254.

[8] *KPSS v rezol.*, pt. I, 414–15; N. Bukharin and E. Preobrazhensky, *Azbuka kommunizma* (Petrograd, 1920) 140; M. Ilin, *New Russia's Primer*, tr. G. Counts and N. Lodge (Boston, 1931) 150; Halle, *Woman*, 366. See also Winter, *Red Virtue*, 110.

far more individualistic kolkhoz. Since then, although full public catering has survived as an ideal, the tendency has been away from communal feeding, living, and housekeeping. In recent times, with the ever growing tendency for the "separate apartment" (*otdelnaya kvartira*) to replace that expedient combination of socialism and urban overcrowding, the "multiple family apartment" (*kommunalnaya kvartira*; or, in everyday speech, *kommunalka*), the tendency away from residential collectivism appears irreversible. The quiet and continuing abandonment of communal living was due partly to the Party's decision to reinforce the separate nuclear family, and partly to the obvious lack of enthusiasm among most Russians for this particular feature of classical socialism.[9]

Communal or collective upbringing of children has met a similar fate. Kollontai's dream—shared by a recent disciple, the eminent economist Strumilin—of having all Soviet children cared for almost full-time in state nurseries has never come true. Nor has there ever been agreement as to how child care duties ought to be divided between the state and the parents, though the regime has always cherished the goal of a "complete" network of preschool institutions capable of allowing all women to work. The network was begun right after the Revolution when only a handful of nurseries existed, and it grew slowly during the 1920's, taking a big jump during the first plan, tapering off after the mid-1930's, and taking a downward swing—relative to the need—during and after World War II. At the present time, only about 10 percent of the children under two and about 20 percent of those between three and seven are enrolled in nursery schools and kindergartens, the largest numbers being found in the big cities. Though the cost is reasonable and based on earnings, many women would prefer not to put their very small children in them and would rather entrust them to a *babushka*-in-residence, if they have one. Nevertheless, the demand for daycare centers far exceeds the supply. The result is that many women who do not enjoy the use of such facilities are kept out of the economy or in jobs unsuited to their skills.[10]

The woman continues to bear the chief responsibility for looking after the children, as well as most of the housework, whether or not she has access to a day care center. Official statements proclaim that it is the husbands' socialist duty to honor sexual equality by helping with domestic chores and with the children. In a recent poll of young men and women, 75 percent agreed that the

[9] For some accounts of early efforts at collective feeding: Sokolov, *Spasite detei!*, 23; *Petrokommuna* (Petrograd, 1920); *Kommunistka*, 8–9 (Jan.-Feb. 1921) 26–30; Krupskaya, *Zavety*, 39–40; Dillon, *Russia*, 230. The *Pravda* article is cited in Stavrakis "Women," 70, n. 36. The *kommunalka*, still the norm in large cities, is a formerly one-family (but large family) apartment now divided among two or three families or multiple individuals who share kitchen, toilet, bath, and hallway. The *otdelnaya* is equivalent to our one-family apartments.

[10] Bilshai, *Sov. demok.*, 49; Stavrakis, "Women," 249; Dodge, *Women*, 76–83, 241; Susan Jacoby in *Saturday Review* (August 21, 1971) 41–43, 53; Starodub, *Zhenshchina-truzhenitsa i mat* (Leningrad, 1967), 80. For Strumilin's position and a refutation: Laptënok, *Moral*, 232–35, and Starodub, *Zhenshchina*, 90.

husband should partake of housework. But a Leningrad study revealed that 81.5 percent of the wives interviewed did all the housework themselves. And a 1962 Soviet book reprinted a cartoon showing a wife up to her neck in housecleaning being teased by her reclining husband with the words: "You haven't read Remarque? God you are backward!" The official status of Soviet woman is unashamedly summarized in a recent book devoted to women's progress throughout the world. "The working woman fulfills a number of social functions," it says. "As a worker she participates in the production of goods and services needed for the sustenance of society; as a citizen she partakes of state and public life; as a mother she bears and rears a new generation; and besides that she runs the house which also possesses social significance, for in it is the normal environment for living and leisure for the members of the family who work and study."[11] But who possesses the leisure? Although the housework time of the average Moscow woman has fallen since 1923 from 6.02 hours to 3.20 hours per day, and the difference between the amount of her time and her husband's has diminished, she still works more and rests less than anyone else in the family. Women spend twice as many unproductive hours as do men. Shopping consumes about 40 percent of the time used for household concerns, and there is a relative lack of electrical appliances and of household auxiliary services such as take-out food shops, laundromats, cleaners, and the like. For most married women, it all adds up to either staying home from work, over-work, or employment at a nearby job which might not meet their qualifications.[12]

How do women feel about it? On one side there are those like "Vera" who, in an interview with Susan Jacoby, rejected state raising of children with the following comment. "They [the old Bolsheviks] weren't realistic about everything. That idea has been pretty much discredited in our country. It just isn't in human nature to carry it out. I consider myself a good communist, but it's not up to the Party to bring up my son." Another of Jacoby's interviewees voiced the desire to stay home all the time and be paid as a professional mother,[13] an idea that has won some academic support from the demographer Perevedentsev. But this is certainly a minority view. Perevedentsev's solution has been characterized by the jurist Berëzovskaya as "no better than slavery,"[14] Another woman writer holds that turning engineers, doctors, and scientists into "universal kitchen machines" would hurt not only production but also the position of women.[15] This is a judgment that, in the light of Western experience, can hardly be denied. A recent questionnaire—no doubt made

[11] Figures: Stiernlöf, *Kvinnor*, 119; Cartoon: *Chistyi istochnik*, 32. Quotation: *Zhenshchiny mira v borbe za sotsialnyi progress* (Moscow, 1972) 65.

[12] Dodge, *Women*, 91–99; Madison, *Social Welfare*, 70; Stiernlöf, *Kvinnor*, 76–80; Starodub, *Zhenshchina-truzhenitsa*, 74–77.

[13] Jacoby, "Women's Lib—Russian Style," *Sunday Times* (London), (August 20, 1972) 25–26.

[14] Stiernlöf, *Kvinnor*, 102–103.   [15] Tolkunova, *Pravo*, 170.

from a very selective sampling—indicated that 90 percent of the women polled desired to fulfill all three roles of the ideal Soviet woman: in the economy, in public activity, and in the family.[16] The fact is few women have much time for public activity. Yet most Russian women are convinced that although work does not automatically confer liberation, true liberation is impossible without it—a belief that is gaining wide credence in many societies.

Whatever measures the regime may take in the near future, short of mandating that males share housework and child care on an absolutely equal footing with their wives, they are not likely to solve the problem. Efforts to increase household services and child care facilities will alleviate the problem but will not remove it. The double shift, as long as it prevails, means less time and job continuity for females; and this in turn means less opportunity for promotion and thus, ultimately, less power for women. This is the fruit of the politics of sex in Soviet society. Its most fundamental cause may be simply the determination of men to run things; but its institutional basis is the solution of the family question reached in the 1930's and modified and improved in the decades since Stalin. The resultant inequality is inscribed upon the sociological face of the Soviet pyramids of political power.

If one were to align the main institutions of Soviet life in a spectrum according to female participation in leading positions, one would find that the army, the Party, and the bureaucracy on the side having fewest women in responsible positions, with the economic, scientific, welfare-health, and educational hierarchies gradually filling up with women. The professional military is almost purely male, as in most other societies past and present. Not since the Civil War has a woman studied at the General Staff College or commanded a sizable regular unit. After the War, women were demobilized and the armed services reverted to a traditional male composition. Amazonism was a fellow casualty of other euphoric military innovations of the stormy years, and it shared its grave with military democracy and egalitarianism.

Prejudices are often shattered by necessity. In World War II, the Party recalled the war-like talents of the female population, and students, schoolgirls, workers, and volunteer women snipers were welcomed into the Red Army where they served as machine-gunners, tank-drivers, partisans, pilots, and navigators. They also staffed the communications, medical, and political branches of the service. Partisan women were the most colorful and their exploits often recalled those of the revolutionary past. One *partizanka* destroyed a nest of Germans by blowing up herself and them with a grenade; another posed as a chamber maid and slew Wilhelm Kube, the governor of Belorussia, in his bed. Zoya Rukhadze, as she stood before a German firing squad, invoked the name of Vera Figner. And the most famous of them all, Zoya Kosmodemyanskaya—an eighteen-year-old Komsomol—summoned up

---

[16] *Soviet Life* (March 1974).

recollections of Bardina, Perovskaya, and a dozen others as she reenacted their stoic valor and stood upon the gallows in December 1941 crying "You hang me now but I am not alone. We have two hundred million and you cannot hang them all." But having women permanently in the army, and especially leading it, was not considered a part of normal procedure, and after the War women again returned to peaceful work and the army became practically *Frauenrein*.[17]

Women's position in the Party and the government, in terms of numbers, percentages, or places of influential leadership, has not changed significantly since it assumed the pattern of the 1930's. Female membership in the Party hovers around a fifth of the total. Few women hold high-ranking positions: none has ever occupied any of the three top posts in Soviet political life; and the Party's inner sanctum, the Politburo or Presidium, was entered by a woman (Furtseva) only in the time of Khrushchëv. At that time also, women were seen as ministers for the first time since Kollontai, and, although Soviet women are certainly more numerous in the various legislative bodies than they are in most other countries, their presence at the top of administration is rare. The same pattern holds for almost every pyramid of Soviet life: the factory, the collective farm, the unions, Party affiliates, and the social, cultural, and educational establishments. Managers, directors, chief-surgeons, rectors, chairmen are almost always men. As Dodge and others have pointed out, although women do rise in Soviet career channels that are closed to them in most of the world, the peaks of these are generally denied to them.[18]

It would appear, then, that the male leaders of Soviet society share Aristotle's view that "although there may be exceptions to the order of nature, the male is by nature fitter for command than the female, just as the full-grown is superior to the younger and more immature."[19] Whether or not Soviet women could, indeed, be made totally fit "to command" and to operate the decision-making machinery of their society at the highest levels is still an open question. But the fact remains that, by the resolve of male leadership past and present, women have been deprived—by virtue of their one-sided role in the family—of the chance to compete equally for high administrative positions. No one can prove that women lack the ability and the energy for

[17] For these events, see: *Svetlyi put*, 211–20; Figner, *V borbe*, 226; *Geroini*, 2 v. (Moscow, 1969), I, 283–92 (quotation, 286). For more on the subject: *Zhen. Gorod*, 207–75; T. Logunova, *O dnyakh partizansikh* (Moscow, 1969); V. Gordeeva, *Lyudmila Donskaya* (Moscow, 1973); Stiernlöf, *Kvinnor*, 9–19; *La femme*, 59; *The Diary of Nina Kostërina*, tr. M. Ginsburg (New York, 1968).

[18] Tolkunova, *Pravo*, 102; Dodge, *Women*, 213–14, 243. For the way this is reflected in fiction, see Gasiorowska, *Women*, 12, 169, 210. Valuable analyses of women's political functions at the local level may be found in Joel Moses, "Indoctrination as a Female Political Role in the Soviet Union," *Comparative Politics* (July 1976) 525–47; and Jerry Hough, "The Impact of Participation: Women and the Women's Issue in Soviet Policy Debates" in his *The Soviet Union and Social Science Theory* (Cambridge, Mass., 1977).

[19] Aristotle, *The Politics*, ed. B. Jowett (Oxford, 1921) I, 1259[b].

even the most arduous tasks of sustaining and developing socialism in the Soviet Union; but such tasks require total dedication, long hours of uninterrupted and concentrated work, a continuity and an alertness that does not brook frequent interruptions for queuing up to buy salami and cucumbers. The time and continuity required for such intensive activity is robbed from them in order that they will perform a social function which the state, again by male decision, has chosen not to undertake in large measure.

Beyond that, and at the root of it, Soviet men are also not really ready to grant complete equality to women. The actions of Soviet leaders suggest this strongly; and conversations with Soviet men confirm it. Men—not only in Russia—still have a fear of Amazonism. Their ideal of the Soviet woman is a highly successful career woman (but an engineer, a doctor, a cosmonaut, or cultural figure; not a manager, premier, or commander) who also has a husband and a well-adjusted family life. The ideal in the case matches the reality. It is as far as the Soviet woman has gone. And, though women have achieved more parity in Soviet society than in most other societies, it cannot be called equality.

How do Soviet women answer the eternal question "What is to be done?" The most frequent answer, when applied to women's equality, is: "done about what?" A few who answer this way are simply skeptics who believe, with Otto Weininger, that the woman question will be with us as long as there are two sexes; and specifically that there is an insoluble tension between women's need to care for home and children and the revolutionary tradition of women in production and in social activity. If the woman works, she is doomed to exhaustion; if not, to boredom. But many insist that there is no woman question in Russia any more, that it has been solved by the Revolution. Successful revolutions—as Americans and Russians should both know—tend to cast a self-satisfied pall over efforts at constant improvement. Or, as one writer describing Israeli women's "flight from feminism" put it, the "smoke-screen of past achievements" convince women that they are fully liberated.[20] And far more of the Israeli liberation—largely a product, incidentally, of the Russian-Jewish intelligentsia—has eroded in recent years than has the Soviet, however else one might compare the relative merits of each. The average urban woman in Russia is so concerned with the everyday questions of study and work, prices, housing, and child facilities that she tends to smile ironically (as do men) at the very words "woman question" (*zhenskii vopros*) as at something quaint and out of the distant past.

Since the early 1960's, spontaneous and at first unofficial "women's soviets" have sprung up in factories, schools, and other institutions with the purpose of "bettering the condition of life" by means of inspections, evalua-

[20] Carol Clapsaddle, "Flight From Feminism: the Case of the Israeli Women," *Response* (Summer 1973) 157–75.

tions, and recommendations for improvement of this or that aspect of women's life. And in 1967 a "women's commission" was established in the Central Trade Union Council. These may be seen as a partial revival of the old delegate system within Zhenotdel. But the main national organ, the Committee of Soviet Women, is far from being a reincarnation of Zhenotdel itself. Founded in 1941 as the Anti-fascist Committee of Soviet Women, it helped give birth four years later in Paris to the International Democratic Federation of Women, and has since then been far more interested in the international concerns of that body—fighting "fascism," supporting liberation struggles in the Third World, and promoting peace movements—than it has in the domestic problems of Soviet women. Its recent President, Tereshkova, writing on International Women's Day in 1970, reiterated the duties of Soviet women and urged a "thoroughgoing scientific study of" the problem of blending these roles and of "maximizing the liberation of women from unproductive housework and reordering our everyday life." But beyond holding symposia and making declarations such as this, the Committee has displayed few signs of independent feminist activity.[21]

This is not to say that there is no activity and no program for reform; only that it tends to be dispersed and to take the form of journalistic agitation. One of the strongest statements in this agitation was that made by the writer on women's affairs, Tolkunova. "Compared to the number of women engaged in the economy and the number of specialists among them, too few of them are promoted to positions of independent administrative responsibility in various governmental organs at the regional, territorial, republican, and Union levels." What she recommended as a solution to this and other shortcomings in women's life, was a moral remodeling of people and their ideas about women, more public feeding, laundry and other facilities, and a correspondence of the work hours of husbands and wives.[22]

In all of this there is a little trace of what in the West is now called a "women's liberation movement," and nothing at all of Radical Feminism which, according to one American vision, "is working for the eradication of domination and elitism in all human relationships."[23] If the regime itself wished to push directly toward total equality, it would either have to promote and co-opt women to the top of all Soviet hierarchies on a par with men, thus demoting many men and sending them home to mind the house, or to do so by socializing all housework and releasing women to rise to their highest natural levels. Neither one appears likely to occur. And, it seems that most Soviet women—even the most conscious and talented among them—would not soon avail themselves of the opportunity to climb all the way up to the denuded

[21] *Svetlyi put*, 209–210, 227; S. T. Lyubimova, *Oktyabrskaya revolyutsiya i polozhenie zhenshchin v SSSR* (Moscow, 1967) 25; *Zhenshchiny mira*, 71–82. Tereshkova's remarks are from *Pravda*, (March 8, 1970) 3. See Starodub, *Zhenshchina*, 51 on the commissions.

[22] Tolkunova, *Pravo*, 102–103 (quotation), 184–85.

[23] Ware, *Woman Power*, 1.

peaks of power and decision making. Apparently, they are not overly anxious to assume the highest responsibilities. They would rather have a situation where the few who wished to could rise and where all women would enjoy more leisure and study time and greater opportunity for professional and scholarly self-development than is now afforded them by the lopsided inequities of the double shift. This is as high as a "feminist" consciousness has risen at present.

Should, however, the Party renege on its recent promises of more facilities, more free time, and more opportunity for women's advancement and renege for any reason other than a military emergency, the nature of the dissatisfaction may be altered. "I believe," wrote Elena Dyakonova as far back as the 1890's, "that in the future the role of women in Russia will be important. The idea of higher education for women will be firmly rooted in society and a whole series of women capable of helping to run the country will appear. But what if, after future historical events, we are again pushed down, and our precious rights taken from us? Shall we submit without a struggle? No! No, comrades! If life vetoes work for me—then let this diary remain and serve as a monument to my self-consciousness."[24]

3. THE NATURE OF THE LIBERATION

How did the Bolshevik liberation of women differ from what is commonly called their "emancipation" in the West? First, the essential ingredients of the liberation include: the release and mobilization of energies, talents, and skills, previously stored up and unused, among the female population of a then backward society; a freeing of the forces within women for the general good and the development of a sense of purpose; and an institutionalization, of this process by the legal establishment of sexual, educational, economic, and political equality. Of these declared equalities, those absolutely essential to the full utilization of women's labor and women's mental power have come closest to realization: educational and economic equality. Through the portals of schools, factories, and institutes women have passed in an endless stream, thereby gaining much and giving much in return; the doors leading to the corridors of power and influence are technically open to all women, but in reality can be pried open by only a few. At the base of this arrangement is a social myth of Soviet life that teaches: Women are equal to men in ability and creativity.

This freeing of energies—customarily called "careers open to talent" by historians—was at the center of the original European feminism that came into the world at a time when only the few were convinced that constitutionalism, representative government, and democracy were to be the wave of the future. In places like Russia, the feminism of education and op-

[24] Dyakonova, *Dnevnik*, 289.

portunity (initially for some; eventually for all) flourished for decades in an environment where legal political life was no more than a dream. It was natural everywhere that early feminists, surrounded by hordes of voteless subjects and citizens, were initially concerned with clearing away obstacles to the professional advancement and full development of women as human beings. Marital and juridical reforms were ancillary to this central mission. But as suffrage began to widen in the late nineteenth century, and since men continued to place obstacles along the path to equality in professional life, women just as naturally focused on the vote, though this was originally seen by many as simply an indirect method of achieving their main design. As the century turned, the mystique of the franchise obscured all others, and the bulk of feminist energies was channeled into the suffrage movement. The movement itself was transformed into a crusade that, it was fervently believed, would finally endow the woman with her human rights.

Winning the vote turned out to be a hollow victory for the Western feminists. It did not bring in its wake any large-scale benefits in terms of women's work or professional and educational opportunity, or even much of importance in the way of legal and sexual equality. And since almost everywhere in the West, the women's movement was divided sharply into a prominent bourgeois feminism and a weaker working-class women's movement, a division often further complicated by the presence of ethnic and confessional subgroups, the continuing efforts to secure the opening of public life to women on an equal basis were dissipated in wastefully repetitive and mutually hostile activities. Thus, deprived of unity, of power, of the support of men in power, and of an integrated program, Western feminism failed even to achieve its original goal: massive opening of the doors to opportunity. Neither direct action nor the indirect device of the franchise had effected this. England and the United States—by no means the worst examples—were as much a man's world in the 1960's as they had been in the days when Suffragettes were forcibly fed.

The Bolshevik liberation differed from the Western experience on two major counts: it was effected in a backward society and it was effected by revolutionary forces. But it was also preceded and prepared by generations of theoretical rumination and social movement. The continuity between these pre-revolutionary movements and the Bolshevik liberation has never found full acceptance in the sparse literature on Russian women. The feminists, in particular, have been virtually ignored until very recently. Soviet writers tend to trace things back only as far as the proletarian women's movement of the Bolsheviks, dating from 1913–1914; while strongly pro-Soviet Western writers, such as Halle and Mandel[1] preface their accounts of Soviet women by references to the great heroines of the populist movement in the 1870's. The feminists, properly speaking, are hardly mentioned as part of this process.

[1] See Chapter XII, 1, n. 3.

417

But it is precisely the feminists, the generation of the 1860's as well as that of 1905, who must be credited with making the woman question a larger public issue than the intelligentsia had done; with publicizing its complexities, with agitating for and winning higher education and other rights for women. It was the Russian feminists, not Bebel, who taught Russians how difficult the problem was and who outlined all of its dimensions including some, like prostitution, which the Marxists refused to study seriously until forced to do so in a post-revolutionary environment. There were in fact three strands in the pre-revolutionary women's movement: the legal feminist movement; the proletarian women's movement; and the tradition of women playing prominent roles in the broader revolutionary movement. Each of these, in different and sometimes conflicting ways, contributed greatly to women's consciousness before the Revolution and to the fact that on the day after the Revolution a woman's movement was possessed of a program, an embryonic organization, and a mystique.[2]

Bolshevik liberation itself also came in three overlapping waves—each characterized by a different relationship of the sexes. The first was the flow of basic legislation in the years 1917–1920 that gave women suddenly and almost permanently all the civic, legal, and political rights which they would receive in Soviet times. The decrees were signed mostly by masculine hands, but their contents were inspired at least by women—the relationship being symbolized by such programmatic and operational partnerships as Goikhbarg-Kollontai, Semashko-Lebedeva, and Lunacharsky-Krupskaya. The second wave, historically congruent with the Zhenotdel, was by far the most interesting and the most important in terms of women's auto-emancipation—and the most different from Western experience. It was the deliberate, painstaking effort of hundreds of already "released" women injecting their beliefs and programs and their self-confidence into the bloodstream of rural and proletarian Russia. It was classical social revolution—a process not an event, a phenomenon that cannot be fused, triggered, or set off by a mere turnover of power which confines itself to the center and confines its efforts to decrees and laws enunciating the principles of equality. True social revolution in an underdeveloped society does not end with the reshuffling of property any more than it does with the reshuffling of portfolios; it is the result of social mobilization. Put in plain terms, it means bodies moving out among the people with well-laid plans, skills, and revolutionary euphoria; it means teaching, pushing, prodding, cajoling the stubborn, the ignorant, and the backward by means of the supreme component of all radical propaganda: the message and the conviction that revolution is relevant to everyday life.

[2] It is instructive here to contrast the continuity of the women's movement in Russia from 1860 to 1930 with the episodic character of women's revolutionary ferment in France in 1789, 1848, and 1871. For the roots of the problem, see the recent article by Jane Abray, "Feminism in the French Revolution," *American Historical Review*, LXXX, 1 (Feb. 1975) 43–62.

The movement of Bolshevik women and men through the Russian country-side in the early years of the Revolution, the Agit-trains, the reading cabins, the literary and sanitation drives, cannot help but recall to the student of Russian history that bygone "movement out to the people" of the revolutionary populists. But in the twentieth-century version, the naïve will of the *narodnik* was buttressed by the self-confidence of political organization; and the subjective personality of the romantic populists was replaced by the hard objectivity of political power. Zhenotdel, combining the old revolutionary messianic fervor with the modern machinery of political and social mobilization, was able to lay the foundations of the first genuine social women's liberation in history. "The process of emancipation now going on in Russia," wrote Fanina Halle in 1932, "differs from all earlier ones in the recorded history of mankind in that it is carried out according to plan and on an unprecedented scale. And however that process may turn out in the course of historical development, one thing has already been attained: the humanization of women."[3]

This wave of the movement was led by the women themselves, often without the moral and political support of men. In the next wave, however, the women's self-emancipatory impulse was largely missing, and the decisions affecting them were made almost wholly by men. This was the industrialization drive that began in the late 1920's and lasted through the following decade. In reading the sources and the accounts of the period, it is hard not to gain the impression that, as impressive as Zhenotdel had been, the big victories in opportunity, full employment, and affirmative action really date from the first Five Year Plan and reach their apogee after the liquidation of Zhenotdel, in the full flush of industrialization. The equality and scope of activity sought by women fitted in with the needs of the regime—the need for the labor and mental power of the entire population. This put an undeniably manipulative stamp upon the Soviet experience, and this manipulative tendency also accounted for many of the regressive measures enacted in the last decade of Stalinism. In perspective, the liberation of women in Soviet Russia came about in the way it did because of the congruence of some of the interests of women and of the ruling men—or, put in a different way, the congruence of a humanistic ideology with the requirements of a rapidly developing economy.[4]

If the Soviet experience is viewed as a historical or sociological model for women's liberation elsewhere, its methodology and its achievements ought to be treated as two separate—though not always easily separable—components of such a model. In affluent developed societies exhibiting no signs of a serious and viable Marxist-Leninist or Maoist oriented movement—in other words in the West—interest in the Soviet model will tend to focus on the results rather than the process and the original revolutionary style of the libera-

[3] Halle, *Woman*, ix.
[4] The best and most recent treatment of this theme is Lapidus, *Women in Soviet Society*.

tion. Such societies will see more parallels in the first wave (legislation) than in the second (mobilization) or the third (industrialization). Western feminists will want to examine the Soviet experience—negative as well as positive—with policies of affirmative action in job and school, equal curricula, the opening of professions, and the consequent cultivation of respect and self-respect for women; with maternity programs for working women accompanied by a greater measure of general medical and social welfare, networks of child care centers, shared housework, and the changed sex attitudes attendant upon these reforms; and finally, in the context of their own societies, with the possibilities—after sufficient psychological preparation in connection with all these innovations—of the gradual movement of women into positions of responsibility and power at first in the private pyramids of social life and then in the state itself.

National liberation movements in the developing world will probably display more immediate interest in the role of women in revolutionary action—in their ability to fight and organize; in the use of female cadres in mobilizing masses of women in support of a general liberation program, national or social; in their post-revolutionary role in drawing the backward elements of the population (women, peasants) into the orbit of modernity—however that may be defined; and, finally, in the value of women as technicians and workers when the time arrives to move that revolutionary society toward industrialization. In fact, examples of such utilization of women, whether consciously adopted from a so-called Marxist-Leninist model or not, already abound in the experience of some developing and insurrectionary nations of recent decades even in places where primitive economic levels and religious peculiarities do not always permit this model to be emulated effectively.[5]

It is to be hoped that women and men, in remaking the relations of the sexes in order to achieve a richer existence for women and thus a healthier environment for both sexes, will find something of value in the history of the Russian

[5] Little of a comparative nature on women in twentieth-century revolutions, Communist or otherwise, has been written. For some individual cases, see: M. Wolf and R. Witke, eds., *Women in Chinese Society* (Stanford, 1975); M. Young, ed., *Women in China* (Ann Arbor, 1973); C. K. Yang, *Chinese Communist Society: the Family and the Village* (Cambridge, Mass., 1959); Ruth Sidel, *Women and Child Care in China* (Baltimore, 1973); D. Marr, "The 1920's Women's Rights Debate in Vietnam," *Journal of Asian Studies*, XXV, 3 (May 1976) 371–89; *Women of Vietnam*, 1966- (periodical); *Vietnamese Women* (Hanoi, 1966); Arlene Bergman, *Women of Vietnam* (San Francisco, 1974); M. Randall, *Cuban Women Now* (Toronto, 1974); Fidel Castro and Linda Jeness, *Women and the Cuban Revolution* (New York, 1970); S. Purcell, "Modernizing Women for a Modern Society: the Cuban Case," in A. Pescatello, ed., *Female and Male in Latin America* (Pittsburgh, 1973); *Žene hrvatske u radničkom pokretu* (Zagreb, 1967); J. Tomasevich, "Yugoslavia During the Second World War," in W. Vucinich, ed., *Contemporary Yugoslavia* (Berkeley, 1969) 59–118; D. Živković, "O učešću žena Boke u narodoosloboditačkoj borbi," *Istorijski časopis*, XIV-XV (1963–1965) 465–81; *Slovenke v narodo-osvobodilnem boju: zbornik dokumentov, člankov, in spominov*, 2 v. in 3 (Ljubljana, 1970); B. S. Denich, "Urbanization and Women's Roles in Yugoslavia," *Anthropological Quarterly* 49, 1 (Jan. 1976) 11–19; *idem.*, "Sex and Power in the Balkans," in M. Rosaldo and L. Lamphere, eds., *Women, Culture, and Society* (Stanford, 1974) 243–62.

women's struggle for a place in society equivalent to their enormous potential as productive and creative members of that society. Adopting styles, techniques, and slogans worked out in a culture of such obvious historical specificity as Russia's is a perilous business at best; and there is no call to believe that local equivalents of a Figner, a Kollontai, or a Zhenotdel are the prerequisites for a successful liberation effort, revolutionary or otherwise, in one's own society. Nevertheless, there is in the opulent and often flamboyant history of the Russian women's movements and their ultimate fate an extraordinary quantity of social experience and theory that can reveal much about the nature of social movements—not only of Russia's past but also, by way of very careful analogy, of the present time and of other places. Most important, the revolutionary settlement of women's role in Russian life—its distortions and shortcomings as well as its glittering achievements—will hold lessons for women and men for some time to come.

APPENDIX

Note on Kollontai's *Social Bases of the Woman Question* (1909)

Kollontai's *Social Bases of the Woman Question*, the biggest book ever written by a Russian on the subject, was planned to serve as the theoretical underpinning of the labor delegation to the All-Russian Women's Congress of 1908, perhaps as a handbook for the tutors (certainly not for the workers themselves), and perhaps also as a lure for the more socially minded feminists. But Kollontai had difficulty in finding a publisher, and when she did, the manuscript was sent for comment to Gorky who was then living on Capri. Gorky approved the work but the manuscript was lost for several months and the book only appeared in early 1909. By that time, not only was the Congress over, but almost everything else as well: the feminists and socialists were both in disarray and the issue of women's emancipation temporarily out of fashion. Since the main focus of the book was an analysis of the Russian feminist movement as of 1908, these circumstances robbed it of some historical influence. Since it was too long for agitational purposes, too learned for ordinary workers, and too topical to have relevance at a later stage in the movement, *Social Bases* found itself hanging in a historical limbo and was rarely cited by activists in the socialist women's movement. But since it remains the major work on the subject by a Russian Marxist, and thus likely to be used extensively by historians of the woman question, some commentary on it is in order.[1]

The book's historical and economic analysis closely follows Bebel, Engels, and other German writers, and it suffers from excessive abstractness. When Kollontai attempts to comment on the origin of the women's movement in Russia, she either exaggerates the importance of early female mutinies in factory and field or retreats into such commonplaces as "the emancipatory efforts of the Russian bourgeois women were synchronized with the awakening of the economic and political life of Russia in the 1860's." But she strikes a more cogent note when she proclaims that the woman question is much broader and deeper than the problem of education and professional opportunity. "The woman question," she writes, employing one of her favorite figures, "is in the last analysis a question of a morsel of bread. Its roots lie deep in economics. In order to enjoy real equality with man, the woman must

---

[1] The circumstances of the book's publication are given in Kollontai, "Avtbiog. ocherk," 277.

423

first of all become economically independent." And in a passage which owes much to Bebel and more to Zetkin, she sums it all up:

Followers of historical materialism deny the existence of a special woman question separate from the general social question of our day. Certain definite economic factors have brought about the subjugation of woman; her own natural peculiarities played only a *secondary* role in this. Only the disappearance of the economic causes and the transformation of those economic modes which enslaved her can fundamentally change her status. In other words, the really free and equal woman can make her appearance only in a world reorganized along new social and productive lines.[2]

There was little new in all this. Tkachëv, as early as the 1860's had said much the same thing.[3] The main enemy was feminism, and Kollontai's assault upon it occupies most of the book. Quoting Zetkin, she describes the European feminist movement as "the last echo of the Third Estate's struggle for emancipation." It is not meant as a compliment, for the burden of her argument—buttressed with quotations from resolutions of international feminist congresses and parties—is that the "bourgeois" women's movements (her pages are littered with terms like *burzhuazki* and *ravnopravki*) desire only the enfranchisement of women of their own class either in order to help stop the spread of popular suffrage or to open up professional opportunities for women of means. The allegation was partially correct, as many feminists were willing to admit. But it was *not* true for all feminists, either in Europe or in Russia.

Kollontai did not blame women who wanted the vote "within the framework of the existing structure of social classes" for their "involuntary sin." This was a natural class position. What angered her was the feminists' stepping outside the boundaries of their class in order to lure their "poor younger sisters" of the proletariat, whose energies were thus being plundered and deflected from their "class" mission. "Ought working women answer the call of the feminists and play an active, direct role in the struggle for women's equality or, remaining true to their class traditions, ought they march along their own road and fight with whatever means at their disposal for the liberation not only of women but of all humanity from the yoke and enslavement of the contemporary modes of social existence?" The unequivocal answer was a quotation from the Gotha Program: "The emancipation of the proletarian woman cannot be the business of women of all classes. This task can only be accomplished by the common effort of the entire proletariat without distinction of sex."[4]

[2] Quotations, in order; 49, 34, 4 (italics in the original). An excerpt, with all the main points in the argument, may be found in Kollontai, *Stati*, 61–81.

[3] See Chapter II/3 above.

[4] Quotations: Kollontai, *Sots. osnovy*, 235, 27, 3 and 235 again. This arrangement of Kollontai's passages does not violate or exaggerate the sense of her argument.

The Russian feminists bore the brunt of Kollontai's assault. For women of the philanthropic societies, she had nothing but contempt. "They cannot," she wrote, harnessing an old cliché of the intelligentsia to Marxist purposes, "empty out the ocean of pain and misery created by the capitalist exploitation of hired labor with the teaspoon of charity." Though recognizing that the Mutual Philanthropic Society had graduated into politics, Kollontai paid little attention to it except to deride its senseless dream of an all-women's movement. The Progressive Party came in for more abuse, not only for its isolation from the masses, but for its pretensions to social concern. But most of Kollontai's attention was riveted on the Union for Women's Equality, the most democratic, the most social, and therefore the least vulnerable to attack. Since the entire left wing of the Union supported universal suffrage and a strong labor reform platform, Kollontai had to focus on the schism in the Union and on its consequent refusal to choose the Social Democrats as their "own" party. The wooing of the Trudoviks and of the Kadets was proof enough to Kollontai that this was the product of "an instinctive recognition of class antagonism, a gulf, based upon economic interests."[5]

Much of the anti-feminist polemic in *Social Bases* is overdone. The author is incapable of giving any credit whatsoever to the feminist movement either in having contributed to electoral victories elsewhere, in supporting universal suffrage, or in showing concern for social problems at home. When she does concede a social dimension to a feminist group, she sees it only as a demonstration of ulterior motives. In the last analysis, it would seem that the major offense of the feminists, which Kollontai claims to forgive, is that they were not socialists. A different kind of weakness is that Kollontai gives very little attention to burning problems within the proletarian movement itself. Claiming that male and female workers (and socialists) are yoked to a common struggle, she sheds no light on the problem of male proletarian hostility towards women workers and socialist women emancipators; though in fairness it should be said that she made up for this shortcoming in her future writings. And in claiming that "educated" bourgeois women were alienated from women in the factories, she tells us nothing of the problems faced by the socialist *intelligentka* in communicating with that same stratum of women. On top of all this, the book is meandering, repetitive (often to the point of dullness), and hastily put together. And it is certainly mistitled.

But in spite of these weaknesses and disappointments, the book has merit. In scope and erudition, if not in clarity, it compares with Bebel's *Woman and Socialism*; Zetkin never found the time to write a study of comparable length. Had it appeared earlier, *Social Bases* might have held a more prominent place among the landmarks of the literature. Yet even as it stands it has great value as a chronicle of feminism in the years 1905–1908. The pages dealing with

[5] Quotations: Kollontai, *Sots. osnovy*, 109, 311. Her remarks on individual feminist groups are spread throughout the book.

these events possess a vibrancy rarely encountered in works of this sort. Because of its numerous passages quoting feminist sources now difficult to obtain, Kollontai's account—notwithstanding its petulant distortions—is a valuable source for the history of Russian feminism. Furthermore, Kollontai's general conclusions about the feminist movement at home and abroad, though frequently marred by excessive verbal abuse, are on the whole sound. Hers is the only critique in the literature which throws clear light on the fundamental weakness of the narrowly feminist approach to the problem which had come to dominate the movement by 1908. The fact that she was able to perceive this long before the issue became clearer and the approaches to it more sharply defined (in the years after 1910) show that Kollontai, for all her flamboyant rhetoric, was quite capable of penetrating to the roots of a social issue.

BIBLIOGRAPHY

In order to make this bibliography as useful as possible for scholars, it has
been restricted largely to works bearing directly on the problem. This has
meant, regrettably, ruling out many standard works on Russian history that
were indispensable to my over-all understanding of Russian culture and society, secondary works of a marginal sort (even those cited in the notes), most
works on European feminism, *belles-lettres*, and translations. There are a
number of important exceptions to this. Comments on many of the works
listed below will be found in the notes. In a study of this sort, it is not always
easy to distinguish precisely between sources and secondary materials, but an
attempt to do so has been made in each of the chronological periods into
which the bibliography is divided. Some overlapping is inevitable; and many
works listed in Section V could have been put in Section IV—particularly
biographical materials. The major periodicals for the subject are not listed
separately but are to be found in the appropriate section of the bibliography.
Abbreviations for them and other items are at the front of the book. Those
planning to work through the maze of pre-revolutionary periodical literature
are advised to have the following reference works at hand: V. A. Popov, *Sis-
tematicheskii ukazatel statei pomeshchennykh v nizhepoimenovannykh peri-
odicheskikh izdaniyakh s 1830 po 1884 god.* (SPB, 1885); S. A. Vengerov,
Kritiko-biografischeskii slovar russkikh pisatelei i uchenykh, 2 ed., 3 v. (Petrograd, 1915); I. F. Masanov, *Slovar psevdonimov russkikh pisatelei*, 4 v.
(Moscow, 1956–1960).

I. ARCHIVAL SOURCES

A. *Leningrad*

Tsentralnyi Gosudarstvennyi Istoricheskii Arkhiv, Leningrad (TsGIAL).
Central State Historical Archives in Leningrad:

1. "I Vserossiiskii S"ezd po Obrazovaniyu Zhenshchin" 1912. Fond
751, op. 1, No. 1.

2. Papers of Anna Filosofova and records of Rossiiskoe Vzaimno-
Blagotvoritelnoe Obshchestvo v S. Peterburge (Russian Mutual Philanthropic Society of St. Petersburg). Fond 1075.

3. Records of Rossiiskoe Obshchestvo Zashchity Zhenshchin (Russian
Society for the Protection of Women). Fond 1335, op. 1.

4. "Po zakonodatelnomu predpolozheniyu 40 chlenov Gos. Dumy ob
izbiratelnykh pravakh zhenshchin" 1912. Fond 1405, 1912, op. 532, d.
321.

B. *Amsterdam*

International Institute of Social History.
1. Brupbacher Archive. Folder "Wera Figner."
2. Archive "Menševiki, 1917–1918."
3. Archive Robert Grimm. Zimmerwald Bewegung, H-19 and I-30 (1915).

C. *Cambridge, Massachusetts*

Harvard University, Widener Library. Smolensk Archive, Zhenotdel documents, 1922–1934.

II. GENERAL AND BIBLIOGRAPHICAL

A. *Sources*

Amerigo, N. *Zhenshchina v russkikh poslovitsakh*. Moscow, 1908.

Mikhailova, V. *Russkie zakony o zhenshchine*. Moscow, 1913.

Milovidova, E. *Zhenskii vopros i zhenskoe divzhenie*, Ed. K. Tsetkin. Moscow, 1929.

Shchepkina, E. N. *Iz istorii zhenskoi lichnosti v Rossii*. SPB, 1914.

Svod zakonov rossiiskoi imperii. Ed. I. D. Mordukhai-Bolkovskii. 16 v. SPB, 1912.

Zhenskoe pravo. SPB, 1973. A collection.

B. *Secondary*

Amfiteatrov, A. V. *Zhenshchina v obshchestvennykh dvizheniyakh Rossii*. Geneva, 1905.

Atkinson, D. "Society and the Sexes in the Russian Past." Ed. Atkinson *et al. Women in Russia* (see V/B under Atkinson).

Davydov, N. V. *Zhenshchina pered ugolovnym sudom*. Moscow, 1906.

Dudgeon, Ruth. "Women Students in Russia, 1860–1905." Ph.D. thesis, George Washington University, 1975.

Glickman, Rose and R. Stites. Eds. Women in Nineteenth Century Russia. A collection of articles (unpublished).

Kantorovich, Ya. (Orovich). *Zhenshchina v prave*. 3d ed. SPB, 1895.

Kovalëva, K. N. *Istoricheskoe razvitie byta zhenshchiny, braka, i semi*. Ed. S. Volfson. Moscow, 1931.

Likhachëva, Elena. *Materialy dlya istorii zhenskago obrazovaniya v Rossii*. 4 pts. in 2 v. SPB, 1890–1893.

Melnikow, N. M. *Die gesellschaftliche Stellung des russischen Frau*. Berlin, 1901.

Neumark, Noralyn. "The Consciousness of Women in the Russian Women's Movement, 1860–1914." Ph.D. thesis, University of Sydney, 1976. With an exceptionally rich bibliography.

Satina, Sophie. *Education of Women in Pre-Revolutionary Russia*. New York, 1966.

Sinaisky, V. I. *Lichnoe i imushchestvennoe polozhenie zamuzhnei zhenshchiny*. Dorpat, 1910.

Stern, Bernhard. *Geschichte der öffentlichen Sittlichkeit in Russland*. 2 v. N. p. 1907–1920 (V. II is 2d ed.).

"Ukazatel literatury zhenskago voprosa na russkom yazyke," *SV*, VI (July 1887) 1–32 (s.p.); VIII (Aug. 1887) 33–35.

Vysshie zhenskie (bestuzhevskie) kursy: bibliograficheskii ukazatel. Moscow, 1966.

III. TO 1881 (PARTS I AND II)

A. *Sources*

Annenkov, P. V. *Literaturnye vospominaniya*. Moscow, 1960.

Annenskaya, A. "Iz proshlykh let (vospominaniya o N. F. Annenskom)," *RB* (Jan. 1913) 53–81; (Feb. 1913) 36–65.

Babikov, K. I. *Prodazhnyya zhenshchiny (prostitutsiya)*. Moscow, 1870.

Bakunina, Ekaterina. "Vospominaniya sestry miloserdiya krestovozdvizhenskoi obshchiny (1854–1860 gg.)," *VE* (March 1898) 132–176; (May 1898) 55–105.

Belinsky, V. G. *Polnoe sobranie sochinenii*. 13 v. Moscow, 1953–1959.

Breshko-Breshkovskaya, Ekaterina. *Hidden Springs of the Russian Revolution: Personal Memoirs*. Ed. L. Hutchinson. Stanford, 1931.

———. "Iz vospominanii (S. A. Leshern, N. A. Armfeld, T. I. Lebedeva, M. K. Krylova, G. M. Gelfman)," *GM* (Oct.-Dec. 1918) 169–235.

———. *The Little Grandmother of the Russian Revolution*. Ed. Alice Stone Blackwell. Boston, 1930.

Cabet, Etienne. *La femme*. 8th ed. Paris, 1848.

Chernyshevsky, N. G. *Chto delat?* Moscow, 1963.

———. *Polnoe sobranie sochinenii*. Ed. B. P. Kozmin *et al*. 15 v. Moscow, 1939–1950.

Chudinov, A. N. *Ocherki istorii russkoi zhenshchiny*. 2 ed. SPB, 1873. A series of lectures.

Daul, A. *Zhenskii trud*. Tr. P. N. Tkachëv. SPB, 1869.

Deich, L. "Yuzhnye buntari," *GM*, IX (1920–1921) 44–71.

Deniker, I. E. "Vospominaniya . . . ," *KS*, No. 3 (1924) 20–44.

Deriker, V. V. *Fiziologiya zhenshchiny*. SPB, 1854.

Destunis, Nadezhda. "Chemu my, zhenshchiny uchilis?" *Russkaya beseda* (March 1859) 21–50.

Dobrolyubov, N. A. *Sobranie sochinenii*. Ed. B. I. Bursov *et al*. 9 v. Moscow, 1961–1964.

Dostoevsky, F. M. *The Diary of a Writer*. Tr. Boris Brasol. 2 v. New York, 1949.

Dostoevsky, F. M. *Pushkin (ocherk) Rech proiznesennaya F. M. Dostoevskim, 8 Iyula 1880 g.* SPB, 1899.

Druzhinin, Aleksandr (Alexander Drouginine). *Polinka Saxe.* Tr. Alphonse Claëys. Brussels, 1872.

Dzhabadari, Ivan. "Protsess 50-ti (Vserossiiskaya Sotsialno-Revolyutsionnaya Organizatsiya) 1874–1877 gg.," *Byloe* (Aug., Sept., Oct., 1907) 1–26, 169–192, 168–197.

Enfantin, B. P. and C. H., Count de Saint-Simon. *Oeuvres.* 47 v. Paris, 1865–1878.

Engel, Barbara and C. Rosenthal, Eds. and Tr. *Five Sisters: Women Against the Tsar.* New York, 1974.

Figner, Vera. *Memoirs of a Revolutionist.* Tr. C. C. Daniels *et al.* London, n.d.

————. "Studencheskie gody (1872–1873)," *GM*, X (Oct. 1922) 165–181.

————. *V borbe.* Leningrad, 1966.

————. *Zapechatlënnyi trud: vospominaniya.* 2 v. Moscow, 1964.

Fourier, Charles. *Oeuvres complètes.* 3d ed. 6 v. Paris, 1846–1848.

Gan, E. A. *Polnoe sobranie sochinenii.* SPB, 1905.

Gere (Guerrier), V. "Teoriya i praktika zhenskago obrazovaniya," *VE*, XII (Mar. 1877) 645–700.

Gertsen (Herzen), A. I. *Sobranie sochinenii.* 30 v. Moscow, 1954.

————. *Sochineniya.* 9 v. Moscow, 1955–1958.

Goncharov, I. A. *Polnoe sobranie sochinenii.* 12 v. SPB, 1899.

Grigorovich, D. V. *Literaturnye vospominaniya.* Leningrad, 1961.

Héricourt, Jenny (Eugénie) d'. *A Woman's Philosophy of Woman: an Answer to Michelet, Proudhon, Girardin, Legouvé, Comte and other Modern Innovators.* New York, 1864.

Ilinsky, P. A. *Russkaya zhenshchina v voinu 1877–1878 g.: ocherk deyatelnosti Sestër Miloserdiya, feldsherits i zhenshchin-vrachei.* SPB, 1879.

Karnovich, E. O *razvitii zhenskago truda v Peterburge.* SPB, 1865.

Khvoshchinskaya, Nadezhda Dmitriena (V. Krestovsky-psevdonim). *Povesti i rasskazi.* Moscow, 1963.

[Koltsova-Masalska, Elena (Ghica)] Dora d'Istria. *Les femmes en orient.* 2 v. Zurich, 1860.

Koni, A. F. *Na zhiznennom puti.* 5 v. Reval, 1914–1929.

Kovalevskaya, Sofiya V. *Sonya Kovalevsky: Her Recollections of Childhood.* Tr. Isabel Hapgood. New York, 1895.

————. *Vospominaniya detstva i avtobiograficheskie ocherki.* Moscow, 1945.

————. *Vospominaniya detstva; Nigilistka.* Moscow, 1960.

Kovalskaya, E. N. "Moi vstrechi s S. L. Perovskoi," *Byloe*, XVI (1921) 42–48.

Kravchinsky, S. M. (Stepniak). *A Female Nihilist*. 3d ed. Boston, 1886.

⸺. *Sofiya Perovskaya*. Berlin, 1903.

Kropotkin, P. A. *Memoirs of a Revolutionist*. Ed. Jas. A. Rogers. New York, 1962.

Krupskaya, A. "Vospominaniya sestry krestovozdvizhenskoi obshchiny, 1854, 1855 i 1856 gg.," *Voennyi sbornik*, XX (August 1861) 417–448.

Kusheva, E., ed. "Ot russkogo revolyutsionnogo obshchestvo k zhenshchinam," *Lit. nasled.*, XLI–XLII (1921) 147–150.

Kuznetsov, Mikhail. *Prostitutsiya i sifilis v Rossii: istoriko-statisticheskiya isledovaniya*. SPB, 1871.

Lavrov, P. L. *Izbrannye sochineniya*. Ed. I. S. Knizhnik-Vetrov. 4 v. Moscow, 1934–1935.

⸺. *Narodniki-propagandisti, 1873–1878 godov*. SPB, 1907. Primary source for Zurich period.

Lukanina, A. L. "God v Amerike: iz vospominanii zhenshchiny-medika," *VE*, XVII (Apr. 1882) 495–538.

⸺. "Iz detstva i shkolnykh let," *SV* (Feb., Mar., Apr. 1886) 65–96, 91–129, 87–144.

Lyubatovich, Olga. "Dalëkoe i nadavnee," *Byloe* (May, June 1906) 208–248, 108–154.

Michelet, Jules. *Oeuvres complètes*. 40 v. Éd. définitive. Paris, 1893–1899.

Mikhailov, Mikhail Larionovich. *Sochineniya*. Ed. B. P. Kozmin, 3 v. Moscow, 1958.

⸺. *Zhenshchiny: ikh vospitanie i znachenie v seme i obshchestve*. SPB, 1903.

Mikhailovsky, N. K. *Sochineniya*. 6 v. SPB, 1896–1897.

Mill, John Stuart. *Dissertations and Discussions*. 4 v. Boston, 1865–1868.

⸺. *O podchinenii zhenshchiny*. Tr. G. E. Blagosvetlov. SPB, 1869.

Miller, Orest and N. N. Strakhov, eds. *Biografiya, pisma, i zametki iz zapisnoi knizhki F. M. Dostoevskago*. SPB, 1883.

Mordovtsev, Daniil. *Russkiya zhenshchiny novago vremeni: biograficheskie ocherki iz russkoi istorii*. 3 v. SPB, 1874.

Morozov, N. M. *Povesti moei zhizni*. 3 v. Leningrad, 1947.

Moser, Charles. *Antinihilism in the Russian Novel of the 1860's*. The Hague, 1964.

Muzhchina i zhenshchina vroz i vmeste v razlichnya epokhi ikh zhizni. SPB, 1859.

Nekrasova, Ekaterina. "Zhenskie vrachebnye kursy v Peterburge: iz vospominanii i perepiski pervykh studentok," *VE*, XVII (Dec. 1882) 807–845.

Nikoladze, N. "Vospominaniya o shestidesyatykh godakh," *KS*, IV (33), 1927, pp. 29–52.

Odoevsky, V. "Dnevnik V. F. Odoevskogo, 1859–1869 gg.," *Lit. nasled.*, XXII–XXIV (1935) 79–308.

Oshanina, Mariya and E. S. "K istorii partii Narodnoi Voli," *Byloe* (June 1907) 1–10.

Panaeva, Avdotiya Yakovlevna (Bryanskaya). *Vospominaniya.* Ed. K. Chukovsky. Moscow, 1956.

Panteleėv, L. *Iz vospominanii proshlago.* SPB, 1905.

[Perovsky]. "Iz vospominanii brata S. L. Perovskoi," *Na chuzhoi storone,* X (1925) 204–209.

Pirogov, N. I. *Sevastopolnye pisma i vospominaniya.* Moscow, 1950.

———. *Sobranie sochinenii.* 8 v. Moscow, 1957–1960.

———. *Sochineniya.* 2 v. SPB, 1900.

Pisarev, D. I. *Izbrannye pedagogicheskie sochineniya.* Moscow, 1951.

———. *Sochineniya.* 6 v. SPB, 1894.

———. *Sochineniya.* 4 v. Moscow, 1955–1956.

Pomyalovsky, N. *Meshchanskoe schaste; Molotov.* Moscow, 1957.

Prizvanie zhenshchiny. SPB, 1840.

Proudhon, Pierre-Josephe. *Oeuvres complètes.* 12 v. Ed. Celestin Bouglé *et al.* Paris, 1923–1946.

Razsvet. Monthly. SPB, 1859–1862.

Sazhin, M. P. "Russkie v Tsyurikhe (1870–1873 gg.)," *KS* (No. 10, 1932) 20–78.

Sechenov, I. M. *Avtobiograficheskiya zapiski.* Moscow, 1907.

[Shabanova, Anna Nikitichna] Sh. "Zhenskie vrachebnye kursy," *VE,* XXI (Jan. 1886) 345–357.

Shashkov, S. S. *Istoricheskiya sudby zhenshchiny: detoubiistvo i prostitutsiya.* SPB, 1871.

———. *Istoriya russkoi zhenshchiny.* 2d ed. SPB, 1879.

———. *Ocherk istorii russkoi zhenshchiny.* Rev. ed. SPB, 1872.

———. *Sobranie sochinenii.* 2 v. SPB, 1898.

———. *Zhenskoe delo v Amerike.* SPB, 1875 (a reprint).

Shchapov, A. P. *Sochineniya.* 3 v. SPB, 1906–1908.

Shelgunov, N. V. *Izbrannye pedagogicheskie sochineniya.* Ed. N. K. Goncharov. Moscow, 1954.

———. *Sochineniya.* 3 v. 3d ed. SPB, 1904.

Shelgunov, N. V., L. P. Shelgunova, and M. L. Mikhailov, *Vospominaniia.* 2 v. Moscow, 1967.

Shelgunova, L. P. *Iz dalëkogo proshlogo.* SPB, 1901.

Shestidesyatye gody: materialy po istorii literatury i obshchestvennomu dvizheniyu. Ed. N. K. Piksanov. Moscow, 1940.

Shtakenshneider [Stackenschneider], Elena. *Dnevnik i zapiski.* Moscow, 1934.

Skabichevsky, A. M. *Literaturnye vospominaniya.* Moscow, 1928.

Skalkovsky, K. "Zhorzh Zand," *Razsvet,* XI (1861) 355–380.

Sleptsov, Vasily. *Sochineniya.* 2 v. Moscow, 1957.

Sokolov, D. P. *Naznachenie zhenshchiny po ucheniyu slova Bozhiya*. SPB, 1884 (1st ed., 1862).

Strakhov, N. M. *Iz istorii literaturnago nigilizma*. SPB, 1890.

———. *Zhenskii vopros: razbor sochineniya Dzhona Styuarta Millya 'O podchinenii zhenshchiny.'* SPB, 1871. A reprint.

Tkachëv, P. N. *Izbrannye sochineniya*. 7 v. Moscow, 1932–1937.

Tsitovich, P. *Chto delali v romane 'Chto delat?.'* 5th ed. Odessa, 1879.

Turgenev, I. S. *On the Eve*. Moscow, n.d.

Uspenskaya, Aleksandra Ivanovna. "Vospominaniya shestidesyatnitsy," *Byloe* (No. 18, 1922) 19–45.

Ustav obshchestva dlya posobiya bednym zhenshchinam v S.-Peterburge. SPB, 1865.

Vasilev, Ilarion. *Femida*. Moscow, 1827.

Vernadskaya, Mariya Nikolaevna. *Sobranie sochinenii*. SPB, 1862.

Vodovozova, Elizaveta Nikolaevna. *Na zare zhizni i drugie vospominaniya*. Ed. B. I. Kozmin. 2d ed. 2 v. Moscow, 1934. 3d ed., 1964.

Volkenshtein, Lyudmila. *13 let v Shlisselburgskoi kreposti*. SPB, 1905.

[Vorms. N.] "Belyi terror," *Kolokol* (Jan. 1, 1867) 1889–1895.

Yunge, Elizaveta. "Iz moikh vospominanii, 1843–1860 gg.," *VE*, XL (May 1905) 256–291.

Zasulich, Vera Ivanovna. *Vospominaniya*. Ed. B. I. Kozmin. Moscow, 1931.

Za zhenshchin! 2d ed. SPB, 1886.

Zhenskii vestnik. Journal. SPB, 1867–1868.

"Zhenskii vopros," *Vsemirnaya illyustratsiya*, V (Feb. 20, Mar. 6, and Mar. 13, 1871) 122–123, 158–159, 171–174.

Zhukovskaya, Ekaterina. *Zapiski*. Ed. Kornei Chukovsky. Leningrad, 1930.

Zlatkovsky, Mikhail Leontevich. *Zhenskoe spetsialnoe obrazovanie v Peterburge*. SPB, 1875.

B. *Secondary*

Abramov, Ya. "Zhenskie vrachebnye kursy," *SV* (Feb. 1886) 117–142.

Arkhangelsky, V. G. *Katerina Breshkovskaya*. Prague, 1938.

Asheshov, Nikolai. *Sofiya Perovskaya: materialy dlya biografii i kharakteristiki*. SPB [sic], 1920.

Ashevsky, S. "Russkoe studenchestvo v epokhu shestidesyatykh godov (1855–1863)," *Sovremennyi mir* (Aug. 1907) 19–36.

Bazanov, V. *Iz literaturnoi polemiki 60kh godov*. Petrozavodsk, 1941.

Bogdanovich, Tatyana A. *Lyubov lyudei shestidesyatykh godov*. Leningrad, 1929.

Chanson, Paul. *Le droit à l'amour selon George Sand*. Paris, 1943.

Chemëna, O. M. "I. A. Goncharov i semeinaya drama Maikovykh," *Voprosy izucheniya russkoi literatury*. Ed. B. P. Gorodetsky. Moscow, 1958.

Chukovsky, K. I. *Lyudi i knigi shestidesyatykh godov: staty i materialy.* Leningrad, 1934.

Claus, Claire. *Die Stellung der russischen Frau von der Einführung des Christentums bei den Russen bis zu den Reformen Peter des Grossen.* Munich, 1959. Ph.D. thesis. Basel University.

Curtiss, John Shelton. "Russian Sisters of Mercy in the Crimea, 1854–1855," *Slavic Review* (Mar. 1966) 84–100.

Deich, Lev. *Rol Evreev v russkom revolyutsionnom dvizhenii.* Moscow, 1926. 2d ed. Vol. I (only).

Dolléans, Edouard. *Féminisme et mouvement ouvrier: George Sand.* Paris, 1951.

Dzhanshiev, Grigory A. *Epokha velikikh reform: istoricheskiya spravki.* 6th ed. Moscow, 1896.

Engel, Barbara. "Women Revolutionaries, 1855–1881," to appear in Glickman and Stites, *Women.*

[Evgenev-Maksimov, V.] V. Evgeiev. "Goncharov i ego otnoshenii k nigilizmu," *Kniga i revolyutsiya,* II (Jan. 1921) 16–22.

Fateev, P. S. *Mikhail Mikhailov.* Moscow, 1969.

Figner, V. N. *Shlisselburgskaya uznitsa Lyudmila Aleksandrovna Volkenshtein.* Moscow, 1906.

Filippova, L. D. "Iz istorii zhenskogo obrazovaniya v Rossii," *Voprosy istorii* (Feb. 1963) 209–218.

Footman, David. *Red Prelude: the Life of the Russian Terrorist, Zhelyabov.* New Haven, 1947.

Gershenzon, M. O. *Istoriya molodoi Rossii.* Moscow, 1923.

Geschichte der Frauenbewegung in den Kulturländern. Ed. Helene Lange and Gertrud Bäumer [Handbuch der Frauenbewegung, I]. Berlin, 1901.

Grimal, P., ed. *Histoire mondiale de la femme.* 4 v. Paris, 1965–1967.

Iokhelson, Vladimir and R. M. Kantor. *Gesya Mironovna Gelfman.* Petrograd, 1922.

[Ivanov, Razumnik Vasilevich] R. V. Ivanov-Razumnik. *Istoriya russkoi obshchestvennoi mysli.* 2 v. SPB, 1909–1911.

Kan, S. B. *Istoriya sotsialisticheskikh idei.* 2d ed. Moscow, 1967.

Karenin, V. [Komarova]. *Zhorzh Zand.* 2 v. published. SPB, 1899–1916.

Kara-Murza, S. "Geroi i geroini romana 'Chto delat?'," *Krasnaya niva,* VI (July 22, 1928) 8–9.

Khmelevskaya, E. M. "A. N. Lukaninoi," *Literaturnyi arkhiv,* IV (1953) 346–373.

Knight, Amy. "The Fritschi: a Study of Female Radicals in the Russian Populist Movement," *Canadian-American Slavic Studies,* IX; 1 (Spring 1975) 1–17.

Knizhnik-Vetrov, I. S. *Russkie deyatelnitsy Pervogo Internatsionala i Parizhskoi Kommuny*. Moscow, 1964.

Kostomarov, N. I. *Ocherk domashnei zhizhi i nravov velikorusskago naroda v XVI i XVII sloletiyakh*, SPB, 1860.

Kotlyarevsky, N. A. *Kanun osvobozhdeniya, 1855–1861*. Petrograd, 1916.

Kupreyanova, N. "Shelgunov," *Istoriya russkoi kritiki*. Ed. B. P. Gorodetsky, *et al*. 2 v. Moscow, 1958. Vol. II, 226–242.

Librovich, Zigizmund. *Pëtr Velikii i zhenshchiny: istoricheskii ocherk*. SPB, 1904.

Lipinska, Mélina. *Les femmes et le progrès des sciences médicales*. Paris, 1930.

Lyadov, V. N. *Istoricheskii ocherk stoletnei zhizni Imperatorskogo Vospitatelnago Obshchestva Blagorodnykh Devits i Sanktpeterburgskogo Aleksandrovskogo Uchilishcha*. SPB, 1864.

Malia, Martin. *Alexander Herzen and the Birth of Russian Socialism, 1812–1855*. Cambridge, Mass., 1961.

Mazour, Anatole. *Women in Exile*. Talahassee, 1975.

McNeal, Robert H. "Women in the Russian Radical Movement," *Journal of Social History*, v. 2 (Winter 1971–1972) 143–163.

Meijer, J. M. *Knowledge and Revolution: the Russian Colony in Zuerich (1870–1873); a Contribution to the Study of Russian Populism*. Assen, The Netherlands, 1955.

Nechkina, M. V. *Dvizhenie Dekabristov*. 2 v. Moscow, 1955.

Ostrogorsky, V. P. "Dvadtsatipyatiletie zhenskikh gimnazii: istoricheskaya zametka," *VE*, XVIII (Apr. 1883) 826–838.

Ovsyaniko-Kulikovsky, D. N. *Istoriya russkoi intelligentsii*. 2d ed. 2 v. Moscow, 1907–1908.

Ovtsyn, Vladimir. *Razvitie zhenskago obrazovaniya*. SPB, 1887.

Peskovsky, M. "Ocherk istorii vysshago zhenskago obrazovaniya v Rossii (za 20 let)," *Nablyudatel*, I (Apr., May, Jun. 1882), 74–92, 166–177, 117–136.

Peunova, M. N. *Obshchestvenno-politicheskie i filosofskie vzglady N. V. Shelgunova*. Moscow, 1954.

Pinaev, M. T. *Kommentarii k romanu 'Chto delat?'* Moscow, 1963.

Plotkin, L. A. *Pisarev i literaturno-obshchestvennoe dvizhenie shestidesyatykh godov*. Moscow, 1964.

Pustvoit, P. G. *Roman I. S. Turgeneva 'Ottsy i deti' i ideinaya borba 60-kh godov XIX veka*. Moscow, 1964.

Riasanovsky, N. V. "Fourierism in Russia: an Estimate of the Petraševcy." *American Slavic and East European Review*, XII, 3 (1953) 289–302.

Sankt-Peterburgskie vysshie zhenskie (bestuzhevskie) kursy (1878–1918 gg.): sbornik statei. Ed. S. N. Valk *et al*. Leningrad, 1965. 2d ed. 1973.

Segal, Elena. *Sofya Perovskaya*. Moscow, 1962.

Semënov, D. "Stoletie Smolnago Monastyrya," *OZ*, CLIC (May, 1864) 388–409.

Semevsky, V. "N. D. Khvoshchinskaya-Zaionchkovskaya," *RM*, XI (Oct., Nov., Dec. 1890) 49–89, 82–110, 124–148.

Shchegolev, V. N. *Zhenshchina-telegrafist v Rossii i za granitseyu*. SPB, 1894.

Shulgin, V. *O sostayanii zhenshchin v Rossii do Petra Velikago*. Kiev, 1850.

Sidorov, N. N. "Statisticheskie svedeniya o propagandistakh 70-kh godov v obrabotke III Otdeleniya." *KS* (No. 1, 1928) 27–56.

Skaftymov, A. *Stati o russkoi literature*. Saratov, 1958.

Sleptsov, Zhosefina, "Vasilii Alekseevich Sleptsov v vospominaniyakh ego materi, 1836–1878," *Russkaya starina*, LXV (Jan. 1890) 233–241.

Smirnov, Aleksandr. *Pervaya russkaya zhenshchina-vrach*. Moscow, 1960. A biography of Suslova.

Sourine, Georges. *Le fourierisme en Russie*. Paris, 1936.

Sposobin, A. D. *O razvode v Rossii*. Moscow, 1881.

Stanton, Theodore, ed. *The Woman Question in Europe: a Series of Original Essays*. New York, 1884.

Stasov, Vladimir Vasilevich. *Nadezhda Vasilevna Stasova: vospominaniya i ocherki*. SPB, 1899.

Stillman, Beatrice. "Sofya Kovalevskaya: Growing up in the Sixties." *Russian Literary Triquarterly*, 9 (Spring 1974) 277–302.

Stites, Richard. "All-Russian Socialist-Revolutionary Organization," *Modern Encyclopedia of Russian and Soviet History*. Gulf Breeze, Fla., 1975. I.

——. "Bardina, Sofya Ilarionovna," *ibid.*, III (1977).

——. "M. L. Mikhailov and the Emergence of the Woman Question in Russia," *Canadian Slavic Studies*, 3 (Summer 1969) 178–199.

Venkstern, N. *Zhorzh Sand*. Moscow, 1923.

Venturi, Franco. "Anna Kuliscioff e la sua attività rivoluzionaria in Russia," *Movimento operaio*, new series, IV (Mar., Apr. 1952) 277–287.

Veselovsky, Aleksei. *Zapadnoe vliyanie v novoi russkoi literature*. 5th ed. Moscow, 1916.

Vilenskaya, E. S. *Revolyutsionnoe podpole v Rossii (60-e gody XIX v.)*. Moscow, 1965.

Vsesoyuznoe Obshchestvo Politicheskikh Katorzhan i Ssylno-Poselentsev. *Deyateli revolyutsionnogo dvizheniya v Rossii: biobibliograficheskii slovar*. Ed. Feliks Kon, *et al*. Many vols. Moscow, 1927–.

Whittaker, Cynthia. "The Women's Movement During the Reign of Alexander II," *Journal of Modern History*, XLVIII (June 1976).

Zelnik, Reginald E. "The Sunday-School Movement in Russia, 1859–1862," *Journal of Modern History*, XXXVII (June 1965) 151–170.

IV. 1881–1917 (PART III)

A. *Sources*

Abramovich, N. Ya. *Zhenshchina i mir muzhskoi kultury*. Moscow, 1913.

Adov. *Bezumnoe povalie*. SPB, 1914. A reply to Elets, *Povalnoe bezumie*.

Albitsky, P. *Khristianstvo i sotsializm*. Nizhny Novgorod, 1907.

Aleksandrova, Vera. *Perezhitoe (1917–1921 gg.)*. New York, 1962.

Amfiteatrov, A. V. *Zhenskoe nestroenie*. 3d ed. SPB, 1908.

Anzimirova, M. N. *Prichiny nravstvennoi fizionomi zhenshchiny*. SPB, 1901.

Ardashëv, N. *Velikaya voina i zhenshchiny russkiya*. Moscow, 1915.

Argamakova, S. *K voprosam etiki v sovremennom brake*. Polotsk, 1895.

Armand, Inessa Fedorovna. *Stati, rechi, pisma*. Moscow, 1975.

Artsybashev, M. *Sanin*. Berlin, 1911 (In Russian).

Balabanova, Anzhelika (Angelica Balabanoff). *Iz lichnykh vospominanii tsimmervaldtsa*. Moscow, 1925.

Baranov, A. *V zashchitu neschastnykh zhenshchin*. Moscow, 1902.

Beatty, Bessie. *The Red Heart of Russia*. New York, 1919.

Bebel, August. *Gosudarstvo budushchego*. Rostov-na-Donu, 1906. Excerpt from *Zhenshchina i sotsializm*.

―――. *Zhenshchina i sotsializm*. Tr. from 34th ed. Odessa, 1905.

―――. *Zhenshchina i sotsializm*. Moscow, 1959. Tr. from 55th ed. (Berlin, 1946).

Belikov, B. D. *Zhenshchina v promyshlennoi inspektsii zapada*. Tver, 1914.

Bentovich, B. *Torguyushchiya telom*. 2d ed. SPB, 1909.

Bezobrazov, P. V. *O sovremennom razvrate*. Moscow, 1900.

Bilshai, Vera, ed. *K. Marks, F. Engels, V. I. Lenin o zhenskom voprose*. Moscow, 1971.

Bobrovskaya (-Tselikson, Tsetseliya; Bobrowskaja, Z.). *Bolschewiki im zaristischen Russland*. Hamburg, 1932.

―――. *Lenin and Krupskaya*. New York, 1940.

―――. *Zapiski podpolshchika, 1894–1917*. Moscow, 1957.

Bochkarëva, Mariya (Marie Botchkareva) and Isaac Don Levine. *Yashka: My Life as Peasant, Officer, and Exile*. New York, 1919.

Bolkvadze, M. G. *Ne razvrashchaite zhenshchin! ili "vragi chelovechestva."* SPB, 1908.

Brandt, B. F. *Sovremennaya zhenshchina*. SPB, 1896.

Breshko-Breshkovskaya, Ekaterina (Breshkovsky, Catherine; Katherine). *For Russia's Freedom*. Tr. E. Poole. Chicago, 1905.

―――. *A Message for the American People*. New York [1919 or 1920].

Broido, Eva. *Memoirs of a Revolutionary*. Tr. and ed. Vera Broido. London, 1967.

―――. *V ryadakh R.S.-D.R.P.* Ed. V. V. Nevsky. Moscow, 1928.

―――. *Wetterleuchten der Revolution*. 2d ed. Berlin, 1931.

Bryant, Louise. *Six Red Months in Russia*. London, 1918.

Chebysheva-Dmitrieva, E. A. *Rol zhenshchin v borbe s alkogolizmom*. SPB, 1901.

Chego khotyat sotsial-demokraty. Odessa, [1917].

Dan, Lidiya. *Iz vstrech s Veroi Nikolaevnoi Figner*. New York, 1961.

Dneprov, P. *Zhestokii gorod*. SPB, 1907.

Dolgorukaya (Stephanie Dolgorouky). *La Russie avant la débacle*, Paris, 1926.

Dreksler, Karl. *Kak predupredit beremenost u bolnykh i slabykh zhenshchin*. 6th ed. SPB, [1910].

"Droit de suffrage pour les femmes, Le," *La revue socialiste*, XLIV (Aug. 1906) 145–166.

Dubnova-Erlikh, S. *Obshchestvennyi oblik zhurnal "Letopis."* New York, 1963.

Dubovskaya, P. *Zhenskaya dolya v razreshenii sotsialnykh zadach*. Moscow, 1906.

Dyakonova, Elizaveta. *Dnevnik Elizavety Dyakonovoi na vysshikh zhenskikh kursakh (1895–1899 g.)* 2d ed. SPB, 1905.

Elets, Yu. L. *Povalnoe bezumie*. SPB, 1914.

Eletsky, M. *Svobodnaya lyubov*. SPB, 1908.

Eliseev, V. *Programmy i pravila zhenskikh gimnazii* . . . 21st ed. Moscow, 1913.

E. M. *Golos russkoi zhenshchiny po povodu gosudarstvennago i dukhovnogo-religiozno-nravstvennago vozrozhdeniya Rossii*. SPB, 1906.

Engels, F. *The Origin of the Family, Private Property, and the State*. Moscow, 1952.

Ermansky, A. "Vserossiiskii zhenskii s"ezd," *Sovremennyi mir*, Pt. II (Jan. 1909) 103–112.

German, B. *Biologiya i sotsializm*. Geneva, 1904.

Gippius, Z. *Sinyaya kniga: peterburgskii dnevnik, 1914–1918*. Belgrade, 1929.

Glebov, P. *Politicheskiya prava zhenshchin v mestnom samoupravlenii*. Moscow, 1906.

Gleichheit, Die. 1890–1925. Organ of the German Social Democratic women's movement.

Goldberg, G. "Zhenskii trud v russkoi promyshlennosti," *Russkiya vedomosti*, CCLXXXV (Nov. 17, 1910), 4.

Gordon, G. "Brak i prostitutsiya v suzhdeniyakh sovremennoi molodëzhi," *Novaya zhizn* (February 1913) 190–205.

Govorov, A. V. *Zhenskii vopros*. Kazan, 1907. Liberal-religious.

Gromozova, Lyudmila. *Rech*. Geneva, 1904.

Gryaznov, K. *Prostitutsiya kak obshchesvennyi nedug*. Moscow, 1901.

Gumilovich, V. *Brak i svobodnaya lyubov*. 3d ed. Moscow, 1907.

Gurevich, Lyubov. *Pochemu nuzhno dat zhenshchinam vse prava i svobodu.* SPB, 1906.

Gvozdëv, S. *Zapiski fabrichnago inspektora.* Moscow, 1911.

Isaev, A. A. *Chego ozhidat zhenshchine ot sotsializma?* Stuttgart, 1903.

Ius Suffragi. Monthly, Organ of the IWSA. 1904–.

Ivanov, P. *Studenty v Moskve.* 2d ed. Moscow, 1903.

Kablukov, K. A. *Studencheskii kvartirnyi vopros v Moskve.* Moscow, 1908.

Kage. *Svedeniya dlya zhenshchin poluchivshikh srednee obrazovanie o vysshikh i professionalnykh uchebnykh zavedeniyakh i kursakh.* SPB, 1905.

Kalmanovich, Anna A. *Otchët o Zhenskom Mezhdunarodnom Kongresse 1904 g.* 2d ed. Saratov, 1905.

————. *Pretenzii k zhenskomu dvizheniyu voobshche i k 1-mu Vserossiiskomu zhenskomu s"ezdu v chatnosti.* SPB. 1910.

————. *Suffrazhistki i suffrazhetki.* SPB, 1911.

————. *Zhenskoe dvizhenie i ego zadachi.* SPB, 1908.

————. *Zhenskoe dvizhenie i otnoshenie partii k nemu.* SPB, 1911.

Kechedzhi-Shapovalov, M. V. *K svobode: etyud po zhenskomu voprosu.* SPB, [1905].

————. *Zhenskoe dvizhenie v Rossii i zagranitsei.* SPB, 1902.

Khvostov, V. M. *Zhenshchina i chelovecheskoe dostoinstvo.* Moscow, 1914.

————. *Zhenshchina nakanune novoi epokhe.* Moscow, 1905.

Klingen, I. *Rol zhenshchin kak obrazovannoi selskoi khozyaike v obnovlenii russkoi derevni.* SPB, 1903.

Kollontai, Aleksandra (Alexandra Kollontay). *Den första etappen.* Tr. T. Nordström-Bonner. Stockholm, 1945.

————. (A. K.). *Komu nuzhna voina?* 1916; Helsinki, 1917.

————. *K voprosu o klassovoi borbe.* SPB, 1905.

————. (A. K.). *O soveshchatelnom predstavitelstve.* SPB, 1906.

————. *Po rabochei Evrope.* SPB, 1912.

————. *Rabotnitsy i Uchreditelnoe Sobranie.* Peterburg, 1917.

————. *Sotsialnyya osnovy zhenskago voprosa.* SPB, 1909. For more titles by this author, see Section V,A of the bibliography.

Krupskaya, N. K: *Memories of Lenin.* Tr. E. Verney of 2d ed. London, 1930. Subsequent editions under title: *Reminiscences of Lenin.*

————. "Pyat let raboty v vechernykh smolenskikh klassakh," in *Leninskie ustanovki v oblasti kultury.* Moscow, 1934, pp. 222–239.

————. (Sablina). *Zhenshchina-rabotnitsa,* n.p. 1901.

Kryzhanovskaya-Tuchapskaya, V. G. "Iz moikh vospominanii," *Katorga i ssylka,* VI, 67 (1930) 18–50.

Kudashëva, E. *Umstvennyya sposobnosti zhenshchiny.* Ekaterinoslav, 1897.

Kudrin, N. (Rusanov). *O ravnopravosti zhenshchin.* SPB, 1905.

Kuskova, E. "Zhenskii vopros i zhenskii s"ezd," *Obrazovanie,* 1–2 (Jan.–Feb. 1909) 74–99, 33–43.

Kuzmin, S. *Zhenshchina v osveshchenii sotsial-demokratov*. SPB, 1907.

Lesnevskaya, A. *Po neprotorënnoi doroge*. 1901; SPB, 1914.

Lozinsky, E. *O nastoyashchem i budushchem zhenskago dvizheniya v svyazi s problemoi tselomudriya i zadachami materinstva*. N.p. 1903 or 1904.

Lukhmanova, N. A. *Nedochety zhizni sovremennoi zhenshchiny*. Moscow, 1904.

Margulies, M. S. *Reglamentatsiya i svobodnaya prostitutsiya*. SPB, 1903.

Mariya, Princess of the House of Romanov (Marie, Grand Duchess of Russia). *Education of a Princess*. Tr. Russell Lord *et al*. New York, 1931.

Matyushensky, A. I. *Polovoi rynok i polovyya otnosheniya*. SPB, 1908.

Mavritsky, V. *Pravila i programmy zhenskikh uchebnikh zavedenii . . . na 1909–1910 g*. Moscow, 1909.

Mikhail (Archimandrite). *Zakonnyi brak*. SPB, [1908].

———. *Zhenshchina-rabotnitsa*. SPB, 1906.

Mikhnevich, V. *Yazvy Peterburga*. SPB, 1886. An anatomy of Petersburg crime and vice.

Mikhnov, S. D. *O zhenshchine s biologicheskoi tochki zreniya*. Yurev, 1904.

Mirovich, N. (pseud. for Zinaida Ivanova). *Iz istorii zhenskago dvizheniya v Rossii*. Moscow, 1908.

———. *Pobeda zhenskago dvizheniya v Finlyandii*. *Moscow. 1904.*

———. *Zhenskoe dvizhenie v Evrope i Amerike*. Moscow, 1907.

Mizhuev, P. G. *Zhenskii vopros i zhenskoe dvizhenie*. SPB, 1906.

M. L. "Une utopie rare: l'utopie du Ruvarebohni." *Bulletin of the International Institute of Social History, Amsterdam*, I (1937) 26–36.

Mukalov, M. K. *Deti ulitsy: maloletniya prostitutki*. SPB, 1906.

Nedësheva, V. *Nevskii prospekt*. SPB, 1906.

Novik, I. D. *Borba za politicheskiya prava zhenshchin*. Moscow, 1906.

Novopolin, G. S. *Pornograficheskii element v russkoi literature*. SPB, [1909].

Oboznenko, P. E. *Podnadzornaya prostitutsiya S.-Peterburga*. SPB, 1896.

Omelchenko, A. P. *Svobodnaya lyubov i semya*. SPB, 1908.

Orlovskaya, M. V. *O zhenskom dvizhenii v Rossii*. SPB, 1911.

Otchët o deyatelnosti Rossiiskoi Ligi Ravnopraviya Zhenshchin za 1913 god. SPB, 1914.

Paley, Princess. *Memoirs of Russia: 1916–1919*. London, 1924.

Pervye zhenshchiny-inzhenery. Leningrad, 1967. Memoirs.

Pervyi zhenskii kalendar. Annual. 1899–1916 (?).

Petrazhitsky, L. I. *Rech*. SPB, 1907. Duma speech.

Pokrovskaya, M. I. *Vrachebno-politseiskii nadzor za prostitutsiya sposobstvuet vyrozhdeniyu naroda*. SPB, 1902.

———. *Zashchitniki i protivniki ravnopraviya zhenshchin v pervoi gosudarstvennoi Dume*. SPB, 1907.

Polovoe vospitanie. Moscow, 1913.

Polyansky, A., ed. *Russkaya zhenshchina na gosudarstvennoi i obshchestvennoi sluzhbe*. Moscow, 1901.

Prodazha devushek v doma razvrata. 4th ed. Moscow, 1901.

Rabotnitsa. Journal. 7 issues. 1914.

Rossiiskoe Obshchestvo Zashchity Zhenshchin v 1913 godu. Petrograd, 1914.

Rozanov, V. V. *Semeinyi vopros v Rossii*. 2 v. SPB, 1903.

Sabinin, A. Kh. *Prostitutsiya*. SPB, 1905.

Samoilova, K. *V obedinenii*. Moscow, 1921.

Semeinaya zhizn v eya radostyakh i pechalyakh. SPB, 1888.

Shabanova, Anna Nikitichna. *Ocherk zhenskago dvizheniya v Rossii*. SPB, 1912.

Silov, V. *Zhenshchina zamuzhem*. 2d ed. Moscow, 1897.

Slushatelnitsy S.-Peterburgskikh vysshikh zhenskikh (bestuzhevskikh) kursov. SPB, 1912. Questionnaires of 1909.

Soyuz zhenshchin. Monthly, SPB, 1907–1909. Organ of the Union for Women's Equality.

Sprudina, T. *Russakaya zhenshchina nashego vremena*. 2d ed. SPB, 1908.

Studencheskaya zhizn. Semimonthly, Moscow, 1910–1911 files.

Trudy Pervago Vserossiiskago S"ezda po Borbe s Torgom Zhenshchinami i Ego Prichinami . . . 1910 goda. 2 v. SPB, 1911–1912.

Trudy I-go Vserossiiskago S"ezda po Obrazovaniyu Zhenshchin. SPB, 1914.

Trudy Pervago Vserossiiskago Zhenskago S"ezda . . . 1908 g. SPB, 1909.

Tsebrikova, M. K. *Katorga i ssylka*. SPB, 1906 (written, 1890).

——. *Pismo k Aleksandru III*. SPB, 1906 (written, 1890).

Tyrkova-Vilyams, Ariadna (A. Tyrkova-Williams). *From Liberty to Brest-Litovsk*. London, 1919.

——. *Na putyakh k svobode*. New York, 1952.

——. *Osvobozhdenie zhenshchiny*. Petrograd, 1917.

——. "Strashnyi vopros," *Zaprosy zhizni*, 17 (April 1910) 5–10.

——. *To, chego bolshe ne budet*. Paris, 1954.

Ustav Obshchestva Okhraneniya Zdorovya Zhenshchiny v g. S.-Peterburge. SPB, 1898.

Ustav Obshchestva pod nazvaniem "Rossiiskaya Liga Ravnopraviya Zhenshchin." SPB, 1911.

Ustav S.-Peterburgskago Obshchestva Izyskaniya Sredstve Tekhnicheskago Obrazovaniya Zhenshchin. SPB, 1905.

Ustav S.-Peterburgskago Zhenskago Kluba. SPB, 1908.

Vakhovskaya, V. I. *Zhizn revolyutsionerki*. Moscow, 1928.

Vladimirov, V. *Mariya Spiridonova*. Moscow, 1905.

Volkenshtein, Olga. *Komu i zachem nuzhno vseobshchee izbiratelnoe pravo?* SPB, 1906.

——. *Osvobozhedenie zhenshchiny*. Petrograd [1917].

Vrachebno-politseiskii nadzor za gorodskoi prostitutsiei. SPB, 1910.

BIBLIOGRAPHY

Woman Question: Selections from the Writings of Karl Marx, Frederick Engels, V. I. Lenin, Joseph Stalin. New York, 1951; reprinted 1972.
Yuzhakov, S. *Zhenshchina-izbiratelnitsa*. Moscow, 1906.
Zasulich, Vera. "O voine," *Samozashchita: marksistskii sbornik*. Petrograd, 1916, I, 1–3.
Zetkin, Clara. *Arbeiterinnen-und Frauenfrage der Gegenwart*. Berlin, 1889.
———. *Woman Suffrage*. Tr. J. B. Askew. London, 1906.
Zhenshchina i voina. Ed. A. K. Yakovleva. Semimonthly. Moscow, 1915–?
Zhenshchina v semeinoi i sotsialnoi zhizni. Ed. I. P. Goldberg. SPB, 1901.
Zhenskaya dolya. Geneva, [1905?]. An *Iskra* publication.
Zhenskaya mysl. Semimonthly. Kiev, 1909–1910 (?).
Zhenskii almanakh. Odessa, 1901.
Zhenskii vestnik. Monthly. SPB, 1904–1917. Organ of the Women's Progressive Party. No continuity with journal of the same title (1867–1868) cited in Section III of this bibliography.
Zhenskii vopros v Gosudarstvennoi Dume. SPB, 1906.
Zhenskoe delo. Monthly. SPB, 1899–?.
Zhenskoe delo. Weekly. Moscow, 1909–1917. Semiofficial organ of the League for Women's Equality.
Zhenskoe dvizhenie poslednykh dnei. Odessa, 1905.

B. *Secondary*

Bobroff, Anne. "The Bolsheviks and Working Women, 1905–1920," *Soviet Studies*, XXVI, 4 (October 1974) 540–567.
Borman, Arkady. *A. V. Tyrkova-Vilyams*. Louvain, 1964.
Clements, B. "Women and Social Democracy, 1905–1914," Typescript of paper read at American Historical Association conference, Atlanta, 1975.
Drumm, Robert. "Feminists and Women Workers in Petrograd, 1917." As above.
Edmondson, Linda. "Russian Feminists and the Women's Congress of 1908," *Russian History* (scheduled for 1977).
Fréville, Jean. *Une grande figure de la Révolution russe: Inessa Armand*. Paris, 1957.
Giffin, F. G. "The Prohibition of Night Work for Women and Young Persons: the Russian Factory Law of June 3, 1885," *Canadian Slavic Studies*, II, 2 (Summer 1968) 208–218.
Glickman, Rose. "The Russian Factory Woman, 1880–1914," in Atkinson, *et al. Women in Russia*.
Ilberg, Ganna. *Klara Tsetkin*. tr. A. Shtekli. Moscow, 1958.
Karpetskaya, N. D. *Rabotnitsy i Velikii Oktyabr*. Leningrad, 1974.
Knight, Amy. "Women in the Russian Revolutionary Movement, 1881–1917." In Glickman and Stites. *Women*.
Kollontai, A. M. *Mezhdunarodnye sotsialisticheskie soveshchaniya rabotnits*. Moscow, 1918.

Krupskaya, N. K. *Klara Tsetkin*. Moscow, 1933.

Madison, Bernice. "Russia's Illegitimate Children Before and After the Revolution." *Slavic Review*, XXII, 1 (March, 1963) 82–95.

Meyer, A. G. "Marxism and the Women's Movement." in Atkinson *et al.* *Women in Russia*.

M. I. Ulyanova. Moscow, 1965.

Pachmuss, Temira. *Zinaida Hippius*. Carbondale, Ill., 1971.

Petropavlovskaya, L. *Lyusik Lisinova*. Moscow, 1968.

Pieck, Wilhelm (Vilgelm Pik). *Klara Tsetkin*. Moscow, 1957.

Podlyashuk, P. *Tovarishch Inessa*. 2d ed. Moscow, 1965.

Ruthchild, Rochelle. "Russian Feminists, 1905–1917." Ph.D. thesis. University of Rochester, 1976.

Sbornik pamyati Anny Pavlovny Filosofovoi. 2 v. Petrograd, 1915.

Serditova, S. *Bolsheviki v borbe za zhenskie proletarskie massy (1903-Fevral 1917 g.)*. Moscow, 1959.

Shinn, W. T. "The Law of the Russian Peasant Household," *Slavic Review*, XX, 4 (Dec. 1961) 600–621.

Shishkin V. F. *Tak skladyvalas revolyutsionnaya moral*. Moscow, 1967.

Sobolev, M. *Zhenskii trud v narodnom khozyaistve XIX veka*. SPB, 1901.

Steinberg, I. *Spiridonova*. Tr. G. David and E. Mosbacher. London [1935].

Stites, R. "Women's Liberation Movements in Russia, 1900–1930," *Canadian-American Slavic Studies*, VII, 4 (Winter 1973) 460–474.

Tyrkova, *Filosofova*: see *Sbornik* above.

Zabludovskaya, E. D. "Odna iz pervykh zhenshchin vrachei-pediatrov v Rossii: A. N. Shabanova," *Pediatriya*, 6 (1957) 71–78.

Zhikharëva, A. "Anna Sergeevna Milyukova," *Poslednye novosti*, April 5, 1935 and following Sunday.

Zinovieva, Z. (Lilina). *Soldaty tyla: zhenskii trud do i posle voiny*. (1916); Petrograd, 1918.

V. SINCE 1917 (PART IV)

A. *Sources*

Arbore-Ralli, Ekaterina. *Mat i ditya v sovetskoi Rossii*. Moscow, 1920.

Balabanova (Angelica Balabanoff). *Impressions of Lenin*. Tr. Isotta Cesari. Ann Arbor, 1964.

———. "Note autobiografiche," *I buoni artieri*. 3 pts. Ed. Alessandro Schiavi. Rome, 1957, pt. I, pp. 7–56.

———. *Minnen och upplevelsen*. Tr. Leif Björk. Stockholm, 1927 (Eng. ed.: 1938; Bloomington, 1973).

———. *Ot rabstva k svobode*. Moscow, 1920.

Beryushin, A. *Pochemu ya stala kommunistkoi*. Moscow, 1919.

Bez nikh my ne pobedili by. Moscow, 1975. Memoirs.

Bilshai (Bilshai-Pilipenko), Vera. *Sovetskaya demokratiya i ravnopravie zhenshchin v SSSR*. Moscow, 1948. As opinion.

Bobryshev, I. *Melkoburzhuaznye vliyaniya sredi molodëzhi*. Moscow, 1928.

Brak i semya. Moscow, 1926.

Bryant, Louise. *Mirrors of Moscow*, New York, 1923.

Bystryansky, V. *Kommunizm, brak i semya*. Petrograd, 1921.

———. *Revolyutsiya i zhenshchina*. Petrograd, 1920.

Byulleten [number] *Otdela TsKRKP po Rabote Sredi Zhenshchin*. Moscow. Irregular. 1919–1930. Internal organ of Zhenotdel.

Chernyavina, Tatyana (Tchernavin). *We Soviet Women*. Tr. N. Alexander. New York, 1936.

Chistyi istochnik. Moscow, 1962.

Docheri revolyutsii. Moscow, 1923.

Doklad Otdela po Rabote Sredi Zhenshchin TsKRKP. Moscow, 1922.

Femme et le communisme, La: anthologie des grands textes du marxisme. Paris, 1950.

Fridland, L. *S raznykh storon: prostitutsiya v SSSR*. Berlin, 1931.

Gelman, I. *Polovaya zhizn sovremennoi molodëzhi*. Moscow, 1923.

Ginzburg, B. S. *Sud nad materyu podkinuvshei svoego rebënka*. Moscow, 1924.

Ginzburg, Evgeniya. *Into the Whirlwind*. Tr. P. Stevenson and M. Harari. Harmondsworth, 1968.

Goikhbarg, A. G. *Brachnoe, semeinoe i opekunskoe pravo sovetskoi respubliki*. Moscow, 1920.

———. *Novoe semeinoe pravo*. Moscow, 1918. Earlier ed. of above.

Grigorov, G. and S. Shkotov. *Staryi i novyi byt*. Moscow, 1927.

Grinfeld, [Yuliya ?]. *Iz vospominanii o borbe za svobodu i narodovlastie v Odesse, 1918–1920 gg*. New York, 1962.

Halle, Fanina. *Woman in Soviet Russia*. Tr. M. Greene. New York, 1933.

Kabo, E. O. *Ocherki rabochego byta*, I. Moscow, 1928.

Kalmanson, S. M., ed. *Polovoi vopros*. Moscow, 1924.

Ketlinskaya, Vera and Vladimir Slepkov, eds. *Zhizn bez kontrolya (polovaya zhizn i semya rabochei molodëzhi)*. Moscow, 1929.

Kolbasina-Chernova, Olga (Kolbassine-Tchernoff). *Les prisons soviétiques*. Paris, 1922.

Kollontai, Aleksandra. *The Autobiography of a Sexually Emancipated Communist Woman*. Ed. Iring Fetscher. Tr. Salvator Attanasio. London, 1972.

———. "Avtobiograficheskii ocherk," *Proletarskaya revolyutsiya*, 3 (1921) 261–302.

———. "Avtobiografiya," *ES* (Granat) XLI, 1, 194–201.

———. *Bolshaya lyubov*. Moscow, 1927. Tr. Lily Lore as *A Great Love* (New York, 1929) 3–153.

———. *Bud stoikim bortsom!* Moscow, 1919.

―――. *Communism and the Family*. London, n.d.

―――. "Dekret na stene," *Nemerknushie gody*. Leningrad, 1957, 209–211.

―――. *Free Love*. Tr. C. Hogarth. London, 1932.

―――. "Gigant dukha i voli: golos Lenina," *Oktyabr*, XL (Jan. 1963) 4–6.

―――. *Izbrannye stati i rechi*. Ed. I. M. Dazhina *et al*. Moscow, 1972.

―――. *Iz moei zhizni i raboty*. Moscow, 1974. Assorted autobiographical works.

―――. *K istorii dvizheniya rabotnits v Rossii*. Kharkov, 1920.

―――. *Lyubov pchël trudovykh*. Moscow, 1923.

―――. *Obshchestvo i materinstvo*, I (only). Petrograd, 1916.

―――. *Novaya moral i rabochii klass*. Moscow, 1918.

―――. "Pisma k trudyashcheisya molodëzhi," *Molodaya gvardiya*, 1–2 (Apr.-May, 1922) 136–144; 6–7 (Oct.-Dec., 1922)128–136; 3 (May, 1923) 111–124. The last, and most famous, is "Dorogu Krylatomu Erosu!"

―――. *Polozhenie zhenshchiny v evolyutsii khozyaistva*. Moscow, 1922.

―――. *Prostitutsiya i mery borby s nei*. Moscow, 1921.

―――. *Rabotnitsa i krestyanka v Sovetskoi Rossii*. Petrograd, 1921.

―――. *Rabotnitsa-mat*. 1914; Moscow, 1918.

―――. *Rabotnitsa za god revolyutsii*. Moscow, 1918.

―――. *Red Love*. New York, 1927.

―――. "Ruka istorii: vospom. A. Kollontai," *Krasnoarmeets*, 10–15 (1919) 68–71.

―――. *Semya i kommunisticheskoe gosudarstvo*. Moscow, 1918.

―――. "Skoree v Rossii!" *Sovetskie arkhivy*, 2 (1967) 23–33.

―――. *Vospominaniya ob Iliche*. Moscow, 1959.

―――. *Workers Opposition in Russia*. Chicago [1921].

―――. *Zhenshchina na perelom*. Moscow, 1923.

Kommunistka. Monthly-irregular. 1920–1930. Organ of Zhenotdel.

Kostërina, Nina. *The Diary of Nina Kostërina*. Tr. Mirra Ginsburg. New York, 1968.

K perevyboram delegatskikh sobranii 1929–30 goda. Moscow, 1929.

Krupskaya, N. K. *Izbrannye pedagogicheskie proizvedeniya*. Moscow, 1965.

―――. *Zhenshchina, ravnopravnyi grazhdanin SSSR*. Moscow, 1937.

Laptënok, S. D. *Moral i semya*. Minsk, 1967.

Lenin, V. I. *On the Emancipation of Women*. Moscow, n.d.

―――. *Polnoe sobranie sochinenii*. 5th ed. 55v. Moscow, 1960–1965.

―――. *Women and Society*. New York, 1938.

Leningradki: vospominaniya, ocherki, dokumenty. Leningrad, 1968.

Lunacharsky, A. *O byte*. Moscow, 1927.

Lyadov, M. N. *Voprosy byta*. Moscow, 1925.

Na puti k novomu. Moscow, 1925.

Nesterev, V. G. *Trud i moral v Sovetskom obshchestve*. Moscow, 1969.

Oktyabrëm rozhdënnye. Moscow, 1967.

Olitskaya, E. *Moi vospominaniya*. 2 v. Paris, 1971.

Otchët o pervoi mezhdunarodnoi konferentsii kommunistok. Moscow, 1921.

Pravda, stavshaya legendoi. 2d ed. Moscow, 1969.

Programmy dlya kursov perepodgotovki rabotnikov sredi zhenshchin, 1928. Moscow, 1928.

Rabotnitsa. Weekly. Petrograd; later Moscow, 1917– with gaps. A revival of the 1914 *Rabotnitsa*.

Reich, Wilhelm. *The Sexual Revolution*. Tr. Theo. Wolfe, 4th ed. New York, 1969.

Ryazanov, David. "Marks i Engels o brake i seme," *Letopis marksizma*, III (1927) 13–35.

Sbornik instruktsii Otdela TsKRKP po Rabote Sredi Zhenshchin. Moscow, 1920.

Schlesinger, Rudolf, ed. *The Family in the U.S.S.R.* London, 1949. Documents.

Skvoz gody i buri. Moscow, 1969.

Smith, Jessica. *Women in Soviet Russia*. New York, 1920.

Sokolov, Boris. *Spasite detei!* Prague, 1921.

Sputnik organizatora krestyanok. 2d ed. Moscow, 1927.

Stasova, Elena. *Stranitsy zhizny i borby*. Moscow, 1960.

———. *Vospominaniya*. Ed. V. N. Stepanov. Moscow, 1969. Amplified edition of the above.

Tri goda diktatury proletariata: itogi raboty sredi zhenshchin Moskovskoi organizatsii RKP. Moscow, [1921].

Trotsky, L. D. *Problems of Life*. Tr. Z. Vengerova. London, 1924.

Velikii Oktyabr i raskreposhchenie zhenshchin Srednei Azii i Kazakhstana (1917–1936 gg.). Moscow, 1971. Documents.

Vinogradskaya, Polina. *Pamyatnye vstrechi*. 2d ed. Moscow, 1972.

———. "Voprosy morali, pola, byta, i tovarishch Kollontai," *Krasnaya nov*, 6 (10), (Oct.-Nov., 1923) 179–214.

Volfson, S. Ya. *Semya i brak v ikh istoricheskom razvitii*. Moscow, 1937.

———. *Sotsiologiya braka i semi*. Minsk, 1929.

Vospominaniya o Nadezhde Konstantinovne Krupskoi. Ed. A. M. Arsenev *et al*. Moscow, 1966.

Winter, Ella. *Red Virtue*. New York, 1933.

Woman and Communism: Selections from the Writings of Marx, Engels, Lenin, and Stalin. London, 1950.

Zalkind, A. B. *Revolyutsiya i molodëzh*. Moscow, 1925.

Zetkin, Clara. *Lenin on the Woman Question*, New York, 1934.

———. (Tsetkin). *Vospominaniya o Lenine*. Moscow, 1968.

Zhenshchiny goroda Lenina. Leningrad, 1963.

Zhenshchiny i deti SSSR. Moscow, 1969, Statistics.

Zhenshchiny russkoi revolyutsii. Ed. L. P. Zhak *et al*. Moscow, 1968.

Zhenshchiny v revolyutsii. Moscow, 1959.

Zinovieva, Z. (Lilina). *Ot kommunisticheskoi semi k kommunisticheskomu obshchestvu*. Petersburg, 1920.

B. *Secondary*

Arenshtein, A. *Rannim moskovskim utrom*. Moscow, 1967. On the Smidoviches.

Astakhova, N. and E. Tselliarius, *Tovarishch Olga*. Moscow, 1969.

Atkinson, D., A. Dallin and G. Lapidus, eds. *Women in Russia*. Stanford, 1977.

Bailes, Kendall. "Alexandra Kollontai et la Nouvelle Morale," *Cahiers du monde russe et soviétique*, VI, 4 (Oct.–Dec. 1965) 472–496.

Barulina, A. T. "Rabota petrogradskoi i moskovskoi partorganizatsii sredi zhenshchin-rabotnits (mart-oktyabr 1917 g.)." *V borbe za pobedu Oktyabrya*. Moscow, 1957, 184–208.

Bestuzhevki v ryadakh stroitelei sotsializm. Moscow, 1969.

Bochkarëva, E. and S. Lyubimova, *Svetlyi put*. Moscow, 1967.

Body, Marcel. "Alexandra Kollontai," *Preuves*, II, 14 (April 1952) 12–24.

Bolshevikov, P. and G. Gorbunov. *Olga Afanasevna Varentsova*. Moscow, 1964.

Breslav, E. I. "A. M. Kollontai v 'Pravde' 1917 goda," *Zhurnalistika i zhizn*. Leningrad, 1967, 96–118.

Bronner, V. M. *La lutte contre la prostitution en URSS*. Moscow, 1936.

Brown, Donald, ed. *The Role and Status of Women in the Soviet Union*. New York, 1968.

Clements, Barbara. "Emancipation through Communism: the Ideology of A. M. Kollontai," *Slavic Review*, XXXII, 2 (June 1973) 323–338.

———. "Kollontai." 1976. Unpublished ms. Biography.

———. "Kollontai's Contribution to the Workers Opposition Movement," *Russian History*, II, 2 (1975) 191–206.

Dodge, Norton. *Women in the Soviet Economy*. Baltimore, 1966.

Dridzo, Vera. *Nadezhda Konstantinovna*. 2d ed. Moscow, 1966.

Dunham, Vera, "Sex: From Free Love to Puritanism," in *Soviet Society*, ed. A. Inkeles and K. Geiger (Boston, 1961) 540–46.

Egalité de la femme en U.R.S.S., L'. Moscow, 1957.

Emelyanova, E. D. *Revolyutsiya, partiya, zhenshchina*. Smolensk, 1971.

Ershov, D. A. *Mariya Ilinichna Ulyanova*. Saratov, 1965.

Eubank, Carol. "The Bolshevik Party and Work Among Women." *Russian History*, 1977.

Farnsworth, Beatrice. "Bolshevik Alternatives and the Soviet Family," in Atkinson *et al. Women in Russia* (Stanford, 1977).

———. "Bolshevism, the Woman Question, and Alexandra Kollontai," *American Historical Review* (Summer 1976) 292–316. A reworking of the above.

Fitzpatrick, Sheila. "Sex and Revolution: Sexual Mores of Soviet Students in the 1920's." Paper read at the American Association for the Advancement of Slavic Studies, Atlanta, October, 1975.

Frauen der Revolution. Berlin (East), 1960.

Gasiorowska, Xenia. *Women in Soviet Fiction, 1917–1964*. Madison, 1968.

Geiger, H. Kent. *The Family in Soviet Russia*. Cambridge, Mass., 1968.

Goreva, E. and M. Sumenkova, "Zhenotdely," *V edinom stroyu*. Moscow, 1960, pp. 150–175.

Halvorsen, Carsten. *Revolutionens Ambassadør: Alexandra Kollontays Liv og Gerning (1872–1917 aarene)*. Tr. G. Thomsen. Copenhagen, 1946.

Hough, Jerry. "The Impact of Participation: Women and the Women's Issue in Soviet Policy Debates." To appear in his *Soviet Union and Social Science Theory*, Cambridge, Mass., 1977.

Igumnova, Zoya. *Zhenshchiny Moskvy v gody grazhdanskoi voiny*. Moscow, 1958.

Isbakh, A. A. *Tovarishch Absolyut (Elena Dmitrievna Stasova)*. Moscow, 1958.

Itkina, Anna. *Revolyutsioner, tribun, diplomat: ocherk zhizni Aleksandry Mikhailovny Kollontai*. Moscow 1964. 2d ed. 1970.

Ivanova, N. A. *et al. Novoe zakonodatelstvo o brake i seme*. Moscow, 1970.

Juviler, Peter. "Family Reforms on the Road to Communism," *Soviet Policy-Making*. Ed. Juviler and H. W. Morton. London, 1967.

Kharchëv, A. G. *Brak i semya*. Moscow, 1964.

Krovitsky, G. A. *Put starogo bolshevika: k shestidesyatiletiyu E. M. Stasovoi*. Moscow, 1933.

Krupskaya, N. K. *Zavety Lenina o raskreposhchenii zhenshchiny*. Moscow, 1933.

Kunetskaya, L. and K. Mashtakova. *Stranitsy prekrasnoi zhizni*. Moscow, 1969. On Krupskaya.

Kurganov, I. A. *Zhenshchiny i kommunizm*. New York, 1968.

Lapidus, G. "Occupational Segregation and Public Policy: A Comparative Analysis of American and Soviet Patterns," *Signs: Journal of Women in Culture and Society*, I, 3 pt. 2 (Spring 1976) 119–136.

―――. *Women in Soviet Society*. Berkeley, 1977.

Lenczyc, Henryk. "Alexandra Kollontai: essai bibliographique," *Cahiers du monde russe et soviétique*, XIV, 1–2 (Jan.–June, 1973) 205–241.

Levidova, S. M. and E. G. Salita. *Elena Dmitrievna Stasova*. Leningrad, 1969.

Levidova, S. M. and S. A. Pavlotskaya. *Nadezhda Konstantinovna Krupskaya*. Leningrad, 1962.

Lyubimova, S. T. *Oktyabrskaya revolyutsiya i polozhenie zhenshchin v SSSR*. Moscow, 1967.

Madison, Bernice. *Social Welfare in the Soviet Union*. Stanford, 1968.

Mandel, William. *Soviet Women*. New York, 1975.

Massell, Gregory. *The Surrogate Proletariat*. Princeton, 1974.

McNeal, Robert. *Bride of the Revolution: Krupskaya and Lenin*. Ann Arbor, 1972.

Mindlin, E. L. *Ne dom, no mir: povest ob Aleksandre Kollontai*. Moscow, 1969.

Morozova, Vera. *Rasskazy o Zemlyachke; Klavdichka; Konkordiya*. Moscow, 1970.

Palencia, Isabel de. *Alexandra Kollontay*. New York, 1947.

Pierre, André. *Les femmes en Union soviétique*. Paris, 1960.

Starodub, V. I. *Zhenshchina i obshchestvennyi trud*. Leningrad, 1975.

———. *Zhenshchina-truzhenitsa i mat*. Leningrad, 1967.

Stavrakis, Bette. "Women and the Communist Party in the Soviet Union, 1918–1935." Ph.D. thesis, Western Reserve University, 1961.

Stiernlöf, Sture. *Kvinnor i Sovjet: yrkesliv och könsroller i första socialiststaten*. Stockholm, 1970.

Stites, Richard. "Balabanova, Anzhelika," *Modern Encyclopedia of Russian and Soviet History*, III (1977).

———. "Bobrovskaya, Tsetsiliya," *ibid*., IV, 1978.

———. "Kollontai, Inessa, Krupskaia," *Canadian-American Slavic Studies*, IX, 1 (Spring 1975) 84–92.

———. "Zhenotdel: Bolshevism and Women, 1917–1930," To appear in *Russian History*, 1977.

Tolkunova, V. N. *Pravo zhenshchin na trud i ego garantii*. Moscow, 1967.

Wolfe, Bertram. "Lenin and Inessa Armand," *Slavic Review*, XXII, 1 (March 1963) 96–114.

Zetkin, Clara (Tsetkin). *Zavety Lenina zhenshchinam vsego mira* (1933). Moscow, 1958.

"Zhenotdely," *BSE*, 2d ed. XVI, 62.

Zhenshchiny mira v borbe za sotsialnyi progress. Moscow, 1972.

INDEX

education (*cont.*)
32-34, 36, 39, 43-45, 50, 59, 64, 73, 89,
93, 113, 115-16, 149, 158-59, 166-73,
176-77, 191, 218, 283-84, 293, 393-400,
409, 416; congress on 223-24; and
radicalism, 126-38; secondary, 4, 10, 15,
43, 45, 50, 52, 76, 134-35, 144, 167-68,
217, 398; university, 4, 52-54, 73, 75-83,
87, 93, 96, 101, 109, 149, 168-73, 217,
221, 283, 295, 398-99, 418. *See also* Bestuzhev Courses, childrearing, medicine
Efimenko, A., 174, 301
Egorova, Zh., 302
Eichorn, H., 313
Ekaterinodar, 298
Elena Pavlovna, Princess (Grand Duchess),
30-31
Elizabeth, Empress, 14
Elizarova, A., 254, 256-57, 302
Ella, Grand Duchess, *see* Sergei, Grand
Duchess
Emelyanova, E., 331
Enfantin, B.-P., 18-19, 21, 97, 110, 133, 353,
378-79
Engelhardt, Aleksandr, 68-69
Engelhardt, Anna, 68, 193
Engels, F., 57, 59, 233-34, 247, 258, 260,
262-64, 268, 375, 388, 400, 409, 423; *Ori-
gin of the Family, Private Property and the
State*, 233, 265
England, xvii, 62n, 70n, 74, 164, 175, 178,
180, 212, 225, 281-82, 307, 403-404, 417;
feminists in, 64, 181n, 214, 228, 338. *See
also* suffragettes
English Women's Journal, 37
Epstein, A., 150
Ermansky, A., 216, 218-19
Estonia, 307
Ethical-Social Movement, 197
Eubank, C., 342
European Economic Community, 400
Evreinova, A., 106, 176
Evropeus, P., 117

Fabian Society, 237
Fadeev, R., 24
family, 3, 6-11, 22-23, 34-35, 44, 49, 56, 72,
99, 101, 117-18, 120, 125, 126n, 141-42,
158, 160-61, 170, 181-82, 188-89, 224,
229-30; Kollontai on, 349-58; Lenin on,
378-79; Marxism and, 258-69; rebellion in,
48, 105-107; Soviet, 362-71, 381-91, 402-
406, 413
Fanon, F., 84
Fatherland Union, 208
Fawcett, M., 212, 228, 282
feminism, xvii, xviii, 23, 42, 47, 62-90, 93,

101, 108, 112, 125, 138, 154, 159, 162-63,
166, 173-74, 176, 180-81, 188, 190, 191-
237, 239, 243, 246, 250-52, 255, 257-58,
269-70, 281-84, 286-88, 310, 328, 331-33,
338, 341-42, 399, 416-17, 418, 420, 423-
26; and the Russian Revolution of 1917,
293-301, 303, 306-308. *See also* charity,
education, suffrage
Fénelon, F., 3
Feuerbach, L., 111
Fichte, J., 16
Figner, L., 135, 357n
Figner, M., 309n
Figner, V., 84, 87, 127, 130n, 134-38, 141-
47, 151-53, 194, 229, 292-93, 309, 357n,
412, 421
Filippov, A., 135
Filosofov, D., 67, 194, 225
Filosofov, V., 67
Filosofova, A., 66-70, 80, 83, 87, 176, 193-
97, 216, 218-19, 229, 252, 281, 291, 298
Finland, 198, 249-50, 274, 300; feminists in,
198
Finnish Women's Association, 198
First Congress on Prostitution, 226
First International (International Work-
ingmen's Association), 132, 238, 240
First Women's Calendar, 198
Flaubert, G., 11, 350; *Mme. Bovary*, 23
Flaxerman, G., 277
Fleishits, E., 175
Fourier, C., 90, 95, 118, 234, 266, 353
France, xvii, 62n, 175, 237, 404; ideas of,
17-20, 38-41, 43. *See also* French Revolu-
tion of 1789, Paris Commune
Free Labor Artel, 407
free love, 45, 97, 136, 187, 189-90, 229,
260-61, 269, 361, 374, 379, 383
French Revolution of 1789, xvii, 153, 247,
309, 317
Freud, S., 42
Fridland, L., 376, 384
Fritschi Circle, 134-37, 141-42
Frommett, B., 268
Furtseva, E.

Gan, E., 23-25; *Ideal*, 24
Gapon, G., 245
Ge, K., 321
Geiden, P., 209
Gelfman, G., 147n, 148, 150
Geneva, 124, 137
gentry, 3-11, 14, 30, 33, 35, 56, 60-61, 68,
72, 79, 83, 88, 98-99, 105, 119, 128-30,
132, 134-35, 143, 145, 167, 170n, 195,
204, 215, 217, 220, 228, 372
Georgians, 124, 137, 393

459

socialism and women, 233-77. *See also* Bol-
sheviks, Proletarian Women's Movement,
radical movement
Socialist Revolutionaries, 140, 154, 203-204,
206, 210, 250, 268, 270-73, 294, 304-305,
308-13, 327, 336, 338, 393; Left Socialist
Revolutionaries, 294, 311-13, 363
Society for Aiding Women Students at the
Medical and Pedagogical Courses, 85
Society for Assisting Young Girls, 192
Society for Cheap Lodgings, 69
Society for Circulating Useful Books, 70
Society for Helping Needy Women, 70
Society for Providing Means of Support for the
Higher Women's Courses, 70, 83
Society for Stimulating a Love for Work, 70
Society for the Struggle Against Alcohol, 197
Society for the Training of Well-Born Girls, 4
Society for Women's Work, 69-70
Society of Cotton Dresses, 68-69
Sofia, 204, 246
soldatki (soldiers' wives and daughters), 61,
83, 141, 288-91, 304-305, 322
soldiers' wives, *see soldatki*
Sollogub, F., 185
Sollogub, V., *Life of a Woman of the World*,
11
Solntseva, E., 129-30
Solovëv, S., 78, 81
Solovëv, V., 194, 273, 354
Soloviëv, N., 96-97
Sorokin, P., 289, 300, 346, 364, 371
Spencer, H., 273
spinsters, 8-9, 36, 56, 190
Spiridonova, M., 272-73, 294
Stackenschneider, E., 29, 33, 70, 76
Staël, Mme. de, 350
Stal, L., 246, 254, 302
Stalin, I., 313, 325, 376, 385-87, 390-92
Stankevich, N., 16-17
Stanton, E., 228
Stasov, V., 65, 67, 69, 78, 274
Stasova, E., 67, 256, 274-75, 323-26, 334
Stasova, N., 34, 62, 66-68, 70-71, 77, 83, 87,
168, 193, 274
Stasovs, 249
Stasyulevich, 53
Stavrakis, B., 339-40
Stead, W., 184
Steinberg, I., 311, 363
Stepniak-Kravchinsky, S., 128, 142, 147;
Career of a Nihilist, 151
Stockholm, 221
Stone, L., 140n, 228
Stoyunin, V., 44
Strakhov, N., 74-75, 99
Strakhova, M., 247-48
Strauss, R., 279

Strumilin, S., 410
Struve, P., 176, 204, 205, 239, 249
Stuchka, P., 369-70
Sture, L., 272
Stuttgart, 237, 242, 251
Subbotinas, 136
suffrage, women's, xviii, 44, 158, 175, 191,
194-95, 198-224, 234, 236, 238, 253, 256,
282-84, 292-94, 332-33, 345, 417, 424-25
suffragettes, English, 212, 229, 256, 281,
297, 417
Sukhanov, N., 277
Sukhumi, 339
Sullerot, E., 400
Sunday Schools, 71-72, 117, 240, 248, 273-
74, 340
Sun Yat-sen, 84
Suslova, N., 55, 84, 117, 135
Sutner, B., 283n
Suvorova, M., 337
Sverdlov, G., 389
Sverdlov, Ya., 323, 330
Sweden, 60, 174, 189, 285-86, 302, 325, 333
Switzerland, 55-56, 82, 124, 131-38
Sychova, M., 102n

Takhtarëv, K., 244
Tambov province, 208, 292
Tarnovskaya, P., 85
Tashkent, 364
Tatars, 205, 393
Tatlina, P., 23
Taylor, H., 44, 73
teaching, 60, 81, 119, 151, 173-74, 224,
271-73, 275, 283, 295, 301, 339; as gover-
ness, 57, 93, 119, 173
technical education, 176, 198, 396, 398-99
temperance, *see* alcohol
Terem, 13
Tereshchenko family, 192
Tereshkova-Nikolaeva, V., 396, 415
terror, 143-48, 248, 271-73, 308-310, 312-13,
327
Third Women's Club, 254
Thoreau, 101n
Tiflis, 248, 254
Tikhomirov, L., 131, 151
Tkachëv, P., 58-59, 67, 72, 78, 118, 126n,
424
Tkachëva, S., 118
Tolkunova, V., 415
Tolstaya, L., 119
Tolstoy, D., 76, 80, 82, 84, 174
Tolstoy, F., 96
Tolstoy, L., 33, 74, 159, 176-78, 189, 194,
213, 220; *Anna Karenina*, 9, 159n, 182,
231; *Infected Family, An*, 111; *Kreutzer
Sonata, The*, 159, 170, 188, 229, 365, 381;